Marketing Management:
A Cultural Perspective

Edited by
Lisa Peñaloza,
Nil Toulouse and
Luca M. Visconti

Routledge
Taylor & Francis Group

LONDON AND NEW YORK

First published 2012
by Routledge
2 Park Square, Milton Park, Abingdon, Oxon OX14 4RN

Simultaneously published in the USA and Canada
by Routledge
711 Third Avenue, New York, NY 10017

Routledge is an imprint of the Taylor & Francis Group, an informa business

British Library Cataloguing in Publication Data
A catalogue record for this book is available from the British Library

Library of Congress Cataloging in Publication Data
Marketing management : a cultural perspective / edited by Lisa Peñaloza, Nil Toulouse and Luca M. Visconti.
p. cm.
Includes bibliographical references and index.
ISBN 978-0-415-60682-0 (hardback)
1. Marketing–Management–Cross-cultural studies. 2. Export marketing–Cross-cultural studies. 3. Marketing–Cross-cultural studies. I. Peñaloza, Lisa. II. Toulouse, Nil. III. Visconti, Luca M.
HF5415.13M352315 2012
658.8–dc23   2011019409

ISBN: 978-0-415-60682-0 (hbk)
ISBN: 978-0-415-60683-7 (pbk)
ISBN: 978-0-203-35726-2 (ebk)

Typeset in Times New Roman
by Cenveo Publisher Services

Marketing Management: A Cultural Perspective

Culture pervades consumption and marketing activity in ways that potentially benefit marketing managers. *Marketing Management* provides a comprehensive account of cultural knowledge and skills useful in strategic marketing management.

In making these cultural concepts and frameworks accessible and in discussing how to use them, this edited textbook goes beyond the identification of historical, socio-cultural, and political factors and their effects on market outcomes. It builds understanding of the cultural symbols, world views, and practices at the heart of organizations and consumer collectives to better comprehend their relationships in markets. This book highlights the benefits managers can reap from applying interpretive cultural approaches across the realm of strategic marketing activities including: market segmentation, product and brand positioning, market research, pricing, product development, advertising, and retail distribution, among others.

With global contributions grounded in the authors' primary research with companies such as General Motors, Camper, Prada, Mama Shelter, the Kjær Group, Hom, and the *Twilight* community, this edited volume delivers a truly innovative marketing textbook. *Marketing Management: A Cultural Perspective* brings a timely and relevant learning resource to marketing students, lecturers, and managers across the world.

Lisa Peñaloza is Professor of Marketing at EDHEC Business School, Lille, France. Her work exploring interpellations of cultural meanings and economic valuation in credit/debt, migration, community formation, and retailing is published in the *Journal of Consumer Research, Journal of Marketing*, and *Consumption, Markets and Culture.*

Nil Toulouse is Assistant Professor of Marketing at Université Lille Nord de France and Skema Business School, France. Her research on sustainability, consumer ethics, immigration and fair trade appears in over 20 articles and chapters in periodicals and books, including the *Journal of Macromarketing, Journal of Business Research*, and *Journal of Business Ethics.*

Luca M. Visconti is Associate Professor of Marketing at ESCP Europe, Paris. His work appears in books and journals, including the *Journal of Consumer Research, Journal of Advertising, Industrial Marketing Management, Journal of Business Research, Journal of Consumer Culture*, and *Consumption, Markets and Culture.*

Marketing Management: A Cultural Perspective

Contents

Figures

Tables

Notes on contributors

Laurie Anderson is Associate Professor of Marketing at the W.P. Carey School of Business and Research Faculty at the Center for Services Leadership at Arizona State University, USA. Her research focuses on consumer well-being, collective goods, and collective efficacy especially related to poverty, culture, immigration and health, along with creativity, consumer co-creation, and transformative services research. One of her most current research project focuses on using community action research methods in a subsistence community dealing with a very high rate of diabetes. She is looking at issues of hope and hopelessness in particular. Additional projects look at consumer-centric service innovations and customer collaboration in health organization, space as a public good, ethnic groups going back and forth between the mainstream world and the ethnic world, and the self-socialization of teens on the internet. Her research has been published in the *Journal of Consumer Research*, *Journal of Public Policy and Marketing*, *Journal of Advertising*, *International Journal of Research in Marketing* and the *Journal of Consumer Behaviour* among others.

Eric Arnould, PhD, is Professor of Marketing at the University of Bath and Visiting Professor at the University of Southern Denmark in Odense. Eric also has benefited from teaching students at the Universities of Arizona, Nebraska, South Florida, Colorado-Denver, Cal State University Long Beach, Southern Denmark University, University of Ljubljana, IAE-Sorbonne, Dauphine University, and EAP-ESCP, all in Paris, France, and Lille 2 University. He has consulted for Abt & Associates, Chemonics, CVS, TransFair USA, H J Heinz, USAID, United Nations Environmental Program, Rainbird, CARE, Vertical Communications and a number of other entities. Eric's research on sustainability, economic development, services marketing, consumer culture theory, and marketing channels in developing countries appears in over 90 articles and chapters in major social science and managerial periodicals and books, including the *Journal of Consumer Research*, *Journal of Marketing*, *Journal of Public Policy and Marketing*, *Human Organization* and the *Journal of Marketing Research*.

Søren Askegaard is Professor of Marketing at University of Southern Denmark in Odense. His research interests generally lie in the field of analyzing consumption from a cultural perspective. Current research projects include the mixing of global and local cultural capital in branding, the consequences of reflexive culture on consumption processes, consumption of self-actualizing techniques and the social construction of health, governmentality and consequent consumer anxieties. Past research topics include consumer desire, acculturation processes, cosmetic surgery and life style. He has received three major Danish research awards. He has published in numerous anthologies as well as in journals such as *Consumption, Markets, and Culture, European Journal of Marketing, International Business Review, Journal of Consumer Culture, Journal of Consumer Research, Marketing Theory and Psychology and Marketing*. He is an associate editor at the *Journal of Consumer Research*, the co-author of a leading European textbook in consumer behaviour and a founder of the university–business collaboration project, Brand Base.

Deniz Atik, PhD, is Assistant Professor of Marketing at Izmir University of Economics. Her PhD was awarded in Bocconi University, Milan, Italy. She also spent one academic year at the University of Texas Pan-American as Visiting Assistant Professor, teaching marketing and international business courses. Her academic research focuses on consumer culture theory, especially the interagency between consumers and producers, consumer freedom, low-income consumers, authenticity, and fashion theory. Some of her work is forthcoming in the *International Journal of Consumer Studies* and the *Journal of International Consumer Marketing*. She also has done several years of professional work experience besides her academic work, in different sectors such as tourism, graphic design (product package/label planning), and tobacco.

Jill Avery, DBA, is an Assistant Professor of Marketing at Simmons College. She holds a DBA from Harvard Business School and an MBA from the Wharton School. Her research focuses on brand management and customer relationship management. Her research on online brand communities won the 2006 Harvard Business School Wyss award for excellence in doctoral research, and the best paper award at the Association of Consumer Research conference on gender, marketing, and consumer behavior. Her work has been published in the *Journal of Consumer Research, Harvard Business Review, Sloan Management Review, Business Horizons* and the *Journal of Marketing Communications*. Her branding insights have been cited in *Advertising Age, The Economist, The New York Times*, and *The Financial Times*. Prior to her academic career, Dr Avery spent nine years in brand management, managing brands for Gillette, Braun, Samuel Adams, and AT&T, and spent three years on the agency side of the business, as an account executive for Pepsi, General Foods, Bristol-Myers, and Citibank.

Domen Bajde started his career in advertising at STB Saatchi & Saatchi. Currently he is Assistant Professor of Marketing at the Faculty of Economics, University of Ljubljana, Slovenia. His current research projects delve into creative online communities' engagement with copyright and general consumer response to anti-piracy advertising. In the past he has researched charitable gift giving and consumer altruism, publishing his work in journals such as *Consumption, Markets, and Culture, Economic Business Review* and *Managing Global Transitions*.

Amina Béji-Bécheur is Professor of Marketing at the Université Paris Est and Affiliated Researcher at IRG-Prism Research Center, France. Her current research projects explore the diffusion of innovation and more particularly social innovations such as fair trade or corporate social responsibility, the role of creative consumer or lead user, the role of social entrepreneurs, or network of actors, the construction of markets through institutional and cultural approaches. Her research has been published in the *Journal of Macromarketing, Journal of Business Ethics, Décisions Marketing, Finance Contrôle Stratégie, Management et Avenir*, and *Revue Française du Marketing*.

Russell Belk is a pioneer. His *Possessions and the Extended Self* is one of the seminal papers in consumer behavior. Other contributions include 117 journal articles (25 in JCR –*Journal of Consumer Research*), 21 books, and 78 chapters. Belk's contributions have received several awards, such as the 2005 Sheth Foundation/JCR Award for Long Term Contribution to Consumer Research, the 2004 Paul D. Converse Award, and Fellow in the Association for Consumer Research (ACR). He initiated the Consumer Behavior Odyssey, the ACR Film Festival, and the Consumer Culture Theory Conference. His current research projects include Envy and Social Comparison, Sharing, Naming, The Enigmatic Smile, Clean & Dirty Consumption, Shangri-La China, Global Consumer Ethics, and Skin Colour and Beauty in Asia. He is Kraft Foods Canada Chair in Marketing at the Schulich School of Business, York University, Canada. He also holds honorary professorships at universities in North America, Europe, Asia, and Australia. He is the co-editor for two forthcoming titles also by Routledge, *The Routledge Companion to Identity and Consumption* and *The Routledge Companion to Digital Consumption*.

Gaël Bonnin is Professor of Marketing at Reims Management School, France. His research interests pertain to store design, with a specific focus on gesture and movements, market orientation and technology. His previous research has been published in *Recherches et Application Marketing*, *Décisions Marketing*, and *Sciences de la Société*.

Sammy K. Bonsu is Associate Professor of Marketing at the Schulich School of Business, York University, Canada. He is a student of consumption and identities, with a focused interest on Africa and diaspora experiences that inform theoretical developments in contemporary consumer cultures and markets. Sammy was a management consultant for several years. These days, when he is not partying with his two older children who left the nest, he spends the bulk of his time playing with the remaining two not-so-young ones who still live at home – a good excuse for staying away from conferences! Nobody reads his research that has been published in the *Journal of Consumer Research*, *Journal of Consumer Culture*, *Journal of Macromarketing*, *Journal of Contemporary Ethnography*, and *Consumption, Markets and Culture*, among others… really, who cares?

Stefania Borghini is Associate Professor of Marketing at Università Bocconi, Milan. Her research interests are related to consumer behavior in the marketplace and its connections with brands and retail spaces in particular. The construction of meaningful bonds with place is at the intersection of many of her studies both in consumer and industrial contexts. Her current projects focus in particular on children's and women's behavior. In her studies she adopts a consumer culture perspective and privileges ethnographic methods. She has published her works in books and academic journals such as the *Journal of Consumer Research*, *Journal of Marketing*, *Journal of Retailing*, *Journal of Advertising*, *Journal of Business Research*, *Industrial Marketing Management*, *Journal of Business & Industrial Marketing*, and *Journal of Knowledge Management*.

Antonella Carù is Professor of Marketing at Università Bocconi, Milan, where she is Director of the Master of Science in Marketing Management. Her traditional research interests are focused on services marketing and innovation; in the past few years she has been working on the experiential perspective in consumption and marketing. She is involved in various research projects on the arts and cultural marketing field. She is also one of the promoters of a research group on Mediterranean Marketing together with Italian and French colleagues. She published books and articles in various national and international journals, including the *International Journal of Services Industry Management, Marketing Theory, Journal of Consumer Behaviour, European Management Journal, European Accounting Review* and *International Journal of Arts Management.*

Judith Cavazos is Marketing PhD Program Coordinator in UPAEP Business School, Puebla, Mexico. Her most recent research projects focus on the impacts of Mexican migration on family consumption and the adjustment processes, cultural adaptation and consumption of Mexican expatriates in Brazil; another research subject targets analysis and marketing strategies of electronic and mobile commerce in Mexico. She has participated in several international events including the Congreso Internacional de Investigación de la Academia de Ciencias Administrativas (ACACIA), Association for Consumer Research Conference, the International Conference on Immigration, Consumption and Markets, and the Macromarketing Seminar. She has published two books in Spanish, one related to electronic commerce, and the other oriented to paths and strategies for mobile commerce in Latin America.

Isabelle Collin-Lachaud is Associate Professor of Marketing at the Université Lille Nord de France–Skema Business School, France. Her main current research projects explore retailers' loyalty strategies: first, loyalty programs and especially the role of intangible advantages on consumers' valorization of the loyalty programs, and second, other retailers' loyalty strategies based on the social dimension of consumption. Previous research has examined the dynamic relationship between satisfaction and loyalty in the cultural sector as well as the impact of experiential value on loyalty. Her research has been published in *International Journal of Arts Management, Décisions Marketing* and *Gestion 2000* and several congress proceedings.

Bernard Cova is Professor of Marketing at Euromed Management, Marseilles, and Visiting Professor at Università Bocconi, Milan. A pioneer in the consumer tribes field since the early 1990s, his internationally influential research has emphasized what he calls "the Mediterranean approach" of tribal marketing. His work on this topic has been published in the *International Journal of Research in Marketing*, the *European Journal of Marketing, Marketing Theory*, and the *Journal of Business Research*. He is also known for his research in B2B marketing, especially in the field of project marketing. His work on this topic has been published in the *European Management Journal, Industrial Marketing Management, International Business Review,* and the *Journal of Business and Industrial Marketing.*

Véronique Cova is Professor of Services Marketing at the Paul Cezanne University of Aix-Marseille III. Her research interests focus on servicescapes design, consumer experience and postmodern consumption. She has been conducting extensive research in the areas of consumer behavior and service experience. She is specialized in service design and the way the consumers reappropriate the offering through diversion tactics. She has published books and articles in various French and international journals, including *International Journal of Service Industry Management, European Journal of Marketing, Journal of Business Research,* and *Marketing Theory.*

Samantha N. N. Cross is an Assistant Professor in Marketing at Iowa State University. Her current research examines household decision-making and food consumption in culturally diverse families; immigrant, bi-national and bi-cultural consumer behavior; innovations in methodology and consumption; and social and consumption networks. Her research has been presented in several forums, including the Association for Consumer Research (ACR) Conference, the Consumer Culture Theory (CCT) Conference and the Academy of Marketing Science (AMS) Conference, where she was awarded the Jane K. Fenyo Best Paper Award for Student Research. She has also received several awards for her research, including the American Marketing Association Foundation (AMAF) Valuing Diversity PhD Scholarship, UC Irvine's Ray Watson Doctoral Fellowship and the ACR/Sheth Foundation Dissertation Award. She received her PhD in Marketing from the University of California, Irvine; her MBA in International Business from DePaul University and a BSc in Management Studies from The University of The West Indies.

Daniele Dalli is Professor of Marketing and Consumer Behavior at the University of Pisa, Italy. He does research in the field of consumption culture, the role of consumers in the process of market value creation, consumption communities, brand culture. He has published in the *Journal of Business Research*, *Journal of International Market Research*, *Marketing Theory*, and *Advances in Consumer Research*.

Benét DeBerry-Spence is an Assistant Professor of Marketing in the Liautaud Graduate School of Business at the University of Illinois at Chicago (UIC), USA. Her current research interests are retailing, cultural consumption, social entrepreneurship and subsistence markets, and her work has appeared in such publications as the *Journal of Retailing*, the *Journal of Consumer Research*, the *Journal of Business Research* and the *Journal of the Academy of Marketing Science*. She has significant managerial experience in marketing, strategy and business development, with a focus in global commercialization. She has worked with both Baxter and Monsanto/G.D. Searle as a member of senior management and is the past President of StreetWise, a leading advocacy group for the homeless and the largest North American Street Newspaper. In 2005, Dr DeBerry-Spence founded MASAZI®, a social venture operating in Ghana, West Africa. Currently she is on the Board of Directors of Royal Neighbors of America and a member of the Executive Committee of the UIC Senate. Dr DeBerry-Spence received a PhD in Marketing from the Kellogg School of Management at Northwestern University, an MBA from the University of Chicago and a Bachelor of Science from the University of Notre Dame.

Nikhilesh Dholakia is Professor of Marketing and International Business in the College of Business Administration at the University of Rhode Island (URI), USA. He is also a Fellow of caQtus collaborative, a poststructural research group based at University of Texas – Pan American (UTPA). Dr Dholakia's research deals with globalization, technology, innovation, market processes, and consumer culture. He is author of several books and his articles have appeared in, among other places, *Journal of International Management*, *Journal of Marketing*, *Journal of Marketing Management*, *Marketing Theory*, *Consumption Markets and Culture*, *Columbia Journal of World Business*, *Journal of the Academy of Marketing Science*, *European Journal of Marketing*, *Journal of Business Research*, *Journal of Interactive Marketing*, *Journal of Macromarketing*,

Journal of Electronic Commerce in Organizations, Electronic Markets and *Information & Organization*.

Delphine Dion is Assistant Professor at the Sorbonne Graduate Business School, France. Her current research projects explore luxury brand legitimacy, material culture and ethnicity. Her research has been published in the *International Journal of Service Industry Management*, *Recherche et Applications Marketing*, *Décisions Marketing*, *Revue Française de Gestion* and *Revue Française de Marketing*. Her last book *A la Recherche du Consommateur* received the 2008 best marketing book award.

Souad Djelassi is Assistant Professor of Marketing and Researcher at the Université of Lille Nord de France–Skema Business School, Francee. Her current research interests include waiting time, sales promotion misuse, budget arbitration and deviant consumer behavior. Previous research has examined the role of perception of time in retail choice behavior and the shopper relationship with time. Her research has been published in *Revue Française de Gestion*, *Revue Française de Marketing*, *Décisions Marketing* and in several congress proceedings.

Susan Dobscha is Associate Professor of Marketing at Bentley University, USA. Her current research focuses on three main areas: gender, sustainability, and anti-consumption. Recent work with the VOICE Group has focused on the transition of new mothers into motherhood. Her sustainability work examines the complexities of potential solutions to the global environmental crisis. Her work in gender has employed feminist theory to better understand issues such as wedding gown shopping and women's relationship to nature. Her research has been published in the *Journal of Public Policy and Marketing*, *Journal of Macromarketing*, *Consumption, Markets, and Culture*, *Qualitative Market Research*, and the *Harvard Business Review*.

Güliz Ger is Professor of Marketing and Director of the Center for Research in Transitional Societies at Bilkent University, Turkey. She has been a former president of the International Society for Marketing and Development and is a member of its Board of Directors. She serves on the editorial boards of various journals. Her research interests involve the socio-cultural and global dimensions of consumption and marketing, particularly in transitional societies/groups. Her recent projects include the acculturation in home furnishings of rural-to-urban migrants, historical origins of consumer culture in different geographies, and the relationship between a mundane practice such as tea-drinking and modernity and temporality. Her research has been published in the *Journal of Consumer Research*, *California Management Review*, *Journal of Economic Psychology*, *Journal of Consumer Policy*, *Journal of Public Policy and Marketing*, *Journal of Material Culture*, *Journal of European Ethnology*, and in various edited volumes.

Mary C. Gilly is Professor of Marketing at the Paul Merage School of Business, University of California, USA. Her research currently focuses on consumers and technology, internal marketing and cross-cultural issues in marketing. Professor Gilly's recent work on seniors' adoption of the Internet and her study of technology's role in the household decision-making of deployed naval personnel and their spouses has been supported with research grants. Her work on consumer-generated advertising has received a grant from the Marketing Science Institute (MSI) and includes the cooperation of a member company, P&G. Her research has appeared in the *Journal of Consumer Research*,

Journal of Marketing, Journal of Retailing, Journal of the Academy of Marketing Science, and other venues. Professor Gilly is active in her professional associations, having been President of the Academic Council of the American Marketing Association and currently the Academic Director for the Association for Consumer Research.

Silvia González Garcia is director of the Center for Retailing, and Professor of Marketing at Business School of ITESM, Monterrey, Mexico. Her research interest includes consumer decision-making, in particular in-store decision-making, customer satisfaction, and loyalty. She has been visiting professor in France, Peru, Chile, Guatemala, Honduras, and El Salvador. Her work has been published in the *International Journal of Consumer Marketing* and the *Advances of Consumer Research*. She is on the board of Centre d'Etudes et Recherche Amérique Latine-Europe in Paris.

Denis Guiot is Professor of Marketing and Research Director at Dauphine Recherche Management Center, University of Paris-Dauphine, France. He heads the Master of Research in Marketing and Strategy Program (first year PhD program). He has carried out research on the influence of time on consumer behavior. His current research projects explore alternative forms of consumption including the second-hand market and the use of virtual communities by consumers. Previous research has examined the challenges of marketing to senior consumers and young consumers which highlight the use of the subjective age concept to segment the elderly and the adolescent markets. Denis Guiot has advised theses and lead surveys for companies on these topics. His research has been published in numerous books and in the *Journal of Retailing*, *Psychology & Marketing*, *Advances in Consumer Research*, *Recherche et Applications en Marketing* (English edition), *Décisions Marketing*, *Sciences de Gestion* and *Management & Avenir*.

Gabriela Head earned her MBA from the University of Arizona's Eller College of Management, where she studied under Professor Hope Schau. Thanks to Professor's Schau's tutelage, Ms. Head became deeply interested in brand communities. This interest led Ms. Head to continue working with Professor Schau on the research of brand communities and with Dr Gaurav Bhalla on the research of Brand-Consumer value co-creation. She serves as Strategy Planer for [wire]stone, an international digital media agency, where she helps brands develop models in which they can engage their consumers via social media and gaming and identify co-creation opportunities.

Morris B. Holbrook is the recently retired W. T. Dillard Professor Emeritus of Marketing in the Graduate School of Business at Columbia University. From 1975 to 2009, he taught courses at the Columbia Business School in such areas as Marketing Strategy, Consumer Behavior, and Commercial Communication in the Culture of Consumption. His research has covered a wide variety of topics in marketing and consumer behavior with a special focus on issues related to communication in general and to aesthetics, semiotics, hermeneutics, art, entertainment, music, jazz, motion pictures, nostalgia, and stereography in particular. His books and monographs include *Daytime Television Game Shows and the Celebration of Merchandise: The Price Is Right* (Bowling Green University Popular Press, 1993); *The Semiotics of Consumption* (with Elizabeth C. Hirschman, Mouton de Gruyter, 1993); *Consumer Research* (Sage, 1995); *Consumer Value* (edited, Routledge, 1999); and *Playing the Changes on the Jazz Metaphor: An Expanded Conceptualization of Music-, Management-, and*

Marketing-Related Themes (Special Issue of *Foundations and Trends in Marketing*, 2008).

Dannie Kjeldgaard is Professor of Marketing at the University of Southern Denmark. Before joining academia he worked for four years in a London-based PR consultancy. Published in a numerous international journals and books, Dannie's work analyzes change processes of market-based glocalization in domains such as place branding, branding, media and identity construction, global consumer segments, body culture, ethnicity and qualitative methodology. His research has been published in the *Journal of Consumer Research*, *Journal of Consumer Behaviour*, *Consumption, Markets and Culture*, *Marketing Theory*, *Journal of Macromarketing* and in several anthologies.

Olga Kravets is Assistant Professor of Marketing at Bilkent University, Turkey. She holds a PhD from the University of Sydney, Australia. Her research interests lie with the historical, socio-cultural, and political aspects of consumption and markets in transitional societies. Her current research explores marketing practices in the Soviet Union and post-socialist Russia, and the intersection thereof with the state politics. Previous research examined materialities of branding and the dynamics of materiality and signification in brand iconization processes. Olga worked at A.C. Nielsen Australia, a market research company, and her research has been published in the *Journal of Material Culture*, *Advances in Consumer Research*, and an edited book.

Marius Luedicke is Assistant Professor of Marketing at the University of Innsbruck, Austria, and an interim Professor of Marketing at Witten/Herdecke University, Germany. His research focuses on consumer cultural myths, ideologies, and practices that pose socio-cultural barriers to progressive societal change. Topics under study include (un)sustainable consumption, brand-based discrimination, brand community conflict, and the dynamics of consumerist morality. His work has been published in academic outlets such as the *Journal of Consumer Research* and *Advances in Consumer Research*, and in international media including the *New York Times*, *Time Magazine*, and *Wired*.

Pauline Maclaran is Professor of Marketing and Consumer Research at Royal Holloway University of London, UK. Her research interests focus on cultural aspects of contemporary consumption, and she adopts a critical perspective to analyze the ideological assumptions that underpin many marketing activities. In particular, her work has explored socio-spatial aspects of consumption, including the utopian dimensions of fantasy retail environments, and how the built environment mediates social relationships. Her publications have been in internationally recognized journals such as the *Journal of Consumer Research*, *Psychology and Marketing*, *Journal of Advertising*, *Journal of Strategic Marketing* and *Consumption, Markets and Culture*. She has co-edited several books including *Marketing and Feminism: Current Issues and Research*, *Critical Marketing: Defining the Field* and the *Sage Handbook of Marketing Theory*. She is also Editor-in-Chief of *Marketing Theory*, a journal that promotes alternative and critical perspectives in marketing and consumer behavior.

Pierre McDonagh, PhD, is Senior Lecturer in Marketing at Dublin City University Business School and a Fellow of caQtus collaborative. He is best known for his work on Green Management and Advertising – in 1997 along with Andrea Prothero he edited one of the first texts on *Green Management: A Reader* with Dryden, now International

Thomson Business Press. In 1995, his three-act play "Q: Is Marketing dying of Consumption? A. Yes and the answer is consumption!" won the best paper at the Marketing Eschatology international gathering of marketers organized by Professors Brown, Carson and Bell at the University of Ulster. In 1997, he produced and directed "The Fable of Joseph the Pig Farmer," screened at the Marketing Illuminations Spectacular in Belfast, which provoked debate and controversy within the interpretive consumer research community. He has won the *Journal of Macromarketing* Charles C. Slater Memorial Award for best article in 1997–98. Pierre researches Sustainability Marketing and Consumption Studies. He has published in the *Journal of Marketing Management, Journal of Managerial Psychology, Greener Management International, Business Strategy & the Environment, Consumption Markets and Culture, European Journal of Marketing, Journal of Strategic Marketing, Built Environment, Journal of Euromarketing, Irish Marketing Review, Marketing Intelligence and Planning, International Journal of Contemporary Hospitality Management, British Food Journal* and the *Journal of Consumer Behaviour*.

Johanna Moisander, PhD, is Professor of Business Communication at Aalto University, Aalto School of Economics, Helsinki. She is also an active adjunct professor at the University of Helsinki, Department of Economics and Management, and the University of Lapland, Faculty of Business and Tourism. She has served as the president of the Finnish Association for Consumer Research (FACR) and as the Editor-in-Chief of the peer reviewed journal that FACR publishes. Her research interests center on cultural and practice-based approaches to business research, media studies, and qualitative research methodology. She has published, for example, in *Organization Studies, Organization, European Societies, Consumption, Markets & Culture, Management Decision, International Journal of Consumer Studies*, as well as *Business Strategy and the Environment*.

Sofie Møller Bjerrisgaard is Assistant Professor at Department of Marketing and Management, University of Southern Denmark. Her current research explores how marketplace realities of advertising practitioners are embedded in particular culture ideologies and enacted through practices of global market research. It adds to the understanding of markets as producer and consumer co-creation by focusing on the ideological orchestration and socio-historic conditioning of market research practices. Further projects are concerned with marketers' strategic use of the body in market communication in cultivating intimate relations between consumer and brands.

Philippe Odou is Assistant Professor of Marketing and Researcher at University Lille Nord de France, and SKEMA Business School, France. His main current research projects explore consumer resistance to marketing techniques: first, through defensive stereotyping and, second, through deviant practices within the marketplace. Previous research has examined the influence of national stereotype attached to brands. His research has been published in *European Journal of Marketing, Décisions Marketing, Revue Française de Marketing, Recherche et Applications en Marketing* and in several congress proceedings.

Jacob Ostberg is an Associate Professor at The Center for Fashion Studies, Stockholm University, Sweden, and holds a PhD in marketing from Lund University, Sweden. His current research projects explore discourses of masculinity in advertising and popular culture and how these discourses, alongside representations of class, are utilized in consumers' identity projects. Previous research has looked into consumers' handling of contrasting discourses of food and health as well as brands as cultural resources, and consumer tribes. His work has appeared in *Advances in Consumer Research, Consumption, Markets and Culture and Marketing Theory* as well as in several books. To capture the visual element of contemporary consumer culture he has worked with videography and presented award-winning films at the ACR film festival and in CMC.

Laura Oswald's areas of expertise include cross-cultural consumer research, brand strategy, and semiotics – a social science discipline that anchors sign theory in the culture of consumers. In her research and consulting practice she applies semiotics to advertising response theory, brand discourse, and cross-cultural consumption settings. Her research among Haitians in North America, blacks in the inner city of Chicago, and Chinese consumers in the French luxury market examines the role of meaning production strategies in consumer acculturation. Dr Oswald is currently conducting comparative ethnographic research among affluent consumers in Paris and Shanghai to determine the cultural variables underlying consumer perceptions of luxury brand advertising, and to identify the role of advertising in developing "brand literacy" among consumers in emerging markets. She has published in the *Journal of Consumer Research, Semiotica,* the *Journal of Marketing Communication, Advances in Consumer Research Design Issues, Poetics Today,* and the *Journal of Popular Culture.* Her second book, *Marketing Semiotics: Signs, Strategy, and Brand Value,* is forthcoming (Oxford University Press).

Nacima Ourahmoune is Assistant Professor in Marketing at Reims Management School (RMS, France). Prior to the PhD (ES SEC, Paris, France), Nacima obtained a MSc in Politics (IEP and Exeter Univ.), a MSc in Management (HEC Paris), a MSc in Research in Marketing (Paris 1 La Sorbonne Univ.) and an MBA focused on the luxury sector. Nacima was previously a consultant in strategy, and a marketer in the luxury industry in Paris. She contributes on a regular basis to various consultancy projects, using qualitative methods and bringing a cultural focus to managerial issues. Her academic research tackles socio-cultural aspects of consumption and of branding, especially the way masculinities are constructed by the fashion market and reshaped by consumers' discourses and practices. Her work has been presented in 15 international conferences and published in *Advances in Consumer Research.*

Julie L. Ozanne, PhD, is the Sonny Merryman Professor of Marketing at Virginia Tech's Pamplin College of Business, USA. Professor Ozanne specializes substantively in the area of transformative consumer research and on new forms of market exchange based on sharing. Her research has focused on the problems of poverty and health care access in rural Appalachia, the struggles of low literate adults in the marketplace, illegal consumption among juvenile delinquents, environmentally sensitive consumption, and consumer activism. She specializes in alternative methodologies for the study of social problems, such as interpretive, critical, feminist, and participatory action research methods. Her work has appeared in the *Journal of Consumer Research, Journal of Public Policy and Marketing, Journal of International Business Studies, Consumption, Markets & Culture, Journal of Marketing Management,* among others. She is co-editor of a new book, *Transformative Consumer Research for Personal and Collective Well-Being*.

Lisa Peñaloza is Professor of Marketing, EDHEC Business School, Roubaix and Nice, France. Her current research projects explore the intricate mix of cultural meanings of freedom, security, and national interest in the use of credit in the US white middle class, and the bittersweet impacts of remittances in Mexican families. Previous research has examined the challenges of ranchers and consumers maintaining cultural memories and traditions at a western stock show, the mutual market adaptation of Mexican immigrant consumers and retailers doing business in the US, and the development of urban community among subsequent generations of Mexican Americans. Her research has been published in the *Journal of Consumer Research*, *Journal of Marketing*, *Consumption, Markets and Culture*, *Public Policy and Marketing*, *International Journal of Research in Marketing*, *Marketing Theory*, *Journal of Strategic Marketing*, and the *International Journal of Sociology and Social Policy*.

Andrea Prothero is Associate Professor of Marketing at University College Dublin, Ireland. Prior to moving to UCD in 1999, Andy lectured at Universities in Wales and Scotland and she gained her PhD from the University of Cardiff. Andy's research broadly explores the area of Marketing in Society. Specific research projects have focused on, for example, advertising to children, motherhood and consumption, and sustainable consumption. The area of sustainability marketing has been a key focus of Andy's work since the early 1990s and she has published widely in this area. Andy was the Guest Editor of a special issue on Green Marketing in the *Journal of Marketing Management* in 1998 and she currently serves as Associate Editor for the "Global Policy and the Environment" Track for the *Journal of Macromarketing*, and as Associate Editor for the "Sustainability" Track for the *Journal of Marketing Management*. She has published in *Consumption, Markets and Culture*, *European Journal of Marketing*, *Journal of Business Research*, *Journal of Consumer Culture*, *Journal of Macromarketing*, the *Journal of Marketing Management* and the *Journal of Public Policy and Marketing*.

Simona Romani is Associate Professor of Consumer Behavior and Marketing at Department of Economics and Business, LUISS Guido Carli University in Rome. She does research in the field of consumption culture, branding and emotions. She has published in *Journal of Product and Brand Management*, *Journal of Brand Management*, and *Advances in Consumer Research*.

Dominique Roux is Professor at Paris-Sud. She is currently leading a project on "Information and communication to consumers" with the 17 French consumer organizations and was previously coordinator of the ANR/NACRE project (New Approaches to Consumer Resistance). Her main research area is consumer behavior, second-hand consumption and consumer resistance. She has studied the links between the self, used objects and their symbolic dimensions. This research field has been extended into the area of other alternative and controversial behavior in the marketplace. Her research has been published in the *Journal of Retailing*, *Advances of Consumer Research* (2005–11), *Recherche et Applications en Marketing* (English edition) and *Décisions Marketing*. She served as guest editor of a special issue on Anti-Consumption and Consumer Resistance of the *European Journal of Marketing* and as editor of the French book *Marketing et Résistance(s) des consommateurs* (2009, Paris: Economica).

Özlem Sandıkcı is Assistant Professor of Marketing at Bilkent University, Faculty of Business Administration, Turkey. Her research addresses socio-cultural dimensions of consumption and focuses on the relationship between globalization, marketing, and culture. Her current research projects explore the dynamics of the Islamic consumption-scape, identity-space-consumption interaction, and histories and stories of branding in emerging markets. She is the co-editor of the forthcoming *Handbook of Islamic Marketing*. Her work has been published in *Journal of Consumer Research*, *Journal of Business Research*, *Fashion Theory*, *Advances in Consumer Research*, *Place Branding and Public Diplomacy* as well as in several edited books. In 2003, she received The Franco Nicosia ACR Competitive Paper Award.

Hope Jensen Schau is an Associate Professor of Marketing and Susan Bulkeley Butler Fellow at the Eller College of Management, University of Arizona. She earned her PhD from the University of California Irvine. Her research interests are: the role of consumption and brands in consumer identity projects, collective consumption, collaborative value creation, technology and the marketplace, and the impact of new media on marketing communications and brand strategy. Her research has been published in journals including, the *Journal of Marketing*, *Journal of Consumer Research*, *Journal of Retailing*, *Journal of Advertising*, and *Journal of Macro-marketing*.

Avi Shankar is Senior Lecturer in Marketing and Consumer Research in the School of Management at the University of Bath, UK. His research interests focus on critiques of contemporary consumer culture, the dynamics of marketplace cultures and studies of identity and consumption. Examples of his work can be found in the *Journal of Consumer Research*, *European Journal of Marketing*, *Journal of Marketing Management*, *Feminism and Psychology*, *Marketing Theory and Consumption*, *Markets and Culture*. He recently co-edited with Bernard Cova and Robert Kozinets the ground-breaking bestseller *Consumer Tribes*.

Lionel Sitz is Professor at EM LYON Business School, France, and a member of the Center of Research OCE. His research revolves mainly about the articulation between brand strategy and consumer behavior with an emphasis on the communal and socio-cultural aspects of brand consumption. He is also interested in the resistance displayed by consumers, alone or in groups and by regional aspects of consumption.

Lorna Stevens is a Lecturer in Marketing at the University of Ulster. Prior to becoming an academic she spent ten years working in the book publishing industry in Ireland and the UK. Her work is primarily focused on feminist perspectives and gender issues in marketing and consumer behavior, with specific interest in experiential consumption, consumer culture and media consumption, particularly advertising and women's maga-zines. Her research adopts a qualitative, consumer-focused approach, drawing in particular on reader response theory and feminist literary theory. Whilst there is a consumer focus in her research, she also endeavors to address the wider social, cultural, historical and political aspects of our interactions with the marketplace. She has published her work in a range of journals in the field, including *Journal of Advertising*, *Journal of Strategic Marketing*, *Journal of Consumer Behaviour* and *Journal of Marketing Management*, and she is co-editor of *Marketing and Feminism: Current Issues and Research*.

Katherine A. Thompson is a 2009 graduate of the University of Arizona's Eller College of Management with a BSc in Business Administration and focus on marketing. She is currently working at a digital agency while pursuing a Master's degree in Business Administration and then potentially a PhD in Marketing. Her current research projects explore collective engagement, femininity, and consumer-generated content through the cultural phenomenon, The *Twilight* Saga. Her research interests include collective consumption, brand communities, nutritional advertising and perception of nutrition, integrated new media and consumer experience, and consumer-generated content. Her research has been presented at the Association for Consumer Research North American Conference.

Natalia Tolstikova teaches at the School of Business of Stockholm University, Sweden. She is also a Director of the Centre for Consumption Culture Studies at the Department of Marketing in the Stockholm University. Her research interests are Western and Soviet/Russian consumer cultures in historical perspective, visual culture, immigration and emigration studies, societies in transition, and media studies. Currently she works on the project studying how Russian immigrants in Sweden maintain identity through food consumption. Her chapter on Soviet media and consumption was published in *Marketing and Feminism: Current Issues in Research* (ed. by M. Catterall, P. McLaran and L. Stevens). Her research has been published in *Advances in Consumer Research* and *Journalism History*.

Simon Torp is Head of Department of Marketing and Management at the University of Southern Denmark and Director of Research in Strategic Communication Management. He has a PhD in Business Administration and a Master's degree in Philosophy and Organizational Culture and Communication. Simon has published articles on integrated marketing communications, leadership and management. He has acted as a consultant in the sphere of communication, management and intercultural understanding in Danish and international companies.

Nil Özçaglar Toulouse is Professor of Marketing at Université Lille North de France and Skema Business School, France. She currently leads a research project on Ethnicity and Consumption (Ethnos) that has been granted a two and a half year funding from the French National Research Agency (ANR). She is Visiting Professor at the Wuhan University – WTO (China). She primarily carries out research in the field of consumption, including analyzing consumer ethics, immigration, sustainable development and or promising niche markets such as fair trade. Her work has been published in *Décisions Marketing, Recherches et Applications – Marketing, Journal of Macromarketing, Journal of Business Ethics, International Journal of Consumer Studies, Advances in Consumer Research*, etc. She is also co-author of several books. She has also presented her research findings at international marketing conferences (ACR, EACR, CCT, AFM, AM). Nil is a co-founder and president of FairNESS (Network on Exchanges in Social Sciences) and a member of the ACR and AFM.

Mine Üçok Hughes is an Assistant Professor of Marketing at Woodbury University in Burbank, California. Dr Üçok Hughes aligns her academic work with the Consumer Culture Theory and her research interests include globalization, transnationalism, and transnational immigrants in relation to consumption. In her doctoral studies she examined the transnational immigrant phenomenon and studied the consumption practices of the transmigrants from Turkey to Denmark through a multi-sited ethnography. She has presented at various international conferences and has published mainly on the topic of transmigrant consumer research.

Anu Valtonen is Professor of Marketing at the Faculty of Social Sciences, University of Lapland, Finland. Her research interests relate to cultural theories and methodologies in consumer research and tourism research (cultural studies, practice theory, anthropology of consumption, sensory anthropology, new forms of ethnographies). Her current research projects explore embodiment, sleep, and senses in consumer culture, and weather in outdoor recreation. She has co-authored, with Johanna Moisander, *Qualitative Marketing Research: A Cultural Approach* (Sage, 2006). Her research has been published in *Annals of Tourism Research*, *Consumption, Markets and Culture*, *Tourist Studies*, and the *International Journal of Consumer Studies*.

Luca M. Visconti, PhD, is Associate Professor of Marketing at ESCP Europe, Paris. His interpretive research investigates the liberatory and/or marginalizing role of markets on consumers, including in particular first generation migrants, second generations, gays, Mediterranean consumers, and the elderly. Current research also deals with the consumption of public goods, and public space more specifically. Overall, his work deeply shares the concerns highlighted by Transformative Consumer Research in the way marketing research is called to improve its responsiveness and relevance for consumers also. His work has been published in several books, edited books, and book chapters as well as in journals, including the *Journal of Consumer Research*, *Journal of Advertising*, *Industrial Marketing Management*, *Journal of Business Research*, *Journal of Consumer Culture*, *Consumption, Markets and Culture*, and the *Advances in Consumer Research*.

Detlev Zwick is Associate Professor of Marketing at the Schulich School of Business, York University, Canada. His research focuses on cultural and social theories of consumption and the critical cultural studies of marketing and management practice. His works has been published widely in marketing, communication, media culture, and sociology journals, as well as in several edited collections. His book (edited with Julien Cayla), entitled *Inside Marketing*, is published by Oxford University Press. His current book project explores the role of marketing in the making of a culture of personal investing. He holds a PhD in Marketing from the University of Rhode Island, USA.

Preface

Dear readers, you are invited to join us in this pedagogical adventure. This book was launched in a café in Lille in the north of France where the three of us – Lisa, Nil, and Luca – were discussing the state of the art of teaching materials in the field of marketing. Over glasses of wine we talked about the headway made in consumer cultural theory (Arnould and Thompson 2005; see also Belk 1991 and Peñaloza, Moisander and Valtonen 2009, for a sense of the chronology of this burgeoning international intellectual community). Steadily, conceptualizations of meaning, desire, and value, and elaborations of their joint production processes in discourse and practice by consumers, marketers, and other stakeholders are providing valuable strategic insights and understandings regarding contemporary market development, with many more promising contributions to come!

We wish to thank many people, for their early work providing the foundations upon which we have assembled the current volume and for the support of many more colleagues and dear friends in making this endeavor possible. Thanks Mike Solomon (1991), since the early 1990s you've been making accessible interpretive research findings that document and comprehend cultural consumption and marketing activities, artifacts, and marketplace forms by drawing from the work of this loosely defined group of scholars and practitioners in the US spearheaded by the likes of Russell Belk, Elizabeth Hirschman, Morris Holbrook, Melanie Wallendorf, John Sherry, Grant McCracken, Fuat Firat, Alladi Venkatesh, and so many others, certainly more than we can mention here. Thanks, too, Eric Arnould, Linda Price and the late George Zinkhan (2002), for carrying this momentum forward in your consumer behavior texts through the first decade of 2000 that have featured second and third generation scholars including Craig Thompson, Douglas Holt, Linda Scott, Eileen Fischer, Julie Ozanne, Laurel Anderson, Rob Kozinets, Al Muñiz, and Hope Schau, again to name but a few. Journals have played and continue to play another vitally important role in fostering interpretive scholarship and practice. We thank Richard Lutz and Kent Monroe for enabling the early entry of interpretive work at the *Journal of Consumer Research*, and John Deighton for championing this work over the past decade in its pages and for bridging to marketing practitioners via the Marketing Science Institute. We express our gratitude to Bob Lusch for fostering the initial forays of interpretive scholarship in the *Journal of Marketing*; to Nikhilesh Dholakia, Fuat Firat, and Alladi Venkatesh for their innovative vision in anticipating the importance of culture in bridging across consumption and markets in *Consumption, Markets & Culture* and Jonathan Schroeder in continuing this important work there, and to Pauline MacLaran for her leadership at *Marketing Theory*. We also thank our publisher, Routledge, and the leadership of Stephen Brown and the late Barbara Stern. Over the years through your interpretive series you have published in book and monograph format so many of the European contributions that have provided an equally important foundation upon which interpretive consumption and market scholarship has flourished. Such pioneering scholars as Evert Gummesson, Dominique Bouchet, Richard Elliott, Pauline Maclaran, Güliz Ger, and Michelle Bergadàa have fostered streams of interpretive work on consumption and market phenomena in Europe. We especially thank all the contributors for their work and enthusiasm in pushing us far beyond our initial hopes and expectations. Without you this volume simply would not have been possible. In turn, a cadre of second, third, and fourth generation interpretive scholars, including many of the authors in this volume, form a critical mass contributing to this growing, world wide network of researchers who examine in-depth consumer and marketer interfaces, activities, and shifting balances of power within increasingly techno-commercial marketplaces across the globe.

We discussed the many opportunities and challenges in bringing interpretive, cultural perspectives and knowledge to marketing management and strategy classes for undergraduate and MBA students. In addressing these challenges and opportunities, we build upon the managerially oriented work of Grant McCracken (2005) and Douglas Holt (2004) that have provided intellectual foundations for redirecting consumer cultural scholarship from its home base in consumer research to marketing practice. Also helpful were the earlier edited books by John Sherry (1995; 1998), Janeen Costa and Gary Bamossey (1995), Robert Hefner (1998), and Michael Solomon (2003) that impressed upon us the importance of providing managers with cultural insights and specific tools for understanding consumers' priorities and life concerns. Edited volumes by Yoram Carmeli and Kalman Applbaum (2004), Michael Saren *et al.* (2007), and Marc Tadajewski and Douglas Brownlie (2008) have been helpful to us as well in strengthening our commitment to the development of critical approaches to marketing practice that maintain at the fore a sense of the impact of marketing activity upon consumers and cultures. Such approaches are ever more important as connections between consumers and marketers in markets and cultures become more tightly interwoven, even as maintaining a sense of their distinctions is critical in forging what we here call CMM, that is, Cultural Marketing Management.

Perhaps it was the French wine that emboldened us to act. Yet the timing was also crucial, as today work stemming from these interpretive, cultural approaches makes its way steadily from the field of consumer behavior into the mainstream of marketing strategy in academic courses as well as the carrels, offices, and boardrooms of businesses worldwide. Following in the rich tradition of cultural sensitivity in interpretive scholarship and giving concerted attention to the interests of multiple stakeholders in these pages, the authors grapple explicitly with the lucrative opportunities pursued by managers, as well as their most difficult challenges. Throughout our careers most of us have taken an active interest in examining what economists refer to as the negative externalities and imperfections of markets, finding here a rich field of material from which to glean valuable research findings and practical directives. Simply put, we become more effective learners and teachers when we orient our work around the social contract that is the foundation of firm legitimacy. In taking a discerning, challenging posture to marketing practice, markets, consumers, and other stakeholders in this book, we hope to foster in our students greater understanding regarding the many rewards, compromises, and hard choices dealt with by marketing managers.

Have we kept an edge in editing this book? We hope so. We believe the cultural approach offers distinct advantages and challenges as it is more fully leveraged in business school classrooms. With a few notable exceptions, interpretive consumer behavior and critical marketing research contributions have remained on the sidelines in the top selling marketing texts, tucked away in boxes of marketing insights/editorials in ways that support traditional ways of thinking and teaching marketing (Solomon 2008; Bagozzi and Ruvio, 2010). In bringing interpretive work to the front and center in this book, the authors question basic assumptions, perspectives, and fundamental concepts and techniques, such as relations between marketers and consumers, processes of organization and market development, and ways of conceptualizing and implementing marketing strategies. Its aim is to provide a robust toolkit with which to develop greater understandings of consumers and managers in the homes, neighborhoods and organizations which they inhabit, as impacting and impacted by market development. In consolidating and making more accessible interpretive, cultural concepts, approaches, and insights, we have sought to write this book with a minimum of academic jargon and illustrate it with photographs and rich excerpts from field study. Hopefully it will help enable readers – students, professors, practitioners, and others – to realize new possibilities in together envisioning and enacting a truly sustainable cultural marketing management.

References

Applbaum, Kalman (2003) *The Marketing Era: From Professional Practice to Global Provisioning*, New York: Routledge.

Arnould, Eric J., Price, Linda and Zinkhan, George M. (2002) *Consumers*, New York: McGraw-Hill.

Arnould, Eric J. and Thompson, Craig J. (2005) "Consumer Culture Theory (CCT): Twenty Years of Research," *Journal of Consumer Research*, 31(March), 868–82.

Bagozzi, Richard and Ruvio, Ayalla (eds) (2010) *The Wiley Encyclopedia of Marketing, Volume 3 Consumer Behavior*, New York: Wiley-Blackwell.

Belk, Russell W. (ed.) (1991) *Highways and Buyways: Naturalistic Research From the Consumer Behavior Odyssey*, Provo, UT: Association for Consumer Research.

Carmeli, Yoram and Applbaum, Kalman (2004) *Consumption and Market Society in Israel*, Oxford: Berg.

Costa, Janeen and Bamossey, Gary (eds) (1995) *Marketing in a Multicultural World: Ethnicity, Nationalism, and Cultural Identity*, Thousand Oaks, CA: Sage, pp. 209–30.

Hefner, Robert W. (1998) *Market Cultures*, Boulder, CO: Westview Press.

Holt, Douglas (2004) *How Brands Become Icons: The Principles of Cultural Branding*, Boston, MA: Harvard Business School Press.

McCracken, Grant (2005) *Culture and Consumption II*, Bloomington, In: Indiana University Press.

Penazola, Lisa, Moisander, Johanna, and Valtonen, Anu (2009) "From CCT to CCC: Building Consumer Culture Community," *Explorations in Consumer Cultural Theory*, Eileen Fischer and John Shery (eds) Routledge, pp. 7–33.

Saren, Michael, Maclaran, Pauline, Goulding, Christina, Elliott, Richard, Shankar, Avi, and Catterall, Miriam (eds) (2007) *Critical Marketing: Defining the Field*, London: Butterworth-Heinemann.

Sherry, John F. Jr. (1995) *Contemporary Marketing and Consumer Behavior: An Anthropological Sourcebook*, Thousand Oaks, CA: Sage.

—— (ed.) (1998) *ServiceScapes: The Concept of Place in Contemporary Markets*, Chicago, IL: NTC Business Books, pp. 591–617.

Solomon, Michael R. (1991) *Consumer Behavior: Buying, Having and Being*, Boston: Allyn and Bacon.

—— (2003) *Conquering Consumerspace: Marketing Strategies for a Branded World*, New York: American Management Association.

Tadajewski, Mark and Brownlie, Douglas (eds) (2008) *Critical Marketing: Issues in Contemporary Marketing*, New York: John Wiley & Sons.
Zwick, Detlev and Cayla, Julien (eds) (2011) *Inside Marketing*, Oxford: Oxford University Press.

Lisa Peñaloza, Nil Toulouse, and Luca M. Visconti
Boulder, Colorado, USA; Lille, France; and Milan, Italy, April 2011

Introduction

Lisa Peñaloza, Nil Toulouse, and Luca M. Visconti

Introduction

This book was put together by marketing professors – who are also marketing researchers, students, and practitioners – seeking to develop materials that make the cultural approach to market development more accessible. Our aim is to incorporate cultural skills and understandings more fully into the canon of pedagogical material available for MBA and undergraduate classes in marketing management and strategy. We do this now, twenty-plus years after rich and edgy interpretive studies first appeared in the top consumer behaviour and marketing journals, to help managers make sense of, and adapt to the unrelenting pace of global competition and financial market pressures amidst technological developments in production, distribution, services, and social media. Such technological, socio-cultural, and market developments in consumption and marketing practice and in the corporate and media landscape require that we call into question our basic marketing concepts and techniques. Such basic concepts as product development, pricing, distribution, and promotion made a lot of sense in a bygone era characterized predominantly by the distribution of material products by firms for their consumption by consumers. And yet each of these basic concepts requires radical rethinking when reconceptualized as the joint production of consumers, marketers, and other stakeholders. Even such core concepts as the marketing concept no longer make sense when consumer satisfaction is viewed as a collective, enacted accomplishment.

Because the cultural approach offers tools relevant to marketers in firms worldwide, we seek to further diffuse this work in places where marketing is taught, such as business schools, and where it is practised, such as marketing departments, advertising agencies, and consulting firms worldwide. The book is distinct among marketing management texts in bringing to the fore the importance of culture in marketing practice. In contrast, other MBA/undergraduate text and case books that make reference to culture do so by featuring it in a separate chapter at the end or by including culturally oriented consumer behaviour and marketing scholarship – often by many of the contributors to this volume – in boxes or cases on the sidelines. By bringing cultural work to the fore, this text conveys the concepts, ways of thinking, and skills at the levels required to carry out this work in research and marketing strategic development and practice.

To elaborate, most conventional marketing texts treat culture as an *influence on* consumption and marketing practice. Most typically, cultural differences in perception, attitudes, or values are used to explain differences in consumption and marketing decisions or choices. These perceptions, attitudes, or values are characterized as the essential basis for culture and understood as fairly universal qualities that determine consumption behaviour and marketing practice even as they vary somewhat across peoples and places.

Teaching students cultural variations in consumption and marketing phenomena across nations is both fascinating and entertaining. Yet doing so disseminates the misleading views that consumption and marketing activity are best comprehended as an *effect of* culture, and that culture is something that exists prior to, and apart from consumption and marketing practice. Following from these views are the directives to catalogue cultural values and attitudes and profile consumers as the best way of understanding consumer behaviour in order to develop "pure" forms of marketing strategy devoid of these cultural variations. The consequences of this traditional canon to managers are doubly serious in undermining the significance of cultural knowledge and capabilities inherent in consumption and marketing practices, and encouraging the development and implementation of marketing research and strategy that minimize these cultural distractions.

In contrast, the chapters in this book proceed from the view that culture pervades consumption and marketing phenomena. From this perspective it makes no sense to speak of cultural influences on consumption and marketing, as culture cannot be separated from either activity. These writings document the cultural forms inherent in what consumers and marketers say and do, and provide guidance enabling marketing students and managers to begin to unravel the joint cultural production by consumers and firms that comprises market activity.

Cultural marketing management operates as an assemblage of marketing techniques – product/service offerings, pricing, distribution, and promotion/communication – finely honed to specific cultural categories. Among the chief tasks for managers is to understand these cultural categories and the relational principles organizing them, with attention to how these cultural categories and relational principles are accorded economic valuation by consumers and marketers in tandem. Thus, these cultural categories and the relational principles organizing them become fundamental to consumption and to marketing practice as they work together in the development of markets.

This cultural marketing management text emphasizes the symbolic character of consumption and marketing. Culture is evident in consumers' use of foods in celebrating holidays and colours in home décor and national flags. For marketers, cultural conventions are recognizable in the words selected for brand names and the symbols comprising brand logos. The text employs various cultural concepts, techniques, and approaches in addressing the symbolic character of consumption and marketing. A key concept is culture, a term which we use to encompass the system of shared signs, meanings, activities, social relationships, and forms of organization of a group of people. In Chapter 1, Russell Belk uses the category of food to review the basic characteristics of culture. Such characteristics of culture include its shared and transmitted qualities and dynamism. Culture in this sense serves as a template for living and a lens through which people experience and make sense of their lives and the world around them. In Chapter 8, Laura Oswald explains additional terms useful in understanding literacy as a fundamental process in consumption and marketing. Key in such literacy is the knowledge and grammar of signs as the basic building blocks of the cultural systems sustaining consumption and marketing practice. Thus, attention is directed to how consumption and marketing signs convey meaning by referring to objects, ideas, persons, even other signs, and how they are interpreted as a relational system of conventions, practices, and rules.

The text also emphasizes the constitutive properties of culture. As we will see in the chapters that follow, consumers use cultural signs in the form of products, services, and brands to convey their sense of who they are, who they want to be, or not be, what's important to them, and how they relate to others. More subtle are the ways in which such consumption practices configure consumers, in orienting and structuring their lives. In turn, marketers use signs in developing products, advertisements, packages, places and logistics of distribution, etc., to appeal to consumers in providing them with important resources for living and to distinguish themselves from others. Such marketing practices narrow the field of what is available and possible for consumers. Together, consumers and marketers draw from and reproduce the cultural conventions and material that form the larger marketplace. Does that mean by emphasizing symbols and meanings, the cultural approach to marketing management is opposed to function? Absolutely not; we view function as symbolic activity. Knowing what product, service, or brand serves for what purpose, in managing identity and social relations or competing with other firms, falls well within the scope of this book.

One of the pioneers in recognizing the cultural nature of the marketplace was Sidney Levy in his article, "Symbols for Sale" (1959) that has become a classic in marketing. Another important contribution to this work was Dennis Rook (1985), who pointed out the importance to marketing managers of appreciating the ritualistic character of such consumption activities as grooming, preparing meals, and celebrating special occasions. Douglas Holt (2004) has contributed to the toolkits of marketing managers as well in detailing the cultural work in advertising in showing how brands tap into and articulate the myths and stories of cultural groups in ways that resonate with consumers by expressing their priorities, relations with others, and sense of being in the world. In another foundational work, McCracken (2005) posits the necessity of understanding culture to marketing managers, encapsulating meaning management as an increasingly important part of product development, pricing, promotion, distribution, etc.

Yet while important, meaning-making by consumers and marketers does not in itself make markets. Emerging work is drawing attention to transpositions between cultural meaning and economic valuation as the basis of markets (Callon *et al.* 2002; Cochoy 2008; du Gay and Pryke 2002; Peñaloza and Mish 2011; Zwick and Cayla 2011). For marketers, understanding the transpositions between cultural meaning and economic valuation must be seen as an essential strategic skill in developing markets.

Finally, we note the agency and power in such transpositions. The MasterCard series of advertisements proceed by listing items and their prices, suggesting that while some things are priceless, MasterCard is appropriate for everything else. We assert the importance to managers of developing marketing strategies more sensitive to those difficult personal, social, organizational, and environmental challenges in assigning an economic valuing to what is most difficult, even troubling, to value in monetary terms. Only by understanding how cultural meanings are valued economically and how economic value intervenes in cultural meaning-making as both become institutionalized in markets will we understand the intended and unintended "effects" of market development.

Extending from this emphasis on culture, the chapters in this text review fundamental marketing topics and strategic directives and modify them as appropriate to the cross-fertilization of cultural meanings and economic values by consumers and marketers in increasingly intense inter-relations, with attention to how these cultural meanings and economic values are negotiated and produced with various other stakeholders. Such modifications are carried through in ways of conceptualizing and implementing marketing strategies, in matters of organizational leadership, in processes of market development, and in the role of business schools in marketing pedagogy.

Another contribution of this book is to bring to the fore the importance of interpretive research methods. These methods, and the ways of thinking they are based upon, are valuable additions to the skill sets of managers in developing and implementing strategic marketing insights because they access fundamental cultural aspects of market phenomena inaccessible with other methods.

To detail the difference, most MBA and undergraduate marketing strategy texts rely upon and reinforce a canon of conventional content and perspective drawn predominantly from quantitative studies, in which market phenomena are divided up and compartmentalized into attitudes, perceptions, values, and needs, to examine their effects on other variables, such as motivations, decisions, and choices. Underlying these constructs is the explicit or implicit emphasis on cognitive activity as the most relevant determinant of the behaviour of consumers, marketers, and other market agents generally understood as relatively autonomous individuals.

While this all seems innocuous enough, it becomes a problem when students steadfastly proceed to deal with cultural differences in consumption and marketing activity as primarily a matter of cognition. Reducing culture to a cognitive attitude, value, or choice in turn reduces the strategic imagination and toolkit of managers. Instead, the chapters in this volume assert that developing culturally attuned marketing strategy requires understanding that culture operates in discourse and practice and forms the conditions upon which such cognitive concepts as attitudes, values, and choices are recognizable.

The interpretive approach utilized in these pages treats the marketplace as a collective system and gives emphasis to the cultural discourses and practices that stabilize and destabilize that system. In examining the elements and logic structuring the conditions of possibility for consumption and marketing discourse and practice, this approach illuminates the ways these logics produce consuming and marketing subjects, not as autonomous individuals, but rather as entities subject to these logics in intricate inter-relationships to each other. This approach further highlights the ways in which relations between consumers, marketers, competitors, and other stakeholders are forged and modified in the negotiation of cultural meaning and economic value in markets. Because interpretive work examines explicitly the intricate weavings of market agents and activities within global and local cultural domains, it is adeptly suited to contribute valuable understandings of how marketing managers and organizations develop effective courses of action as members of firms and industries, with consideration to pressing cultural concerns, such as social relations among groups, distribution of resources, and environmental wellbeing.

Each day managers are challenged in learning about and adapting to consumers and markets in developing appropriate marketing strategies. Cultural insights regarding market offerings, co-creation of value by consumers and marketers, consumer and organization identity, brand community, sustainable development, ethics, and market justice, to name a few, are invaluable in the development of practical tools and insights in meeting these challenges. While practical, the interpretive tools and cultural insights in the chapters that follow are innovative in calling into question assumptions and perspectives long accepted in the field regarding basic separations between consumers and marketers, and fundamental marketing topics such as the 4Ps of product, price, promotion, and distribution (place). Even marketing segmentation, targeting, positioning, and consumer satisfaction are necessarily revised in the increasingly interactive, service-dominated marketplace when we acknowledge that it is obsolete to comprehend marketing activity as something marketers do to consumers. While this book may not in itself change the climate of undergrad and MBA classes and business schools steeped so heavily in traditional ways of thinking, its chapters do offer the fresh views and concepts so badly needed by managers globally in dealing with economic uncertainty, cultural volatility, and political flux.

Scope and organization of the book

The book pairs each subject developed in marketing management books with persons, junior and senior, doing work in the area. The title, *Marketing Management: A Cultural Perspective*, encapsulates our goals to educate students and managers of the importance of culture in marketing management and what the interpretive approach to managing market development entails. Regarding format, in each chapter authors draw from their work in questioning definitions of seminal topics, strategic directives, and characteristics of marketers, firms, consumers, competitors, and their activities to help foster more culturally attuned understandings of market development.

The book is organized into five Parts: global-local cultural domains; consumer and marketer identity and community politics; researching consumers, marketers, and markets; refashioning marketing practices; and institutional issues in the marketing organization and the academy.

Part I overviews the characteristics and processes of a selected subset of global and local cultural domains inhabited by consumers, marketers, and market organizations. In particular, the chapters by Russell Belk; Güliz Ger, Olga Kravets, and Özlem Sandıkçı; Daniele Dalli and Simona Romani; and Delphine Dion and Lionel Sitz frame the overarching scenario for cultural marketing. By exploring the intricacy between global and local market cultures, they attribute new meanings and potentialities to marketing management. The chapters by Natasha Tolstikova; Benét DeBerry-Spence, Sammy Bonsu, and Eric Arnould; Judith Cavazos Arroyo and Silvia González García; and Laura Oswald contextualize cultural marketing to given geographical regions, including Latin America, Africa, and the post-Communist economies of China and Russia.

In Chapter 1, Belk overviews the importance of the cultural approach in surveying the breadth and depth of cultural differences in consumption and marketing practices by focusing on the food industry. Suggesting that foods are good to think, he elaborates the characteristics of culture relevant to marketing strategy and proceeds to track cultural dimensions of social class, age, gender, religion, and ethnicity distinguishing food consumption and to address consumption practices across a range of daily, holiday, and restaurant domains in showing how they unite and divide groups of people on matters of morality, health, safety, pleasure, profit, and politics.

In applying the cultural approach to international marketing strategy, in Chapter 2, Ger, Sandıkçı, and Kravets challenge the over-emphasis on similarities and differences and the oppositional logic directing standardized strategies to homogeneous cultures and prescribing adaptive strategies for heterogeneous cultures. Instead, these authors show that both local and transnational companies can be better off when integrating globalization with localism instead of framing them as opposite strategies. Drawing from the case studies of Green Mama cosmetics and Cola Turka as well as other examples, the authors discuss important insights to be gained in leveraging the cultural distance of the outsider and the intimate knowledge of insiders to better understand the play of the alluring foreign, the comforting local for status, community affiliation, nostalgia, and authenticity that come together as consumers negotiate domestic and international products and services.

Dalli and Romani's Chapter 3 elaborates cultural branding possibilities for firms, in a process they label locbalization. While geography often is treated as a universal influence related to climate or is reduced to country of origin effects of product location on consumer preferences, their work offers an account of how Camper has globalized local values and priorities. Majorca, Spain, is where brand consultant Shubhankar Ray leveraged the company's "mindstyle," its slower, more conscientious way of life oriented around people and place in building community, supporting livable wages for workers, and using energy and materials wisely in ways that have resonated among consumers worldwide otherwise living in the fast lane. Extending from Holt's (2004) work specifying the firm's reauthorization of myth markets, these authors question whether meanings for Camper are best understood as a myth or as a belief in meaningful work and consumption.

Dion and Sitz's Chapter 4 offers a veritable primer in strategically leveraging regional cultural resources that fall between the global and the local domain. Their work emphasizes culture as a toolkit for consumer identity and for firm's strategic use in market segmentation and positioning. Providing examples of distinct cultural signs and competencies in brands for a range of French firms in Alsace and Brittany, the authors highlight the creative and dynamic interactions of consumers and marketers not explained in terms of nationality or national origin, but rather more clearly understood in terms of joint learning and adaptation processes of acculturation, assimilation, resistance, and reappropriation.

The other chapters in Part I apply the cultural approach to specific geographical areas. The chapters emphasize emergent and post-communist markets including Russia, Africa, Latin America, and China.

Chapter 5 by Tolstikova builds cultural understandings of contemporary advertising practices by contrasting essentialist and constructivist conceptualizations of how culture "works" in advertising. The author presents the "Real Beauty" campaign by Dove soap in Russia, and invites students to explain and remedy its failure by applying the two approaches. In contrast to profiling national characteristics as guided by the work of Geert Hofstede, Tolstikova situates consumers' reception of the campaign in tracing the development of ideals of women's beauty from the Bolshevik revolution, through the Stalinist era, to present post-Soviet commercial developments.

Chapter 6 by DeBerry-Spence, Bonsu, and Arnould applies the cultural approach to market development in Africa. The authors contrast the cooperation, small-scale, and loosely coupled social networks characterizing vibrant market activity in this oldest of human civilizations with the privatization, economies of scale, and vertically integrated organization forms endorsed by liberal economic policies and they acknowledge the legacy of colonialism in the region. DeBerry-Spence, Bonsu, and Arnould provide several mini-cases demonstrating the importance of cultural understanding for the simultaneous development of consumer tastes and market infrastructure. Their argument is compelling in encouraging managers to direct attention to the particular patterning of consumption and production in leveraging local resources in the interest of both companies and social formations.

Cavazos-Arroyo and González García in Chapter 7 emphasize that cultural insights and approaches are imperative for organizations and managers in developing appropriate and effective marketing strategies in the Latin American region. The authors review some of the particularities of market development in Latin America, with attention to its blend of tradition, modernity, and postmodernity; its informal and formal distribution channels; reality of corruption in market infrastructure; and issues of identity, agency in consumer culture and offer strategic directives relating each to the strategic marketing concerns of distribution, market segmentation and targeting.

Finally, in Chapter 8, Oswald highlights important skills for managers in reading and manipulating cultural signs and meanings at the heart of developing marketing strategies for luxury products in China. She explains key concepts from semiotics regarding the structure and workings of cultural symbolism and contrasts this particular cultural approach to more conventional approaches emphasizing brand equity and value added. The author proceeds to carry out a brand audit comparing the meanings that the Chinese and the French assign to luxury products. Using these comparisons Oswald provides guidance to managers in gaining and applying cultural insights in advertisements and social media in facilitating consumers' brand literacy.

Part II focuses on the complex inter-relations forged by consumers and marketers in identity and community politics. This section features chapters by Jill Avery; Antonella Carù and Bernard Cova; Bernard Cova and Avi Shankar; Gabriela Head, Hope Jensen Schau and Katherine Thompson; and Søren Askegaard and Simon Torp.

Part II opens with Chapter 9 by Avery that provides an excellent overview of the cultural approach to consumers' relationships with brands. The author contrasts the explicit attention to the ways consumers employ brand meanings in consumer identity projects and socialization processes with the traditional focus in loyalty programs of evaluating consumers based on the economic resources they potentially generate for firms. Rather than "managing" customer relationships Avery counsels managers to become more conscientious of the ways they negotiate relationships with consumers to foster specific relationship building processes and formulate appropriate criteria in negotiating culturally appropriate rules that vary over the course of the relationship.

By viewing consumers as heroes in novels, in Chapter 10, Carù and Cova highlight the active role played by consumers in authoring their experiences and their skills and competencies in employing symbolic resources towards their identity and community projects. They contrast this cultural approach with a more conventional approach emphasizing consumer emotions and marketplace atmospherics. The authors expand upon work and pleasure as tyrannical and euphoric forces in consumers' lives and encourage managers to "guide" consumers and collaborate with them in jointly producing the market-social places they inhabit.

In Chapter 11, Cova and Shankar elaborate the phenomenon of tribes as a key concept in comprehending consumption and brand community. Tribes include communities but entail a more diffused and loosely organized social formation, since they are not necessarily built around a given brand or even consumption. The authors provide explicit guidelines to managers to reformulate their segmentation strategies in ways that account for the collective, competent, and empowered subject represented by tribes. Rather than using demographic information to define and determine market segments, Cova and Shankar caution managers to instead use demographic information to facilitate media webs of collective creativity and to address the ongoing challenges of authenticity for these consuming groups in developing marketing strategies that help members deal with these challenges.

Head, Schau, and Thompson go in depth in Chapter 12 into the workings of the brand communities that have formed around the *Twilight* book series in drawing important lessons for managers. These authors emphasize the strategic marketing activity of developing themes in the books that provide ample means for readers to connect with the author and with other readers in expressing key issues in their lives. As such, the *Twilight* community accounts for the role of consumption and brands in elaborating social ties, gender identities, and intimate relationships in collective narratives that transcend the narrow confines of the market.

Finally, in closing the section on identity and community, in Chapter 13, Askegaard and Torp detail the cultural challenges in corporate brand management in balancing the identity concerns of consumers with those of employees and managers in the organization. The authors track the transition of the Kjær Group, a Danish company that has had an impact worldwide in delivering transportation services in times of environmental disasters, in their shift from Maslowian notions of culture based on the hierarchy of individual needs to more collectively and collaboratively attuned concerns regarding organizational identity and community.

Part III elaborates distinct techniques of interpretive consumer and marketer research. Interpretive research methods are the hallmark of cultural strategic marketing insights, and it is important to note that each of the methods follows from distinct ways of thinking, distinct philosophies. Chapters by Sofie Møller Bjerrisgaard and Dannie Kjeldgaard; Johanna Moisander and Anu Valtonen; Samantha Cross and Mary Gilly; and Julie Ozanne and Laurie Anderson elaborate distinct interpretive processes, with attention to how these various methods generate insights for marketing strategy.

In Chapter 14, Møller Bjerrisgaard and Kjeldgaard lead off this section by updating conventional understandings of the ways research informs marketing strategy by emphasizing the ways research methods structure their findings and define strategic possibilities. The authors contrast the strategic insights produced with the cultural approach and the interpretivist/constructivist philosophy guiding it with those insights produced with the functional approach and the positivist/logical empiricist philosophy guiding it. The authors guide readers through the case example of SignBank in detailing the symbolic processes, interactions, and experiences between customers and firms that result from cultural marketing research in comparison to the cognitive thoughts and decisions that characterize functionalist research findings, and they show how such cultural insights are useful in reformulating marketing strategies to feature greater understandings of the ways consumers experience products and services in their lives.

Moisander and Valtonen, authors of the book *Qualitative Marketing Research*, explicate the strategic marketing use of the cultural research technique of ethnography in Chapter 15. They discuss the importance of exploratory, data-driven research that taps into collective ways of thinking and acting regarding consumption phenomena in naturally occurring settings in deriving resonant and actionable marketing strategies. In detailing the conduct of such methods in examples of branding and coolhunting, the authors emphasize: the immersion of researchers in the field in bricks-and-mortar and online settings for observation and participation with those under study, attention to relevant cultural priorities and patterns of daily life surrounding the consumption or market phenomena of interest, and the use of structured and unstructured interviews in deriving marketing strategies from explicit, practical cultural knowledge of consumers and marketers.

Cross and Gilly detail the nature of innovative cultural research in Chapter 16. The authors review a rich array of examples and provide practical guidance for each in data collection, analysis, and in developing innovative marketing strategies. They also provide some examples of innovative multi-method marketing research and discuss the advantages and challenges in combining different methods.

Ozanne and Anderson close Part III in providing a useful overview of action research in Chapter 17. This work traditionally has been used for social intervention, as the authors note, and its attention to social formations, such as tribes and communities, and priorities such as sustainability and well-being render it useful to firms seeking to collaborate with consumers. The chapter details the action research processes of setting agendas and developing solutions with various interest groups, and the data collection and analysis techniques of oral history, collage, web, and photovoice, in generating collaborative, action-oriented consumer and marketing insights.

Part IV explicates the use of the cultural approach in specific marketing strategic techniques. Chapters by Luca M.Visconti and Mine Üçok Hughes; Marius Luedicke;

Domen Bajde; Philippe Odou, Souad Djelassi, and Isabelle Collin-Lachaud; Nacima Ourahmoune; Amina Bécheur and Deniz Atik; Lorna Stevens and Jacob Ostberg; Stefania Borghini, Pauline Maclaran, Gaël Bonnin, and Veronique Cova; Dominique Roux and Denis Guiot; Detlev Zwick and Nikhilesh Dholakia bring interpretive, culturally focused perspectives to bear in rethinking basic marketing techniques including segmentation, pricing, product design, advertising, positioning, retailing, sales promotion, and database marketing.

Part IV opens with a thoughtful essay by Visconti and Üçok Hughes on market segmentation and targeting in Chapter 18. The authors question the traditional assumptions of market segmentation, and observe how customers' belonging to multiple cultural milieux jeopardizes the stability of market targeting efforts. Drawing from their research on migrants' market adaptation in the US and Europe, the authors contrast various examples of ethnic targeting both from the US and Europe. The authors conclude that the cultural perspective suggests considering the multiplicity of cultural ties each consumer holds as well as the implications for segmentation put forward by environmental, political and social forces.

In Chapter 19, Luedicke focuses on the ways managers must consider deeply rooted cultural meanings cutting internal and external to brand communities in positioning brands. This cultural approach contrasts with the traditional, individually oriented demographic measures used to profile consumers and position brands. Drawing from his field and net research on Hummer vehicles, the author details the advertising trajectory of this American icon, from the hypermasculine emphasis of the H2 on militarism, rugged security, sophistication, and individual achievement, to the H3, targeting women. Brand positioning turns bad, the author warns, when not attuned to cultural sentiments and contradictions. In the case of Hummer, the company abandoned successful strategic positioning efforts that tapped into the American national identity and adopted humorous appeals that treated all too lightly the state of war of the country, and overlooked seeming contradictions between free choice, unfettered self-expression, and benevolent good guys.

Establishing the cultural foundations for price as a culturally accepted way of measuring and formalizing the value in market exchanges, in Chapter 20, Badje questions well-established truisms in the field that price is the only marketing mix element that produces revenue, and points to the implications in such thinking that limits managerial practice to short term profit maximization. Instead Badje advances a holistic understanding of price that emphasizes its role with other elements in the marketing mix in co-creating value, and directs attention to the ways price strategies draw from and impact consumers' access to products and services, their social relations, and on more general resource allocations in societies.

In Chapter 21, Odou, Djelassi, and Collin-Lachaud direct attention to cultural dimensions of sales promotion. Highlighting consumers' negative reactions and associations of such programs with feeling tricked or manipulated, the authors provide guidelines for managers featuring alternative representations of the consumer to yield more dignified, intelligent relations with consumers and accomplish more trustworthy sales promotional programs.

In Chapter 22, Ourahmoune discusses cultural aspects of product design. Drawing from her research into HOM men's underwear, the author educates students and managers on the importance of balancing the dual priorities of function and meaning in pointing to distinct styles and meanings. She shows how product design is not only a matter of aesthetics or functionality, but also the company's ability to enter a cultural discussion on consumption and the brand. In so doing, marketers should be able to involve their customers in the co-creation and co-design of the product.

Bécheur and Atik, in Chapter 23, generate insight into product development by taking a cultural perspective on the diffusion of innovations. Drawing attention to social norms, customs, and social relations, these authors document culturally specific practices not addressed in cognitive models of trial, adoption, and attitude change. They show that interagency, that is, the collective participation of multiple actors – designers, consumers, engineers, distributors, etc. – is key in innovating, and they elaborate important cultural skills in anticipating, even bringing about social change in diffusing innovations. The authors conclude that viewing innovation as culturally embedded better explains and enables successful inventions.

In Chapter 24, Stevens and Ostberg approach advertising as a cultural artifact and activity, as compared to more traditional, cognitive perspectives emphasizing the presentation and processing of information for problem solving. Seeking to attune students and managers to the inherently cultural character of advertising, the authors explain gender representations in terms of Cartesian dualistic thinking and historical patterns of specialization and division of labor in the family. They provide several examples of ad campaigns to show the pervasive social constructions of gender in images of masculinity and femininity, in portrayals of sexual desire, and in legal limits defining what is pornographic. In charting complacent and subversive strategic options for managers in proceeding from the cultural or traditional approach, the authors demonstrate that advertising is not culturally neutral. Rather, it stands as a powerful, agentic element that draws from and shapes people's sense of themselves and of others, as consumers and beyond in reproducing social relations.

Borghini, Maclaran, Bonnin, and Cova address the cultural intricacies of marketplace design in Chapter 25. These authors trace the historical background of contemporary imagination-provoking, experience-oriented places including the Prada Epicenter in New York and Mama Shelter in Paris. Turning to contemporary marketplace design, the authors emphasize the importance of adapting retail store and mall design to changes in the social landscape regarding identity and social interaction and note that these very same marketscapes alter such social relations.

Roux and Guiot elaborate cultural aspects of retailing in Chapter 26. Providing a brief history that links changes to retail sites to changes in consumption and shopping, these authors situate the development of second-hand retailers within the larger trajectory of retail market development. They identify four profiles of consumers for second-hand markets, and trace connections between traditional and emergent forms of retailing in developing managerial guidelines applicable for all retail formats.

In the last chapter in this section, Zwick and Dholakia emphasize cultural aspects of database marketing. These authors detail marketers' production of consumers in contemporary database marketing practices in a complete reversal of how segmentation and targeting have been taught. Instead of seeking to know consumers as they are, to profile them and tailor products to them, marketers use databases to track and model changes in consumers' purchase patterns, lifestyle preferences, and psycho- and socio-demographics, and to make sense of these changes in developing ongoing relationships with consumers regarding various products and services.

The final section, Part V, addresses institutional issues in the marketing organization and the academy. Chapters feature Susan Dobscha, Andrea Prothero, and Pierre McDonagh on sustainability and retailing; Nil Toulouse on sustainable development; Morris Holbrook on consumer orientation and experiential marketing in the business school; and Lisa Peñaloza on ethics and credit. While cultural insights are useful in understanding and developing successful marketing strategies at the level of individual consumers and for the households, organizations, and communities in which they inhabit, students and managers benefit as well in appreciating macro, institutional perspectives on market development.

In Chapter 28, Dobscha, Prothero, and McDonagh address a relevant missing element in the retailing discussion, that is, reverse logistics. The authors show that traditional companies and retailers do not take into account what happens to products after their purchase. Relying on an extensive set of empirical exemplifications, they describe various forms of consumer-driven innovations in distribution and contrast emerging consumer-citizens and their politics with more traditional notions of the consumer and producer–middlemen– consumer channels. By means of The Inverted Pyramid of Sustainability (TIPS), they list and contrast several forms of product disposition that constitute a more environment-friendly alternative to throwing away.

In Chapter 29, Toulouse documents how the sustainable market is traditionally seen by companies. Because a segment of consumers views sustainability as important, and because this market is judged to be really attractive, companies are involved in sustainability in order to improve their profitability. Based on her case study of fair trade in France, the author details the institutional challenges involved in developing sustainable markets. This chapter proposes that managers see sustainable development as a social construct from the viewpoint of social legitimacy.

Reflecting on a successful career as one of the most published scholars in the field after retiring from one of the nation's premier business schools, in Chapter 30, Holbrook works to set the record straight regarding the adoption of, ironically, some of his own work on experiential marketing and consumer orientation as the basic business plan in teaching marketing. Attributing the emphasis on business interests and "satisfying" customer-students to the resulting myopic focus in business schools on entertainment, camaraderie, and credentials over intellectual excellence and curiosity, the author cautions that such problems hamper firms' efforts as well. Because providing stimulating learning materials that challenge marketing and consumer behavior concepts and practices is the purpose of this book, we are well advised to heed Professor Holbrook's musings in our classrooms!

Finally, in Chapter 31, Peñaloza elaborates characteristics of cultural market ethics in ways that build upon previous work on ethics in marketing. The chapter reviews the definition of ethics, distinguishes it from laws and highlights ethical issues for specific marketing activities. It then elaborates the cultural approach to ethics in discussing the importance of representation, discourse and practice, and in emphasizing the importance of multiple actors in various fields within an overall market system. The chapter closes with a case study of the financial crisis in the US, in providing various perspectives, agents, and institutions and inviting students to take a position and do more than role "play" to actively participate in the ongoing and collaborative determination of market ethics.

References

Callon, Michel, Méadel, Cécile and Rabeharisoa,Vololona (2002) "The Economy of Qualities," *Economy and Society*, 31(2): 194–217.

Cochoy, Frank (2008) "Calculations, Qualculation, Calqulation: Shopping Cart Arithmetic, Equipped Cognition, and the Equipped Consumer," *Marketing Theory*, 8(1): 15–44.

du Gay, Paul and Pryke, Michael (eds) (2002) *Cultural Economy*, London: Sage.

Holt, Douglas (2004) *How Brands Become Icons: The Principles of Cultural Branding,* Boston: Harvard Business School Press.

Levy, Sidney (1959) "Symbols for Sale," *Harvard Business Review*, July–August: 117–24.

McCracken, Grant (2005) *Culture and Consumption II*, Bloomington, IN: Indiana University Press.

Peñaloza, Lisa and Mish, Jenny (2011) "Leveraging Insights from Consumer Culture Theory and Service Dominant Logic: The Nature and Processes of Market Co-Creation in Triple Bottom Line Firms," *Marketing Theory*, 11(1): 9–34.

Rook, Dennis (1985) "The Ritual Dimension of Consumer Behavior," *Journal of Consumer Research*, 12(December): 251–64.

Saren, Michael, Maclaran, Pauline, Goulding, Christina, Elliott, Richard, Shankar, Avi, and Catterall, Miriam (eds) (2007) *Critical Marketing: Defining the Field*, London: Butterworth-Heinemann.

Zwick, Detlev and Cayla, Julien (eds) (2011) *Inside Marketing*, Oxford: Oxford University Press.

Part I

Global–local cultural domains

1 Cultures, consumers, and corporations

Russell Belk

Overview

When a product or service marketer attempts to market in different cultures, there is inevitably the question of whether to attempt localized versions of its offerings as opposed to more standardized global offerings. There is no fixed answer to this question, but it should always be based on an understanding of local cultures. This chapter uses the example of food consumption to illustrate the way in which a cultural (interpretive) perspective can help inform these decisions. It introduces some key concepts such as cosmopolitanism, sacrifice, and prestige, as well as some key cultural considerations such as class, gender, age, and religion to help in analyzing the effect that marketing offerings are likely to have in different cultures. And it shows how an interpretive approach to researching and understanding markets provides a more informed and complete understanding of food preferences.

In early 1999, construction began on a fast food outlet in Mutare, Zimbabwe. Local residents looked forward to the store with great anticipation. A rumor was widely circulated that it was to be Zimbabwe's first McDonald's restaurant – a possibility that was eagerly and hopefully embraced because it would mean that Zimbabwe had arrived. It was believed that McDonald's employed a formula that calculated a country's economic development and that a certain level had to be reached before McDonald's corporate headquarters would entertain selling a franchise. When it turned out that the fast food outlet was instead a Nando's – a Portuguese chicken chain from South Africa – the disappointment was palpable. This was in spite of the fact that chicken is more common in Zimbabwean diets than beef, although both were a stretch from the local staple of a white corn mash called sadza that is normally served with greens and condiments like tiny dried kapenta fish.

The would-be welcome of McDonald's in Zimbabwe contrasts sharply with the restaurant's reception in many other parts of the world. Schlosser (2002: 243–4) records some other global activity involving McDonald's during the same time period:

1995   400 Danes loot a McDonald's in downtown Copenhagen.
1996   Indian farmers ransack a McDonald's in Bangalore.
1997   A McDonald's in Cali, Colombia, is destroyed by a car bomb.
1998   Bombs destroy two McDonald's in St. Petersburg, Russia, and one in Rio de Janeiro.
1999   Belgians set fire to a McDonald's in Antwerp and more than a dozen McDonald's are attacked in Beijing.
2000   Protesters destroy a McDonald's in London's Trafalgar Square.

It is evident from these very divergent examples of embracing and rejecting the American fast food chain McDonald's that there is something very basic about global foods to precipitate such strong reactions. Yet looking inside most textbooks on marketing management and strategy and searching for the topics of food and eating produces very little on this. Perhaps there is an account of food labeling requirements in the EU or a study by the Food Marketing Institute of how consumers move through a supermarket. Maybe there is a nod to ethnicity being a relevant segmentation variable in various food product categories. But we learn nothing of the role that food plays in our lives, what it symbolizes, the roles that fine dining and family meals play in socializing, the meanings that local and global foods hold for us, or the impacts of consumer movements like vegetarianism, slow food, or the 100-mile (kilometer) diet (consisting of only locally grown foods in order to avoid the environmental and economic cost of transshipping). Interpretive consumer research has a great deal to say about these and related topics.

This chapter takes an interpretive or cultural approach and uses food as a context in which to better appreciate how considerations of the global and the local should influence strategic and tactical international marketing management. This approach differs from non-interpretive approaches to understanding culture, because rather than quantitative survey research, it uses qualitative observations, ethnography, and depth interviews to provide a richly textured understanding of the influences of culture. An example of the alternative survey-based approach to culture and consumption is a book by Marieke de Mooj (2004) called *Consumer Behavior and Culture*. She attempts to understand consumption of eating and other consumption patterns by correlating national consumption levels of various products with measures of four cultural values: power distance, individualism/collectivism, masculinity/femininity, and uncertainty avoidance, following Hofstede (1991). Thus, we are told, for instance, that people consume more soft drinks in masculine cultures like the US and the UK and people drink more tea in high uncertainty avoidance cultures like Japan and China. The objective of the present interpretive chapter is to provide a richer approach to understanding how culture – including rituals, symbols, hierarchies, and norms (Geertz 1973) – influences our everyday consumption behavior. Such knowledge can be of enormous use to marketing managers in understanding how to market globally.

Because food consumption is a critical component of culture and national identity, it is an important context in which to consider how marketing strategies, globalization forces, and consumers influence one another, our environment, and human well-being. That is, what we put on our table has a great deal to say about how culture, consumption, and corporations interact in today's world and what sorts of issues we might think about in buying, selling, and regulating trade in a global context.

Food for thought

> Food and eating have become prominent topics in social research. According to a recent appraisal, one could argue that the anthropology of the second half of the twentieth century was practically founded on food studies, with Lévi-Strauss's *The Raw and the Cooked* (1969/1983) and *The Origin of Table Manners* (Lévi-Strauss 1978/1990) occupying pride of place.
>
> (Farquhar 2006: 147)

Food and beverage taste preferences are not primarily biological or universal. Our tastes and distastes are instead largely a matter of culture (Wilk 1997). We begin to learn these preferences as children and they become deeply ingrained in our notions of home, family, and personal as well as group identity (Lupton 1996). It is no surprise that ethnic and regional foodways have been characterized as "the performance of group identity" (Brown and Mussell 1984; Swislocki 2008). The foods we eat are like the language we speak in distinguishing "us" from "them." Just as we can learn another language or marry someone who speaks a different language, we can learn to like other foods or marry someone from a different food culture. But generally speaking, our initial food culture is like our mother tongue in that it feels natural and totally comfortable. When children are adopted from another culture, their new parents often try to make them familiar with food from their culture of birth (Bergquist 2006), as if not doing so would deprive them of a birthright. When immigrants lack the language of their birth culture, food can become the primary sign that identifies their cultural and group identity (Mankekar 2002; Threadgold 2000). In other words, food is not only good to eat, it is good to think with (Tambiah 1969). It is constitutive of our identities. Sharing food forges and reinforces bonds with family, friends, and neighbors, while being excluded from such sharing, especially during ritual holiday meals, is a mark of otherness (e.g. Shuman 2001).

Beyond actual exclusion, food likes and hates help to distinguish group membership based on tastes. Wilk (1997: 185) gives four examples based on food preferences:

1   Like/inclusion – We like red beans.
2   Like/exclusion – They like black beans.
3   Dislike/inclusion – We hate black beans.
4   Dislike/exclusion – They hate red beans.

Thus, what we hate can be as powerful a basis for group boundaries as what we love. So strong can these aversions be that the thought of certain foods that are perfectly acceptable to others can provoke feelings of revulsion and disgust (Miller 1997; Pillsbury 1998; Rozin and Fallon 1987). Moreover, it is not only cultures that have different tastes. Groups can also form as consumption communities that share food tastes and distastes. Prominent examples includes vegetarians (e.g. Twigg 1983; Fiddes 1991), health food aficionados (e.g. Thompson and Troester 2002; Warde 1997), and opponents of genetically modified foods (e.g. Paarlberg 2000). Such taste cultures can also form around particular brands, as with lovers and haters of Starbucks (e.g. Roseberry 1996; Thompson and Arsel 2004).

Other symbolic aspects of food consumption encode meanings related to more structural variables like gender and class. Although there are cultural differences in what is regarded as masculine, feminine, high class, or low class food (e.g. Farquhar 2002; Feirstein and Lorenz 1982; Goody 1996; Wu and Chee-beng 2001), the ability of food, beverages, and eating habits to make statements about gender and class is widespread. Bourdieu's (1984) study of cultural capital in France acknowledges the role of eating in distinguishing the refined and distinguished from the common and vulgar. These traits of people are directly reflected in food choices that are light, refined, and delicate versus heavy, fatty, and coarse. Levy (1981, 1986) finds similar class-based patterns in American food and beverage choices and describes further distinctions that can be detected with regard to differing preferences according to gender and age. For example, food and beverages that are bitter rather than sweet, consumed in small quantities rather than large quantities, and that are intense in flavor rather than bland, are found in Levy's American studies to be associated with higher social class, older, male consumers. Not only is what we eat or drink important, but where and how

concern with purity meant that they would not cook rice and cakes in the same rice cooker. They failed again. Purity is an important cultural category in cultures like those of Japan and India. And like most food rules and taboos, it is culturally inscribed and highly salient (Douglas 1966).

Our focus on food as an expression of culture is especially evident in holiday feasts and on other special ritual occasions. As Farb and Armelagos (1980) emphasize, the foods on such occasions should be scarce, expensive, and take time to prepare. These luxury foods are not arbitrary, but there are differences between cultures, regions, religions, and families as well as further differences according to age and gender (Wallendorf and Arnould 1991). While drinks are a part of feasting, it is the sharing of food (in abundance and with a prescribed order of dishes) that more closely binds those at the table. It is perhaps for this reason that beverage consumption has homogenized more within Europe than have diets (Smith and Solgaard 2000). As Mary Douglas puts it, "Drinks are for strangers, acquaintances, workmen, and family. Meals are for family, close friends, honored guests" (1972: 66). Inclusion and intimacy are strongly symbolized in holiday meals, where exclusion and distance mark the Other. According to Lévi-Strauss (1969), the sharing of food is the most significant process in human evolution after the sharing of women between families. The two are not unrelated, however, as the preparation of meals in the home, whether everyday food or holiday food, is still largely the domain of women (e.g. Wallendorf and Arnould 1991; Warde 1997).

So food both unites and divides us. Not only how and what we eat, but how and what we do not eat may signal our nationality, ethnicity, gender, age, class, personality, and sophistication. Because prominent foods like McDonald's hamburgers and French wines are so emblematic of culture, they can become a target for protests and boycotts that are ultimately directed at their nations' political ideologies and actions. The cuisine of any group is never static, however. The changes in eating patterns brought about, in part, by global foods and restaurants may be resisted, but they are more often incorporated, creolized, bracketed (i.e. marked as "foreign"), and ultimately accepted. We might well ask how rising consciousness of the healthiness of food will affect future food consumption practices around the world and why, in spite of these trends, unhealthy fast food consumption continues to grow, especially in rapidly economically developing countries.

Food, pleasure, and pain

On the surface, our indulgence in global foods, whether through culinary tourism, through the patronage of ethnic and foreign restaurants, or in our daily meals at home, can be thought of as the playful pursuit of cosmopolitanism (Cheah and Robbins 1998; Thompson and Tambyah 1999). When we pursue "sophisticated" French food or Belgian chocolates, this may indeed be an apt description (e.g. Basil and Basil 2009; Wooliscroft and Ganglmair-Wooliscroft 2009). But when we seek out the "primitive" as with African-American soul food or Ethiopian cuisine, we may be engaging in commodity racism or what bell hooks (1992) calls "eating the Other." For this and other reasons, food has a long history of being read as part of a moral discourse (Coveney 2000). As Tiger puts it:

> Surrounding food is an endless battle involving pleasure, calories, vanity, the fear of early death, lust for taste, and sociability. It has come to seem ever more theological, particularly in North America. The higher the death rate from food-induced diseases goes and the more rampant becomes the information about the extermination model of

food, the more pervasive is the explicit conflict between meat and morality and between pleasure and prudence. Traditional supermarket products such as pastas irrelevantly boast that they are cholesterol- and sodium-free.

(1992: 179)

While the health and weight-related concerns in Tiger's account may be relatively recent, the emphasis on pleasure was certainly a part of ancient feasts like those of the Romans and Greeks. But even then, food was part of a moral discourse. Visser (1991) notes that between dinner and drinks at an ancient Egyptian feast, a wooden corpse in a coffin was carried around to remind diners that they were all too mortal. But like the *memento mori* (e.g. skulls, flickering candle flames) in seventeenth-century Dutch still life paintings (see Bryson 1990), these reminders of death may have introduced a more somber tempering of pleasures, but they did not raise nutritional issues. As Coveney (2000) documents, such health concerns did not arise until the nineteenth century in the West. The concern with nutrition and health arose for several reasons. People began to have more choice in what to eat. With curbing of most infectious diseases like tuberculosis in the West, attention began to turn to chronic diseases like heart disease, diabetes, and cancer. With greater affluence and more sedentary lifestyles, people started to become more obese. And with the rise in processed branded foods, diets once rich in local foods that had sustained people in "eating regimes" of the past (Giddens 1991) began to give way to less nutritious "risky" foods in terms of health consequences.

A case in point is the twentieth-century changes that have taken place in the diet of Mexico. Pilcher (2002) details how a combination of global food brands and local cuisine – a hybridized mix that he calls "half-baked globalization" – resulted in a diet that has wreaked havoc on the health of Mexico's poor. Originally their diet of beans and home-ground corn tortillas was an ideal combination with the amino acids each complementing what was missing in the other. But the substitution of industrially processed tortilla flour, soft drinks, the Mexican equivalent of Wonder Bread (brand name: Bimbo), and junk foods that are high in fats and sugars, have led to dramatically rising incidences of heart disease, diabetes, hypertension, cancer, and arteriosclerosis, combined with serious malnutrition and anemia. While the rich can afford to replace vegetable protein with meats, the rural poor attempt to compensate by dumping heaping spoonfuls of sugar in their weak coffee. Besides, global food consortiums like Pepsico, the Mexican government, members of the middle class, and even the clergy have helped accelerate these trends through subsidies, giving cases of Pepsi Cola as wedding gifts, and even substituting Pepsi Cola for wine in communion ceremonies, insisting that it drives off evil spirits and cleanses the soul (Pilcher 2002).

Nor is Mexico alone in substituting mostly unhealthy processed and branded foods for healthier local food items. Among India's urban elite, fast foods and soft drinks have been replacing local offerings since the economic liberalizations of the 1990s (Narayan 1995). Similar changes in the diets of native Americans have led to diabetes rates as high as 50 percent among those over 35 (Joos 1984). Equally dramatic changes have been observed in the South Pacific and among indigenous groups in Canada, Australia, and New Zealand. Ger and Belk (1996) report incidents in Turkey where mothers sell their milk-producing cow in order to afford candy for their insistent children. The latter example suggests that even the poor are not immune to the seduction of processed and branded food commodities. The sacrifice of "necessities" to afford "luxuries" is no longer unusual and has been termed "leaping luxuries" (Belk 1999). Many other cases like these could be cited. The lure of powerful global brands like Coca-Cola can be extremely strong (see Foster 2008). Given the lengths to which some people will go to afford these exotic and highly touted global brands, McDonald's economic calculus for determining when to enter a developing nation may be shortsighted. But on the other hand, perhaps Zimbabweans are better off in foregoing Big Macs for spicy Nando's chicken. It is partly the health consequences and partly the challenge to traditional local foods that cause protests against the introduction of some global brands. This is the case with Coca-Cola and Pepsi Cola in India, for example, where activist groups campaign to instead drink local products like *lassi*, *sherbat*, and *nimbu paani* (Varman and Belk 2009; Wolf 2005).

Besides direct health concerns stemming from global food brands, the other major part of the moral discourse surrounding eating involves the indirect health consequences as well as aesthetic concerns with obesity, slimness, and food. While the slim body we are obsessed with today would have been considered anemic and unhealthy a little over a hundred years ago, the massive investment in diet plans, dieting books, gym memberships, weight loss clinics, and various self-help groups all testify that we, and especially the upper middle classes, have become obsessed with being thin rather than fat (Moisio and Beruchashvili 2010). One vocabulary characterizes eating excessively and lacking a regular program of exercise as being evil, sinful, deviant, and transgressive (e.g. Turner 2004; Warde 1997). But while anorexia nervosa and bulimia were once considered a pathway to liberating the Christian soul (Bell 1985; Turner 2004), both are now considered deviant self-abnegation. Still, the vocabulary persists and weight loss is sometimes considered to be a secular path to salvation (Leiwica 2000). Paralleling the methods of Alcoholics Anonymous, we give ourselves over to a higher power in order to help overcome our weakness. We seek to resist the "temptation" of fattening foods and control our "evil" impulses to indulge. Rather than external sanctions against these "sins," we self-govern our desires and learn to control our impulses toward self-gratification (Foucault 1979). A slim body becomes a sign of self-discipline. But this internalization of responsibility for our weight may be reversing. As suggested by health-based lawsuits against McDonald's, boycotts against the chain, and exposés about what a diet of McDonald's is doing to our health (Probyn 2000; Spurlock 2004), we may be externalizing our concern. The challenge to McDonald's and other fast food chains has been to transform at least a portion of their menus into healthier offerings so that the presence of health-relevant choices can once again place the burden back on consumers.

But it is worth noting that the whole movement toward self-denial in eating fattening, unhealthy, and sugary foods and the avoidance of chocolates, sweets, and other "treats," flies in the face of consumer culture. Consumerism is all about indulgence, pursuing pleasure, and seeking out irresistibly good things. While there are other reasons for food consumption (e.g. sustenance, sociality), food consumption is perhaps the distilled essence of consumer culture. With the partial exception of Dubai's annual Shopping Festival, most of us would be loathe to explicitly advocate self-indulgence, conspicuous consumption, and unbridled hedonism. But at the same time few of us would denigrate the ritual feasting and frequent over-indulgence in eating that takes place at holidays like Christmas, New Year, Valentine's Day, Chinese New Year, Mother's Day, Halloween, Thanksgiving, Divalli, Passover, and the Eid and Iftar celebrations of Ramadan. By cloaking many of these feasts in the garb of religion and family, they take on anything but a sinful character. We relish eating out not just at fast food places, but at a wide variety of ethnic and gourmet restaurants. We revel in our cosmopolitan globalism in celebrating special occasions with exotic meals. We tell the birthday child that he or she may eat anything they wish on their special day. And we reward ourselves, our children, and even our pets with small treats of food and drink that we know deep down are not good for us.

Conclusion: cultures of food

As we have seen in this brief tour of food, what we eat says a great deal about how we regard ourselves, our culture, and our world. What a global food item or fast food restaurant means in one culture may be completely different in another culture. Thus hamburgers in China (Watson 2000) and pizza in India (Eckhardt 2003) are thought of as prestigious snacks, but are not considered to be a meal. Even though food and beverages almost always have associations with social class, gender, age, and personality, the relationships of these categories to specific foods may be markedly different between cultures, subcultures, and ethnic groups. Because food tastes and distastes mark boundaries between such groups, what we dislike may be as important as what we like in signaling our identity. Increasingly we are becoming more concerned with the health consequences of what we put in our bodies, but conflicting scientific reports and loose usage of terms like "natural," "organic," "green," and "healthy" make for a great deal of confusion in the marketplace. Nevertheless, because food is a moral discourse, we may be highly concerned with such claims. And we should be. Likewise marketers should be increasingly concerned not only with health factors but with the extent to which they can or should localize their offerings.

This has necessarily been a quick tour of a very broad topic. It has neglected many cultural concerns with food including climate, food shopping patterns, food purity concerns, home food preservation and preparation equipment, other food classification systems like the hot and cold yin/yang medicinal system of Chinese cultures, convenience preferences, and food retailing institutions. Because we eat not just food, but socially constructed meanings, it is critical to understand not just what people eat, but what it means. This is precisely the sort of question that interpretive consumer research is good at answering.

One suggestion for a take-away (no pun intended) from this admittedly diverse chapter is to divide a piece of paper or the electronic equivalent into two columns. In one column list the factors by which cultural differences affecting eating might be described (e.g. class, gender, subculture, region, religion, age, nation, occasion). In the second column list some of the concepts this chapter has brought up for understanding the impacts of such cultural variables (e.g. pleasure, prestige, health, luxury, sacrifice, cosmopolitanism, likes/dislikes, globalism/localism, need for marketing adaptation). To attempt linkages between the entries in the columns in terms of food would be too easy. So use another consumption context like clothing, transportation, homes, or sports. The challenge is to discuss how the various cultural differences impact behaviors in the chosen context, with attention to the conceptual variables as lenses for understanding these impacts. The answers may not always be self-evident, but you will then be asking the right sort of question.

Review and discussion questions

1 What does McDonald's mean? How might the answer to this question differ in different cultures?
2 Besides nourishment, why do humans eat and drink?
3 How do distastes, the things we *don't* like, help in expressing our identity and differentiating ourselves from others?

Figure 1.1 The owner and chef at a fixed-price restaurant in Tokyo with seven set courses and a wide
selection of free Saki. It is booked up more than a year in advance.
Source: Photo credits: Russell Belk.

Figure 1.2 An all-garlic restaurant in San Francisco.
Source: Photo credits: Russell Belk.

4   What do the things we eat say about our age, gender, class, and religion in different cultures?
5   How is holiday and festival food different from everyday food?
6   Why does Chinese food inside and outside of China often differ?
7   As the world becomes a more global place, how does this impact the diversity or homogeneity of our diets?
8   If consumers know that most fast food is bad for them, why do we continue to eat and drink so much of it?
9   Consider the food consumption discussed in Figures 1.1 and 1.2. To what extent are these food consumption patterns local versus global in character? How well would they travel between these different cultures?

Keywords

consumer well-being, culture, globalism, health, holidays, localism, ritual, symbolism

References

Allhoff, F. (ed.) (2008) *Wine and Philosophy: A Symposium on Thinking and Drinking*, Oxford: Blackwell.
Banerji, C. (2006) *Feeding the Gods: Memories of Food and Culture in Bengal*, Oxford: Seagull Books.
Basil, M. and Basil, D. Z. (2009) "Reflections on Ultra-fine Dining Experiences," in A. Lindgreen, J. Vanhamme, and M. B. Beverland (eds), *Memorable Consumer Experiences*, Ashgate: Gower.
Belasco, W. and Scranton. P. (eds) (2002) *Food Nations: Selling Taste in Consumer Societies*, New York: Routledge.
Belk, R. (1999) "Leaping Luxuries and Transitional Consumers," in R. Batra (ed.), *Marketing Issues in Transitional Economies*, Boston: Kluwer.
Belk, R and Groves, R. (1998) "Luxury Beverage Consumption in Hong Kong," *Asia Pacific Advances in Consumer Research*, 3: 36–7.
Bell, R. (1985) *Holy Anorexia*, London: The University of Chicago Press.
Bergquist, K. J. S. (2006) "From Kim Chee to Moon Cakes: Feeding Asian Adoptees' Imaginings of Culture and Self," *Food, Culture, and Society*, 9(2): 141–53.
Bestor, T. C. (2000) "How Sushi Went Global," *Foreign Policy*, 121(December): 54–63.
Bourdieu, P. (1984) *Distinction: A Social Critique of the Judgment of Taste*, London: Routledge and Kegan Paul.
Brannen, M. Y. (1992a) "'Bwana Mickey': Constructing Cultural Consumption at Tokyo Disneyland," in J. Tobin (ed.), *Re-Made in Japan: Everyday Life and Consumer Taste in a Changing Society*, New Haven, CT: Yale University Press, pp. 216–34.
—— (1992b) "Cross-Cultural Materialism: Commodifying Culture in Japan," in F. Rudmin, and M. Richins (eds), *Meaning, Measure, and Morality of Materialism*, Provo, UT: Association for Consumer Research.
Brown, L. K. and Mussell, K. (eds) (1984) *Ethnic and Regional Foodways in the United States: The Performance of Group Identity*, Knoxville, TN: University of Tennessee Press.
Bryson, N. (1990) *Looking at the Overlooked: Four Essays on Still Life Painting*, London: Reaktion Books.
Buitelaar, M. (1993) *Fasting and Feasting in Morocco: Women's Particpation in Ramadan*, Oxford: Berg.

Cheah, P. and Robbins, B. (1998) *Cosmopolitics: Thinking and Feeling Beyond the Nation*, Minneapolis: University of Minnesota Press.

Chow, K. and Kramer, I. (1990) *All the Tea in China*, San Francisco: China Books.

Coe, A. (2009) *Chop Suey: A Cultural History of Chinese Food in the United States*, Oxford: Oxford University Press.

Coveney, J. (2000) *Food, Morals and Meaning: The Pleasure and Anxiety of Eating*, 2nd edn, London: Routledge.

De Mooij, M. (2004) *Consumer Behavior and Culture: Consequences for Global Marketing and Advertising*, Thousand Oaks, CA: Sage.

Douglas, M. (1966) *Purity and Danger: An Analysis of the Concepts of Pollution and Taboo*, London: Routledge and Kegan Paul.

—— (1972) "Deciphering a Meal," *Daedalus*, 101(Winter): 61–81.

Eckhardt, G. M. (2003) "Building a Local Brand in a Foreign Product Category in India: The Role of Cultural Interpretations," *European Advances in Consumer Research*, 6: 9–10.

Farb, P. and Armelagos, G. (1980) *Consuming Passions: The Anthropology of Eating*, Boston: Houghton-Mifflin.

Farquhar, J. (2002) *Appetites: Food and Sex in Post-Socialist China*, Durham, NC: Duke University Press.

—— (2006) "Food, Eating, and the Good Life," in C. Tilley, W. Keane, S. Küchler, M. Rowlands, and P. Spyer (eds), *Handbook of Material Culture*, London: Sage.

Feirstein, B. and Lorenz, L. (1982) *Real Men Don't Eat Quiche*, New York: Pocket Books.

Fiddes, N. (1991) *Meat: A Natural Symbol*, London: Routledge.

Fields, G. (1983) *From Bonzai to Levi's, West Meets East: An Insider's Surprising Account of How the Japanese Live*, New York: Macmillan.

Finkelstein, J. (1989) *Dining Out: A Sociology of Modern Manners*, New York: New York University Press.

Fischler, C. (1999) "The 'McDonaldization' of Culture," in J.-L. Flandrin and M. Montanari (eds), *A Cultural History of Food*, New York: Columbia University Press.

Flandrin, J-L. and Montanari, M. (eds) (1996) *Food: A Culinary History*, New York: Columbia Unversity Press.

Foster, R. J. (2008) *Coca-Globalization: Following Soft Drinks from New York to New Guinea*, New York: Palgrave Macmillan.

Foucault, M. (1979) *Discipline and Punish: The Birth of the Prison*, London: Tavistock.

Gabaccia, D. R. (2002) "As American as Budweiser and Pickles? Nation-Building in American Food Industries," in *Food Nations: Selling Taste in Consumer Societies*, London: Routledge, pp. 175–93.

Geertz, C. (1973) *The Interpretation of Cultures*, New York: Basic Books.

Ger, G. and Belk, R. (1996) "I'd Like to Buy the World a Coke: Consumptionscapes of the Less Affluent World," *Journal of Consumer Policy*, 19: 271–304.

Giddens, A. (1991) *Modernity and Self-Identity: Self and Society in the Late Modern Age*, Stanford, CA: Stanford University Press.

Gillette, M. B. (2000) "Children's Food and Islamic Dietary Restrictions in Xi'an," in J. Jing (ed.), *Feeding China's Little Emperors: Food, Children and Social Change*, Stanford, CA: Stanford University Press.

Goody, J. (1996) *Cooking, Cuisine, and Class: A Study in Comparative Sociology*, Cambridge: Cambridge University Press.

Heldke, L. (2003) *Exotic Appetites: Ruminations of a Food Adventurer*, London: Routledge.

Hofstede, G. (1991) *Cultures and Organizations: Software of the Mind*, London: McGraw-Hill.

hooks, b. (1992) "Eating the Other," in b. hooks, *Black Looks: Race and Representation*, Boston: South End Press.

Joos, S. K. (1984) "Economic, Social, and Cultural Factors in the Analysis of Disease: Dietary Change and Diabetes Millitis among the Florida Seminole Indians," in L. K. Brown, and K. Mussel (eds),

Ethnic and Regional Foodways in the United States: The Performance of Group Identity, Knoxville, TN: University of Tennessee Press.

Korsmeyer, C. (ed.) (2005) *The Taste Culture Reader: Experiencing Food and Drink*, Oxford: Berg.

Lee, J. (2009) *The Fortune Cookie Chronicles: Adventures in the World of Chinese Food*, New York: Twelve.

Leiwica, M. M. (2000) "Losing Their Way to Salvation: Women, Weight Loss, and the Salvation Myth of Culture Lite," in B. Forbes and J. Mahan (eds), *Religion and Popular Culture in America*, Berkeley, CA: University of California Press.

Lévi-Strauss, C. (1969) *The Elementary Structures of Kinship*, Boston: Beacon Press.

—— (1969/1983) *The Raw and the Cooked, Vol. 1 of Introduction to a Science of Mythology*, New York, NY: Harper & Row (edition reprinted in 1983 by University of Chicago Press).

—— (1978/1990) *The Origin of Table Manners, Vol. 3 of Introduction to a Science of Mythology*, New York, NY: Harper & Row (edition reprinted in 1990 by University of Chicago Press).

Levy, S. J. (1981) "Interpreting Consumer Mythology: A Structural Approach to Consumer Behavior," *Journal of Marketing*, 45(Summer): 49–61.

—— (1986) "Meanings in Advertising Stimuli," in J. Olson and K. Sentis (eds), *Advertising and Consumer Psychology*, 3, New York: Praeger.

Lozada, E. P., Jr. (2000) "Globalized Childhood? Kentucky Fried Chicken in Beijing," in J. Jing (ed.), *Feeding China's Little Emperors: Food, Children, and Social Change*, Stanford, CA: Stanford University Press.

Lupton, D. (1996) *Food, the Body, and the Self*, London: Sage.

Ma, E. K. (2001) "The Hierarchy of Drinks: Alcohol and Social Class in Hong Kong," in G. Mathews and T. Lui (eds), *Consuming Hong Kong*, Hong Kong: Hong Kong University Press, pp. 117–40.

Mankekar, P. (2002) "'India Shopping': Indian Grocery Sores and Transnational Configurations of Belonging," *Ethnos*, 67(1): 75–98.

Miller, W. (1997) *The Anatomy of Disgust*, Cambridge, MA: Harvard University Press.

Moisio, R. and Beruchashvili, M. (2010) "Questing for Well-Being at Weight Watchers: The Role of the Spiritual-Therapeutic Model in a Support Group," *Journal of Consumer Research*, 36(February): 857–75.

Montanari, M. (1994) *The Culture of Food*, Oxford: Blackwell.

Nakano, Y. (2009) *Where There are Asians, There are Rice Cookers: How "National" Went Global via Hong Kong*, Hong Kong: Hong Kong University Press.

Narayan, U. (1995) "Eating Cultures: Incorporation, Identity and Indian Food," *Social Identities*, 1(1): 63–82.

Paarlberg, R. (2000) "The Global Food Fight," *Foreign Affairs*, 79(3): 24–38.

Pilcher, J. M. (2002) "Industrial Tortillas and Folkloric Pepsi: The Nutritional Consequences of Hybrid Cuisine in Mexico," in W. Belasco and P. Scranton (eds), *Food Nation: Selling Taste in Consumer Societies*, London: Routledge, pp. 222–39.

Pillsbury, R. (1998) *No Foreign Food: The American Diet in Time and Place*, Boulder, CO: Westview Press.

Probyn, E. (2000) *Carnal Appetites: Food, Sex, Identities*, London: Sage.

Ritzer, G. (1993) *The McDonaldization of Society*, Thousand Oaks, CA: Pine Forge Press.

Roseberry, W. (1996) "The Rise of Yuppie Coffees and the Re-imagination of Class in the United States," *American Anthropologist*, 98(4): 762–75.

Rozin, P. and Fallon, A. E. (1987) "A Perspective on Disgust," *Psychological Review*, 94(1): 23–41.

Schlosser, E. (2002) *Fast Food Nation: The Dark Side of the American Meal*, New York: Harper Perennial.

Shaw, S. A. (2008) *Asian Dining Rules: Essential Strategies for Eating Out at Japanese, Chinese, Southeast Asian, Korean, and Indian Restaurants*, New York: William Morrow.

Shuman, A. (2001) "Food Gifts: Ritual Exchange and the Production of Excess Meaning," *Journal of American Folklore*, 113(450): 495–508.

Smart, J. (2005) "Cognac, Beer, Red Wine or Soft Drinks? Hong Kong Identity and Wedding Banquets," in T. M. Wilson (ed.), *Drinking Cultures, Alcohol and Identity*, Oxford: Berg, pp. 107–28.

Smith, B. C. (2007) *Questions of Taste: The Philosophy of Wine*, Oxford: Oxford University Press.

Smith, D. E. and Solgaard, H. S. (2000) "The Dynamics of Shifts in European Alcohol Consumption," *Journal of International Consumer Marketing*, 12(3): 85–109.

Smith, S. R. (1983) "Drinking Etiquette in a Changing Beverage Market," in J. Tobin (ed.), *Re-Made in Japan: Everyday Life and Consumer Taste in a Changing Society*, New Haven, CT: Yale University Press.

Spurlock, M. (director) (2004) *Supersize Me*, 100-minute video, Los Angeles, Roadside Attractions.

Swislocki, M. (2008) *Culinary Nostalgia: Regional Food Culture and the Urban Experience in Shanghai*, Stanford, CA: Stanford University Press.

Tambiah, S. (1969) "Animals are Good to Think and Good to Prohibit," *Ethnology*, 8(4): 423–59.

Thompson, C. J. and Arsel, Z. (2004) "The Starbucks Brandscape and Consumers' (Anticorporate) Experiences of Glocalization," *Journal of Consumer Research*, 31(December): 631–42.

Thompson, C. J. and Tambyah, S. K. (1999) "Trying to be Cosmopolitan," *Journal of Consumer Research*, 25(December): 214–41.

Thompson, C. J. and Troester, M. (2002) "Consumer Value Systems in the Age of Postmodern Fragmentation: The Case of Natural Health Microculture," *Journal of Consumer Research*, 28(March): 550–71.

Threadgold, T. (2000) "When Home is Always a Foreign Place: Diaspora, Dialogue, Translations," *Communal/Plural: Journal of Transnational and Crosscultural Studies*, 8(2): 193–217.

Tiger, L. (1992) *The Pursuit of Pleasure*, Boston: Little Brown.

Tobin, J. (1992a) "A Japanese-French Restaurant in Hawai'i," in J. Tobin (ed.), *Re-Made in Japan: Everyday Life and Consumer Taste in a Changing Society*, New Haven, CT: Yale University Press.

Tobin, J. (ed.) (1992b) *Re-Made in Japan: Everyday Life and Consumer Taste in a Changing Society*, New Haven, CT: Yale University Press.

Tuan, Y.-F. (1993) *Passing Strange and Wonderful*, Washington, DC: Island Press.

Turner, B. S. (2004) *The Body and Society*, 2nd edn, London: Sage.

Twigg, J. (1983) "Vegetarianism and the Meaning of Meat," in A. Murcott (ed.), *The Sociology of Food and Eating*, Cardiff: Gower.

Varman, R. and Belk, R. (2009) "Nationalism and Ideology in an Anti-Consumption Movement," *Journal of Consumer Research*, 36(December): 686–700.

Visser, M. (1986) *Much Depends Upon Dinner: The Extraordinary History and Mythology, Allure and Obsessions, Perils and Taboos, of an Ordinary Meal*, Toronto: McClelland and Stewart.

—— (1991) *The Rituals of Dinner: The Origins, Evolution, Eccentricities, and Meaning of Table Manners*, New York: HarperCollins.

Wallendorf, M. and Arnould, E. J. (1991) "'We Gather Together': Consumption Rituals of Thanksgiving Day," *Journal of Consumer Research*, 18(June): 13–31.

Warde, A. (1997) *Consumption, Food and Taste*, London: Sage.

Warde, A. and Martens, L. (2000) *Eating Out: Social Differentiation, Consumption, and Pleasure*, Cambridge: Cambridge University Press.

Watson, J. (ed.) (1997) *Golden Arches East: McDonald's in East Asia*, Stanford, CA: Stanford University Press.

Watson, J. (2000) "China's Big Mac Attack," *Foreign Affairs*, 79(3): 120–34.

Watson, J. and Caldwell, M. (eds) (2005) *The Cultural Politics of Food and Eating: A Reader*, Malden, MA: Blackwell.

Wilk, R. (1997) "A Critique of Desire: Distaste and Dislike in Consumer Behavior," *Consumption Markets and Culture*, 1(2): 175–96.

Wolf, S. (2005) "Thanda-Hearted Matlab: Coca Cola in India," unpublished thesis, University of Wisconsin.

Wooliscroft, B. and Ganglmair-Wooliscroft, A. (2009) "Co-Production in Memorable Service Encounters: Three Hot Chocolates in Belgium," in A. Lindgreen, J. Vanhamme, and M. B. Beverland (eds), *Memorable Consumer Experiences*, Ashgate: Gower.

Wu, D. Y. H. and Chee-beng, T. (eds) (2001) *Changing Chinese Foodways in Asia*, Hong Kong: Chinese University Press.

Wu, D. Y. H. and Cheung, S. C. H. (eds) (2002) *The Globalization of Chinese Food*, Honolulu: University of Hawai'i Press.

Yan, Y. (2000) "Of Hamburger and Social Space: Consuming McDonald's in Beijing," in D. S. Davis (ed.), *The Consumer Revolution in Urban China*, Berkeley, CA: University of California Press.

Yang, M. M.-H. (1994) *Gifts, Favors and Banquets: The Art of Social Relationships in China*, Ithaca, NY: Cornell University Press.

2 International marketing at the interface of the alluring global and the comforting local

Güliz Ger, Olga Kravets, and Özlem Sandıkcı

Overview

This chapter highlights the poles of global/local and standardization/adaptation and calls for a focus on the specific interaction between a local context and the global forces while forming a glocalization strategy. It focuses on a key question managers try to answer: what is the right marketing approach for a firm operating in international markets? The decision of if and how to tailor their marketing offerings to global/local market dynamics is fundamental in defining the marketing strategy of both transnationals and local companies in emergent markets. We describe how emergent market companies can successfully compete with transnational giants by developing brands that serve consumers bridge various sociocultural tensions in their daily lives. We focus on one such tension: the alluring global and the comforting local. Two cases – a Russian brand of cosmetics, Green Mama and a Turkish brand of cola, Cola Turka – demonstrate effective business solutions that bridge the desire for both the local and the global. These cases also underscore that the specifics of the design and implementation of glocalization as well as cultural analysis of the sociohistorical context of a national market are vital for successful marketing.

Cultural positioning: overcoming the dualities of standardization/adaptation and global/local

Firms have been grappling with the trials and tribulations of global standardization, local adaptation, and recently, glocalization. Standardization indicates operating "as if the world were one large market" (Levitt 1983: 92). The proponents of this approach note that with globalization the world becomes homogeneous; in particular, technology, media and tourism cause the convergence of consumer tastes and preferences across geographies. Thus, companies can and should capitalize on this homogeneity to attain economies of scale, scope, and rapid diffusion of products. This approach also allows a company to establish its reputation as a global player and to build/maintain a coherent brand image across the world, thus to increase its brand equity.

The opponents of standardization point to the persistent differences in cultural, political, legal, and economic environments worldwide; hence they advocate adaptation of the marketing mix to suit local market conditions and characteristics. They argue that the rationale for standardization lies primarily with supply issues and lacks sufficient consideration of demand: consumers, cultures, purchasing power, and market infrastructures. Hence, by offering a standardized marketing program, a transnational company would lack the proximity to local cultures and consumers, and lose on opportunities that a local market presents, or face consumer resistance and fail.

Currently, glocalization, a blend of global standardization and local adaptation, is the common recommendation for global marketers. This involves finding an optimal combinatory solution – a glocal solution – that would reflect and respond to the complex array of factors pertaining to the company, brand, consumers and local cultures. Glocalization entails local adaptation of global strategies. For example, Coca-Cola runs special advertising campaigns aligning the beverage with local holidays, such as the Chinese New Year and Muslim Ramadan (http://popsop.com/31409). McDonald's offers locally customized flavors in addition to its standard menu, such as Aussie Burger in Australia, McTurko (http://www.mcdonalds.com.tr/Urun_Detay.asp?mainId = 1&subId = 0&CatID = 1&ItemID = 10) in Turkey and soy burgers in South-East Asia.

Glocalization is a major concern not only for transnational but also the local firms competing with them. With the influx of foreign companies and brands, managers of domestic firms need to decide on how to respond to the internalization of their markets. Many "smart" local companies in emerging markets such as Brazil, Mexico, China, India, Indonesia, Thailand, Turkey, and Russia not only defend their market shares against the transnationals, but also have become market leaders. For example, in Brazil the local computer manufacturer Grupo Positivo commands more market share than global giants such as Dell and HP. Mexican hypermarket chain Grupo Elektra competes head on with Wal-Mart. The biggest dairy manufacturer of Russia, Wimm-Bill-Dann Foods sells more milk than Danone. And in Turkey, the local baby shampoo brand Dalin enjoys market leadership while Johnson and Johnson and Nivea are followers.

Commonly recommended and pursued means for local companies to compete with transnationals are to capitalize on their economic, human and technological competitive assets and capabilities, position in the domestic industry, and familiarity with the local infrastructure and preferences. For example, the Philippines-based fast-food chain Jollibee pursued standardization by benchmarking transnational fast-food chains' operations to devise their own operation system. The company also implemented adaptation by developing a Philippino cuisine-based fast-food menu. By successfully glocalizing, that is, combining standardization and adaptation, Jollibee expanded its business beyond the Philippines to South-East Asia and even the US.

Overall, standardization, adaptation and glocalization can each be effective strategies under specific market conditions. In essence, these strategic options relate to the debates on globalization: the socio-cultural homogenization and heterogenization or convergence and divergence. Just as technology, media and tourism create and promote a transnational culture of sameness, they also highlight and reify differences among nations, regions, and ethnic groups and the peculiarities in local cultures, traditions, and lifestyles. Many managers take international marketing to be about deciding on a degree and balance of localness and globalness in their activities. Then, the decision becomes whether and to what extent to employ a particular strategy. To that end, companies are conventionally advised to consider cultural differences and similarities. When similarities are prevalent, standardization and when differences are prevalent, adaptation seem to be preferred. However, rather than being opposites, homogenization and heterogenization co-exist, react to, and shape each other. Globalization is about the coexistence and interpenetration of the global and the local (Appadurai 1990). That interpenetration unfolds in a specific manner in different times and spaces.

The cultural perspective considers the coexistence and interpenetration of the global and the local, and hence it goes beyond viewing culture as a set of differences and similarities. As such, it attends to cultural resources, forces and tensions and negotiations thereof. Adopting a cultural perspective enriches the arsenal of managers by making apparent the not-so-easily seen opportunities. Cemex México's *Patrimonio Hoy* program illustrates this business logic. As part of the program, Cemex, a building material producer, sets up clubs to organize self-financing of home building and improvement projects for low-income families (Leteller *et al.* 2003). These clubs are modeled after the long-existing *tanda* groups, where each member contributes money weekly and a different member receives the yield of the week in cash. In Cemex's clubs, members receive building materials instead of cash. Thus, Cemex uses the *tanda* group practice as a cultural resource to create a market for its products among low-income consumers. Cemex's marketing draws on a situated understanding of cultural values. It addresses the tension between the local value of a community spirit and the global desire for improved living conditions for an individual family. Mexicans want a social identity as respected members of their community by, for example, contributing financially to communal celebrations. They also want to be individuals who provide well for their own households. These opposing cultural forces create a tension for low-income consumers. Cemex helps them negotiate and resolve that tension. The company enables community affiliations by, for example, sponsoring communal celebrations of family achievements in building their house and the meetings of *Patrimonio Hoy* clubs. It also enables an individual family to own a house by organizing affordable financing and providing technical advice, delivery, and warehousing services. Thus, Cemex created a unique customer value by identifying and mobilizing cultural resources, forces and tensions. Cemex leveraged its cultural capital[1] in a product category where foreign companies lacked such capital and was able to differentiate cement – a prototypical commodity and become the world's number three cement producer. The success of Cemex provides one example of the merit of the mobilization of cultural resources in generating customer value (Ger 1999).

Attending to cultural resources, forces and tensions often requires a reflexive distance to the local culture, that is, taking an outsider's as well as an insider's perspective to question taken-for-granted understandings. A reflexive distance can be attained by being a foreigner or having been acculturated to a different culture. Consider the reinvention of traditional root dyes in Turkey after their disappearance in early twentieth century from the scene of traditional carpets. They were rediscovered in the 1970s by individuals who were either foreigners or Turks educated abroad. Another example is Inca Cola in Peru, invented by an immigrant British family based on an ancestral concoction. It has been so successful that it commands a 31 percent share of the soft drink market, followed by Coca-Cola's 26 percent. Perhaps it is difficult for local entrepreneurs to notice the taken-for-granted value of a cultural resource that outsiders can see more readily. Thus, reflexive distance is of great use in the ability to detect and imagine the potential market value in a particular cultural resource, a potential to be capitalized on by cultural entrepreneurship.

Understanding of cultural resources, forces and tensions also requires managers to get even closer to consumers than possible by conducting cross-cultural surveys. While these surveys magnify and over-generalize differences and similarities, they overlook cultural tensions and negotiations. However, in their daily lives consumers encounter the coexistence and interpenetration of the local and the global, and often have to deal with the related tensions and contradictions. Marketing solutions that help negotiate such tensions are likely to succeed. Among these tensions, we now focus on a specific one experienced by consumers who encounter the global within a particular local.

The allure of the global and the comfort of the local

Consumers relate to global products in diverse ways. They can embrace global(ized) goods for the sake of modernity or status, or reject them in pursuit of nostalgia and authenticity, or connect global products to local consumption practices and give them local meanings (Ger and Belk 1996). Underlying such consumer strategies in emergent markets is the co-presence of two seemingly opposing desires – the desire for the seductive foreign and the desire for the authentic and familiar local (Wilk 1999). On the one hand, consumers enjoy an intimate connection to local goods. The familiarity with local products provides a sense of comfort and security; their history assures a sense of continuity and tradition (Ger 2005), perhaps poignantly illustrated by enduring preference for Russian-made vodka in Russia. On the other hand, consumers are attracted to the foreign – as they drink Starbucks coffee or walk the streets with iPods, they feel they are a part of a global community and modernity. Even if they cannot afford iPods, poorer consumers feel closer to the rest of the world when enjoying the little luxury of drinking Coke or eating a Mars bar.

The "allure of the foreign" (Orlove 1997) is prominent globally. There is widespread enthusiasm for Western/Northern goods across all classes in Latin America, Africa, and Asia. Compared to consumers in developed countries, consumers in developing countries have more favorable attitudes toward foreign products. European or North American goods signify quality and mark status, modernity, and global commonality. In addition, the preference for the foreign over local equivalents is driven by the desire to know more about the world, to become more sophisticated, and to create a "local identity on a global stage" (Wilk 1999: 253).

This consumer preference for the foreign in developing countries is also reflected in the adoption of foreign or foreign-sounding names for domestic products. For example, two major Turkish snack producers, Ülker and Eti, often use foreign languages (Finger, Petit Beurre, Rio Black) and foreign-sounding/-looking names (Haylayf – "high life" in Turkish phonetics; Alpella – reminiscent of the Alp mountains) in branding. Similarly, middle-class neighborhoods in Turkey and Russia frequently feature stores with foreignified names.

However, such glocalization, in the form of international associations, can turn against a firm due to some political or cultural incidents. For example, the allusion to Italian style and association to Italian culture exercised by Bellona, a furniture manufacturer and retailer in Turkey, backfired when a political crisis broke out between Turkey and Italy in 1998. At the time, the leader of Kurdish terrorists was in hiding in Italy. Hostile reaction against Italy arose in Turkey and many Turkish consumers boycotted Italian brands, to which Italian firms in Turkey tried to respond through various declarations. Although it was not an Italian firm, Bellona also ran an advertising campaign during the period stating that 100 percent of its capital was Turkish and that its products were not made in Italy. Thus, while the allure of the foreign is strong, it necessarily plays out in the delicate scene of international politics and, hence, may backfire, even if temporarily. In addition to cultural forces and tensions, broader political, economic, and social events also set the frame and impact the success of glocalization. Socio-historical conditions, either long-standing or recent, shape the meanings attributed to "foreign" and Western versus domestic brands and motivate choices in a specific market. A set of particular historical political and economic relations between one developing country and the "West" plays a crucial role in shaping the opposing desires for the local and the global in that country. So, standardization, adaptation, or glocalization decisions pertain to and thus should consider not only a desired cultural fit based on differences and similarities but also the specific international interactions.

Regardless of and in addition to particular short-lived or long-standing international interactions, there is the "eternal struggle" between and the "dance" of "seductive globalism" and "authentic localism" (Wilk 1999). The tension between seductive globalism and authentic localism relates to issues of social identity. Individual consumers use the global consumer culture together with the local culture to navigate and position themselves in local identity hierarchies. Rather than merely clash, the seemingly opposing desires talk to each other, interact, and transform each other. The companies that find a way to ease the tension between the two desires by mingling the global and the local win. Implementation of glocalization will be effective to the extent that a particular design of the marketing mix and positioning help different consumer segments carry out their own identity projects.

The cultural perspective offers various advantages over conventional approaches to international marketing. By focusing on cultural resources, forces, and tensions, it reveals innovative marketing solutions, from new product development to creating new markets, financing systems and distribution networks. This is in contrast to the conventional approaches which emphasize cultural similarities and differences and concentrate on adjusting an existing marketing mix to a particular market depending on the extent of the cultural fit between home and host markets. Furthermore, analysis of culture based on similarities and differences assumes a static national culture and static life-style segments, such as traditional and modern lifestyle segments or ethnocentric and cosmopolitan consumers. However, analysis of culture based on the cultural resources, forces, and tensions brings to the fore the coexistence and the interpenetration of the global and the local and the dynamism thereof. Attention to such dynamism enables managers to create new markets and receptive segments, rather than merely cater to existing markets and segments.

Adapting such a cultural perspective requires a new mindset and methods of market research and consumer intelligence. The conventional recommendation to international firms is that, in order to make adjustments in their marketing mixes according to "cultural differences," they should measure the degree of difference found across countries on a standard set of cultural values such as individualism–collectivism or masculinity–femininity. In this approach, culture is treated as a factor that influences marketing decisions. As such, this approach reduces culture to a static set of stand-alone characteristics that are supposed to represent the whole country. Moreover, seeking to measure and compare cultures according to a limited set of values is too reductive to discover uses and meanings of consumption. The focus on preferred end-states ignores the very essence of consumption: how consumers reach these end-states in particular contexts. Consumers act differently in different situations and their actions are by no means always consistent (Holt 1994). Conventional comparative approaches to studying "cross-cultural behavior" have become increasingly inadequate to capture the complexity of cultural dynamics in the global world (Askegaard *et al.* 2009; Nakata 2009). Instead, the globally interconnected political, economic and cultural forces that constitute local and global markets call for innovative forms of ethnographic research and multi-sited ethnographies.

In sum, the cultural perspective highlights that managers of transnational and domestic companies should not view global and local as opposites and strive merely for more or less localness and globalness. International marketing in general and glocalization in particular should be about enabling consumers to resolve their daily tensions with a specific global/local composition of a market offering. Companies which find ways to reflect various possible resolutions of the alluring globalism–authentic localism tension through their positioning and differentiation strategies are likely to win the hearts and minds of consumers.

The following cases illustrate how a Russian cosmetics and a Turkish beverage company have benefited from the cultural perspective. They both tapped into complex global–local tensions in different localities and have generated business successes.

Mingling the foreign and the familiar: two cases

Green Mama cosmetics: with a scent of home

In the early 1990s Russia, all things "foreign" were invariably heralded as stylish and pres-tigious and of superior quality and value. After years of product shortages, long queues and what many Russians considered poor quality products, foreign goods, previously forbidden to the general public and accessible only to a few, were embraced as tangible signs of the country's Westernization and democratization. However, the mid-1990s witnessed a shift in consumer preferences toward local products. Some interpreted this as an expression of Russian nationalism. In "The Taste of Nationalism," Caldwell (2002) suggests that Moscovites prefer local products because of the concern with national integrity, arising from market-oriented reforms and the influx of foreign goods. Through their choice of local products, consumers in Russia strove to (re)assert their national cultural identity, sense of belonging, and the uniqueness of Russia in an increasingly transnational world.

Although compelling, this reasoning does not account for the differences in preferences among different categories of goods and among different social groups (Patico 2003). The "apparent ethnocentrism" of Russian consumers is best understood when considered along the following lines of tensions. The first tension centers on consumers' concerns with quality and their experiences of the post-Soviet free market. In the 1990s transition from a socialist to a market economy, counterfeiting was rampant; an army of one-night entrepreneurs manufactured goods in garages and decorated them with foreign labels. There were many small-scale producers seeking to capitalize their home-grown know-how within the newly liberalized production system. The flood of forged and genuine imports and new local goods created a sense of a chaotic market – a space out of control where producers rule and anything goes as long as it is profitable, where consumers should take care not to be duped or poisoned. In that context, consumers chose domestic (often former Soviet) goods because they offered shoppers a sense of familiarity, safety and security. In Soviet times, the state guaranteed and enforced product safety through a system of quality standards. The system implied that all goods were produced to "scientific standards" developed in research institutes independent of an individual producer's capabilities and external to its interests. In contrast, the workings of the free market with its self-regulation ethos was less understood, and, given their initial market experiences, people were skeptical of a market's quality control system. Thus, consumers often opted for the familiar guarantees of the state, choosing seemingly state-endorsed products (e.g., Kenneth 2003a).

The second tension centers on the country's perceived position within a global hierarchy of economic development. For many in Russia, Gorbochev's *perestroika* (reconstruction) was a promise of "finally catching up with the rest of the (Western) world" and becoming a European country, particularly in terms of lifestyle and consumption. However, due the economic instability in the 1990s, specifically the 1998 currency devaluation, Western goods became too expensive, hence out of reach for many. That exposed as a fantasy the imagery of the West as a place of abundance and comfort *for all* which many Soviet people believed. Also, in Soviet times, Western goods were believed to be superior in every way – better quality and healthier, more aesthetic and technologically advanced, and above all, they were seen as magical, capable of making a person happy. Thus, disillusionment was inevitable. However, that disillusionment was not attributed to unrealistic initial expectations, but to the "fact" that Western firms were not selling their best products in Russia. There was a pervasive belief that firms designated some cheap, low quality, even harmful goods for "export to Russia," because Russia was becoming a poor "Third World" country (Patico 2003). The belief was corroborated by the observations that Russian factories were closing, the economy was being sustained on raw materials exports and the public believed "nobody wants our goods." In short, underlying the tension was the concern that the changes were transforming Russia into a "Third World" country, thus driving people further away from the desired "Western way" of living.

The third tension is the *perestroika*-induced disjuncture between economic and cultural capital experienced by some social groups in Russia. The study of teachers in St Petersburg (ibid.) found that reforms led to the economic impoverishment of these formally "respectable representatives of mass intelligentsia" – a social class of well-educated people engaged in intellectual labor directed at the development and dissemination of culture. As their incomes shrank in absolute and relative terms, teachers found themselves marginalized, unable to enjoy the long-desired Western goods or partake in shaping the newly emergent market culture. Thus, many adopted a cynical and critical stance towards the market economy; notably, teachers often drew on the global discourses of ethical consumption to advance their criticism and explain their (local-oriented) consumption patterns.

How is it possible for a firm to tap into these complex global–local tensions in Russia and become a success? Let's look at one example. Green Mama is among Russia's top five manufacturers and marketers of cosmetics. Recently nominated "the best Russian brand" (Green Mama n.d.), it competes in the $4 billion Russian cosmetics market alongside the former Soviet giants (e.g., Kalina and Novaya Zarya) and transnational corporations (e.g., Proctor & Gamble and L'Oréal). The company is "a family-owned corporate entity" that was established in 1996 by Oleg and Irina Nasobin (Green Mama n.d.). From the beginning, the company promoted itself as *international* with operations in the Czech Republic, France and Russia and specialist employees from Russia, France, Japan, Ukraine, and South Africa. Later, the company set up headquarters in Grass (France) and production facilities in Russia, and presented itself as "Russian company with a French address" (*The New York Times*, 2000). The French connection was crucial for the company's initial success, because former Soviet consumers believed that the best quality cosmetics came from France, and more generally, the allure of the foreign was still strong (ibid.) Equally important for the company was to assert its Russian "roots." It did so in a powerful way – the company's positioning was based on the use of native Russian plants as active ingredients. In his interviews, Mr. Nasobin noted that the ribwort, a Russian roadside weed or a daisy are "our own, close to a Russian heart," hence more suitable for a Russian than foreign jojoba. In a sea of foreign-made products with attractive packaging but strange ingredients, Green Mama offered consumers what they were looking for – familiar ingredients that had the smell of childhood and/or Russian nature, in a foreign package. Similarly, the company's name – Green Mama – maintains a local–foreign duality: although written in English it is understandable to anyone with minimal knowledge of English and the word "mama" is Russian for "mother," implying home and care. Thus, as the *New York Times* (2000) writes, the company's winning formula was "homegrown extracts with a made-in-France label."

In a market plagued by distrust, as a small company with an unknown name, Green Mama had to establish a reputation as a quality producer. It addressed the challenge in several ways. First, it linked itself to the geographical area, known as "the global capital of cosmetics and perfumery and the center for global research into essential oils and a venue for top scientific conferences" (Kenneth 2003b: 2). Second, it set its research laboratories in France away from the mass production facilities in Russia, thereby creating the perception of external quality standards, i.e. to a degree, replicating the Soviet model (described above). Significantly, to reassure concerned consumers, the company explained that its standards differ from those of transnational corporations. For instance, the color of a cream may vary from tube to tube because, unlike many transnationals, the company produced only *natural cosmetics*; it used all natural ingredients, characteristics of which can change depending on the season. Third, the company emphasized that it conducted research and manufacturing for some well-known foreign brands, and exported its own "Russian-made products" to 34 countries (Green Mama n.d.).

Green Mama defines its target audience as the "representatives of intelligentsia," educated people with "high cultural level," and someone "who pays attention to his or her health and body, and is not susceptible to direct effects of aggressive advertising ... someone who knows exactly what s/he wants, or someone who thinks before buying anything" (ibid.). Throughout the years, the company has been successful in aligning its marketing strategy with the sensibilities of this consumer group. Green Mama does not advertise nationally, instead it uses local newspapers, radio, television and a multi-language web-page. Indeed, Mr. Nasobin insists that he does not believe in marketing, market competition, and operational figures since the company has "a different orientation on the market." He states:

> Unlike typical US companies our aim is not to control everything in the sector by absorbing or swallowing others.... We are in the business of cosmetics production. Therefore, our central aim is to produce quality products, try to sell them, and whatever we get is all ours. We also don't have a goal of making all women use our products, etc.
>
> (Kenneth 2003b: 22)

Such rhetoric echoes the sentiments of the "representatives of intelligentsia," who have been hit the hardest economically and socio-culturally by the reforms and are critical of "the Western market" with its predatory competition and in-your-face marketing tactics.

Consistent with the ethos of this target audience, the Green Mama's "quality products" are natural, ethical and eco-friendly. The company followed an intricate path to assert this "natural" image. It distanced itself from transnational, industrialized producers, while communicating that Green Mama was not a home-based operation with grandmother's pots either (Green Mama n.d.). Green Mama claims to use cutting-edge technologies, engage in scientific research and employ top experts, to create superior quality recipes and produce on a modest scale. The company's publicity materials educate consumers about production processes and characteristics of active ingredients used. Furthermore, Green Mama's advertising and packaging are dominated by a soft-green pallet and draw on associations with the local nature and sensory experiences of native plants. Yet, Green Mama is grounded in the global concern with ethical production. For Green Mama, "ethical" includes a sustainable use of natural ingredients accompanied with a lack of animal testing, no animal-derived products, no preservatives, not using genetically modified ingredients, or chemical enhancers of color and scent. Moreover, "ethical" means honesty (hence, the detailed product labeling) and a fair price for consumers, whose "ethical concerns is a part of the company's ethical image" (ibid.).

Green Mama's mission is similar to that of many other international companies – a developer of "eco-friendly & chic cosmetic products for the idealists of the world, for all those who read the label before choosing a cream" (ibid.). However, the company achieved its success by responding to the global–local tensions as they play out in the post-socialist Russia. Green Mama used the foreign side to distance itself from the ills of the reform era market in Russia, while endorsing the quality of its products. It used the local side to differentiate itself from foreign competitors, which have been dominating the hearts of consumers in Russia since Soviet times, and to appeal to the sensibilities of those locals, who have been disenfranchised by the market. Overall, Green Mama managed to bridge the foreign–local tension by linking the local anxieties with global concerns.

You can find out more information and take a look at some of Green Mama's products on their website: http://www.greenmama.ru.

Marketing Cola Turka in Turkey

Until recently, the cola market in Turkey, similar to many other countries, was dominated by two giants, Coca-Cola and Pepsi Cola. Coca-Cola was the market leader with more than 60 percent share, and Pepsi Cola commanded around 25 percent share (Thompson 2005). In July 2003, a local brand, Cola Turka, entered the market with significant advertising support and ambition to become a key player. Cola Turka is manufactured and marketed by Ülker, a giant Turkish company that operates in fields as diverse as food and beverage, information technologies, logistics, packaging, and real estate. Ülker was established in 1944 as a small manufacturer of cookies; over the years it developed into a global firm that now exports its products to over 110 countries (www.ülker.com.tr/en). In 2007, the group purchased Godiva Chocolatier. Although Ülker has never projected an Islamic image in its marketing communications, the company is well known for its ties to Islamist politics in Turkey. The group's entry to the cola market signaled a direct attack on Coca-Cola.

All over the world there are several local brands that position themselves as "anti-Coca-Cola" and resist Coca-Cola as a symbol of American colonization and cultural imperialism. Brands such as Mecca Cola, Zam Zam Cola and Qibla Cola target Muslim consumers and attempt to position themselves as morally superior alternatives to Coca-Cola. For example, Mecca Cola communicates with its audience through the tag lines "No more drinking stupid – drink with commitment" and "Don't shake me, shake your conscience!" The company publicizes that it donates 10 percent of its profits to charities in the Palestinian territories. Like Mecca Cola, Qibla Cola aims to offer "real alternatives to global consumer brands that support unjust policies" (Qibla Cola). In addition to Qibla Cola, the company sells Qibla Fantasy (orange and mango) and Qibla 5 (lemon and lime, named after the five pillars of Islam). There are other Muslim colas dedicated to taking market shares from Coca-Cola. However, they face distribution problems and typically remain as "niche" products. With their low market shares, they pose little threat to Coca-Cola.

Unlike other Muslim colas, Cola Turka did not position itself as "anti-cola" and emphasize its religious connotations. On the contrary, Cola Turka claimed to be the cola that not only Turks but also Americans would prefer to drink. The launch commercials aimed to convey the idea of "Drink Cola Turka, become Turkish." The commercials were produced by the Istanbul affiliate of Young and Rubicam and featured American actors Chevy Chase and Bob Brown. In the first commercial, Chase walks through Times Square as a car full of Turkish men, wrapped in their national flag, drive by celebrating a soccer victory. Perplexed by what he saw, Chase enters a diner only to realize that a New Yorker (Bob Brown) in a cowboy hat, sitting at the counter, speaks to him in Turkish after drinking Cola Turka. In the second commercial, Chase returns to his suburban home to discover his wife preparing a traditional Turkish meal for the children and their grandparents. At dinner, everyone drinks Cola Turka and begins singing the Turkish anthem of the youth, a popular song associated with Turkish national independence. Chase can't resist any more and sips Cola Turka. In the last scene Chase wears a bushy black mustache, a stereotypical symbol of Turkishness and finally becomes "Turkishized." The slogan "Cola is the usual coke, Turka is our Turka" appears at the end.

The commercials were an immediate success. Brand name awareness increased rapidly and, by October 2003, Cola Turka had captured 20 percent of the market share (Thompson 2005). However, in the coming months, the share dropped to around 10 points. There were several reasons for the drop. Coca-Cola responded swiftly and aggressively and engaged in a price war. Some consumers who initially tried the product claimed that they did not like its taste. And some others, who learned that Cola Turka was produced by Ülker, a company associated with Islamist politics, did not want to purchase the brand (Sandıkcı and Ekici 2009). Nonetheless, Cola Turka was able to capture a loyal and substantial group of consumers who believed that Cola Turka offered a strong, tasteful, and ideologically correct alternative to Coca-Cola. According to company officials, Cola Turka now commands a 13 percent market share and competes head on with Pepsi Cola for the number two position in the market. Ülker exports Cola Turka to more than 15 countries, including the USA and France, and has extended the product line by offering new varieties such as Cola Turka Sıfır (Zero).

What are the reasons underlying Cola Turka's success? In order to understand how Cola Turka became a key contender in the cola market, one needs to examine the socio-cultural underpinnings of the brand's marketing strategy. Similar to Inca Cola, Cola Turka stayed away from an explicit "anti-cola" positioning. Instead, it mobilized both nationalist pride and cosmopolitan subjectivity and sought to appeal to consumers by projecting a model of "global Turkishness." It claimed to be as good as the foreign and yet national at the same time. However, Cola Turka did not simply exploit Turkish consumers' nationalist feelings. Rather, it articulated the neoliberal nationalist discourse and offered its consumers a way to reconcile the tension between the local and global.

Until the 1980s, Turkey's economic development strategy was based on the import-substitution model. The semi-controlled mixed economy consisted of a domestically oriented publicly and privately owned industrial sector and mostly privately owned small agricultural businesses. With many restrictions on foreign direct investment and high import tariffs, local companies were protected from global competition. The range of consumer goods was limited and their quality was mediocre and the country frequently suffered from product shortages. In the 1980s, the economy went through a neo-liberal restructuring. With the opening up of the country to global competition, Turkish consumers found themselves bombarded with foreign brand name products that they either had not heard of before or could only have purchased on the black market. Given the relative developmental status of the country and the prices and standing of its products in both domestic and world markets, respect and esteem for national identity and national products had been low. Similarly, pride in local culture and local products had dissipated and respect in what the locals could do had diminished. In such a context, except for elite cosmopolitans, most consumers' reactions to foreign products were mixed. On the one hand, foreign brands were regarded as prestigious and of high quality and hence much more desirable than the local ones; but on the other hand, foreign brands lacked the familiarity and the casual comfort of local products.

In the late 1990s, there was a greater variety of products, both local and imported, along with a greater quality range for both. Along with such proliferation, there has been a reinterpretation of the local and the traditional. Products that offered a sense of Turkishness but with a global sensitivity began to achieve significant success. For example, a show entitled *Sultans of the Dance* (the title *is* indeed in English) has become hugely successful. It is a Turkish version of the Irish Riverdance show and consists of stylized folk dances and music from various regions of Turkey with allusions to ancient Anatolian myths. Many proud viewers comment that "it is great to see that *we* can accomplish such a professional, world class show." Products that successfully blend Turkishness with globalness, such as Ottoman-inspired luxury hotels and spas or Starbucks-like Turkish coffee chains, have begun to enjoy increasing shares and profits. That has been the case even for electronics which started to sell globally and advertise their global sales successes, depicting Western consumers using Turkish electronics. They convinced many consumers that Turkish brands are now as good as the global ones, and that "*we* can produce electronics as well as anyone else." Similarly, Cola Turka skillfully responded and took advantage of the tension between Turkishness and globalness. From the very beginning, it has strategically and successfully articulated a sense of global Turkishness. However, while Cola Turka emphasized its local roots in its marketing communications activities, it sought to distance itself from projecting a hardcore nationalistic image. By emphasizing self-respect at the national level and seeking recognition at the global level, Cola Turka has won the hearts and minds of many consumers.

The website for Cola Turka can be found at: http://www.colaturka.com.tr

Managerial implications

Green Mama (Russia) and Ülker's Cola Turka (Turkey) devised unique marketing strategies in their respective internationalized markets in order to compete in industries dominated by transnational giants. Both companies managed to successfully compete by attending to complex global–local tensions and taking advantage of their cultural capital. Green Mama and Ülker's Cola Turka serve as models for transnational giants as well as other emergent market companies. Their marketing solutions respond to complex global dynamics within a specific market and pertain to the company's capabilities, industry's structure and competition. Also, the solutions are built on nuanced understandings of historical cultural sensibilities and socio-political contexts that shape consumer preferences. Thus, the solutions are sensitive to the existing cultural forces and tensions and incorporate them to ease the associated consumer anxieties. Accordingly, as with Cemex México (discussed above), the key issue of successful glocalization is the specification of how it is to be implemented rather than solely about deciding on the extent and balance of localness and globalness in marketing activities. These cases illustrate: (1) the usefulness of the mobilization of cultural resources in generating customer value and thus competing with transnational giants; and (2) the merits of attending to the coexistence and interpenetration of the global and the local forces.

In today's interconnected world, business success lies in dialogue within the global–local encounters. The local companies are best positioned to succeed by engaging with the global as they experience it in their markets, rather than merely imitating transnationals or being anti-global. The transnational companies are likely to win by understanding and responding to the global/local cultural forces and tensions, rather than imposing a global uniformity.

To do this, managers need to go beyond considering only the differences and similarities between foreign and local cultures. They need to understand the tensions and negotiations among significant cultural forces that might appear to be poles. Transnationals and emergent market companies that attend to the interactions among apparently opposing cultural forces gain knowledge of various tensions local consumers face and deal with in their daily lives. To uncover such tensions, marketing managers should develop a reflexive distance to both local and global cultures. In other words, they must look at the local through the lens of the global and at the global through the lens of the local. Such knowledge allows companies to craft innovative marketing solutions that help consumers negotiate and solve cultural tensions. The emphasis on tensions suggests that consumers do not live on the poles of global or local, ethnocentric or cosmopolitan, or traditional or modern, but rather they navigate these dimensions. Thus, as the Green Mama and Cola Turka examples show, some consumers want to have both "the alluring global" and "the comforting local" and prefer marketing solutions that promise both. Companies catering to this desire for both the local and the global stand to win the hearts and minds of consumers.

Review and discussion questions

1 Compare and contrast standardization, adaptation and glocalization approaches.
2 Discuss the major strengths and weaknesses of the cultural perspective over conventional approaches to international marketing.
3 Explain what "the allure of the global" is.
4 Explain what "the comfort of the local" is.
5 What is the notion of "cultural tension" in marketing management from a cultural perspective?
6 Examine marketing practices of a transnational company such as McDonald's and discuss whether and to what extent the company attends to the cultural tensions in your country. Explain the tensions consumers face. Discuss the specific strategies that the company has or should devise to help consumers solve these tensions.
7 Find examples of companies that base their international marketing strategies primarily on standardization, adaptation or glocalization. Discuss the strengths and weaknesses of each approach.
8 Identify a cultural tension experienced by a particular consumer segment in your country (for example, the disjuncture between economic and cultural capital experienced by the intelligentsia in Russia) and discuss the implications for a transnational firm that plans to market its products to this consumer segment.

Keywords

adaptation, allure of the global, comfort of the local, consumer ethnocentricity, cultural resource, cultural tension, global marketing strategy, glocalization, historical specificity, nationalism, local marketing strategy, religion, standardization

Note

1 Bourdieu's (1986) concept referring to knowledge, cultural competencies and orientations, and social connections.

References

Appadurai, Arjun (1990) "Disjuncture and Difference in the Global Economy," in M. Featherstone (ed.) *Global Culture: Nationalism, Globalization and Modernity*, London: Sage, pp. 295–310.

Askegaard, Søren, Kjeldgaard, Dannie, and Arnould, Eric J. (2009) "Reflexive Culture's Consequences," in Cheryl Nakata (ed.), *Beyond Hofstede: Culture Frameworks for Global Marketing and Management*, London: Palgrave Macmillan, pp. 101–24.

Bourdieu, Pierre (1986) "Forms of Capital," in J. G. Richardson (ed.), *Handbook of Theory and Research for the Sociology of Education*, New York: Greenwood Press, pp. 241–58.

Caldwell, Melissa (2002) "The Taste of Nationalism: Food Politics in Postsocialist Moscow," *Ethos*, 67(3): 295–319.

Ger, Güliz (1999) "Localizing in the Village: Local Firms Competing in Global Markets", *California Management Review*, 41(4): 64–83.

—— (2005) "Warming: Making the New Familiar and Moral," *Ethnologia Europea: Journal of European Ethnology*, 35(1–2): 19–22.

Ger, Güliz and Belk, Russell (1996) "I'd like to Buy the World a Coke: Consumptionscapes of the 'Less Affluent World'," *Journal of Consumer Policy*, 19(3): 271–304.

Green Mama (n.d.) www.greenmama.ru

Holt, Douglas B. (1994) "Consumers' Cultural Differences as Local Systems of Tastes: A Critique of the Personality/Values Approach and an Alternative Framework," *Asia Pacific Advances in Consumer Research*, 1: 178–84.

Kenneth, Christopher (2003a) "Russia's World of Cosmetics and Fragrance," *The Russia Journal*, 524 (May 15).

—— (2003b) "Heading a Family Empire," *The Russia Journal*, 528 (July 1).

Leteller, M. F., Flores, F. and Spinosa, C. (2003) "Developing Productive Customers in Emerging Markets," *California Management Review*, 54(4): 77–103.

Levitt, Theodore (1983) "The Globalization of Markets," *Harvard Business Review*, 83(3): 92–102.

Nakata, Cheryl (ed.) (2009) *Beyond Hofstede: Culture Frameworks for Global Marketing and Management*, London: Palgrave Macmillan.

New York Times (2000) "International Business: Russians Want Beauty with Scent of Home," July 29.

Orlove, Benjamin (ed.) (1997) *The Allure of the Foreign*, Ann Arbor, MI: University of Michigan Press.

Patico, Jennifer (2003) "Consuming the West but Becoming Third World: Food Imports and the Experience of Russianness," *Anthropology of East Europe Review*, 21(1): 31–6.

Sandıkcı, Özlem and Ekici, Ahmet (2009) "Politically Motivated Brand Rejection," *Journal of Business Research*, 62(2): 208–17.

Thompson, Donald (2005) *Marketing Management in Turkey: Cases and Challenges*, Ankara: Gazi Kitabevi.

Wilk, Richard R. (1999) "'Real Belizean Food': Building Local Identity in the Transnational Caribbean," *American Anthropologist*, 101(2): 244–55.

3 Mediterranean shoes conquer the world

Global branding from local resources: the Camper case

Daniele Dalli and Simona Romani

Overview

Brand management literature is often based on the implicit assumption that there are general rules and common principles for globally building and exploiting a brand's potential. According to this view, brand meanings and values can be "adapted" to the international setting according to the target markets' characteristics. Moreover, adaptation usually presupposes domestic (country of origin) and international markets' intrinsic characteristics.

In this section, we describe the Camper case: this company succeeded in positioning the brand according to its local meanings and values, influencing the market to accept them, thus contradicting the "adaptation" paradigm (*glocal*: think global, act local) and following the opposite way (*locbal*: think local, act global). Furthermore, this experience demonstrates that management rules, especially when they involve cultural interaction, can be critically assessed and "transformed". Subsequently, original, innovative, and successful strategies can be developed by interpreting the brand's role in its cultural background and in the target market.

Introduction

This chapter aims to demonstrate that, following a cultural orientation in brand management, effective international marketing strategies can be based on local values and meanings that can be successfully extended towards the global market. This is the situation at Camper, originally a small company on the island of Majorca, Spain – geographically and culturally a small area compared with the large economies of North America, continental Europe and Japan. The company has successfully exported its products using the brand as an ideological and cultural carrier (Holt 2004; Schroeder *et al*. 2006) representing ethnic and ethical issues, even critical ones. An example of the latter is the company's famous "walk don't run" slogan that seems targeted at global footwear brands that encourage jogging. Hence, a cultural orientation in marketing can be promising for many small and medium-sized companies, not necessarily located in wealthy economies, but still aiming at competing on a global scale, "out-localizing" transnational corporations (Ger 1999).

Traditional strategic brand management often follows the implicit assumption of branding as a universal technique and the use of common principles across cultures to build a strong brand. It ignores the crucial aspect of brand as a cultural form; in practice, the traditional approach to brands and branding assumes that the cultural context has a marginal role in determining the brand architecture and the model of the brand development.

Kapferer (2008), for example, minimizes the importance of the brands' historical, geographical and cultural roots in the creation of a strong global brand identity and positioning. He affirms that the geographical roots (Premium vodka and Finland) or the native soil's values (Apple and California) can help the process of brand building, but deems many other elements to be more important in this process, such as a brand's typical products, symbols, logotypes, etc.

From another point of view, Keller (2008) focuses on brand value creation (building). According to this perspective, companies create value starting from zero and/or exploiting extant cultural and symbolic resources. In this process, nothing is said about the ideological dimension of the market process: brands and branding are not neutral cultural tools and their development often implies ideological, if not even ethical, decisions. Branding strategies and their extension to international markets can be seen as acts of reproduction of the dominant ideological values (Arnould and Thompson 2005). In fact, often consumers react negatively to corporate communication and try to resist (Holt 2002). Companies are not necessarily constrained to carry on and reproduce extant market ideology: they can also challenge mainstream values and differentiate their positioning in ideological and ethical terms. This means paying attention to the target consumers' cultural characteristics in a more profound, critical, and interactive way than the usual "adaptation" paradigm (Cayla and Arnould 2008).

In this section, unlike in the above-mentioned approaches, we accept the idea of a brand as a specific symbolic form, a particular way of talking about and regarding the world. Consequently, it is essential to examine branding from deep historical, geographical and socio-cultural contexts in order to acknowledge the diverse way of branding and thinking about brands across different situations. If branding is viewed as a culturally malleable mode of communication, this allows us to think more productively about the way the cultural context influences branding activities – even its ideological dimension.

The interpretive tradition in consumer research has shown how important the knowledge of local culture can be in order to compete successfully against global players (Ger 1999): the intrinsic advantage of local companies is their "local identity and culture". This can be improved to compete with "local" strategies aimed at defining goods and services' "authentic" value. Traditional international marketing approaches focus brand management's attention on the search for similarities at the global level to turn them into local, adapted marketing programs, whereas in a more culturally oriented fashion, local companies could and should focus on local idiosyncrasies and extend them on a global scale (Askegaard and Kjeldgaard 2007).

As the case of Camper will demonstrate, companies can also consider the socio-cultural setting in critical ways, proposing new and unexpected cultural and marketing programs, in which "local" resources are employed to change the "global" cultural and competitive scenario.

Consider the Camper case in a specific segment of the footwear market:

- Camper "criticized" the market's dominant logic: Walk, don't run!
- Camper chose concerned and committed consumers: *no los compres, si no los necesitas!* (Don't buy the product, if you don't need it!)
- Camper has changed (self-criticism) its positioning and communication by trying to select and link groups of consumers with similar cultural and ideological orientations toward the same core concept: the Med (the Mediterranean) is the Net!

In this section we analyze the emergence of Camper's footwear as a successful international brand to contribute to this research stream. In particular, we discuss the ways in which historical, cultural, social and geographical configurations could influence brand activities and become precious resources that the company can use to define diverse and particular identities and positioning.

In 2000, with a view to competing against well-funded global fashion brands in the global market, Camper launched its campaign, "The Walking Society". By building on its established origins and on the David and Goliath story (with its compelling binaries), Camper was portrayed as "small", "friendly", "authentic" and rooted in a traditional "Mediterranean spirit". This unique positioning stood in clear contrast to the "cool" and "placeless" global fashion brands and produced results in terms of sales and revenues.

To explain Camper's success, we need to explore the complex relations between different forms of brand building strategies, myths and authenticity.

The company and its history

To understand the Camper phenomenon, we must start with its origins. The company's history began in 1877 when Antonio Fluxà, on returning from a trip to England, brought together a group of craftsmen in his birthplace, Majorca,[1] and set up the island's first shoe factory. The manufacturing tradition was handed down from father to son to Antonio Fluxà's grandson, Lorenzo, who, in 1975, created the Camper brand with the idea of introducing design in the company and producing casual wear products.

In a Spain where the Franco dictatorship had recently ended and which was characterized by a strongly conservative spirit, Camper's decision to introduce casual shoes was no coincidence. The project emerged as a yearning for liberty and change – a yearning which marked the post-Franco period in Spain, an example of the desire for a radical transformation after years of isolation and the country's closed attitude towards the rest of the world.

Camper had anticipated the explosion of creativity that would characterize the country a few years later, particularly in the city of Barcelona, with which Camper has always had close and strong relations. It was precisely here that the first mono-brand shop was opened in 1981, and here that, 23 years later, Camper initiated its business diversification in the catering (with Camper FoodBall) and hospitality (with Casa Camper) sectors.

In 1992, the international expansion of the brand began with the opening of branches (offices and shops) in the main centres of European fashion (the UK, France, and Italy).

However, the crucial turning point for Camper came after a meeting with the young copywriter Shubhankar Ray[2] who discovered the brand in 2000 during a trip to Majorca.

> I thought it had the potential of Apple. There is something friendly about it; I thought it was slightly idiosyncratic and had more to do with industrial design than fashion. Also, they weren't based in London or New York, but Majorca. I thought the location had a psycho-geographical impact on the brand. But the image was not really an international standard.
>
> (Interview recorded by the authors at the Camper headquarters in Majorca in July 2006. This holds for other excerpts, unless otherwise stated.)

Ray managed to meet with Lorenzo Fluxà, who immediately decided to employ him to develop Camper's image:

I asked to be put up in an old finca on the hill to achieve the same psycho-geographical effect. I started to look at what this culture comprised. They are not confident with outsiders; there are fences everywhere. They are insular, Spartan. There is a reluctance to waste money … I started photographing the countryside, the farmer playing a card game called "truco", people on Vespas, horse-trap racing in which the horses aren't allowed to run. I started to define another Majorca, one that wasn't about tourists getting drunk on the beach.[3]

The result of this experience was the identification of something "unique" about both the brand and the island. It was something that had always been there, but that had never been defined. Ray decided to use this exclusivity, together with other elements, to conceive the Camper brand that, right from the start, he considered as something very distant from traditional, US-based models of globalization and consumerism.

In contemporary social and cultural conditions, brands can have several potential meanings and can be used and interpreted in unexpected ways in local contexts, where they are re-territorialized, appropriated and transformed in surprising ways. For example, Cova *et al.* (2007) highlight many variations in the meanings that American and French players give to a battle re-enactment game called Warhammer. Again, Kates and Goh (2003), using the Absolute Vodka brand case, illustrate that brand meanings "morph" across social, community and national groups, facilitated by marketers who understand plurality and cultural diversity. However, while certain global brands might be characteristically fluid, others are more culturally and affectively fixed. Crucially, Holt (2006) recognizes that brands cannot generate meanings to which people will subscribe regardless. Such brands should rather tap into broader sensations, desires, opinions and identities, often aligning themselves with mythical notions produced by different cultural forms such as movies, novels, music, popular discourse, etc. Brands may thus be conceived as "ideological parasites" that depend on tapping into pre-existing discourses and feelings, into "myth markets" (ibid.).

Here we can identify a popular myth associated with the Camper case that taps into popular pre-existing structures of feeling, belief and identity and through which individuals acquire meaning for their social life and experiences. It is, in fact, by building on its established origins and the David and Goliath story – dynamized by the compelling mini/ giant, local/global and south/north binaries – that the Camper brand emerges as "small", "friendly", "authentic" and rooted in a traditional "Mediterranean spirit". This is very distant from the prefabricated glossy images that advertisers traditionally associate with global fashion brands.

This myth is often used whenever a small, weak party takes on a giant. In most contexts, smallness and weakness are not advantages as such. Goliath killed many other Israelites who were smaller and weaker. David's sling and five stones taken from a brook were simple technology, especially when employed against the armour that made Goliath seem invulnerable. However, David's one stone hit him on the forehead and the giant fell face down.

Similarly, Ray identified in the normally devalued local (in comparison to the global) possible strengths. These strengths could be grasped when combined, in new dynamic ways, with the island's precious historical, geographical and cultural resources. Together with the family's know-how of the product, the austerity and simplicity of the rural world, as well as the Mediterranean history and culture, all of these influence the brand's aesthetics and values. These phenomena represent several forms of brand rooting that the company uses to successfully create a distinctive and authentic image.

Rooting Camper in the rural Mediterranean world

Rurality and old traditions

> Camper means peasant, and the simplicity of the rural world is one of the brand's most important roots. … My previous work at Levis and Caterpillar had all been about global-ization and the urban; I began to conceive Camper as the opposite: local and rural. I was thinking about an alternative and opposite viewpoint to construct its brand image. I was lucky that the brand owner wanted to create something different and indulged me in my particular line of thinking, which was based more on 'mindstyle' than on lifestyle.

As Ray passionately and rigorously stresses, given its geographical origin (Majorca), the Camper brand had the possibility of being rooted in an honest and simple rural spirit. This is an alternative way of thinking – the opposite of the great themes of modernization and development.

Pasini (2005) observes that the geography of this brand forms part of its DNA, to the point that, from time to time, one has the impression that Camper's rural roots are as important as the product itself. This particular brand would not have been possible, or would have been quite different, had it not been conceived in Majorca.

The present cultural context – having left the phase of triumphant modernity behind and now witnessing the affirmation of postmodern thought – clearly favours this type of very "traditional" rooting. Owing to postmodernity's rediscovery of aesthetic and emotive aspects, its sense of openness toward others and those who are different, and the end of the great narratives, it can accommodate the rise of new approaches in branding and marketing in general.

As several authors note (Firat and Dholakia 2006), postmodernism, precisely because it succeeds modernism, does not demonize tradition as a simple and obtuse resistance to modernity. It rather considers tradition as a resource, a store of symbols and meanings that can be reinterpreted in a new phase and on the basis of new requirements. Some groups of consumers actually perceive the need to distance themselves from the fundamentalism of modernity. They therefore transfer new values from rural traditions (honesty, austerity, simplicity) in order to regain the quality of life. These values can provide different concepts of wealth than the dominant ones, which are limited to a mere private accumulation of goods as a possible solution to present-day needs.

Camper crucially emphasizes respect for tradition and its rural origins, reinterpreting these on the basis of present needs, and giving them a new meaning in the light of changes brought about by progress and innovation:

> The spirit of the brand is transmitted through the product. Our shoes are a link between our origin and tradition and our markets' urban reality. They evoke the stable values of the rural Mediterranean world – durability and simplicity – and incorporate them into the urban world by means of a sophisticated informality, a careful design, a rhetoric that does not discard irony and, particularly, imagination.
>
> (Camper internal document)

We are thus faced with a postmodern, not a pre-modern interpretation of traditions. Rural values such as sobriety and respect for nature and the environment have endured the modernity that had reduced and confined them. However, by bearing the experience of this period and having acquired certain elements from it, these values are now transformed in respect of their origin. This signifies a reworking of traditions on the basis of their continuous interaction with modernity.

Hence, the pre-modern interpretation of austerity (reduce, re-use, repair) is re-taken from a contemporary viewpoint with recourse to new production processes that favour material and energy savings, to recycled and recyclable materials, to simple, basic and modest products. In addition, respect for nature and the environment is reconsidered through the use of ecological and natural materials. It is not by chance that Lorenza Fluxà, the actual owner, considers Camaleon (Figure 3.1), the first shoe model produced by Camper in 1976, to be the real symbol of the company. The reason is because this shoe was inspired by an authentic peasant model made in an artisan way with pieces of truck canvas, leather offcuts and rubber tire. Camaleon was the "original recycled" shoe.

As reported by Pasini (2005):

> Working toward health and sustainability, today, means adding value to a project, starting with a design that leans toward the essential that backs the idea of eliminating components and simplifying products rather than adding new and redundant elements. The experience of comfort is a simple idea that can be given concrete representation through materials and the production process if one is capable of applying a new concept of technology, in which the vision of a long-term future is sustained by the need to reduce and simplify rather than add elements. Reducing is the great hope of the future since reducing means diminishing our dependency on products and raw materials, which are clearly less and less compatible with the idea of sustainable development.
>
> (Interview with Juana Martorell, Camper Product Manager at that time)

The Camper product that perhaps best represents this philosophy is the "Wabi" (Figure 3.2). This shoe's name is a Japanese word from the verb "*Wabiru*" (to ask for forgiveness). The shoe was developed according to the concepts of simplicity, modest living, comfort and pure satisfaction. Ergonomic and environmentally friendly, the shoe was launched on the market with the slogan "healthy for your feet, good for the planet" and "healthy + clean = Wabi". The main trait of this model is that whereas the majority of shoes need an average of 10 production phases and 60 components, the Wabi merely requires four phases and three independent components (external protection, inner sole and sock) using natural, recyclable materials such as rubber, jute, felted wool or coconut fibre.

Figure 3.1 Camaleon shoes.

Figure 3.2 Wabi shoes.

The rural root of this brand is also recreated in advertising. Showing super-real, contradictory images of a simple and traditional Mediterranean reality is an alternative to the US-based models of globalization and consumption in which everybody is sexy and cool. Some examples from the campaigns include old men playing a local bowling game, small cars photographed in Naples, camels, Bedouins, and a contemporary Cleopatra in Cairo.

The Mediterranean history and culture

Another central element in the rooting of the Camper brand is the Mediterranean history and culture. Ray maintains that it is necessary to reappraise the Mediterranean, its dignity and identity and, accordingly, the need to disrupt the modern North's dominance. In particular, Ray's ideas are based on the desire to get rid of the clichés and stereotypes that have been attributed to the Mediterranean area by dominant thinking and that associates it with either the mafia, and other criminal activities, or with images of an idyllic tourist paradise. He strongly perceives the need to go beyond these perceptions and to focus on those values that constitute Mediterranean wealth, such as creativity, openness to others, fantasy, imagination and tolerance. These are the positive and valuable characteristics that should contribute to the brand-building process and form Camper's identity all over the world.

Ray's point of view on the role of the Mediterranean area is very aligned to that claimed in several books by Franco Cassano (1996, 1998, 2001, 2002), the Italian sociologist who takes on the challenge of trying to come up with a true discourse capable of illustrating Mediterranean thinking and culture. As he clearly affirms in *Paeninsula (Peninsula)* (1998: 90):

> Today, it is possible to rediscover the South, the Mediterranean, to restore the value of its innate polytheism, the relish of a moderation that arises from this ancient destination at the crossroads of nations. This is the only right thing to do here and not only here.

Mediterranean values are therefore not only a cultural proposal for the South, but a resource for contemporary thinking in general. These values can be of central importance in the South's integration into a global culture to which it can contribute creatively. This differs radically from its long-assigned role as a depressed area and obstacle to development. This means reformulating "alternative conventions of poverty and wealth, taking into account the dignity of another way of living" (Cassano 1996: 5). It means re-examining these points by dispelling the myths generated by modernity. For example:

The desert was not destined for the motorized idiocy of the Paris–Dakar. It has been a founding location of a part of spirituality, divine transits, marches, fasts, temptations and fears. It was much richer when crossed by these travellers than today when it has become the stake of consumerist followers of the foreign legion. Only a clouded mind could consider the desert as something awaiting progress, to fill, to develop for tourism and normalisation.

(ibid.)

One of the Mediterranean values given most attention is that of slowness. Cassano entitles the first chapter in *Pensiero meridiano (Meridian Thinking)* "go slowly" and certain texts contained in *Modernizzare stanca (Modernizing makes you tired)* are veritable eulogies to slowness. He observes that:

[T]he man of speed, *homo currens*, undoubtedly gains certain faculties, but loses others, primarily attention for others …, the passion, caring or tenderness that comes from having not merely aims, but also sentiments, not only competitors, but also friends, ties, prohibitions or troubles.

(2001: 154)

Regaining slowness can favour the contemporaneous presence of different temporalities (fast and slow) and therefore enable the individual to choose from these various contexts. As Firat (2005) observes, if only a small elite of trendsetters were to be inclined towards slowness, the majority of people would find pleasure in immersing themselves in different ways of living and consuming without limiting their choice to just one.

The defence of slowness is central for Camper with its motto "Walk, don't run" and "The Walking Society" advertising campaign that Ray created in 2001. Camper intends to restore the pleasure of walking to counter speed, which is one of modernity's greatest obsessions. Indeed, Camper's communication advises individuals to re-appropriate slower rhythms, rediscover reflection, calmness, pauses, a sense of sociality and contact with nature.

For Camper, walking also means travelling, going from one place to another. In fact, "The Walking Society" campaign takes the consumer to a different Mediterranean country each season. This is meant to reference (and reinforce) the cultural *Zeitgeist* underpinning the Camper brand.

Each campaign is rooted in a specific location (Majorca, Morocco, Italy, Greece, Egypt, etc.), with certain people and their customs, and seeks to illustrate some of the values found in the David and Goliath story that strongly inspire the brand-building process.

All in all, The Walking Society represents a virtual society of people who share the Mediterranean spirit, but come from different social, cultural, economic, or geographical realities and who dedicate their imagination and their efforts – individually or collectively – to contributing useful, positive ideas and solutions to improve the world.

(Camper internal document)

Moreover, as part of the campaign, Ray initiated a low-budget *magalog* (magazine + catalogue); this publication features provoking and often controversial photographs, amusing images from Moroccan landscapes, and of Bedouins in Egypt at the time of the American invasion of Iraq. Besides the images, Ray also features politically charged articles on subjects like the oil trade, the anti-car movement, slow food and free software in the *magalog*. The *magalog* can thus be seen as Camper communication's ideological vector.

The result: authenticity with "realism"

Camper attempts to deeply root its brand by using historical, geographical and cultural themes to attain authenticity – the key concept. The rural Mediterranean area becomes the site of claims for authenticity as a marker that distinguishes this area from the non-authentic urban global North.

On Lovemarks, Brenda from the United Arab Emirates writes:

> When you're in an elevator, do you press the button manically in the hope the doors will close quicker? Walk don't run. When you're passing by a garden do you put your head down, immersed in your thoughts? Walk don't run. Do you have to stop and talk to people or do you rush around from one chore to the next? Walk don't run. Do you take the time to savour the goodness in your food? Walk don't run. That is the Camper's spirit – open, authentic and refreshing.
>
> (September 7, 2006, www.lovemarks.com)

Authenticity is a central element in branding (Alexander 2009) because it serves as a form of cultural distinction that can be projected onto objects, places and institutions through which consumers can "express themselves and fix points of security and order in an amorphous modern society" (Spooner 1986: 226). Consumers look for brands that contribute to the creation of their identity by providing important symbolic and cultural elements (Arnould and Thompson 2005). Successful brands are those that best realize this project, that succeed in creating worlds that stimulate, provoke and inspire the consumer's imagination, that help him/her interpret the surrounding culture and find an acceptable position within it (Holt 2004; Beverland and Farrelly 2010).

However, this is not always enough to ensure long-lasting success, since in a situation of equality in terms of cultural contribution, consumers prefer the brands of companies that demonstrate their ability to fulfil their civic obligations, "that act like a local merchant, as a stalwart citizen of the community" (Holt 2002: 88). Camper has made a real contribution to this process of constructing a new form of authenticity that places increasing importance on the ethical and cultural qualities of the company that markets the brand, and which has to transform this brand into a veritable cultural resource that can inspire and stimulate consumers.

As illustrated above, by emphasizing the Mediterranean's re-evaluation and the recovery of tradition with moderation and also taking into consumers or citizens' increasing request for respect into consideration, Camper represents a true authentic brand – a "citizen artist brand" according to Holt's (2002) definition.

As Laura writes on Lovemark: "I love Camper because they love nature, while being innovative. Because they radiate happiness. Because they are fashionable, but they are out of the fashion system. Because I like what they believe in" (September 14, 2005, www.lovemarks.com).

Not all brands are made by "money-grabbing capitalists" selling products that consumers probably don't need. Some brands can project an honest reality with social responsibility and ethics. Camper is one of them.

However, this is not the end of the story. Since Camper faces more competition, Ray's task, in 2005, became to transform the rural Mediterranean positioning by including cities from the emerging world, to do so with humour and to extend the company image across the globe.

Transforming the rural Med positioning to include more international images

In Camper's language, walking is a metaphor for travel. In 2005, a new exciting journey in search of new cultural experiences and new possible relationships started for this brand.[4] The first destination was India with the Autumn/Winter 2005 campaign, which was immediately followed by China. Ray explains this decision:

> After the 2000–2004 period when the focus was on the Mediterranean and on the opposition between north and south, I had the feeling that there was a way to propose the same strategy, the same concept to a bigger world outside the Mediterranean. I considered the possibility of playing with the same idea, playing with the same things (slowness, walking, etc.) but inside a new setting, a new world.
>
> And I realized that there were relationships between the South (Spain, Italy, the Arabic countries and the East) that were far more than between the West and the South.

The East is synonymous with civilization, ease and comfort; it is the place of the community, of the hierarchy; it is the place where rules (natural, social, etc.) come before individuals whose freedom mainly lies in the interpretation of their roles in society (Cassano 1998: 50–1).

But the interesting point in this transformation from the rural Mediterranean to a more international positioning is the creation of a new type of opposition, based not only on the North–South binary this time, but also on alliances: on one side, the strong North-West characterized by innovation, technologies, and economics and, on the other side, the weak South-East with its backwardness, fatalism, and deficit. Again, David versus Goliath story emerges, although in an extended version.

Ray talks about "creative pollination" outside the Med and he tries to generate new cultural experiences associated with the brand, choosing the different cultures' essential and truly authentic elements and combining them in an original way. The images of holy cows in India, or of farmers and rice paddies in China are a way to reinforce Camper brand values – such as rurality, slowness, irony, naturality – and to enrich them with diversity (Figure 3.3).

The result of this activity is a new type of creative language open to experimentation and contamination, in which the experience of difference stops being a defensive barrier and become a stimulus for new contact. According to Ray, Camper "moves from the rural Mediterranean with reality to the international emerging world with diversity".

This movement to the East is also associated with an important Camper sales growth in the Asian Pacific, especially in Korea and Japan. The brand started to perform really well, much better than in other areas of the world, such as the US. However, the idea of the new South-East alliance was soon replaced by the South in the Autumn/Winter 2006 campaign. In this case, not the Mediterranean South, but the Latin American South as represented by Brazil and the city of São Paulo (Figure 3.4). Ray stresses "the passage from the old world

Figure 3.3 Camper advertising.

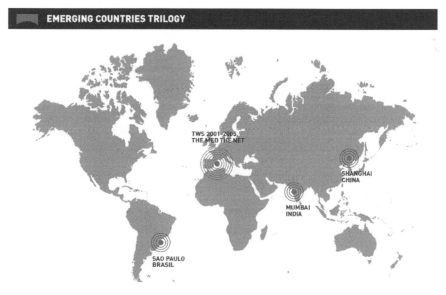

Figure 3.4 Emerging countries and Camper.

cities of influence – London, Paris, New York – to the new world cities of relevance – Mumbai, Shanghai, and São Paulo".

São Paulo is a location that emphasizes the brand's new international status, and the idea of movement from the Mediterranean to the rest of the world. The city's multicultural mix can specifically help deliver diversity as the new core brand value. The samba friends, the graffiti artists, the flower growers and the football players are the visual expression of the association between the rural Mediterranean Camper values and the social groups featuring Brazil's rich diversity of Brazil (Figure 3.5).

The emerging country trilogy closes Camper's journey around the world. As competition increases and the brand becomes more visible around the world, there is the need to protect the brand's mindstyle, values and personality. What next strategy will allow Camper to continue being a "special" brand?

The analysis of the diverse ways of branding and thinking about brands across different contexts is very limited. These issues are strongly related to the idea of a brand as a cultural form, which is generally detached from the traditional strategic brand management approach. Conversely, when a brand is accepted as a specific cultural and symbolic form, as a particular way of talking about and seeing the world (Cayla and Arnould 2008), it is crucial to consider it from deep historical, geographical and socio-cultural contexts. Thus, the diverse ways of branding and thinking about brands across situations can be acknowledged, and the idea that all over the world brands are evolving in the same way, can be rejected.

Conclusion and managerial recommendations

The Camper experience seems promising in the light of a cultural appraisal of marketing models and tools. Without a clever and committed concern for the cultural dimension of the company's background, actual setting, and final market, Camper would have not been able to compete against global players in the footwear market. In this case, symbolic and mythic elements of local culture have been processed and transferred to a larger setting (the international market), adapting brand image to and positioning in one country at a time, but following the same "ideological" framework: rurality, tradition, authenticity, moderation, etc.

In a sense, the company has employed both flexibility and modesty with regard to the cultural settings at which the brand has been targeted. Modesty means that Camper has not taken the actual market conditions for granted and the company has been willing to take a critical stance toward them, even towards its own values and past experiences. In a period in which "running" seemed a mainstream trend, Camper decided to ask its customers not to run, just walk. When global marketing communication had been focused on product performance, endorsement, and massive campaigns, Camper chose traditional and sustainable product attributes, peasants and farmers as endorsers, and their own customers as communication agents.

This history has been told by means of an open(-minded) cultural framework: flexible, modest, and – mostly importantly – open. The Med-is-the-Net metaphor stands for a flexible, soft, permeable and inclusive tool that the company used to intelligently "endear" their customers in different countries, and win their attention and attachment.

In a sense, Camper has turned the "glocal" (think global, act local) slogan into its opposite: "locbal" (think local, act global). The company has been able to apply a self-reflexive, self-critical, even critical assessment to assign the most value to the local symbolic and

Figure 3.5 Camper advertising.

cultural resources employed in an international setting (Askegaard and Kjeldgaard 2007; Ger 1999).

The Camper experience can be located in Cova's (2005) idea of a Mediterranean approach to marketing. Using Cassano's model of Meridian Thinking (Cassano 1998), he proposes a moderate marketing approach capable of avoiding the excesses that characterize the typical traditional view of marketing. Cova's moderate position of a company vis-à-vis its consumers generates:

> a more comprehensive and less utilitarian approach that does not invoke simplistic reflections phrased in terms of market actions or responses to consumers, but instead calls for a more complex understanding both of how companies fit into society, and also of their interrelations with all of its actors. In other words, this is a socially relevant perspective of the interface between clients, firms and all of their market-oriented or non-market-oriented stakeholders.
>
> (Cova 2005: 211)

Camper fits very well with this sense of proportion regarding the company's product offer, marketing approach and relation with society.

The company took a critical stance toward extant models about how to run the business and engage with customers. Starting from internal job conditions and relationships with employees, Camper developed a general positioning in terms of ethics and ideology. Employment contracts, services, and even manufacturing options (outsourcing, delocalization, materials, etc.) have been considered in the light of a mature and socially responsible attitude. Starting from this, Camper took a humble perspective about how to approach the market and its customers without imposing or projecting a pre-defined model of consumer behaviour to which customer could or should adapt. Besides, Camper offerings have been proposed as an opportunity, a resource, "just in case" it could prove to be interesting and/or attracting: *no los compres, si no los necesitas!* (Don't buy it, if you don't need it!). Moreover, the company took a pedagogical stance towards its customers and the market, trying to defend and support ideals of sustainability, openness, tolerance, and integration, creating a welcoming bundle of products, services, platforms, and meanings.

However, it is important that applying the associations between ways of thinking and managerial actions is not limited to the Med area, but can be extended to other areas of the world. An interesting case is represented by the Celtic approach to marketing (Brown 2006; McAuley *et al.* 2006) that stresses the valorization of the typical Celtic traits of being "spontaneous, creative, dangerous, mystical" and the opposition to the more Anglo-Saxon ones of being "methodical, rule-seeking, circumspect, rational" (Hackley 2006: 69). In terms of marketing practices, the focus here is on the use of Celtic symbols, designs, myths, and legends as part of the product, packaging, promotion, etc. The marketing of Guinness, the popular Irish beer, provides an useful successful example: in spite of being brewed in 50 countries and marketed in 150 regions, the "black stuff" continues to be quintessentially Irish because the Celtic myths and symbols have been central in the development of the brand identity during its long history (Simmons 2006).

Cayla and Eckhardt (2008) present interesting experiences about Asian companies that are trying to Asianize their positioning, situating brands as belonging less to a specific country and more to a region. Again, as in the Camper case, and in general in the construction of iconic American brands, as illustrated by Holt (2004), brand managers draw from different local stories and myths to create powerful brands. This is specifically true with these regional Asian brand managers' need to create a new synthesis of cultural referents (East and West, future and present, etc.). With these referents, they construct a new identity myth for Asian consumers that is more appealing than the traditional representation of an exotic Asia. Similar to the Camper experience, these brands try to combine tradition and modernity, and to construct a different type of modernity that does not imitate the West and that "escape the Western and orientalist gaze representing Asia as exotic" (Cayla and Eckhardt 2008: 226).

Review and discussion questions

The Camper experience suggests the need for a more plural, self-reflexive, culturally conscious, even critical reasoning about the way in which marketing managers approach branding decisions. The following elements can be employed to stimulate collective discussion:

1   Local cultural values are not necessarily marginal, even if, from a merely quantitative point of view, they represent a small portion of the whole market. Camper meanings and values are rooted in a micro-culture that lies at the crossroad between Spanish, Catalan, and Majorcan traditions, all of which share common Mediterranean origins. Regardless of the size of this cultural background, these values can be extended to and re-interpreted for a larger, multi-cultural setting.
2   Local, even marginal, cultural meanings and values prove attractive for various profiles/ segments of global consumers. Different markets have appreciated Camper shoes for different reasons – from the design to the company's communication, from its cultural values to its ethical stances. Local values can be conjugated according to different final market characteristics.
3   The development of local cultural values towards global branding strategies can be improved by employing managerial capabilities and competences that come from outside the cultural milieu: outsiders' cultural framework assists in identifying the most important issues in a local culture that can be better employed in the global branding strategy.
4   Given that brands can be conceived as cultural and ideological carriers, it is necessary to carefully identify and select appropriate symbols and values, starting from local and specific ones, and seeing whether and how they can be "translated" for a wider market;
5   In the Camper case, elements of the communication mix are markedly idiosyncratic compared to traditional marketing approaches: for instance, the endorsers of the brand differ from traditional ones. Which other elements in Camper's communication can be considered from the same perspective?
6   Camper aimed at building an iconic brand. Usually iconic brands benefit from premium price strategies. Is this true? If so, should it be accepted? Is it possible to conceive iconic brands as convenience brands?

Keywords

authenticity, critical marketing, cultural branding, hybridization, iconic brand, Mediterranean, myth, responsibility, simplicity, sustainability

Notes

1 Majorca is the largest of the Balearic Islands, Spain. It is located in the Mediterranean Sea, approximately 200 km south of Barcelona.
2 Shubhankar Ray was born in Calcutta, India, in 1968. After graduating from Manchester University with a Chemistry BSc, he worked for numerous global brands: G-Star, Camper, Caterpillar, Levi's, Stride, and Travel Fox.
3 McCracken (1988, pp. 11–12) describes the relationship between the researcher and the culture and observes that the "intimate acquaintance with one's own culture can create as much blindness as insight. It can prevent the observer from seeing cultural assumptions and practices." Ray, as a stranger to the local culture, was able to minimize the dangers of familiarity. Excerpt from Iconeye. com (http://www.iconeye.com/index.php?option = com_content&view = article&id = 2622:mallorca – icon-024--june-2005).
4 In 2005, in addition to the brand's internationalization phase, the company decided on a diversification phase. Camper FoodBall, an ecological and healthy alternative to fast food, and Casa Camper, a new concept hotel, are the results of this diversification. The company realized these projects internally and manages them under the motto "Producing for the three fundamental needs of man: feet, home and food, the rest is a bonus."

References

Alexander, N. (2009) "Brand Authentication: Creating and Maintaining Brand Auras", *European Journal of Marketing*, 43: 551–62.
Arnould, E. J. and Thompson, C. J. (2005) "Consumer Culture Theory (CCT): Twenty Years of Research", *Journal of Consumer Research*, 31: 868–82.
Askegaard, S. and Kjeldgaard, D. (2007) "Here, There, and Everywhere: Place Branding and Gastronomical Globalization in a Macromarketing Perspective", *Journal of Macromarketing*, 27: 138–47.
Beverland, M. B. and Farrelly, F. J. (2010) "The quest for authenticity in consumption: Consumer's purposive choice of authentic cues to shape experienced outcomes", *Journal of Consumer Research*, 36(6): 838–56.
Brown, S. (2006) "Tiocfaidh a´r la´: Introduction to the Special Issue", *Journal of Strategic Marketing*, 14: 1–9.
Cassano, F. (1996) *Il pensiero meridiano* [*Meridian Thinking*], Bari: Laterza.
—— (1998) *Paeninsula. L'Italia da ritrovare* [*Peninsula: Finding Italy Again*], Bari: Laterza.
—— (2001) *Modernizzare stanca: perdere tempo, guadagnare tempo* [*Modernizing Makes You Tired: Lose Time, Gain Time*], Bologna: Il Mulino.
—— (2002) *Il ritmo meridiano* [*Meridian Rhythm*], Lecce: Aramirè.
Cayla, J. and Arnould, E. J. (2008) "A Cultural Approach to Branding in the Global Marketplace", *Journal of International Marketing*, 16: 86–112.
Cayla, J. and Eckhardt, G. M. (2008) "Asian Brands and the Shaping of a Transnational Imagined Community", *Journal of Consumer Research*, 35(2): 216–30.
Cova, B. (2005) "Thinking of Marketing in Meridian Terms", *Marketing Theory*, 5: 205–14.
Cova, B., Pace, S., Park, D. J. (2007) "Global Brand Communities across Borders: The Warhammer Case", *International Marketing Review*, 24: 313–29.
Firat, A. F. (2005) "Meridian Thinking in Marketing? A Comment on Cova", *Marketing Theory*, 5: 215–19.
Firat, A. F. and Dholakia, N. (2006) "Theoretical and Philosophical Implications of Postmodern Debates: Some Challenges to Modern Marketing", *Marketing Theory*, 6: 123–62.
Ger, G. (1999) "Localizing in the Global Village: Local Firms Competing in Global Markets", *California Management Review*, 41: 64–83.

Hackley, C. (2006) "A Celtic Crossing: A Personal, Biographical Exploration of the Subjective Meaning of the Celtic Brand and its Role in Social Identity Formation", *Journal of Strategic Marketing*, 14: 69–76.

Holt, D. B. (2002) "Why Do Brands Cause Trouble? A Dialectical Theory of Consumer Culture and Branding", *Journal of Consumer Research*, 29: 70–90.

—— (2004) *How Brands Become Icons: The Principles of Cultural Branding*, Boston: Harvard Business School Press.

—— (2006) "Jack Daniel's America: Iconic Brands as Ideological Parasites and Proselytizers", *Journal of Consumer Culture*, 6: 355–77.

Kapferer, J -N. (2008) *The New Strategic Brand Management: Creating and Sustaining Brand Equity Long Term*, London: Kogan Page.

Kates, S. M. and Goh, C. (2003) "Brand Morphing Implications for Advertising Theory and Practice", *Journal of Advertising*, 32: 59–68.

Keller, K. L. (2008) *Strategic Brand Management: Building, Measuring, and Managing Brand Equity*, Upper Saddle River, NJ: Pearson/Prentice Hall.

McAuley, A., Carson, D., Gilmore, A. (2006) "Celtic Marketing: The Fusion and Companionship of Art and Science", *Journal of Strategic Marketing*, 14: 89–98.

McCracken, G. D. (1988) *The Long Interview*, Newbury Park, CA: Sage Publications.

Pasini, E. (2005) "From an Ethics of Process to an Ethics of Concepts", *Experimenta*, 55–106.

Schroeder, J. E., Salzer-Mörling, M. and Askegaard, S. (2006) *Brand Culture*, London: Routledge.

Simmons, J. (2006) "Guinness and the Role of Strategic Storytelling", *Journal of Strategic Marketing*, 14: 11–18.

Spooner, B. (1986) "Weaver and Dealers: The Authenticity of an Oriental Carpet", in A. Appadurai (ed.), *The Social Life of Things*, Cambridge: Cambridge University Press.

4 Regional affiliations

Building a marketing strategy on regional ethnicity

Delphine Dion and Lionel Sitz

Overview

In the traditional perspective, the frame of analysis of international marketing most of the time is the nation. In this regard, culture is understood as national and uniform countrywide. Completing this vision this chapter focuses on infra-national referents, e.g. regions. We show that regions are not only the products' place of origin, but rather an identity device that individuals use to build their identity and to show it to their social environment. According to this perspective, we propose four marketing strategies based on regional affiliations: (1) drawing on regional cultural resources (legends, traditions, heritage); (2) positioning the brand in resistance to globalization; (3) inscribing the region in the globalization process; and (4) allowing consumers to express their regional affiliation. These practices can allow the brand to successfully differentiate itself on the market. The chapter ends with a discussion on conditions of applicability concerning market size and target heterogeneity issues.

From a utilitarian to a cultural consideration of the region

Dealing with international issues, the frame of analysis is generally the country as a nation-state: countries are easy to identify and are believed to be quite homogeneous from an administrative and political standpoint, despite the fact that this can often mislead the political strategies in some countries. This national frame of analysis can be completed by a supra-national classification (Europe, North America, South-East Asia) because of an alleged homogenization internationally, especially for some market segments (Kjeldgaard and Askegaard 2006). However, this nation-focused division does not make it possible to take the heterogeneity that is developing locally into account. A particularly pertinent level of analysis can be found at the infra-country regional scale.

Today, the regional level of analysis is particularly important because of the (re)emergence of regions that has been witnessed throughout the world in recent years. This phenomenon can be explained by the rise of economic uncertainty, the globalization process, and the creation of supra-national actors such as the European Community which have led individuals to turn to the re-appropriation of local cultures in order to define their identity. However, regional, national, or supra-national logics are not incompatible: usually these identities are intertwined and coexist peacefully (Thiesse 1999). A person can feel Basque, Spanish and European at the same time. In this regard, the logic of various identities could be compared with the notion of role. Behaviours and beliefs are linked with the level of identification.

Table 4.1 Traditional and cultural perspectives of regionalism

	Traditional perspective	Cultural perspective
Culture definition	An administrative classification determined by geographical factors (e.g. the American, the Chinese, etc.) and a given set of symbols, norms, and experiences	A social construction that has a relational nature and is constantly constructed by individuals
Frame of analysis	Geographical borders (e.g. Spain, European Community, Asia, etc.) within which the given set of cultural tools is uniformly shared by individuals	Cultural affiliations through the analysis of the boundary work of the individuals who must display, justify and legitimize their affiliation
Marketing practices	Creating labels to signal the country of origin (e.g. an outstanding *savoir-faire*, a traditional recipe)	Providing cultural resources in order to allow individuals to experience their various affiliations

Facing the emergence of regionalism, a number of companies have integrated this dimension in their marketing practices. In traditional marketing approaches, marketers focus on products' place of origin (Table 4.1). They manipulate regional emblematic representations to highlight specific product characteristics in congruence with the regional heritage. Other companies develop innovative marketing strategies based on consumers' experience of their regional affiliations (Table 4.1).

The region as a product's place of origin

In the traditional vision of marketing, the region is considered as a product's attribute to highlight specific characteristics and/or qualities of the product such as traditional craftsmanship, a specific *savoir-faire*, a famous recipe, customary local commodities, and so on. This is mainly used when the region is well known for a product category, e.g. Scottish whisky, Burgundy wine, Sichuan pepper, Alsatian sauerkraut, etc.

In this perspective, regional stereotypical representations such as folkloric costumes, emblematic animals, typical landscapes, and/or official representations are used to enable a rapid identification of the origin and possibly the characteristics of the product. Mobilizing these symbols is the easiest way to represent a region in advertising or on packaging because of their taken-for-granted nature and their blatancy. Thus, these symbols are mobilized as heuristics in situations of uncertainty and, as such, reduce the cognitive effort for the individual consumer evaluating the offer. For example, the horseradish brand Raifalsa is associated with numerous emblematic representations of Alsace (Figure 4.1): a stork (the emblematic bird of Alsace), the traditional Alsacian costume, and Gothic script. The brand name mixes the two words *raifort* (horseradish) and *Alsace* in order to underline the links between the traditional images of Alsace as a horseradish producer and as a gastronomic region. Another example is the brand *Ker Cadélac* (Figure 4.2) with a logo that mixes numerous Breton stereotypes that French consumers are familiar with and can easily decipher: the folkloric Breton costume and the word *Ker* which is a typical Breton word. These elements are reinforced by the message *Mes recettes bretonnes* meaning "My Breton recipes". All these elements are used to reinforce the authenticity

Figure 4.1 Raifalsa.

Figure 4.2 Ker Cadélac.

of the products and to build on the gastronomic heritage of Brittany (famous for its butter cookies).

Similar to regional country of origin, many regional labels have been created in Europe. For instance, the label *Produit en Bretagne* ("Made in Brittany") was founded in 1993 and intended to make local business more dynamic and stimulate local employment. Today, the label covers 200 companies from various industries (food processing, retailing, engineering, culture and creation, services, etc.). These companies generate a €15 billion consolidated turnover and employ 85,000 people. At first, the *Produit en Bretagne* label was put only on food products. Today, it covers all the product categories (sportswear, cosmetics, banking, insurance). As the ad says, there are "2,300 products to enjoy, wear, read, and listen to". It is, for instance, placed in the bottom right-hand corner of the Ker Cadélac packaging (Figure 4.2).

In the two situations, the emphasis is placed on the origin of the products. The regional referents are used to highlight an outstanding *savoir-faire*, a traditional recipe, etc. In the example of the *Produit en Bretagne* label, regional referents are used to put the emphasis on the local production conditions. Rather than considering the region as a product's place of origin, brands can become cultural entrepreneurs by using and circulating regional referents to make individuals experience their regional affiliations. The emphasis is no longer on the origin of the product but on consumers' experience of their regional affiliations. Thus, it is important to understand regional affiliations.

Regional affiliations

In a cultural perspective, culture is not a given set of defined elements. Nor is it transmitted once and for all as a crystallized bundling of norms and knowledge. Rather, culture is a relational construct: it is constructed through one's experiences, social relationships, life events, etc. In this respect, culture becomes visible through its relationships with other cultural backgrounds. As a sociologist put it, "people become aware of their culture when they stand at its boundaries" (Cohen 1982: 3). For this reason we have to struggle to ascertain the dynamics of cultures and societies *in* time as on-going systems and *through* time as emergent sequences. Thus, it is particularly useful to study cultural variation with meticulous attention to co-variation, *both* regionally and through time. Culture is relational, historical, and constructed. Hence, one is not born a Scottish person or a Sicilian but becomes one. One can be born, live, and work in one region without defining oneself in relation to it. Others can feel and express a very strong regional feeling and construct their identity in relation to that region, even though they were not born and did note live there. The key is not to know if one *is* Scottish or Sicilian but if one *feels* Scottish or Sicilian. Beliefs and experiences become essential to understanding regional affiliation and the actual region of birth or residence turns out to be anecdotal. Regions are considered a set of resources and identity competencies representing a toolkit with which individuals manage their personal and social identity.

Integrating regional affiliations in marketing make it possible to develop innovative and competitive marketing strategies that break with traditional marketing approaches. Rather than considering the region as a product's place of origin, brands can become cultural entrepreneurs by using, circulating, and providing cultural resources to make individuals experience their regional affiliations. Although some global firms like McCain's, Coca-Cola and Société Générale use regionalism in their marketing strategies, the transnational strategies using regional symbols are mainly conducted by regional SMEs.

Because France is symptomatic of the re-emergence of regions and because regional marketing initiatives are abundant here, this chapter focuses on two French regions: Brittany (located in the West of France, with a total population of 3.1 million and a land area of 27,200 km^2) and Alsace (located in the East of France, with a total population of 1.8 million and a land area of 8,280 km^2).

Regional marketing

Despite the growing importance of regional affiliation and the strength of local particularities, marketing scholars have been reluctant to take into account the regional level. The focus on the national scale is useful but some opportunities can also be found in regional marketing. We identified four types of actions: (1) drawing on regional cultural resources;

(2) resisting globalization; (3) linking the local and the global by inscribing the region in globalization; and (4) helping consumers to display their regional affiliation.

Drawing on regional cultural resources

France has a long tradition of regional particularism. In many border regions, people still speak a distinct regional idiom and the traditional regional costumes are very specific. Also, French regions are often symbolized by some distinguishable monuments or landscapes that crystallize the image of the region as well as its culinary heritage. For these reasons, every region has a specific cultural heritage made of heterogeneous elements which do not have the same particularity.

The alcohol brand Sommer uses regional cultural resources heavily. In its brand history, Sommer specifically mentions its "Alsatian culture": "Sommer … highlights its savoir-faire and its Alsatian culture" (http://www.amersommer.com/). Linked with regional habits of drinking beer with a bitter aroma, the brand strives to prove its particularity by using regional cultural codes. Alsatian culture is marked by "stammtish," a moment of sociality when friends gather to share stories and drink beer. Sommer insists on this particular moment of consumption and links the taste of its product with local culinary specialties like pretzels and flammeküeche. These symbols of regional culture allow the brand to position itself as traditional and authentic. Thanks to this strategy the brand is able to forge deep emotional links with the regional consumers.

It is always possible to uncover or to revive a forgotten element to rejuvenate a facet of the regional image. For example, this is the case of the Lancelot brewery that sells a range of beers inspired by Breton history and Celtic legends. Created in 1990, the Lancelot brewery manufactures and markets a range of traditionally brewed beers. The brewery tries to immerse consumers in the magical universe of Celtic legends and historical events of Brittany. The company exploits various Breton stories, mythical heroes, and stereotypical representations of the region. It is interesting to note that some of them are popular among the Breton, the French and even the European population while others are really limited to the region. For instance, they called one product Bonnets Rouges, referring to a peasants' rebellion in 1675 against the central power of the French Crown that tried to raise new taxes on the notarial acts. This rebellion was overlooked and almost forgotten for many years until the launch of the beer. The bottle is decorated by a drawing representing a group of peasants armed in front of a typical Breton church; a short description of the event enables the brand to revive the memory of this event and the text of the first article of the Peasant Code that started the rebellion (in Breton and in French) that sheds a light on the reasons for the rebellion (Figure 4.3).

The Lancelot brewery also exploits forgotten rituals dating from the Celtic period. One beer refers to the Samhain Night, an ancient feast that preceded Halloween. This dark, strong beer (11.1° alcohol) is called *XI.I – the beer of the Samhain night* referring to the first day of the eleventh month. During the Celtic period, the Samhain Night was a feast when local communities gathered together and brewed a special beer. Today, the Lancelot Brewery organizes a brand fest around this event in order to revitalize this Celtic symbol and to create an aura for the brand. Brewed at sunset on October 31st, the beer is available after six weeks of fermentation, for the winter solstice (Figure 4.4). The Lancelot brewery combines regional narratives and local events in order to legitimize the regional character of the brand. For example, it created the *Bogue d'Or*, a chestnut-flour flavoured beer celebrating the Teillouse day (celebration of the chestnut occurring in the Redon County in October). Through these

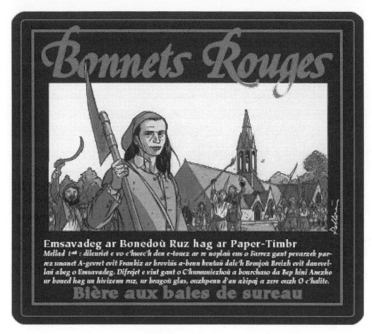

Figure 4.3 Label of the Bonnets Rouges beer.

(a)   (b)

Figure 4.4 The XI.I beer (a) and the Samhain Night at the Lancelot brewery (b).

actions, Brasserie Lancelot revives old legends and positions its brands at the heart of old and current rituals.

This is resonant with a movement of micro-brewery openings that started around the 1990s and gave rise to many artisanal breweries throughout Brittany. Although the production of beer in Brittany is a new industry, one producer even defined Brittany in one commercial as "beer's second home" (Figure 4.5). Breton beers are becoming important challengers for the national and international brands on the Breton market. As the Lancelot brewery example demonstrates, marketers are not only ideological parasites, using existing

Figure 4.5 Brands as cultural entrepreneurs.

cultural symbols (Holt 2006), but are also cultural entrepreneurs who can literally create cultural symbols through branding strategies and communication.

Resisting globalization

Through the globalization of media and brands, individuals can be in touch with faraway information, have discovered new ways of life and have found new consumption practices. Anthropologists have documented how regional affiliations have become a way for individuals to deal with globalization: regional particularism resurfaces as a side-effect of globalization.

Facing this change, many regional brands position themselves as symbols of resistance to globalization. This regional resistance is based on the protection and rejuvenation of the region's cultural specificities. Wattwiller, a mineral water brand, is a good case in point. This product is part of a very competitive market in which brands strive to find exploitable and durable points of differentiation. The mountain origin is traditional in the mineral water market. Wattwiller insists on its regional personality: "the name Wattwiller is derived from the Alsatian words for water, 'Wasser', and village, 'Weiler'. Wattwiller means the water village." Wattwiller is deeply committed to the Alsatian language and defends its use by offering a version of their Internet site in the language. This emphasis on the regional tongue is a way for Wattwiller to distinguish itself from the various brands acting on the market. Alsatian people are deeply committed to their idiom and appreciate the brand for its dedication to the dialect. This regional commitment is an efficient way of positioning the brand as an alternative to those with a more national-based image.

Another example can be found in the positioning of the Meteor Brewery. Meteor is an Alsatian brewery located in Hochfelden (Bas-Rhin), in the heart of Ackerland, a growing region for Alsatian hops, between Saverne and Strasbourg. Today Meteor is

(a)   (b)

Figure 4.6 Meteor, proud to be Alsatian.

the biggest independent family brewery in France with a 560,000 hectolitres production and a €45 million turnover. The Haag family, head of the brewery for seven generations, is deeply rooted in economic and local cultural networks. The brewery is committed to perpetuating three fundamental values: richness of flavour, tradition and modernity, and the attachment to the Alsatian land. This attachment makes the brewery favour local raw materials (water, malt, hops), thus defending its location. The brewery is proud to be Alsatian and emphasizes this in the foreground of its communication (Figure 4.6). The first ad, showing a traditional Alsatian café (*"bierstuebe"*) stuck between two modern buildings symbolizing globalization says "Alsatian we are and Alsatian we stay". The second one states "We are Alsatian" and then, in graffiti style, is added "And proud to be so".

The resistance to globalization can also appear through the misappropriation of global iconic brands. The objective is to distance oneself from global brands that are symbols of globalization such as Coca-Cola or Nutella by creating resistant regional brands: Corsica Cola, Breizh Cola, Breizhella. For instance, in 2002, the company Phare Ouest launched Breizh Cola, a Breton cola (Breizh means Brittany in the Breton language) (Figure 4.7). The company currently sells over 5 million bottles per year and has a 10–14 per cent market share in Brittany across the region. The brand resistant positioning is explicitly stated on their website:

> For quite some years, the significance of cultural diversity has increased. Don't we talk, for instance, about the need to save regional languages? And in the environmental domain, no one questions the absolute necessity to maintain the diversity (the bio-diversity) of animal and vegetal species; only the solution to think about

Figure 4.7 Breizh Cola ad.

sustainable development. Yet there is a cultural model that is imposed on everything. And there are products, which planetary dissemination leads to a unique consumption model. Thus, here and there, some individuals gather, without any vehemence, and react in order not to lose their identity. Some are irreducible declaring: "We will re-empower ourselves, let's take a universally known product … the cola, and appropriate it. We decided without any complex to manufacture and market in Brittany: *Breizh Cola*, Le cola du Phare Ouest."

(www.breizh-cola.fr)

Inscribing the region in globalization

Regional affiliations do not necessarily challenge globalization. Rather than resisting globalization, brands can try to make regional representations part of global icons. This strategy requires the brand to position itself as a part of a somewhat global culture (Kjeldgaard and Askegaard 2006) while remaining authentic to its regional affiliation. Hence, this is another way of drawing attention to cultural diversity and the emergent nature of cultural arrangements. This is, for instance, the strategy of Breizh Punisher's, a Breton sportswear brand. Tee-shirt designs convert regional representations into national and international referents (Figure 4.8). For instance, the Clint Eastwood tee-shirt mixes regional symbols (e.g. the flag used as a cape, the traditional Breton hat and jacket), with national references (e.g. the message is a wordplay derived from a popular French proverb) and American

Figure 4.8 Humorous tee-shirt designed by Breizh Punisher's.

symbols (e.g. Clint Eastwood, Western-style writing, English brand name). This design inscribes the regional culture in the globalization movement and thus regenerates the culture.

This is often the case in the food industry where consumers have valued the notion of world food. The restaurant chain Flam's, offering *Flammekueche* (a traditional Alsatian meal consisting of a pie with cream, onions, and diced bacon) positions itself as "the No. 1 flammekueche restaurant". It explains the Alsatian origins of the meal, underlying its cultural value and authenticity. In order to establish restaurants outside Alsace and to widen its target, Flam's proposes some *Flam's creations* such as a *New-Yorker flamme-kueche* or an *Indian flammekueche*, etc. which have some success with consumers but break with the Alsatian tradition. This culinary DIY that mixes Alsacian and international gastronomy enables the restaurant chains to offer new tastes.

Non-French companies also use similar practices. In order to appear more local, they include regional representations in their offer. For instance, in order to counter Breizh Cola, Coca-Cola tried to inscribe their brand in the region by adapting its national communication to the region using emblematic regional representations (e.g. waves, the Breton flag, seagulls, lighthouses, traditional Breton hats, Celtic triskeles) (Figure 4.9). This is emphasized by a welcoming sentence in Breton (*Degemer mat!*) and a sentence in French, *Coca-Cola vous rafraîchit en Bretagne* (Coca-Cola refreshes you in Brittany). Coca-Cola does not want to be considered as local, which would not be truthful but as a way of enjoying Brittany and the Breton culture. The brand is presented as a facilitator to enjoy Brittany and the Breton culture.

delicatessen trade brand, is a good example of this strategy. The firm started in 1946 in a small Alsatian village. At that time, it was a pork butcher's shop and delicatessen. It then started to sell delicatessen products in supermarkets throughout Alsace. In the 1980s, the brand started to produce sauerkraut, then flammekueche, etc. The brand exploits its regional legitimacy by slowly expanding its product range to other regional products. To show its regional legitimacy while targeting consumers outside the region, the brand launched advertising showing a consumer from another region talking about its product and describing its authenticity.

Export of the cultural expertise to other regions

Once a company has developed a specific regional expertise, it can try to develop a similar business model in other regions. The challenge is to construct legitimacy not in one region but in a regional-oriented authenticity. For instance, Ouest-France publishing began its activity in Brittany and published books about Brittany, for Breton consumers. Gradually it succeeded in becoming the "publisher of the regions". Created in 1975, the Ouest-France publishers, currently an independent subsidiary, occupy an important position in the French publisher landscape. With 150 new products a year and an 1,800-title catalogue, it generates a €17 million turnover. The Ouest-France publishers define themselves as *the publisher of the regions*. Far from confining itself to Brittany, it is now multi-regional:

> Ouest-France actively participates in the development of the local, regional and national inheritance. The aim is to give a large audience access to a region through its various dimensions, a range of quality books at affordable prices (from 2 to 15 euros, except art books) and translated in several languages.
>
> (www.edilarge.fr)

Ouest-France publishers offer for each French region various books organized into thematic collections: regional cooking, memoirs, discovery itineraries, history, atlas, literature, monographs, regional languages. For instance, the company can publish a book on the fairy tales and legends in Lorraine (North-Eastern France), a book teaching the Breton language (Western France) and a book of recipes from Savoy (Eastern France). This example clearly shows the mechanism of expanding its legitimacy to other regions. A brand that has a genuine legitimacy in one region can position itself as a specialist of regional heritage. This relies on the capacity to defend more general cultural elements: regional languages (rather than one specific regional language), regional heritage (rather than the heritage of a region), regional *savoir-faire* (and not the traditional practices of a region).

Going beyond the region

A third strategy is to change the scope of the regional references. A company can focus on a very local culture linked to a county or can search for common roots with other regions. Sociologists have long demonstrated how localities are linked together by specific cultural traditions. Brittany has particular traditions and a strong regional culture, but also shares many common elements with Ireland, Galicia, Scotland, etc. through the Celtic culture. This is also true for Alsace, which shares many cultural traits with other parts of the Rhine Valley (Switzerland, Germany). Hence, marketers could leverage their regional positioning by

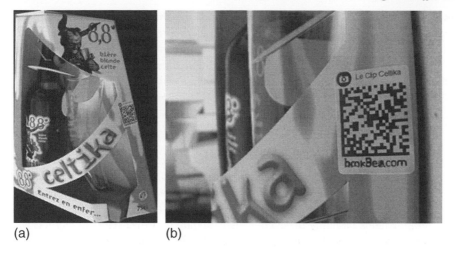

(a)　　　　　　　　　　　　(b)

Figure 4.11 Celtika packaging.

addressing the cultural heritage shared by various regions (cf. Chapter 3 in this volume). This is the current strategy of *Brasserie de Bretagne*. Founded in 1998 in Brittany, the company is today the seventh largest French brewery with an annual production of 2.5 million litres of beer. So far, the company has been focused on Breton culture. In 2010, they released a new product based on the Celtic culture, Celtika. With this product, the aim of the company is to target the eight Celtic countries: Brittany, Ireland, Cornwall, Scotland, Wales, the Isle of Man, Galicia, and Asturias. The product is based on a Celtic legend they translated into the eight Celtic languages that tells of an episode in the wars between Celtic and Viking tribes. The beer is sold with a horn glass to reference the Celtic history. By using a flashcode stuck on the packaging, consumers can download on their iPhone a 5-minute video narrating the legend (Figure 4.11). This video, made by the employees of the company and volunteers, presents a remix of the legend mixing Celtic references (traditional Celt music and landscapes), historical references (medieval costumes) and modern references (Harley-Davidson motorcycles).

Target heterogeneity

The target can be quite heterogeneous in terms of regional affiliation. We can identify three relevant kinds of consumers for a segmentation strategy based on regional affiliation: the locals, the cowbirds and the wannabees.

Locals are consumers who live in their region of origin. For them, regional affiliation is lived as obvious and is experienced in ordinary situations. They generally do not question their regional affiliation and look for taken-for-granted elements. For these consumers, it is important to position the brand on traditional elements and to ensure its legitimacy. The brand and its products must be part of a taken-for-granted regional background. The brands targeting these consumers should highlight not only regional culture but also their taken-for-granted dimension. Coop Alsace is a good example of a brand targeting these consumers: this retailer is Alsatian and is present in almost every Alsatian village and its presence seems obvious.

Cowbirds are consumers living in a region different from their region of birth but who have a strong regional affiliation. They are emotionally involved with their region of adoption. They are actively engaged in showing and demonstrating their regional affiliation. These people are eager to enrich their regional cultural capital and look for regional traditions and *savoir-faire*. For these consumers the (re)discovery of regional traditions is something important. Hence, they look for brands that revive and/or rejuvenate regional traditions. The brand Pâté Henaff is a good example of a brand that is popular nationwide but has a strong appeal for people moving to Britanny, *because* it is known outside Brittany.

Wannabees are consumers who strive to be part of the region but do not have an important regional cultural capital. In contrast to *cowbirds*, the regional affiliation of these consumers is not necessarily long-lasting. On the contrary, their affiliation is generally unsettled and changes over time. These consumers wish to have a taste of the region through their consumption. Brands targeting these consumers should mobilize regional stereotypes that can be understood by people with a weak regional cultural capital. Using stereotypes is a way of targeting people that have only a vague idea of the regional culture. For instance, *Momo le Homard*, a Breton company, sells T-shirts with simple messages such as *Petite Bretonne* (Little Breton) or *Papa Breton* (Breton Dad).

Ability to decode the symbolic representations

Because these three types of consumers do not have the same cultural background, some symbolic representations may not make any sense for some of them or may not have the same meaning for them all. In contrast to official representations (flag, national anthems), representing regional institutional frameworks, picturesque spots (culinary, architectural elements) and mythical representations (legendary characters and places) are not imposed. If these symbolic representations are to make sense for consumers, they have to be known and appropriated. In other words, the significance of regional cultural capital structures the consumers' interpretation process: the comprehension of the deployed meaning depends on consumers' regional cultural capital. It is necessary to know how to handle symbolic representations of the region according to the target, in order to adapt the level of generality according to one's knowledge. Thus it is important to adapt symbolic and cultural representations handled according to the level of the collective representations of the target. The broader the target, the less specific its regional cultural capital and the greater the need to use simple, widely shared stereotypes. The more expert the target, the greater the need to refine the representation elements used in order to avoid appearing non-authentic and made for tourists. A few years ago, the bottled water brand Carola decided to reinforce its legitimacy among Alsatian *locals*. In so doing it launched a communication campaign using the Alsatian language. This strategy succeeded in strengthening the ties with local consumers. However, consumers who did not speak the regional language did not understand the campaign, and thus it had no impact on them.

Managing authenticity

The three segments of consumers look for different things and do not share the same cultural codes. The traditional regional culture is generally lived as a natural thing and taken for granted. Nonetheless, it can appear folkloric and unappealing to outsiders. This highlights a fine line between authenticity and folklorization that is between real and fake (Visconti 2010). The Corsican brewery Pietra put forward an interesting strategy by launching a "Corsican beer", even though beer is not a traditional product. To authenticate the brand, the brewery used a legitimizing discourse about the ingredients used to produce the beer. Also, this example vividly illustrates the role of marketing in the production of culture and the importance of cultural entrepreneurship in the success of a brand. Marketers using regional affiliations have to manage the authenticity of their strategy. In order to do so, they have to reflect on the symbols and cultural resources used: they have to be understandable by a large number of consumers and should meanwhile appear specific enough to target them. This is linked with complex authentication strategies that legitimate the regionalist aspect of the brand. Since authenticity is a social and cultural construction, it is important that marketers constantly display the authenticity of their brand. In so doing, they should use the regional symbols cautiously and be aware of the importance of the context in which they use them.

This chapter traces the possible use of regional affiliation in a marketing strategy: regional marketing. It underlines the interpretive flexibility of regional symbols and the various ways consumers can connect with these symbols. Regional positioning can be an effective strategy. First, it resonates emotionally with local consumers' expectations and can thus be more effective than nation-based positioning. Second, regional marketing can present itself as a way of resisting hegemonic global brands. Third, it interlaces the region with globalization by presenting it in comparison with global brands. Fourth, regional marketing helps consumers to exhibit their regional affiliation publicly. In order to expand their business, companies using regional marketing could extend their product ranges. Entrepreneurs could also draw on other regions in order to multiply their positioning strategies. Businesses exploiting regional affiliations also have the possibility of going beyond the region by linking the regional culture with broader cultures. Because of consumer targets heterogeneity, managers should develop a special ability to decode cultural codes and understand the subtleties of regional culture and its links with national culture. A key issue for companies is to manage authenticity by legitimizing their regional genuine nature.

Review and discussion questions

1   Is the use of identity symbols possible in other domains of life?
2   The process outlined here changes the work of marketers and the place of marketing. In what respect? What knowledge and tools do marketers need to adapt?
3   Class discussion could revolve around the sociocultural construction of the regional imaginaries. It would be interesting to draw the genealogy of regional particularities by historicizing them and by showing what role marketing plays in this process. After debating the ethical dimension of the use of regional affiliation, the class could discuss the heterogeneity of individuals' tactics toward identity symbols, especially those provided by marketers.
4   Choose a region with cultural specificities (the great figures of its history, famous landscapes and monuments, etc.); then define a marketing strategy to use to position its offer.
5   Imagine a foreign product and imagine a marketing strategy that could bring this product into regional culture (i.e. indigenize it).

Keywords

brand, communication, culture, ethnicity, globalization, packaging, regionalism

References

Askegaard, S., Arnould, E. J. and Kjeldgaard, D. (2005) "Postassimilationist Ethnic Consumer Research: Qualifications and Extensions", *Journal of Consumer Research*, 32: 160–70.

—— (2009) "Reflexive Culture's Consequences", in N. Cheryl (ed.), *Beyond Hofstede: Culture Frameworks for Global Marketing and Management*, London: Palgrave Macmillan.

Cayla, J. and Arnould, E. (2008) "A Cultural Approach to Branding in the Global Marketplace", *Journal of International Marketing*, 16: 86–112.

Cayla, J. and Eckhardt, G. M. (2008) "Asian Brands and the Shaping of a Transnational Imagined Community", *Journal of Consumer Research*, 35: 216–30.

Cohen, A. P. (1982) "Belonging: The Experience of Culture", in A. P. Cohen (ed.), *Belonging: Identity and Social Organization in British Rural Cultures*, Manchester: Manchester University Press, pp. 1–18.

Craig, C. S. and Douglas, S. (2006) "Beyond National Culture: Implications of Cultural Dynamics for Consumer Research", *International Marketing Review*, 23: 322–42.

Dion, D., Rémy, E. and Sitz, L. (2010) "Le Sentiment régional comme levier d'action marketing", *Décisions Marketing*, 58: 15–26.

Dion, D., Sitz, L. and Rémy, E. (2011) "Embodied Ethnicity: The Ethnic Affiliation Grounded in the Body", *Consumption Markets & Culture* 14, 3: 311–31.

Hirschman, E. C. and Panther-Yates, D. (2006) "Problematizing Consumer Ethnicity", in R. W. Belk (ed.), *Handbook of Qualitative Research Methods in Marketing*, London: Sage.

Hobsbawm, E. and Ranger, T. (1983) *L'Invention de la tradition*, Paris: Editions Amsterdam.

Holt, D. B. (2006) "Jack Daniel's: Iconic Brands as Ideological Parasites and Proselytizers", *Journal of Consumer Culture*, 6(3): 355–77.

John, A. and Silk, M. (2010) "Transnational Organization and Symbolic Production: Creating and Managing a Global Brand", *Consumption, Markets & Culture*, 13: 159–79.

Kjeldgaard, D. and Askegaard, S. (2006) "The Glocalization of Youth Culture: The Global Youth Segment as Structures of Common Difference", *Journal of Consumer Research*, 33: 231–47.

Özçağlar-Toulouse, N., Béji-Bécheur, A., Fosse-Gomez, M. H., Herbert, M. and Zouaghi, S. (2010) "L'éthnicité dans l'étude du consommateur: un état des recherches" ("Ethnicity in Consumer Behavior: A State of the Art"), *Recherche et Applications Marketing*, 24, 4: 57–76.

Peñaloza, L. (2001) "Consuming the American West: Animating Cultural Meaning and Memory at a Stock Show and Rodeo", *Journal of Consumer Research*, 28: 369–98.

Rao, H. (2009) *Market Rebels: How Activists Make or Break Radical Innovations*, Princeton, NJ: Princeton University Press.

Thiesse, A -M. (1999) *La Création des identités nationales. Europe XVIIIe–XXe siècle*, Paris: Editions du Seuil.

Thompson, C. and Tambyah, S. K. (1999) "Trying to Be Cosmopolitan", *Journal of Consumer Research*, 26: 214–41.

Thompson, C. and Tian, K. (2008) "Reconstructing the South: How Commercial Myths Compete for Identity Value through the Ideological Shaping of Popular Memories and Countermemories", *Journal of Consumer Research*, 34: 595–613.

Varman, R. and Belk, R. W. (2009) "Nationalism and Ideology in an Anti-consumption Movement", *Journal of Consumer Research*, 36: 686–700.

Venkatesh, A. (1995) "Ethnoconsumerism: A New Paradigm to Study Cultural and Cross-Cultural Consumer Behavior", in J. A. Costa and G. J. Bamossy (eds), *Marketing in a Multicultural World: Ethnicity, Nationalism and Cultural Identity*, Thousand Oaks, CA: Sage.

Visconti, L. M. (2010) "Authentic Brand Narratives: Co-Constructed Mediterraneaness for l'Occitane Brand", in R. Belk (ed.), *Research in Consumer Behavior*, vol. 12, Bingley, UK: Emerald.

Online resources

http://www.amersommer.com/sommer.htm
http://www.brasseriedebretagne.com/
http://www.brasserie-lancelot.com/
http://www.celtika.eu
http://www.produitenbretagne.com/

5   Dove in Russia

The role of culture in advertising success

Natalia Tolstikova

Overview

> Since I've tried the new Dove, my skin has become younger and softer. The pores opened up.
> I felt a surge of energy … I was surprised, because it tasted like regular soap.
>
> (Russian advertising humour)

This chapter analyses the Russian version of Dove's Campaign for Real Beauty and the audience's reactions to it. It explores reasons for the failure of Dove's campaign in Russia by examining factors that have influenced Russian perceptions, such as cultural history, attitudes, gender norms, and cultural expectations, among others. It demonstrates versatility and the richness of cultural approaches to marketing problems.

Introduction

The attractiveness of Russia

Recently, a number of new lucrative players have emerged on the world market. Some established economic leaders, such as the United States and Japan, are being challenged, in particular, by four countries: Brazil, Russia, India and China (BRIC). Despite the global financial crisis, these emerging markets are developing with such speed and fervour that they are predicted to become the world's most dominant economies by 2050 (O'Leary 2008). The four countries differ from each other in history, economic orientation, religion and political systems. Their cultural make-up could not be more different. What unites them, however, is brisk economic growth and robust consumer demand. A more detailed look at Russian economic history and realities will help to set the background for the Dove advertising case study.

After the fall of Communism and the switch from a production economy to an economy of consumption, there were dramatic changes in the Russian ideological orientation. For 70 years, the population was deprived of the ability to enjoy 'casual' shopping: choice was very limited, brand names were non-existent, and retail outlets were finite. Since the fall of Communism, Russians have been overwhelmed with consumer goods such as the 50 different brands of yoghurt now always available. After being the country of supposed equals, Russia is now home to almost 90,000 hard currency millionaires. Russia is now among the world's top luxury markets as the new rich want to signal their affluence (ibid.). The bulk of the new market, however, is occupied by the developing middle class who have smaller incomes and less ostentatious buying habits. Nevertheless, it is estimated that Russians spend almost three-quarters of their wages on retail shopping (ibid.). Yet about one-fifth of Russians often can barely afford basic goods (ibid.); the difference in life style and opportunities between the very rich and the very poor is dramatic.

For Russia, the status of an emerging market means that the country's economy has not yet reached so-called 'First World' status but the growth in consumption has outpaced many developed countries. As such, Russia represents a lucrative potential market for foreign brands, especially in the FMCG (fast moving consumer goods) category with high competition and fast sales. Above all, a successful entry into a market depends on marketing communication through which the company reaches its audiences and stakeholders and engages them in a meaningful conversation.

The importance of advertising in winning new markets

Marketing communication professionals know that advertising is one of the critical marketing communication tools in global competition. It makes the brand visible and distinct through carefully designed brand identity. Textbooks on international marketing advise that there are two main approaches to advertising in foreign countries: standardization or adaptation. For obvious reasons of limitation and risks of misunderstanding, few companies choose a standardized message that is disseminated unaltered in each market. The majority adopt the adaptation approach where the message is transformed in various degrees, conforming to the norms of the country where it is distributed. Advertising operates in languages, images and sounds and so in order to be understood, it has to be based on social behaviour and cultural symbols. Cultural comprehension is crucial when a company decides to advertise in a foreign country. Understanding the cultural make-up is the key to market success through intelligent adaptation to local contexts.

There are several schools of thought regarding the way advertising works, in particular, the Strong Theory and the Weak Theory. According to the Strong Theory, advertising's primary aim is to generate profits so there is a direct connection between advertising and sales. Advertising is seen as being capable of changing attitudes, beliefs and behaviour, thus influencing the audiences through persuasion. Weak Theory, on the other hand, postulates that advertising works by frequent exposure and reassurance, creating favourable impressions on consumers over time. According to this framework, consumers are active participants in communication who, together with the advertiser, co-create meanings attributed to the brand. These meanings are driven by internalized brand values combined with individual past experiences. This meaning is personal but it is shaped by broader socio-cultural influences and contexts (Hackley 2010). Advertising is seen as a complex cultural text. The way a text such as advertising is encoded by the sender and decoded by the receiver is guided by culture and involves individual negotiations and interpretations (Hall 1973). Members of a culture must share a common key to interpret their social surroundings in order to participate in working communication. The verbal, visual and acoustic language of advertising has to be understood by its intended target audience in order to be persuasive. In the context of the Weak Theory, 'understanding' means getting personal relevant meanings out of a text, which might more or less overlap with the intended meanings of the advertiser; however, sometimes, in more post-modern advertising, there is no intended meaning, but the process of subjectively making meanings becomes even more relevant according to the Weak Theory.

Traditional marketing management philosophy subscribes to the Strong Theory. The cultural interpretative approach shares the perspective with the Weak Theory.

Research tools for appraising international cultures

For a brand to succeed, marketing managers need to access, learn and adequately respond to the local culture and conditions, incorporating appropriate elements of culture into marketing communication. Culture is a lens through which the world is perceived but also is a blueprint for behaviour; factors such as language, history, geography and time influence it. So there are immaterial dimensions of culture, but there is also a material aspect of culture. Materially manifested cultural symbols, such as the shamrock in Ireland or an apple pie in the United States, help to establish rules and patterns. Learning this enormously complicated material requires time that a marketing manager usually does not have. There are, however, short cuts. To ensure advertising success, marketing textbooks, among other steps, recommend determining cultural motivations and drivers, as well as broader cultural values relevant to the product marketed internationally (i.e. Doole and Lowe 2008). Traditional research tools suggested in the textbooks are the cultural dimensions developed by the Dutch sociologist Geert Hofstede.

The foundation for Hofstede's cultural dimensions construct (1980) was the study of work-related values across countries. Through surveys and questionnaires Hofstede identified four universal binary dimensions of culture: individualism, power distance, uncertainty avoidance and masculinity/femininity. He argued that the dimensions explain cross-cultural differentiations in people's behaviour and beliefs. Although it was a revolutionary approach in his discipline, sociology and organizational behaviour, its direct application to marketing and consumer behaviour presents some problems. One problem is that Hofstede equates culture with a nation state which might be useful in cross-cultural research but is problematic when studying a single country with its multiple subcultures. Another issue is that Hofstede's primary research tool, a questionnaire with structured and prearranged questions, prohibits any deviations from the research scenario and also averages individual responses. Hofstede has a different concept of culture, seeing it as the collective programming that distinguishes members from one group from those of another (ibid.). It is an essentialist position where a specific phenomenon possesses a number of properties which each entity of this kind possesses, so in this way such a phenomenon has only one definition or meaning. However, culture itself is a complex living phenomenon that is constantly changing so it is difficult to measure it. Cultural manifestations also depend on their context so culturally driven interpretations will depend on the contextual environment (Craig and Douglas 2006).

To appraise the successes and failures of marketing communication efforts, a different methodological approach is needed. The cultural approach combines a number of non-essentialist interpretive approaches to view culture as broader varied phenomena where multiple cultural groups overlap and produce complexity in interaction, action and meaning (Table 5.1) (Arnould and Thompson 2005). Unlike traditional essentialist and realist perspectives, cultural research design lacks a grand overarching theory, seeing culture as fragmented, fluid and intermingling manifestations of ways of life (ibid.). The interpretive position allows us to analyze the phenomenon in question from a historical perspective and take into account contextual settings. Cultural research studies analyze the phenomenon using in-depth interviews or open-ended questionnaires in an attempt to comprehend contextually bound complexities. The cultural research agenda does not reject traditional approaches but complements them by opening up new ways for exploration. Thus if we want

Table 5.1 Essentialist vs. interpretive research on consumer culture

Assumptions	Essentialist approach	Interpretivist approach
Culture	A set of rules that govern consumer behaviour	Dynamic and complex phenomenon that can be understood in context
Categories	Clear set of independent categories	Fragmentation and fluidity
Goal	To identify dimensions common across cultures to predict consumer behaviour	To analyze various manifestations in the socio-historical context in order to understand consumer behaviour
Research tools	Statistical surveys, Likert scale questionnaires	In-depth interviews, observations, textual analysis
Knowledge generated	Time-free, Context-independent	Time-bound, Context-dependent
View of causality	Causal effect logic	Multiple, simultaneous shaping events

Source: Based on Solomon *et al*. (2007: 26).

to analyze the successes and failures of the Dove advertising presence in Russia we have to consider not only traditional statistical performance data but also look at the factors that are likely to influence the perception of the Dove advertising campaign, such as the history of and attitudes to advertising in Russia, gender relations, consumer culture, and other elements as well as exploring these factors in qualitative research setting.

This chapter illustrates the advantages of the cultural approach in the case of an advertising campaign for a global FMCG, Dove. It demonstrates the importance of analyzing the complex cultural reality in emerging market countries, such as Russia, when attempting to communicate with the local target market. It also suggests that if Dove had employed a cultural approach, it might have had a more favourable reception of its Campaign for Real Beauty in Russia.

Advertising case study: Dove in Russia

The personal care brand Dove, owned by Unilever, is the third largest brand in their portfolio after Lipton and Knorr. Reportedly, Dove's core product, moisturising soap with added cream, was developed in the US during the Second World War to help burn patients with damaged skin. After the war it found its application in cosmetics and the core advertising image for Dove, at the time, depicted cream being poured into the beauty bar of soap. In 2004, Dove launched a new advertising campaign called the 'Campaign for Real Beauty' aimed at women aged 18–64. Reportedly, it was created in response to research commissioned by Unilever from Harvard Business School and the London School of Economics about women's attitudes toward body image that found that only 2 per cent of women consider themselves beautiful. This attitude was thought to be influenced by mass media images of standardized beauty ideals. In collaboration with Ogilvy & Mather, in this campaign traditional airbrushed thin models were replaced with 'real women' presented without airbrushing (Maksimova 2006). Spread globally, the campaign caused a significant public reaction and was extensively analyzed both in the popular media and in academic studies (i.e. Fournier and Lee 2009).

In Russia, the campaign began in May 2006. Similar to its launch in Arab countries, it attempted to reduce problems with national religious and cultural traditions and beliefs by altering its images. In Russia's case, in order to reduce cultural shock, the implementation had to significantly curtail its core message: breaking female stereotypes. Unlike Europe and the US, the older population in Russia did not appeal to Dove as a lucrative target market (Maksimova 2006). Thus, Irene Sinclare, aged 96 (Figure 5.1), the oldest model in the global campaign, was replaced by Larisa Sysoeva, aged 57 (Figure 5.2), the oldest model in the Russian campaign. Original images of a woman with a mastectomy and a woman with an

Figure 5.1 Dove advertisement with Irene Sinclare, 96.

Figure 5.2 The image of Muscovite Larisa Sysoeva, 57, used for the Dove website.

abnormally large nose as beauty ideals were omitted as being too shocking for Russian women. Only a redhead with freckles (Figure 5.3) and a slightly plump but conventionally attractive woman (Figure 5.4), images which only slightly deviated from glossy beauty standards, found their way into Russia. Mass media advertisements were supported by the Russian version of Dove's internet site, print articles by specialists, an exhibition by famous female photographers entitled 'Beauty through women's eyes' as well as roundtables with experts and regular consumers on the essence of beauty (ibid.).

Figure 5.3 A freckled model from the www.dove.ru website. The text reads, 'Can only women with ideal skin be beautiful? Agree or Disagree.'

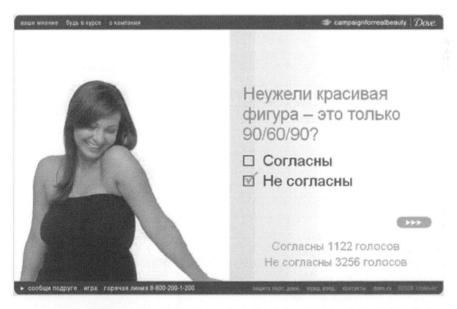

Figure 5.4 A woman used on the Russian website for Dove. The text reads 'Is the only beautiful figure 90/60/90? Agree or Disagree.'

In Europe, the positive reaction to the 'Campaign for Real Beauty' was matched by profits: Dove's sales grew by 20 per cent (Euromonitor, cited in Maksimova 2006). In Russia, sales numbers and market share, traditional marketing indicators of advertising success, remained low. Dove's market share in 2006 was less than 1 per cent (Provotorova 2006). According to one Russian marketer, in 2007, Dove's profits fell despite extensive marketing efforts (Tamberg 2010).

Public reaction to the campaign: findings

At the time of the writing of this chapter, the central event was already a historical entity. In order to access the reactions of the audiences occurring after the launch of Dove, I had to use the internet, as historically bound reactions have been captured in this medium.

The data below are taken from several Russian internet forums and articles describing the public perception and reception of the Dove marketing attempt. Generally there was a positive welcome to Dove's creative concept to introduce 'normal-looking' female images into advertising. As reported by the Russian journal *Advertising Industry* (Anon 2007), female Russian consumers were mostly sympathetic to the images of 'regular' females as necessary for self-esteem, allowing women not to be embarrassed about cellulite or about a modest stomach bulge. If women were happy to see typical females as advertising models, men wanted to admire idealized women like the ones found in the regular glossy magazines (sostav.ru). A (male?) discussant (Tamberg 2010) mistook freckles for pimples and was repulsed by the model; he also thought that the plump model had a 'horrible' figure. A (female) user pointed out the mistake about the freckles and asserted her admiration for the campaign. But reactions were not as simplistic and clear-cut along the gender divide. A female web forum participant reacted somewhat negatively to the Dove campaign saying than she did not want to look at average, common people in the adverts; instead, she needs to aspire to an ideal that the adverts present (Anon 2006). For her, the phrase, 'I am beautiful even with a pot belly, my husband loves me anyway', is the death of all principles; she believed that a woman should never stop trying, otherwise she will stop being a woman. Another female discussant admitted to liking the campaign but not having any intention of trying the brand (ibid.).

On a forum specializing in marketing, participants discussed and analyzed the Dove campaign from a professional position (Tamberg 2010). One of them pointed out that the purpose of anti-aging products is to postpone old age so choosing old models for these products is silly because there is no ad motivation in such strategy. He added that advertising should create ideals and concluded that the Dove campaign was not a success.

Continuing the same sentiment, a Russian creative director from Leo Burnett, Moscow, did not consider Dove's Campaign for Real Beauty's creative concept to be globally applicable (Danilina 2008). He unfavourably compared it with the creative concept for Axe deodorants, 'If you smell good, women will like you', that has a universal appeal.

The Russian office of Unilever attempted to place a Dove advertising billboard with the slightly plump model on a building in St. Petersburg, Russia and the owner of the building strongly rejected it, saying that the image was 'anti-aesthetic' (Provotorova 2006).

Thus both females and males questioned the effectiveness and appropriateness of Dove's Campaign for Real Beauty's images, sometimes being unable to see them as advertising normative inspiration for the audiences.

Secondary research considerations

The images of real beauty for Russian women were embodied by representations of a freckled and of a moderately corpulent young women and an older woman, which slightly deviated from standardized glossy beauty images. Dove appealed to women's values of naturalness, equating beauty with charisma. Because of the marketing buzz and mass media discussions, the unintended male market was also exposed to the campaign. The Russian response to the message and the images was strong and unexpected. In order to understand and appreciate the reaction to the campaign, we need to outline the factors that influenced the Russian cultural perception, such as attitudes to advertising, the nature of consumer and consumption, the perception of beauty, gender relations, etc. Since the female target market selected by Dove comprised both the older generation whose views were formed by Soviet conditions and younger women, some of whom were born after 1991, two different perspectives, Soviet and post-Soviet, have to be taken into account.

Attitudes toward advertising in Russia

As in many other industrialized nations, professional advertising has existed in Russia since at least the eighteenth century. Although its steady development was interrupted by the 1917 Communist revolution, the new regime promptly adopted advertising as one more tool in building a new society. But even though advertising, in some form, was present throughout the whole of Soviet history, its role was mainly of an ideological and political nature rather than a business one. For instance, after the Second World War when the economy had to be rebuilt, advertising was used to placate the public by propagating the myth of already existing consumer abundance as an argument in the ideological war with the West. Advertising techniques were mainly employed to spread the messages of furthering the construction of the Communist society, as well as used as propaganda weapons during the Cold War. To assist the trade, advertising was utilized when a particular product, such as sewing machines or double-breasted suits, had been over-produced due to the incorrect centralized planning and needed to be sold quickly. The population regarded Soviet advertising with suspicion and cynicism, realizing its deceptive goals (Humphrey 1995). Perhaps due to the absence of Western goods on the Soviet consumer market, Western advertisements were absent as well and were maligned by the Party as tools of capitalist ideology.

After Gorbachev's *perestroika*, advertising exploded. Foreign companies rushed to win the new market and at first it created havoc. In the 1990s, when marketing techniques such as targeting and positioning were absent, the new advertising created a lot of confusion among the population. Often it promoted specialized niche products to mass consumers. On a typical day in the early 1990s, state television 'dizzyingly' showed a commercial for German dialysis machines followed by adverts for banks, cat food and even weapons (Kelly 1998). Mostly Western-made early post-Soviet advertisements were not adapted to the Russian realities and consumers could not help but draw parallels between the new advertising and Soviet propaganda. Historically, the unfavourable attitudes were already predetermined; in Russian, the word 'advertising' has a negative connotation: to advertise means 'to praise without shame' (Tolstikova 1994).

Nevertheless, marketing communication continued to expand in Russia. The increased volume of advertisements in the mass media and outdoors was initially met with animosity. Russians were often annoyed and distracted by advertising especially when it interrupted

TV programming. However, their attitudes toward advertising have been complex and perpetually evolving. A recent study (Savel'eva 2007) found that Russians started to feel mostly neutral or positive toward advertising, with the majority of respondents wanting advertising to stay, which means that they have accepted advertising as a part of their culture. Russians have absorbed advertising-speak into their daily language; they discuss striking and poor advertising examples, critically analyzing them and exchanging anecdotes like the one taken as an epigraph to this chapter. Not surprisingly, the same study discovered that younger Russians have adapted most to the new social conditions and therefore have more positive attitudes toward advertising. The reasons for this are complex and probably include factors such as growing availability of goods advertised, adverts more precisely targeting audiences, the audiences learning to read ads, changed generation influence in public media infrastructure, etc.

Along with Western advertising, post-Soviet marketing communication is gaining ground. Contemporary Russian advertising illustrates a chaos in value systems: Soviet values have been discredited yet the post-Soviet ones are still in a formative stage while Western values are intensely debated in the Russian discourse (Sal'nikova 2001). In the mid-1990s, when Russian-made advertisements first appeared on the scene, culturally they were hybrids that combined the symbols of the romanticized West and the emblems of imperial Russia (Boym 1994). According to social surveys, after the disintegration of the Soviet Union, Russians primarily favoured spiritual values while power and success represented negative values (Salmi and Sharafutdinova 2008). In the mid-1990s there was an apparent shift in favour of material values. In 2002, the top preferential value was to be well-off (ibid.). Thus in Russia advertising is deemed to be aspirational so consumers can emulate images and lifestyle. Understanding this socio-cultural factor is relevant to advertising and its creative message. If your approach to culture is founded on essentialist premises (see Table 5.1), you could easily misinterpret or avoid factors described above; the result could lead to problems with advertising communication as happened with Dove: an essentialist cultural conception is not working because of cultural complexity and fluidity.

Attitudes toward consumption in Russia

The economy of the Soviet Union was driven by production, not consumption. Consumption *per se* in the Soviet Union was not an evil, consumption of spiritual and culture-enhancing artifacts – books, museums and such – was greatly encouraged. Consumerism equated with irrational acquisition of things was, however, considered to be immoral (Pilkington 1996). In Soviet times, shopping was a chore rather than a pleasure. The goal of shopping was to obtain as much as possible of what limited goods were available. Brand products were virtually unknown. Shopping was mostly done by women and often included visits to several stores to procure the basic items. The consumer had to be prepared to spend considerable time, to meet a number of challenges and in the end not even to find the goods in question. Retailing methods were cumbersome and inefficient; a customer had to stand in several lines to examine, pay for, and finally receive the merchandise (Tolstikova 2001).

After the collapse of the Soviet Union, Russians had to learn about conspicuous consumption and became expert shoppers fast. In the twenty-first century, Russians are sophisticated shoppers familiar with most global brands. Now a trip to the store is a pleasure rather than a chore although it still may be painful because of the high prices. Russian men rarely do everyday shopping but wealthier men now enjoy buying luxury products themselves. Yet the old Soviet habits remained. Soviet consumers bought consumer goods – non-perishable food or shoes, in multiple quantities 'just in case'. Less wealthy Russians still hoard goods as they did in the times of the distributive economy (Shevchenko 2002). This strategy has proved to be useful in the unsettling continuous financial crisis that Russians endure.

Thus the situation has evolved and, although attitudes toward the West are still complex, consumption is now perceived as a new everyday norm. Moreover, there is even a tendency to over-consume. This trend can be explained due to the uncertainty and instability of the country but also due to the Russian characteristic generosity, which is one of the basic character traits of Russians who are ready to give gifts on any occasion (Salmi and Sharafutdinova 2008). New consumption realities meet at the intersection of 'old' expectations, 'new' contextual environment and traditional gender roles.

Attitudes toward gender

Pre-revolutionary Russia was patriarchal; the public sphere belonged to males while the private was the female realm. Soviets wanted to construct a different set of gender relations where both genders serve the state and additionally women served men. Women were expected to perform the roles of worker, mother and housekeeper while men were expected to be workers and soldiers. Despite the Soviet attempts, the society remained patriarchal in reinforcing traditional gender roles and male supremacy. The woman was always suspected of flirty behaviour, a propensity for petty interests and personal values which clashed with the Communist foundations.

Although, in post-Soviet times women have gained more economic power and often occupy the role of breadwinner, the cultural idea that the man should be in control is still prevalent (Ashwin 2000). Hence, the new (old) cultural norm is that women are expected to look their best to please a man and men are expected to pay for everything even if a woman earns more. Russian females make intensive and extensive efforts to look glamorous. Reportedly, in 2006, about 80 per cent of Russian women used decorative cosmetics (compared to 68 per cent in other countries) and a manicure was a norm for 70 per cent (compared to the world average of 46 per cent) (Provotorova 2006). Complex, driven by contradictions, the Russian gender sensibilities must be taken into account especially when designing a marketing communication campaign involving gender considerations.

Attitudes toward beauty

Traditionally, beauty in Russia has been associated with physical attractiveness, so it was firmly based on gender. Russian attitudes toward beauty are closely connected with historical and economic changes. Immediately after the revolution, the state proclaimed equality between sexes. Attempts at gender differentiation, such as use of cosmetics fashion were frowned upon. The Soviet woman, the 'tough equal of the man' (see Figure 5.5), was even expected to look like him with a short haircut and efficient clothes. In the spirit of the Party ideology, the notion of beauty was equated with naturalness, physical sport and health, not with cosmetic embellishment (Tolstikova 2001).

From the 1950s on, the Party position on beauty held that beauty is in the eye of the beholder but conventionally women were encouraged to look attractive and to use cosmetics. Soviet women's magazines promoted beauty parlours, cosmetics, and even cosmetic surgery thus suggesting that attractiveness requires some additional efforts (ibid.).

Figure 5.5 The December 1937 cover of the Soviet women's magazine *Rabotnitsa* [Working Woman].

Russian beauty standards were not restrictive to any particular body type, hair colour or specific features but general pleasantness (outside) and 'solid character' (inside). Still the images in those magazines were of low quality and lacked the glossy retouched glamour. With the appearance of the Western glossy women's press, the Russian population joined the rest of the world and became exposed to commonly thin models with unnaturally long legs and flawless faces.

Women's glossy magazines in Russia

In the 1990s, the new Western product that proved to have a great influence on women's lives and, more importantly, brought new norms and values, was the glossy magazine. Unlike traditional Soviet-style women's magazines printed on yellowing paper with bland illustrations and homely content, the new publications were awash with different ideology and high definition photos of stylish models. It signalled the departure from mostly verbal culture to visual. Through reading but mostly through looking, Russian women joined other females around the world who would buy into the allure of the material world that has been assembled through advertisements and editorials (Stephenson 2007).

The product transposed directly from the West, functions as disseminator of fantasy and aspirational ideals for women (Ballaster *et al.* 1991: 173). As a fantasy machine, women's magazines put an ideological lens on female perception of reality and create a need to emulate the ideals presented on its pages.

Arguably, for some females, glossy women's magazines have been the largest factor influencing their cultural norms. The old Soviet norm of a patriotic mother and a hard worker was being replaced with a glamorous domestic goddess and a fashion plate. Not all women could afford pricey glossies but they were still being exposed to them in public places and girlfriends' houses. Dozens of titles catered to different segments of females constructing lifestyles and ploughing the ground for marketers.

Globalization

The foreign brands widely available in Russia are not the only results of globalization. Brands like Gucci and Bentley arrived accompanied with specific values and ideologies. From the essentialist point of view, the process of globalization is often equated with cultural imperialism and the dominance of Western cultural values. The cultural perspective suggests looking at the contextual base and specific configurations of the global and local. In the early post-Soviet Russia there was a feeling that Western consumption norms somehow were contaminating the culture (Humphrey 1995). The first apparent sign was foreignization of the Russian language with 10,000 English words invading the speech (Ustinova 2006). It became especially noticeable in advertising language with slogans often translated verbatim and seldom making much sense to a Russian. However, a cultural researcher sees culture as always dynamic and evolving and a complex result of a varied set of influences, rather than assuming a pure, clean, natural local culture and something bad/foreign attacking its 'authentic' values. Russian advertising language utilized English or even English-sounding words to signal prestige, novelty and high quality (ibid.). Attitudes to the foreign influence on the Russian language are complex and contradictory, some call it vulgarization, others hail it as the enrichment, yet others consider it a natural process (ibid.). Understandably, some Russians equate the process of language change with the change in norms but the norms are perpetually involving and cultures mutually influence each other.

Dove's products produced and promoted by Western companies bear the mark of foreignness which might be appealing to some Russians and also might be perceived negatively by others. The marketing managers should be aware of such complex attitudes toward the West and should design the promotional message with that in mind.

Primary research considerations

From the cultural perspective, Dove's main research instrument – the questionnaire – should be enhanced with interpretive research such as in-depth interviews; this will allow more complex results and richer data. Primary research for Dove's campaign is beyond the scope of this chapter for the reasons that several years have passed since its launch and the historical context has changed, so the results obtained through primary research at this point in time would be biased. However, considering research methods is crucial for a marketing manager. When preparing the Russian Campaign for Real Beauty, in addition to collecting and analyzing secondary sources, Dove would have benefited from qualitative primary research. It would have helped to unpack statistical data and understand the meaning of the numbers. In a setting of in-depth interview or a focus group, researchers are able to access the participants' own perspective. Also, qualitative research methods used by the cultural approach allow researchers to ask additional questions to clarify the meanings of the responses. Therefore, Russian women would have shared their own meaning of beauty or the importance of consumption in their lives or their feelings about globalization.

Discussion and managerial implications

In the reality of global marketing there is always a temptation to replicate successful branding efforts onto another culture, unchanged. Dove's Campaign for Real Beauty had been exemplified as an almost perfect communication message in Western markets. However, in order to make an impact in other culturally different markets, marketing managers must fight this temptation and approach the process from fundamentals, trying to appraise and comprehend the local history, beliefs, expectations and norms. The brand might be well established elsewhere but it is important to communicate the message that will be understood and interpreted appropriately by local audiences.

The cultural approach illustrated by the Dove advertising case above is a creative research tool to investigate marketing problems. The cultural approach philosophy provides a good managerial support system but also helps a better understanding of the phenomenon of the Dove ad campaign and the responses to it. The factors selected for secondary research sources were chosen because of cultural considerations: beliefs are crucial cultural components and glossy magazines and globalization are recent phenomena that greatly influence Russian everyday life. However, these factors are not exclusive and may be expanded to reflect a different cultural research design.

Dove based its marketing strategy on the survey, finding that only 2 per cent of women consider themselves beautiful. However, the reasons for this number are probably different in different countries. Statistical numbers of the Dove survey in Russia and other countries might look similar but, as the secondary research of factors suggest, the meaning of beauty and the relationship between genders are more conservative there than in other countries. Russia is undergoing dramatic external changes that affect its cultural make-up. Only a decade ago consumers needed to adapt from the shortage economy to the abundance economy. With the availability of unlimited global brands, the ideology of consumption had to undergo a rapid change. This process involved developing different attitudes toward consumption driven more by economic factors than by ideology. However, gender and understanding of beauty, deeper cultural components, remained more or less unchanged. If in the West glossy beauty standards put a strain on ordinary women, Russian women consider them as something to aspire to (Provotorova 2006). In Russia, every woman wants to be Claudia Schiffer; the country is still in the process of building new ideals and is not ready to break with the conventional beauty stereotypes, partially because the Western mass media beauty ideals are still being exalted.

Armed with the secondary study results, a cultural researcher will be able to develop discerning questions for primary research – in-depth interviews with Russian women – and this would have helped to understand the meaning they associate with the core marketing communication message of the Dove Campaign for Real Beauty. Cultural research philosophy enriches not only academic but also managerial advertising research. With the cultural perspective you can access and analyze dynamics and the complexity of various cultural phenomena that can only be understood as a part of context, both contemporary and historical, regarding issues like beauty, the portrayal of women in mass media or looking flawless with the help of airbrushing.

Review and discussion questions

1   Identify the types of research that Dove performed in order to create the Campaign for Real Beauty in Russia.

2   What are the ways of retaining the core message of the campaign and reaching the
     Russian target market?
3   What are the implications for Dove regarding the entry into the Russian market of *not
     launching* the campaign in Russia?
4   What do you think Dove should have done differently in order to create a favourable
     reception for the core marketing communication message?
5   You are a marketing manager for Mountain Dew and you are in charge of entering the
     Russian soft drink market in 2011. How will you approach this task using cultural
     research methods?

Keywords

beauty, cultural approach, gender, research methods, Russian market

References

Anon (2006) Responses to the Article Dove Prolongs the Summer, Discussion. Available at: http://
    www.kleo.ru/items/fashion/summer_light.comments.shtml?37 (accessed August 2010).
Anon (2007) Beauty, the Russian Style Dove Decided Not to Shock Russian Women, *Everything
    about Advertising*. Available at: http://www.printmagazine.ru/news/222 (accessed August 2010).
Arnould, E. and Thompson, C. (2005) Consumer Culture Theory (CCT): Twenty Years of Research,
    Journal of Consumer Research, 31: 868–82.
Ashwin, S. (ed.) (2000) *Gender, State and Society in Soviet and Post-Soviet Russia*, London:
    Routledge.
Askegaard, S., Kjeldgaard, D. and Arnould, E. J. (2009) Reflexive Cultures Consequences, in
    C. Nakata (ed.), *Beyond Hofstede: Culture Frameworks for Global Marketing and Management*,
    Chicago: Macmillan.
Ballaster, R. *et al.* (1991) *Women's Worlds: Ideology, Femininity and the Woman's Magazine*,
    Basingstoke: Macmillan.
Boym, S. (1994) *Common Places: Mythologies of Everyday Life in Russia*, Cambridge, MA: Harvard
    University Press.
Craig, C. S. and Douglas, S. P. (2006), Beyond National Culture: Implications of Cultural Dynamics
    for Consumer Research, *International Marketing Review*, 23(3): 322–42.
Danilina, N. (2008) We Are Not in the Top League Yet, in Russian. Available at: http://www.
    kommersant.ru/doc rss.aspx?DocsID = 1034655 (accessed August 2010).
De Mooij, M. (2005) *Global Marketing and Advertising: Understanding Cultural Paradoxes*, London:
    SAGE.
Doole, I. and Lowe, R. (2008) *International Marketing Strategy: Analysis, Development and
    Implementation*, London: Cenage Learning.
Fournier, S. and Lee, L. (2009) Getting the Brand Communities Right, *Harvard Business Review*,
    April: 105–11.
Geertz, C. (1973) *The Interpretations of Culture*, New York: Basic Books.
Hackley, C. (2010) *Advertising and Promotion: An Integrated Marketing Communication Approach*,
    2nd edn, London: Sage.
Hall, S. (1973) *Encoding and Decoding in the Television Discourse*, Birmingham: Birmingham
    University.
Hofstede, G. (1980) *Culture's Consequences: International Differences in Work-Related Values*,
    Beverly Hills, CA: Sage.
Humphrey, C. (1995) Creating a Culture of Disillusionment: Consumption in Moscow, a Chronicle of
    Changing Times, in D. Miller (ed.), *Worlds Apart: Modernity through the Prism of the Local*,
    London: Routledge, pp. 43–8.

Kelly, C. (1998) Creating a Consumer: Advertising and Commercialization, in C. Kelly and D. Shepard (eds), *Russian Cultural Studies: An Introduction*, Oxford: Oxford University Press, pp. 223–46.

Maksimova, L. (2006) Мыльная опера. Как Dove делал мир чище [Soap Opera. How Dove Was Making The World Cleaner]. *Adme.ru*. Available at: http://www.adme.ru/articles/mylnaya-opera-kak-dove-delal-mir-chische-11719/ (accessed August 2010).

McCracken, G. (1988) *The Long Interview*, Newbury Park, CA: Sage.

—— (2002) *New Approaches to Symbolic Characters of Consumer Goods and Activities*, Bloomington, IN: Indiana University Press.

—— (2005) *Markets, Meaning and Brand Management*, Bloomington, IN: Indiana University Press.

Nakata, C. (2003) 'Culture Theory in International Marketing: An Onthological Research and Epistemological Examination', in S. C. Jain (ed.), *Handbook of Research in International Marketing*, Northampton, MA: Edward Elgar Publishing, pp. 209–29.

O'Leary, N. (2008) 'How Brazil, Russia, India and China Are Reshaping the Marketing World', *Adweek*, Feb 1. Available at: http://www.adweek.com/aw/content_display/specialreports/other-reports/e3ibd2a4d5f94f9578bb5e64247c12ae3b1?pn = 5 (accessed August 2010).

Pilkington, H. (ed.) (1996) *Gender, Generation and Identity in Contemporary Russia*, London: Routledge.

Pilkington, H. *et al.* (eds) (2002) *Looking West? Cultural Globalization and Russian Youth Cultures*, University Park, PA: University of Pennsylvania Press.

Provotorova, E. (2006) 'Действительно страшная сила. Дов насаждает новые представления о красоте [Indeed powerful. Dove promotes new ideology of beauty]', *Oilworld.ru*. Available at: http://www.oilworld.ru/news.php?view = 13612 (accessed August 2010).

Salmi, A. and Sharafutdinova, E. (2008) Culture and Design in Emerging Markets: The Case of Mobile Phones in Russia, *Journal of Business and Industrial Marketing*, 23: 384–94.

Sal'nikova, E. V. (2001) Эстетика рекламы: культурные корни и лейтмотивы *[Advertising Aesthetics: Cultural Roots and Leitmotifs]*, Moscow: Ministry of Culture of RSFSR.

Savel'eva, O. (2007) 'Prospects of Change in Russians' Attitudes toward Advertising', *Sociological Research*, 46: 47–61.

Shevchenko, O. (2002) In Case of Fire Emergency. Consumption, Security and the Meaning of Durables in a Transforming Society, *Journal of Consumer Culture*, 2(2): 147–70.

Solomon, M., Bamossy, G., Askegaar, S., Hogg, M. *et al.* (2007) *Consumer Behaviour: A European Perspective*, Englewood Cliffs, NJ: Prentice Hall.

Sostav.ru (2006) 'Advertising forum'. Available at: http://www.sostav.ru/columns/weekend/2006/0003/ (accessed August 2010).

Stephenson, S. (2007) The Changing Face of Women's Magazines in Russia, *Journalism Studies*, 8: 613–20.

Tamberg, V. (2010) Discussion of the Dove Campaign. Available at: http://tamberg.livejournal.com/95684.html (accessed August 2010).

Tolstikova, N. (1994) Signs from the Other World: Russian Attitudes toward American Advertising, in *Proceedings of American Academy of Advertising*, p. 62.

—— (2001) Reading *Rabotnitsa*: Ideals, Aspirations, and Consumption Choices for Soviet Women, 1914–64, PhD Diss., Urbana, IL, University of Illinois.

Ustinova, I. (2006) English and Emerging Advertising in Russia, *World Englishes*, 25: 267–77.

6 Market development in the African context

Benét DeBerry-Spence, Sammy K. Bonsu, and Eric J. Arnould

Overview

Africa has moved from the periphery of interest to global business to the center as Euro-American concerns re-evaluate its potential and emerging market actors in China and India continue to expand their presence there. African "market development" contains a two-part dynamic. The first involves transforming markets into effective avenues for the economic empowerment of African businesses and consumers to purchase both foreign and domestic products. The second revolves around export market development intended to generate revenues for African exporters and to support an economically robust consumer base on the continent. Africa has a long history of participation in global markets as well as some unique commercial forms and structures. Africa contends with a legacy of colonial extraction-based economic policies, and a post-colonial legacy of ineffective commercial policies. Commercial infrastructure in Africa is underdeveloped generally, but this provides many new opportunities for market development as our case studies suggest. Entrepreneurship is alive and well on the African continent. Many African consumers are quite poor, but this does not mean that they are unattractive markets, given the right mix of products, prices, and distribution strategies. Opportunities exist to participate in a renaissance of African marketing systems in both the so-called informal sector, as well as the formal sector of the economy for multinational firms, local firms and NGOs.

Cultural positioning

Pundits and scholars alike have recently become interested in Africa, proclaiming the continent as a potential global commercial center: a diamond in the rough that could be polished for the simultaneous benefits of financial profits and poverty alleviation. This is a dramatic shift from the 1980s and 1990s, when strategists actively advocated neglect of the world's second-largest continent because they perceived African markets as offering little or no value to firms' bottom line. At that time, Africa's market value was perceived to lie only in the meager potential of its wealthy minority. Global firms developed this wealthy segment at the expense of other local markets. The resulting niche market's appeal was considered comparable to other segments in the world in tastes and financial resources and thus required no extra marketing design for success. This perspective was grounded in an economic analysis that understated the marketing implications for the neglected 900-million-plus population. Such analysis also failed to consider the latent implications of the often tenuous engagement among markets, marketing, and society.

In the face of contemporary globalization, the status quo that gave Euro-America priority in African trade is being challenged by China, India and other countries, forcing all parties to consider new ways of approaching African markets and marketing. Progress toward transforming Africa into a commercial center requires a more holistic approach that recognizes African markets as sites for socio-economic development. An emerging consensus toward such an approach revolves around Hart's model that perceives tripartite benefits by way of firm profitability, environmental sustainability and poverty alleviation. Evidence from the field, however, suggests that business emphasis in African markets remains on financial profits without much reference to local culture, poverty alleviation, and environmental sustainability. Developing such an approach suggests the need for an enterprise-driven market structure in contemporary Africa; one that also recognizes the ideological implications of related strategic actions.

Toward this end, this chapter proposes an approach to African market development premised on the view that globalization – that which affords enhanced free mobility of resources around the world – portends an increasing role for Africa and its markets in the future world economy. To be an effective agent of change for the benefit of Africa, however, the market should close the income gap that perpetuates poverty by realizing the latent value of local economic and cultural resources (Stiglitz 2002). That is, the much emphasized focus on demand (Africans as *consumers* of global products, e.g., Prahalad 2004) should be supplemented by the supply side (Africans as *producers* for global markets).

From this perspective, African "market development" may be seen as a two-part dynamic. The first element involves transforming markets into effective avenues for the economic empowerment of African businesses and consumers to purchase both foreign and domestic products. The second revolves around export market development intended to generate revenues for African exporters and to support an economically robust consumer base on the continent. Thus, our view of market development in Africa highlights the need to understand how local resources, such as market structures, socio-cultural bonds outside the market, and latent domestic knowledge, combine with global tools to provide opportunities for crafting African-relevant strategies for long-term socio-economic sustainability.

In this chapter, we stress the need to understand local conditions within historical and contemporary developments of African business. Africa is by no means a homogeneous continent. It is a diverse set of peoples and cultures that do not respond similarly to market stimuli. Indeed, this is one major reason why a cultural approach to African markets and marketing is necessary. We recognize that our attempt to paint a general picture of African market development is oversimplified, but we offer a common set of market features that can be adapted for use in any specific African community.

African markets: then and now

Evidence of African business enterprises pre-dates the arrival of the first Europeans (Takyi-Asiedu 1993), and commerce extends deeply into the historical record (e.g., Lovejoy 2002). Most African economies today contain market systems that correspond to different historical epochs in their development, often organized around discrepant economic principles. For example, contemporary markets seem to have supplemented old forms of market relationships that relied on neighborly, kin and ethnically rooted trust with the contract-based form introduced by European colonizers (i.e., Portuguese, Dutch, English, and French) who long ago established themselves along the West African Coast to trade in gold, ivory, pepper and, later, slaves (Osae *et al.* 1973).

Colonial-era African markets were specialized and of limited access to ordinary Africans; later under cosmopolitan influence, they opened up to the exchange of all manner of goods and services (Meillassoux 1971). On the abolition of slave trade in the 1850s, local markets reverted to trading in foods and other essentials, expanding to embrace the exports of raw materials and the trading of increasingly diverse imports. To support the export market for local raw materials (e.g., cocoa, coffee, diamonds, bauxite, gold), most of Africa's colonial era railroads were built to transport raw materials from the interior to the coasts, where they were exported to Europe and other areas. The architecture and direction of growth of the Kumasi Central Market in Ghana, for example, and the network of transportation infrastructure in the country are testaments to these colonial developments.

The colonial strategy was designed to maximize benefits to the colonizer, with little concern about the well-being of the locals. The structural dynamics of colonial control and its systematic stripping away of legitimate access to markets for locals, especially export markets, ensured that colonial expatriates were the primary owners of most market and marketing resources (Rodney 1981). It is no accident then that colonial-era companies, such as Unilever and Barclays Bank, are still key business players on the continent. Post-independence Africa is colored by its colonial legacy.

Government policies for market development in much of Africa have also been modeled on the colonial system that favored the establishment of centralized marketing boards that controlled the movements of goods and services. Although most of these state monopolies have disappeared in the wake of World Bank structural adjustment reforms in the 1980s and 1990s, some trading relationships remain. For example, in Ghana, the Cocoa Marketing Board (CMB) was rebranded COCOBOD and allowed to compete for farmers' harvest along with a few private firms. By reason of its pioneering and other structural advantages, COCOBOD remains the dominant force in the trading of cocoa in the country (Amoah 1995). Similarly, the Tanzania Telecommunications Company, a privatized offspring of the state-owned version, inherited the political power of its predecessor and uses this leverage to control the market (Maddy 2000).

The colonial market development strategy brought about significant local mistrust of foreigners, especially in its effort to dispossess locals of wealth and opportunities. The mistrust seemed mutual as colonial powers encouraged an increasing role for Indian commercial actors in East Africa and Lebanese traders on the West Coast at the expense of locals. Good commercial relationships with Indian and Middle Eastern merchants facilitated African colonizers' access to networks of commercial interests that extended beyond Africa and Europe (Rodney 1981).

In sharp contrast to the colonial practice of defining markets relationships by written contracts, traditional African markets relied more on cultural networks (e.g., kinship, friend-ships) for performance. Market systems such as the extended household commercial enterprise (Yusuf 1975) still exist along with various others that encourage long-term commercial partnering between actors. Rules in this market are akin to the structure and organization of the prevailing socio-cultural order that makes non-commercial relationships a significant undercurrent for market dynamics. These domestic market relationships were reproduced in cross-cultural marketing when merchants from North Africa presented their wares (e.g., salt, dates) in Sub-Saharan markets and returned home with other items (e.g., cereal crops). Many branches of indigenous marketing were managed by geographically dispersed ethnic trading diaspora (Lovejoy 2002).

More recent market development in Africa has been influenced by increased globaliza-tion and the presence of Chinese businesses that, unlike earlier foreign investors, actively encourage local input into marketing practices. Wary of the status quo that privileged Euro-American ideals, Africans have responded favorably to Chinese views of the market that offer flexibilities for local engagement and mutual benefits, without political interference. Although China's involvement, especially its continued engagement with Sudan and Zimbabwe, has caused some concern in Euro-America, African traders have welcomed China's approach, perceiving it as a cheaper alternative and as a possible opposite to the colonial engagement. Chinese personnel often attempt to learn the local African languages and cultures, and study the local market to develop products specifically for them (see Brautigam 2009).

The historical and contemporary influences on African markets have resulted in hybrid market systems that try to preserve the cultural components while adopting the benefits of markets afforded by global capitalism. However, there is still a high level of trust among actors in traditional markets: formal contracts are rare and informal credit (social and pecuniary) is still abundant. This trust is not easily extended to foreign merchants who operate on a system of contracts. The dual system (traditional versus contemporary) and its related hybrid can pose barriers to market development, but it also provides a rich resource (e.g., market intelligence, local skills and knowledge) for improving market efficiency and offering socio-economic benefits to the parties involved.

In what may be regarded from a Western perspective as unsuitable or unstable economic environmental conditions, African entrepreneurs survive by drawing on available local resources. The driver behind most business start-ups is "enforced entrepreneurship," rather than the "pull of market opportunities" (Rogerson 2001: 117). The challenge for many African enterprises is "to turn the miracle of survival into the miracle of growth" (Steel 1994: 4). A major hurdle for firms, especially foreign firms, is overcoming the preconceived notion that the continent lacks the necessary infra- and supra-structures for effective marketing. This line of reasoning implies that Africa should follow the same path to marketing as the West, suggesting superiority undertones that are reminiscent of the imperialist argument that places the foreign business in a position of power over the African (Bonsu 2009). Overcoming this notion requires a keen eye for the African market and a willingness to abandon conventional indicators in assessing market opportunities (Arnould 2001; Arnould and Mohr 2005). Then, the marketer can seek local knowledge and other resources that can serve as a foundation for marketing success. It is this foundation that should direct market development in contemporary Africa.

Market development in Africa

Developing African markets begins with understanding the role of local small and medium-sized businesses in the market. The significance of entrepreneurship, indigenous private enterprise, and micro- and small-scale enterprises (MSEs) to both economic and social development in Africa is well established. Less than 3 percent of all African businesses have 10 or more employees (Spring and McDade 1998), and those with one to three employees constitute the majority (Daniels *et al.* 1995). The presence of small enterprise economies contributes to areas of employment creation and to poverty alleviation (Rogerson 2001); thus, continued market development in Africa must involve African entrepreneurs as important agents of change and growth. However, these businesses together will not support market development if the barriers to entry are not addressed.

Local manufacturers and exporters in many Sub-Saharan countries face other issues, including limited foreign market knowledge, product quality and production capacity problems, and government and exogenous economic export problems. The small size of economic units, the dependence on market exchanges for most resource allocation, and the fragmented nature of transactions all impede market development in Africa (Fafchamps 1997). Perhaps the most important impediment is the failure to recognize the cultural underpinnings of African markets as a valuable resource. African markets are often perceived as "informal" and thus inefficient. However, the realities that African market actors and institutions face are similar to those faced by their Western counterparts, including supply, demand and the allocation of resources to address market needs, even if the mechanisms employed in the African context are less formal (ibid.). African market development efforts are more likely to succeed if they capitalize on the strengths of existing market forms and structures, rather than attempting to transform local markets to fit Western forms and function.

Informal business networks encourage collaboration and collective action, a necessary strategy in Africa where market fragmentation is the norm, and individual initiative does not ensure efficiency (ibid.). Through collective action, micro-business entrepreneurs are able to meet both social and economic needs (DeBerry-Spence 2010). Working with people linked by socio-cultural background provides entrepreneurs with access to resources and complementary investments (Helmsing 2003). For example, the benefits from a peasant farmer's limited investment in an innovative production facility toward meeting market requirements may be stifled without complementary investments from others in support services areas, such as packaging and transportation. The degree of specialization of investment in African markets – due to limited resources – suggests the need for cooperative efforts among specialized players in the entire value chain (Arnould and Mohr 2005). Marketing under these conditions calls for unique adaptive strategies on both domestic and export market fronts.

Adaptive strategies for domestic market development

Africa's domestic market base is over 900 million potential customers. As markets in Europe, Japan, and North America become saturated, businesses are turning their attention to poorer regions such as Africa with an eye toward building them up as possible new markets (Prahalad 2004). Approximately 3 percent of the African population (about 24 million people) is wealthy enough to afford all the luxuries a consumer culture offers (Burgess *et al*. 2002), and multinational consumer product companies have often targeted this group. However, because the vast majority of people in Africa are poor, strategies for developing the African market must necessarily focus on the poor. We anchor our discussion of how this might be done in the experiences of MTN, a telecommunications company with operations in 16 African countries.

Case study 1: MTN

Mobile phones have single-handedly redefined the ways consumers and businesses around the world communicate with each other. According to AfricaFocus (2004), Africa has the highest annual growth rate in mobile subscribers: an estimated one in three Africans have access to a mobile phone. This is in sharp contrast with the landline telephone, which remained rare in Africa at the end of the twentieth century (de Bruijn *et al*. 2009). At the heart of Africa's mobile exchanges are companies such as the MTN Group, a South African-based telecommunications company started in 1994 with reported revenues in 2009 of R111.9 billion, or US$16.159 billion (MTN Group 2009). With licenses across 16 African countries and a subscriber base exceeding 115 million, MTN is the leading telecommunications company in Africa.

Driving market growth in Africa

Several factors have contributed to MTN's rapid market presence. Some pertain to market dynamics, such as drops in the cost of cellular technology, the affordability of mobile phone usage, and the development of mobile phone cottage industries, which has led to growth in jobs and incomes. Other factors are more directly linked with MTN company initiatives, one of which is the strategic acquisitions of both existing cellular businesses and local/domestic fixed-line operators. The latter was particularly effective because it afforded quick expansion in tightly regulated markets.

MTN also redefined the market. MTN accomplished this in Uganda by emphasizing: (1) that subscriber lines were technology insensitive, and the technology choice was a market competition strategy; (2) that all people, including the affluent and the poor, had the right to access cellular service; and (3) that the cellular service was a business tool similar to the existing fixed lines (Mureithi 2003). This strategy enabled MTN to alter market dynamics and to begin a paradigm shift in the mind-set of both consumers and governments regarding the rights of all people to have access to cellular communications and its potential technology uses.

To extend voice services to underserved markets (e.g., the poor), MTN used existing distribution outlets where many Africans get their everyday products. As with foods, toiletries, and clothing, consumers purchase MTN products from vendors selling in large open markets, along roadsides, in traffic, in kiosks, at neighbors' houses, and so on (see Figure 6.1). Becoming an MTN retailer requires a mere purchase of MTN products (i.e., pre-paid phone cards) from a wholesaler, while becoming an MTN wholesaler and/or selling "transfer credits" (i.e. mobile-to-mobile pre-paid units) is only slightly more complex. If the entrepreneur sets up a kiosk/shop, MTN usually provides promotional support with posters, decal stickers, umbrellas and vendor jackets. The cost of the MTN start-up is so low and relatively easy that many retailers add the firm's products to their lines; a diversification strategy of sorts for many African micro-business operators. This distribution strategy's low barriers to entry are well suited to Africa's micro-business entrepreneurial landscape.

Challenges to continued growth

MTN reports that significant growth opportunities remain in African markets, with mobile penetration below 50 percent in the 16 markets in which it operates. However, there are several challenges to the firm's future growth. First, the success of African telecommunications markets has attracted significant foreign investment that has driven both industry growth and consolidation (Mureithi 2003). Market consolidation has also led to more intense competition from fewer but large players, making the brand and brand loyalty critical. Consolidation can be problematic since rapid growth in its mobile cellular consumer base has resulted in network congestion and recurrence of poor customer service. The MTN brand continues to hold cachet, but many consumers have become less patient and are no longer willing to rely solely on one carrier for their cellular services. With the cost of SIM cards

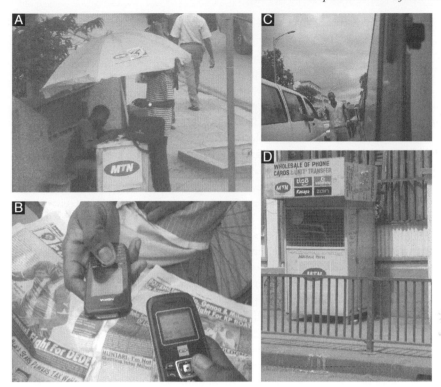

Figure 6.1 MTN distribution outlets. (A) Streetside: Tabletop, (B) Neighbors: Mobile-to-mobile, (C) In-traffic, (D) Roadside: Kiosk.
Source: Photo credits: James Koomson.

often less than US$1 in most markets, brand switching is inexpensive, and consumers often own more than one SIM card brand to avoid service interruptions or to take advantage of promotions. Here, they can choose to use MTN or one of its competitors, such as Vodafone, Glo, or Tigo, depending on which firm has the best promotional pricing on a particular day or week.

Second, in addition to an increasingly competitive marketplace, MTN and other telecommunications companies must deal with challenges posed by continued environmental hostilities (e.g., unreliable power, lack of infrastructure, security threats) common to many Africans. For example, frequent power outages pose significant problems for MTN wholesale distributors who rely on money counters to execute sales transactions. Money counters are essential for MTN wholesalers operating in Africa, which are primarily cash-based, because the low-value currency makes counting large volumes of money necessary on a daily basis. In addition, money counters own a counterfeit currency detection feature, which is critical to the MTN wholesaler's profitability because of the low profit margins associated with phone cards/credit transfers. The impact of environmental hostilities on businesses such as MTN helps emphasize that technology is often still an expectation rather than a reality (de Bruijn *et al.* 2009).

Lessons from the MTN case study

The MTN case study illustrates the need for adaptability of strategy based on local market conditions to develop African markets. MTN recognized that the poor are sophisticated and demanding in their market choices. This is contrary to the prevailing belief that the poor are too focused on the pursuit of basic necessities that they will not spend on seeming luxuries like cell phones. Although encumbered by financial problems, African consumers manage to get their communications needs met, with the help of MTN who have designed products and matching prices to appeal to these targets. Notice the seeming democratization of mobile phone use that does not discriminate on the basis of wealth. MTN's offer is a matter of scale as the rich buy more of the same services provided for the poor as well.

Like MTN and other private enterprises seeking to meet the needs of the poor in Africa, governments will do well to consider innovative means of serving consumers. Consider the government of Uganda's effort to address the portable water needs of low-income residents in small towns. The government brings several communities together and coordinates activities such as site location, borehole drilling and community land purchasing. A private operator is hired to distribute water and ensure safety of supply. A community water board sets tariffs and policies. This collaborative model has brought portable water to 490,000 people in 57 communities through coin-operated water kiosks. In 2006, the 18,944 water connections yielded a turnover of 2 billion Ugandan shillings ($1.2 million) (UNDP 2008: 109).

One of the most ingenious market development strategies is finding alternative uses for existing products. Confronted with new technologies, African consumers often adapt them to their own purposes. For example, banks and mobile phone users were quick to transfer the phone into a banking tool. *Sente* is the informal practice of sending and receiving money that leverages public phone kiosks and trusted networks in Uganda. Instead of sending money directly from phone to phone, anyone with phone access can send airtime credit to a kiosk operator over the cellular network. The kiosk operator then converts the credit into cash and gives the cash to the recipient who lacks access to a phone or a bank account. In effect, the kiosk operator and the phone take the place of an automated teller machine. This example highlights how business and grassroots adaptation can build on each other to develop new domestic markets (ibid.: 48). It would seem then that the need for education for developing African markets really means marketers educating themselves about grassroots innovativeness.

Other adaptive strategies

- *Adapting communications*: Communicating marketing information requires adaptation to the means and modes that will readily reach the targeted audience. Radio is an important channel all over the continent. The innovative multi-use of products can be transferred to communication strategies. Consider MTN's modes of communication: clothing, umbrellas, kiosk painting and other things of pragmatic value to their retailers and customers. The company's advertising is strongly connected to providing some of the locals' necessities.

  In other contexts, marketing promotions and communications can be coupled with consumer education as was the case in Botswana where advertising and other traditional communication tools were used to foster awareness of basic consumer rights and responsibilities (Makela and Peters 2004). However, lack of access to media in many

African communities calls for innovative avenues. In Ghana, Nigeria, Tanzania, and other countries, religious organizations are the ultimate source of practical life. Pastors and Imams are directly involved in the everyday lives of their congregations. Some have become exemplars of business leadership, spreading the word of capitalism and entrepreneurship from their pulpits (Bonsu and Belk 2010). Their roles also accord them significant authority as opinion leaders whose choices are emulated by adherents. Firms may consider working with religious leaders. This was the case when, in Madagascar, the firm Bionexx partnered with a local religious radio station to spread information about its *artemisia annua*, a medicinal plant used in malaria treatments. (UNDP 2008: 81). The ubiquity of religious movies in many African countries (Ukah 2003) also provides an opportunity for tapping this medium as an effective avenue for communicating market and other information.

- *Adapting prices*: It is indisputable that prices must be reduced in low-income markets through innovative product formulation and packaging systems. However, businesses must be cautious in their approach. Most Africans are farmers and thus purchasing power fluctuates dramatically from season to season. Much creative work to adapt prices and consumer credit schemes to the seasonal availability of cash is needed. Further, remittances from migrants are an important source of cash for many Africans. Developing three-way payment plans between local consumers, wage-earning migrants, and local firms remains an untapped element of local pricing strategy. In addition, resource pooling among extended family members to support significant expenditures is not uncommon, thereby significantly increasing the purchasing power of family network agents.

  Finally, many firms assume that the poor will buy only if products are cheap. As the MTN case suggests, this is not always the case although consumers prefer lower price options if the perceived quality across alternative products is the same. Some commentators have argued that the poor are more likely to buy expensive items not only because they last longer but also because conspicuous expenditure conveys prestige on the consumer or the recipient of a gifted item. That is, the poor sometimes buy global products because of their reputational value in local social systems. Therefore, adapting prices to local markets may have a negative impact on that reputation as well as a declining impact on the market/sales. If reduced prices were always provided, no distinction could be made between those who use expensive cars, expensive homes, imported materials, and so on in local systems of prestige, and those who are unconcerned with the image expensive items accord them.

- *Adapting distribution*: As the MTN case suggests, recognizing actual resources available for distributive activities (e.g., informality, social ties, trust) and accounting for these realities can be productive in African markets (Arnould 1985). Adding to that, consider that approximately 70 percent of Africa's population is rural and spread over a vast geographical area. This can create distribution challenges for Western firms serving this market if local relevance is overlooked. To deal with this problem, Barclays Bank embraced the traditional "susu" system and worked with the Ghana Susu Collectors Association to benefit all parties involved. Susu is a centuries-old traditional system in many African countries in which collectors pick up savings from participating households and individuals. The susu associations offer small, short-term loans that rotate among members of the group. Ghana has about 4,000 susu collectors, each serving between 200 and 850 clients daily. Overcoming its neglect of local knowledge to adopt what had long been deemed inefficient, Barclays can now reach clients who were previously out of reach. Collectors also benefit by keeping their collections safely at Barclays' branches, where they and their clients may earn interest on their deposits (UNDP 2008: 82). The mutual benefit derived from this cooperation contributes to market efficiency and makes more local financial resources available for investments.

Another example of successful adaptive distribution is one that relied on technological leapfrogging to deliver services through innovative marketing channels. Celtel International entered the Democratic Republic of Congo in 2000, when the civil war was still raging. It faced a market with widespread insecurity, poverty, depleted human capacity, and political uncertainty. There was little or no infrastructure, no regulatory framework, and no banking network. The potential customer base seemed very small, with few ways to reach them. Despite these obstacles, Celtel has gained more than two million customers in the country, allowing communities previously isolated by war and poor infrastructure to exchange information. Celtel also established Celpay (previously part of Celtel and now owned by FirstRand Banking Group) as a mobile banking system to compensate for the lack of a national banking network. Celpay proved so efficient that the government is now using it to pay its soldiers. Moreover, many women have gained financial autonomy by reselling Celtel mobile phone airtime (ibid.: 45, 93, 111).

Developing export markets

Developing export market opportunities for Africa is an essential component of long-term economic sustainability, especially because the level of economic growth needed in these developing countries cannot be achieved from serving domestic demand alone. The lack of exports and growth in exporting markets is associated with the poor economic performance of many African countries. For example, between 1974 and 1998, only two Sub-Saharan countries, Mauritius and South Africa, experienced substantial growth in manufacturing exports (Söderbom and Teal 2001). In contrast, Botswana experienced significant growth from exporting natural resources.

The Kenya cut flower export industry is considered one of globalization's success stories: an export growth market that leverages Kenya's climatic advantages and provides a remedy for low incomes, bringing thousands of employment opportunities to poor rural women. Kenya enjoys 5 percent of the global cut flower market that generates £130 million of export earnings a year. Ethiopia's cut flower industry export sales are now reaching half of Kenya's. Over the past few years, however, the industry has been the target of NGO campaigns and media exposés for poor labor practices (Dolan and Opondo 2005; Orton-Jones 2008). Starbucks, the nation of Ethiopia, and Oxfam, the NGO, waged a recent battle over the right to trademark regional coffee varietal names, Yirgacheffe, Harrar and Sidamo. The struggle concerned the right to extract a greater share of the retail value of these regionally branded coffees either for Ethiopian subsistence producers or Starbucks, respectively. A court and public relations battle eventuated in a "win" for Oxfam activists and the Ethiopian side that may now retain the lucrative branding rights (Faris 2007; Perera 2007).

The export of natural resources has been identified as a cause of economic impoverishment in some African countries because resource extraction industries are vulnerable to boom and bust cycles, they have a limited multiplier effect, and royalty payments to governments often do not trickle down to the benefit of local populations. In some cases these problems have led to serious civil strife as in Congo. In the Niger Delta of Nigeria, governmental misallocation of oil extraction money and serious pollution have fueled a local guerrilla movement.

The case of the Ideal Providence Farms exemplifies the movement from survival to growth and shows how local products can be developed to economically empower the very poor while providing a profitable export business for the entrepreneur.

Case study 2: Ideal Providence Farms (shea butter)

Georgina Koomson, a young entrepreneur with experience in the US chemical and pharmaceutical industry, established Ideal Providence Farms in 1998. The ultimate goal of this venture was to alleviate poverty through business and market development. Koomson's choice of location was ideal for this goal. The Upper West Region of Ghana is one of the poorest regions in the country. Agriculture is the region's major economic activity and is often operated on a subsistence scale. The region faces staggering levels of poverty and unemployment, and women are two to three times more likely to be unemployed than men. These challenges, coupled with the long dry season, cause many people to leave the area to find work in other parts of Ghana and even in the bordering country of Burkina Faso. However, the region is rich in at least one renewable natural resource – shea nut (*Vitellaria paradoxa*). This resource is popular in pharmaceutical production, medicines, and cosmetics in particular.

Valuing local resources

Koomson saw an opportunity to market shea butter from the shea nut, which grew wild in the area. With a low population and a large number of unemployed women, this region provided a base level of local resources from which Koomson could convert this seemingly unmarketable product. Now, shea butter is an important and versatile product that the locals use in several ways, from cooking oil to body lotion to skin moisturizer. Ideal Providence mobilized local women to collect and organize the shea nut and then process the nuts as shea butter for export. The resulting product was packaged and readied for shipping to overseas markets. Knowing the value of the product in the overseas pharmaceutical market, Koomson sought buyers for her products in North America and Europe. She found willing partners in Canada and Germany that paid market prices for the shea butter. Because the shea nut grew in the wild, Koomson could label her brand as "organic," which became a competitive advantage over other sources of the product. By developing a market for this natural product, Koomson was able to mobilize the local population to support her business, and in doing so, she improved their incomes and skills. In turn, these should support domestic market development in the future.

The core business idea for Ideal Providence Farms is local production of high-quality organic shea butter for foreign cosmetics companies. However, although the local population had experience with shea butter, they still needed to be trained to appreciate the requirements of target markets in Europe and North America. Therefore, local inhabitants are trained in all aspects of the production process, from collecting the nuts to producing high-quality shea butter for export. They are encouraged to be creative and to propose solutions as operational problems arise. Through this initiative, local innovators developed packaging material for the finished products that mobilized the skills of traditional handicraft producers. Various other businesses have emerged to serve the needs of those who live and work around Ideal Providence Farms. A complete system of goods and services has emerged to support the needs of the company and its workers. Koomson can now leave some of the women in charge of the production facility when she travels abroad for extended periods to find new buyers for the shea butter.

Working with local culture

A Ghanaian of southern ethnic extraction, Koomson is to all appearances a "foreigner" in the Upper West Region. Developing her product in the region required a delicate balance of marketing and political skill. She has demonstrated respect for the local culture while working to influence it, and through her firm's employment of mostly community women, she has empowered them beyond their dependence upon their fathers, brothers, and husbands. Women in the community have little self-worth, and it is generally considered a bad investment to send a female child to school. Thus, most of the women working at Ideal are illiterate with little or no confidence in their abilities, and with minimal support from their male counterparts. With the cooperation of local leaders, Koomson secured land and other facilities to set up a place where the women could be trained to convert their domestic expertise into marketable skills. The women are trained in marketing, production, and financial management. They are allowed to contribute to a savings plan for their children's education and send their daughters to school. Koomson's success in the market and community has enhanced her local reputation. This example demonstrates the value of mobilizing local resources for market.

One of the strategic objectives of Ideal Providence Farms is to alleviate poverty, especially among women. The informal sector, which is the driving force in most African economies, relies on 40–65 percent female participation. There is a long history of women as primary sources of income for their families (e.g., Clark 1994). Although these women engage in what is often considered mere extensions of domestic activities (e.g., cooked foods, textiles, and household goods), their roles in developing export markets, as the Ideal Providence Farms case suggests, should not be overlooked. Women constitute a major part of the labor force and should be tapped for transforming markets.

Companies seeking to develop export markets may do well to seek alliances with such powerful, local women who have extensive trading contacts, local knowledge, and other skills. Their strategic networks and other intangible resources can support export and domestic market. Often, firms overlook these women as resources because they do not fit into the formal practice of marketing. In addition, women are deemed to lack the general set of requirements that foreign multinational companies use to assess market opportunities (e.g., limited formal education, infrastructural shortcomings in their locations). Through the use of woman as female role models, firms can tap into Africa's strong kinship-based business network structures to enhance their marketing outcomes.

Most local African producers are so small that they cannot derive economies of scale. The uniqueness of Ideal Farms makes its volume less of a factor, but for many others, production volume is important for market performance. The highlighted brief case study on the Integrated Tamale Fruit Factory exemplifies a way to address this problem. This firm brings together farmers and supports them in several ways to help maintain supply of raw materials. Here, too, the market is better served when the firm works with local producers to improve the socio-economic well-being of all involved.

Case study 3: Export marketing: Integrated Tamale Fruit Company

The Integrated Tamale Fruit Company – operating in the Savelugu-Nanton District in Ghana's Northern Region, an area of widespread poverty – cultivates certified organic mangos for local and export markets. To boost its power in the export market with higher production volumes, the company established a scalable business model that includes local farmers. Instead of acquiring a large piece of land, which is physically and financially impractical, the company produces high volumes through an outgrower scheme, which began in 2001 and today includes 1,300 outgrower farmers. Each has a farm of about one acre, with 100 mango trees that supplement the nucleus farm of 160 acres. The company provides an interest-free loan to the outgrowers through farm inputs and technical services, and farmers begin paying for the loan from selling mangos only after the trees yield fruit. The cost of the loaned inputs is repaid, without interest, beginning in the fifth year. Approximately 30 percent of sales go toward repayment.

The company also provides education to the outgrowers, whose ability to repay the loans depends on their ability to produce good crops. Because illiteracy makes it difficult for the farmers to meet international standards, the company began training the farmers in best practices.

This arrangement allows the company to reliably source a large volume of quality organic mangos, and the farmers can enter mango production with long-term income prospects. The nucleus farm's profits are on track to reach $1 million a year by 2010. The case study examines the key challenges of the outgrower scheme and its implications for the company's business (UNDP 2008).

Other examples of this cooperative approach are found in shea butter export business of Ghana's Tungteeya Shea Butter and Honey Care Africa, which develops honey for European and American markets. Honey Care Africa is a noteworthy example because it conforms to the Sustainable Local Enterprise Network model of development, which combines a financial anchor firm (usually a foreign firm or non-governmental organizations) with a social mission for local investments in stakeholder well-being.

In African domestic markets, small enterprise success relates to business proximity to growing markets (McPherson 1995), suggesting that export market efforts include expanded intra-African trade (see case study 4). The difficulties associated with expanding global social networks make consideration of intra-continental markets a necessary component of African market development. This is especially pertinent given that most Sub-Saharan African countries (excluding Nigeria, South Africa, and Ethiopia) have relatively small populations and, thus, limited customer bases (McDade and Spring 2005). There are tremendous export market development opportunities within Africa. With a population of over 900 million and free trade agreement among its countries, African producers can target other African producers with their goods and services. Case study 4 provides an example of how Niger used this approach. As incomes among African consumers improve and technology allows for improvements in banking facilities across the continent, intra-Africa export markets are likely to grow.

Case study 4: Intra-African Onion Export Marketing

An indigenous agricultural export industry has emerged in the Niger Republic that suggests the potential for intra-continental export growth. More than 10,000 people were directly involved in this business, in which onion exports increased by one-third in the five years between 1989 and 1993 alone. This business was organized in a variety of ways. A network of producers, small-scale traders, and bulking agents funnel product to Nigerian export wholesalers, foreign importers' agents, and foreign exporters. Ivoirian and the smaller-scale Burkinabé, Togolese, and Béninoise women wholesalers send agents to buy from the bulking agents or small traders. In the consuming countries, the channel structure is essentially the inverse of this.

Profitability in this business is limited primarily by five factors: limited storage and holding capacity for onions, a perishable crop; the physical length of the channel of distribution; poor telecommunications facilities; a lack of short-term credit to invest in buying and marketing; and illicit rent seeking by government agents. Though lucrative for both producers and channel intermediaries at the wholesale level, like many entrepreneurial initiatives, the study identified disincentives for expanded investment. Insurance is not available. Local bank credit is not available. Fear of exposure to illicit rent seeking by government agents induces successful market participants to minimize investments in storage, other commercial infrastructure, and improved packaging. Since this research was conducted, the cell phone revolution has probably resolved the issue of telecommunications. Banking facilities have also improved in some countries, such as Ghana (Arnould 2001).

Conclusion

Marketing and international business strategists commonly assume that markets in Africa are constrained by factors that thwart efforts to build these markets. Although the lack of infrastructure, low levels of education, high levels of corruption, and other negative factors are indeed present in the African context, poor market development by firms appears to be grounded more in neo-colonial misconceptions than the realities of business operations in Africa (Bonsu 2009). What is important is that people find effective ways to circumvent or control these problems in their business dealings. For example, there are many successful multinational corporations with long histories in African markets (e.g., Barclays Bank, Unilever, Guinness). These firms have found ways to succeed and have been well rewarded financially for their investments. Developing African markets has become an important future for firms as the developed markets' potential stagnates. Firms that try to understand the continent and overcome negative perceptions and roadblocks stand to gain in diverse ways.

This chapter suggests that the development of export markets for African products is a necessary ingredient for sustaining local markets for foreign goods and services. In the absence of such development, local capacity to generate income through domestic productive ventures can be stifled. If Stiglitz (2002) is correct in arguing that the "income gap" is the most significant contributor to business and socio-economic development, the lack of effective income-generating activities in Africa – regardless of what else may be done for the purposes of human development – may count for nothing. Creating local capabilities and support for both export and domestic markets development requires a careful understanding of African market structures, as well as cultural and other resources that can be tapped for efficiency. The case studies in this chapter offer examples of how this can be done and done well.

Traditionally, Western economic perspectives have identified the informal market sector in Africa as an impediment to market efficiency. However, this sector employs the vast majority of people and has survived in the face of significant threats over a long time.

Therefore, the informal sector seems to be a repository of market knowledge which firms can tap into. Indeed, the informal sector market is important because of its ability to employ local knowledge systems to increase market dynamics and efficiency. These systems provide a strong socio-cultural basis for trust and relationships among partners, dimensions that in most "developed" markets depend more on contractual agreements. International companies attempting to develop their domestic African markets would do well to abandon their traditional prejudices and plug into the informal market system, if only to gain access to the wealth of relationships and knowledge it provides. In other words, firms trying to develop African markets should employ adaptive strategies that recognize the specific nature of the African continent and the unique resources it offers – the social, cultural, political, and economic factors that contribute to creating conditions for market efficiency.

Review and discussion questions

1 Outline briefly some of the elements of African culture referenced in the chapter. Why are these and other aspects of culture important in African markets?
2 What are some of the local resources in Africa (tangible and intangible) that the global firm might tap for market development? How might these resources be used?
3 Compare and contrast the nature of markets in your home country to the African environment described in the chapter. To what extent do the differences and similarities inform global market development?
4 You have been asked by the President of your company to investigate and advise on the best ways to break into the African market with your product. Focusing on one African country, develop a plan for your boss. What are your primary considerations?

Keywords

Africa, development, domestic markets, exports, poverty, strategic adaptation

References

AfricaFocus (2004) "Africa: Mobile Renaissance?", *AfricaFocus Bulletin*, Available at: http://www.africafocus.org/docs04/han0405.php (accessed October 22, 2009).

Amoah, J. E. K. (1995) *Development of Consumption, Commercial Production and Marketing*, Takoradi: Jemre Enterprises.

Arnould, E. J. (1985) "Evaluating Regional Economic Development: Results of a Regional Systems Analysis in Niger", *Journal of Developing Areas*, 19(2): 209–44.

—— (2001) "Ethnography, Export Marketing Policy, and Economic Development in Niger", *Journal of Public Policy & Marketing*, 20(Fall), 151–69.

Arnould, E. J. and Mohr, J. J. (2005) "Dynamic Transformations of an Indigenous Market Cluster: The Leatherworking Industry in Niger", *Journal of the Academy of Marketing Science*, 33(Summer): 254–74.

Bonsu, S. K. (2009) "Colonial Images in Global Times: Consumer Interpretations of Africa and Africans in Advertising", *Consumption Markets & Culture*, 12(1): 1–25.

Bonsu, S. K. and Belk, R. W. (2010) "Marketing a New African God: Pentecostalism and Material Salvation in Ghana", *International Journal of Nonprofit and Voluntary Sector Marketing*, 15(4): 305–23.

Brautigam, D. (2009) *The Dragon's Gift: The Real Story of China in Africa*, Oxford: Oxford University Press.

Burgess, S., Harris, M. and Mattes, R. (2002) *SA Tribes*, Claremont, SA: New Africa Publishing.

Clark, G. (1994) *Onions Are My Husband: Survival and Accumulation by West African Market Women*, Chicago: University of Chicago Press.

Daniels, L., Mead, D. and Musinga, M. (1995) "Employment and Income in Micro and Small Enterprises in Kenya: Results of a 1995 Survey", GEMINI Technical Report No. 92, Development Alternatives Inc.

DeBerry-Spence, B. (2010) "Making Theory and Practice in Subsistence Markets: An Analytic Autoethnography of MASAZI in Accra, Ghana", *Journal of Business Research*, 63(6): 608–16.

de Bruijn, M., Nyamnjoh, F. and Brinkman, I. (2009) "Mobile Communications and New Social Spaces in Africa", in M. de Bruijn, F. Nyamnjoh and I. Brinkman (eds), *Mobile Phones: The New Talking Drums of Everyday Africa*, Bamenda, Cameroon: Langaa Research and Publishing Common Initiative Group.

Dolan, C. and Opondo, M. (2005) "Seeking Common Ground", *Journal of Corporate Citizenship*, 18 (April): 87–98.

Fafchamps, M. (1997) "Introduction: Markets in Sub-Saharan Africa", *World Development*, 25(5): 733–4.

Faris, S. (2007) "Starbucks v. Ethiopia", *Fortune*, February 26. Available at: http://money.cnn.com/magazines/fortune/fortune_archive/2007/03/05/8401343/index.htm (accessed June 11, 2008).

Helmsing, A. H. J. (2003) "Local Economic Development: New Generations of Actors, Policies and Instruments for Africa", *Public Administration and Development*, 23: 67–76.

Lovejoy, P. E. (2002) *Salt of the Desert Sun: A History of Salt Production and Trade in the Central Sudan*, Cambridge: Cambridge University Press.

Maddy, M. (2000) "Dream Deferred: The Story of a High-Tech Entrepreneur in a Low-Tech World", *Harvard Business Review*, 78(3): 56–69.

Makela, C. J. and Peters, S. (2004) "Consumer Education: Creating Consumer Awareness among Adolescents in Botswana", *International Journal of Consumer Studies*, 28(September): 379–87.

McDade, B. E. and Spring, A. (2005) "The New Generation of African Entrepreneurs: Networking to Change the Climate for Business and Private Sector-Led Development", *Entrepreneurship & Regional Development*, 17(January): 17–42.

McPherson, M. A. (1995) "The Hazards of Small Firms in Southern Africa", *Journal of Development Studies*, 32 (1): 31–54.

Meillassoux, C. (ed.) (1971) *The Development of Indigenous Trade and Markets in West Africa*, London: Oxford University Press for the International African Institute.

MTN Group (2009) *Annual Report*, Cresta, South Africa: MTN Group. Available at: http://www.mtn-investor.com/mtn_ar09/book1/or_coo.html (accessed October 2, 2010).

Mureithi, M. (2003) "Self-Destructive Competition in Cellular: Regulatory Options to Harness the Benefits of Liberalization", *Telecommunications Policy*, 27(February/March): 11–20.

Orton-Jones, C. (2008) "Bloom and Bust", *Financial Management*, February: 18–21.

Osae, T. A., Nwabra, S. N. and Odunsi, A. T. O. (1973) *A Short History of West Africa: A.D. 1000 to the Present*, New York: Hill and Wang.

Perera, A. (2007) *Starbucks Campaign: Anatomy of a Win*. Available at: http://www.oxfaminamerica.org/articles/starbucks-campaign-anatomy-of-a-win.

Prahalad, C. K. (2004) *The Fortune at the Bottom of the Pyramid: Eradicating Poverty through Profits*, Upper Saddle River, NJ: Wharton School Publishing.

Rodney, W. (1981) *How Europe Underdeveloped Africa*, Washington, DC: Howard University Press.

Rogerson, C. M. (2001) "In Search of the African Miracle: Debates on Successful Small Enterprise Development in Africa", *Habitat International*, 25(1): 115–42.

Söderbom, M. and Teal, F. (2001) "Can African Manufacturing Firms Become Successful Exporters?", CSAE-UNIDO Working Paper No. 4, paper presented at Third United Nations Conference on the Least Developed Countries, Brussels.

Spring, A. and McDade, B. E. (1998) *African Entrepreneurship: Theory and Reality*, Gainesville, FL: University of Florida Press.

Steel, W. F. (1994) "Changing the Institutional and Policy Environment for Small Enterprise Development in Africa", *Small Enterprise Development*, 5(2): 4–9.

Stiglitz, J. E. (2002) *Globalization and Its Discontents,* New York: W.W. Norton.

Takyi-Asiedu, S. (1993) "Some Socio-Cultural Factors Retarding Entrepreneurial Activity in Sub-Saharan Africa", *Journal of Business Venturing*, 8: 91–8.

Ukah, A. F. K. (2003) "Advertising God: Nigerian Christian Video-Films and the Power of Consumer Culture", *Journal of Religion in Africa*, 33(2): 203–31.

UNDP (2008) *Creating Value for All: Strategies for Doing Business with the Poor*, New York: United Nations Development Program.

Yusuf, A. B. (1975) "Capital Formation and Management among the Muslim Hausa Traders of Kano, Nigeria", *Africa*, 45: 167–82.

7 Market development in the Latin American context

Judith Cavazos-Arroyo and
Silvia González García

Overview

This chapter develops an overview of how cultural marketing strategic insights and approaches are now an imperative for organizations and individuals who require efficient tools and better understandings of the Latin American context.

Introduction

Latin America is considered a region of great contrasts, as it possesses multiple resources and at the same time faces immense differences. The cultural identity of the region is derived from the confrontation, penetration and integration of the different world cultures, mainly indigenous, European, African and, to a lesser degree, Asian cultures, and this has had repercussions on aspects which have permeated the economic, political, legal, cultural and social spheres (Picotti 1998; Leme 2000; Chang-Rodríguez 2008). However, in order to understand the cultural dynamics of the Latin American region it is necessary to develop thought patterns which comprehend the cultural differences beyond the opposite bipolar conceptions, as these differences are based essentially on the multiculturalism resulting from many of the changing and interactive hybrids which go beyond the uniform representations of the continent (Morales 2008; Villavicencio 2008).

It is true that most Latin American countries share different linguistic, religious, economic, philosophical, and political ties, but in cultural terms they present regional, class and ethnic nuances which distinguish them (Chang-Rodríguez 2008) and which are reflected in the recent visible recognition of diversity and cultural differences (García-Canclini 2001; Gimson 2006) and which should be taken into consideration by experts wishing to develop trade strategies in the region. It is not enough to acknowledge these differences it is also necessary to understand what they consist of and how they are involved in the consumers' lives, as stated by Bartra (2002: 27):

> We still partially hold the illusion that the institutions which are good in some countries will also be good in our own, without making them undergo any modifications; and sometimes, out of insufficient research, we candidly believe that foreign organizations can be copied and placed over a national organization in a perfect manner, when we know that a simple suit which fits a Saxon cannot be donned by a Mexican without being altered considerably.

Evolution of market development and the consumer culture

Markets were created by humans and many factors interact in them and influence the different institutions and facets of life (Grossbart 2002). When the Spaniards reached the so-called New World, several pre-Hispanic cultural and socio-economic institutions were modified in order to adapt to the new paradigms. The traditional market, street vendors, *tianquiztli* or *tianguis* (in Náhuatl) were pre-Hispanic institutions that were trans-formed in response to new food requirements, and to ethnic and commercial movements (Mosquera 2005). In the pre-Conquest era, the market also played social and religious roles (for example, social interaction through bartering, the acquisition of jade, copal or idols for rituals), making street vendors useful in the reconfiguration of cultural, social, economic and political aspects, according to Christian, social standards. These were used as control mechanisms for deritualization by means of new market regulations. For example, the indigenous, established mainly in urban settlements, were only supposed to go to the market to buy food, and it was forbidden to sell pre-Hispanic religious articles; and the schedule was modified by going from five indigenous days to seven indigenous days according to the Christian calendar, and there were also modifications to the practices pertaining to the supervision, production, and transportation of goods (Hassig 2001).

Markets were places where the pre-Conquest cultural capital was reformed and redirected toward the introduction of Christian cultural capital. In colonial times, the marketplace was mostly a socio-spatial reference where ties were created between the indigenous and non-indigenous peoples. The traditional market represented goods, knowledge and technologies which were regulated, produced, exchanged and reproduced with great emphasis on symbolic Catholic objects and practices (Mosquera 2005).

Up until the first decades of the twentieth century, the Latin American region was considered to have lived as an incipient consumer culture, stimulated by small establish-ments and the beginning of catalog sales. Establishments were later opened by immigrants, particularly Europeans, who initiated a change in the consumption of the elite, thus stimulating the consumption of European and American products (Buchenau 2004). The "consumer revolution" reached several countries of the region after World War II, strongly influenced by the "American way of life" which broadened the variety of alternatives of products, practices, and messages available to the elite, who started to focus on consumption and material prosperity (Moreno 2003; Volpi 2007). The material and immaterial culture represented by imported and domestic products and services has played a key role in Latin American history in connection with class, race, civilization, citizenship and modernity where the global process of growth in consumption becomes a local experience through the cultural filters in keeping with the specific conditions of the host culture (Bunker 2009).

Academically, the study of the importance of goods and consumption in Latin American societies began at the end of the 1990s, due to the economic focus on exportation, scarce research regarding the growth of domestic markets and the appreciation of imported goods (Bunker 2009). In many regards, Latin America is still undergoing truncated and mixed cultural times (Calderón 1987), centering on production and postmodernity, the latter of which is characterized by the appreciation of consumption over production (García-Canclini 1995), which has involved many changes, both in the manner in which people are prepared and educated to adopt their social identity and in the way in which groups are inserted into consumption (Bauman 2000). As stated by Brunner:

In their contemporary development, Latin American cultures do not express an order – as a nation, or class, or religion, or state or charisma, or tradition, or of any other sort – but rather reflect in their organization, the contradictory and heterogeneous processes of a belated modernity, built on conditions of accelerated internationalization of symbolic markets worldwide.

(1995: 276)

Cultural diversity and consumer culture

Cultural diversity is a socio-historical construction which makes it possible to understand the heterogeneity of what cultural representations signify and involve in the coexistence of groups, societies or peoples with cultures that are their own, diverse and valuable (Briones 2007). Diversity has multiple aspects, characterized by pluralities which are ethnic as well as indigenous, mestizos, white or black or differentiated based on their own socio-cultural characteristics which may simultaneously converge in time and space. "Otherwise, how can we explain the coexistence of a society, such as the Mexican society, and a community such as the *Huicholes* where girls are given away to the elder cantors and young women may be traded for beer?" (Arenas 1999: 102). Similarly, acts of consumption are in keeping with different forms of logic which are motivated and justified by the context (Sassatelli 2007).

Another way of analyzing diversity, which goes beyond ethnic background, is by means of establishing what is one's "own" and what is "foreign," "us" and the "others" in the cultural representation, recreating asymmetric relations between those who have and those who do not have access to the array of products and services, capital and material and immaterial exchanges available on the market. There may be many choices, yet they are not available to all consumers. Those who are excluded by virtue of their income, religion, ethnic background, education, shared values, gender, etc. in consumer societies generally coexist in a cultural world created for those who do have access to the goods (Seabrook 1988; Bauman 2000). Due to the growth in urbanization and the emergence of megacities such as Mexico City, São Paulo, Buenos Aires, Rio de Janeiro, Bogotá, Lima and Santiago, there has been an accentuation of forms of social exclusion and urban segregation depending on the type of household or neighborhood, access to security, shopping centers and transportation, which affect work, leisure and consumption (De Caldeira 2000; Tironi 2003). Localization and mobility are key aspects in the socio-cultural differentiation marked by the use and access to areas of consumption. One example is the migration of families from the countryside to the cities. Mobility to large cities generates expectations of increasing the possibility of acquiring more and better food products, as well as access to a house and goods for the home, health, education, potable water, transportation, information technology and electricity; and also increases the possibilities of having the luxury of acquiring a refrigerator and a television, despite living in the marginalization of a Brazilian *favela* or an unplanned urban settlement of any other large Latin American capital city (Briceño-León 2002; Guesalaga and Marshall 2008).

In some countries such as Mexico, Venezuela or Brazil only approximately 20 percent of the population possess a large amount of material possessions. However, the beginning of the twenty-first century has been characterized by the development of a culture of intense consumption among low-income consumers, particularly those living in urban areas. In Brazil, for example, expanding trade for several companies involves developing marketing strategies that focus on increasing purchasing power despite a family's low household income, which generates a certain inclusion by means of consumption.

Unlike rural consumers, many inhabitants of urban areas make their purchases in supermarkets and shopping centers, receive a salary, are able to plan their purchases and have more options for comparing products and prices, whereas rural consumers are faced with poor distribution systems, a limited supply of products and services and complications in terms of mobility. Möller (1993) describes an example when studying consumption in the Agua Blanca *ejido* in the Mexican state of Chiapas. This place is located in the jungle and is a hot and humid area in the southern part of the country. Given the topographical conditions of the place, there is poor communications reception. The population, characterized by low income, works mainly in agricultural activities and river fishing and in the *ejido*, there is only one store which brings products from the state capital and transports them to the *ejido* by truck and then by motor boat. The merchant only transports goods which he believes will sell, those are generally not the inexpensive goods sold by bulk. The results of the study indicated that what makes an impact is not only the efficiency of distribution to remote areas, but also the image, and strength of the brand, as well as how the perceived image relates to quality, prestige and performance of the product. In Agua Blanca, as elsewhere, the purchasing decisions regarding what is consumed in the household are the women's territory and account for up to 70 percent of the income, and thus a great degree of responsibility, concern and awareness is attached to the products purchased by those who buy them and make them available to the family.

Differences do not prevent us from recognizing and directly or indirectly interacting with others, particularly if the others are nearby (Bauman 2008). However, some companies prefer to exclude certain groups from their marketing programs either because they are a minority (Cui and Choudhury 2002), because they appear to be markets that are not very profitable or even because the market in question is located in areas considered to be dangerous or "tough." It is precisely in the exclusion that some organizations have found opportunities to develop strategies that are sufficiently creative and differentiated to access and satisfy these segments. In Venezuela, in an attempt to penetrate poor neighborhoods, Polar (www.empresas-polar.com), the leading brand of beer, opted for multi-level marketing strategies whereby truckers are independent distributors who initiate their sales close to their shantytown homes. Polar later decided to use homes in those neighborhoods as points of sale, installing thousands of refrigerators where housewives supplement their income with the sale of beer, and the salespeople are women from the neighborhood, people known to the neighbors (Ireland 2008). Given Polar's success, another strategic business unit of the same company, Pepsi Cola (www.empresas-polar.com/pepsi.php), decided to use rustic vehicles and mini-depots with electric cars to facilitate access to poor neighborhoods, areas with high density and a lot of traffic. After studying 3,500 poor neighborhoods, Coca-Cola (www. coca-cola.com.ve) decided to use a strategy similar to Polar's, called Productive Households (*Hogares Productivos*) and installed 30,000 refrigerators in 500 poor neighborhoods in the first two years of operation (Gutiérrez 2005).

Despite the accomplishments of these and other companies, the reality is that both establishing and penetrating markets in different locations of the region requires consideration of aspects that go well beyond just offering jobs, being able to find cheap labor, or massively penetrating low-income markets. The socially responsible firm needs to consider health risks, environmental issues, and possible human right abuses that might be related to the production, distribution, consumption, and disposal of the product as well. For example, in the floriculture industry where countries such as Colombia, Ecuador, and Mexico stand out as producers, there have been reports about serious adverse effects on human health and on the environment with inadequate reinvested profits in local economies by the multinational corporations which distribute the flowers around the world (Donohoe 2007).

On the other hand, Polar, Pepsi Cola and Coca-Cola were able to raise the income of various families in extreme poverty with innovative distribution systems. But at the same time, alcoholism, obesity, and diabetes are on the rise in Latin America. The average annual alcohol consumption in the Americas is 8.7 liters per person, whereas the global average is 6.2 liters (Pan American Health Organization 2007; BBC 2011). This excess of alcohol consumption within the region is associated with the increase in physical and emotional violence towards women and children (Herrera and Arena 2010). In 1995, the diabetes prevalence rate in Latin America was 5.7 percent among the general population, by 2025, it is expected to reach 8.1 percent with 39 million cases, 50 percent of which will be concentrated in Brazil and Mexico (Andrade 2009). This has turned into such a serious public health issue that in Mexico, the government has given priority to the development of public campaigns concerning weight control, since seven out of ten adults and four out of ten children aged 5–11 in Mexico are overweight. If not reversed, this tendency might cause the collapse of the public health system due to cardiovascular and diabetes concerns in the population. The rise of fast food options, the high consumption of carbonated beverages, the decrease in physical activities due to the high crime rate in the streets, video game entertainment, and the absence of regulations on the commercialization of junk food, have left a trail of malnourishment, obesity and a sense of urgent changes required regarding consumer habits and strategies with a greater degree of social responsibility from the companies involved and stronger government regulations regarding the food industry (Durán 2010).

Implications for the organization of consumption alternatives

Consumer societies continue to expand and be reconfigured in the everyday activities of Latin American cultures and, as a consequence, complex consumer logic and combinations have arisen. It is, however, possible to identify some consequences which are shaping the future of the organization of several consumer alternatives. Although there are undoubtedly many more, we have considered five of these implications here (Table 7.1).

Construction of an identity combining the traditional, modern and postmodern

The transition of the traditional way of life, dependent basically on agriculture for self-consumption, to modernity has had considerable effects on economic development, on social structures and traditional values, involving development based on the industrialization and expansion of science and technology, the promotion of capitalist expansion worldwide,

Table 7.1 Implications in the organization of consumption alternatives in Latin America

1. Construction of an identity combining the traditional, modern and post-modern
2. Understanding the nuances of cultural diversity in market segmentation
3. Cultural tension and legitimacy of corruption
4. Consumption between formal/informal trade
5. The role of the consumer agency

urbanization, the emergence of a modern identity of self-development and the representation of the consumer as an agent which is mostly cognitive (Featherstone 1991; Firat and Venkatesh 1995). Postmodernity, or the second modernity, questions the approach of modernism involving changes in the cultural sphere and the manner in which they affect modes of production, consumption, circulation of symbolic goods, as well as the everyday practices and experiences of the different groups, their regimes of significance, means of orientation and identity structures (Featherstone 1991; Miller 2005).

Postmodernity is characterized by accelerated change, complexity, and uncertainty, where the space in which the market agents interact is interpreted more than as a physical territory, as a symbol, a dynamic concept which is open, changing, flexible, multilinear, and historical. The postmodern consumer never completes his/her construction process, and rather becomes a participant in production of the self, but based on transcultural coexistence (Firat and Venkatesh 1995; Arnould 2007).

As previously stated, most of the Latin American countries are, within themselves, cultural mosaics separated mainly by enormous inequalities on which collective identities are built and which are distinguished and distanced among themselves by social status, conflicting values, education, lifestyle, and world vision (Almeida 2007). Understanding these differences involves changing the form of perception and validating what is perceived as "outside" cultures and the manner in which meanings and everyday living practices interact in popular culture, the cultures of the masses and the culture of consumption (Featherstone 1991).

Many inhabitants of Latin America live in conditions which can be described as an unequal modernity, rather than as postmodernity (Vargas-Hernández 2005). Modernization in these societies has produced anxiety due to the increase in consumption standards which are not really connected to local levels of productivity, and created market niches capable of participating in modern consumption but at the same time interacting with large markets which are aware of their exclusion from certain goods and forms of consumption. The Latin American migratory phenomenon can also be explained by this perspective, since the material prosperity of those who have left exerts pressure on those who remain behind, wishing access to goods and services, and all of this leads to modified consumer habits and lifestyles; social and consumer networks which operate transnationally are formed (Portes 1997; Lawson 1998; Durand and Massey 2010).

Understanding the nuances of cultural diversity in market segmentation

Organizations need to respond more efficiently to changing market conditions, in such a way that the more assertive the segmentation is, the better use the organizations can make of their marketing resources to develop insights (Yankelovich and Meer 2006). In order to take the time to identify the peculiarities of the consumer groups and understand the meanings and relations among the cultures and subcultures, it is necessary to develop methods which allow the researcher to become immersed in the social constructions of the markets and their development (Peñaloza and Venkatesh 2006) and thus have an in-depth understanding of the system of symbols, the spatial organization of the community and the subject–subject relations between marketers and consumers.

Among the non-demographic traits of Latin American segmentation, in addition to the psychographic aspects, there are ethnic and class characteristics linked to consumption. For example, the multiplicity of ethnic groups may be differentiated by skin color, gender, relationship, birth context and even by how they are perceived in certain artwork

(Zolfagharian 2010). The lifestyle, language, conduct, and values tied to the acquisition and use of products may also vary between segments. For example, given the lack of sufficiently favorable conditions to meet educational and health needs, socio-economic levels respond differently to these needs. The highest levels in the Latin American social hierarchy tend to be the purchase of education insurance plans for children and health insurance. In regard specifically to health, the Brazilian market heads the insurance acquisition sector, followed by Mexico (Datamonitor 2008a, 2008b) as a means of avoiding the uncertainty of the quality of service of public health. Among the lower classes, however, in addition to the fact that it is common for children not to complete their education, it is also common to self-medicate, use natural medicine and visit government health infirmaries or health clinics.

In terms of cultural diversity, in practice, the symbolic implications take on transcendental importance and goods take on a language of their own (Sassatelli 2007). For example, with globalization and the commodified culture it is possible to find Coca-Cola in most countries of the world; however, beyond efforts to standardize the presentation of the product and even the advertising, not all consumer groups share the same meaning of the product. In small towns in Latin America, during courtship, a gentleman takes his chosen one out to drink a Coca-Cola and not a Pepsi Cola; they may both cost the same, but one has a more "elegant" image than the other; once she has become his girlfriend, he may drink the soda he truly prefers.

Cultural tension and legitimacy of corruption

Corruption is a phenomenon which is mostly studied from the legal, political, moral and economic disciplines, however, it is also a phenomenon which interacts with social and cultural aspects and becomes a part of everyday life, of institutional relations and of public–private interaction. Few studies regarding the social mechanisms of corruption have been made and to understand corruption involves looking at the legitimization processes from the players' point of view, in other words, how the value systems and cultural codes enable the justification of practices of corruption in everyday life (Olivier de Sardan 1999).

Societies may have different moral, political and administrative views regarding what constitutes corrupt practices. A corrupt practice generally includes a public agent and a private agent, however, it may also exist among private agents. Some of the acts included are outright theft, the inappropriate allocation of state funds or property, nepotism, the abuse of public authority, and cronyism in exchange for payment or personal benefit (Harch 1993).

In the case of Latin America, the governments of several countries continue to adopt plans and programs to combat corruption and Latin Americans themselves agree that there are four major problems which put economic development and quality of life at risk: insecurity, unemployment, corruption, and drug trafficking, combined with citizens' distrust of police, government, and political parties (Barómetro Iberoamericano 2010). However, in practice there is the perception that many of the legal precepts are structured in a confusing and ambiguous manner, leading many people to ignore formal rules and favor solutions which appear to be more realistic (Husted 2002); many think that the law is applied in a discretionary manner, favoring or chastising people based on their place in the social hierarchy and the merits achieved vis-à-vis the authorities, which is why social corruption and bribery are a way of life inserted in a culture of corruption (Sarquis 2008).

Corruption operates based on a logic of meanings so that even when it is presented in a veiled manner, concealing its presence and extent from the average spectator (Etkin 1993), despite the legal condemnation of certain practices, it may be culturally legitimate and interacts in the systems of relations and forms of exchanges and exerts continuous pressure on the social players (Olivier de Sardan 1999). Thus, in some Latin American spheres it is common for the agents involved, both corruptor and corrupted, to produce exchanges in order to obtain what one of the parties considers to be a greater value, and even use highly valued relations such as friendship, family solidarity and trust (Lomnitz 1992). The manner in which corruption operates is through forms of exchange and reciprocity based on networks of personal contacts and local practices of corruption, such as the "*mordida*" (bribe) which is a way of facilitating processes in the public administration system, "*compadrazgo*" (cronyism) which implies a tacit system of connections and personal relations in order to obtain a favor or mutual help by means of the continuous exchange of favors without involving money but which is very sensitive to social position, or the "*jeitinho*" (way/solution) which acts as an instrument that makes it possible to obtain a favor by breaking the rules, using emotional, social or economic resources (Lomnitz 1988; Almeida 2007).

Thus, this and multiple other local practices are inserted into the cultural systems, interacting with the tension among subjects or between the subject and the institution, and are resolved by means of different forms of negotiation, at the same time making it difficult to legally gain access to services, justice, education and health in Latin American spheres (Huber 2008).

Consumption between formal/informal trade

In the complexity of purchasing and consumption practices, in Latin America, confrontations, combinations and even complementarity have developed among the formal and informal modalities of trade, which have been strengthened by their spatial dissemination and meanings in urban and semi-urban areas, even overcoming social differences (Figure 7.1, Figure 7.2).

Macro and micro informal methods of trade have gradually adapted to the phenomenon of the mobility of urban consumers and have settled in the form of established, semi-established and street vendors, mainly in areas where there is a lot of pedestrian and vehicular traffic, offering products for daily consumption, for personal and household use, whether they are original or counterfeit. Formal and informal trade practices come together in organized physical spaces as large as *Tepito* in Mexico's Federal District, *Los San Andresitos* in Colombia, *Ciudad del Este* in Paraguay, *Centro de Compras Popular, Shopping Popular o Camelódromo* in different cities in Brazil or *Rua 25 de março* in São Paulo, the latter of which brings together over one million shoppers on holidays (Figure 7.3).

Organized formal trade practiced in large areas and supermarket chains which catered to the middle and upper classes in the 1960s and 1970s, and which in the 1980s initiated the implementation of new formats, has become more flexible, particularly when targeting the lower-income market segment (Duhau and Giglia 2007; Da Silva and Moura 2009). Thus, these areas become meaningful for consumption activities, rituals for expressing affection and reaffirmation of family ties, entertainment and lifestyle (García-Canclini 1995).

Understanding consumption in informal markets requires reflection beyond legal and political aspects. The system of illicit trade, such as drug trafficking, and the dynamics of the informal market share certain characteristics such as corruption, the importance of trust and

Figure 7.1 Street market in Mexico City.
        Source: Photo credits: Cavazos and González.

Figure 7.2 Mall in Buenos Aires.
        Source: Photo credits: Cavazos and González.

Figure 7.3 A *San Andresito* in Bogotá, Colombia.
    Source: Photo credits: Cavazos and González.

reciprocity (Lomnitz 1988). However, illicit trade stands out because it involves illegitimate violence and the corruption of public agents (Lins 2006, 2008). On the other hand, in the dynamics of the informal market, trust and certain principles of reciprocity prevail between the supplier, the merchant and the client. As expressed by a woman interviewed by Duhau and Giglia (2007: 38), regarding her consumption practices in informal trade in Mexico City:

> Coca-Cola and Pepsi cover for them (the street vendors); they give them the tarps ... the tables and everything: they make their life easier and they feel protected ... in this city there have always been *tianguis* (farmers' markets), it is a tradition that is in our blood, we like to buy things on the street, that's the way we are ... [The only thing is that] we need to make it more orderly, there's no way of avoiding it. And the people who work in this entire area, that don't have the means to walk into a restaurant, or even have a fixed menu meal, because the prices are extremely high, because of the rent, because costs have increased a lot; well, we are going to eat there in peace, right? In an orderly way.
>
> (Woman, approximately 40 years old, civil servant,
> Antigua shopping plaza, Santa Fe, Cuajimalpa, Mexico)

Although informal sales are generally considered illicit because they contravene the stand-ards and regulations established by formal authorities, the suppliers, intermediaries, and consumers involved in the transactions could be considered licit, in other words, they are legitimized by society or by certain groups (Heyman and Smart 1999; Abraham and van Schendel 2005). There are common examples in the acquisition of certain counterfeit products such as pirated movies and music, as well as the purchase of products from street vendors who are unlicensed to carry out commercial activity (Figure 7.4, Figure 7.5). In the city of Este, right on the border of Paraguay and Brazil, Latin American consumers, mainly Brazilians, purchase cigarettes, beauty products, electrical appliances, CDs, counterfeit medication, toys and other products in shopping centers, galleries and in the street for personal use and for re-sale. It is commonly considered dangerous, even heroic, to bring these products back into Brazil (Pinheiro 2004).

The role of the consumer agency

There have been many debates and theories regarding consumer agencies in the social sciences, however, in order to understand the implications of the Latin American consumer agency, we will consider that the agency is linked to the consumer's capacity to act in his/her socio-cultural context. Through the globalization process, in emerging markets, the consumer has gradually turned into an active participant in the selection of products and among local, transnational and government organizations (Eckhardt and Mahi 2004). The way in which the consumers in these markets interact with agents tends to be by negotiating consumption processes and by the manner in which many of the products take on localized meaning and are even transformed into symbols of modernity and status (Ger and

Figure 7.4 Informal trade in Mexico.
    Source: Photo credits: Cavazos and González.

Figure 7.5 Informal trade in Honduras.
  Source: Photo credits: Cavazos and González.

Belk 1996). The reasons behind consumption are many and their coherence may be incomprehensible at first where the implications not only have an impact on the local consumer but also on the companies and on the significance of their products and brands and on the manner in which the consumers adopt them.

Despite the fact that in Latin America the variety and supply of products are relatively more limited than in other contexts and that many of the imported products were not designed with the local culture in mind, it is much more common for the consumers to accept and undergo a meaning transformation or opt to reject the goods (Eckhardt and Mahi 2004). On the other hand, the co-creation of meaning and value between the company and the consumer generates benefits for the agents involved. *Casas Bahia* (www.casasbahia.com.br) in Brazil and *Cemex* (www.cemex.com) with their programs "*Patrimonio Hoy*" (Heritage Today) and "*Centros Productivos de Autoempleo*" (Self-employment Productive Centers) in Mexico, Colombia, Costa Rica, and Nicaragua, are examples of Latin American business models whose meaning and value to consumers have impacted market development from the base of the pyramid in both countries (Prahalad 2005). *Casas Bahia* became the largest retail furniture and electrical appliance chain in Brazil and is characterized by selling at low prices and by creating an innovative financing system which considers aspects pertaining to consumers' payment history rather than their formal income. The company has even set up points of sale in *favelas* with populations of over 80,000 people and 20,000 homes (*Exame* 2008).

Cemex, the third largest cement company in the world, has developed two innovative programs with social implications, "*Patrimonio Hoy*" (Heritage Today) and "*Centros*

Productivos de Autoempleo" (Self-employment Productive Centers) that promote community development and are increasingly significant both for the organization and for the program participants. "*Patrimonio Hoy*" is a micro-financing program for construction material and services, targeting low-income urban families. The company believes that value is generated by families obtaining specialized technical assistance and access to the supply of construction material (Figure 7.6, Figure 7.7). The "*Centros Productivos de Autoempleo*"

Figure 7.6 Self-constructed house in Mexico.
        Source: Photo credits: Cavazos and González.

Figure 7.7 Self-constructed house in Mexico with the *Patrimonio Hoy* program.
        Source: Photo credits: Cavazos and González.

(Self-employment Productive Centers) are an initiative for low-income families to produce basic material for construction or renovation of their homes. In order to do so, the company provides a plot of land approved by the community, a cement mixer and a cement block maker. After training the group of workers, the company provides the raw material and begins production whereby half of what is produced becomes the property of the group members and the remaining material is channeled through the self-employment productive center for sale (*Expansión* 2009). The innovations of these businesses are based both on the processes and on the way in which value is passed on to the low-income clients by generating inclusive solutions, providing meaning, simplicity, and access to the purchase and use of the product.

Strategic marketing insights

To design marketing strategies oriented to the development of markets in the Latin American region implies an understanding of the historic evolution of the context and the cultural awareness by marketing management. Given that traditional, modern, and postmodern daily cultural aspects are strongly connected, it is therefore advisable that the development of marketing proposals avoids a possible conflict with the value and pride that many Latin Americans have for their historic and cultural legacy.

The complexity between the traditional, modern, and postmodern must be considered in the commercialization strategy, the access and use of technologies, and the way in which consumers rationalize their decision-making of their purchases, have an impact on the development of products and services, the choice of the distribution channels, and the integration of the communication strategy.

An example of how these elements have combined is the evolution of the supply of the culinary options of pre-Hispanic origin and the colonial fusion with other culinary tendencies such as ingredients, tools, preparations, presentations, and the transformation of the production, distribution, and consumption spaces of these elements (Curiel 2005).

Using research techniques that allow more in-depth knowledge of the characteristics and needs of the consumption groups and their cultural diversity can contribute to the development, redesign, and the promotion of goods and services that will better satisfy the unrequited needs and value proposals that are aligned with the lifestyle, values, and symbolic aspects which are characteristic of the cultural groups. These elements have an impact on the position strategy and relocation of products and brands in their construction and communication with the audiences.

Marketing researchers should also recognize negative social aspects that may directly affect the marketing activities. This chapter emphasizes the practice of corruption among the region, even though perceptions on the matter may vary, and it is influenced in part by cultural values (Scholtens and Dam 2007).

It is difficult to understand all the mechanisms, the way they operate and what their effects are. Nevertheless, we know that the well-being of the workers, consumers and other market agents are affected, as well as the performance of political, social, and economic institutions. This demands ethical behavior from the marketing researchers as well as the organization itself.

The strategic directions may include the incorporation of transparency of the process linked to the supply chain of the organization (which includes commercialization), respect of and compliance with local laws, preserving human rights, incorporating a corporate social responsibility plan (CSR), based on trustworthy long-term relationships, as well as policies and actions that exhibit integrity and fairness to consumers, employees and communities and other stakeholders (Murphy *et al*. 2005).

Trademarks and copyrights are not enough to protect brands that provide differentiation, linking it to status and distinction. We have shown how informal salesmen and counterfeiters utilize the brand as an own resource that capitalizes itself in exchange practices, the production of meanings and relationships where the brand becomes accessible to mass markets, despite the fact that it may not be the original product.

Some companies have found in the diversification of products and markets a lower risk for the false imitation of the brand (Campuzano 2003), others work intensely on the qualities associated with the product, design, manufacture, use, recycling, and so forth (Cordell *et al*. 1996). Even though we need to recognize the fact that the quality of imitations has improved over the years and that in many cases, it is increasingly difficult to distinguish them from an original product (Gentry *et al*. 2006).

Brands may conceptualize themselves as socio-cultural entities that charge localized meanings and even transform themselves into different symbols for the consumer groups. These meanings are dynamic and are highly influenced by the context in which the brand is being tested (De Berry-Spence 2008).

With the present use of brands and slogans, consumers reproduce the lifestyles that the brand embraces (Arvidsson 2005), they create and share meanings, social relationships, affective bonds, and have the power to stabilize products. This is why marketers must convert the creativity and the consumer agency into strong sources of surplus value (Foster 2007).

The orientation and co-creation of value based on cooperation between producers and consumers sustained in a long-term relationship of intimacy, respect and reciprocity can be seen in cases like *Casas Bahia* and *Cemex* with outstanding attributes in quality, price, micro-financing, cooperation, as well as unique value experiences.

It is necessary to recognize the outspoken consumer, acknowledging that consumers are active agents, with their own identities, capable of judging the products, as well as criticizing, sharing feelings, and interacting with other consumers (Foster 2007). As seen in the case of the Equatorial Amazon residents affected by the oil company Chevron. Many communities organized themselves in an assembly of those affected demanding through legal action the restoration of the damages caused by the polluting production practices and the disposal of toxic waste over the years, impacting rivers and the lives of various local area native groups. Despite the decision given in 2011 by a judge in Ecuador demanding the payment of more than US$9 billion in damages to the communities, both Chevron and the assembly of the communities affected appealed against the verdict (Romero and Krauss 2011).

Finally, the strategies in cultural marketing operate better when they are based on a sustainable entrepreneurship focus. Taking into account protection of natural resources and green space, the preservation of natural life, and, if they sustain communities, where the culture and the natural and social capital are inseparable from the economic aspects. This orientation allows the attainment of economic and non-economic gains for both individuals and organizations, such as:

- *Economic gains*: enhancing the socio-economic status of people, improving subjective well-being and emotional, psychological, and physical health.
- *Non-economic gains to individuals*: increasing child survival rate, education, equity, and equal opportunities.

- *Non-economic gains to society*: in this chapter, it means the well-being of each Latin American country as well as the life satisfaction and degree of happiness of the inhabitants of the total region. Crime, low interpersonal trust, corruption, violence and environmental decline mean obstacles for the social development of the region.

(Shepherd and Patzelt 2011)

Conclusion

Several cultural aspects have played a predominant role in market development in the Latin American context. The market has facilitated the interaction and transformation not only of economic capital but also of social, cultural and symbolic capital in Latin American societies. Recent years have been characterized by strong dynamics in consumer culture, focusing on increasing the consumption of goods and services. However, in many cases, access to consumption is closely linked to certain mechanisms related to socio-cultural differentiation.

Efficient marketing must be based on creativity and innovation, considering the complexity and the implications involved in markets. Meeting the needs of cultural groups requires the development of strategies that generate greater value for the agents involved in the exchange processes. The cultural implications are dynamic, shaped by socio-cultural representations of the consumer groups and thus require constant, in-depth reviews by the market experts in an effort to avoid stereotyping diversity.

The implication of the meanings in the acceptance or transformation of products and services with the local culture is a complex process not only among Latin American countries, but within each one as well. It is necessary to understand that what is conceptualized as "traditional" does not mean obsolete, nor does it necessarily imply that it is contrary to what is modern, and understand what a cultural practice considers to be legitimate as part of its own evolutionary process within a framework of conceptions that people produce in their social structure. The challenge that marketing experts face is to understand the dynamics in which subjectivities interact and how the meanings involved in consumption are developed, as well as the manner in which the subjects incorporate products and services into their lives, accepting the fact that they have the power to give them new meaning in ways that are even unanticipated by the organizations.

Review and discussion questions

1   The text mentions some implications related to the organization of consumption alternatives in the Latin American context. Think about other implications which might be considered.
2   How is cultural diversity related to the development of Latin American markets? Is this concept useful for segmenting purposes beyond class or rural–urban distinctions?
3   Reciprocity is a common element in the development of exchange relations in Latin cultures. Consider a Latin American context and discuss how you would incorporate it into a strategy based on cultural administration.
4   "With the local culture in mind, it is much more common for consumers to accept and undergo a meaning transformation or opt to reject the goods." Explain this argument based on the characteristics of the Latin American consumer agency.
5   How can the concept of consumer agency be applied when targeting consumers?

Keywords

deritualization, *ejido*, *huicholes*, informal trade, lifestyle, modernity, postmodernity

References

Abraham, I. and Van Schendel, W. (2005) "Introduction: The Making of Illicitness," in W. Van Schendel and I. Abraham (eds), *Illicit Flows and Criminal Things*, Bloomington, IN: Indiana University Press.

Almeida, A. C. (2007) *A cabeça do brasileiro*, Rio de Janeiro: Record.

Andrade, F. (2009) "Estimating Diabetes and Diabetes-free Life Expectancy in Mexico and Seven Major Cities in Latin America and the Caribbean," *Pan American Journal of Public Health*, 26(1): 9–16.

Arenas, N. (1999) "Globalización, integración e identidad: América Latina en las nuevas perspectivas," *Revista Venezolana de Coyuntura*, V(1): 89–108.

Arnould, E. (2007) "Can Consumers Escape the Market?," in M. Saren, P. Maclaran, C. Goulding, R. Elliot, A. Shankar and M. Catterall (eds), *Critical Marketing: Defining the Field*, London: Butterworth-Heinemann, pp. 139–55.

Arvidsson, A. (2005) "Brands: A Critical Perspective," *Journal of Consumer Culture*, 5(2): 235–58.

Barómetro Iberoamericano (2010) *El barómetro Iberoamericano de gobernabilidad 2010.* Available at: www.cimaiberoamerica.com (accessed September 22, 2010).

Bartra, R. (2002) *Anatomía del Mexicano*, México: Plaza Janés.

Bauman, Z. (2000) *Trabajo, consumismo y nuevos pobres*, Barcelona: Gedisa.

—— (2008) *Múltiples culturas, una sola humanidad*, Barcelona: Katz Editores.

BBC (2011) "El alcoholismo, una enfermedad muy democrática," *BBC World.* Online. Available at: www.bbc.co.uk/mundo/noticias/2011/02/110209_adiccion_alcoholismo_america_latina_pea. shtml (accessed February 19, 2011).

Briceño-León, R. (2002) "La nueva violencia urbana de América Latina," *Sociologías*, 8: 34–51.

Briones, C. (2007) "La puesta en valor de la diversidad cultural: implicancias y efectos," *Revista Educación y pedagogía*, XIX(48): 38–56.

Brunner, J. J. (1995) "Tradicionalismo y modernidad en la cultura latinoamericana," in J. L. Reyna (ed.), *América Latina a finales de siglo*, México: Fondo de Cultura Económica.

Buchenau, J. (2004) *Tools of Progress: A German Merchant Family in Mexico City, 1865–Present.* Albuquerque, NM: University of New Mexico Press.

Bunker, S. (2009) "First Approaches toward Understanding Mexico City´s Culture of Consumption," *Journal of Urban History*, 36(1): 111–15.

Calderón, F. (1987) "América Latina: identidad y tiempos mixtos. O cómo tratar de pensar la modernidad sin dejar de ser indios," *David y Goliath*, XVII(52): 4–9.

Campuzano, S. (2003) *El universo del lujo*, Madrid: McGraw-Hill.

Chang-Rodríguez, E. (2008) *Latinoamérica su civilización y su cultura*, Boston: Thomson Heinle.

Cordell, V. V., Wongtada, N. and Kieschnick, R. (1996) "Counterfeit Purchase Intentions: Role of Lawfulness Attitudes and Product Traits as Determinants," *Journal of Business Research*, 35: 41–53.

Cui, G. and Choudhury, P. (2002) "Marketplace Diversity and Cost-effective Marketing Strategies," *Journal of Consumer Marketing*, 19(1): 54–73.

Curiel, G. (2005) "Ajuares domésticos. Los rituales de lo cotidiano," in A. Rubial (ed.), *La ciudad Barroca, (Tomo II) Historia de la vida cotidiana en México*, México, DF: Fondo de Cultura Económica, El Colegio de México, A.C.

Da Silva, L. and Moura, C. J. (2009) "Faces atuais do espaço comercial em Campina Grande/PB: Algumas considerações sobre a coexistência de formas modernas e tradicionais do comércio na 'Nova' Dinâmica sócio-espacial," *Revista de Geografia*, UFPE-DCG/NAPA, 26(2): 40–60.

Datamonitor (2008a) "Insurance in Mexico," *Industry Profile*, November: 1–29.

—— (2008b) "Insurance in Brazil," *Industry Profile*, November: 1–29.

De Berry-Spence, B. (2008) "Consumer Creations of Product Meaning in the Context of African-style Clothing," *Journal of the Academy of Marketing Science*, 36(3): 395–408.

De Caldeira, T. (2000) *City of Walls: Crime, Segregation and Citizenship in São Paulo*, Berkeley, CA: University of California Press.

Donohoe, M. (2007) "Flowers, Diamonds, and Gold: The Destructive Public Health, Human Rights, and Environmental Consequences of Symbols of Love," *Human Rights Quarterly*, 29: 164–82.

Duhau, E. and Giglia, A. (2007) "Globalización e informalidad en la Ciudad de México. Prácticas de consumo y movilidad," *TRACE*, 51: 28–43.

Durán, M. (2010) "México, primer lugar mundial en obesidad," *Radio Nederland Weeldomroep*. Available at: www.rnw.nl/espanol/article/mexico-primer-lugar-mundial-en-obesidad (accessed February 19, 2011).

Durand, J. and Massey, D. S. (2010) "New World Orders: Continuities and Changes in Latin America Migration," *The Annals of the American Academy, AAPSS*, 630: 20–52.

Eckhardt, G. and Mahi, H. (2004) "The Role of Consumer Agency in the Globalization Process in Emerging Markets," *Journal of Macromarketing*, 24(2): 136–46.

Etkin, J. (1993) *La doble moral de las organizaciones: Los sistemas perversos y la corrupción institucionalizada*, Madrid: McGraw-Hill.

Exame (2008) "Casas Bahia abre sua primeira loja em," *Revista Exame*. Available at: http://portalexame.abril.com.br/ae/economia/casas-bahia-abre-sua-primeira-loja-favela-175446.shtml (accessed October 10, 2010).

Expansión (2009) "Cemex gana premio otorgado por la ONU," *CNNExpansión*. Available at: http://www.cnnexpansion.com/negocios/2009/07/07/la-onu-otorga-premio-habitat-a-cemex (accessed October 10, 2010).

Featherstone, M. (1991) *Consumer Culture and Postmodernism*, London: Sage.

Firat, A. F. and Venkatesh, A. (1995) "Liberatory Postmodernism and the Reenchantment of Consumption," *Journal of Consumer Research*, 22: 239–67.

Foster, R. (2007) "The Work of the New Economy: Consumers, Brands, and Value Creation," *Cultural Anthropology*, 22(4): 707–31.

García-Canclini, N. (1995) *Consumidores y ciudadanos. Conflictos culturales de la globalización*, México: Grijalbo.

—— (2001) *La globalización imaginada*, Buenos Aires: Paidos.

Gentry, J. W., Sanjay, P. and Clifford, J. S. (2006) "The Effects of Counterfeiting on Consumer Search," *Journal of Consumer Behavior*, 5(3): 245–56.

Ger, G. and Belk, W. R. (1996) "I'd Like to Buy the World a Coke: Consumptionscapes of the 'Less Affluent World'," *Journal of Consumer Policy*, 19(3): 271–304.

Gimson, A. (2006) "Nuevas xenofobias, nuevas políticas étnicas en la Argentina," in L. Grimson-Jelin (ed.), *Migraciones regionales hacia la Argentina: Diferencia, desigualdad y derechos*, Buenos Aires: Prometeo.

Grossbart, S. (2002) "Editorial," *Journal of Macromarketing*, 22(1): 3.

Guesalaga, R. and Marshall, P. (2008) "Purchasing Power at the Bottom of the Pyramid: Difference across Geographic Regions and Income Tiers," *Journal of Consumer Marketing*, 25(7): 413–18.

Gutiérrez, S. (2005) "Perspectivas de Mercado para los próximos años: ¿Las transnacionales están subiendo los cerros?," *Prisma*, 1(1): 1–5. Available at: http://www.cuft.tec.ve/cuft/publicaciones/barquisimeto/revistacuft/paginas/revista/prisma_1/articulos/samuel_gutierrez-perspectivas_de-mercado.pdf (accessed September 14, 2010).

Harch, E. (1993) "Accumulators and Democrats: Challenging State Corruption in Africa," *Journal of Modern African Studies*, 1(31): 31–48.

Hassig, R. (2001) *Time, History and Belief in Aztec Colonial Mexico*, Austin, TX: University of Texas Press.

Herrera, J. M. and Arena, C. A. (2010) "Consumo de alcohol y violencia doméstica contra las mujeres: un estudio con estudiantes universitarias de México," *Revista Latino-Americana de enfermagem*, 18: 557–64.

Heyman, J. and Smart, A. (1999) "States and Illegal Practices: An Overview," in J. Heyman (ed.), *States and Illegal Practices*, Oxford: Berg, pp. 1–24.

Huber, L. (2008) *Romper la mano. Una interpretación cultural de la corrupción*, Lima: Instituto de Estudios Peruanos.

Husted, B. W. (2002) "Culture and International Anti-Corruption Agreements in Latin America," *Journal of Business Ethics*, 37(4): 413–22.

Ireland, J. (2008) "Lessons for Successful BOP Marketing from Caracas´ Slums," *Journal of Consumer Marketing*, 25(7): 430–8.

Lawson, V. (1998) "Hierarchical Households and Gendered Migration in Latin America: Feminist Extensions to Migration Research," *Progress in Human Geography*, 22(39): 39–53.

Leme, M. T. (2000) "Gerenciando a diversidade cultural: experiências de empresas brasileiras," *Revista de Administração de Empresas*, 40(3): 18–25.

Lins, G. (2006) "Other Globalizations, Alternative Transnational Processes and Agents," *Série Antropologia*, 389: 1–47. Universidade de Brasília. Available at: http://vsites.unb.br/ics/dan/Serie389empdf.pdf (accessed October 1, 2010).

—— (2008) "El Sistema Mundial No-Hegemónico y la Globalización Popular," *Alambre. Comunicación, información, cultura*. 1 March. Available at: www.revistaalambre.com/Articulos/ArticuloMuestra.asp?Id = 7 (accessed October 1, 2010).

Lomnitz, C. (1992) *Exits from the Labyrinth: Culture and Ideology in the Mexican National Space*, Berkeley, CA: University of California Press.

Lomnitz, L. A. (1988) "Informal Exchange Networks in Formal Systems: A Theoretical Model," *American Anthropologist*, 90(1): 42–55.

Miller, D. (2005) "Materiality: An Introduction," in D. Miller (ed.), *Materiality*, Durham, NC: Duke University Press, pp. 1–50.

Möller, H. (1995) "Hábitos del consumidor mexicano," *Entrepreneur*: 22–26.

Morales, M. R. (2008) "Serving Two Masters, or Breathing Artificial Life into a Lifeless Debate (a Reply to John Beverley)," *Journal of Latin American Cultural Studies*, 17(1): 85–93.

Moreno, J. (2003) *Yankee Don´t Go Home! Mexican Nationalism, American Business Culture, and the Shaping of Modern Mexico, 1920–1950*, Chapel Hill, NC: University of North Carolina Press.

Mosquera, D. (2005) "Consecrated Transactions: Of Marketplaces, Passion Plays and Other Nahua-Christian Devotions," *Journal of Latin American Cultural Studies*, 14(2): 171–93.

Murphy, P. E., Laczniak, G. R., Bowie, N. E. and Klein, T. A. (2005) *Ethical Marketing*, Upper Saddle River, NJ: Pearson Prentice Hall.

Olivier de Sardan, J. P. (1999) "A Moral Economy of Corruption in Africa?," *The Journal of Modern African Studies*, 1(37): 25–52.

Pan American Health Organization (2007) "Alcohol, Gender, Culture and Harms in the Americas," *Pan American Health Organization*. Available at: http://new.paho.org/hq/dmdocuments/2009/AGCHA_ENG.pdf (accessed 19 February 2011).

Peñaloza, L. and Venkatesh, A. (2006) "Further Evolving the New Dominant Logic of Marketing: From Services to the Social," *Marketing Theory*, 6(3): 299–316.

Picotti, D. (1998) *La presencia africana en nuestra identidad*, Buenos Aires: Serie Antropológica, Ediciones del Sol.

Pinheiro, R. (2004) "'A garantia soy yo': Etnografía das práticas comerciais entre camelôs e sacoleiros nas cidades de Porto Alegre (Brasil) e Ciudad Del Este (Paraguai)," Rio Grande do Sul, M.A. Thesis, Graduate Program in Social Anthropology, Federal University of Rio Grande do Sul.

Portes, A. (1997) "Neoliberalism and the Sociology of Development," *Population and Development Review*, 23(2): 229–59.

Prahalad, C. K. (2005) *La oportunidad de negocios en la base de la pirámide*, Bogotá: Grupo Editorial Norma.

Romero, S. and Krauss, C. (2011) "Ecuador Judge Orders Chevron to Pay \$9 Billion," *The New York Times*. Available at: http://www.nytimes.com/2011/02/15/world/americas/15ecuador.html?partner = rss&emc = rss (accessed February 27, 2011).

Sarquis, D. (2008) "Raíces históricas del problema de la corrupción en México," *Razón y Palabra*, 62. Available at: http://www.razonypalabra.org.mx/n62/varia/dsarquis.html (accessed October 2, 2010).

Sassatelli, R. (2007) *Consumer Culture: History, Theory and Politics*, London: Sage.

Scholtens, B. and Dam, L. (2007) "Cultural Values and International Differences in Business Ethics," *Journal of Business Ethics*, 75: 273–85.

Seabrook, J. (1988) *The Race for Riches: The Human Cost of Wealth*, Basingstoke: Marshall Pickering.

Shepherd, D. A. and Patzelt, H. (2011) "The New Field of Sustainable Entrepreneurship: Studying Entrepreneurial Action Linking 'What Is to Be Sustained' with 'What Is to Be Developed'," *Entrepreneurship Theory and Practice*, 35(1): 137–63.

Tironi, M. (2003) *Nueva pobreza urbana. Vivienda y capital social en Santiago de Chile, 1985–2001*, Santiago: Ril Editores.

Vargas-Hernández, J. (2005) "Modernidad y postmodernidad en América Latina," *Estudios Centroamericanos*, 61(696): 999–1022.

Villavicencio, S. (2008) "Republic, Nation and Democracy: The Challenge of Diversity," *Diogenes*, 55(4): 83–9.

Volpi, A. (2007) *A História do consume no Brasil. Do mercantilismo à era do foco no cliente*, São Paulo: Campus, Elsevier.

Yankelovich, D. and Meer, D. (2006) "Rediscovering Market Segmentation," *Harvard Business Review*, 84(2): 122–31.

Zolfagharian, M. A. (2010) "Identification, Uniqueness and Art Consumption among Bicultural Consumers," *Journal of Consumer Marketing*, 27(1): 17–25.

8 What do affluent Chinese consumers want?

A semiotic approach to building brand literacy in developing markets

Laura R. Oswald

Overview

This chapter examines the limitations of Western luxury advertising to engage affluent consumers in the People's Republic of China. The approach is based on a theory of brand literacy drawn from a theory of language acquisition. The study illustrates how semiotics, a social science discipline devoted to the study of signs and meanings in cultural perspective, can be used to identify the cultural tensions between consumers and brands in emerging markets and provide direction for correcting the problem. In the following sections, the chapter reviews the basics of brand equity, illustrates the role of marketing communication for brand strategy, and outlines some of the challenges facing Western companies as they target consumers in developing consumer societies such as China. A case study is then presented where marketing semiotics research in Shanghai exposed differences between the ways Chinese and European consumers perceive luxury and luxury advertising.

Brand equity

Brands are sign systems that form the identity of specific products or services and distinguish them from other brands in a product category. This, the semiotic function of brands, defines the strategic management process. Managers develop the brand positioning by laying claim to a distinctive semantic territory carved out of the broad field of meanings consumers associate with a product category. They reinforce these associations in consumers' minds by representing them consistently in specific words, stories, and images in advertising. For example, Coke and Pepsi both belong to the carbonated cola beverage category, but they each claim different semantic territories. Coke's positioning as "the real thing" speaks to the brand's authenticity, consistency, and tradition. By contrast, Pepsi, "for the new generation," is positioned as a trendy, young, and evolving brand. Brands succeed or fail in direct proportion to the strength and clarity of these positionings in consumers' minds.

The range, consistency, and force of the meanings consumers associate with brands over time contribute measurable value to brands – their brand equity. Brand equity defines an intangible asset on the company's annual report, but has tangible strategic value for the firm. For example, in 2010, the Interbrand Group valued the Coca-Cola brand – the meanings consumers associate with the name and logo – at over $70 billion (Foster 2010).

Simply put, the semiotic value of the name, logo, and other proprietary signs consumers associate with the brand is fundamental to brand equity, not just a value-added. The semiotic value transcends the functional "use value" of goods and contributes substantially to the bottom line of companies. Brands draw higher prices, higher profit margins, and stronger customer loyalty than generic products because they appeal to the unsatisfied emotional needs of consumers.

Consumer needs and wants

Consumers draw upon the semiotic resources of brands when they use name brands to build self-confidence, extend their personal identity (Belk 1988), or use brands to enhance their self-presentations (Goffman 1956). Consider the weekend athlete who is motivated to perform by wearing Nike sportswear, inspired by the brand message – "Just Do It!" Consumers may also use brands to mark their identification with social groups and subcultures. Consumers immigrating to the United States, for instance, may choose iconic American brands to blend into their new culture, though they may resort to familiar ethnic traditions to feel the comfort of the homelands they left behind (Peñaloza 1994; Oswald 1999).

The brand equity hierarchy

Consumers develop brand perceptions in stages, beginning with the very general, cognitive awareness of a brand name or logo, to very specific, emotional brand relationships based on repeated experiences with the brand (Aaker 1991; Aaker 1997; Fournier 1998). This process forms a kind of brand equity hierarchy consisting of five stages:

1 awareness
2 perception of quality
3 recognition of emotional and social benefits associated with the brand
4 identification with the brand persona
5 loyalty, when consumers experience a personal relationship with their brands.

Brand value increases as consumers move up the hierarchy and become increasingly engaged in the brand world (Figure 8.1). Awareness is the most rudimentary measure of a brand's value, and defines the ability of consumers to recall the brand's name, whether they have used the brand or even know what the brand stands for. The perception of quality refers to the brand's reputation for using good materials, working properly, or delivering good service. As consumers begin to know the brand because of repeated exposure to advertising or the product itself, they gain an appreciation of what the brand stands for – is it timeless and traditional, or trendy and changing? They may even be able to personify the brand, giving it human personality traits.

Though brand characters such as Tony the Tiger or the Mr. Clean may facilitate brand personification, repeated association of the brand with events and characters that consumers relate to, such as Coke's association with Santa Claus, contributes to the brand personality. The brand personality stage is critical to the final stage, brand loyalty, inasmuch as the relationship is based upon finding an emotional connection to the brand that parallels a human relationship. At this stage, consumers form a kind of personal stable of brands that they choose consistently over competitors. Their stable of brands may include a range of personal relationships from intimate to formal (Fournier 1998).

The challenge of global branding

At each stage of the brand hierarchy, brand meaning relies increasingly on matching the brand heritage to the social and cultural contexts of the marketing event and communicating

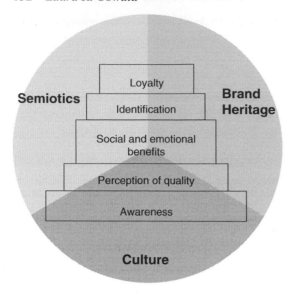

Figure 8.1 The brand equity hierarchy.
      Source: Photo credits: Laura Oswald.

the brand message in signs and symbols that consumers can relate to. In order to move consumers up the hierarchy, from logo recognition toward personal engagement, brand strategy must be focused on calibrating brand meanings to the evolving culture of the target market and the changing needs, wants and identity projects of consumers. This process is particularly important for global branding strategies in developing markets.

As sign systems, brands face the same tensions in foreign markets as tourists who do not speak the local language. For example, in non-Christian cultures, how do consumers interpret Santa Claus? Do Arab consumers compare the Mr. Clean genie to the *jinns* from Arabic folklore? Such cultural differences are likely to create ambiguity and even barriers to brand acceptance abroad, particularly in developing consumer societies where brand culture may be an emerging phenomenon. To succeed in the global marketplace, managers must adapt the brand message, not just the language, to the local culture – without losing the core brand identity in the process. Translating brands from one culture to the next may be as simple as changing the cultural references in a print ad or as complex as creating a new communications strategy built upon new media, special events, and/or educational forums.

Case study 1: What do affluent Chinese consumers want?

This section reviews the design and implementation of a semiotics research project in China with affluent consumers. I have chosen a semiotics methodology to solve a marketing problem because semiotics research bridges the social sciences and communication theory, connecting the dots between consumer insights and brand communication. Semiotics, sometimes called, "the science of signs," extends linguistic theory to non-verbal media such as the images, myths, and archetypes that abound in popular culture. Unlike classical rhetoric, semiotics embeds the study of signs in the cultural context, explaining the meaning of myth and archetype in terms of the history and ideology of the consumer setting.

Furthermore, semiotics extends the work of anthropologists by identifying the underlying codes, patterns and figures structuring the categories of culture, and articulating the meaning of consumer behavior as a kind of language or sign system. By identifying the "language" structuring a consumer setting, product category, or advertising campaign, management can track the consistency of brand communication over time and its relevance for consumers in foreign markets. In addition, semiotics can be used to adjust brand communication to a local setting, to "translate," as it were, the brand system into the terms appropriate for a specific market.

Background

Newly rich consumers in cities like Beijing or Shanghai have contributed to the double-digit growth of the European luxury sector in the past decade, and economists project that China will surpass Japan in the next decade as the leader in the consumption of luxury goods, or 29 percent of the world consumption pie (Eurostaf Report 2003; USDA Reports 2006). Though the financial data on luxury consumption in China is straightforward, we propose looking beyond the numbers to understand the factors motivating brand choice, the unmet emotional needs and wants of consumers, and the influence of Chinese history and culture on their perception of luxury and luxury brands.

As mentioned earlier, the emotional and cultural dimensions of a category tend to influence long-term brand loyalty, so this information could have important implications for management over the long term. Brand relationships, like interpersonal relationships, develop and grow based on identification with some aspect of the story, personality, and cultural context associated with the brand in marketing communication. If Western companies speak to consumers in China without changing the tone, style, and even strategy of their brand communication, it is very likely that they will create barriers to forming lasting relationships between their brands and local consumers.

Luxury manufacturers from Europe such as Louis Vuitton, Armani, Chanel, and Dior, generally employ the same communications strategy and even the same ads in China as they do in Western markets. They may take for granted the universal appeal of brand symbols and stories, and target consumers in China without a clear understanding of the cultural frames that shape consumer perceptions of luxury and luxury brands. They pin their communications strategy on the traditional, single image magazine ad, use European models for the most part, and evoke an interpretation of luxury that cues into Western values for ostentation, individuality, and fantasy.

Findings from consumer research in Shanghai suggest that affluent consumers in China may purchase famous luxury brands for their basic recognition factor, may not engage with brands on a personal, emotional level, and therefore may blur distinctions among luxury brands in the marketplace.

Study design

With the help of Chinese interpreters, I conducted on-site ethnographic research with 16 affluent consumers in Shanghai between 2007 and 2008. The first phase, conducted in June 2007, was exploratory and included both consumers and professionals in the luxury industry, including fashion and interior designers and fashion editors. The second phase included only consumers and focused more on luxury brands and advertising. The study was limited to research on European fashion categories, from leather goods to couture, watches, and cosmetics. Consumers discussed their own experiences of luxury, their understanding of Chinese luxury traditions, their perception of European brands, and their interpretation of brand communication in magazine advertisements for global brands such as Louis Vuitton, Dior, and Patek Philippe. In this discussion, I will focus on a section of the study devoted to eliciting emotional responses to the questions, "What is luxury?" and "What does this brand stand for?"

Findings summary

Early stage findings suggest that Chinese consumers stop short of identifying the emotional associations that distinguish luxury brands from each other and, as a result, often lack a visceral, personal connection to the brands they purchase. Since brand value on the marketplace is founded on nothing less than the personal and emotional associations consumers associate with brands, these findings have serious implications for the growth of the European luxury sector and also raise important questions about brands in translation, consumer cultures in contact, and the limits of consumer assimilation to global consumer culture.

The "next generation" of the new rich in China may expect more of their luxury brands than to display their money and success. They expect luxury brands to both express and inform their *savoir-faire*, personality, and taste. They also expect advertising to assist them in learning how to "read" and appreciate brand meanings. Respondents moving up the economic ladder with their new MBAs and rich husbands consistently expressed disappointment with their expensive purchases because they did not identify with the persona of the brand or the emotional dimensions of luxury that were suggested in luxury advertising. They had trouble making qualitative distinctions between luxury brands and failed to connect with brands in a "visceral" way (Wetlaufer 2001). Although they sought brands that would reflect their personalities, the brands they bought did not satisfy this need. Their luxury bags and shoes did not extend their personal identities much beyond the meanings of "status" and *savoir-faire*. Several respondents reported losing interest in their Louis Vuitton bags once they got them home, leaving them in the closet with indifference.

As the goods piled up in their closets, these same consumers expressed strong interest in finding a "match" with a brand that satisfied their need for self-expression and met their expectations, fueled by advertising, that luxury consumption would enrich their fantasy life.

Consumers struggled to move beyond the somewhat generic interpretation of luxury brands as "expensive" and "high quality." They also interpreted luxury through the lens of Confucian values, associating luxury consumption with a noble character and, ironically, the simple life.

The historical context

Specific historical and ideological conditions in China have interfered with local traditions of luxury, not only since the victory of Communism in 1949, but for the past 150 years as the result of colonial invasions, wars, and the frugal ideology of Confucianism. More recently, Mao Tse Dong repressed luxury traditions and values in China, tortured rich property owners, destroyed or stole their luxury possessions, and banished them to the countryside during the Cultural Revolution.

This may explain why respondents did not draw upon local traditions and values related to luxury as means of interpreting and assessing the meaning and value of European luxury brands. The signs and symbols of luxury represented in European ads were thus meanings that lacked a referent in a deep, context-rich experience of luxury. As a result, Chinese consumer responses to European luxury focused on the most general meanings of luxury, such as price. In linguistic terms, their responses betrayed tensions between the meaning and reference of brand symbolism: the CC (Coco Chanel) logo signifies "expensive," Louis Vuitton must be successful because they are "so well known." However, these brands fail to conjure up any emotional experience, fantasy, or image that the consumer can relate to. Consumers struggle to find a brand that links brand symbolism to their personal values, lifestyles, and fantasies.

Brand literacy

Thus, the unique history and ideology of Chinese consumers have shaped their appreciation of luxury and luxury brands in the popular consciousness. Consumers grasped the general meanings of luxury, such as "expensive," "successful," and "royal" ("like the British royal family"). They also interpreted luxury through the lens of Confucianism, a philosophy that values personal virtues and filial piety over materialism. Several respondents actually stated that people who purchased luxury fashion brands probably had good characters and "took care of their parents." Giving luxury brands as gifts can also "make other people happy."

The distinct cultural heritage of consumers in the People's Republic of China forms a contrast with Western concepts of luxury that is no less dramatic than the contrast between the Chinese and English languages. One cannot expect Chinese consumers to be "fluent" in the codes structuring Western luxury any more than one can expect them to be fluent in French or English without specific training. The large luxury companies have nonetheless charged into this market using the same creative strategies they employ in the West, heedless to the resistance of their target market to the nuances and distinctions of their brands. As long as the revenues flow in, for the moment at least, they are ignoring deep-seated cultural conflicts that may eventually impede long-term brand loyalty and market growth.

Stages of brand literacy

Research findings suggest that consumers in emerging markets pass through various stages of brand literacy in order to recognize and identify with the precise meanings and worlds associated with brands. These stages parallel the stages in the brand equity hierarchy, and are related to specific experiences of consumers.

1 The New Rich

    (a) Awareness: Louis Vuitton is a famous luxury brand from France.
    (b) Perception of Quality: Louis Vuitton products are expensive and well made.

2 Passionate Trendsetters

    (a) Awareness: Louis Vuitton is a famous luxury brand from France.
    (b) Perception of Quality: Louis Vuitton products are expensive and well made.
    (c) Social and Emotional Benefits: Louis Vuitton is a badge of status and wealth.

3 The Mature New Rich

    (a) Awareness: Louis Vuitton is a famous luxury brand from France.
    (b) Perception of Quality: Louis Vuitton products are expensive and well made.

(c)   Social and Emotional Benefits: Louis Vuitton is a badge of status and wealth.
(d)   Brand Identification.
(e)   Loyalty.

Consumers' levels of brand literacy correlated positively with social experiences, work, and life projects. The newly rich housewife had very low emotional investment in luxury brands, but used them to show off her husband's success. The passionate trendsetters wanted to show off their *savoir faire* about Western luxury, like the new rich. In addition, they also sought to express their personal tastes and identities by means of brands, but they were disappointed to say that they could find no connection with their brands. Finally, a small group of consumers who regularly travel outside of China, to Hong Kong, Japan, or the West, or worked in marketing, engaged with brands in ways very similar to consumers in the West.

Barriers to engagement

The majority of the respondents in this study were either "new rich" or "passionate trendsetters." Though passionate trendsetters are deeply motivated to find an emotional connection to their brands, and though many of them had obtained MBAs from prestigious schools in China, they do not move up the brand equity hierarchy much further than the new rich, who use luxury brands as badges and nothing more. Furthermore, the lack of emotional connection and identification with these brands resulted in their reducing all luxury brands to a few universal attributes, such as expensive, good quality or character, and high class. In other words, they failed to differentiate brands on the basis of their distinctive character-istics. Even when recall was aided by showing them several print ads for each brand, they came up with the same generic associations for them all. This lack of differentiation forms a barrier to brand loyalty and competitive strength in the marketplace, and presents a critical challenge for marketers in China.

To summarize, when exposed to advertisements for Western luxury brands, most respondents in Shanghai produced a limited repertoire of emotional associations with the advertisements, which led to their difficulty differentiating one brand from the other on the basis of qualitative values.

By contrast, consumers in the West are able to differentiate between brands and even articulate distinct cultural contexts for them. I demonstrate these findings with a brand audit exercise conducted in Paris in 2006.

Brand audit exercise: a semiotic analysis of luxury perfume ads

I exposed MBA students in Paris[1] to a similar exercise in order to initiate the class in the practice of semiotic analysis. The exercise involved sorting, classifying, and analyzing brand distinctions in a set of advertisements for luxury perfume. The exercise displays the complexity of the semiotic systems at work in advertising that contribute to brand distinc-tiveness, appeal, and cultural relevance, all of which contribute to the value of brands. It also demonstrates the parameters of the kinds of meanings that consumers, with some prodding, can identify in advertisements. Students in the class, whether they consumed luxury brands or not, were able rather quickly to enter into the analysis of the ads, highlighting a range of semiotic operations and levels of meaning that structure differences and similarities between major brands and contribute to consumer distinctions between brands as personalities.

The binary analysis

Luxury perfume advertisements are distinct from everyday brands inasmuch as they rein-force the fantasy of the woman set apart from the mundane details associated with shopping and saving money. A quick binary sort of the ads produced a binary set of images: one set included only black and white photography, the other stack only used color photography. The black and white ads employed metonymy to engage the spectator in the narrative depicted in the image – we see a part of a story and must fill in the details; the color ads employed metaphor to make comparisons between the perfume and the feminine icon in the image. Further analysis revealed a paradigmatic set of oppositions, beginning with rhetorical style and extending to the kinds of characters, their points of view in the image, the camera angles, and cultural cues.

Like works of art, luxury brands tap into the myths and icons of culture, and promise the consumer access to transcendent experiences such as beauty, limitless wealth, and immortal-ity. Since perfume itself is ephemeral and impermanent, the brand benefits of the luxury perfume category are entirely based on the delivery of intangible esthetic associations of the brands with idealized representations of women at personal, social, and existential levels of discourse. The strategic question, then, was how different luxury brands were positioned with reference to the question, "What is Woman?"

Students were exposed to two dozen print ads for luxury perfumes and were asked to sort them by their esthetic styles, their emotional tone, and the relationship they suggested for consumers. Students inevitably drew an initial distinction between ads that were executed in black and white photography from those executed in color. From there, they found that the black and white images all had couples or families in them in a realistic setting, whereas the photos in color showed women alone on an undefined background. From this initial binary, a paradigmatic series of oppositions were generated that extended to other cultural catego-ries such as esthetic style, social identity, and national culture. These binaries could be linked in turn to two distinct interpretations of feminine ideal. The black and white photos all leaned toward a more casual representation of women as "the girl next door," in everyday settings that resembled prose. The colored photos leaned toward a more formal representa-tion of Woman as Goddess in iconic representations that resembled poetry. These stylistic distinctions were evidence of deeper cultural differences between the two sets of ads, since without exception the ads in black and white represented American brands; the ads in color represented French brands.

Brand literacy and cognition

Though a longer summary of this exercise would draw attention to the broad and complex range of meanings communicated in the ads in this exercise, this cursory analysis reveals the cognitive processes involved in the interpretation, integration, and identification with brands. It highlights how, with some probing, consumers identify and differentiate the cultural cues that distinguish brands. It also forms the basis for understanding how consumers acquire preferences and emotional attachments to some brands rather than others.

This exercise also illustrates how reading brand identity is culture-specific. It also accounts for the limitations facing consumers in non-Western markets who try to enter into this semiotic game, missing the nuances and emotional meanings that define brand equity and identity. While French students could identify a range of semiotic dimensions and cultural cues in these European ads, whether or not they had personal experience with luxury brands, respondents in Shanghai displayed, for the most part, limited abilities to elaborate upon the distinctions among brands or the culture these brands represent. Such consumer responses are symptomatic of a deep divide between the culture of the target market and the culture of the brand, and threaten the perceived value of the brand for these consumers. Yet advertisers in the luxury sector have so far failed to recognize the need to address this cultural conflict.

Brand literacy in semiotic perspective

The very notion of brand literacy is grounded in the assumption that non-linguistic sign systems such as advertising are structured like language, by means of codes or conventions that are embedded in the culture of consumers. Structural semiotics, like linguistics, offers a rigorous, repeatable methodology for analyzing the codes underlying the structure of meaning and reference to the cultural context in discourses such as advertising and consumer behavior. Semiotic analysis brings forth objective criteria such as codes, rhetorical operations, and other formal dimensions of data. Semiotics has the advantage over content analysis by identifying structural systems, patterns, and rules that transcend the content of the message itself. These structural elements organize phenomena into meanings under the rubric of cultural categories such as gender, power, or identity. (See McCracken 1986 for a discussion of cultural categories.)

Structural semiotics transcends its origins in Russian Formalism (Lemon and Reis 1965) by moving beyond the simple formal analysis of texts and taking account of the implication of form and meaning in a given cultural context, such as the family meal. Though meals have a beginning, middle, and end, the meal preparation, the disposition of the family members around the table, and the foods brought to the table are inseparable from the cultural values, priorities, and traditions of the family.

The notion that discourses are structured both by the internal organization of signs and the external references to the context of the communication, originates with the linguistic theories of Swiss linguist, Ferdinand de Saussure (1983/1971/1913) in the nineteenth century. This notion has been refined and expanded over the years by experts in the areas of semantics and culture theory. These experts emphasize the importance not only of the structure of discourse but the reference of discourse to the context of the communication.

Brand literacy operates on at least two levels: the *structural* level associated with the literal, "dictionary meaning" of signs; and the *semantic* level associated with the relation between the dictionary meaning to the context of discourse. Writers such as Eco (1979), Greimas (1983/1966), and Benveniste (1971) extend structural semiotics by emphasizing that discourses are not only meaningful because of *structural* codes responsible for the coherence of the sign system itself, but also because of *semantic* codes that embed discourses in the context of the communication event. Irony is a good example of the importance of context. For example the utterance, "What a beautiful day!" taken at face value, signifies meanings one associates with good weather. When someone utters this same statement in order to remark on yet another cold and rainy day in Chicago, the meaning becomes an ironic comment on the bad weather. In other words, two distinct levels of semiotic organization – the internal structure of signs and the reference to a semantic context – drive meaning production.

The distinction between the meaning and reference of discourse, we shall see, has great importance for understanding the dynamics of brand literacy. Though I will elaborate in more detail on this dynamic further on, suffice it to say that consumers must be able not only to understand the meaning of brand signifiers (e.g. "this is an expensive brand") but also to relate them to the semantic context of the brand world, the product category, and their own lifestyles (e.g. "this brand reminds me of people who are fun, sexy, and free"). In the present study in China, the brand communication failed to elicit these kinds of associations with luxury brands, so consumers did not personalize, differentiate, or identify with one brand over another. They did not relate to the European culture of luxury in the ads, and could not fill in the brand world suggested by the images.

Brand literacy and language learning

Brand literacy affects various levels of brand semiotics, from the logo to the broad system of associations brands communicate over time. These levels include:

- *Denotation*, or the literal association of a signifier with a signified, the way logos stand for the company. The CC logo references the Coco Chanel brand.
- *Connotation*, the association of a signifier with an esthetic signified, such as the association of the logo with the brand's quality, positioning, and benefits for consumers. The sign /CC/ stands for exclusivity, high status, and classic beauty.
- *Symbolism*, the association of brand signifiers, from the logo to celebrity endorsers, with the brand culture and identity. The Chanel woman is classic, intelligent, assertive, and sophisticated.

As meaning production moves from the literal or denotative function to the symbolic function, the importance of the cultural context increases. The CC logo may be universally recognized, but consumers' responses to the Chanel brand would be dramatically different if they were living in austerity-prone China during the Cultural Revolution in the 1960s and 1970s.

By drawing upon structural semiotic theory, I propose that consumers learn the codes structuring brand meaning in a sequence that resembles language acquisition. Russian linguist and semiotician Roman Jakobson (1956/1990) discovered that language literacy occurred in stages and that not all people followed these stages in the same way. By studying the stages of language loss experienced by aphasics and comparing findings with the stages children pass through in language acquisition, Jakobson developed a binary schema for mapping the literacy process in terms of a double axis formed by associations by similarity (the paradigm or set of all possible replacements) and associations by contiguity (the syntagm or concatenation of all terms in a given message). These semiotic structures, in Jakobson's schema, parallel cognitive operations of substitution and alignment in the mind.

Jakobson also identified two distinct types of aphasia, distinguished by the relative emphasis on the ability to create associations by similarity and the ability to create associations by contiguity. He finds that one set of aphasics gradually loses the ability to combine signs on the basis of their similarity – they can define a word, for instance, but they cannot replace it with something like it, as in the paradigmatic association of a knife with similar tools using a blade. The other set of aphasics gradually loses the ability to combine signs on the basis of their contiguity – their logical or physical association with each other, as in the linear or syntagmatic association of the table knife with all other utensils in a serving set.

In typical Structuralist fashion, Jakobson extrapolates these findings about two types of aphasic disturbances to a general theory of "two aspects of language" that account for

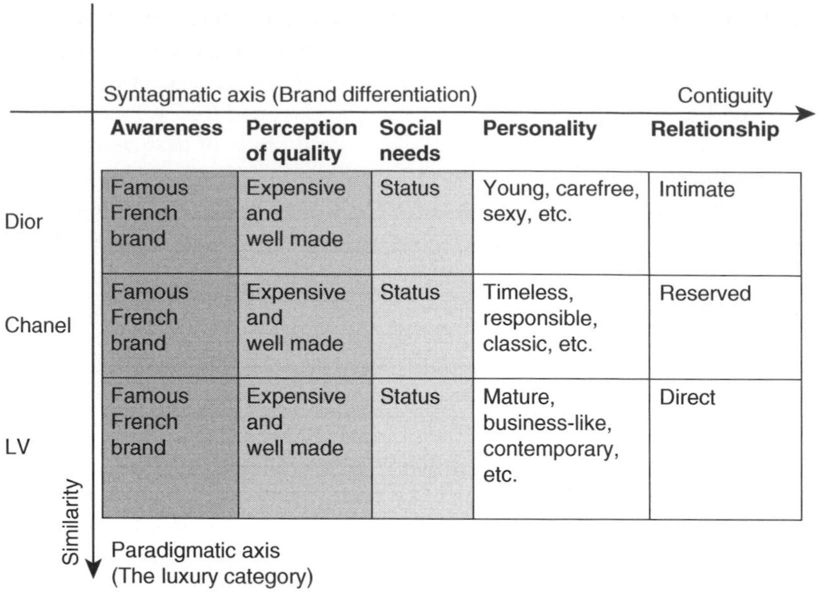

	Syntagmatic axis (Brand differentiation) Contiguity				
	Awareness	**Perception of quality**	**Social needs**	**Personality**	**Relationship**
Dior	Famous French brand	Expensive and well made	Status	Young, carefree, sexy, etc.	Intimate
Chanel	Famous French brand	Expensive and well made	Status	Timeless, responsible, classic, etc.	Reserved
LV	Famous French brand	Expensive and well made	Status	Mature, business-like, contemporary, etc.	Direct

Paradigmatic axis
(The luxury category)

Similarity

Figure 8.2 Two dimensions of brand discourse.
        Source: Photo credits: Laura Oswald.

non-linguistic forms of literacy associated with cultural systems other than language, such as prose and poetry. In Figure 8.2, I plot the two axes of meaning on a grid, then demonstrate how this can be applied to advertising research.

On the paradigmatic axis, moving top to bottom, I have listed a set of famous luxury brands – Dior, Chanel, and Louis Vuitton – that share qualitative attributes associated with the luxury category as a whole. These attributes include awareness of a famous French brand, perception of quality and high price, and status. These attributes contribute to the set of all qualities that French luxury brands have in common. On the syntagmatic axis, moving from left to right, the attributes of each brand become increasingly distinct. Research findings suggest that as consumer perceptions move *from* awareness of generic brand attributes such as price and status, *to* identification with the personality and relationship style of the brand, their ability to differentiate and develop preferences for one brand over another increases.

Implications for consumer research

Jakobson's schema has important implications for consumer learning and brand literacy because it enables the researcher to separate the paradigmatic set of attributes that define a product category from the unique associations on the syntagmatic axis that define the world of specific brands. The paradigmatic associations join brands together by similarity; the syntagmatic associations differentiate brands by means of a chain of signifiers that form the context. By mapping findings from the research in Shanghai on this grid, we observe that Chinese consumers readily recognize the set of brand attributes that all luxury brands share (the paradigmatic axis) but have greater difficulty recognizing differences among brands based on their contexts (the syntagmatic axis).

There are at least two conclusions that can be drawn from this finding. First of all, since the cultural context forms the distinct meanings, rituals, and personal identities that define the brand's positioning in the marketplace, the cultural incompatibility between the Western advertising and the culture of consumers limits Chinese consumers' interpretation of the brand world.

Second, it is possible that Chinese and Western consumers acquire semiotic codes in different ways. Future research may reveal that brand literacy, like language acquisition, follows two distinct paths, determined by culture – association by similarity and association by contiguity. It is possible that Chinese consumers initially lean toward associating brands along lines of similarity, while Western consumers may initially lean toward differentiating brands along the lines of contiguity. Managing brand meanings to account for these differences in learning styles may be critical for translating brands across borders.

Ultimately, language learners acquire skill in making both associations by similarity and contiguity in order to master language. However, language learning, like branding, does not develop in a vacuum, but is formed by means of the ongoing practice of associating meanings with the context of discourse. Continuing the analogy with language, in order to develop engaged, loyal consumers in China, marketers must understand the local culture and establish a brand world that is calibrated to the cultural context.

Implications for marketers

Findings from this study suggest that the strong growth in the luxury sector in China may obscure underlying tensions between the culture of consumers and the meaning of brands. In the first blush of affluence, consumers in developing markets such as China may purchase luxury brands regardless of their personal identification with particular brands. As emerging markets mature, affluent consumers demand more of their brands than simple ostentation and status. To grow long-term value and consumer loyalty over the long haul, marketers must focus on building brand literacy in these markets by innovative research and communication strategies.

The culture factor

Luxury manufacturers in the West rely on the double-digit growth in emerging markets such as China, but have rushed into this market without adapting the brand message to the culture of local consumers. The first generation new rich in China may have been content to show off famous, expensive brand names even if they did not engage with the brand on a visceral level. However, the current research suggests that second and third generations of affluent Chinese consumers will not be satisfied with the current, somewhat generic association of luxury brands with money and success seek brands that satisfy their needs for personal expression and relationship. In order to develop a more personal relationship to Western luxury brands, Chinese consumers must relate brand meanings to their culture and their unique identity projects.

The role of advertising

Management itself is responsible for creating barriers to consumer engagement with luxury brands, if not to the luxury category as a whole, by assuming that Chinese consumers already know the "rules of the road" relating to luxury goods, rituals, and culture in the West. The Western images used in advertising are structured by cultural as well as linguistic and esthetic codes, and these cultural codes interfere with the brand recognition and identification process. In similar fashion, reading Chinese would present problems for the untrained American tourist.

The present research identified several broad areas in which luxury advertising came into conflict with the cultural values of Chinese consumers:

- Western luxury advertising tends to focus on the individual model isolated from her lived environment. By contrast, Chinese consumers traditionally interpret the individual as a cell in a larger organism, subject to the forces of nature, fate, and the social group.
- Furthermore, Chinese consumers have a rather short history of branded market culture, so they cannot "connect the dots" between what the advertisement shows in the image and what it infers about the luxury context in the same manner as Western consumers.
- For the most part, luxury advertisements in Asia reproduce the one-page fashion shot that characterizes fashion advertisements in Europe, even reproducing the photographs, replacing the language with Chinese. Though consumers may be able to relate to the verbal text, they may not relate to the visual "language" structuring the meaning of woman, beauty, and luxury in the West.

The challenge for advertisers is to adapt brand communication to the culture of local consumers without losing the essence and meaning of the brand across markets (Sherry 1987; Cayla and Eckhardt 2008). Ogilvy & Mather took steps in this direction in the "Journey" campaign for Louis Vuitton luggage. They embedded the product in scenes, sometimes two pages across, that highlighted substantial, highly achieving personalities that included Mikhail Gorbachev, Madonna, and David Beckham. They replaced the single page ad featuring anonymous bodies on a black backdrop with texture, history, and high values. Whether the campaign was targeted specifically to the Chinese market or not, it in fact responded to Chinese consumers' need for context, notable characters and noble actions.

However, marketers may have to go a step further and replace the traditional magazine ad with a new creative strategy altogether, one that would include different forms of consumer contact and non-traditional media. In addition to celebrity endorsers (see Wicks *et al.* 2007), luxury marketers may have to abandon the assumption that luxury transcends time and culture (Wetlaufer 2001) and find ways of weaving their brands into the lifestyles and values of Chinese consumers. They need to move beyond the single image print ad and the iconic fashion model in order to initiate Chinese consumers into the luxury brand culture. They may also have to follow the lead of marketers in other categories, such as household appliances, where brand recognition has been built upon personal selling, shopping mall tutorials, trade shows, and other non-traditional media to educate consumers about a new category or brand.

Conclusion

Brands grow in value to the extent that consumers engage with brands at personal, visceral levels and grow in brand loyalty (Yankelovich1964; Aaker 1991; Fournier 1998). The brand literacy of consumers in emerging consumer markets has important economic implications, not only for particular companies but also for the global economy, since emerging markets are driving global economic growth. In this brief study I demonstrated the usefulness of marketing semiotics in building global brand strategy.

Furthermore, advertising forms the symbolic site for the intersection of cultures in contact and a medium for translating cultural meanings from one market to another. With the market opening in China in the 1980s, global advertising also has the potential to exceed its marketing function and serve as a moderator for consumer acculturation in developing consumer markets such as China. Moderating consumer acculturation has relevance not only to build successful brands in these markets, but also has the potential to build understanding and dialogue between nations.

The objection could be made that brand strategy built upon growing brand literacy in developing markets may be a form of indoctrination to Western culture. However, as we found in the present study, translating brands is a two-way, dialectical process moderated by the intersection of the marketing message and the perceptions of consumers (Zhang and Schmitt 2001). This research suggests that consumers in developing markets are not likely to be assimilated easily or completely into a monolithic global consumer culture, because they demand more relevant communication that matches their own cultural priorities and even filter brand messages through the lens of local values and ideology. The brand-literate consumer, in China or any other market, would not simply "assimilate" to the codes and values of Western brands, but would be able to manipulate these codes to express their personal tastes or "extend" their personas (Belk 1988). Ongoing research into the culture, poetics, and history of Chinese culture will open the way to create brand literacy in the luxury sector, improve long-term brand value for European luxury brands, and enhance cultural understanding between consumers in the global marketplace.

Review and discussion questions

1   What does Coco Chanel mean? How might the answer to this question differ in different cultures?
2   How can the concept of brand literacy be applied in targeting consumers in advertising?
3   Outline briefly some of the elements of Chinese culture referenced in the chapter. Why are these and other aspects of culture important in the Chinese luxury market?
4   You are a marketing manager for a luxury brand and in charge of entering the Chinese luxury market. How will you approach this task by means of semiotic methods?
5   Make a list of your favorite luxury brands. Compare and contrast the website of those brands in your home country with those of brands in an emerging country.

Keywords

advertising, affluent consumers, brand equity, brand literacy, China, global branding, luxury consumption, luxury, semiotics

Note

1 ESSEC Business School, Paris, France, 2005–6.

References

Aaker, David A. (1991) *Managing Brand Equity*, New York: Free Press.

Aaker, Jennifer (1997) "Dimensions of Brand Personality," *Journal of Marketing Research*, 34(3): 347–56.

Belk, Russell (1988) "Possessions and the Extended Self," *Journal of Consumer Research*, 15: 139–68.

Benveniste, Emile (1971/1966) *Problems in General Linguistics*, trans. Mary Elizabeth Meek, Coral Gables, FL: University of Miami Press

Cayla, Julien and Eckhardt, Giana M. (2008) "Asian Brands and the Shaping of a Transnational Imagined Community," *Journal of Consumer Research*, 35: 216–30.

de Saussure, Ferdinand (1983/1913) *Course in General Linguistics*, trans. R. Harris, London: G. Duckworth Publishers.

Eco, Umberto (1979) *Theory of Semiotics*. Bloomington, IN: Indiana University Press.

Eurostaf Report (2003) *La Fabrication des produits de luxe*, Vol. 1–2, Paris.

Foster, Stephen (2010) "Coke Still World's Biggest Brand as BP Drops out of Interbrand's Top 100." Available at: www.moreaboutadvertising.com /2010/09 (accessed September 16, 2010).

Fournier, Susan (1998) "Consumers and Their Brands: Developing Relationship Theory in Consumer Research," *Journal of Consumer Research*, 24: 343–73.

Goffman, Erving (1956) *The Presentation of Self in Everyday Life*, New York: Anchor Press.

Greimas, Algirdas Julien (1984/1966) *Structural Semantics: An Attempt at a Method*, trans. Ronald Schleifer, Daniele McDowell, and Alan Velie, Omaha: The University of Nebraska Press.

Jakobson, Roman (1956/1990) "Two Aspects of Language Two Types of Aphasic Disturbances," in Linda R. Waugh and Monique Monville-Burston (eds), *On Language*, Cambridge, MA: Harvard University Press, pp. 115–33.

Lemon, Lee T. and Reis, Marion J. (1965) *Russian Formalist Criticism: Four Essays*, Omaha, Nebraska: University of Nebraska Press.

McCracken, Grant (1986) "Culture and Consumption: A Theoretical Account of the Structure and Movement of the Cultural Meaning of Consumer Goods," *Journal of Consumer Research*, 13: 71–84.

Oswald, Laura (1999) "Culture Swapping: Consumption and the Ethnogenesis of Middle-Class Haitian Immigrants," *Journal of Consumer Research*, 25 (March).

Peñaloza, Lisa (1994) "Atravesando Fronteras/Border Crossings: A Critical Ethnographic Exploration of Consumer Acculturation of Mexican Immigrants," *The Journal of Consumer Research*, 21(1): 32–54.

Sherry, John (1987) "Advertising as a Cultural System," in J. Umiker-Sebeok (ed.), *Marketing and Semiotics*, New York: Mouton de Gruyter, pp. 441–61.

United States Department of Agriculture Reports (2006) *Historical Real Per Capita Income Values ; Projected Real GDP Values, Historical GDP Shares Value*. Available at: webadmin@ers.usda.gov. Updated December 26, 2006.

Wetlaufer, Suzy (2001) "The Perfect Paradox of Star Brands: An Interview with Bernard Arnault of LVMH," *Harvard Business Review*, October: 117–23.

Wicks, Gaya, Nairn, Agnes and Griffin, Christine (2007) "The Role of Consumption Culture in Children's Moral Development: The Case of David Beckham," *Consumption, Markets and Culture*, 10(4).

Yankelovich, Daniel (1964) "New Criteria for Market Segmentation," *Harvard Business Review*, March–April: 83–90.

Zhang, Zi and Schmitt, Bernt (2001) "Creating Local Brands in Multilingual International Markets," *Journal of Marketing Research*, August: 313–25.

Part II
Consumer, marketer identity, and community politics

9 The relational roles of brands

Jill Avery

Overview

In contemporary culture, brands play important relational roles, linking consumers to others and serving as relational partners. This chapter provides a cultural understanding of the relational roles of brands to illuminate why and how consumers connect with brands and how those connections enable consumers to relate to each other. Moving away from an economic conceptualization of marketing relationships as exchange-based, the chapter provides a more nuanced understanding of consumer–brand bonds and highlights the core processes that drive customer relationship development. It cautions managers not to try to manage their customer relationships, but rather, to negotiate them with consumers, providing a cultural approach to customer relationship management (CRM).

Relating to customers

Consumers engage in relationships with brands and with the firms that sell them. As a result of this, a key strategic initiative for firms is to establish and maintain strong, profitable relationships with their customers. Since the mid-1990s, firms have invested significant amounts of financial and managerial resources into developing sophisticated CRM systems and processes. These systems are designed to collect individualized information on each consumer, such as how much the customer buys, how frequently the customer buys, and what the customer buys, and disseminates it to all customer-facing personnel in the firm. This enables customer service representatives, salespeople, and other managers to enter into each customer encounter armed with a background of historical purchasing information about the customer's interactions with the firm so that they can personalize a relationship with a particular consumer.

Despite the vast resources spent on CRM over the past decade, many managers remain disappointed with the return that they are receiving from their CRM investment. Forty-five percent of firms who have executed large-scale CRM systems are dissatisfied and more than half of all CRM projects fail to achieve the economic and relational objectives firms had for them (Dignan 2002). Herb Hunt, chief technology officer for Siebel, one of the largest suppliers of CRM software, blames firms themselves for the failures, claiming that it is the lack of a customer relationship strategy that dooms CRM systems, rather than the lack of data or the technology to use it: "The big question is whether a company is implementing a technology or a strategy. For CRM to be a success, it is critical [that] customers have a strategy" (ibid.: 3). Firms have gathered reams of CRM data but still do not understand how to relate to their customers. Consumer researchers Susan Fournier, Susan Dobscha, and David Glen Mick claim that:

> Ironically, the very things that marketers are doing to build relationships with customers are often the things that are destroying those relationships. Why? Perhaps we are skimming over the fundamentals of relationship building in our rush to cash in on the potential rewards of creating close connections with our customers. Perhaps we do not understand what creating a relationship really means.
>
> (Fournier *et al.* 1998)

Although managers want to forge relationships with their customers, they remain puzzled how to do so, given that they have a largely economic, rather than cultural, understanding of their customers. This economic perspective causes most firms to view customers as assets to be managed, rather than as relationship partners with whom the company must negotiate. Most managers do not understand the types of relationships consumers form with brands, and/or the processes that drive customer relationship development. It is this cultural understanding which is necessary to develop customer relationship strategy and to implement activities that create, nurture, and grow relationships with consumers. Collecting data on your customers is the easy part; the hard part is figuring out what to do with it!

Relating to brands

Before we can determine how to best manage consumer–brand relationships, we must first step back and understand why it is that consumers form relationships with brands. This chapter is designed to provide an anthropological understanding of the relational roles of brands to illuminate how consumers connect with brands and how those connections enable consumers to relate to each other.

Why consumers form relationships with brands

To effectively steward consumer–brand relationships, we must first understand what brands mean to and do for their consumers. Consumers often buy products not for what they do, but to capture the meanings contained within them. The symbolic value of brands often outweighs the functional or utilitarian value to consumers (Levy 1959). In today's world, brands are cultural artifacts, tangible objects which contain and store more abstract cultural meaning (McCracken 1986). As such, brands play an important role in documenting culture and making it concrete by encapsulating our cultural ideologies, beliefs and values. As consumers form relationships with brands, they extract the meanings embedded within them and use them in their own lives (Fournier 1998).

Considering brands in this way illuminates the fact that customer relationship management (CRM) at its core involves meaning management. Consumers search for brands to relate to that will fill meaning voids in their lives; therefore, brands that experience strong consumer–brand relationships are those that consistently and reliably deliver meanings that are culturally resonant to consumers.

Relating to others through brands

The relationships consumers have with brands are embedded in the greater web of social relationships that entangle the consumer. This web includes relationships between consumers and other people in their lives and relationships between consumers and their fellow consumers of the brand. Our relationships with brands help us manage our social relationships with others because brands help us establish our social identities and because brands help us manage our loyalties to other people who are important to us.

Consumers use their relationships with brands to create their social identities, to fit in and stand out from others. Consumers choose brands that signify who they are or who they would like to be, and avoid brands that are "not me" (Kleine *et al*. 1995) or which are used by undesirable others (Berger and Heath 2007). Our relationships with brands help us express our personalities, statuses, lifestyles, social class, ideologies, and many other social identities. We can be whoever we want to be, merely by changing the brands with which we share relationships. As cultural studies author James Twitchell explains, many of our social identities are defined by the brand relationships that help us inhabit them: "Without soldiers, King Lear is no king. Without a BMW there can be no yuppie, without tattoos no adolescent rebel, without big hair no Southwestern glamour puss, without Volvos no academic intellectual" (1999).

Consumer researchers Avinash Malshe and Linda Price (2004) view brands as solutions that consumers use to solve relational problems that arise in their lives. Brands help their consumers service relationships with their family members, friends, colleagues, and acquaintances. When a mother brings home a cereal brand preferred by her children, she facilitates her relationship with them. When a husband stops at Best Buy to purchase a Nintendo Wii for his family, he facilitates his relationship with them. Malshe and Price remind us to always view consumers' devotion to brands in the context of their devotion to others. Brands are tools we use to build and maintain our relationships with others.

Brands as social glue

Brands function as social glue, bringing people together. Through our use of brands, we form bonds with others who share our preferences. In today's society, it is our consumption which connects us to others, as expressed by cultural anthropologist Daniel Boorstin:

> The modern American was tied if only by the thinnest of threads and by the most volatile, switchable loyalties to thousands of other Americans in nearly everything he ate or drank or drove or read or used ... Americans were increasingly held to others not by a few iron bonds, but by countless gossamer webs knitting together the trivia of their lives.

(1974)

Communities of consumers have formed around consumption items and brands (Muniz and O'Guinn 2001). In these communities, consumers come together to celebrate the brand during brandfests or major brand events like new store openings. For example, Saturn owners travel to the birthplace of Saturn to celebrate a Saturn "homecoming" and Apple devotees line up one day in advance to be the first ones to enter a new Apple store. Virtual brand communities are also flourishing with consumers congregating in online spaces to meet others who share their passion for a brand. Anti-brand communities have also emerged, drawing consumers who are opposed to a brand together and making it easier to organize brand boycotts and other consumer activism. Anti-brand communities for Starbucks and Nike actively work against the brand.

Thus, consumer–brand relationships are purposive: they provide meaning that consumers use to create and manage their identities, negotiate important relationships, and forge bonds with others who are like them. Relating to brands helps consumers relate to themselves and to others. The brands which best serve these purposes are the ones with which consumers will form strong relationships.

Types of consumer–brand relationships

What types of relationships do consumers form with their brands? Historically, marketers have viewed consumer–brand relationships as economic exchanges. According to psychologists Margaret Clark and Judson Mills, we typically have exchange relationships with strangers or mere acquaintances and the purpose of these types of relationship is often business. People in exchange relationships expect quid-pro-quo for everything they put into it, "members assume that benefits are given with the expectation of receiving a benefit in return" (Clark and Mills 1979: 12). In exchange relationships, consumers engage with a brand to receive something from the brand that is equal to or exceeds the consumer's investment in the relationship. Following neoclassical economic theory, consumers are viewed as rational, self-interested, economic beings who engage in relationships with brands purely to maximize the utility they receive from them.

However, consumer behavior in the marketplace tells quite a different story. Consumer anthropologists have documented relationships with a much different flavor; consumers of brands such as Harley-Davidson, Apple, Porsche, *Star Trek*, and Krispy Kreme donuts are much more passionate about their brands than the exchange relationship model predicts. The relationships these consumers have with their brands more closely resemble communal relationships we have with important people in our lives, like our family and our closest friends. In communal relationships, consumers are less self-interested and more interested in the brand as a relationship partner, demonstrating concern for the brand and its needs and for the continuation of the relationship (Aggarwal 2004). Communal consumer–brand relationships are sometimes described as marriages, in which the consumer loves the brand, is highly loyal and committed to it over time, and derives great psychological and social benefit from the relationship. Consumers with communal brand relationships usually demonstrate high levels of brand loyalty, a strong emotional attachment to the brand and frequent and/or exclusive purchase of it. Communal relationships represent nirvana to marketers, as these types of relationships are deemed most valuable to the firm; hence, the goal is to create communal customer relationships with as many of their customers as possible.

What are the factors that make up a strong consumer–brand relationship? Consumer researcher Susan Fournier developed a six-faceted Brand Relationship Quality scale (Fournier 1998) to measure the six factors which combine to make relationships strong and enduring. The six factors demonstrate that strong relationships between consumers and brands involve much more than traditional definitions of brand loyalty which focus on brand liking and brand purchase have allowed:

- *Love and passion*: Consumers feel a strong emotional attachment to the brand and feel anxious when the brand is not available to them.
- *Self-connection*: Consumers feel a strong connection between the brand and their personal identity. The brand represents an important aspect of the consumer's self.

- *Interdependence*: Consumers have a high level of interaction with the brand. Interactions are emotionally important to the consumer. The brand has become part of important rituals in the consumer's life.
- *Commitment*: Consumers feel and demonstrate commitment to the brand in the face of adversity. Consumers may also derogate competing brands.
- *Intimacy*: Consumers know a great deal about the brand or the brand firm. Brand knowledge is highly personalized and connected to the self.
- *Brand partner quality*: Consumers believe that the brand is a worthy relationship partner. Consumers believe the brand cares about them and that the brand will act in their best interest to protect their relationship. Consumers believe the brand is reliable, trustworthy, dependable, and predictable.

Strong consumer–brand relationships create brand fans, whose passion for the brand leads them to tattoo the brand on their skin or carve it into their hair, name their children after the brand, stand outside for days to be the first to acquire a new product from the brand, or launch brand fan clubs. YouTube is filled with videos made by avid brand fans. Songs written about brands by fans are on the web. Consumers' Facebook pages are dotted with the logos and widgets of their favorite brands.

Despite marketers' wishes, not all customers will become brand fans! Customers do not form strong, enduring bonds with all of the brands they use, just as they do not form strong personal bonds with every person they encounter in their lives. Consumer–brand relationships, just like human relationships, take many different forms, which are more or less valuable to the firm. Many more kinds of relationships exist between consumers and their brands beyond the exchange/communal distinction. After studying a myriad of relationships consumers have with their brands, consumer researcher Susan Fournier contends that consumer–brand relationships take many of the relational forms we see in human relationships, including friendships, flings, and marriages of convenience (ibid.). Fournier identified 15 different types of relationships which are summarized in Table 9.1.

These varied relational types indicate that consumer–brand relationships vary along many more dimensions than just weak versus strong. Consumers have positive relationships with brands, but they can also have negative relationships with brands. Consumer–brand relationships can be imposed upon consumers or entered into willingly. Consumer–brand relationships satisfy the functional needs of the consumer or their emotional needs. Consumer–brand relationships are intense or superficial and they exist for short durations or endure over time. Consumers can keep their brand relationships private or publicly acknowledge them to others.

The types of relationships differ across the six factors which define a strong relationship, indicating that some relational forms are stronger than others. For example, some relationships, such as committed partnerships and secret passions, involve love and passion and some, such as adversaries and enslavements, do not. Some relationships invoke a strong connection with the self, such as childhood friendships and kinships, while others, such as rebounds and arranged marriages, do not. In some types of relationships, such as best friendships and dependencies, consumers are highly interdependent on the brand, while in others, such as compartmentalized friendships or flings, the interdependence is minimal. Commitment is crucial to some relationships, such as best friendships and committed partnerships, but less important to others, such as flings and marriages of convenience. Some relationships include intimacy, such as best friendships, some, such as courtships, do not.

Table 9.1 Typology of consumer–brand relationship forms

Type of relationship	Example
Arranged marriages	I use Verizon for my cell phone service because my parents have a family plan that we are all on
Casual friends/buddies	I like Pepsi and drink it occasionally
Marriages of convenience	I shop at Stop-n-Shop because it is the closest supermarket to my house. I prefer Shaw's, but it is too far away
Committed partnerships	I love my Mac and would never think about using a PC
Best friendships	My MINI and I are so much alike. I know I can count on my MINI to be fun and reliable
Compartmentalized friendships	I have three different jean brands that I wear for different occasions. 7 is my brand for casual weekends, Diesel is my brand for going out to clubs, and True Religion is what I wear to school
Kinships	I use Tide detergent because that is what my mother used and the smell reminds me of her
Rebounds/avoidance-driven relationships	I wear Reeboks because I find Nike's labor practices to be morally reprehensible
Childhood friendships	On Halloween, I always buy Snickers because that was my favorite candy when I went trick-or-treating when I was young
Courtships	I bought a trial size of Herbal Essence shampoo to see if I like it
Dependencies	I can't live without my Starbucks latte
Flings	I drink Harpoon Winter Warmer beer during the holidays, but go back to my Sam Adams the rest of the year
Enmities	I won't use Crest because my ex-boyfriend used it
Secret affairs	I love to watch *Dancing with the Stars*, but I hide it from my friends because they will laugh at me
Enslavements	I have to purchase my Internet connection from Comcast because they are the only ones who offer high speed Internet in my area

Importantly, consumers have different types of relationships with different brands: a consumer who uses Crest toothpaste just because his wife likes it (arranged marriage) may use Dial soap because it reminds him of his father (kinship), and may have signed a short-term lease (fling) on a Volkswagen Beetle to regain his memories of driving around in one when he was a child (childhood friendship). He may be deeply committed to his iPhone and refuse to even consider another cell phone provider (committed partnership) and may feel like he cannot live without his nightly Oreo binge before bedtime (dependency).

Consumer researchers Linda Price and Eric Arnould argue that relationships between customers and firms are different from relationships between two people. They studied service providers and their clients and uncovered a unique relational type they labeled "commercial friendships." Although commercial friendships share many of the same attributes as human friendships, such as affection, intimacy, social support, loyalty, and gift giving, commercial friendships are constrained to the commercial setting in which they are enacted. Importantly, Price and Arnould find that customers who are engaged in commercial friendships with their service providers have high levels of satisfaction, loyalty, and generate positive word of mouth for their "friend" (Price and Arnould 1999). This work illustrates that managers should not blindly apply human relationship forms and practices to consumer–brand relationships, but rather, that they should strive to understand consumer–brand bonds as somewhat different from, but related to, the bonds between people. For example, in real life, we may be restricted by custom and by law to be married to just one person at a time; in brand life, we can be married to several brands simultaneously!

Managerial implications

Firms manage a portfolio of many different kinds of relationships with their customers. One of the first things managers must do is understand the type of relationships their brand has with its customers. Here are some ideas on how to get started:

- *Listen to your customers and how they talk about your brand.* Consumers in communal relationships will use more emotional and social language, while consumers in exchange relationships will use more rational language. What relational metaphors do customers use to describe how they feel about the brand and your firm? These metaphors can point the way to the type of relationship consumers experience; for example, a consumer who uses the terms "love," "loyalty," and "commitment" may be in a committed partnership, a consumer who uses the terms "addicted" or "obsessed" may be in a dependency relationship, while a consumer who uses the terms "hate," "disgusted by," or "enemy" may be in a relationship based on enmity.
- *Do not limit yourself to human relational forms.* Although you should leverage what you know about human relationships to try to make sense of what consumers are saying about your brand, do not try to categorize all of your customer relationships into a human equivalent. You may discover some relational forms that are unique to commercial settings. Consumer researcher Pankaj Aggarwal warns: "It is likely that the commercial context creates its own norms of behavior that lay on top of the social relationship norms that ultimately determine consumers' attitudes and behaviors" (2004: 99), reminding us that all consumer–brand relationships have an element of exchange at their core since they involve commercial transactions.
- *Remember that each consumer may have a different type of relationship with your brand.* Any customer portfolio contains multiple relationship types. Look for differences across customer segments and consider segmenting your customers by relational form (cf. Chapter 18 in this volume on segmentation and targeting). What are the commonalities that define customers who have a specific type of relationship with the brand, and how are these customers different from those who have other types of relational bonds with the brand?

Customer relationship management (CRM)

Why are relationships missing from CRM?

Unfortunately, the type of information that is collected by most CRM systems does little to inform firms about their customer relationships. Most CRM systems collect and calculate economic data on customers, such as the cost to acquire and retain them, their cross-selling potential, and their customer lifetime value to the firm. None of this data provides relational insight. Firms use this economic data to separate customers into economic tiers, depending on their level of profitability to the firm. The customer pyramid, developed by researchers Valarie Zeithaml, Roland Rust, and Katherine Lemon (Zeithaml *et al.* 2001), organizes customers into four profitability segments: lead, iron, gold, and platinum. Lead customers generate the least amount of profit for the firm; they tend to buy low-margin products or demand excessive customer service attention from the firm which makes the cost to serve them high. Platinum customers generate the most profit for the firm because they buy high-margin products, they buy frequently and in high quantities, and/or they have a lower cost-to-serve than other customers. The customer pyramid enables managers to identify those customers who provide value to the firm and to customize customer service and promotional offers to them to maximize profitability. For example, managers wring increased profitability from the customer base by mining CRM data to identify and to nurture "platinum" customers with extra services, customized products, and loyalty programs. These customers are offered opportunities to increase their economic spending with the firm through the cross-selling of other products and services the firm offers. The data is also used to weed out unprofitable "lead" customers, customers whose cost-to-serve exceeds their benefit to the firm.

By using the customer pyramid, firms believe that they are differentially managing their relationships with customers, providing the good ones with extra service and attention and reducing or eliminating contact with the bad ones. However, what the firm is doing in these instances has very little to do with relating to its customers. CRM, instead of enabling relationships between firms and customers, has become a database and a series of resource allocation practices that enable firms to treat their customers like other economic assets (Fournier and Avery 2011). Firms use their CRM data to increase their profitability by rationalizing service and marketing efforts towards customers who are most likely to deliver value to the firm and away from those who are too costly to serve. Increasingly, a practice that used to be used only in extreme cases is becoming a more common occurrence: firing your customer. Once unheard of in a world where "the customer is king," firing your customer is becoming standard business procedure: a recent survey of 900 consumers found that 30 percent of consumers claimed to know someone who has been fired by a firm. Table 9.2 recounts the stories of three fired customers. Ironically, these customers were originally identified and cultivated by the firm's CRM systems as "good" customers because of their frequent purchasing, and were rewarded by the firm with special discounts, upgrades, and events: Filene's Basement invited Norma to join its Insiders Club and Royal Caribbean recognized Brenda and Gerald as Platinum members before they were fired.

Rather than using CRM systems to segment and fire their customers, managers need to study the relational processes that lead to customer profitability issues and to take responsibility for the role the firm plays in the fabrication of a lead or a platinum customer (Fournier and Avery 2011). Relationships take two, so if a customer is in a less profitable relationship with a firm, both the consumer and the firm share the blame. Firms are in the dark as to how the actions they take positively and negatively affect customer relationships. Gains from customer resource allocation are a short-term way to wring profitability out of the firm's customer base; long-term gains will only come when managers truly understand the relational processes by which customers come to be in the lowest tiers (or highest tiers) of profitability in the customer pyramid. The first step towards greater understanding comes from envisioning your brand as a relational partner.

Table 9.2 Firing your customer

Inside a customer relationship	Norma considered herself a "best customer" of Filene's Basement, a retail chain selling designer labels at discounted prices. Norma was a long-time customer of the store, spending tens of thousands of dollars over 30 years. She brought hundreds of friends to the store and did special favors for the store employees whom she viewed as her personal friends, providing them with merchandising and selling advice. These friends often bent the rules for Norma, acknowledging her as one of the "The Regulars," a group of women well-known because of their frequent shopping activity and first-in-line position for new store openings and special events. Norma was invited to join the Insiders Club, a group created to reward the store's "best customers" with invitations to special events.	Brenda and Gerald were frequent customers of Royal Caribbean Cruise Lines and Diamond level members. The couple had enjoyed over 20 cruises with the company. After experiencing customer service problems ranging from being locked out of their stateroom due to a faulty door latch to dealing with overflowing sewage in their stateroom, Brenda and Gerald complained to Royal Caribbean, who apologized and offered them cash refunds and discounted fares for future cruises.	Michael shopped frequently at Home Depot. As a carpenter, the store supplied many of the materials he needed to do his job. After buying over $100 worth of lumber for a project he was working on, Michael absent-mindedly walked away from the checkout counter with the clerk's pencil in his hand.
The firing of a customer	After asking a manager to extend a sales price on a set of flatware, Norma was fired by Filene's Basement for excessive returns and excessive complaints. She was warned never to enter a Filene's Basement store again.	Brenda and Gerald were fired by Royal Caribbean after posting information about their customer service issues on an online forum. Royal Caribbean asked the couple to remove their negative posts, and when they refused, the company banned them from their cruise lines for life.	Michael was banned from shopping at any Home Depot store after an employee stopped him outside the door to the store and accused him of shoplifting the pencil. He was escorted out of the store by four employees.
The customer's response	After being screamed at by the store manager, Norma received a call from headquarters. She recounts her memory of the phone call: "I honestly thought they were going to send me flowers! And then this gruff voice says, 'You are never to call Filene's Basement again, you are never to set foot in any of our stores again,' I was so flabbergasted. I honestly don't think they knew how much I spent. I honestly don't think they knew I was such a good customer" (Avery and Fournier 2011).	Fighting back tears, Brenda says, "I'm just trying to help people out and this is what this bunch does to me. I'm not interested in cruising with them at all" (Anon 2008).	Although Home Depot later apologized to Michael and invited him to return as a customer, Michael claims, "I have no intention of going back in there. Why should I put money in someone's pocket when they treat me like this?" (Samuels 2005).

Brands as relational partners

In human relationships, we interact with a human partner; in brand relationships, we interact with an inanimate object. Consumers transform brands into enlivened relational partners through a process of anthropomorphism, by attributing human characteristics, traits, motivations, and behaviors to brands to animate and humanize them. Consumers can easily describe the brand personality, the human traits consumers associate with the brand such as gender, age, lifestyle, and interests, of their favorite brands. Consumer researcher Jennifer Aaker shows that brands can be perceived by consumers as sincere, exciting, competent, sophisticated, and/or rugged (Aaker 1997). Each different brand personality lends itself to the development of a different kind of relationship with its consumers, for example, exciting brands are ripe for flings, while sincere brands are more appropriate for friendships and committed partnerships.

Marketers help shape the brand personality of their brands through advertising imagery, product design, retail environments, and customer service. Brand management involves paying attention to every detail pertaining to the brand to make sure that, through all of your actions, you are developing a relational partner persona that is working to create the type of relationship you want with your customers. Once your brand has developed a relational persona, you are ready to begin the process of negotiating your consumer–brand relationships. The next section dives into the processes that drive the creation, growth, deepening, and failure of consumer–brand relationships.

The rules of consumer–brand relationships

In an ethnographic study of consumer–brand relationships and their trajectories over time (cf. Chapter 15 in this volume on ethnographic methods), consumer researchers Susan Fournier, Jill Avery, and Andrea Wojnicki found that each type of consumer–brand relationship has its own unique set of rules which guide consumers' actions and expectations within the relationship – telling the consumer how to behave during interactions with the firm and, also, what behavior to expect from the firm (Fournier *et al.* 2009). Rules govern all aspects of the consumer–brand relationship. Interaction rules govern how the firm and consumer will interact with one another. Reward rules arbitrate what the consumer and the brand will give to and get from the relationship. Relational rules govern the development of intimacy, trust, and commitment. A summary of the various types of relational rules found in consumer–brand relationships is contained in Table 9.3. All types of relationships come with rules, so brands are bound by the rules associated with the type of consumer–brand relationships their consumers believe they have.

Many of the rules that govern person-to-person relationships transfer to consumer–brand relationships. The type of relationship consumers have with a brand affects their expectations of the rules governing the brand and therefore, shapes their satisfaction with the brand and attitude towards it. For example, one of the rules of communal relationships is that the two parties freely give and receive help from each other. The exchange of money tends to complicate communal human relationships. What is the role of money in consumer–brand relationships? Consumer researcher Pankaj Aggarwal (2004) shows that consumers in communal relationships with brands are angry when a brand charges them an incremental fee for helping them resolve a service issue, while consumers in exchange relationships do not care as much. Why? Aggarwal explains: "People in an exchange relationship expect to receive

Table 9.3 The rules of consumer–brand relationships

Rule type	Rule categories	Rules that govern
Reward rules	Give and get rules	How rewards will be transmitted from one to other How satisfaction is measured The level and degree of investment of each party
	Help and support rules	Legitimacy of requests for help Expected sacrifices
	Reciprocity rules	Emotional/financial support Repayment of debt Equity and distributive justice
Interaction maintenance rules	Boundary rules	Degree of independent functioning Amount of shared activity Interaction domains and spheres
	Regard and respect rules	Critical expressions of the other Acceptance of the other "as they are" Privacy and secrets
	Communication rules	How parties will contact each other Listening
	Power and control rules	Allowable influence Controls in decision-making Mutual influence vs. compliance
	Conflict rules	Accommodation/flexibility Acquiescence Transgression tolerance
Relational rules	Intimacy rules	Information sharing Authentic self-presentation Mastery of intimate details Actions celebrating specialness of partner
	Trust rules	Basis for trust Reliability, dependability, being counted on Willingness to assume risk for the other
	Commitment rules	Respects plans/promises Barriers to exit encouraged Solidarity

monetary payments for providing help … Conversely, people in a communal relationship do not expect monetary payment for helping their partner" (ibid.: 89).

Understanding the role of money in relationships can help firms shape their loyalty programs to offer rewards that are consonant with the type of relationships consumers share with the firm. For example, customers in exchange relationships may value rebates, discounts, or coupons, while customers in communal relationships may prefer status designations with which the firm recognizes them as distinctive from other consumers.

In an experiment, consumer researchers Jennifer Aaker, Susan Fournier and Adam Brasel created an online photography processing service where consumers could send their disposable cameras in for photo processing (Aaker *et al.* 2004). The researchers randomly assigned consumers to two groups and exposed each group to the same photography processing service, but with two different fictional brand personalities: the first group interacted with a brand that consumers found "sincere" and the second group interacted with a brand that consumers found "exciting." The researchers then let relationships develop between consumers and the brands. Consumers with sincere brand partners developed stronger relationships with their brand which increased in intensity over time and which resembled friendships. Consumers with exciting brand partners developed weaker relationships with their brand which decreased in intensity over time and which resembled flings. Then, after six weeks, the photography processing service told consumers that it had accidentally lost their photographs. Interestingly, consumers with sincere brand partners were significantly more upset at this transgression than consumers with exciting brand partners and their relationships suffered accordingly. Consumers with exciting brand partners were initially less upset and the transgression acted to positively intensify their relationship with the brand. The type of relationship (and its associated rules) the consumers had with the brand determined whether losing their photographs weakened or strengthened their relationship.

As these studies show, the type of relationship a consumer has with a brand affects how he or she responds to the brand's actions. On the one hand, a strong, highly committed relationship can elicit relationship-saving biases that protect the relationship from brand transgressions, allowing it to endure. On the other hand, a strong relationship creates expectations for the brand's behavior. These expectations are shattered when the brand commits a transgression, creating emotional distress for the consumer and reducing her commitment to the brand. These two forces work against one another to shape the consumer's response – one force pushing the consumer closer to the brand and the other pulling the consumer away from the brand relationship.

Understanding the rules guiding each of the firm's customer relationships is critical for managers of the brand because the rules indicate what the brand can and cannot do. The rules governing a consumer–brand relationship help determine the potential profitability of the relationship for the firm. By understanding what the firm is relationally obligated and forbidden to do, managers can better match their marketing efforts to consumer expectations and desires.

Negotiating consumer–brand relationships

Relationships are negotiated between two parties and not managed by one. Hence, CRM is a misnomer: firms need to *negotiate* their relationships with customers, not *manage* them (Fournier *et al.* 2009). But negotiating any kind of relationship is not easy, as those of us who struggle to maintain good relationships with our siblings, our parents, and our friends can attest. Just like human relationships, consumer–brand relationships follow an evolutionary path which is forged by each and every interaction between the consumer and the brand. When negotiating a relationship, everything matters.

Consumer–brand relationships are dynamic and constantly changing. Consumer researchers Susan Fournier, Jill Avery, and Andrea Wojnicki found that consumer–brand relationships progress through four distinct phases in which the relationship is explored, initiated, negotiated, and renegotiated over time (Fournier *et al.* 2009).

Phase 1 *Relationship exploration.* During the relationship exploration phase, consumers are exploring a potential relationship with the firm. Within initial interactions, simple rules emerge to guide the exchange of benefits between the two parties. As interactions between the consumer and the firm increase, more rules develop to maintain an efficient and effective working relationship. All of the firm's behaviors in this stage are intensely scrutinized by the consumer, as the consumer makes inferences about the rules of the relationship based on the way the firm acts. Finally, as interactions over time develop into a burgeoning relationship between the consumer and the firm, more sophisticated rules governing intimacy, trust, and commitment emerge. The emergence of these types of rules is an important inflection point in consumer–brand relationships, in that they signal the beginning of a more communal relationship, rather than just a series of exchange interactions.

Phase 2 *Relationship expansion.* During the expansion phase, consumers label their relationship with the brand as a way of understanding it. The rules that have developed between the consumer and firm become pieces of a puzzle, which when assembled, form a picture of a certain type of relationship. Once consumers figure out what kind of relationship they have with the firm, they transfer rules from that type of human relationship to the consumer–brand relationship. Thus, if consumers believe they are in a "friendship" with a brand, they will expect the brand to adhere to the rules of human friendship, which include being supportive, being able to ask for and receive help from each other, and showing positive regard for each other.

Phase 3 *Relationship commitment.* The transition from the relationship expansion phase to the relationship commitment phase involves the willful performance by the consumer of behaviors that go beyond what is required in the negotiated relationship. For example, consumers may spread positive word-of-mouth about the brand or actively work to recruit customers to it. Consumers may try to help the brand by sending in suggestions to help the firm develop new products or refine existing ones. Consumers may resist competitive sales pitches and switch all of their business to the brand. These extra-role actions provide no direct rewards to the consumer, yet are usually executed with expectations of reciprocation by the firm. This is a signal of the consumer's desire to change the relationship to one with deeper requirements and entanglements. When a firm recognizes this behavior and reciprocates with its own extra-role actions, such as giving the consumer special recognition or incremental rewards like discounts or access to customized products, the firm sets the scene for a virtuous cycle of increasing loyalty and a deepening relationship. However, when a firm neglects to reciprocate a consumer's behaviors, the relationship reverts back to its less committed level.

Phase 4 *Relationship disengagement.* In this final evolutionary phase, relationships either terminate, roll back to a less committed state, or settle into a static state. Relational interrupts, both positive and negative, bring the relationship between the consumer and the brand into focus, causing the consumer to stop and evaluate the state of the relationship. These pivotal events are a motivating force for relationship redefinition. One type of relational interrupt is a breach of the rules of the relationship. A breach usually forces relationship disengagement or dissolution. Breaches include basic rule violations or more severe violations which indicate that the firm does not uphold the same definition of the relationship that the consumer does.

Managerial implications

Understanding relationships as process phenomena enables managers to take a longitudinal and evolutionary approach to negotiating their customer relationships. Rather than segmenting customers by their current profitability to the firm, a static measure, managers who understand consumer–brand relationships can segment their customers based upon the type of relationship that has evolved, and then execute CRM programs that recognize and maximize the value of those relationships. Once managers realize that relationships are not static, they can begin to put plans in place to move customers up to more profitable types of relationships. Here is how this can work:

- *Rework your CRM systems to collect relational data* in addition to economic data about customers. What rules are at play in your relationship with a customer? Market research studies such as focus groups and depth interviews can be used to uncover the relational rules in play. Tracking customer complaints can also shed light into what customers expect from the firm. Clusters of rules can help identify the type of relationship you have with a customer. What actions by the firm and by the customer have led to these rules? This allows the firm to better understand how its actions affect the trajectory of its customer relationships.
- *Identify most profitable relationship types* and then work to implement customer management programs that help create these types of relationships with new customers. Surprisingly, the most profitable relationship types are not always "committed partnerships." Why? Committed partnerships come with lots of complex rules to which the firm must adhere, which may drive down profitability. For many firms, best friendships are more profitable than committed partnerships.
- *Understand where you are in the relational cycle* with each customer and act accordingly. Firms have the most influence on how a relationship develops in the relationship exploration phase. Make sure that you interact with new customers in ways that reflect the relational rules you want established. Do not make exceptions to rules that are important to you in this early stage. Negotiations get tougher as rules become established and taken for granted by the consumer. As your relationship with a customer progresses, watch for examples of supra-contracting which can indicate that the relationship has entered the relationship commitment phase, and if the relationship is important and profitable to the firm, reciprocate with some extra effort on the firm's part to push the relationship into a more committed state.
- *Take care of your profitable relationships.* Nurture your most valuable customers by adhering to the rules underlying the most profitable types of relationships in order to avoid relationship transgressions which may lead to relationship dissolution. Once managers know which relationships are most profitable, they can dissect them to understand the rules at play.
- *Negotiate new terms for your unprofitable relationships.* Actively negotiate new relationship rules with consumers in less profitable relationships to change the rules to be more beneficial to the firm. Rather than firing these customers, renegotiate the terms of the relationship to obtain better terms for the firm.

In this way, firms can transform the customer pyramid from an economic tool to a relational tool, focused on identifying the processes by which the firm can move all customers up towards higher levels of profitability by negotiating better relationships with them.

Conclusion

To effectively steward brands, we must first understand what brands mean and do for their consumers. In contemporary culture, brands play important relational roles, linking us to ourselves and to others, and serving as relational partners. Moving away from an economic definition of marketing relationships as exchange-based, this chapter provided a more nuanced cultural understanding of consumer–brand bonds which is summarized in Table 9.4.

Highlighting the core processes and social rules that drive relationship development, the chapter shows that consumer–brand relationships are jointly created, negotiated, and lived by consumers and by the firms that own their brands. The relationships that are formed are multifaceted, reciprocating, dynamic, and evolutionary, making customer relationship management a culturally embedded, complex, and ongoing task for marketers.

Review and discussion questions

1   Why do consumers pursue relationships with brands?
2   What types of relationships do consumers have with their brands? How are these types of relationships similar to and different from human relationships?
3   What factors define a strong consumer–brand relationship?
4   What are some of the rules governing consumer–brand relationships?
5   What are the stages through which consumer–brand relationships progress?

Table 9.4 Adding a cultural perspective to customer relationship management

Traditional approach to CRM	Adding a cultural perspective
Consumers buy brands for what they do	Consumers buy brands for what they do and for what they mean
Consumers connect with brands for utilitarian purposes	Consumers connect with brands for utilitarian purposes and for relational purposes: to create and manage their identities, to negotiate important relationships, and to forge bonds with others like them
Consumer–brand relationships are exchange relationships	Consumer–brand relationships can be either exchange relationships or communal relationships
There are only two types of consumer–brand relationships: exchange relationships and deeply committed partnerships	There are a myriad of consumer–brand relationship types, including friendships, flings, enmities, secret affairs, and others
Consumer–brand relationships are built by the firm via customer relationship management programs	Customer–brand relationships are jointly determined by firms and their customers in everyday interactions
Firms can *manage* their customer relationships	Firms must *negotiate* their customer relationships with consumers
Economic data, including acquisition costs, retention costs, purchasing history, and customer lifetime value, indicate the health of a customer relationship	Relational data, including love and passion, self-connection, interdependence, commitment, intimacy, and brand partner quality, indicate the health of a customer relationship

6   Why must customer relationships be negotiated rather than managed by the firm? Think about the brands with which you have relationships. How would you characterize them by relationship type? What are the major rules that define each of your types? What happens when your brands break these rules? What happens when you do?

7   What types of customer–brand relationships are the most valuable to firms? Why? What do firms have to do to build, nurture, and maintain these types of relationships?

8   Evaluate the prevalent practice of firing your customers. How does a cultural understanding of consumer–brand relationships inform this practice? Should firms fire their customers? Why or why not?

Keywords

brand relationship quality scale, brands as relational partners, communal relationship, consumer–brand relationship, customer pyramid, customer relationship management, exchange relationship, firing your customer, interaction maintenance rules, relational rules, reward rules

References

Aaker, J., Fournier, S. and Brasel, S. A. (2004) "When Good Brands Do Bad," *Journal of Consumer Research*, 31(1): 1–16.

Aaker, J. L. (1997) "Dimensions of Brand Personality," *Journal of Marketing Research*, 34(3): 347–56.

Aggarwal, P. (2004) "The Effects of Brand Relationship Norms on Consumer Attitudes and Behavior," *Journal of Consumer Research*, 31(1): 87–101.

Anon (2008) "Banned from Royal Caribbean for Complaining Too Much," *Expert Cruiser.com*. May 19, 2008. Available at: http://www.expertcruiser.com/advice/royal-caribbean-says-get-out-of-here-to-couple.

Avery, J. and Fournier, S. (2011) "Firing Your Best Customer," in M. Fetscherin, S. Fournier, M. Breazeale and T. C. Melewar (eds), *Consumer–Brand Relationships: Theories and Applications*. London: Routledge.

Berger, J. and Heath, C. (2007) "Where Consumers Diverge from Others: Identity Signaling and Product Domains," *Journal of Consumer Research*, 34(2): 269–79.

Boorstin, D. (1974) *The Americans: The Democratic Experience*, New York: Vintage Books.

Clark, M. S. and Mills, J. (1979) "Interpersonal Attraction in Exchange and Communal Relationships," *Journal of Personality and Social Psychology*, 37(1): 12–24.

Dignan, L. (2002) "CRM: Dream or Nightmare," *ZDNet News*, April 3, 2002.

Fournier, S. (1998) "Consumers and their Brands: Developing Relationship Theory in Consumer Research," *Journal of Consumer Research*, 24(4): 343–73.

Fournier, S. and Avery, J. (2011) "Putting the 'Relationship' Back into CRM," *MIT Sloan Management Review*, 52 (3): Spring 2011, pp 63–72.

Fournier, S., Avery, J. and Wojnicki, A. (2009) "Toward a Dynamic Theory of Consumer–Brand Relationships: Content and Process from a Relationship Contracting Perspective," Working Paper.

Fournier, S., Dobscha, S. and Mick, D. G. (1998) "Preventing the Premature Death of Relationship Marketing," *Harvard Business Review*, 76(1): 42–51.

Kleine, S. S., Kleine, R. E. and Allen, C. T. (1995) "How Is a Possession 'Me' or 'Not Me'? Characterizing Types and an Antecedent of Material Possession Attachment," *Journal of Consumer Research*, 22(December): 327–43.

Levy, S. J. (1959) "Symbols for Sale," *Harvard Business Review*, 37(4): 117–24.

Malshe, A. and Price, L. (2004) "Embedded Loyalties: A Customer Centric View," in *Proceedings from the ACR North American Conference*, Portland, OR.

McCracken, G. (1986) "Culture and Consumption: A Theoretical Account of the Structure and Movement of the Cultural Meaning of Consumer Goods," *Journal of Consumer Research*, 12: 71–84.

Muniz, A. and O'Guinn, T. C. (2001) "Brand Community," *Journal of Consumer Research*, 27: 412–32.

Price, L. L. and Arnould, E. J. (1999) "Commercial Friendships: Service Provider–Client Relationships in Context," *Journal of Marketing*, 63(4): 38–56.

Samuels, A. P. (2005) "A Sharp Apology in Store Pencil Case," *The Boston Globe*, November 21, B2.

Twitchell, J. (1999) "Two Cheers for Materialism," *Wilson Quarterly*, 23(2): 16.

Zeithaml, V.A., Rust, R. T. and Lemon, K. N. (2001) "The Customer Pyramid: Creating and Serving Profitable Customers," *California Management Review*, 43(4): 118–42.

10 Experiencing consumption

Appropriating and marketing experiences

Antonella Carù and Bernard Cova

Overview

This chapter analyzes the different marketing approaches used by companies to manage consumption experiences. Ever since the seminal article by Holbrook and Hirschman on the subject (1982), consumer research has considered experience to be central to today's consumers, looking for meanings to associate with in their lives (Holbrook 2000). Here, the consumption experience is understood as the set of phenomena whereby a consumer comes into contact with a product, service, brand, event or place, and this generally occurs in the company of others who may or may not also be consumers. The cultural approach has led to an in-depth understanding of the consumption experience (Arnould and Price 1993; Firat and Dholakia 1998) that is in contrast to the better-known models in the areas of experiential marketing (Schmitt 1999) and the experience economy (Pine and Gilmore 1999). The aim of this chapter is to illuminate the contributions of different approaches to experience management in order to support managers in their everyday activities.

The chapter begins with an overview of the prevailing experiential marketing models that seek to generate extraordinary and unforgettable consumer experiences through the creation of thematized, secure, enclave environments that emphasize sensory stimulation (Pine and Gilmore 1999; Schmitt 1999; Hetzel 2002). Creating experiential contexts generally means generating a set of stimuli (product, environment, activity) that allow access to the experience: not only points of sales (cf. Chapter 25 in this volume) but also, for example, brand plants, events and websites.

Adopting a cultural approach, the chapter then raises questions about the limitations of focusing on models of emotional induction which tend to overestimate the influence of sensory factors on consumer experiences. These approaches represent just one of the ways of examining the topic of consumer experiences because these experiences occur in people's daily lives and cannot simply be considered exceptional events. Moreover, they occur in a variety of contexts that are not exclusive to the market, and are produced not just by companies, but also by the consumers themselves. Finally, access to experience is not instantaneous, but instead requires a process of progressive appropriation.

The chapter identifies ways in which companies can develop marketing approaches capable of supporting the appropriation of experiences by the consumer. Specifically, the chapter offers tools and methods by which marketers can support the consumer in the appropriation process: (1) support systems, including guides and referents; (2) collective actions involving communities and rituals; and (3) self-determination, including training and autonomy, eliciting autonomous participation.

The prevailing managerial approaches to experiencing consumption

At the beginning of the 1990s, Arnould and Price (1993) showed that a sporting activity such as river rafting provides absorption and integration, personal control, joy and valuing, a spontaneous letting-be of the process, and a newness of perception. Such an activity involves consumers in an unforgettable process, transforming them through experiences in which they are immersed. It is clear why this study has inspired so many scholars working on experience in marketing – scholars who, as they have gone along, have tended to replace the concept of "experience" with that of "extraordinary experience", as every experience ought to be memorable. Indeed, there is a shared belief among marketing experts that consumers are simply not what the rational model of marketing wants them to be; emotion is often cited as the heart of the consumption experience. Thus, for experiential marketing, a good experience is "memorable" (Pine and Gilmore 1999) and exploits all of the senses (Schmitt 1999). This type of experience produces emotions and also supports the consumer's self-image. Offering experiences can be a solution to the commodity trap for any kind of business, including pure retailing where the aim is to build up a set of strategies that offer the consumer physical and emotional sensations during the shopping experience. For marketing (Schmitt 1999; Hetzel 2002) and economy (Pine and Gilmore 1999), an experience is an offering that is in addition to merchandise (or commodities), products, and services – a fourth type of offering that is particularly suited to the needs of the contemporary consumer.

The achievement of these experiences has been the main area of discussion for various authors (Pine and Gilmore 1999; Schmitt 1999, 2003; Hetzel 2002), who have developed different experiential marketing approaches. According to Pine and Gilmore (1999), staging is at the core of the creation of experiences, just as production and supply are central to goods and services production, respectively. They identify specific actions for the staging of experiences. The first is the preparation of the stage, which varies according to the area to which the experience belongs (entertainment, education, escapism, and aesthetic experience) and to the different opportunities offered by each area. Once the stage is set, the experience is turned into a show by giving it a specific theme. For this purpose, they identify a list of possible functional themes. Again, it is necessary to personalize the experience, to search for a sole value for customers that is based on the ability to surprise them, as emphasized by Hetzel (2002). In this experience-creation process, the metaphor evoked is that of theatre, which, in its various forms, represents the model. In his first book, Schmitt (1999) establishes that the goal of experience creation is to induce specific customer behaviours and reactions. Thus, customer experience management (CEM) (Schmitt 2003) is the process of strategically managing a customer's entire experience of a product or a company. Common among these experiential approaches is the concept of entertainment (Wolf 1999), which encapsulates show, theatre, intrigue, etc. This is particularly evident in the case of experiential shopping, during which the purchase of products is accompanied by opportunities for entertainment or "hedonistic experiences" (Hetzel 2002).

Experience is, however, a subjective process, and thus firms cannot offer experiences but rather experiential platforms or contexts. Indeed, even though the "experience economy" school asserts (Pine and Gilmore 1999) that firms offer experiences, firms actually only offer devices and stimuli that consumers mobilize to realize their own experiences. There are three qualities that constitute the underlying foundations of the experiential context (Figure 10.1):

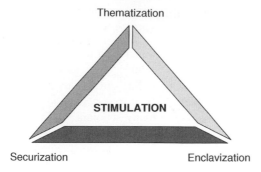

Thematization

STIMULATION

Securization   Enclavization

Figure 10.1 The three qualities of an experiential context.

- The experience must be enclavized within specific boundaries, allowing consumers to break with (and step outside of) their daily lives, bringing them into a separate world of entertainment where all of the usual worries and hardships that they face in their ordinary lives disappear.
- The context must be secure and closely monitored in order to eliminate the need to pay attention to oneself, to one's children or possessions, or any other concerns that people have in their daily lives. Consumers would rather not have to deal with hard realities, preferring environments and activities that are more watered-down and controlled, and in which risks are minimized.
- The context must be thematized. This acts as a sort of symbolic packaging of the context, notably by ascribing meaning to the act of consumption. A theme can be an activity, era, region, population, or any combination of these elements, and must be very distinctive.

The company must then work to enunciate and materialize the theme. This involves creating theatre effects and *staging* the company's product or service offering, effectively putting the consumer *on stage* through careful attention to décor, environmental design and store atmospherics (ibid.). These efforts revolve around sensory and imaginary devices that serve to stimulate consumers' senses and imagination, thereby fostering entertainment:

- The stimulation of the senses is achieved through a multisensory layering of visual, auditory, olfactory, gustatory, and kinaesthetic stimuli (Schmitt 1999).
- The stimulation of imagination involves a constantly renewed introduction of narratives, stories, images, and intrigue – all part of a playful approach known in retail circles as "shoptainment".

In many well-known cases of experiential marketing, including Rainforest Café, Starbucks, Sephora, Club Med, and Diesel, the theme is the brand. Thus, the creation and management of brand experience contexts have become one of brand management's main activities. When a firm or brand only delivers products and not services, it is advisable that it creates its own premises (theatres of consumption) so that the consumer can experience its products without the intrusion of any competing influences. This is what happens in Nike Towns or in other concept or flagship stores such as those of Adidas, Armani and Ferrari. Of course, consumers can experience a brand outside of such contexts (for example, at home using the brand's products), but for the company, the key experiential contexts are the ones that will allow it to closely manage not only the experience but also the processes by which people access the experience. Four major types of brand experience contexts have been identified:

1   *Brand stores*, such as Apple Store, Nike Town and Audi Forum, which lead to highly "branded" shopping experiences. These are likely to echo Pine and Gilmore's injunctions (1999) concerning the need to promote shopping experiences that are increasingly fun and which can be assimilated with the types of experiences people have at theme parks such as Disney World.
2   *Brand plants*, such as Volkswagen's Autostadt in Wolfsburg, the Crayola Factory in Pennsylvania, the Guinness Brewery in Dublin, or the Heineken Experience in Amsterdam, where people can have a *factory experience*. Today, the line between a tourist attraction and a factory has become increasingly blurred, to the extent that people often have to pay to visit brand plants and the brand museums frequently found on their premises. The distinction can also be very blurry in the case of theme parks that double as retail experiences, such as the Legoland chain.
3   *Brand fests*, including the various celebrations and outings organized by such companies as Harley-Davidson and Ducati to evoke a *festival experience*. These brand-related events are opportunities for consumers to have an embodied experience of the brand by having direct contact with it. Here, the customer experience is facilitated by the possibility of developing or reinforcing physical contact with staff or products. At such events, the experiential context is ephemeral and constantly changing.
4   *Brand websites* (for example, those of Fiat 500 and Nutella) are now being designed to provide virtual experiences. Most experiential approaches are implicitly grounded in real contexts, whether natural or artificial, but with the rise of the Internet, people have come to accept the possibility that the context of their experience will be virtual in nature, driven by advances in so-called "immersion technologies", notably those of online games.

A critical approach to experiential marketing

Alongside the development of approaches to experiential marketing, research in consumer culture has sought to understand consumer experiences, highlighting some links with the managerial elements described above. The entertainment aspect is made explicit in the work on "spectacular consumption" at Nike Town, Chicago (Sherry 1998; Peñaloza 1999). Enclavization is emphasized as a major condition for eliciting memorable experiences because it limits the intrusion of elements that do not belong to the theme, thereby enhancing the intensity of the experience (Firat and Dholakia 1998). Enclavization is also analyzed in the case of *flagship stores*, which are typically enclaves where people can focus on everything a brand is offering without any intrusion from external elements, such as other brands (Kozinets *et al.* 2002). In the same vein, the securization provided by hyper-real contexts is stressed (Goulding *et al.* 2002). The impact of thematization in flagship stores on consumers is a product of "lavish decor, sleek finishes and attention to the smallest details" (Kozinets *et al.* 2002: 20). The brand-specific experiential context of brand fests is studied in the case of Harley-Davidson (McAlexander and Schouten 1998). All this shows that the cultural approach is not completely in contrast to experiential marketing approaches. However, the overall consumption-centred vision developed by cultural researchers also points to significant incoherencies between the two approaches. Indeed, a reading that starts from consumption reveals some discrepancies with regard to the production of experience, its extraordinary nature, and how it is accessed.

Production of experience

For researchers in consumer culture, when considering the consumption experience, it is essential to go beyond a view of experience that is totally dependent on what the market offers. The sociology of consumption (Edgell *et al.* 1997) has highlighted four typologies of consumption experience in function of the mode of provision. These are: (1) family experiences resulting from family ties; (2) friendship experiences resulting from reciprocal relations within a community; (3) citizenship experiences linked to relations with the state; and (4) consumer experiences connected to exchanges with the market. Three of these typologies of individuals' daily consumption occur outside the context of the market; thus, an instance of consumption is not necessarily a "consumer experience". The consumption experience of a meal at a friend's house is linked to a sphere outside the market, even if products from the market may be consumed. In the same way, the communal consumption of a self-produced show is outside the notion of a consumer experience (consider, for example, the experiences of attendees at the Burning Man Festival) (Kozinets 2002). Moreover, marketing is only interested in the specific social context of the market, in which the individual is a consumer living experiences with the supplier and with other consumers. In this specific context, the experience is produced by the company.

The cultural approach (Carù and Cova 2007) outlines a continuum of consumption experiences that consumers undergo and the associated activities of marketers:

- At one extreme are experiences that are mainly constructed by consumers and which can involve products or services provided by a company. Here the firm pursues a traditional product or service marketing approach and it is the consumer who organizes his or her own experience. Consumption of traditional products like pasta, the small items that populate our daily lives, and most particularly organic products and those of non-profit and local associations are prime examples here.
- In the middle we find experiences that have been co-developed by companies and consumers. Here the firm provides an experiential platform upon which consumers can develop their own experiences. The firm imbues the experience with potential, turning it into a veritable raw material composed of certain diffuse elements that the consumer can mould, and which will therefore assume the shape of the resulting experience. Sports tourism, adventure packages, rock concerts and cultural events are part of eliciting such experiences.
- At the other extreme, we find experiences that have largely been developed by companies and where consumers are immersed in a context that is frequently hyper-real in nature. Here the firm is pursuing a total experiential marketing approach and plans all the details of the experience for the consumer. Nowadays, fashion, sports brands, toys and other forms of entertainment specialize in this approach. In fact, experiential marketing has focused on this type of experience.

The extraordinary nature of experience

What is seen in the work of Schmitt (1999) and of Pine and Gilmore (1999) is a vision of experience that is anchored in Romanticism (Holbrook 1997). Romanticism underlies our present model of consumption, a model which moves increasingly away from the pure functionalism of responding to needs (Addis and Holbrook 2001).

This obsession in our society with the extraordinary experience that marketing proposes has recently provoked a strong reaction that may help managers to rethink the concept of the consumption experience in a broader way. Bruckner (2000) attacks the mysticism of the peak points and the search for perpetual euphoria that permeate the ideology of contemporary society. The author criticizes the enemies of boredom and the society of continual entertainment, sustaining a vision of existence in which experiences of differing intensity co-exist. Consumer culture researchers have adopted this critical way of looking at everyday experiences (Carù and Cova 2003) and proceed to question whether entertainment should be seen (Wolf 1999) as the main characteristic of experiential marketing. On the one hand, such an idea is puzzling and seems to suggest an excessively unilateral marketing approach, while on the other, it cannot be denied that many elements of this approach are found in numerous offering systems.

Access to experience

Once the context has been enclavized, secured and thematized, and after the theme has been dressed in theatre effects and staged, the consumer is supposed to be able to dive seamlessly into the context, thereby accessing the experience. It is here that the approaches of experiential marketing are incompatible with the cultural approach. For researchers interested in consumer culture (Ladwein 2003), there is nothing straightforward or systematic about accessing the consumption experience, which requires competencies or aptitudes that consumers do not necessarily have at their disposal. In fact, this is a construct that mainly applies to consumers who are already "experts" in a theme or context and can therefore dive straight into it, but not to "novice" consumers who feel distant from a theme and its staging, a disposition that impedes their immersion, thus killing the experience. Spectacular staging like enclavization can even create threshold effects for consumers in this situation. As a result, the immersion of people who are new to a brand or a context much more frequently assumes the sequence of nesting, exploration and stamping, rather than a dive into something (Carù and Cova 2006). It is not enough that a company simply creates a good experiential context – it must above all develop the means to facilitate people's immersion in this context. In marketing, the immersion concept suffers from the sense of immediacy that is conveyed by the often associated image of a consumer diving into something – an image that presents immersion as nothing more than a model of instantaneous emotional induction, wherein it seems sufficient that one simply be present to experience immersion (ibid.).

The image of the diver infers that immersion is tantamount to consumers being plunged into a hyper-reality that has been introduced through the agency of the firm alone, implying that consumers lose their freedom of choice due to pressure exerted on their emotions and sensations. The idea of appropriation, on the other hand, suggests that access to experience comes about through operations that consumers carry out to produce the experience by negotiating to their own advantage whatever is being done to manipulate them. To achieve immersion, consumers will use the tools, competencies and aptitudes that they develop during the course of the experience (Ladwein 2003).

In short, there are two very distinct ways of envisaging the process of accessing the experience:

- as something total and instantaneous, like being plunged into water, as sought in experiential marketing;
- as something partial and progressive, achieved through a series of appropriation operations, as it is understood by researchers in consumer culture.

A cultural approach to the management of consumption experiences

It is in the second view above that a more consumer-centric approach to the management of consumer experience has emerged. This approach suggests that, rather than being a sudden and involuntary occurrence, immersion in a consumption experience is more a process, and to facilitate it, greater attention must be paid to the management of those experiential elements that will have an impact on the operations of appropriation. The goal of appropriation is to make something one's own, to adapt it and thereby transform it into an extension of one's own self-expression. Appropriation can be moral, psychological and affective in nature. In this view, the role of the company is to support customers in the process of appropriating experience. This support must take account of consumers' different levels of competence and familiarity with the type of experience in question, and can be divided into three categories of action: support systems, collective action, and self-determination (Figure 10.2).

Support systems

Using guides and referents is an effective way of providing support. The very idea of having a facilitator who is there to ease consumer access to the experience pervades cultural research (Price *et al.* 1995).

Some evoke the figure of a *guide* to convey the subtle role that should be played by the particular staff member who will be present during the course of the appropriation. Interactive media can also play this consumer guidance role. Moreover, a novice's appropriation depends strongly on the guide's ability to act as a quasi-friend, even going so far as to share some intimacy, thereby exceeding consumers' expectations of this type of service (ibid.). Achieving this requires the development of contact personnel to facilitate

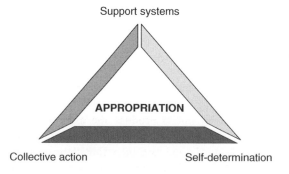

Figure 10.2 The three categories of actions to support consumers in the appropriation process.
Source: Photo credits: Antonella Carù and Bernard Cova.

novices' appropriation. The notion of perceived authenticity is very important here; appropriation is better facilitated when staff members appear to be genuine, i.e., when consumers believe that staff members are doing what they do because they are passionate or feel a sense of vocation, not just because they want to make a sale. In addition, contact staff members have increasingly come to experience the brands and products that they are promoting in a frenetic manner. These "passionate salespersons" are in a better position to respond to customer demands and, above all, to facilitate appropriation by substituting traditional sales talk (of attributes, advantages and benefits) with personalized discourse anchored in their own experiences with the brand (Rémy and Kopel 2002). The more guides give of themselves, the more they elevate the experience from the confines of a purely commercial exchange, which reassures the novice consumer. In short, contact staff members play a guide's role, but this should not be confused with the role of a simple master of ceremonies ensuring that the show goes on. Much has been written about the Apple Store experience and what can be learned from its successful retail execution (www.apple.com/retail/). However, there is a forgotten dimension: that of contact persons acting as guides. Mac Specialists (as Apple's front-line sales talent are known) are trained to take on individual clients, as opposed to moving among multiple customers. This allows the Specialist to delve into the customer's life and comfortably build rapport. It does not absolve the Specialists from the responsibility of selling, but it does focus their attention on the customer. It encourages them to develop strong listening skills. It is rare for a retailer's sales approach to successfully serve both the customer experience and the employee's professional development, as Apple's does.

The role of reference points corresponds to what we find today in other fields such as cinema, which is highly self-referential and where appropriation is facilitated by the recycling and re-utilization of referents taken from past films, sometimes even involving a total remake or pastiche of a movie (Belfiore and Bennett 2007). What can be recycled are all the signs and symbols relating to a brand or a company – its past, products, key moments and leading personalities – all of which the consumer recognizes easily. Depending on the consumers' individual histories, which provide a structure for analyzing reference points that are being revealed in a particular context, they will engage in decoding behaviour and progressively appropriate the experiential context. This suggests that a firm should mobilize elements derived from other contexts. For example, when one is introduced to classical music, the guide might use images and terms from more familiar areas such as pop or film music so that the novice consumer has a basis for understanding. This utilization of external elements softens the excessive thematization of the context, corresponding to the views of those who advocate a moderate usage of thematization (Ritzer 1999).

An example of this is the film, *Night before the Exams* (*Notte prima degli esami*), which was a great success in Italy, with the tenth-highest box-office takings (fifth among Italian films) for the 2005/06 season. The film presents two reference levels. The first is linked to the experiences of the majority of people of all ages in Italy, recounting a particular moment in their lives: the school exit examination. This experience is momentous and one of the events in people's lives that is remembered with the greatest intensity. The second level is the period in which the film is set, the late 1980s, a period with which it is easy to identify and which has been raised to a mythical status by the younger generations who did not directly experience it. The film sought to facilitate the identification of a broad public with the period by using many references to the common heritage of different generations, e.g., the songs (the title of the film is the same as a famous song by a well-known singer-songwriter) that were all popular successes and 20 years later have become cult music. The film was a cross-generational success both among the young who are still close to the events and among older people who took their exams in those years and could recall their own memories and the myths that marked their adolescence (Gilmore and Pine 2007).

Collective action

Collective action involves the development and preservation of communitarian-flavoured connections within an experience, thereby allowing mutual learning and shared emotions. It also means supporting an understanding of (and participation in) the collective micro-rituals that structure all activities. Firms that think in terms of one consumer's behaviour often neglect the collective dimension of an experience (Peñaloza 1999; Schouten *et al.* 2007). And yet the consumption experience needs to be explicit, explained and shared if it is to really exist. This is because the attribution of meaning to an individual experience calls for the creation of a narrative that is itself inseparable from the power to articulate one's own thoughts. An experience is never really complete if it has not been expressed, i.e. if it has not been communicated in linguistic or other forms. Whether one has the experience in the home or elsewhere, it cannot be separated from ideas like sharing and collective enjoyment.

Companies have recently started to work on the collective dimension of experience by using group interactions to facilitate it. Many firms have understood the power of *communities* or tribes in the novice consumer's appropriation (Muñiz and O'Guinn 2001), trying to develop get-togethers where expert, advanced, fluent and novice consumers join forces to enable one another, reassured by the collective atmosphere, to engage themselves. The concepts applied here include mutual learning (with the more educated training everyone else) and imitation (with novices copying experts' gestures). Certain brands such as Ducati and Harley-Davidson focus specifically on creating and preserving brand communities in which novices are taken under the wing of experts, due to the moral obligation of mutual assistance that is *de rigueur* in such communities (ibid.). In the same vein, experiential contexts should be thought of as places where connections and meetings occur (Kozinets *et al.* 2002), meaning they cannot be characterized by smooth and transparent forms, as is the case with supermarkets that are places where buying activities are central. Quite the contrary, they should be intricate and discontinuous, full of private areas and quiet corners that facilitate discrete immersions and small groups of people sharing their emotions.

One example, the North Face Ultra-Trail du Mont-Blanc (www.ultratrailmb.com) is a spectacular and very tough race: 163km long and a vertical climb of 9,500m around Mont Blanc, starting and finishing in Chamonix. In 2008, 2,300 contestants of more than 40 different nationalities participated. The race is a typical brand festival that brings together ultra-trail enthusiasts, competitors and spectators alike. Even the start of the race is a moment of collective emotion, and people follow the event throughout, both day and night. From the arrival of the winners to that of the back-markers, support and encouragement are continuous. There are often opportunities for exchanges between the long-time spectators and the newbies, such as tourists in Chamonix who come across the race by chance and are initially surprised but easily enticed by the pervasive and intense festive atmosphere. The vibrant heart of the event is the square in Chamonix, where the runners on the circuit can be monitored on a giant screen, and where spectators have another opportunity to interact.

Even more recently, companies have rediscovered the power of *rituals*, despite the fact that consumer behaviour research has for 20 years (Rook 1985; Otnes and Lowrey 2004) been emphasizing the importance of rituals for consumers' individual (and especially collective) experiences. This has given us a new vision of consumption, presenting it from the standpoint of participation in rituals in which individuals act jointly in a symbolic manner. It remains that the ritual aspects of an experience appear to have a relatively minimal impact on appropriation. For example, many of the applause rituals of a classical music concert make for a real headache among novices, who do not know whether to applaud at the end of a piece. Rituals are vectors of appropriation, both positive and negative, and consumers will only immerse themselves in an experience if its rituals help them to advance instead of increasing the sense of distance caused by failing to understand the rituals.

Difficulty in getting tickets has always been a feature of the Teatro alla Scala (www. teatroallascala.org), and even today with much higher prices, it is still not at all easy. However, since the end of the Second World War, there have been 200 inexpensive standing places in "the gods" (the second circle in the opera house), which cannot be booked in advance. The aim of this tradition, which is regulated by a specific directive of the theatre, is to allow all opera-lovers to attend a performance without spending a fortune. Today, the Accordo association draws up a list of eligible recipients and distributes the vouchers to buy a ticket at the box office on the evening of the opera. The interesting thing is the way in which the list is put together, following various "calls" throughout the day. On the opening night of the Scala, an extremely important occasion in Milan, the first call is at 6.00 in the morning, followed later by another two. People queue up all night long to be on the list for the first call, and have to return for each subsequent call to avoid losing their places. Each person receives just one ticket. Despite the difficulty, the cold, the long wait and the scant possibility of getting a ticket, this is a ritual that opera-lovers have been repeating for years. Another unwritten but accepted rule is that of the old aficionado who lives in a car outside the opera house on via Filodrammatici and collects the names of those interested even before the first call. In the early hours of the morning, Mr Gianni sits beside his little dog in his Polo outside the box office, taking down the names of the people who will be the first on the Accordo association's list when the counting starts.

Self-determination

Self-determination refers both to training actions (e.g., workshops, internships and seminars) that enhance consumers' competencies, and to consumers' agency once they are given the means to apply their own specific competencies. Self-determination is rooted in a concept that equates consumers with protagonists who are traditionally considered to be operating in reaction to something. The idea here is that consumers are trying to be less passive, injecting a personal touch into their consumption experiences. This is quite straight-forward for expert consumers who are capable of surmounting any participation proposal that a firm may organize, but it can be a complicated process for novices, who might engage in trial and error to appropriate the experience.

Training is the technique traditionally implemented by companies that rely on consumers' self-determination to facilitate appropriation. In doing so, firms seek to improve the competencies of consumers, who will then be free to implement these competencies in their own way in order to become increasingly immersed in the experience. The issue here no longer involves guiding consumers but instead empowering them so they can achieve appropriation all by themselves. Examples are company-driven proliferation of work experiences, workshops, seminars and distance-learning mechanisms to give consumers the wherewithal they need. Many specialized stores even offer veritable classrooms where experts (who may be company representatives or even expert consumers) come to teach novices. The Home Depot (www.homedepot.com) has launched its series of Do-It-Herself Workshops, which take place at the retailer's more than 1,500 stores. These special clinics help women learn how to use power tools, build a patio, and install outdoor lighting. The events reflect a growing desire among American women for more knowledge and hands-on training in all aspects of home repair. According to John Costello, executive vice-president and chief marketing officer for The Home Depot, "Do-It-Herself Workshops are part of our long-term commitment to be more than a store to our customers who are seeking answers and inspiration." In providing the workshops, The Home Depot creates an emotional connection to its brand through consumer sense of accomplishment. It is about giving consumers the confidence to try a project, instilling in them a sense of personal ownership and empowerment because they actually completed the project themselves.

It appears that the best way forward for any company hoping to incorporate an element of consumer self-determination is to offer the potential for appropriation, providing a veritable smorgasbord of diffuse elements that consumers shape through experience. The purpose of this kind of approach is not to offer customers an experience that has been pre-determined and structured by a scrupulously planned context, but instead to give them an opportunity to achieve *autonomy* by playing a full role in the design and construction of their own experience, something that goes far beyond mere participation and takes the form of a self-serving experience. In other words, a company's vision must transcend simple global programme management approaches that envision experience on a point-by-point basis. Instead, it should pursue an approach that consists of a unifying platform based on which a process, replete with yardsticks and marked here and there by points of reference and readjustment, can unfold in step with the participation of individual consumers and the engagement of their competencies. In short, consumer self-determination forces companies to free up space in the consumption experience and not to organize it in its entirety.

This idea forms the basis for the strategy pursued by the car brand Scion (www.scion.com). When Scion launched in 2003 with 105 California dealerships selling the boxy xB (dubbed "The Toaster" by some clients) and compact xA five-door, many doubted that Toyota's attempt to create an entirely new youth brand would survive. Since then, the brand has spread to 982 of Toyota's 1,231 dealers nationwide and now, five years and 620,000 vehicles later, the division charged with bringing more young people into the Toyota fold is clearly a resounding success. With a line-up consisting only of the new xB, tC coup, and xD five-door (replacing the unloved xA), Scion sells to buyers with the youngest median age in the auto industry (31), and a full 72 percent of whom have never owned a Toyota before. So how does Scion do it? It offers affordable, well-equipped cars with great tuning potential! The brand's strategy is focused on encouraging customization; with many different Scion and TRD accessories on offer, more than 50 percent of buyers spend additional cash to purchase add-ons for their rides. Indeed, most Scion buyers customize their vehicles, and many of the customers come to their dealer's store once a month to purchase a new after-market product such as body-side graphics and roof racks for snowboards or bikes.

Conclusion: in praise of a pluralistic approach

The vision proposed by the cultural approach is based on a wider concept of experience than that used in experiential marketing work, and thus offers greater opportunities in management of the consumption experience. Specifically, by emphasizing access to the experience, the approach encourages managers to work on areas that are underestimated in approaches that consider experience as immediate immersion. This does not mean that the management opportunities based on the cultural approach represent the only frame of reference. Indeed, neither experiential marketing nor cultural approaches are truly predictive; each has limited power to explain reality. And though we are disinclined to propose a Grand Theory combining both views, we feel that a pluralistic approach to the management of experience must be sought. Moreover, the search should be undertaken by managers through practice, rather than by researchers through theory.

Despite the co-existence of different views, the increasingly clear emergence of consumer-driven experience bolsters the relevance of the cultural approach to future marketing efforts. The consumer experience is increasingly designed and produced by consumers, and the opportunities offered by a cultural approach to understand not only how the experience is accessed, but also how it is created, will be of greater value to managers than the self-affirming act of merely directing it. Given the proliferation of consumer-driven web-based experiences (e.g., couchsurfing, geocaching and letterboxing), an understanding of the collective production processes undertaken by consumers is becoming increasingly essential to identify the ways in which companies can accompany the consumer in the experience. The future will be marked much more by consumer-driven experience than by company-driven experience.

Review and discussion questions

1   Make a list of your favourite brands. Could you describe the types of brand experience contexts you have been immersed in for each of these brands?
2   Could you recall your last visit to a museum or an exhibition? Exhibitions and museums are rich and stimulating environments, but visitors often do not enjoy the experience. According to what you lived, could you explain why there is nothing straightforward about enjoying this kind of experience?
3   Concerning a brand of your choice, analyze the three qualities of the brand store context. For the same brand in the same store, analyze the three categories of actions to support consumers in their appropriation process.
4   Look at the Heineken experience website (www.heinekenexperience.com). Do the same analyses as you did for the previous question.
5   Have you ever been involved in a training session dedicated to improving your skills in the use of products and services of a specific brand? Could you develop a short personal introspection of what you experienced during and after this training session?

Keywords

appropriation, experience, guide, immersion, reference point, ritual

References

Addis, M. and Holbrook, M. B. (2001) "On the Conceptual Link between Mass Customisation and Experiential Consumption: An Explosion of Subjectivity", *Journal of Consumer Behaviour*, 1(1): 50–66.
Arnould, E. and Price, L. (1993) "River Magic: Extraordinary Experience and the Extended Service Encounter", *Journal of Consumer Research*, 20(June): 24–45.

Belfiore, E. and Bennett, O. (2007) "Determinants of Impact: Towards a Better Understanding of Encounters with the Arts", *Cultural Trends*, 16(3): 225–75.

Bruckner, P. (2000) *L'euphorie perpétuelle: essai sur le devoir de bonheur*, Paris: Grasset.

Carù, A. and Cova, B. (2003) "Revisiting Consumption Experience: A More Humble but Complete View of the Concept", *Marketing Theory*, 3(2): 259–78.

—— (2006) "How to Facilitate Immersion in a Consumption Experience: Appropriation Operations and Service Elements", *Journal of Consumer Behaviour*, 5(1): 4–14.

—— (2007) *Consuming Experience*, Abingdon: Routledge.

Edgell, S., Hetherington, K. and Warde, A. (eds) (1997) *Consumption Matters: The Production and Experience of Consumption*, Oxford: Blackwell.

Firat, A. F. and Dholakia, N. (1998) *Consuming People: From Political Economy to Theaters of Consumption*, London: Sage.

Gilmore, J. H. and Pine, J. (2007) *Authenticity: What Consumers Really Want*, Boston: HBS Press.

Goulding, C., Shankar, A. and Elliott, R. (2002) "Working Weeks, Rave Weekends: Identity Fragmentation and the Emergence of New Communities", *Consumption, Markets and Culture*, 5(4): 261–84.

Hetzel, P. (2002) *Planète conso: Marketing expérientiel et nouveaux univers de consommation*, Paris: Editions d'Organisation.

Holbrook, M. B. (1997) "Romanticism, Introspection and the Roots of Experiential Consumption: Morris the Epicurean", *Consumption, Market and Culture*, 1(2): 97–164.

—— (2000) "The Millennial Consumer in the Texts of Our Times: Experience and Entertainment", *Journal of Macromarketing*, 20(2): 178–92.

Holbrook, M. B. and Hirschman, E. C. (1982) "The Experiential Aspects of Consumption: Consumer Fantasy, Feelings and Fun", *Journal of Consumer Research*, 9(2): 132–40.

Kozinets, R. V. (2002) "Can Consumers Escape the Market? Emancipatory Illuminations from Burning Man", *Journal of Consumer Research*, 29(June): 20–38.

Kozinets, R. V., Sherry, J. F., Deberry-Spence, B., Duhachek, A., Nuttavuthisit, K. and Storm, D. (2002) "Themed Flagship Brand Stores in the New Millennium: Theory, Practice, Prospects", *Journal of Retailing*, 78(1): 17–29.

Ladwein, R. (2003) "Les méthodes de l'appropriation de l'expérience de consommation: le cas du tourisme urbain", in E. Rémy, I. Garubuau-Moussaoui, D. Desjeux and M. Filser (eds), *Société, consommation et consommateurs*, Paris: L'Harmattan, pp. 85–98.

McAlexander, J. H. and Schouten, J. W. (1998) "Brandfests: Servicescapes for the Cultivation of Brand Equity", in J. F. Sherry (ed.), *Servicescapes: The Concept of Place in Contemporary Markets*, Lincolnwood, IL: NTC Business Books, pp. 377–401.

Muñiz, A. and O'Guinn, T. C. (2001) "Brand Communities", *Journal of Consumer Research*, 27(March): 412–32.

Otnes, C. C. and Lowrey, T. M. (eds) (2004) *Contemporary Consumption Rituals: A Research Anthology*, Mahwah, NJ: Lawrence Erlbaum Associates.

Peñaloza, L. (1999) "Just Doing It: A Visual Ethnography of Spectacular Consumption Behavior at Nike Town", *Consumption, Markets and Culture*, 2(4): 337–400.

Pine, B. J. and Gilmore, J. (1999) *The Experience Economy: Work Is Theatre and Every Business a Stage*, Boston: HBS Press.

Price, L. L., Arnould, E. J. and Tierney, P. (1995) "Going to Extremes: Managing Service Encounters and Assessing Provider Performance", *Journal of Marketing*, 59(2): 83–97.

Rémy, E. and Kopel, S. (2002) "Social Linking and Human Resources Management in the Service Sector", *Service Industries Journal*, 22(1): 35–56.

Ritzer, G. (1999) *Enchanting a Disenchanted World*, Thousand Oaks, CA: Pine Forge Press.

Rook, D. W. (1985) "The Ritual Dimension of Consumer Behavior", *Journal of Consumer Research*, 12 (December): 251–64.

Schmitt, B. H. (1999) *Experiential Marketing: How to Get Customers to Sense, Feel, Think, Act and Relate to Your Company and Brands*, New York: The Free Press.

—— (2003) *Customer Experience Management*, Hoboken, NJ: John Wiley & Sons, Ltd.
Schouten, J. W., McAlexander, J. H. and Koenig, H. F. (2007) "Transcendent Customer Experience and Brand Community", *Journal of the Academy of Marketing Science*, 35(3): 357–68.
Sherry, J. F. (1998) "The Soul of the Company Store: Nike Town Chicago and the Emplaced Brandscape", in J. F. Sherry (ed.), *Servicescapes: The Concept of Place in Contemporary Markets*, Lincolnwood, IL: NTC Business Books, pp. 109–50.
Wolf, M. J. (1999) *The Entertainment Economy: How Mega-Media Forces are Transforming Our Lives*, New York: Random House.

11 Tribal marketing

Bernard Cova and Avi Shankar

Overview

As a marketing manager or student of marketing, you are probably most familiar with the term "tribe" when it is used to describe an ancient, primitive, outdated system of human social organization based on close kinship ties and close geographical proximity. Further, you may think that today tribes only exist in far-flung corners of the world, in isolated communities, barely touched by the modern world. The study of tribes, surely, is the domain of the anthropologist and documentary film-makers for the *Discovery* or *National Geographic* television channels. What do tribes have to do with marketing? And what can you, as today or future business and marketing managers, learn from a tribal marketing approach? These are the questions that we seek to address in this chapter. More specifically the aims of our chapter are:

- to encourage you to think of consumers as tribes and understand the marketing management implications of doing so;
- to show how a tribal marketing approach reverses the immanent logic of one of the cornerstones of traditional marketing – segmentation;
- to show how a tribal marketing approach can be implemented by drawing on a series of case studies with companies that we have engaged with.

Before we start on our journey though, a word of warning: tribal marketing, as we understand it, can never be wholly reduced to a "one-size-fits-all", step-by-step set of management practices that you can simply follow – we cannot tell you how to "do" tribal marketing. Rather, if you embrace a tribal marketing perspective as a lens through which to view marketing, you will begin to see marketing in a non-traditional, culturally embedded manner; one that is grounded in the everyday reality and complexity of the day-to-day lives that people, our potential consumers, lead. Only then can you draw on these insights to inform and then engage in appropriate marketing management practices with your consumers.

"It's a tribe, Jim, but not as we know it"

Many of you will be familiar with the long-running television and film franchise *Star Trek*. In the original television series whenever the *Starship Enterprise* came across a new species somewhere in the galaxy, Dr McCoy or "Bones" would turn to Captain Kirk or Jim and say, "It's life, Jim, but not as we know it." In a similar vein, the tribes that we are concerned with are not the tribes of anthropological study that we began this chapter with: they are quite different; they are everywhere; yet previously we did not have the tools, techniques or opportunities to identify and understand them. To put it another way, as marketing academics and practitioners we were suffering from myopia; we couldn't see them.

Our understanding of tribes takes its inspiration from the work of an eminent French sociologist called Michel Maffesoli. In a landmark book, *The Time of the Tribes* (Maffesoli 1996), he reinforced the argument that the fundamental building blocks of human life are found in the multiple social groups that we all belong to, knowingly or not, throughout the course of our everyday lives. These "little masses", or *tribus* as Maffesoli calls them, are central to our everyday experience and to who we are, our identity. This is especially true of the tribes that we knowingly and actively participate in. And this is where our tribes differ from anthropological tribes; throughout the course of our lives and as who we are, as our identity develops and changes, we can belong to and participate in many little tribes. Our tribal affiliation is no longer limited to the one big tribe that, once upon a time, we were born into and that determined what we could do, be or become.

"Big deal" or "So what?" you might be thinking, but this simple observation is in stark contrast to how people, consumers, are normally portrayed in the business discipline. In economics, and after all marketing is often thought to be just applied economics, the consumer is thought of as an isolated individual, with a group merely an aggregation of individuals. The perspective we subscribe to rejects and therefore fundamentally challenges this assumption. In contrast, we say that there is no such thing as an individual; rather, whether we are aware of it or not, we are always a member of a variety of tribes with, at any one moment in time, some of these tribal affiliations having more significance and meaning for us than others.

This is a big statement for us to make and may run contrary to the way you see yourself and the world beyond you, especially if you are from "the West". However, for people from "the East", brought up in a culture and society that are far more collectivist and less individualistic, this statement will be self-evident. We subscribe to the view that one of the fundamental challenges that faces people today is to make their lives meaningful. Being someone, having an identity, is one of the main ways we achieve this. However, gone are the days when our families, or our relative position in the social and economic hierarchy, determined our identity and life outcomes. Rather, each of us has to make up who we want to be and this is, in part, why some people think of themselves as individuals; they think they are in control of this process. But the identities that we reproduce are always social and relational; in order to be someone, we require that identity to be validated and reinforced by others. Many of you reading this chapter will be students; but the identity of a student is always contingent on and related to others to be meaningful – namely other students and your lecturers. In this way, we see identities to be socially meaning categories descriptive of who we are. Each of you has many identities that come and go as you live your life with, at any one moment in time, some identities being more important to you than others. For example, many of you (or your parents) will have made considerable financial sacrifice to enable your studies. Your student identity will be, therefore, very important to you but, in a few years time, it will be a distant but hopefully pleasurable memory, as you pursue your careers. You are currently part of numerous nascent tribes; you are a member of your MBA, MSc, business school and university tribe; you may have extracurricular interests, perhaps you play sport and are a member of a soccer or tennis tribe; or maybe you regularly frequent the gym and belong to the gym tribe. Close geographical proximity is also no longer a prerequisite for tribal affiliation (cf. Chapter 12 in this volume); indeed when you graduate and become part of your alumni tribe, social media will enable you to maintain tribal affiliation with your fellow tribe members as you and they scatter to all corners of the world.

The tribes we are interested in, though, are naturally occurring groups where: tribe members identify with one another (or alternatively they can be "activated" and encouraged to be linked together by social media or marketing activities); they have shared experiences and emotions; and they are capable of engaging in collective social action – that is, together members of the tribe can "do" things that they would be incapable of doing outside of the collective.

To give you a feel for our understanding of tribes, consider the case of new parents. From a business perspective, new parents represent a highly lucrative market – think of all those new gadgets, prams, toys, furniture, mother and baby clothes, food stuffs, car accessories etc. that they require! To what extent can we consider new parents to constitute a tribe? To be sure, new parents face a bewildering array of new experiences both immensely pleasurable and positive, but also potentially daunting and stressful. New parents clearly can identify with one another because, while they may have their experiences separately, they are also shared in the sense that they are all having the same or similar experiences. In the past, the ability to communicate and share these experiences with other parents was limited. With the advent of the Internet and various social media, this situation has radically changed.

Mums.net, a UK Internet site, was established in 2000 and facilitates parent-to-parent, mainly mum-to-mum interaction and because of its middle-class, affluent user profile, in a relatively short space of time it has established itself as a powerful and influential forum. For example, during the 2010 British General Election, the leaders of the major political parties, Gordon Brown, David Cameron and Nick Clegg, all took part in Mums.net facilitated, live web-chats, with the Prime Minister officially hailing the site as a British institution. The worldwide media attention that the site subsequently received has led to the 2010 General Election being dubbed as the "Mums.net Election" (see: http://www.mumsnet.com/media/mumsnet-election). Clearly then, and through other campaigning activities like their "Let Girls be Girls" campaign that raises awareness of the premature sexualization of young children, the Mums.net tribe is engaged in collective social action (see: http://www.mumsnet.com/campaigns).

Of course, all this mum-to-mum, or from a marketing perspective "potential" consumer-to-consumer interaction has not gone unheeded by the commercial world. Mums.net accepts a range of advertising from large multinationals like Ford to other UK brand and service providers across a range of market sectors. For all these companies the Mum.netters are an ideal tribe or, in conventional marketing terms, an ideal target market.

Tribes and brand communities

The tribal perspective that we have developed so far is limited to community formation around the shared experience of being a new parent. Equally a tribe could form around any leisure-based activity, interest, hobby or passion. If you are passionate about surfing, travelling, a TV show, snowboarding, running, reading books, a band or singer, knitting, fine wine, a film star, rock music, international politics, fossil hunting, or fishing, the rise of social media via the Internet means that you can search for and find other like-minded devotees and *voilà* you will have the basis of a tribe. However, when a tribe forms around one specific company or one of its brands, then we can say we have a brand community and such studies are better developed in the marketing field for this very reason (Muñiz and O'Guinn 2001).

In contrast to a brand community, a tribe, however, is not limited in terms of a specific product or brand. The tribe can be a collective that consumes, but it is much more: tribes can be commercial and non-commercial at the same time. Mums.net, for example, is at its heart a non-commercial space that has been subsequently colonized by the commercial sphere mainly in the form of advertising. Indeed, all tribal gatherings need products, places and services to bolster the collective identity of its members. The tribe may offer a tremendous opportunity for many different products and services, all with a view to supporting the inherent tribal passion but commerce or the commercial realm is not the central objective of the tribe. Brand communities, on the contrary, are grounded in the commercial world because their central object is a specific brand.

However, the similarities between tribes and brand communities are greater than their differences. We have identified three main features of tribes: collective identification; shared experiences, passions and emotions; and the ability to engage in collective action. Similarly, brand communities exhibit three key features too: consciousness of kind or the feeling that you are connected to other like-minded consumers through the brand; shared rituals and traditions that help the community cohere around a brand; and a sense of moral responsibility, duty and obligation to other people in the brand community (ibid.).

Furthermore, some organizations like the Italian motorcycle company *Ducati* blend the two perspectives. They have a brand community called the *Ducatistas* (see http://www.ducatisti.co.uk/) while, during his tenure as CEO of the company, Federico Minoli restructured the organization by drawing on tribal thinking (Table 11.1).

From exchange value and use value to linking value

Hopefully you will remember from your Economics 101 class the concept of exchange and use value. Briefly, in contemporary economic theory (often called neo-classical economics), exchange value has become synonymous with the amount of money that any given product will trade for in any given market. Put in even simpler terms, it represents the price that

Table 11.1 Tribal management model at Ducati

Old model Marketing management	New model Tribal marketing
Recruit	Co-opt
Employee	Member of the tribe
Client	Member of the tribe
Customer–company relationship	Customer–customer relationship
Communicating with customers	Sharing emotions
Marketing activities	Rituals
Factory	Cult Place
Keeping people out	Bringing members in
Discipline	Passion
CEO	Shaman

buyers and sellers negotiate, based on the principles of rational, utility maximization. Use value is the value-in-use of a product, more often than not perceived of as the functional and symbolic benefit(s) a product offers its buyer.

At the time of writing this chapter, what value is and where exactly value resides in any exchange between a company and its consumers are a topic of much debate in marketing and management studies more generally (Prahalad and Ramaswamy 2004). Textbooks tend to reproduce and therefore reinforce the idea that companies create and embed value through their ability to design and manufacture goods and services with utility that is then exchanged in the marketplace, more often than not for money, with consumers subsequently extracting utility from the market offering. However, there is an increasing amount of research that suggests that far more is going on in terms of value creation and exchange than this picture suggests.

From a tribal marketing perspective, consumers are now seen to create their own value – what we call consumer-to-consumer value, and this is, more often than not, independent of the company or its brands. This linking value is also found within brand communities, but here consumers and companies co-create value through the brand (see Schau *et al*. 2009). In both tribes and brand communities, then, what consumers "value" is not primarily the company offering but the communal, social interactions of the tribe or brand community.

The role and function of commercial offerings are to strengthen community links and foster a sense of tribal belonging and membership or "we-ness". Linking value therefore has two distinct yet complementary meanings: for consumers, it is the value (the fun, pleasure, satisfaction, usefulness, sociality, etc.) inherent in communal relations, however ephemeral, fostered by the tribe or brand community; while, for the company, it is the value its products/services/brands have for the construction, development or maintenance of these communal relations (Cova 1997). Companies rarely embed linking value, intentionally, in the value proposition of their products/services but the greater the contribution of a product or service to the development and strengthening of the tribal bond, the greater its linking value will be.

From a company perspective, linking value has to be produced and engineered into the product or service offering and companies are beginning to invest significant resources into this process. However, companies cannot produce linking value without the support of the members of the tribe or brand community who "work" very hard to produce it (Cova and Dalli 2009). Consumers are both creators and users of linking value.

Companies as diverse as Innocent (a drinks and food company specializing in smoothies) and Jeep (the American 4x4 company) host tribal events called brand festivals. At these brand fests consumers of their products have the opportunity to interact and develop relationships with each other and with the company. At these events it is consumers who create the community through their participation in the brand fest with the company facilitating this process.

Consumers can also create linking value that is then attached to the brand or the product, which is consequently perceived as more valuable. New products emerge as a tribal product: the more consumers participate in the new product development process, the more they perceive the product's value, because they regard it as "their" product, from both the individual and the tribal point of view.

Following in the footsteps of the Harry Potter tribe (see Brown 2007), Twilighters (*Twilight* fans), for example, have created many ventures in order to support the development of *Twilight* (cf. Chapter 12 in this volume). *Twilight* is a young-adult vampire-romance novel by Stephenie Meyer. It has generated a worldwide community of fans of the novel and its major characters, Edward Cullen and Isabella "Bella" Swan. The cult of Edward Cullen is especially vivid. Beyond the official Facebook group (12 million members), fans have created dedicated Facebook groups such as "Because of Edward Cullen, human boys have lost their charm" or "Because I read Twilight I have unrealistic expectations in Men", while the first fan website "*HisGolden Eyes.com*" has had more than 40 million visits. Fans have also created the "*Dazzle Award*" (to recall the way Bella speaks about Edward: "His dazzling eyes, his dazzling smile, etc.") which celebrates the Best Twilight fan site of the year (http://www.dazzleawards2009.webs.com/). We can see from this variety of activity that Twilighters produce linking value for the community that adds value to the original novel.

The same value creation process is at play with the "Loggionisti" in Milan, Italy. On 31 January 1973, an association called "Amici del Loggione del Teatro della Scala" (Friends of La Scala Opera) was born. Members soon came to be known as "Loggionisti", after the music lovers who usually prefer watching shows from the famous old opera house's upper lodges instead of its balcony seats. A multitude of reasons explain this preference. First, lodges are better than balcony or circle seats to enjoy the quality of the music. Second, perched on high near the ceiling, they are an ideal stage from where "Loggionisti" can look down upon the whole theatre and judge the proceedings with their customary ruthlessness. Last but not least, there is the ticket price. The point here is not so much that Loggionisti are trying to save money, rather as "real fans" they attend the opera regularly. When La Scala advertises a new show, "real fans" will want to see all of its versions and therefore prefer cheaper seats (and usually season tickets) since this enables them to attend almost every night. These elevated spectators, long-standing fans reputed for their quick judgements and strong emotions, react immediately to any new performance. This is an ongoing concern for everyone on stage at La Scala. Loggionisti are formidable connoisseurs who have no qualms about expressing open and immediate disapproval whenever they feel let down – especially by singers with wavering voices, who miss the high notes or, horror of horrors, go off-key. The French tenor Roberto Alagna was whistled and booed off stage after singing "Celeste Aida". His performance lasted no more than a few minutes, with the incident subsequently creating a real *casus belli* between the singer and La Scala's managers.

Loggionisti are more than just well-informed spectators. Through their association, they produce a slew of events targeting the wider community. The association consists of 1,500 active members but organizes a variety of events for the public's sake: conferences with music specialists, critics and historians to discuss future La Scala productions; meetings with conductors, singers, composers, directors, artistic directors; twice-monthly concerts with young and promising musicians and instrumentalists; competitions featuring an "*Amici del Loggione*" award celebrating La Scala's best decors; an 80-strong choir performing in a variety of locations; an archive, library and media centre featuring innumerable works on opera; training in music and singing; thematic exhibitions organized on-site; culture tours visiting concerts and operas worldwide; academic dissertations in fields relating to the opera. Without becoming a direct partner of La Scala, the Loggionisti association has become a key actor in the Milanese opera market.

Consumers can also create tribal relationships and, hence, linking value even without the participation of companies. Tribes create services like *CouchSurfing* (see http://www.couchsurfing.org/) where fellow travellers and tribe members can get a bed for the night or advice from other fellow travellers. Other examples include the creation of second-hand markets like BookCrossing (see http://www.bookcrossing.com/) where book lovers can swap old books with other members. An Apple Newton brand community exists where devotees of the product that is no longer made by the company, continue to innovate and offer repair services to other members of the community.

Tribal marketing vs. traditional marketing

As hopefully you will be gathering by now, a tribal marketing approach challenges some of the marketing fundamentals that you may have previously come across. One of mainstream marketing's most cherished concepts that is found in every marketing textbook is segmentation (cf. also Chapter 18 in this volume). We will show you how our tribal approach re-conceptualizes this process. But first, we will recap, as succinctly as we can, what you should already know about segmentation.

All companies face the problem of how to leverage their finite resources to meet the needs of their customers as efficiently and effectively as possible. Segmentation is the process of identifying consumers who share similar characteristics. A variety of methods, based on behavioural characteristics, lifestyle or demographics, are used to transform a disaggregated market into a segmented market. The company then chooses which segments it wishes to target, based on its resource capability, segment attractiveness and competitive positioning. In practice, companies rely on extensive research and statistical analysis of complex data sets to generate market segments based on a variety of variables. Clusters or segments are often given names and "personified" to sum up the characteristics of segment, such as "bobos" (bourgeois bohemians) or "metrosexuals" (metropolitan, heterosexual men).

Essentially the company is dividing an assumed heterogeneous market into discrete, bounded and homogeneous segments. Underpinning segmentation therefore is the assumption that the market "out there" is made up of unrelated individuals who can be artificially grouped together to constitute a segment. Our proposition is quite simple: why not just start with "segments", or in our case tribes, that already exist and don't require making up?

We suggest that a tribal approach to segmentation is market- or customer-orientated in its truest sense; after all, marketing purports to structure its management practices around consumers. Segmentation though, as it is currently practised, is an organizationally focused, top-down, activity – matching the needs of the market to the resources of the organization. At its heart is the application of abstract categories (demographics, etc.) to the analysis of markets. The segments that arise from the segmentation process are figments of the marketer's imagination – these segments, after all, do not really exist. On the other hand, a tribal approach to segmentation starts from the bottom up. It concerns itself with naturally occurring groups where various consumption practices often facilitate their coalescing and congregation. A tribe is not necessarily homogeneous in terms of objective characteristics (age, gender, attitudes, etc.), but rather is inter-linked by collective identification, the sharing of emotions with the capability of taking collective action. This contrasts with a "traditional segment" as a group of homogeneous people who share the same characteristics but are not connected to each other in any other meaningful way; a segment is not capable of collective action, its members are simply a collection of unrelated individuals.

How to identify the potential of a consumer tribe

Compared with consumer segments that are made up, tribes are not easy to identify using modern marketing variables, while brand communities are easier to spot. Tribes are fuzzy – more societal sparkle than socio-economic certainty. They are shifting gatherings of emotionally bonded people, open systems to which a person belongs and yet does not quite belong. It takes a disruption in marketing know-how to understand tribes. As we have seen modern, rational analysis such as segmentation tried to describe the specific characteristics of a segment. But tribes will not brook this approach; their logic is too frail.

Tribes convey signs that other members of the tribe can identify with. Such signs, or traces of identity, cannot express the totality of belonging but provide helpful hints and put us on a path towards understanding. We would argue that there are at least two types of "tribal traces": temporal traces and spatial traces. In temporal terms, tribes emerge, grow, reach their zenith, languish, and then may even dissolve. Their underlying logic is timeless and fragmented. For example, in the UK the music festival – the most famous being Glastonbury – has rejuvenated the music industry. The Glastonbury tribe is impossible to define using traditional demographic means, but for one week of the year culminating in the three-day festival the tribe materializes in the Somerset countryside. Tribes therefore also exist spatially and the tribe, or at least some of its members, can gather and perform its rituals in public spaces, assembly halls, meeting places, places of worship or commemoration. These spaces provide a momentary home for the tribe. None of these time and space traces exhaust the full potential of tribes. Tribal belonging exists on a daily basis at home, as well as occasionally and informally with others elsewhere. Some also advocate that a tribe can be just a feeling, a fancy, or a fantasy. Tribal members are never alone because they belong, physically or digitally, to a vast and informal emotional community.

The recognition of tribes requires a different and special effort. The marketer is well advised to cast aside the more traditional mono-disciplinary, systemic approaches. Instead, hunting for tribes requires marketers to look out for tribal traces, detecting signs, foraging for hints and exploring the unusual by undertaking desk research on everything that has been said or written about the tribe in newspapers and books, on chat lines, diffusion lists, Net forums (see Kozinets 2010). Figure 11.1 illustrates somewhat metaphorically the signs that can be found in the environment.

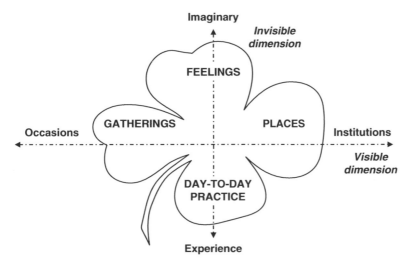

Figure 11.1 The tribal clover.
    Source: Adapted from Cova and Cova (2002).

In this framework, the physical evidence of tribes is located on the horizontal or visible axis (traces or evidences). This includes, on the temporal plane, the moments when tribal members come together for their rituals (occasions), and on the spatial plane, the physical meeting places and virtual spaces (institutions) where tribes convene. On the vertical or invisible axis (hints or shadows), we detect the signs coming from day-to-day activities (the personal and shared experiences) as well as the trends and vogues and other constituents of fantasy and imagination that sweep briskly through society.

As an example, consider the case of a music and dance-based tribe that started in a night-club, in Paris, in 2001. By 2008, the Electro tribe had become a worldwide phenomenon. The music is a blend of techno, house, and electro, combined to make a distinct Euro sound. The Electro tribe's potential (see Figure 11.2) can be analyzed as follows (Cléret and Rémy 2009):

- Cult places are night clubs at the Rivoli Aprem, or Electro and Tecktonik Killers evenings at the Metropolis and are a form of organization and even institutionalization.
- Gatherings occur in most provincial cities as sub-cultural phenomena comprised of shared experiences and knowledge (in areas like dancing or appearance) and battle-like combats (competition between two teams with the winner determined by audience applause).
- Day-to-day practice and gatherings have a tribal dimension since they bring together individuals who are heterogeneous but share certain experiences, emotions and passions.
- The more invisible dimension of this phenomenon is conveyed through the feeling of tribalism that is the movement's fashion effect. Millions of sympathizers adopt accessories to create the Electro look or style and listen to the music.

It is important to note that the visible dimension often accounts for no more than a small proportion of a tribe's potential. There is an imperfect rule of thumb (derived from analyses undertaken over the past ten years) that a factor of 10 to 1 applies in this area. Thus, if a

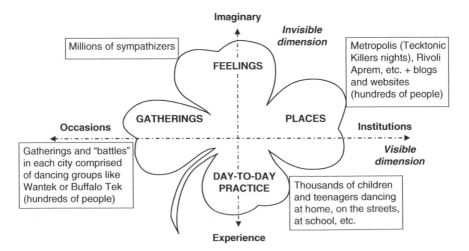

Figure 11.2 The Electro tribe in France in 2008.

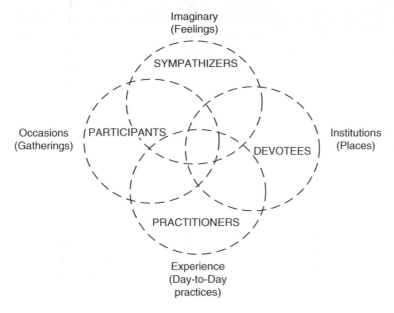

Figure 11.3 Roles of tribe members.
  Source: Adapted from Cova and Cova (2002).

tribe's visible cohort amounts to 100,000 individuals, its invisible total must be around the 1 million mark.

From this, we can work out the roles adopted by tribal members in their dealings with each other and their surroundings. As Figure 11.3 illustrates, tribal members can adopt four roles. These are:

- a member of institutions (associations, religious sects);
- a participant in informal gatherings (demonstrations, happenings);
- a practitioner or adept who has quasi daily involvement in tribal activities;
- a sympathizer or fellow traveller who moves with the vogues and trends and is marginally/virtually integrated to the tribe.

Tribal marketing can target all the members of the tribe at once, or focus on a cross-section with a view (or not) to reaching the whole tribe.

The three major steps of a tribal marketing approach

In order to summarize a possible tribal marketing approach we will use the pioneering strategy developed by Salomon in the 1990s. It remains the best example of a tribal marketing approach.

In 1994, Salomon was a very traditional brand, a little bit outdated, but still a world leader in winter sports equipment. It served people skiing on closed tracks and was completely excluded from new open winter playgrounds where style sports were practised. This also meant it was excluded from new forms of distribution channels. One of these style sports was snowboarding. Snowboarding was not considered a winter game; its roots were to be found in the urban pursuit of skateboarding. Snowboarders represented a specific group, a tribe, which structured itself against the whole universe of skiing (federations, clothes, brands etc.). They wanted to stay apart from traditional skiers. They had their own small manufacturers (more than 150 craftsmen), their own distribution channels (pro-shops), their own cult-brand (Burton) and they hated Salomon which was considered a "daddy's brand".

In 1994, Salomon decided to focus on the snowboarding phenomenon. The watchwords were "be humble", "we are starting from scratch", "we will be low profile", "we will go there to listen". The aim was to build and develop proximity between Salomon and snowboarders. Salomon people mainly did this through participant observation. In 1995, Salomon decided to set up a marketing unit made up of snowboarders. It designed a specific "logo" for its snowboard activities and supported a team of good snowboarders fitted out with non-Salomon boards (Salomon boards did not yet exist!). Some of the tribe members were invited to join the design of Salomon projects.

In 1996, Salomon was ready to launch its snowboard production. No advertising, just physical presence at summer camps and the launching of an advanced batch of 200 boards for pro-shops (not the traditional winter sports channels). At the Grenoble exhibition, Salomon boards were on pro-shop stands, not on Salomon's, clearly showing a different type of approach: Salomon respected the special nature of the tribe. The following year Salomon launched its marketing approach to and with the snowboard tribe:

- huge presence at relevant slopes with boards to be tested by snowboarders without any incentive to buy ("we are just there");
- presence at cult places;
- advertising in tribal media with a great variety of visuals;
- support for contests and events.

By 1999, Salomon had risen to number 3 in the snowboarding market in France. Along with this first foray into the tribal world with the snowboard, Salomon investigated the ways of supporting the in-line roller skate tribe. This approach, however, was more systematic.

Phase 1 (1995–96) consisted of "ethnomarketing", whereby Salomon moved closer and got to know in-line skaters through: an analysis of rituals and practice codes; encounters within the in-line skate milieu; presence at in-line events; and participant observation of in-line skaters.

Phase 2 (1997–98) was all about "co-design" of the product and then launch of its in-line activities and consisted of: design of products in collaboration with skaters; work on the production of distinctive features of the product with skaters; and product testing by a team of skaters supported by Salomon.

By Phase 3 (1999), "tribal support", Salomon had taken root in the in-line skate tribe meaning: Salomon is an embedded actor who shares the values of the tribe; Salomon supports in-line events not by placing an ad (streamer) but by promoting the practice (contests); Salomon creates new events and rituals and helps in the building of in-line structures; and Salomon supports the shared passion of in-line skaters.

By 1999, Salomon had achieved 15 per cent of its turnover in snowboard and in-line skate activities. Salomon became number 3 in the world for in-line products. This has changed the positioning of the brand in the mind of the consumers. Salomon now organizes its marketing approach around the ideas of practices, tribes and passions. It has a new slogan, "Freedom, Action, Sports", a new graphic identity (the logo of the snowboard activities becomes the logo of the brand) and a new type of communication, more non-verbal than verbal.

Can we calculate the return on investment of a tribal marketing strategy? The honest answer is we don't know and, to our knowledge, no one has ever tried. We see a move towards a tribal marketing approach such as Salomon's, first and foremost, as a change in attitudes towards the practice of marketing, followed by a reassessment and redesign of practices that are already being conducted, from new product development through to marketing communications. Philosophy, ethos and approach are hard to account for financially.

According to the new dominant logic of marketing – the service dominant logic (Vargo and Lusch 2004) – the point is no longer to "market to" consumers but to "market with" consumers. Companies co-create value together with consumers and this is the key process in this new marketing logic. In tribal marketing approaches, this erasure of boundaries between consumers and producers has been pushed to the limit insofar as companies play with an intermediary actor – the tribe – which belongs both to the sphere of the offer (the company) and to the sphere of demand (the market) (Figure 11.4).

The limits of tribal marketing approaches: relinquishing control

Consumer tribes are increasingly capable of collective action and prepared to interact in a way that is more and more entrepreneurial, sometimes to the exclusion of the marketer. Indeed, as recently discussed by O'Guinn and Muñiz (2005), within brand communities, one key element in today's tribe–market interactions is that companies can lose part of their control over a brand, to be replaced by a consumer tribe that is trying to re-appropriate the brand (see Cova *et al.* 2007). For Wipperfürth (2005), a "brand hijack" occurs when a group

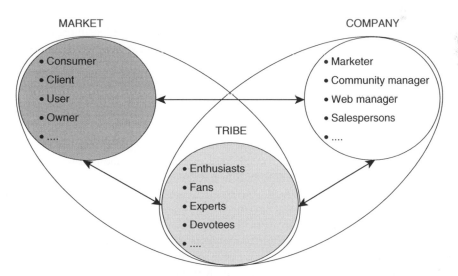

Figure 11.4 The tribe as intermediary actor.
Source: Adapted from Cova (2010).

of consumers takes a brand away from its marketing professionals in an attempt to enhance its further development. Such brand hijack phenomena are accentuated when interactions with the brand tribe occur on-line. Recent research has highlighted the many problems a company can have when interacting with this kind of hard-to-control collective actor whom the Net has spontaneously helped to foster and nurture. On-line consumers would appear to be more active, participative, resistant, militant, playful, yet also social and communitarian than ever before. They want to be influential participants in the construction of experiences. Certain consumers' shared passion for a cult brand will translate, through a range of collective learning systems, into expertise and competency, imbuing on-line tribes with greater legitimacy in production and marketing matters (O'Guinn and Muñiz 2005). As a result, the presence of tribes composed of passionate, united and expert fans has led to a re-balancing of company–consumer power relationships. The strategic options open to an organization are twofold: to try and wrestle back control of the brand; or to engage and collaborate with the tribe in new ways.

When based on a brand hijack, however, this rebalancing of power between brand communities and companies constitutes little more than a passing phenomenon (and one whose importance has been exaggerated by certain researchers and consultants) in a tribal entrepreneurship movement that is in the midst of a broader development process. Tribes are about to become collective actors in the marketplace, much in the same way as companies already are. A tribe's marketing competencies will soon rival a company's. In other words, in the not so distant future, marketing will no longer be the sole domain of a company but a means for acting upon the market that will be available to all communities. In this perspective, "the brand community is not just formed around a brand; it creates the brand. The brand community is not just formed around a product; it is part of the product" (Mairinger 2008: 118). Our final case demonstrates this possibility.

Geocaching is an entertaining outdoor adventure where people use GPS, or maps, to search for hidden containers, called geocaches, that are hidden around the world by other participants in the activity. Caches could be located by proximity to a particular address, postal code, city, or set of geographical coordinates. On 18 September 2010, there were 1,190,933 active geocaches around the world. Geocaches are currently placed in over 100 countries around the world and on all seven continents, including Antarctica. Numerous websites list geocaches around the world. The largest site is www.geocaching.com which began operating on 2 September 2000. With a worldwide membership the website lists hundreds of thousands of caches. Other international websites include NaviCache, OpenCaching, TerraCaching and GPSgames. Geocaching is enjoyed by people from all age groups, with a strong sense of community and support for the environment.

Every geocacher is a producer and a consumer of the game. Gift-giving is central to the development of this game (Boulaire and Cova 2008) as exemplified by the following quote from a geocacher:

> This is my first post and my wife and I have been geocaching since Christmas. We love caching and enjoy all the information available online. The one thing I appreciate is that so much of this info is free and available to members. I would like to do my part and give back to the community. Our first set of caches will be puzzle caches. I first saw online here some members' designs of Cryptex's with many pictures and drawings but I did have to bounce around a lot trying to get the concept. The one thing I found lacking were good quality drawings so I decided to put some of my skills to work and reverse engineered a Cryptex of my own. I used parts available at the local Home Depot but

they could be picked up at any hardware store carrying plumbing supplies. Enjoy and share, that's what there here for. This is my first finished product and will be the final stage of my cache.

(Soxter & Billini, 2 January 2010)

Geocaching is now so well developed in part because of the gift system that some companies are trying to develop partnerships with the community. The US motor manufacturer Chrysler, for example, has started the Jeep 4x4 Geocaching challenge (see http://jeep.geocaching.com/). Jeep has hidden 8,000 small Inferno Red Jeep Commander replicas with a metal tag attached, across 48 states, for participants to find and complete different specific goals every month. Here we see how a company is trying to multiply the opportunities of interactions between its brand community members and tribal members in order to enlarge the former. In doing so, it legitimates the tribe as quasi-business partner.

In these examples as in many others (e.g. CouchSurfing or BookCrossing), we see how a tribe is no longer trying to resist economic actors or the market but instead has itself become a legitimate economic actor in its marketplace, without losing any of its communitarian nature or forms. In particular, note that these tribes' tribal knowledge has given them a significant competitive advantage over their corporate rivals. Tribal knowledge is often tacit and only knowable within a dedicated group of people. It is tantamount to an informal variant of group wisdom. The term is used mostly in management circles when referencing information that other parties operating within a company may need to know if they are to produce a quality product or service. Unlike similar forms of artisan intelligence, tribal knowledge can be converted, albeit with some difficulty, into company property, as demonstrated by Moore (2006) when he describes the thought process underlying decision-making at Starbucks. However, whereas companies are working desperately to develop this type of knowledge, tribal groups are *de facto* able to renew it quite naturally among their members. Tribes work differently: individuals enter social and economic relations knowing ex-ante that giving–receiving is not dictated by somebody, nor can be weighted in a pure, rational way. For example, the (economic) value of coordinating or being part of a tribe is based upon perceptions, feelings and even emotions – beneath the actual output of the tribe and its perceived value from each member (this call for a complex set of inducements and cause–effect relations). Tribes are different: rather than "a new form of organization", they are a new way of thinking about the problem itself, of organizing, and offer a viable solution to manage the duality between individuals and organizations. This gives them an undeniable advantage over companies, one they no longer use today to resist the market but to play with it instead.

Conclusion: a tribal marketing future

The first step in any move towards a tribal marketing future is nothing less than a real re-thinking of the dominant *modus operandi* in marketing management. "KYC" (knowing your customer) may be a crucial concept in marketing, but it is often given the restricted and manipulative denotation that marketers need to know absolutely everything about consumers to satisfy them and secure their loyalty. Seldom has the idea been proposed in marketing that consumers may possess more knowledge that may be of interest to the company than the company itself. We, however, are of the opinion that in future companies will be obliged to incorporate other perspectives, like those put forward by consumers assembled alongside other consumers into tribes. The goal here will not be to use these consumers as a crutch, or leverage them as "loyal customers" but instead to learn from their expertise and experience and for the company to support the sociality inherent to the tribe.

Review and discussion questions

1   During the course of the past week, what groups do you knowingly (and perhaps unknowingly) belong to? Are some of these groups more important to your sense of "who I am", to your identity, than others?
2   Take a closer look at the groups you have identified; are they just groups or can they become a tribe? Which of these groups do you think is capable of taking part in some kind of collective action? Which of your groups could "do" things? And how could these groups be activated and become a tribe?
3   Make a list of the brands, companies, films, books, bands or even famous people that you are most passionate about. Now go on the Internet and see if you can find the existence of a tribe or brand community for each of your choices. How do you feel towards other people who use these sites? Do you feel a connection towards them?
4   Look at the CouchSurfing website (see http://www.couchsurfing.org/). Identify a list of companies or brands that could support this tribe. What issues do you think these companies could face in trying to support the tribe and how could these be overcome?
5   For a brand of your choice, identify the criteria that you think have been used to segment the market. What segments emerge from this process? What "bottom-up" naturally occurring tribes exist or can be "activated" by your chosen brand?

Keywords

community, group, linking value, tribe, value creation

References

Boulaire, C. and Cova, B. (2008) "Attiser le feu du jeu postmoderne : le cas du géocaching et de ses zones liminoides", *Sociétés*, 102: 69–82.
Brown, S. (2007) "Harry Potter and the Fandom Menace", in B. Cova, R. V. Kozinets and A. Shankar (eds), *Consumer Tribes*, Burlington, MA: Elsevier/Butterworth-Heinemann, pp.175–93.
Cléret, B. and Rémy, E. (2009) "Structuration et diffusion des sous-cultures juvéniles: L'Electro Dance et la Tecktonik à partir des Cultural Studies", in *Proceedings of the 14th Journées de Recherche en Marketing de Bourgogne*, Dijon, November.
Cova, B. (1997) "Community and Consumption: Towards a Definition of the Linking Value of Products and Services", *European Journal of Marketing*, 31(3): 297–316.
—— (2010) *Il Marketing Tribale*, 2nd edn, Milan: Il Sole 24 Ore.
Cova, B. and Cova, V. (2002) "Tribal Marketing: The Tribalization of Society and its Impact on the Conduct of Marketing", *European Journal of Marketing*, 36(5/6): 595–620.
Cova, B. and Dalli, D. (2009) "Working Consumers: The Next Step in Marketing Theory?", *Marketing Theory*, 9(3): 315–39.
Cova, B., Kozinets, R. V. and Shankar, A. (eds) (2007) *Consumer Tribes*, Burlington, MA: Elsevier/ Butterworth-Heinemann.
Kozinets, R. V. (2010) *Netnography: Doing Ethnographic Research Online*, London: Sage.
Maffesoli, M. (1996) *The Time of the Tribes*, London: Sage.
Mairinger, M. (2008) "Branding 2.0: Using Web 2.0 Principles to Build an Open Source Brand", *Electronic Markets*, 18(2): 117–29.

Moore, J. (2006) *Tribal Knowledge: Lessons Learnt from Working Inside Starbucks*, Chicago: Kaplan.

Muñiz, A. M. Jr. and O'Guinn, T. C. (2001) "Brand Community", *Journal of Consumer Research*, 27(March): 412–32.

O'Guinn, T. C. and Muñiz, A. M. Jr. (2005) "Communal Consumption and the Brand", in S. Ratneshwar and D. G. Mick (eds), *Inside Consumption: Frontiers of Research on Consumer Motives*, London: Routledge, pp. 252–72.

Prahalad, C. K. and Ramaswamy, V. (2004) *The Future of Competition: Co-Creating Unique Value with Customers*, Boston: HBS Press.

Schau, H. J., Muñiz, A. M. Jr. and Arnould, E. J. (2009) "How Brand Community Practices Create Value", *Journal of Marketing*, 73(5): 30–51.

Vargo, S. L. and Lusch, R. F. (2004) "Evolving to a New Dominant Logic for Marketing", *Journal of Marketing*, 68(1): 1–18.

Wipperfürth, A. (2005) *Brand Hijack: Marketing Without Marketing*, New York: Portfolio.

12 Facilitating collective brand engagement and collaborative production through cultural marketing

Gabriela Head, Hope Jensen Schau, and Katherine Thompson

Overview

In their ground-breaking article, Firat and Venkatesh (1995) question the accuracy and usefulness of the distinction between "producer" and "consumer." Central to their argument is that production and consumption are indistinguishable in time and space. Later, Vargo and Lusch (2004) build on this premise to posit that the traditional goods-driven logic focusing on objects as value repositories has given way to a service-dominant logic or the rise of value in use. Now, new media technologies have enabled momentous consumer empowerment, a cultural desire for co-creation, and innovative branding strategies. These three market conditions promote the blurring distinction between producer and consumer and undermine the traditional assumption that consumption is an individual and/or household level phenomenon, favoring instead the value-creating potential of collective consumer engagement. In essence, marketplace realities have evolved beyond traditional target marketing and brand management strategies. We demonstrate that *Twilight* represents a "perfect storm" of collaborative production and consumption resulting in a highly successful media brand with an enduring value proposition. Specifically, the author, Stephenie Meyer, practices cultural marketing by enabling consumers to collaboratively produce and collectively consume *Twilight* through the narrative's resonating themes, the availability of techno-social communication, and the existence of readily identifiable culturally derived behavioral templates for action. Thanks to the novels' resonating themes and to Meyer's active fan engagement, fans leverage the brand's meanings to craft a brand identity and ultimately collaborate to create a powerful brand community. *Twilight* as a brand is experienced, discussed, and disseminated collectively both online and offline. Within this brand community, consumer-generated content (CGC) is collectively created, circulated, and consumed. Some CGC is not only effective, but it is also comparable to artifacts produced by professionals. Individuals creatively self-express their love and devotion to the *Twilight* saga through a variety of outlets, which are permanent markers of self-expression and identity. There are common attractors to the brand community, and many stem from cultural implications.

What is *Twilight* and why should we care?

Twilight is a series of novels written by Stephenie Meyer and ostensibly marketed by Hachette Book Group toward young adult females, under a genre heading entitled, teenage vampire romances. The book series generated considerable sales and inspired Meyer to pursue movie adaptations of the four novels. From the initial book release in 2005, *Twilight* became a market phenomenon, with frenetic fans awaiting subsequent book releases and the debut of the film adaptations. Peculiar to this media brand is a high level of collective and collaborative engagement; consumers read and discuss the books together in formal and informal reading groups both offline and online, collaboratively create and disseminate marketing communications for the brand, view the films in groups, and engage in collective brand-based activities and events. Also unique to this brand is that its fan base is extremely skewed female.

For the uninitiated, *Twilight* must seem an unlikely topic for a management book. However, *Twilight* is a collaboratively produced marketing phenomenon created through the interplay between and among "producers" and "consumers" which stretches the boundaries of these traditional categories, rendering them almost obsolete. It is fueled by emergent marketing strategies designed by interested stakeholders to capture the logics and passions of contemporary popular culture and to package them into a highly potent value proposition. Consider this consumer response to the *Twilight: Eclipse* film which opened 30 June, 2010:

> We are all so amped! My friends and I bought our tickets for the midnight showing and we started the party at my house at 7pm in anticipation. I had the soundtrack blasting when they arrived. We had red wine flowing in *Twilight* party cups, and a *Twilight* cake I ordered from a local bakery – gorgeous! [Figure 12.1] It was a beautiful evening. The buzz was electric. We discussed the fan trailers we had seen and compared it to the one we created together and the official *Eclipse* material Stephenie [Meyer] and Summit released. We went over every detail. Twice. Three times. We popped *Twilight* and then *Twilight: New Moon*, into the dvd player and watched them on the big screen while we mingled. We were all dressed up in vamp [vampire] and Twi-gear. Two of my friends had gone together to get Twi-tats [*Twilight*-themed tattoos, Figure 12.2]. We examined them. Very tasteful. Very cool. I'm really thinking I want one too … We were happy to be together. Alone waiting for the midnight show would have been an eternity.
>
> (Megan, 27 years old, describing the pre-*Eclipse* party at her house which included 14 female friends aged 22–46)

This interview excerpt is a vivid reminder that *Twilight* is much more than a teenage vampire romance book series. It captures multi-modal fan engagement (books, films, DVDs, soundtracks, clothing, food, tattoos, and themed party supplies) targeted to a wide array of primarily female consumers, far beyond the fickle tween market. The meaning of *Twilight* and the value derived from the brand are collaboratively produced and realized in collective use. The traditional notions of target marketing, especially for a product category like teenage fiction, fail to capture the complexities of the marketplace (cf. Chapter 18 in this volume for a review of targeting). Even suggesting that the brand is targeted toward a conglomeration of individual girls aged 10–18 is unnecessarily restrictive and fails to address the majority of users who have collaboratively infused the brand with value and collectively consumed it in their everyday lives. Echoing this sentiment, Fandango (online ticket retailer) conducted a survey in 2008 of *Twilight* fans who purchased tickets for the first film discovering that nearly 50 percent of the fans were over the age of 25 and more than 60 percent of the fans intended to see the movie with more than three friends. Furthermore, the Fandango survey revealed that more than one-fourth of the fans were planning to see the film with their mothers or daughters. These facts support our assertion that the *Twilight Saga* is not merely a teen sensation, but a female-driven, collaboratively experienced brand.

Figure 12.1 The *Eclipse* party cake.
        Source: Photo credits: Head *et al.*

Figure 12.2 One of the *Twilight* themed tattoos.
        Source: Photo credits: Head *et al.*

Even if we agree that traditional targeting strategies are ineffective for reaching *Twilight* consumers, many skeptics might argue that *Twilight* is a marginal, or offbeat brand, and insights gleaned are too idiosyncratic to transfer to other, more mainstream market offerings. Food for thought, according to Forbes: Stephenie Meyer is the second highest paid author of 2010, earning $40 million in the calendar year despite not releasing a new title since 2008, and the third installment of the *Twilight Saga* films garnered $175 million in the first week of its debut, making it the most successful theatrical release of 2010. *USA Today* claims that one in every seven books sold in 2009 was written by Meyer. These statistics substantiate our rationale that *Twilight* is a highly successful example of a culturally marketed brand.

Through the *Twilight* series (Box 12.1), the author has created an iconic brand (Holt 2004) by presenting her readers with resonating themes: postmodern feminism, romance, and superhuman science fiction. The *Twilight* Saga has captivated millions of readers

---

Box 12.1 The *Twilight* summary

Bella Swan is the story's heroine; a self-conscious yet self-sufficient teen who relocates from sunny Phoenix, Arizona, to overcast Forks, Washington, to live with her father. Forks is the perfect environment for the Cullens, a clan of vampires, in which to dwell. Its overcast skies enable them to blend in with mortals and hide one of their immortal's traits: skin that sparkles like diamonds in the direct sunlight. Forks is also a safe haven for the Cullens because the Quileute's ancestors, a Native American tribe, made a pact with the Cullens that allows them to live in the area as long as they do not feed, harm, or turn humans into vampires. To honor this treaty, the Cullens abide to a strict "vegetarian" diet – feeding on game animals rather than humans. The vampire–werewolf co-existence is severely threatened when Edward Cullen, a dashing 108-year-old vampire "stuck" in the body of a 17-year-old becomes aware of Bella's natural scent. Bella and Edward fall deeply in love, but their love is permeated with constraints that Meyer presents throughout her four novels, *Twilight*, *New Moon*, *Eclipse* and *Breaking Dawn*:

- Victoria, an avenging vampire, has her heart set on killing Bella. When the Quileute sense danger coming, a select few are pre-destined to become shapeshifters who transform into werewolves.
- The oldest vampire clan, the Volturi, have a rigid set of cardinal rules – any human who knows about the existence of vampires must either be converted into a vampire or be killed and vampires must never ever breed.
- Jacob Black is in love with Bella, and he is not only a Quileute, but also a shapeshifter who swears to protect Bella against any harm, including Edward.
- Edward will forever be 17, Bella is getting older, and Edward refuses to convert her into a vampire.
- Bella and Edward eventually get married. Bella gets pregnant, and gives birth to a half-vampire, half-human child Renesmee.
- Childbirth almost kills Bella and to save her, Edward has to turn her into a vampire.
- Renesmee's predestined life-mate is no other than Jacob Black a.k.a Quileute werewolf previously in love with Bella.
- Renesmee's birth beckons the fury of the powerful Volturi.
- In the end, the Cullens, the Quileute, and other vampire clans unite to fight the Volturi. Bella and Edward live happily ever after.

worldwide, and has garnered the interest of multi-generational populations. Readers' interest in Meyer's works has galvanized a significant portion of them to form brand communities whose members celebrate their attachment to these works both offline and online.

What is collective, collaborative consumption and why is it important?

Collective consumption is quite literally when consumers use the brand together. It can take many shapes: sharing a meal or a cup of coffee with friends and family, playing video games with others either proximally or online, enjoying music or television with others, or going to an amusement park. Collaborative consumption is when consumers work together with other consumers and/or producers to construct the brand and its meaning. This can also take many shapes including painting ceramics at a studio like Color Me Mine, producing a fan-made movie trailer, personalizing a shoe on Nike.com, or designing and/or buying a t-shirt on Threadless.com.

One form of collective, collaborative consumption is brand communities. According to Muñiz and O'Guinn (2001), brand communities are enduring (not single use) collectives that are centered on the brand and contain three markers: a consciousness of kind, rituals and traditions, and a sense of moral responsibility for one another. Schau, Muñiz and Arnould (2009) assert that brand community members collaboratively engage in value-creating practises. Brand-community cultures are a phenomenon that calls for a shift in the way brands market to consumers. Traditional marketing and even cross-cultural marketing strategies may not be appropriate as racial, national, and generational markers are no longer what characterize consumers' lifestyles and predict consumption behaviors. The factors that distinguish brand community members from traditional consumers include their connection to the brand's offering, their relation to other brand consumers, and their ability to participate in the evolution of the brand.

Cultural marketing offers an alternative to the process in which an external market analysis is executed because it looks beyond demographics, lifestyle, and usage. Cultural marketing examines the connection between the consumers' lived-in worlds and the tangible and intangible resources on which they depend (Arnould and Thompson 2005). Through cultural marketing, firms learn how consumption helps them to create or reinvent their personal identity (Bonsu and Belk 2003) and form group affiliations. The motivations behind identity and group affiliation are elements that help marketers unearth material, metaphorical, and evocative aspects of consumers' consumption behaviors, and explore how consumers interpret advertisements and other brand messages (Grayson and Martinec 2004).

In this case, cultural marketing manifests itself when resonating themes within the brand foster identification, techno-social spaces nurture connectivity, and behavioral templates motivate active engagement among consumers. Through cultural marketing, brands use the insight provided by community members to outline their strategies, which ultimately allow brands to meet consumers' compelling but as of yet unarticulated needs.

The role of brands in the creation of brand community cultures is critical. Brands need to cultivate the loyal consumer base, provide opportunities for consumer-to-consumer relationship building, and encourage co-creation experiences. When brands achieve this, they can sustain deep levels of connection with consumers where insufficient marketing data, consumer behavior knowledge, etc. are part of bygone eras.

The breadth of *Twilight* merchandise, books, movie tickets, DVDs, etc. provides a window into the market power Meyer commands. These facts do not accurately represent the societal change Meyers has created within the marketplace. Through active engagement, Meyer inspired a loyal fan base to partake in the creation of a female-driven brand community. Interestingly, female-driven consumption collectives are considerably less prominent in the marketplace than gender-balanced collectives and even than male-driven brand communities which are the most common in the marketplace. The diversity in nationalities, socio-cultural backgrounds, and age groups adds to the uniqueness of the brand community as *Twilight* has attracted the attention of young female readers, their older siblings, their mothers, and even their grandmothers from around the globe. The activities conducted by this diverse group of community members set these passionate fans apart from conventional book consumers.

Traditional readers may have read the book series and talked about it with friends, family, and co-workers. They might have passed the books on to someone else to enjoy. However, *Twilight* community members are not simply readers. Community members have read and re-read the books. They will not dare part with them. They happily stood in line for hours for the midnight *Twilight* movie premier, and they returned to the theater to view the movie multiple times. Many held parties to commemorate the *Twilight* movie or DVD release. When community members try to convey to non-*Twilight* lovers the significance of the storyline and characters, they often get blank stares. Thus, for *Twilight* brand community members it is much easier and rewarding to share their passions with others like them who share their meanings and jargon.

Cultural marketing elements

The elements that enable consumers to collaboratively produce and collectively consume *Twilight* are the narrative's resonating themes, the availability of techno-social communication, and the existence of readily identifiable culturally derived behavioral templates for action. Beyond traditional notions of brand management, Meyer leverages these elements to facilitate collective engagement and collaborative production. Resisting the familiar target marketing strategies that would limit brand information dissemination and reduce consumer opportunities for engagement, Meyer actively spurs consumers to produce brand value with her and with one another.

Resonating themes

Meyer offers her *Twilight* readers a rich storyline that contains aspects that deeply resonate with her audience: feminine gender identification, romantic motifs, and superhuman science fiction. These building blocks created not only a unifying bond, but they also foster readership identification with *Twilight* and among readers.

Feminine gender identification

The *Twilight* series presents strong female characters that mirror the traits that twenty-first-century women across several geo-political boundaries value and with which they relate. Her characters depict a range of behaviors that portray women and their distinctive strengths, talents, and vulnerabilities. Bella's mom, although described as "flighty," also has strong intuition that can perceive the strong chemistry between Bella and Edward. The matriarch of the Cullen's family, Esme, renders the role of a resilient and loving mother who despite not birthing any of her "children" is a deeply caring mother. Edward's sister Rosalie, whose antagonistic behavior almost gets Edward killed, guards the safety of Edward's and Bella's child.

Bella's maturity, intelligence, and moral map enable her to be a caretaker to her parents, an accomplished student, and a caring friend to Jacob. Her aversion to being controlled by anyone, including her beloved Edward, prompts her to take risks despite her innate clumsiness. Riding a motorcycle and visiting Jacob's territory, which is forbidden to Edward, show her care-free and independent nature. Bella asserts her sexuality and specifically her need for sexual intimacy by enticing Edward, who tries everything in his power not to give in.

Bella's intelligence and resolve to fight for what she wants position her to be a tenacious fighter and an astute negotiator. Bella knows that in order to be with Edward for all eternity, she has to become a vampire. Yet, Edward fights her on this issue. Bella lobbies Edward's family by presenting the logic behind her request and asks them to take a vote on it. She gains their support and promise to facilitate this transition. Readers witness Bella's ability to exert her leadership through consensus rather than sharp individualism (Rosener 1990). As the storyline progresses, readers witness Bella becoming an even stronger person, and in the end, Bella's assertive leadership shines through as she protects the clan and friends by using a protective shield.

Despite these examples of determination, intelligence, and resiliency, *Twilight* readers do not consider Bella to be a "feminist." In their opinion, the fact that she cooks and keeps home for her mother and later her father exclude her from being considered a feminist. Readers are trapped in the 1960s–1980s expectations for feminism in which women must constantly fight for equality and against male domination. During this period, feminists like Betty Friedman argued that women are victims to the ideal of finding self-identity through their families and home-keeping activities. This theory becomes an obstacle for readers to identify Bella as a feminist since her devotion to Edward is perceived as a loss of self-identity.

Through *Twilight*'s female characters, Meyer captures a key concern for her women fan base: the need to discuss and potentially redefine feminism. Meyer's readers want to be strong and independent females without being classified as traditional "feminists," and derive satisfaction from having a family and home without being stereotyped as "subservient." Meyer addresses this concern by giving readers an alternative to the "feminist" woman. Through *Twilight*'s female characters, Meyer gives readers "postmodern feminist" role models.

These postmodern feminists can select how they find meaning in their lives and define themselves in whatever way they choose. Esme has chosen to care for her "children" advising them not be "show-offs" or cheat during baseball games. Renee doesn't have a home-maker bone in her body, yet, she is constantly trying to learn new things and grow as a human being. Rosalie would give up beauty and immortality to give birth to a child, and uses her strength to defend Bella's choice to continue her pregnancy. Alice loves fashion, fast cars, and Jasper. Bella finds meaning in her life by caring for her parents, falling in love, joining Edward's family, and protecting her reproductive rights. Through these postmodern feminist role models, Meyer presents her readers with a solution to the challenging aspect of balancing their emotional and intellectual needs against society's expectations.

Romantic motifs

Meyer uses characters and concepts to present romantic motifs of deep meaning to her female fan base. Falling in love for the first time is *Twilight*'s initial allure. Through Edward and Bella, older readers recall the experience of their first love without judging the often selfless abandonment and obsessive behaviors that characterize this experience. Younger readers are given a peek into the emotions people experience when they are falling in love for the first time.

The description of Edward, a strikingly beautiful, loving, intelligent, and profoundly faithful vampire who has never felt love until he met Bella, a young mortal female, has proven to be irresistible to female readers regardless of age. Edward epitomizes the traits female readers want to see in their significant others. These traits allow the reader to justify their postmodern feminist attitudes.

Through Bella's and Edward's connection, and Sam, head of the werewolves' "pack" and his life-mate, Emily, Meyers addresses her readers' desire to experience pre-destined monogamy. Edward's ability not to give into the temptation of feeding on her allows Edward to be close to her. A man who is able to conquer his innate need to feed on humans can be a man who is able to be faithful, protective, and completely devoted. Edward articulates his commitment to Bella when he is forced to interact with Jacob, his contender for Bella's love, "You become whatever she needs you to be, whether that's a protector, or a lover, or a friend, or a brother."

Edward's role embodies the positive elements of Hemingway's "Code-Hero" combined with supernatural powers. As a "Code-Hero," Edward has physical power and emotional strength. His speed and intensity enable him to protect Bella against all dangers. Since he doesn't need to sleep, he can watch over Bella while she sleeps. His presence allows Bella's subconscious to rest and prevent her from having nightmares. Unlike a "Code-Hero," Edward only has eyes for Bella. He verbalizes his love for her, and can artistically express this through the lullabies he sings to her. The fact that Edward is an immortal being will enable him to actually deliver on his promise to love Bella forever.

Through these romantic themes, Meyer responds to female readers' needs. The realities of divorce, infidelity, and alienation, etc., have modified our society's outlook on romance and companionship. Yet, female audiences cheer for heroines like *Sex and the City*'s Carrie. This famous heroine refuses to compromise and give up on love. As she breaks up with Aleksandr, her Russian boyfriend, she says, "I am someone who is looking for love … real love … ridiculous, inconvenient, consuming, can't live without each other love." Meyer provides her readers with an ideal love story in which Edward and Bella put all inconveniences aside and determine that they cannot live without each other.

Superhuman science fiction

In the *Twilight* series, the Vampire and Quileute clans possess supernatural powers. These powers set them apart from normal human beings. Fans of superhuman science fiction resonate with *Twilight*'s storyline, and they have become an important part of Meyer's fan base. Female gender identification and romantic motifs are important themes to them as well, and they consider superhuman powers to bring fantasy aspects to the storyline. These characteristics enable *Twilight*'s Leah Clearwater to be the only female who transforms into a wolf. Through Leah's character, readers can observe the insecurities of a female whose unrequited love left her bitter, but whose strength, intelligence, and comradeship positioned her to become a respected leader within the pack. Alice's ability to predict the future coupled with her physicality and bravery makes her a central character. The Cullen clan relies on Alice to alert them of potential dangers, and Edward entrusts her with Bella's safety when he cannot be physically present. The superhuman powers possessed by Leah and Alice allow the readers to experience raw feminine leadership and strength.

Mind reading, future prediction, emotion manipulation, and shape-shifting are topics that have a strong attraction for both male and female fans. During the 1930s and 1950s, superhuman science fiction took shape in Superman and Spider-Man. Superhuman science fiction continues to be in high demand as observed in the *Harry Potter* series. Harry possesses a superhuman power: feeling Voldemort's evil thoughts. Today, shows like *True Blood* portray female characters with a wide range of supernatural powers. Sookie Stackhouse, the heroine in *True Blood*, is a telepath who can read everyone's thoughts except for Bill, the vampire with whom she falls in love. Fantasy plays a key role in superhuman science fiction, and it allows for practically anything to be possible.

Techno-social spaces

Communication spaces

When *Twilight* was released in 2005, it did not debut at number one in the *New York Times'* best-sellers list as *Eclipse* did, the third novel in the series. The first edition of *Twilight* slowly gained popularity thanks to the young readers. The proverbial word-of mouth-effect took off as peer-to-peer reviews were given by readers off- and on-line. The postings of comments on Facebook, MySpace, and other techno-social spaces also influenced other people to pick up the book. Slowly, the fan base within the young female audience began to grow. As older females witnessed this trend, they started reading it too.

Reader-to-reader meeting space

As *Twilight* fans began to experience the emotions they were feeling as they read the books, they sought to connect with other like-minded fans. They began to create techno-social spaces where they could meet other *Twilight* fans with whom they could share their emotions. Young girls listed the reasons why they were falling in love with Edward. Others confessed to be falling in love with Edward. Older fans commiserated with other women in their cohort about their obsession with *Twilight*. They found common emotions such as feeling 16 again, recalling the emotions they felt when they fell in love for the first time, and even lamented the loss of the Edward-like first love they once had with their current partners.

Author-to-reader meeting space

While fans explored the dimensions that connected them to *Twilight*, Meyer was paying attention to what fans were saying. She began to look at the sites that fans had created. She often posted comments and responded to questions. Meyer used MySpace as a techno-social space in which to cultivate her relationship with her fans. One-on-one literary conversations began to take place. Her readers sought to understand character behaviors, and Meyer offered reading book guides to encourage readers to discuss central topics. She prompted readers to evaluate Bella's self-endangering behaviors and explore the Cullens' resolve to feed on animals rather than humans. Since Meyer used literary classics such as *Pride and Prejudice*, *Romeo and Juliet*, and *Wuthering Heights* to contrast *Twilight* themes, she encouraged readers to read these works.

By presenting readers with a map to continue discovering the prism of female personalities and central romantic themes, Meyer further cemented her relationship with her fans. Through Elizabeth Bennet, Juliet Capulet, and Catherine Earnshaw, *Twilight* readers witness the virtues and flaws of each character: Elizabeth's intelligence and prejudice, Juliet's innocence and idealism, Catherine's passion and selfishness. By contrasting the challenges that these protagonists faced with those faced by Bella, Meyer helps readers recognize the multitude of options females have in today's day and age. By the same token, readers can see that these characters are all flawed in one way or another because they are human. Their vulnerabilities and strengths were illustrated through prejudice, suicide, and unrequited love fulfillment in the after-life. Through these interactions, Meyer discovered and applauded her readers' creativity and insight. Meyer's support for her fans coupled with their talents allowed deep levels of connection between *Twilight* and the fans.

In June of 2009, Meyer announced to her fans that she was officially taking down her MySpace page. She stated that the overwhelming volume of emails she received made it impossible for her to continue communicating with them as she had in the past, one-on-one email correspondence. She reminded them that she didn't use Facebook or Twitter, but that she would continue to communicate with them via her personal website. She wished everyone a great summer, and as usual, she suggested summer reading material by a fellow writer. Subsequent communications by Meyer followed thereafter in which she continued to cultivate her relationship with her fans.

Behavioral templates

Consumer-generated content

Meyer's *Twilight* themes offer readers storylines that are not bound to traditional reality. Readers can envision a multitude of possibilities given the presence of powerful female leaders, alternate reality worlds, and superhuman science fiction, together, these elements provide readers with the building blocks to unleash their creativity. Moreover, Meyer's fan engagement positioned her to encourage them to write around her story line and to explore character development. These became invitations for readers to create consumer-generated content. The readers' keen interest in Edward prompted them to pen fan-fiction stories from the perspective of different characters. Fans explored a multitude of "what if" scenarios. For example, Lori Joff's a.k.a "Alphie" wrote "The Lion and the Lamb," which is *Twilight* narrated by Edward, and posted it on fanfiction.net. Meyer found the story and reached out to Alphie because Meyer was working on the same project. She was writing *Midnight Sun*, which was Edward's version of *Twilight*. Other *Twilight*-inspired fanfiction centers mostly on characters' future or past. These include stories about Bella's new life as a vampire and Rosalie's life before being turned into a vampire. Superhuman science fiction also inspires other fans to combine story lines such as "Jane Volturi" goes to Hogwarts. Through these examples we can see that open source literature allows fans to personalize *Twilight*, by engaging in customizing practises within the brand community.

Modeled practises

As a writer, Meyer promoted *Twilight* by going to her fair share of book signings and creating *Twilight* events. The showings were small, but these gave her an opportunity to further connect with her readers. Meyer arranged *Twilight* parties, specifically "I Love Edward" parties. These experiences allowed fans to participate in collective consumption, becoming more involved with the brand community, and realizing more value from the brand experience. As Meyer released *New Moon* and *Eclipse*, her book signings were drawing audiences of up to 3,000. During a book signing for *New Moon*, a college student recommended that Meyer should organize a *New Moon* Prom, and the publishers organized the event. Six hours after Meyer promoted the *New Moon* Prom online, the event had sold out.

The release of the fourth book, *Breaking Dawn*, was considered by Borders to be the biggest book event of the year. Other bookstores like Barnes & Noble coordinated elaborate parties in hundreds of stores in which fans were dressed in *Twilight* costumes and were ready to celebrate the release of the much anticipated book. Meyer encouraged the cult-of-the author by playing up her Mormon housewife identity and making a cameo in the *Twilight* film. She also held events centered on the movie, and most important, she attended those created by the fans. When Meyer issued a call to action promoting the "Save the Book Babe" event, a fundraiser to help a close friend battling cancer, her members showed up with their wallets ready to help.

Meyer reached out to her fans by making herself accessible both online and face-to-face and drawing on cultural marketing to identify her resonating themes. The fact that she coordinated events to connect with her readers allowed them to live the *Twilight* experience on a deeper level. This experience was further magnified as fans began to create their own events. As fans coordinated satellite proms and international proms around the world, *Twilight* traditions began to emerge. As these traditions formed, customs and behavioral protocols followed and these continue to evolve based on the needs of the fans.

The *Twilight* community culture

Resonating themes, connection via techno-social spaces, and behavioral templates gave fans an emotional connection to *Twilight* and Meyer. This connection incited passion in fans, which drove them into making a deeper personal investment which took shape in the form of an active female brand community. The members of this brand community share values, norms, beliefs, and practices that are the integral parts of a culture.

The more than 400 *Twilight* techno-social spaces give community members a space in which to befriend other Twilighters or Twithards, terms that some members use to describe themselves. These spaces become important communication channels and relationship enablers. Fans can share the comprehensive vision of *Twilight*'s importance in their lives. They do not feel as if they have to rationalize their attachment to *Twilight*. They seek others who understand this situation by forming support groups like "Parents Just Don't Understand *Twilight* Life," "The Older Woman Group," and "Bella Moments," which celebrates their identification with Bella's clumsiness.

As with any culture, the *Twilight* brand community has unifying principles that cement the brand, and the elements of cultural marketing, resonating themes, techno-social connectivity, and behavioral templates are manifested through the ideology and norms shared by the great majority of members. At the same time, factions emerge as some members seek like-minded individuals. Groups of compatible friends form and through these, members can express their different beliefs and exercise evocative rituals.

Ideology

Meyer's themes provide *Twilight* members with the opportunity to share cultural ideologies. Female gender identification, romantic motifs, and superhuman fiction provide a common ground for members to connect. The fact that this community is comprised of multi-generational members is not problematic. Different age cohorts identify with different themes and in the different ways they apply these themes to their own lives. For example, for many of the younger audience, Bella's love for Edward and her ultimate sacrifice consecrate her as a strong and independent heroine. For the mature readers, Bella mirrors the traits and behaviors they see in themselves. Bella's intelligence, tenacity, and faith in love call upon the deeply personal sentiments felt by women who, despite personal heart-break, still believe in the magic of loving and being loved. Some members are deeply drawn to Esme. Her maternal instincts touch the needs of some members as they declare that they wish Esme was their mom. Other readers find common ground exploring the superhuman powers. Some forums are devoted to discussing the Quileute tribe. They are drawn to the idea of people developing superhuman powers based on the need to respond to imminent danger.

Norms

Within the brand community, members expect to be involved in the directionality of the brand because the modeled practise cultivated by Meyer has given fans the behavioral template to do so. Thanks to Meyer's open engagement and inclusion of members in key decisions, members feel permitted to make tangible investments in the brand. Fans' investments come in the form of forum discussions, fan-fiction, fan-art, and fan-made videos and movie trailers. Tiffany Dalton, a 19-year-old Australian, is famous for *New Moon*, one of the most viewed fan-made *Twilight* trailers. It has been voted by members as the number one trailer, and fans openly advocate for the movie studio to hire Dalton.

As Summit Entertainment began to cast for *Twilight*'s film adaptation, Meyer asked readers to suggest actors for the parts. She provided them with a special email address in which they could send their nominations. Meyer also called for movie critique, and fans' feedback was instrumental in the modifications made by the director. These invitations to participate and feedback integration cause members to become vested and prompt vigilante marketing behaviors.

Members practice vigilante marketing when they discover anti-*Twilight* sites like Twilightsucks.com. They quickly posted messages condoning the site. There was an open debate in which a member called for a rebellion. Protecting the brand from enemies is not the only responsibility members take upon themselves. A group called "The *Twilight* Zone Rumor Control" takes it upon itself to confirm or deny any rumor about the brand. Members of "A Deeper Look in the *Twilight* Saga" discuss the future of *Twilight*.

Demonstrating affiliation is another important norm with the *Twilight* culture. Members proudly announce which "*Twilight* Character" they are after taking the Facebook quiz – immediately, they tweeted the results for the entire world to read. Creating avatars and Sims (Strategic Life Simulation) computer game characters inspired by *Twilight* are important symbols that represent belonging. At preparatory schools where high school students have a hard time distinguishing themselves from the identical school uniforms of their peers, it is common to find *Twilight* paraphernalia adorning backpacks, decorating lockers, and *Twilight* discussions becoming the last whispers overheard through the halls as the teens head into class.

Beliefs

The beliefs shared by the *Twilight* community stem from their attitudes toward the themes in the storyline and the behavioral templates modeled by Meyer. Fans believe that by participating in discussion groups, they are keeping the brand alive and helping it grow. They explore and argue about these attitudes among each other. Fans also believe that they have the moral right to articulate their opinions through discussions, fan-fiction, fan-art, fan-made videos, and collective practices.

The members exercise their freedom of speech by creating special interest groups. Some members gravitate to discussion groups that explore each book individually. Other groups have formed around a character or characters such as the "Emmett Fan Club" or the "Werewolf Fans." Members have also clustered around age group such as "The Older Woman Group." Other groups form based on members' likes or dislikes in music: "The Paramore Rockers"; "*Twilight* Role Play"; and "Fanfiction". Other groups come together due to their affinity to superhuman science fiction like "Heroes" and "True Blood."

These numerous groups allow members to chime in depending on what they find appealing. In the "*Twilight* Fans who Love Harry Potter" group, members express appreciation for both book series and for having the ability to connect with other people who feel like them – especially within the TwilightSaga.com community. Members in this group discuss their excitement for the *Half-Blood Prince* movie released in the Summer of 2009. They network among the group to enquire about release dates and locations in European countries. Their shared interests and community building within these groups transcend the *Twilight* theme as the platform becomes about the fans.

The community members collectively discuss these topics with fervor. They universally find the vampires sympathetic and their efforts to exist without harming humans to be noble. The vampire quest for legitimacy and acceptance within human society is intriguing and readers compare this to race, ethnicity, and class struggles in contemporary society. Factions emerge when "solutions" to this inequality are vetted. Likewise, strong factions form around the characters and their archetypes. Age cohorts divisions are the least stable as readers readily interact across cohorts to collectively discuss the characters, plot, and interpretations.

Rituals

The shared practices among *Twilight* modeled by Meyer strengthen the bonds between the community and the brand. Members engage in debating their topic of interest and belonging to multiple forums and groups increases their involvement in the brand. *Twilight* members partake in a wide range of discussions with their groups of choice. Knowledge and wit are celebrated within these conversations. Well-informed members who can express their ideas with wit are celebrated by other members. To maintain their status, these members have to demonstrate their strong understanding of the plotline, themes, and character development.

They coordinate *Twilight* events and promote them via multiple techno-social spaces. For example, members organized hundreds of events as the *Twilight* movie and the soundtrack were released. It was not uncommon to see large groups of older women going to the premiere of *Twilight* dressed up in character costumes. Members also organize international events to welcome the much anticipated release of the *New Moon* movie in November 2009. Other groups plan *Twilight* pilgrimages to Forks, WA (where the story takes place).

Within the wall-less community, members organize bi-weekly "Fan fiction" contests in which fans present their own take on *Twilight* ideas and ask the community to vote for them. A group called "The Deeper Look" wrestles with issues about the future of the *Twilight* brand. The members in this group discuss whether the *Twilight* hype is winding down and the appropriate length of the final movie. They also discuss the fact that *Twilight* has become a part of their lives.

The advantages of cultural marketing in *Twilight*

Through *Twilight*, Meyer captured the attention of her female fan base by using key ideological concerns manifested by the actions and vulnerabilities of female characters. Romantic ideas explored within *Twilight* and other works of literature allow the readers to gain a deeper perspective into the complex nature of human relationships and the obstacles society sets forth such as intolerance and prejudice. Superhuman powers possessed by female characters add interesting personality traits and places them in important leadership roles. These themes unite to fulfill an unmet need: modern feminist role models. This solution creates a prevailing bond among *Twilight* fans and between them and the brand.

This bond is fortified by the authentic relationship Meyer has fostered among the fans. Her calls to action have set up behavioral templates to emulate and to enhance. The shared ideologies, norms, beliefs, and rituals bring to life the *Twilight* culture. Through this culture, members consume as a collective, and they have created factions to reinforce their commonalities.

Cultural marketing provides brands with invaluable insight into what consumers want and are willing to purchase. Another major advantage is the opportunity to create new offerings that have a built-in market. Hot Topic is licensed to sell *Twilight* branded merchandise: jewelry, t-shirts, carrying cases, and even "Edward Body Shimmer." Fans eagerly waited for the *Twilight* Sweethearts for Valentine's Day, and they communicated amongst each other to identify the stores that had them in stock. Mattel released *Twilight* dolls, in which Bella and Edward displace the iconic Barbie and Ken duo. Duop Cosmetics released its line of *Twilight* make-up featuring lip-plumping venom. Half of the liquid is red and users have to shake it up before applying to symbolize the human and vampire coming together. *Twilight* fans use this merchandise to show membership affiliation and continue living the *Twilight* experience.

Similar works of fiction: different approaches

The *Twilight* Saga and the *Harry Potter* series have been compared by critics and fans alike since *Twilight* began to gain notoriety. Both works share a number of commonalities:

- appeal to multi-generational readers;
- a multi-volume series allowing reader longevity;
- film versions providing fans with visuals;

- after midnight launch parties;
- superhuman fiction;
- alternate reality worlds;
- active brand communities.

Indeed, the books do share commonalties as their authors also do. However, when it comes to brand community nurturing, Meyer and Rowling have taken drastically different approaches. Rowling has maintained an overt distance between herself and her fans. She has not fostered collaborative opportunities with her brand community members. In fact, she scorns the idea of fan-fiction being commercialized, and she does not hesitate to defend her copyrights through lengthy litigation. She gave her "blessing" for her readers to post their fan-fiction creations online and announced that she wouldn't take legal action as long as they do not profit from its commercialization.[1]

In 2008, Rowling won a court battle against a small publishing house, RDR Books, for attempting to publish *The Harry Potter Lexicon*, a reference work written by school librarian Steven Vander Ark. In his ruling, the presiding judge, Robert Patterson, wrote that Vander Ark's lexicon "appropriates too much of Rowling's creative work for its purposes as a reference guide." However, he also ruled that "while the lexicon, in its current state, is not a fair use of the *Harry Potter* works, reference works that share the lexicon's purpose of aiding readers of literature generally should be encouraged rather than stifled."[2]

Despite Rowling's actions, the *Harry Potter* brand community has bound together to help each other enjoy the series. A "translation collective" group emerged in Germany. Their mission is to enhance communication and education among *Harry Potter* fans. The group had identified errors in the official German translation of the *Harry Potter* books, and the group lists these errors on its website.

The comparison with the engagement between Meyer and the *Twilight* brand community and between Rowling and the *Harry Potter* brand community highlights three important factors. First, products that resonate with consumers' ideologies will garner brand community formation whether supported by the brand or not. Muñiz and Schau (2007) show that the discontinuation of Apple's Newton device did not prevent its brand community from forming a strong, active, and collaborative brand community, which took on traditional brand roles such as service and repair, configuration, and marketing "anti-Steve Jobs" campaigns. Second, brands can choose to have collaborative relationships with their brand communities or antagonistic ones. iPhone users were highly critical of Apple's decision not to open its operating system for user modification. They rallied hard, and Apple eventually budged. This gave way to the user-generated applications, which became the iPhone's powerful value proposition. Third, antagonistic relationships between brands and their brand communities are much more damaging to the brands than the community members. Rowling claimed that the court battles caused her to develop writer's block. Meanwhile, Meyer harvested the insight learned through her brand community and wrote an adult fiction book, *The Host*. This new book presents readers with some of the fundamental elements that made fans fall in love with *Twilight*. *The Host*, a romantic story with a dose of good versus evil is set in a futuristic and dangerous world.

Managerial implications for cultural marketing

Brands that want to employ cultural marketing strategies to reach consumers must first explore how their offerings resonate with their consumers' ideology, norms, beliefs, and rituals. Brands can use cultural markers to provide solutions that help consumers practice their beliefs and engage in rituals that foster connectivity to their ideologies.

The sports world provides a safe masculine environment for men to celebrate their love for sports, male-bonding, etc. Early fall Sunday afternoons mark the beginning of the football season. Fans, of which the majority are male, gather around the television to watch their favorite teams battle it out. Many reasons connect fans to their favorite team, an athlete, hometown or *alma mater* alliance, a childhood memory, etc. Fans share ideologies about the game and its rules, and how players, coaches, and managers should behave. They adhere to behavioral expectations like keeping up with scores during games even while traveling. At the core of their love for the game, they respect the benefits of competition and teamwork. They participate in rituals like watching Super Bowl Sunday, cheering at the right moments, and buckling when the going gets tough.

For today's time-deprived females, the expectation of home-made meal preparation is a stressor. A segment of the female population wants to embrace the notion of domestication; yet their lifestyle circumstances and the constant battle to balance work and life are juxtaposed against contemporary women's ideology. They need a solution that helps them meet behavioral expectations without sacrificing their self-actualization objectives. *30 Minute Meals*, a well-known show on the Food Network, offers women recipes and directions for preparing meals in less than 30 minutes.[3] These programs offer women a solution that helps them meet this social expectation. Consumers can enact the domestication norm of serving a "home-made meal" with the understanding that it has to be something that is quick and easy, and that this cooking template is congruent with today's lifestyles. They can sit with their families and practice the ritual of dining as family and holding true to their social values.

Conclusion

The key advantage for marketing practitioners using a cultural marketing approach is the ability to become a resource to resolve tension in expected modes of behavior, societal roles or other issues critical to the lives of their consumers. *Twilight* resolved the tension in women's view of feminine roles and created a loyal brand community. The co-creation efforts among the brand and its community result in a loyal customer base working to protect the brand. This practice positions *Twilight* as an integral part of the members' lifestyle that can continue to create opportunities for the brand.

Review and discussion questions

1   How does collective, collaborative consumption relate to cultural marketing?
2   In which ways does *Twilight* facilitate cultural marketing?
3   What lessons can be learned from the *Twilight* case?
4   What effect if any did the author's engagement with the fans have on the overall power of the *Twilight* brand?
5   What role does technology play in facilitating collective engagement and collective consumption?
6   What other brands practice cultural marketing and how do they do so?

7   What makes the *Twilight* Saga such a successful brand community? What are the contributing factors?
8   How would you market the *Twilight* Saga in today's marketplace? Come up with a marketing plan/strategy that defines the target market, the promotion/execution strategy, and the metrics that will determine the product's success.
9   How would you leverage brand loyalists and evangelists to promote your product?

Keywords

behavioral templates, brand communities, brand loyalists, brand meaning, collective consumption, collective engagement, consumer collaboration, consumer engagement, consumer-generated content, cult of the author, fan-art, fan-fiction, fansites, user-generated content

References

American Library Association (2008) "J. K. Rowling Wins Copyright Fight," September 10, 2008. Available at: http://www.ala.org/ala/alonline/currentnews/newsarchive/2008/september2008/rowlingwinsrdrsuit.cfm (accessed March 10, 2009).

Arnould, Eric and Thompson, Craig (2005) "Consumer Culture Theory (CCT): Twenty Years of Research," *Journal of Consumer Research*, 31(1): 868–82.

Bonsu, Samel K. and Belk, Russell W. (2003) "Do Not Go Cheaply Into That Good Night: Death Ritual Consumption in Asante, Ghana," *Journal of Consumer Research*, 30 (June): 41–55.

Firat, A. Fuat and Venkatesh, Alladi (1995) "Liberatory Postmodernism and the Reenchantment with Consumption," *Journal of Consumer Research*, 22 (December).

Grayson, Kent and Martinec, Radan (2004) "Consumer Perceptions of Iconicity and Indexicality and Their Influence on Assessments of Authentic Market Offerings," *Journal of Consumer Research*, 31(September), 296–312.

Holt, Douglas (2004) *How Brands Become Icons: The Principles of Cultural Branding*, Boston: Harvard Business Press.

Muñiz, Albert M. Jr. and O'Guinn, T. C. (2001) "Brand Communities," *Journal of Consumer Research*, 27(March): 412–32.

Muñiz, Albert M. Jr. and Schau, Hope Jensen (2007) "Vigilante Marketing and Consumer-created Communications," *Journal of Advertising*, 36(3): 187–202.

Rafferty, Terence (2008) "A Teenage Vampire Tale and Its Careful Retelling," *The New York Times*. October 4.

Rosener, Judy (1990) "Ways Women Lead," *Harvard Business Review*, Nov–Dec: 119–25.

Schau, Hope Jensen, Muñiz, Albert and Arnould, Eric (2009) "How Brand Communities Create Value," *Journal of Marketing*, 73(5): 30–51.

Severson, Kim (1995) "Being Rachel Ray: How Cool is That?," *New York Times*. Available at: http://www.nytimes.com/2005/10/19/dining/19rach.html?pagewanted = print (accessed July 10, 2009).

Vargo, Stephen L. and Lusch, Robert F. (2004) "Evolving toward a New Dominant Logic for Marketing," *Journal of Marketing*, 68(January): 1–17.

Waters, Darren (2004) "Rowling Backs Potter Fan Fiction," BBC News Online Entertainment, May 27, 2004. Available at: http://news.bbc.co.uk/go/pr/fr/-/1/hi/entertainment/arts/3753001.stm (accessed March 7, 2009).

Internet resources for *Twilight* plots

1   Twilightsaga.wikia.com
2   TwilightLexicon.com
3   TwilightersAnonymous.com
4   Twilighters.org
5   TwilightMoms.com
6   BellaandEdward.com

13 Turning a corporate brand upside-down

A case of cultural corporate brand management

Søren Askegaard and Simon Torp

Overview

> We have come on a quest to that famous one,
> the king of the Danes: nothing will be concealed,
> held back when we meet. Now you must know,
> if it has been told truly as we have heard,
> that a foe of the Scyldings[1] – of what sort I know not –
> a mysterious hate-dealer, with terror displays
> unthinkable evil during dark nights,
> humiliation and slaughter. So for this I seek
> to counsel Hrothgar[2] in heart-felt friendship,
> how the wise and good king, may overcome the fiend –
> if ever relief should come to reverse
> the terrible affliction of all these evils –
> and his surges of sorrow then become cooler
>
> (Anon, 2005, *Beowulf*, Chapter IV, lines 270–82)

Branding, it has been stated, is much too important to be left to the marketing department. Whereas the traditional marketing approach to branding is based on single products or lines of products, the marketing value of the brand, not only at the product level but also on the corporate level, has become increasingly obvious. The amount of literature on corporate branding is quickly catching up with the literature on product branding. Branding, whether product or corporate, is increasingly seen not as just a matter of superficial marketing communications but as a profoundly cultural process reflecting both the organization, its role in the marketplace(s) and the cultural symbolism of the brand as interpreted and enacted in use by consumers (Schroeder and Salzer-Mörling 2006). Not surprisingly, then, Schultz (2005) suggests that a profound understanding of corporate branding must include input from at least five different managerial disciplines. First of all, *marketing* provides key concepts such as brand image and brand architecture, as well as the customer relations, that are both generators of the brand image as it exists in reality and the strategic goal of the brand management. *Strategy* as a discipline, then, brings forth notions of not just customer-based corporate reputation and market-based brand positioning but also the brand vision as an expression of the strategic goals of the organization as central for the understanding of corporate branding. *Organization theory*, then, must be brought into the picture, with its focus on the link between corporate identity and brand identity and the necessity of "living the brand culture". Therefore employee branding is also a part of corporate branding process. In circulating narratives of the corporate brand inside and outside the organization, *communication theory* announces itself as an important contributor to corporate branding. Corporate communication is central for legitimizing the link between corporate reality and the corporate brand: in other words for creating and maintaining the link between what the organization really stands for and what it *says* that it stands for. Finally, a central aspect of the corporate communication is the *visual identity*, including the style, the symbols and the aesthetics of the brand expressions.

Here, we focus on the brand universe of a particular Danish corporation, and analyze the link between its corporate identity and the ways in which it has been translated into a corporate brand. We consider this a very compelling case of cultural marketing management, since the relationship between organizational culture, market culture and the ways in which the activities of the organization are translated into brand value are highly strategically reflexive. The strategic goal for the corporate brand simultaneously has been to express and merge the identity of the people of the organization and the people of its markets.

As such, the case study is a perfect example of the lived experience of integrated marketing communication (Torp 2009). In this case study is found not an internal and external communication to different audiences – there is only one communication that permeates the organizational as well as the market reality. Obviously, this does not mean that there are no distinctly internal communicative processes. On the contrary, the case study is filled with seminars and other employer and employee brand-generating activities, but these are always aligned with the corporate existence in the marketplace. From this perspective, corporate identity is not an internal affair and corporate image is a more or less correct interpretation of the corporate identity. All signs, internal and external, contribute to identifying the organization, and all signs, internal and external, are interpreted and recreated in somebody's mind as an image (Christensen and Askegaard 2001).

Corporate history

In 1962, Christian Kjær founded a car sales company in the town of Svendborg, Denmark. The company initially was successful by accepting to deliver cars to customers on the small islands in the archipelago surrounding the town, something other car dealers refused to do. This initial corporate policy about not succumbing to distance or logistical problems contributed to the development of the specialization that has now secured the company a worldwide presence. No longer selling cars in the neighbourhood, what is today known as the Kjær Group Ltd. is a holding company with approximately 200 employees consisting of a number of sub-companies, each with their own name. They specialize in providing and servicing cars and special vehicles in disaster areas (e.g. after earthquakes or other natural disasters) and in developing countries. Consequently, among their most significant customers are the United Nations and Red Cross. Today, the Kjær Group operates in a number of countries where emergency situations and underdevelopment require special equipment and special action. The company was voted the best workplace in Denmark in 2003 and 2004, and in 2004 won a prize for "Diversity in the work place" from the Danish Institute for Human Rights, given to companies who are providing good opportunities for employees regardless of gender, ethnicity, age, handicap, religion or sexual orientation.

The corporate logo includes the company name under a stylized Viking long ship with a crew of seven seafarers (Figure 13.1). The logo refers to the legend of the hero Beowulf, who sailed with his men to save the Danish king's court from the monster Grendel, which was attacking and slaughtering the king's men. In the Kjær Group, Beowulf is interpreted as a symbol of the willingness to expose oneself to risk and trouble in order to help others.

Figure 13.1 Kjær Group corporate logo and mission triangle.

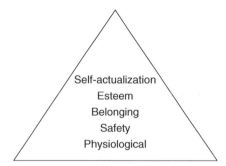

Figure 13.2 Maslow's hierarchy of needs.

In formulating the values of the company, Mads Kjær, son of the founder who became chairman in 1986, had been influenced by Maslow's hierarchy of needs (Figure 13.2), since the company operates mainly in Africa, where satisfaction of the most basic human needs are not something that can be taken for granted.

More than fifty years ago, Abraham Maslow (1954) suggested a theory of human motivation that divided needs into five different levels representing, from the bottom to the top of the pyramid in Figure 13.2: physiological needs, safety needs, needs of belonging, needs of esteem and the need for self-actualization. His point was that needs on a lower level had to be satisfied before the human being would proceed to satisfy needs of a higher order. Thus, the needs are organized in a hierarchy, a pyramid, with the broadest and most basic needs at the bottom and what has sometimes been termed more "luxurious needs" at the top. Maslow, representing the school of humanistic psychology, was keen to underline that the ultimate goal for all of mankind was to reach the self-actualizing state. Rather than seeing self-actualization as "luxurious", Maslow's aim was to plead for welfare politics that could ensure the possibilities of entering the self-actualization stage for the maximum number of people. The humanistic motif is thus central to Maslow's thinking as well as to what we could call the corporate religion of the Kjær Group.

Corporate religion in the Kjær Group

In 1997, the Kjær Group published a small book entitled *Corporate Religion – Kjær Group*, which was reissued in a slightly revised version in 2000. In this book, the company describes

Table 13.1 "Corporate values" of the Kjær Group

You make a difference
We care
Respect and trust
24 hours reply
Pro-active
Red button – help
F1 Fix it right, first time
Win–Win

Source: Kjær Group (2000).

its mission and vision, history and organization, and fundamental value system. The aim of the book, as expressed in the Foreword, is "for all of us to know what it takes be a 100% committed teamplayer" (Kjær Group 2000: 1). The book represents a collection of "all good values that informally described our culture – and was created through the people's creative thinking at several years of summer seminars, education and teamwork" (ibid.: 9). The values and attitudes described in the book (see Table 13.1) derive from and reflect how "we established the company and became successful" (ibid.: 1). As a consequence of the manner in which the company's values came into being – over many years, and with many contributors in many different contexts – these values display great diversity.

As can be seen, there is a general confusion in the list between values, properly speaking ("respect and trust"), prescriptions for action ("24 hours reply", "fix it right") and expected or requested outcomes ("you make a difference", "win–win"). Furthermore, it is clearly stated that the book is not meant to be a manifesto carved in stone. Just like we human beings, it says, the contents will undergo change over time: "our only constant factor is our corporate religion and changes" (ibid.: 1).

A source of inspiration for Kjær's publication was the book *Corporate Religion* by the Danish agency director Jesper Kunde. Among other things, this book deals with the need to secure consistency between the qualitative values of the company and the employee (Kunde 2000: 98). According to Kunde, this is especially important in an organization which, like the Kjær Group, operates internationally and employs staff from many different countries. In multinational companies, according to Kunde, it is crucial that both values and attitudes do not vary, for example, from country to country, and that things should be done in the same way throughout the organization. All staff members should "believe in" or subscribe to the values of the company. Staff should not merely express themselves in conformity with the company's brand and values – ideally, they should also "live out" or, if you like, embody these values in their daily lives. Kunde summarizes his philosophy in the following way:

> The company which has complete control of – and keeps in step with – its international organization can control both the organization and the market with the aid of a strong Corporate Religion. A company's success depends simply on direction … A Corporate Religion ensures that all employees in a company share the same qualitative values … It might sound totalitarian, but with a clearly defined corporate religion, there is nobody who will have problems on the course because everybody's job is connected to the company's Corporate Religion.
>
> (Kunde 2000: 48, 103)

This philosophy is also found in the Kjær Group's book. The description of the company's vision is introduced with the words: "We are all brands: you and me, the companies in the Kjær Group, and the products we represent" (Kjær Group 2000: 5). The symbolic and behavioural dimensions of corporate branding imply that it naturally involves employees (Christensen and Morsing 2005: 52), for it is they who are expected to comply with and redeem the promises made by the brand in their daily work. From a critical perspective, Christensen, Morsing and Cheney (2008) point out that identification is an important part of corporate branding since organizational members are often "expected to align their personal values with the identity of the corporate brand". They must allow themselves to be "incorporated" into the organization and hence to become walking embodiments of the corporate brand. They are expected not merely to communicate about the brand, but to "live" it.

The value explosion and confusion

Through being set out in writing, the company's values changed from being informal to formal. The formalization and formulation of the values in print revealed to the management that the number of values was too large, and that these did not always display internal consistency. Because of its growing involvement in different markets and collaborative partnerships with several car manufacturing companies, a number of sub-companies and sub-brands had been created. Furthermore, the creative spirit within the company had led to something of an explosion in the number of values that were used to express the philosophy of the company. In short, it was no longer very clear what actually constituted the unifying element and the core value foundation of the Kjær Group.

Brand Base

It was at this point, that Mads Kjær contacted Brand Base, a unit at the University of Southern Denmark in Odense. Brand Base is a unit organizing collaborative projects between organizations and corporations, on the one hand, and researchers at the university's Department of Marketing and Management, on the other. Brand Base had been established as a consequence of a number of encounters between representatives of local businesses in Odense and researchers, predominantly from the research units working with consumer behaviour and marketing communications. These units have a distinct developed research profile oriented towards consumer culture theory (CCT) (Arnould and Thompson 2005) and the consideration of strategic communication in organizations as culturally embedded processes. Brand Base today has close to 100 companies and organizations as members, and the explicit goal is to disseminate findings from CCT and other culture-oriented business research domains to the corporate world. Brand Base does so through the publication of newsletters and other written material, through workshops, seminars and conferences, and through collaborative projects with member organizations.

It was obviously not a new experience for the Kjær Group to work with integrated marketing communication and corporate values. Hence, the issue for Mads Kjær was one of theoretical and cultural integrity of the corporate value system. The insistence on a theoretical foundation was what had originally led him to adopt Maslow's perspective, since he considered it a universally valid theory and, as already noted, an appropriate way of thinking about the company's mission and engagement in developing countries and disaster areas. In other words, Mads Kjær saw it as imperative that the basic corporate values could be based on a philosophy, a social theory and a history, and not just the latest advertising agency lingo. In order to ensure a sound theoretical foundation for the reflections on the corporate brand and the corporate values, he contacted a group of researchers at the Brand Base unit at the University of Southern Denmark. Upon contact from Mads Kjær and the Kjær Group, Brand Base created a "task force" consisting of the authors in order to engage in the strategic reflections on and the development of the value profiling of the Kjær Group and its corporate brand.

An encounter between academic research and corporate identity and image

At the first meeting, the company's managing director and brand manager presented the company's existing value universe, vision and mission, and described the challenges as they saw them. It was particularly emphasized that the number of values held by the company had greatly increased, and that the company had gradually differentiated itself into a number of sub-brands. In relation to corporate identity, the question was whether these sub-brands should be allowed to become even more independent, or whether the company should "tidy up its values" and attempt to create a simpler and more consistent brand architecture which would secure continuity and recognizability between the various offshoots. In theoretical terms it was a choice between a monolithic, endorsed group identity and a branded identity strategy (Olins 1989; for a critique of this distinction, see Christensen *et al.* 2008: 65).

The Brand Base taskforce agreed upon the expediency of a simplification process of the corporate brand universe that nevertheless remained respectful to the corporate diversity. In the taskforce, we subsequently decided that we would like to go further than merely fulfilling the brief, which was to propose ways of simplifying the company's value universe and raise its brand profile. Instead, we would challenge the existing ideological and theoretical basis of the corporate value set, and undertake a radical and far-reaching task. In our view, the greatest challenge in relation to the company's marketing communication was that it was out of step with the company's identity. We did *not* claim that what the company practised in the developing countries was in any way incorrect – on the contrary. Our purpose was to refute the belief that a Maslow-based approach is a useful way to include a cultural perspective, although that is standard in much of the brand management literature (Keller 1998; Keller *et al.* 2008). In our opinion, the Maslow-based theoretical perspective and conceptualization which found expression in the company's values, and the hierarchy of which these formed a part, were overly reductionist from a cultural perspective. Frankly speaking, one might say that the application of a Maslowian framework in an international marketing (and branding) perspective presumes a hierarchy of cultures, where the cultural meaning of brands become salient only insofar as lower order needs have been satisfied. Maslow himself would probably have objected to such an interpretation, but this is the way in which his hierarchy of needs has typically been applied in an international marketing context. For example, it is a crucial misunderstanding to communicate to students that "although culture can have an impact on needs at all levels, its impacts tend to be greater where higher-order needs are involved – needs involving emotion and cognition" (de Búrca *et al.* 2004: 69). Just the opening of the phrase and the qualifier "can have" are enough to underline the profound lack of cultural understanding. But also the relative "de-culturalization" of, for example, food and sexuality is an obvious blunder.

One might say that the managing director's political philosophy or view of humanity – in this instance, a highly liberal and individualistic approach – had been transferred to the company's philosophy, at any rate in its formulation. In practice, the company tended to be characterized by a relatively social and meaning-based approach; in other words, it said one thing and did another. There was therefore a disjunction between the company's walk and its talk. We felt that by altering the theoretical foundation and removing the Maslowian aspects, it would be possible to get "the talk" to match "the walk" (Weick 1995) in the Kjær Group.

At the second meeting, we gave a presentation which drew upon a number of theoreticians from French post-structuralists and German sociologists to Danish theologians and ethicists. We attempted to "provoke" the managing director and the brand manager into rejecting Maslow's hierarchy of needs as the basis for the formulation of the company's philosophy and fundamental value system. After some initial debate and a certain (and healthy) scepticism, we were challenged to produce a convincing argument against Maslow as a sound source for a culturally based theory of corporate branding values. Below, we develop the arguments against a Maslow-based approach to understand how meanings and motivations are generated in a cultural context. But let us first throw a little more insight into the process of corporate change that this encounter generated.

From an anthropological and sociological viewpoint we challenged the psychological basis of Maslow's hierarchy of needs that the fundamental purpose in life is survival and that self-actualization only becomes relevant at the "luxury" end of life's goals. We suggested a scrutiny of the values that pervade the Kjær Group in order to find the "social glue" that really keeps the company a coherent, strong unit and makes it a great place to work. The Kjær Group had already played with the relative similarity between their name Kjær (the name is pronounced "care", since the j in the name is almost silent) and "care". Caring for the staff as well as for the people in need of infrastructure and logistics in the world were built-in practices of corporate culture as expressed in the corporate slogan: "Love cars, love life, love people". "Care" was then selected as a central axis for future corporate value and branding processes. Obviously, the notion of care could have been fitted into a Maslowian scheme of, e.g., security needs, but as already stated and as will be explicated in the following, such a Maslowian scheme was deemed to be out of touch with a genuinely cultural perspective on the meaning and value of the Kjær Group's corporate existence.

As already indicated, beyond a certain initial bewilderment concerning our challenge to what the corporate management considered a well-founded theory of human motivation, we encountered openness and curiosity, and a willingness to abandon the usual notions and think outside the box. The result was an exciting dialogue which paved the way for a completely different type of process, and a different kind of interaction between research and practice/management than had been originally conceived of and planned by the company and the Brand Base manager. Both the company's representatives and the researchers increasingly felt that we had created fertile ground for some highly fruitful and mutually inspiring co-operation. The company may have been surprised, in relation to their expectations, by our somewhat different and radical approach, while we for our part were pleasantly surprised by the openness and goodwill we encountered.

Practical co-operation was initiated in a number of areas. Among other things, each of the authors subsequently took part in workshops, meetings, evaluations and presentations, and the company published a folder and an article we had written on the "new" value foundation and approach (Table 13.2). This trajectory led to a reformulation of the Kjær Group's corporate brand, of its core values and of its theoretical foundation. But first, let us explain a little more in depth why Maslow's hierarchy of needs from our perspective is incompatible with a truly cultural approach to marketing management.

Table 13.2 Chronological overview of interaction between researchers and the Kjær Group and articles produced

1   First meeting: Company presentation: The brief (March 2004)
2   Second meeting: Research presentation: Turning the brand upside-down (May 2004)
3   Brochure: Søren Askegaard and Simon Torp: *Kjær is Care – Care in Motion*. Published in connection with the international LIFE-seminar in the Kjær Group A/S (July 2004)
4   LIFE 2004. Simon Torp: Presentation and Value Workshop. Together with Jan Plettner. Kjær Group A/S. Svendborg (August 2004)
5   Article: Søren Askegaard and Simon Torp, "Kjær Group – Corporate Values. In Making a Difference". *Kjær Group Newsletter,* 2nd Issue (September 2004)
6   Article: Søren Askegaard and Simon Torp, "Teorien på hovedet – Historien om et samarbejde mellem Kjær Group og Brand Base". In Brand Base News, Nyheder inden for Symboløkonomi, No. 9 (September 2004)
7   Søren Askegaard: Joint presentation with CEO Mads Kjær, KommitFyn (March 2005)
8   Article: "Corporate Brand: Analyse og Feedback", *Carnation* magazine, the Kjær Group, Svendborg (September 2005)
9   Søren Askegaard: Joint presentation with CEO Mads Kjær, KommitFyn (April 2006)

An economy of symbols

The hierarchy of needs suggested by Maslow makes intuitive sense which is presumably why it is one of the most cited scientific works ever published. Much like Hofstede's cultural index, it represents a fairly simple and understandable framework for including culture and human behaviour in managerial contexts (but see, e.g., Nakata 2009). Needless to say, not all citations have been positive and there have been numerous points of critique raised against the hierarchy of needs. Nevertheless, as is evident from the Kjær case, it is one of those theories that – again like Hofstede's cultural index – have gained a strong "lay foot-hold" in the way business corporations go about reflecting on the complex relationship between society, culture, need and demand. Maslow's humanistic psychology has a strong element of human development, and points to the quest for and the positive influence on life conditions of "ascending the pyramid". It was this humanistic take on the necessity of development, that made the Kjær Group adopt the Maslowian perspective for constructing their corporate value system in the first place.

The problem with Maslow's hierarchy of needs is its individualist and "survivalist" perspective and its relegation of the creation of meaning to a secondary position in the formation of human culture. Consequently, it fails to take into consideration that humans do not individually organize themselves in societies primarily in order to survive, but with respect to the individual and collective meaning, that they can give to their lives (Baudrillard 1970). In an anthropological sense, and beyond the narrow modern form of self-actualization that lies behind Maslow's thinking, it is obvious, that humans as social beings are characterized by being a species that is self-actualizing through all their activities. Even the most basic satisfaction of needs is immersed in social meanings concerning what is edible and what is not (Fischler 1990), which rules and rituals about sexual relationships to obey, and so on. The problem with the hierarchy of needs is that it leads us to believe (and not necessarily in accordance with Maslow's original thinking), that societies and life conditions stricken by poverty equal existential misery, since the level of self-actualization is so far removed from the issues that people have to deal with in their daily lives.

The human being is a species that is organized in societies. Societies constitute patterns of meaning that interweave all levels in the hierarchy of needs. Society provides simultaneously possibilities and frames for satisfying all those needs, and for ranking them in importance, however, not necessarily the same ranking for all social groups. This is quite simply not the way societies work. First of all, it is only when societies have broken down that each man starts to care exclusively for himself. As long as society functions, we are inclined to give up certain individual rights and freedoms in order to respect the laws, God or the spirits, and the community. The hierarchy of needs is a very individualistic model, and, as such, it represents a specific Western thinking. Second, the human being is an animal that is characterized by always being self-actualizing, also when he or she is fulfilling very basic needs. We do not just eat but we communicate a lot about which culture we belong to and which values we have through our likings and dislikings of food. Third, the application of the Maslowian hierarchy of needs maintains a hierarchical structure in terms of social development – there are people who are "closer to" the stage of nature and less culturally developed to the extent that self-actualization in the Maslowian perspective is the epitome of cultural development.

Hence, we can argue that the human world is first and foremost an economy of symbols. As suggested by sociologists Nisbet and Perrin (1980: 47), "The symbol is to the social world what the atom is to the physical world and the cell is to the biological world." Symbols are the building blocks of the social. Hence, the symbolic is not a "luxury" for humans – as one is inclined to think based on the hierarchy of needs – but a constitutive element of society. As pointed out by Frankl (1959), the most significant instrument of survival may be the question of meaning. As stated by Nietzsche (cited in ibid.: 16), "He who has a *why* to live for can bear almost any *how*." In other words, our basic message was that the human being is first and foremost a cultural animal, even in the harshest of conditions. And that rather than considering culture a luxury and a superstructure on top of human societies who have gone beyond the "stage of survival", we concur with French social thinker Edgar Morin, who urges us to go beyond the nature–culture dichotomy by arguing that the human being is a cultural animal because of nature and a natural animal because of culture (Morin 1973). By this cunning inversion, he is suggesting that there is nothing "unnatural" about the development of human culture and that the economy of symbols is rooted in the physical and biological complexity of the human brain. At the same time, he argues, it is this symbolizing and cultural ability that has been our strongest asset in assuring our survival as beings in nature. In other words, human culture and human nature are co-constitutive rather than linked in a hierarchical system of survival and surplus.

It is in this sense, that we would argue against the "economy of survival" logic inherent in the hierarchy of needs, and align ourselves with anthropologists such as Marshall Sahlins, who reject the thesis that non-affluent societies are preoccupied with an endless fight to satisfy their most basic needs, and therefore cannot be considered affluent (Sahlins 1972). Consequently, we also oppose the modern Western apotheosis of economics as the decisive science for understanding social development. The fact that modern, capitalist consumer societies have subjected themselves to a social imaginary permeated by the logic of growth in production and consumption does not permit us to conclude that this is a universal human characteristic. It is, merely, the dominant social logic which we have used to construct our societies and economies through the past centuries. But it is admittedly also a form that has been globalizing to an extent that it today constitutes one of the major challenges to the sustainability of economic activities on this planet.

The present preoccupation with the economy of symbols, through business strategies based on corporate identity, corporate image and storytelling activities, may reflect a growing awareness that culture is not an additional "internal variable" that must be taken into account in the general, economics-based assessment of a firm or an organization, but a "root metaphor" for understanding what an organization is in the first place (Smircich 1983). As such, there is much to be gained from understanding organizations as units for anthropological analysis (Moeran 2005).

Turning the world upside down

What did these reflections on the anthropological nature of any corporate structure, including the Kjær Group and its corporate culture lead to? Just as the emblem of the Kjær Group is a triangle standing on one of its edges, so the researchers of Brand Base suggested that Maslow's hierarchy of needs be turned upside down and expressed in terms of a simplified value universe representing the corporation. Instead of underlining the need, we underlined the positive value of caring, as a fundamental anthropological construct and a fundamental corporate value. Care expresses that humans are always part of a larger context. One cannot fulfil one's own wishes and needs without considering these of the people one cares for. A person becomes who s/he is through the ties with the ones close to him/her: family, friends, colleagues, and so on.

The Kjær Group reformulated the corporate vision and mission and accepted that, for an emergency-oriented corporation like Kjær, care is the basic thing. This is the most fundamental reason for doing what is done: that the corporate employees care and that they are self-actualizing through their caring. With help from the researchers from Brand Base, the Kjær Group translated the upside-down hierarchy of needs to the central values of the company. The central values in the Kjær Group were defined as: care, respect and trust, proactivity, diversity and making a difference. These values were picked from the myriad of existing values that the Kjær Group had developed over years. The rest were abandoned and the remaining five values were reorganized so that "care" was established as the fundamental value of the corporation. The values were organized according to the following logic based not on Maslow's hierarchy of needs but on the perspective that the human being is first and foremost an *animal symbolicum* (Cassirer 1944).

On the basis of mutual *care* (Figure 13.3), for each other and for their customers, Kjær aims at building relationships of *respect and trust*. This is true both inside and outside the organization. There is a basic respect and trust among the different parts of the group, the different nations represented as well as between the various work groups and individuals in the company. Once there is this mutual respect and trust, it is actually not so difficult to go out there and dare, dare to care, dare to do business. This is what Kjær means by *proactivity*.

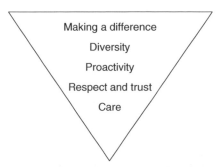

Figure 13.3 Wolsam – a corporate brand turned upside down.

The firm grounding in caring and respectful relations gives the company the courage to go on doing what is difficult, to take chances and to operate even where many others would give up. Proactivity has *diversification* as its logical consequence. The more you try, the more initiatives will actually persist and survive. Opening new markets, including new cultures, joining together people from all corners of the world with very different cultural backgrounds, such is the philosophy of Kjær Group. The result is a win–win situation where the importance is *making a difference*, regardless of what kinds of relationships that the Kjær Group engages in; with customers, with suppliers, with employees and their families and everybody else with a stake in the company.

Consistent with the Kjær Group's self-proclaimed dynamism, it is interesting to note the organizational developments that have taken place since the process was concluded. Mads Kjær, confident that the daily management of the business activities was now well framed, has since stepped down as CEO of the Kjær Group to become chairman of the board. As a consequence, the set of values described above has given way to a reformulated set of values building partially on the prior set. Currently, the value profile is "professionalism, respect, honesty, and dedication". The fundamental principle of care, however, and the priority to the social responsibilities remain, however, as is evident in the current formulation referring to the still valid mission triangle (cf. Figure 13.1).

> We care for our customers, products and the services we provide, for our colleagues and employees, the environment and the society of which we are part. This is expressed with "Love Cars, Love People, Love Life" and the UN 2015 Goals and the UN's Global Compact represent important frameworks for our efforts.[3]

Mads Kjær has engaged in a new project of care, MyC4 (www.MyC4.com), a microfinancing project for starting or developing businesses in Third World countries. MyC4 can be considered a logical strategic result of the attempt to combine the humanism and an economic liberalism that permeates the corporate philosophy of the Kjær Group and which also is expressed in the spirit of the business, profit and meaning relationship that was added to the "Wolsam" triangle and its organization and formulation of the Kjær Group's corporate values.

Managing culture – takeaways?

Referring to Maslow's hierarchy in the formulation of a corporate brand obviously represents an attempt to include a cultural or at least a human dimension in the understanding of the *why* behind the corporation's economic activities. Additionally, brand management is perhaps the managerial domain that is most directly conscious of the centrality of meanings for managerial practices. However, even when such cultural dimensions are taken into consideration, they have a tendency to remain exactly that: a dimensionality, an additional variable to take into consideration. Cultural meaning, much like in Maslow's hierarchy of needs, becomes an epiphenomenon that may indeed be of great importance but inevitably additional to the economic roots of (human and/or corporate) survival. The Kjær Group knew that it is important to take culture into consideration – the use of the humanistic psychology of Maslow, the excellent HRM policies implemented and the reference to the mythological figure of *Beowulf* clearly demonstrate a profound willingness to take culture absolutely seriously in the corporate culture. Our addition was to underline that the cultural roots ought to be based in a notion of meanings rather than needs.

Papadopoulos (1993), elaborating on the complexity of imagery attached to country-of-origin of products draws on the following passage from Umberto Eco's "Foucault's pendulum":

> To each memorable image you attach a thought, a label, a category, a piece of the cosmic furniture, syllogisms, an enormous sorites, chains of apothegms, strings of hypallages, rosters of zeugmas, dances of hysteron proteron, apophantic logoi, hierarchic stoichea, processions of equinoxes and parallaxes, herbaria, genealogies of gymnosophists – and so on to infinity.
>
> (Eco, cited in ibid.: 3)

The quote underlines, among other aspects, that each cultural image, including corporate images, involves elements of classification and hierarchy (what kind of good/ bad company is this?), of symbols that facilitate recall (what do I recognize it from?), of personal imaginations of causality (what made this company what it is?) and chains of beliefs (how does it perform? And why?) as well as potential uncertainties about just about all of these readings. Cultural brand management is not for lovers of simplicity or certainty!

We can now return to Schultz's (2005) five managerial disciplines mentioned above. The Kjær Group was already a well-performing company in many respects. The attempt to turn Maslow's hierarchy upside down by underlining the central importance of meaning for a company promoting self-actualization both for its employees and its (needy) customers was therefore, as such, icing on the cake. But the process did contribute to a clean-up of a mess of values and a clarified corporate brand identity (marketing) while defining the strategic goal – "care" – of the company accordingly. It also facilitated the inclusion of the strong corporate spirit (organization theory) in the self-image of a socially caring rather than individualistically self-actualizing culture and provided a theoretical and cultural rationale for communicating this corporate spirit to internal and external audiences, as a replacement for the Maslow-based logic. Finally, all this was done while retaining the respect for the *Beowulf* narrative and the visual identification with it through the corporate logo. In this sense, the process represents a truly cross-disciplinary and culturally sensitive case of corporate brand management – culturally sensitive both in terms of being respectful of cultural theory and of the corporate culture of the Kjær Group.

Conclusion

We would like to draw three strategic conclusions in terms of how to understand and operate with strategic corporate branding and corporate value universes. First of all, we would like to conclude with some reflections on the relationship between corporate activity and corporate discursivity (the "walking" and the "talking") as discussed by Weick (1995), since our point of departure was some kind of discrepancy between the corporate activity of the Kjær Group and the way it was discursively expressed through the corporate value system and its references to Maslow's hierarchy of needs. Much of the literature on corporate branding and corporate values takes its point of departure that in order to move strategically in the right direction, it is important to first formulate this through the articulation of a corporate value system. In other words, the invitation is usually to sit down around a table and find out, which motivating constructs articulate who we are as a corporation, or even more often who we would like to be and how to get there. Once this is formulated, it can be implemented in the organization – in other words, it becomes a matter of walking the talk. This, however, runs counter to Weick's suggestions. He says:

> Walking is the means to find things worth talking about. People discover what they think by looking at what they say, how they feel, and where they walk. The talk makes sense of walking, which means those best able to walk the talk are the ones who actually talk the walking they find themselves doing most often, with most intensity, and with most satisfaction. How can I know what I value until I see where I walk?
>
> (ibid.: 182–3)

What happened in the collaboration between Brand Base and the Kjær Group was the opposite of asking the corporation to "walk the talk". Instead, the "talking" was reformulated so that it became more expressive of "talking the walk" – the walk was, so to speak, built into the corporate formulation of its own corporate brand. This, according to Weick, has important consequences for the dynamism and the innovativeness of the corporation:

> [P]eople walk in order to find what is worth talking about. When told to walk their talk, the vehicle for discovery, the walking is redirected. It has been pressed into service as a testimonial that a handful of earlier words are the right words. What people forgo is the chance for the walking to uncover something for which the current words are inadequate and for which new words are needed. To "talk the walk" is to be opportunistic in the best sense of the word. It is to search for words that make sense of current walking that is adaptive for reasons that are not yet clear.
>
> (ibid.: 183)

The strategic reflection behind the collaboration was that the "talk" had become outdated and inadequate in order to express the "walk" of the Kjær Group. Hence, the prime contribution was not so much to invent a new "talk" (new corporate values) but to orchestrate the existing value universe into a coherent system that had firm anthropological and culture theoretical roots. It is, however, not the case that "talking the walk" is without problems or challenges either. The talk may lack subtlety in terms of being able to express the logics behind the walking. And, needless to say, the choice of words matters a lot. Ultimately, neither walking the talk nor talking the walk should dominate the formulation of a corporate brand. But since the standard practice is to walk the talk, we would like to make the opposite point here and stress the significance of talking the walk.

The second strategic point we would like to stress draws on practice theory, developed not exclusively but largely by French sociologist Pierre Bourdieu (c.f., Bourdieu 1998; for a good introduction, see Reckwitz 2002). The theory of practice is basically opposed to rational choice theory, arguing that choices are normally not based on rational decisions but in culturally and even bodily embedded practices. It is apparent that this approach, in its focus on the discrepancy between how we talk about our actions and what actually lies behind them, is deeply connected to our reflections on what Weick presented above. This time, however, our point is methodological rather than strategic. Much too often, in strategic analysis of an organization, we are much too dependent on the verbal formulations of corporate programmes, evaluations, strategies, etc. Whereas these textual formulations are of course highly significant, practice theory teaches us that much of what governs the routines and the behaviours in an organization is embedded and embodied in practices, that are not necessarily accessible to the members of the organization themselves. Hence, practice theory challenges models of decision-making in consumer research by underlining that the reasons for our choices in consumption are not clear to us, and also how culture works beyond its presence in cognitive decision rules that will guide choices. In other words, culture is deeper than we can normally account for in verbalized decision rules or decision principles. Consequently, in order to better grasp the organizational being behind the discursive presentations, we need to apply methods of organizational analysis that do not solely consist of verbal material. Since most of our research apparatus is highly verbalized, whether in the form of questionnaires or in-depth interviews, this methodological point challenges much of the existing research and thinking of corporate branding (cf. Chapters 15 and 16 in this volume).

A third strategic point that we would like to stress pertains to the relationship between the notions of culture and economy. Managerial approaches have traditionally considered economic theory in both its general and managerial forms as the most decisive element in explaining the functioning of the corporation (or any other market agent) and neglecting culture or relegating it to secondary importance. In the past few decades, we have witnessed changes in the market that have been interpreted as an increased "culturalization" of the economy. In contemporary managerial theorizing of branding processes, storytelling, corporate culture, and so on, this culturalization has been given increased strategic importance in terms of corporate culture and "cultural orientation", which have become significant assets in the competition in the market. What is overlooked by proponents of this approach to the increasing intertwining of cultural and economic processes, is that such epochal theorization maintains an artificial distinction between culture and economy. If we go back to Sahlins' (1972) economic anthropology, his main point is exactly that we cannot assume an acultural universality of the economic theorizing that has been dominating Western social sciences for two centuries. In other words, all economies are equally cultural.

So, our third and final point can be concluded with the fact, that just as Beowulf came to help the Danes threatened by the monster Grendel and just as the Kjær Group sees it as its mission to bring care (in the form of motor transportation) to the needy in this world, we (and the authors involved in this book in general) would like to help "capturing the markets from the economists" (Slater, in du Gay and Pryke 2002) by pointing out the cultural character of any economic and managerial practice. If we realize this, we will be better off in terms of understanding and navigating the marketplace.

Review and discussion questions

1   What are the most important differences between a classical and a "cultural" perspective on brand values? Which ones are salient in the case of the Kjær Group?
2   What is the relationship between activity and discursivity (the "walking" and the "talking") before and after the change in the corporate value structure? What are the consequences of the activity–discursivity relationship for how you conduct culturally oriented research in organizations?
3   It obviously means a lot whether a society is very poor or very rich – or somewhere in between – with regards to how life and its priorities are organized. However, that does not mean that culture is less relevant or less enriching in poor societies. Try to discuss and explain this based on the arguments concerning Maslow presented here.
4   Discuss the possibilities and difficulties that face the culturally oriented marketing consultant.

Keywords

brand values, consultancy project, corporate branding, critique, Maslow's hierarchy of needs

Notes

1 Another word for Danes, after the mythological founder of Denmark, Scyld.
2 King of the Danes.
3 http://www.kjaergroup.com/about-us/mission-vision-values (accessed October 31, 2010).

References

Anon (2005) *Beowulf*, trans. J. McNamara, New York: Barnes & Noble, Classics.
Arnould, Eric J. and Craig J. Thompson (2005) "Consumer Culture Theory (CCT): Twenty Years of Research", *Journal of Consumer Research*, 31(4): 868–82.
Baudrillard, J. (1970) *La société de consommation*, Paris: Gallimard.
Bourdieu, P. (1998) *Practical Reason: On the Theory of Action*, Stanford, CA: Stanford University Press.
Cassirer, E. (1944) *An Essay on Man: An Introduction to a Philosophy of Human Culture*, New Haven and London: Yale University Press.
Christensen, L. T. and Askegaard, S. (2001) "Corporate Identity and Corporate Image Revisited: A Semiotic Exercise", *European Journal of Marketing*, 35(3/4): 292–315.
Christensen, L. T. and Morsing, M. (2005) *Bagom corporate communication*, Gylling: Samfundslitteratur.
Christensen, L. T., Morsing, M. and Cheney, G. (2008) *Corporate Communications: Convention, Complexity and Critique*, London: Sage.
de Búrca, S., Fletcher, R. and Brown, L. (2004) *International Marketing: An SME Perspective*, Harlow: Prentice Hall.
du Gay, P. and Pryke, M. (eds) (2002) *Cultural Economy*, London: Sage.
Fischler, C. (1990) *L'Homnivore*, Paris: Odile Jacob.
Frankl, V. (1959) *Man's Search for Meaning*, Boston: Beacon Press.
Keller, K. L. (1998) *Strategic Brand Management: Building, Measuring and Managing Brand Equity*, Upper Saddle River, NJ: Prentice Hall.
Keller, K. L., Apéria, T. and Georgson, M. (2008) *Strategic Brand Management: A European Perspective*, Harlow: Prentice Hall.
Kjær Group (2000) *Corporate Religion*: *Kjær Group*, Svendborg: Kjær Group.
Kunde, J. (2000) *Corporate Religion: Building a Strong Company through Personality and Corporate Soul*, London: Prentice Hall.
Moeran, B. (2005) *The Business of Ethnography: Strategic Exchanges, People and Organizations*, Oxford: Berg Publishers.
Morin, E. (1973) *Le paradigme perdu. La nature humaine*, Paris: Seuil.
Nakata, C. (ed.) (2009) *Beyond Hofstede: Culture Frameworks for Global Marketing and Management*, Chicago: Macmillan.
Nisbet, R. and Perrin, R. (1980) *The Social Bond*, New York: McGraw-Hill.
Olins, W. (1989) *Corporate Identity: Making Business Strategy Visible Through Design*, London: Thames and Hudson.
Papadopoulos, N. (1993) "What Product-Country Images Are and Are Not", in N. Papadopoulos and L. Heslop (eds), *Product-Country Images: Impact and Role in International Marketing*, New York: International Business Press, pp. 3–38.
Reckwitz, A. (2002) "Toward a Theory of Social Practices: A Development in Culturalist Theorizing", *European Journal of Social Theory*, 5(2): 243–63.

Sahlins, M. (1972) *Stone Age Economics*, New York: de Gruyter.

Schroeder, J. and Salzer-Mörling, M. (eds) (2006) *Brand Culture*, London: Routledge.

Schultz, Majken (2005) "A Cross-Disciplinary Perspective on Corporate Branding", in M. Schultz, Y. M. Antorini and F. F. Csaba (eds), *Corporate Branding: Purpose/People/Process*, Copenhagen: Copenhagen Business School Press, pp. 23–55.

Smircich, L. (1983) "Concept of Culture and Organizational Analysis", *Administrative Science Quarterly*, 28: 339–58.

Torp, S. (2009) "Integrated Communications: From One Look to Normative Consistency", *Corporate Communications: An International Journal*, 14(2): 190–206.

Weick, K. E. (1995) *Sensemaking in Organizations*, Thousand Oaks, CA: Sage.

Part III

Researching consumers, marketers, and markets

14 The way you see is what you get

Market research as modes of knowledge production

Sofie Møller Bjerrisgaard and Dannie Kjeldgaard

Overview

This chapter addresses the topic of global market research and questions the conventional understanding of market research techniques as managerial devices used to improve marketing decisions. Instead, this chapter considers market research as a cultural practice. This means that market research is no longer understood as a straightforward process of designing the study, collecting the data, interpreting the information and disseminating it throughout the organization in order to enhance decision-making and ultimately organizational profitability. Alternatively, a cultural perspective upon market research addresses the question of *how* the type of insights generated about consumers/markets is structured by the choice of market research method. Based upon an ethnographic study of a global market research technique within the context of advertising, this chapter demonstrates how divergent practices and orientations of market research frame the kind of knowledge generated about consumers, markets, products and brands in global markets. The implications of such a reconceptualization of market research concern the reflexivity of managers upon their own marketplace embeddedness and the strategies involved in mobilizing such reflexivity in order to distinguish between various ways of engaging with market information.

Introduction

Clearly, the type of market research technique used in the search for market and consumer insights matters; the results of market research depend upon the nature of the methods applied. To most marketers this is common knowledge – but the questions of *how* different methods impact on market research outcomes and how organizations should handle this are not equally obvious. In this chapter we examine how divergent practices and orientations of market research structure the type of knowledge generated about consumers, markets, products and brands in global markets. We do this through an ethnographic study of research practices in one particular organizational setting: a global advertising agency.

By viewing market research as a practice that is embedded in particular ways of thinking about markets, organizations and consumers, we present an alternative understanding of the role of market research practices in the development of new products and market communication. This should be seen in opposition to the more traditional understanding of market research stressing its ability to enhance market transparency and thereby permit rational, strategic and profit-maximizing decisions through market orientation and the fulfilment of consumer needs, desires and aspirations. Instead of viewing market research as the transmitter of objective and external market information to the organization, we would argue that markets are constituted by dynamic systems of meaning, co-produced and sustained by consumers and organizations together. This does not mean that market research is useless, invaluable and should be abandoned all together. What it does mean is that organizations should take advantage of understanding their own cultural embeddedness in the global marketplace. By being aware of the ways in which market and consumer knowledge is produced, organizations potentially become capable of challenging dogmatized ways of thinking about their market research procedures and of handling these more strategically.

The chapter first outlines how market research is linked to the basic tenets of the marketing concept and the idea of market orientation and ultimately to the improvement of marketing decision-making and organizational profitability. Then it demonstrates how the literature on market research contains two dominant ways of understanding market research methods. We call these 'modes of knowledge production' to suggest that particular kinds of knowledge are produced by particular understandings of research (what is termed 'paradigms' in the philosophy of science). We illustrate how these two modes circulate in the organizational setting of a global advertising agency and how these different modes of knowledge production influence the type of practical advice given to clients through a number of case studies. Box 14.1 describes the multi-sited ethnography of SignBank. The stories demonstrate how the modes of knowledge production lead to quite different brand positioning strategies and product development processes.

Box 14.1 SignBank

The empirical setting, data and strategies of interpretation

The multi-sited ethnography on which this chapter is based is conducted in the organizational setting of a strategic unit for global ethnographic market research, called SignBank in a global advertising agency. The study is based on several types of data: 20 unstructured interviews were conducted with organizational members engaged in SignBank. Most important were interviews with strategic planners across 11 countries, who had developed and implemented SignBank throughout the organization. Interviews with global top management on the implications of SignBank on new business development, PR, agency creativity and strategy, organizational skills development and corporate culture allow for a more comprehensive understanding of the role of ethnographic and more conventional research techniques in global market research and advertising more generally. The study also builds on the analysis of extensive amounts of documents concerning SignBank, describing both the method *per se* and the use of it in client business. Furthermore notes were made during local, regional and global meetings concerning SignBank.

SignBank: the method

SignBank is, according to its originators, initiated on the basis of a feeling of a lack of market and consumer knowledge relying on conventional qualitative and quantitative market research. This lack is primarily attributed to globalization processes which increase the pressure upon consumer insights across national boundaries. SignBank is based on the idea of using the agency's 13,000 employees worldwide to observe and report on small changes in people's everyday lives. These observations are termed signs and delivered to designated 'Friends of SignBank' who have taken part in formal training sessions of the method. The 'Friends of SignBank' collect and organize the signs into meaningful patterns in accordance with the underlying methodology. On the basis of these patterns, narratives are developed describing present and potential future cultural movements. These stories are initially linked to national settings. Through regional meetings, similarities and differences are detected and cultural narratives at a continental level are formed. The same procedure is followed in the formulation of cultural patterns on a global scale. The insights generated through SignBank are used both at a more general level to direct the attention of agency employees and their clients towards the interconnectedness of broader cultural patterns of meaning and business performance, and at a very concrete level in order to situate clients' businesses within these meaning patterns and develop an elaborate understanding of the market opportunities at hand.

Texts and discourses: the strategy of analysis

The empirical material consisting of interview transcripts, textual documents and field notes are considered pieces of text used for the identification of discourses (Thompson 1998). Analysis of these texts was used to identify the cultural categories and structures of meaning used by informants in their attempts to make sense of their market reality. That is, the analysis identified the taken-for-granted assumptions that were used to give order and predictability to otherwise chaotic and uncertain markets.

Market research: a marketing managerial cornerstone

If the amount of money and energy spent worldwide upon market research is an indicator of the importance of these marketing managerial practices for the conduct of successful businesses, then it is definitely a topic worthy of critical attention and thorough understanding. Each year the global expenditure within the market research industry exceeds \$19 billion and is expected to keep mounting. The significance of market research in organizations is often defined by the importance of improving marketing decision-making. The assumption that knowledge about consumers and markets improves organizational decisions and ultimately contributes to organizational profitability is widespread and taken for granted. 'The overall purpose of marketing research is to assess information needs and provide the relevant information in a systematic and objective manner to improve marketing decision making' (Malhotra and Birks 2006: 28).

The citation from one of the most widely used books on market research exemplifies this relation between market research and marketing decisions. More generally, this understanding of market research is represented in the notion of market orientation (Kohli and Jaworski 1990) which denotes the commitment to organization-wide generation of market knowledge, dissemination of knowledge across departments and organization-wide responsiveness to it. This advocacy in favour of market orientation is based on the premise of continuous change in customer needs and expectations (Jaworski and Kohli 1993: 53) and consequently permanent organizational attention towards consumer satisfaction. Market orientation is explicitly related to the marketing concept which assumes the alignment of organizational aims of profitability with consumer preferences through marketing efforts. This argument is famously promoted by Levitt in his seminal 1960 *Harvard Business Review* article in which he states: 'the organization must learn to think of itself not as producing goods and services but as buying customers, as doing the things that will make people want to do business with it' (Levitt 1960: 149).

The concern for consumers implies a reorientation from short-term tactics of production to long-term strategic marketing in which the needs, wants, desires and aspirations of consumers are pivotal and decisive for the running of the organization as a whole. The direct relation of market research to some of the fundamental concepts of marketing management supports our attention to the ways in which market research is conducted.

Different routes to consumer/market insights

There are many different techniques of market research and the inventiveness and creativity of professionals regarding new ways of getting closer to consumers are impressive. Market research methods in the literature are often divided into groups of quantitative and qualitative techniques in order to point towards a variety of data collection methods. This division equally refers to variations in epistemology, i.e., the way we understand the nature of reality and how we gain access to knowledge about reality (Hudson and Ozanne 1988). Each approach carries implicit assumptions of how and why consumers engage in consumption and about the best ways for companies to acquire market knowledge. We choose to use the term 'modes of knowledge production' to emphasize the practical implications of epistemological differences between positivist/logical empiricist and constructivist/interpretive approaches to marketing research emphasized in the literature (Hunt 1976, 1990; Deshpande 1983; Hudson and Ozanne 1988). We do so in order to demonstrate empirically how such a division structures knowledge about consumers and markets and leads to different marketing decisions. We create the following two categories of market research based upon the epistemological divide predominant in market research literature: (1) the functionalist mode of knowledge production; and (2) the cultural mode of knowledge production. The two modes of knowledge production coexist in the organization and they are equally engaged in market-oriented efforts to represent consumers and markets to organizational decision-makers. Yet it is the aim of the following section to discuss how this task of representation is constituted differently within the two modes of knowledge production depending upon their embeddedness in a positivist/interpretive epistemology, respectively.

To measure needs or to interpret culture – that is the question

A positivist epistemology emphasizes the existence of one single physical reality characterized by discrete elements related through causal relationships. The role of research is to establish objective and value-neutral measures that are representative across time and context. For market research practices, this epistemological stance implies a focus on understanding individual consumer actions as the causal effects of intrinsic preferences. Malhotra and Birks (2006) explain this relation in the following manner:

> The role of marketing research is … the identification and satisfaction of customer needs. To determine customer needs and to implement marketing strategies and plans

aimed at satisfying those needs, marketing managers need information about customers, competitors and other forces in the marketplace.

(ibid.: 5)

The quote clearly reproduces the focus on individual consumer needs as the major determinant for understanding markets and it takes for granted that people are equipped with internal needs which can be articulated, measured and eventually satisfied. The positivist approach understands consumption choices as an outcome of rational decision-making based upon the principles of utility-maximization.

In contrast, in the interpretive approach, the focus is removed from causes and effects to a more holistic understanding stressing, on the one side, the processes through which individuals construct a meaningful life through acts of consumption (seeing the world through the eyes of the consumer – also often called an 'emic' approach) and, on the other, how consumption objects are inscribed with cultural/symbolic meaning through which social life is organized. The interpretive approach puts less emphasis on individual preferences and focus on cultural meanings and their relation to individual and collective consumer perceptions and behaviour (Arnould and Wallendorf 1994; Thompson 1997).

This description of two distinct paradigms in market research addresses the most significant differences between the implicit assumptions about consumer behaviour. It constitutes the background on which the empirical examination of how the two modes of knowledge production play out in our organizational context. Based on close readings of informant interviews and textual SignBank material, the following sections describe how the epistemological assumptions in the market research literature reoccur as modes of knowledge production within organizational practices. The functionalist mode of knowledge production embedded within the positivist paradigm is engaged in the precise depiction of consumer preferences within specific product categories. The cultural mode of knowledge production is embedded within the interpretive paradigm and it is characterized by its attempt to understand consumers through the emic notion of 'people in life' and it structures markets in terms of cultural narratives. Through the identification of the implicit assumptions of the two modes of knowledge production, it becomes evident how market research methods are not just neutral devices which transmit information from the marketplace to the organization. On the contrary, we highlight how market researchers mobilize particular ways of representing consumers and markets and hereby engage in the active co-production of organizational market realities – not within a value-free vacuum but within the web of symbolic meaning (Geertz 1973) of a specific cultural context. Finally, we outline the implications for market communication and new product development.

Product category and consumer preferences: the structures of a functionalist mode of knowledge production

In a functionalist mode of knowledge production, markets are above all organized along structures of product category. The notion of product category occurs in the discourses of informants as an objective and naturalized concept through which the organization can meaningfully reduce complexity by dividing the external world into manageable markets. Product category serves as a means to identify which business/market the organization is operating in. Through this process of complexity reduction, the organization is enabled to direct the attention of their market research effort.

The citation from the global new business manager of the advertising agency below illustrates how he understands markets through a division into product categories. He also assumes that chief marketing officers (CMOs) of agency clients are engaged in the same view upon markets:

> From Brand Capital [the agency's global quantitative survey] we could get very very brand specific, we could go into a number of categories. We could go market by market by market and show a chief marketing officer where his brand tracked on a bunch of attributes versus his competition. So it became very brand-specific. That's the type of thing that to some extent SignBank has to get into, I would love to work with Eva and figure out how we open categories and then use SignBank and say, if you're a pet food manufacturer, these are the observations from SignBank that are very interesting, and then allow that company to have some more in-depth and engagement ... With SignBank, I think we need to zero in on category ... otherwise it's totally ineffective because they [CMOs] just, they screen it out.
>
> (Global new business manager, New York)

With this citation it is suggested that SignBank should be able to deliver marketing insights along the same categories of meaning (the product category in this case) as conventional market research techniques. It is judged through the functionalist mode of constructing knowledge about markets rather than as an alternative way of understanding markets, which limits how it could potentially enrich agency and clients' market understanding.

Beyond the overall division of markets in terms of product category, the functionalist mode of knowledge production amplifies the significance of consumer preferences in conducting market research and understanding markets. As noted earlier, in the market orientation logic and positivist market research, the notions of consumer needs and preferences are assumed to be given phenomena that can be properly revealed and measured through the choice of the right technique and eventually satisfied by marketers and their products.

The importance of understanding consumer preferences in the functional mode of knowledge production came out clearly in our informants' ways of talking about how and why consumers consume. In the functional mode, consumers are represented as individual agents with intrinsic preferences, needs, desires and aspiration which are met through the consumption of specific products. So, regarding practices of market research and the knowledge produced within, the detection of consumer preferences concerning a specific product category is of the essence. The following quote from an executive strategic planner in Malaysia illustrates the contrast of producing market knowledge through a functionalist or cultural mode and equally pays attention to the potentially different strategic outcomes of the two research methods:

> When you are trying to understand liquorice, what normal marketers do in this modernized professional world is that they commission surveys of around 800 to 1000 people, and they ask them every damn question you can imagine about liquorice. Whether they like it in animal shapes or if they like it in alphabet shapes ... I mean, they will ask you 800 questions about liquorice. When you buy liquorice, what you eat, how many grams of liquorice do you eat, all sorts of stuff, because they try to exhort all the information they need on liquorice. They might even ask about other types of sweets like candy, gum, and so on, because it's in the candy category. What they don't do is ask, when you

watch TV, do you like stuff to be very sweet or be medium sweet or do you like stuff to be bitter? They don't ask about your taste in entertainment. What they don't ask you is, how are you treating your children these days? Are you disciplining them or are you not disciplining them, which might affect how often you buy sweets. Those things are what SignBank uses to understand categories. You don't understand categories from that small percentage of time you spend thinking about liquorice. When would you ever think 800 different things about liquorice? You would never. But all the other stuff that you are thinking about … oh, no, my children are getting very spoiled or … I don't like … I have lost my taste for sweet stuff. Or I think I should reward myself more often with small things. All these kinds of ideas have nothing to do with candy, but inform how and when you purchase candy or what kind of candy you like. You might … if you feel like you need to reward yourself more often, you might want to make this liquorice more luxurious, more of a decadent luxury than it is now. If you wanted to … if you are more health conscious obviously, you would have less sugar on it.

(Executive strategic planner, Malaysia)

In this quote, the executive strategic planner illustrates the enormous reflexivity upon the functionalist mode of knowledge production without herself subscribing to this understanding of markets. She nearly ridicules the concern for individual consumers and the trust by conventional market research techniques in the display of consumer preferences upon a request from market researchers. The primary division of market realities by product category is equally brought into play as the informant stresses the fact that potentially 800 questions would be asked about what consumers think about liquorice but not a single one trying to contextualize the answers. SignBank is emphasized as a possible way of contextualizing consumer behaviour and understanding consumers in relation to issues of conducting a meaningful life and not the small percentage of time spent wondering about a certain product and its specific attributes.

Besides the primary division of markets by product category and consumer preferences, the functional mode of knowledge production reproduces particular understandings of the temporal and spatial dimensions of markets. Temporality and spatiality have proved important due to the accelerated processes of globalization (cf. Chapters 2 and 3 in this volume), which fosters an increased demand for market and consumer insights which cut across national boundaries. The reference to space within a functionalist mode of knowledge production becomes relevant in terms of markets as discrete geographical units. These units are repeatedly organized around nationality but may also refer to larger regions such as Asia or Europe. In a world of globalization in which an increasing number of organizations operate across borders, this conception of space requires market research methods capable of representing and mirroring consumer preferences in specific product categories across many countries. Processes of globalization are in a functionalist mode of knowledge production perceived to contribute to a sense of accelerated change in which consumer preferences and lifestyles become increasingly unstable. As a consequence, the date of expiration of market knowledge draws ever nearer. The same global new business manager who earlier advocated for product categories as the best way of understanding markets here addresses the issue of rapid market changes and the challenge this poses for functionalist market research:

There are two problems with Brand Capital. It was a very expensive study for us and once it was, say, one year old, it was, it might as well be ten years. Because prospects and clients say anything over a year old, if in January I start talking about 2005 you might as well be talking about 1910, and whether it's valid or not, the feeling is that the world is moving so fast these days.

(Global new business manager, New York)

The new business manager reflects upon the soundness of his feeling of accelerated change processes whereas he refers to the demand of clients and prospects as legitimization of the continuous renewal of market knowledge. These perceived requirements of globally representative and up-to-date market information form a serious financial and practical challenge to organizations and to the functionalist mode of knowledge production as such.

It has been described how the functionalist mode of knowledge production is framing the process through which organizations are engaged in making sense of their market realities. As an *a priori* reduction of complexity, markets are divided along a structure of product category which determines the relevant area for further market research. In the case study in Box 14.2 it is illustrated how market actors determine the relevance of information in terms of their own position within a specific product category. Hereafter the notion of consumer preferences was identified as an important structure according to which organizations understand consumers and the role of market research and products in respectively

---

Box 14.2 Cultural narrative of micro-sphering

One of the managing directors of the agency's San Francisco branch reported on the development of both market communication and product development for a specific smart-phone brand based on SignBank. The North American SignBank had on the basis of the collection and structuring of signs identified a cultural narrative on people's increased concern with filtering and controlling the character and amount of information and stimuli reaching them. This was labelled micro-sphering. In a broader context micro-sphering was related to feelings of information overload and the intrusion of public/work-related issues into the private sphere and a demand for increased control over one's life. Furthermore this was interpreted as an outcome of consumers suffering from time poverty and stressful lifestyles and aspiring towards a simpler life characterized through popular notions such as 'simple living' and 'downshifting'. In connection to the development of smart phones, this insight pointed towards the importance of being able to control the stream of ingoing information but at the same time being able to use the phone. Existing smart phones in the market would either be turned completely on or off whereas this particular brand was equipped with the feature of being able to use the phone without being disturbed by ingoing calls or e-mails. This feature was also stressed in the market communication for the brand. This example of how cultural narratives transform into concrete product features demonstrates the alignment of demand and supply through the mechanism of lifestyle and identity position. Thus, instead of understanding product innovation as a matter of technological improvement which meets specific and clearly articulated consumer needs, the detection of aspirational consumer lifestyles and identity projects through cultural analysis paves a different way to product development and innovation. This example is much in line with Holt and Cameron's outline of cultural strategy (Holt and Cameron 2010).

detecting and satisfying these preferences. Finally, it has been noted how processes of globalization in terms of, on the one hand, an increasing number of organizations operating across national border and, on the other, a perception of acceleration of changes in consumer preferences and lifestyles display a magnificent challenge to the practices of market research based upon a functionalist mode of knowledge production. This challenge occurs as market research is expected continuously to deliver up-to-date, representative market knowledge on consumer preferences across segments, product categories and national borders.

Structuring markets through cultural narratives

In this section, we describe how changes in the choice of market research techniques and different modes of producing market knowledge lead to alternative understandings of markets. Different techniques and modes of knowledge production not only reshape marketing practitioners' understanding of the market they are operating in but equally open up new opportunities for product development, positioning and market communication. With a cultural mode of knowledge production, represented here by SignBank, markets are primarily understood through the category of 'cultural narratives' which cut across product categories, industries and nations. The following citation from a managing director in Singapore is illustrative of the perception of new opportunities opened through the application of SignBank:

> I think that's what SignBank does, it gives you permission and this is an important point, it gives you permission to look at other, seemingly unrelated areas and allows you to try to make the connection between those things. Other methods don't allow these relations of what's going on with, let's say, the apple business, it's not something related to what's going on in the technology sector or the finance sector, it's all unrelated, but what SignBank does is it allows you to bring that together and it allows you to look at the differences and the changes and the ups and downs of that industry and make analogous connections to something else … SignBank allows us to look everywhere for solutions.
>
> (Managing director, Singapore)

Informants' descriptions of how SignBank facilitates new market perspectives are less precise and characterized by a larger degree of uncertainty and hesitation than the notion of product category organizing the functionalist mode of knowledge production. This should be seen as a consequence of the relative novelty of the method and the vocabulary used in describing and using it. Cultural narratives establish an equivalent *a priori* reduction of complexity to that of product category in the functionalist mode of knowledge production. It is assumed by marketing practitioners ascribing to this kind of ethnographic market research practice that markets are meaningfully divided and understood in terms of underlying cultural streams of meaning. As a consequence, consumption is no longer a matter of satisfying consumer preferences through the acquisition of products specifically targeted towards certain needs, wants and desires. Instead, consumption is evaluated in terms of contributing to a meaningful life of consumers, and products are thought to be inscribed with cultural meaning and hereby play a role as resources for consumer identity projects. The case study in Box 14.2 describes how the insight into specific cultural narratives informed the product development and market communication process of a specific smart phone.

As a consequence of the focus of cultural narratives, practices of market research are no longer primarily concerned with the detection of consumer preferences. Instead cultural modes of knowledge production are bound to the understanding and description of cultural patterns and changes in these. Thus, the cultural mode of knowledge production does not focus solely on acts of consumption but more broadly on the notion of 'people in life' which is supposed to indicate a more general interest in all aspects of human life. This understanding of consumers is reflected in a mantra-like sentence which occurs repeatedly in both interviews and document material. It is stressed that: 'people only spend 3 per cent of their time consuming' and therefore market research should be concerned with a much broader approach to understanding the role of consumption and products in people's lives.

Whereas the functionalist mode of knowledge production is structured by temporal and spatial references shaping markets in terms of discrete geographical units and shorter periods of validity of market knowledge, the cultural mode of knowledge production is, according to informants, related differently to processes of globalization. In the process of uncovering cultural narratives through SignBank, the spatial genesis of specific observations become more or less irrelevant. It is the contribution of market observations to a holistic, coherent and meaningful cultural narrative which counts for its validity and legitimacy and not the degree of statistic representation in a given geographic area. The second case study in Box 14.3, concerning the new product development of a premium beer in Denmark, is based on signs from many different geographical locations but the product was launched only in the Danish market. This means that the spatial configuration of markets is not defined

---

Box 14.3 Implications for new product development

The leading Danish beer brand experienced throughout the late 1990s increasing difficulties in preserving the price premium, and market share, of their major mainstream product. Private labels had taken about 30 per cent of the beer market within a very short time. Two main challenges were defined by the company and the ad agency. On the one hand, the price premium had to be legitimized through increased attraction and trustworthiness of the master brand and, on the other, new market and growth opportunities were sought.

The overall cultural narratives identified through SignBank were creatively applied to the realm of beer business and resulted in two primary insights concerning the challenges of the company:

- The mainstream product was caught in a market position between cheaper private labels and more expensive premium brands. This position appeared unattractive due to cultural changes with, on the one hand, cynicism in consumption choices invisible to others leading to the purchase of cheap private label products, and, on the other, flagging success and identity through consumption of luxury and premium brands.
- SignBank indicates that consumers as they turn towards seriousness and occupation with material success in life reject engaging in market communication just for the fun of it. Instead SignBank indicated the need for brands to 'walk the talk'

(cf. Chapter 13 in this volume), to become real physical manifestations in people's lives rather than remain in 'ad-land'.

The reasoning behind the identification of these cultural changes can be exemplified by a couple of signs used in the process of constructing the cultural narratives. It was noticed that the public heroes and icons celebrated had changed from actors and TV stars to successful CEOs and CFOs. This was termed consumer 'sober-mindedness' with a focus on materialism, bottom line and ambition as opposed to the creativity, curiosity and self-realization of the 1990s. The clear lines drawn between good and evil, enemy vs. hero and friend vs. foe as exemplified in President Bush's rhetoric of the axes of evil were seen as other manifestations of this. The signs used in the formulation of these cultural changes and narratives are derived from a large variety of countries but applied within the national context of Denmark, illustrating well the role and meaning of space at stake in the cultural mode of knowledge production.

Based on the cultural narratives developed through SignBank pointing to the position of the master beer brand between cheap private labels and premium brands as the major challenge, the ad agency formulated the following strategic recommendations:

- Create a truly superior specialty beer carrying all the elements of the master brand: quality, uncompromising attitude to beer, dedication, heritage and pride.
- Make the elements of the master brand a part of people's lives through this beer; re-open the old brewery of the founder, make a superior beer and use exclusive packaging, design, bottle, pricing, distribution and communication.
- Make a beer for the modern part of the consumers who are willing to pay, and are increasingly eager to differentiate themselves, through their ability to appreciate high-quality premium products.

It was noted by the leading strategic planner involved in the project that 'the logical thing to do would have been to enter the discount and private-label category and fight for market shares within the battlefield of price'. Hereby the market knowledge created through SignBank is clearly marked as a crucial source of information leading to different solutions than those generated within a functional mode of knowledge production.

The recommendations of the agency were followed by the brewery and within six months of the launch it was reported that the new product had turned negative growth in sales of the mainstream brand into positive growth rates. The goals for sales and market share of the new brand were both superseded within one year of the launch and the new brand had a market share of more than one-fifth of the market for specialty beer.

This case illustrates the way in which different modes of knowledge production significantly shape the outcome of product development processes. The implications for managers are discussed in the succeeding section.

a priori through reference to particular nation states. Instead market spatiality emerges from the connections and links between places, brought to life through SignBank and its shared cultural narratives. As a part and consequence of processes of globalization, these cultural narratives flow in an increasingly disjunctive way, forming new and unexpected interconnections of similarity and difference across national borders (Appadurai 1990). The following account of how ideas and meanings transcend borders but are manifested differently according to local cultures and the influence hereof on advertising illustrates the understanding of markets in terms of interconnectedness of places through varying degrees of similarity and difference in streams of cultural meaning:

> I think that the idea can be assured globally, I generally think it's maximized when the actual interpretation of that idea is done at the local market level. So I'll give you an example of it; so this brand of cleaning products has always been about these disinfecting products. So both in Latin America and in North America we came up with the idea that it was all about growing happy healthy kids so it wasn't about killing germs, it was about the kids you grow. So that's a North American idea, and you have to look at how that interprets itself in Buenos Aires, it might be really different than how it might manifest itself in China, what is a happy healthy kid?, how is motherhood portrayed?, all of those things have very local cultures associated with them. So, I do believe that ideas transcend, but are interpreted when they're brought to life at the local market level. So in my sense there're some fat things that people will love in every culture, you know, like having healthy kids, right, so the core of the ideas can be the same, but I think the local market interpretations will always be really valuable.
>
> (Managing director, San Francisco)

Spatial references and geography do not become obsolete due to the division of markets through cultural narratives. But instead of organizing markets along lines of separate national boundaries, informants perceive places to be connected through systems of meaning.

The cultural mode of knowledge production also relates in its own way to structures of temporality. As SignBank is assumed to reveal the shared structures of meaning constituting the horizon of conceivable consumer thoughts, actions and aspirations, these are not assumed to change completely overnight. Through continuous observations in the marketplace, SignBank practitioners seek to catch both gradual and more radical changes in the cultural narratives and be able to translate these into new market opportunities.

In market research practices ascribing to a cultural mode of knowledge production, market realities are structured through cultural narratives. These narratives are not thought of as mutually exclusive and independent but interconnected and overlapping. The lack of more clear-cut division of markets into separable units of business is in line with the overall wish to establish a more holistic view of the marketplace. The cultural narratives form coherent discourses representing products as cultural resources of meaning partaking in consumers' continuous engagement in identity projects and performance of a meaningful life. Hence market research practices are thought to operate in order to unveil the underlying streams of cultural meaning in order to strategically apply this market knowledge in the development of products, positioning and market communication.

The challenges of the processes of globalization facing functionalist modes of knowledge production discussed in the previous section are partially overcome through a cultural approach to market research. As cultural narratives are neither defined in terms of discrete geographical units nor fall victim to accelerated processes of change in consumer

Table 14.1 Two modes of knowledge production in market research

	Functionalist mode of knowledge production	*Cultural mode of knowledge production*
Consumption	Fulfilling specific consumer needs	Creation of a meaningful life
Products	Satisfying specific needs	Ascribed with cultural meaning
Market research	Detecting consumer preferences	Identifying cultural patterns
Consumers	Rational agents with inherent needs	People in life
Time	Up to date vs. outdated	Relative stability
Space	Geographical units	Interconnectedness of places
Structuring markets	Product categories	Cultural narratives

preferences, they do not meet identical requirements of representation and freshness. As an alternative, the narratives are imagined as translocal cultural patterns which only change gradually and therefore constitute symbolic flows of meaning across boundaries and hereby become both part and consequence of globalization processes. Table 14.1 summarizes the two modes of knowledge production.

As has been stressed throughout this chapter, organizational commitment to specific techniques and modes of knowledge production in market research practices is by no means value-free. We wish to allude not only to the consequences of different modes of knowledge production for the perception of markets but equally to the marketing implications in relation to product development and market communication.

The implications of the cultural mode of knowledge production on new product development

In the case study in Box 14.3, it is illustrated how the cultural narratives identified through SignBank structured the market reality of the advertising agency in a very specific way and hereby became co-constitutive of a business solution for a large Danish brewery facing declining market share in its core business. The cultural narratives were translated into manageable and meaningful market information concerning the beer business in Denmark. In the advertising agency the beer case is referred to as an example of the superiority and success of SignBank, due to the eye-opening potential of the method as it reconfigured the understanding of the market for this particular company. Furthermore, this case constitutes a success in terms of sales and market share of the product.

Managerial implications

The aim of this chapter has not been to advocate for the superiority of one mode of knowledge production over another. Instead we wish to address how market research practices are embedded in particular ways of thinking of markets and of knowledge about markets and the consequences this has for how marketers ultimately co-produce market realities through market communication and new product development (Peñaloza and Venkatesh 2006). From the discussion in this chapter we can begin to question the depiction of market research in the marketing literature as straightforward and neutral practices of knowledge transmission. Instead market research is a much more messy process of organizational sense-making and co-production of markets. In this sense markets are not discrete units of analysis waiting to be mirrored and unveiled through market research and other marketing activities, but market realities co-produced through modes of knowledge production applied in practices of market research.

The implications of the cultural perspective on market research primarily have to do with organizational introspection. Through critical self-awareness of the market research practices as embedded in particular modes of knowledge production, organizations gain an understanding of their own position and role in the cultural meaning system of the marketplace. This insight can be used in order to engage divergent modes of knowledge production in the strategic and creative process of market communication and (new) product development. Involving different modes of knowledge production in practices of market research sensitizes the organization to its own co-creative resources and serves the purpose of giving a more nuanced view of the nature of markets. Hereby consumer preferences can be demystified and released from the cognitive black box of consumer minds which marketers from a positivist stance desperately need to measure ever more precisely. Instead consumer preferences should be re-interpreted as market opportunities created through the integration of market insight produced through practices of market research. More specifically we recommend that:

- Managers must become more reflexive of the way marketing theory provides normative ideas of practice. Marketing education in business school programmes propagates particular ways of thinking about markets and consumers. Dominant modes of thinking are often communicated without the effort of legitimization.
- Managers must identify what the organization takes for granted about their markets and consumers and facilitate and welcome other ways of understanding. This can happen by ensuring multi-disciplinarity among employees.
- Organizations need to build skills that can identify the variety of modes of thinking so as to make the organization aware of the perspective it employs.
- Marketers analyze *how* the organization is embedded in – rather than situated outside of – the markets they are strategically engaged in.
- The organization must become aware of what kind of mode of market research knowledge they employ, including how the adherence to a specific mode of market research knowledge inflects strategies and practices. That is, at the tactical level, they must be able to identify and make decisions between particular modes of market research knowledge.

These are by no means easy tasks and the solution lies not in searching for 'ten easy steps'. Rather it requires organizations to recruit human resources who have been trained in multiple scientific paradigms and disciplines and that the organization encourages and gives opportunity for self-reflection.

Review and discussion questions

1   What are the most important differences between a cultural and a functional perspective upon market research as presented in this chapter? How does the shift in perspective upon market research alter the understanding of what a market is?

2   How does the shift in perspective upon market research alter the understanding of the consumer?

3   What are the organizational challenges related to the cultural perspective upon market research practices?

4   What kind of new skills and competences do organizations need in order to become (a) more competent in a variety of market research methods; and (b) more reflexive of their market research practices?

5   How are globalization processes involved in the transformation of market research?

Keywords

cultural production, ethnographic methods, globalization processes, market research

References

Appadurai, A. (1990) 'Disjuncture and Difference in the Global Cultural Economy', in M. Featherstone (ed.), *Global Culture, Nationalism, Globalization and Modernity*, London: Sage.

Arnould, E. J. and Thompson, C. J. (2005) 'Consumer Culture Theory (CCT): Twenty Years of Research', *Journal of Consumer Research*, 31: 868–82.

Arnould, E. J. and Wallendorf, M. (1994) 'Market-Oriented Ethnography: Interpretation Building and Marketing Strategy Formulation', *Journal of Marketing Research*, XXXI: 484–504.

Deshpande, R. (1983) 'Paradigms Lost: On Theory and Method in Theory in Marketing', *Journal of Marketing*, 47: 101–10.

Geertz, C. (1973) *The Interpretation of Cultures*, New York: Basic Books.

Hirschman, E. C. (1988) 'Humanistic Inquiry in Marketing Research: Philosophy, Method, and Criteria', *Journal of Marketing Research*, XXIII: 237–49.

Holt, D. and Cameron, D. (2010) *Cultural Strategy: Using Innovative Ideologies to Build Breakthrough Brands*, Oxford: Oxford University Press.

Hudson, L. A. and Ozanne, J. L. (1988) 'Alternative Ways of Seeking Knowledge in Consumer Research', *Journal of Consumer Research*, 14: 508–21.

Hunt, S. D. (1976) 'The Nature and Scope of Marketing', *Journal of Marketing*, 70: 17–28.

—— (1990) 'The Truth in Marketing Theory and Research', *Journal of Marketing*, 54: 1–15.

Jaworski, B. J. and Kohli, A. K. (1993) 'Market Orientation; Antecedents and Consequences', *Journal of Marketing*, 57(3): 53–70.

Kohli, A. K. and Jaworski, B. J. (1990) 'Market Orientation: The Construct, Research Propositions and Managerial Implications', *Journal of Marketing*, 54: 1–18.

Levitt, T. (1960) 'Marketing Myopia', *Harvard Business Review*, 38: 45–56.

Malhotra, N. K. and Birks, D. F. (2006) *Marketing Research: An Applied Approach*, Englewood Cliffs, NJ: Prentice Hall.

Peñaloza, L. and Venkatesh, A. (2006) 'Further Evolving the New Dominant Logic of Marketing: From Services to the Social Construction of Markets', *Marketing Theory*, 6(3): 299–316.

Thompson, C. J. (1997) 'Interpreting Consumers: A Hermeneutical Framework for Deriving Marketing Insights from Texts of Consumers' Consumption Stories', *Journal of Marketing Research*, xxxiv: 438–55.

—— (1998) 'Living the Texts of Everyday Life: A Hermeneutic Perspective on the Relationship between Consumer Stories and Life-World Structures', in B. Stern (ed.), *Representing Consumers: Voices, Views and Visions*, London: Routledge, pp. 127–55.

15 Interpretive marketing research

Using ethnography in strategic market development

Johanna Moisander and Anu Valtonen

Overview

This chapter focuses on interpretive research in marketing. Interpretive research is argued to be particularly well suited for gaining consumer market insight and for developing customer-oriented strategies. Being a data-driven approach, it enables marketing practitioners to keep up with and anticipate the continuous change that is taking place in the market environment, thereby inviting them to make sense of marketing activity in new ways. The chapter starts by discussing the general goals, principles and practices of interpretive research, comparing it with the more traditional approaches to marketing research. Then, the chapter turns to exemplify the interpretive perspective by discussing how *ethnography* – a key methodology in the interpretive research paradigm – might be fruitfully employed in the context of strategic market development, *branding* and *coolhunting* in particular. To conclude, the chapter outlines some challenges that marketing managers face when buying and evaluating interpretive research.

The case for interpretive marketing research

In most well-managed business organizations, marketing is based on research. Marketers systematically gather and analyze data and information about their target markets so as to gain strategic insights into their business environments and to learn about the ways in which they need to relate to their customers, competitors, and other important stakeholders to succeed in the market.

The practice of marketing research is based on various forms of theoretical knowledge and expertise, which typically draw on micro-economics, consumer psychology, sociology of consumption, anthropology, and the methodology of social sciences. Using this knowledge and expertise, marketing practitioners seek to render their target markets and customers knowable and predictable as the objects of marketing activities. The different models and techniques of marketing research are thus important intellectual tools – strategy tools – that enable marketing practitioners to make informed choices and to function effectively in creating and implementing marketing strategies for brands and corporations.

According to the *AMA Dictionary of Marketing Terms*, published and continuously updated by the American Marketing Association (AMA):

> Marketing research is the function that links the consumer, customer, and public to the marketer through information – information used to identify and define marketing opportunities and problems; generate, refine, and evaluate marketing actions; monitor

marketing performance; and improve understanding of marketing as a process. Marketing research specifies the information required to address these issues, designs the method for collecting information, manages and implements the data collection process, analyzes the results, and communicates the findings and their implications.

(American Marketing Association 2009)

As the AMA definition indicates, traditionally the objective of marketing research has been to support managerial decision-making by providing information – facts and figures – for well-defined marketing problems, typically by measuring and monitoring processes, activities and preferences that already exist in the market. Much of the research that is commissioned and carried out today, for example, is based on market surveys of consumer attitudes, values, and lifestyles, or on quantitative studies of consumers' purchase intentions and brand preferences. With fairly simple standardized research instruments, corporations systematically also monitor their performance and measure customer satisfaction, in hotels and restaurants, for example.

In this chapter, we focus on a particular theoretical and methodological approach to marketing and consumer inquiry that is generally referred to as *interpretive marketing research* (Moisander and Valtonen 2006; cf. also Chapter 14 in this volume). We contend that interpretive methods and methodologies are particularly useful for gaining *consumer market insight*, a more holistic understanding of the consumer as a market actor and a member of culture and society. According to the AMA definition, consumer market insight refers to:

An in-depth understanding of customer behavior that is more qualitative than quantitative. Specifically, it describes the role played by the product/brand in question in the life of its consumers – and their general stance towards it including the way they acquire information about the category or brand, the importance attached to generic and specific values, attitudes, expectations, as well as the choice-making process. It refers to a holistic appreciation, which used to be traditionally split by market researchers and brand managers as qualitative and quantitative research.

(American Marketing Association 2009)

By broadening the focus of analysis from the psychology of individual buyers to the social psychology and sociology of groups and communities and their local cultural and spatio-temporal contexts – be they virtual or 'real' – the new interpretive techniques of consumer market insight help marketers to explore and to gain strategic insights into the particular cultural and social categories, distinctions, relationships, and identities through which consumers make sense of their everyday life, construct identities and achieve social order in the marketplace. A particular strength of interpretive methodologies arguably is that they focus attention on the everyday contexts of consumer behaviour and help marketing practitioners better understand the socio-cultural dynamics of marketplace behaviour.

In the sections that follow, we therefore discuss interpretive marketing research as an intellectual technology that is particularly well suited for gaining consumer market insight and for developing customer-oriented strategies in the contemporary multicultural and continuously changing market environments. We begin by briefly explaining what we mean by 'interpretive methodologies' and what makes a study 'interpretive'. Then we elaborate on the nature of interpretive marketing research, using ethnography as a paradigmatic example, discussing the new tools and methods it offers for marketers to learn more about their customers and about ways in which products, brands, and services are used in everyday life.

Finally, we describe the ways in which interpretive inquiry may help companies to improve the effectiveness of their marketing strategies, offering two illustrative cases. First, we discuss the ways in which ethnography can be used to interpret existing markets to develop brand strategies, and then how it can be used together with coolhunting techniques to plan for future.

What makes a study interpretive?

While the interpretive turn in marketing research arguably refers to a fairly heterogeneous body of research that draws on multiple theoretical traditions (Moisander 2008; Moisander *et al.* 2009), what makes a study 'interpretive' is, perhaps, that it is based on theories and methodologies that draw on the *interpretive approaches* to social theory and philosophy of science. From this perspective, social action is intentional and rule governed; it is performed in order to achieve particular purposes and in conformity to some rules (Fay and Moon 1994). Therefore social action such as marketplace activity can only be made sense of or *interpreted* based on knowledge of these intentions and social rules.

To illustrate, if we observe a man lifting his hand, we have no way of knowing what this bodily movement or gesture means unless we also have information about the intentions of this person or about the social context in which it takes place. If the action takes place in a gym, we may interpret that the person is stretching and warming up before a workout. If, on the other hand, the action takes place in a classroom, we might think that the man is asking for permission to speak. In a corporate meeting room he might be voting. And in the street, he might just be happily greeting a friend. Hence, this single bodily movement, lifting of a hand, counts as a vote, a signal, a salute, or an attempt to get warmed up before physical exercise, depending on the set of social rules and conventions that are applicable in the situation and obviously also on the purposes that the actor engaging in the behaviour happens to have for the activity.

Consequently, interpretive approaches to social inquiry are generally based on the idea that the social action can only be interpreted by contextualizing it in the cultural system of concepts, rules, conventions, and beliefs that give meaning to that action. There are different streams of interpretivism (Schwandt 2003), which differ in their conceptualization of the system of rules that give meaning to social behaviour. These rules can be naturalized cultural conventions and social practices, agreed-upon rules and regulations, or discursive systems. But in general, all interpretive approaches to social inquiry would seem to be based on the basic methodological principle that the concepts that are used to theorize and analyze social action (be it physical activities, mental events, or institutions) must capture the specific individual and/or collective meanings that these phenomena have among the social actors that are studied.

In research practice, this means that researchers must try to use the same concepts and meanings that the subjects of their studies themselves use. Interpretive research and empirical analysis are, thus, 'data-driven' and based on 'emergent designs'. The theoretical concepts that are employed in the study are not fixed at the outset but rather drawn from the social life that is being studied – from the empirical context in which the action takes place – and gradually worked out from the data with the help of existing theory. In ethnography, for example, this means that researchers not only conduct open-ended personal interviews but also engage in systematic observation of the ways in which the members of the particular culture or community under study use language and other systems of meaning to make sense of their everyday life and to achieve social order. It also means that the

research problems and the interpretive framework that guide empirical analysis are continuously revised and further developed as the researchers get familiar with and learn more about
the objects of their study.

Furthermore, interpretive research, ethnographic research in particular, is based on
studying people in their natural environments, *in situ*, as active social beings and members
of communities and cultures with particular collectively shared understandings, rituals and
social rules that guide and give meaning to action within the immediate social context of the
activity. It is emphasized, particularly in the cultural streams of interpretive marketing
research, that people live in households, belong to groups and organizations, and define
their identities in relation to ethnic, professional, and other sub-cultural communities. And
therefore they must be studied, addressed, and targeted as members of these groups,
communities, and cultures (Moisander and Valtonen 2006; Peñaloza and Venkatesh 2006;
Moisander 2007; Moisander *et al.* 2009).

The interpretive research differs, hence, from the more traditional research approach in
many ways. While aware of the risk of simplifying, in Table 15.1 we summarize and
compare the two different perspectives and research orientations that the interpretive and
traditional approach to marketing research offer, outlining the corresponding shift in the way
the consumer market is thought of and worked upon. The next section turns to scrutinize in
more detail the benefits, and drivers, of using interpretive research to understand consumer
markets by way of referring to existing business examples and academic studies.

Table 15.1 Comparison of traditional and interpretive perspectives on marketing research

	Traditional perspective	*Interpretive perspective*
Goal of research	To provide generalizable knowledge and 'facts' for decision making	To provide in-depth understanding of a specific consumer market
Research design	*A priori*, theory-driven	Emergent, data-driven
Unit of analysis; how customer markets are understood and conceptualized	The goal-directed individual; individual needs and wants; socio-demographic variables; resources	Individuals as members of culture and community; socially and historically situated actions; meanings, myths and symbols
Examples of marketing problems typically addressed	Measuring brand awareness; monitoring marketing performance; calculating market share; analyzing available income; tracking the effects and outcomes of marketing strategies	Understanding brand meanings; gaining detailed understanding of customer–marketer interaction; understanding marketplace symbolism; building, refining and re-evaluating marketing strategies
Examples of methods used	Experiments, surveys (mail, telephone, personal, internet)	Ethnographic research, interviews, focus groups, observation, projective techniques
Empirical materials	Mostly quantitative: 'facts and figures'; quantitative representations or measurements of preferences, attitudes, perceptions, intentions and behaviours, etc.	Mostly qualitative: interviews; discussions; photographs; videos; drawings; web-based materials; field notes and journals; diaries; stories; first-person narratives; documentary materials, fiction and media texts, etc.

Why interpretive marketing research?

For marketing executives, managers, and other practitioners, the traditional quantitative tools and techniques of marketing research offer valuable 'facts' or measurable information about the topics and issues that they already recognize as important – about something that they know that they need to know more about – to identify problems and opportunities that exist in the market. Drawing mainly on theory-driven methodologies, however, these techniques are largely inadequate for identifying challenges and opportunities that will arise from topics and issues that the practitioners do not recognize or come to think of as important – as it is something that they do not know that they need to know, as the cliché goes.

Quantitative surveys, for example, offer little intelligence for managing the strategic challenges and opportunities that will arise from the currently ongoing technological and cultural market transformations, such as media convergence (Jenkins 2008) and the resulting participatory consumer culture (Jenkins 2006). Such transformations bring about important changes in consumers' hopes, fears, and everyday routines of product use, which will inevitably change the rules of the game in the market in many important ways. In the contemporary global media industry, to illustrate, different new and traditional media technologies and modes of communication are currently melting and morphing into new forms and types of activities, products and services, thus changing the ways in which both corporations and consumers operate and interact with each other in the market. In these turbulent market environments, old industry recipes are losing their relevance and marketers no longer necessarily know what it actually is that they need to measure or monitor, or how to structure well-defined problems for managerial decision-making. The objects of inquiry for which their measurement instruments have been designed are taking new, radically different forms and may eventually even cease to exist, as the basic structures and old realities of the marketplace are rapidly changing. In participatory consumer culture, for example, the media audience may no longer be conceptualized and studied, perhaps, as passive spectators and 'targets' of promotional messages, using the standard methods of measuring media effects. And the conventional techniques of prediction and explanation that marketers have developed and learned to use in strategic planning are losing their validity as the dynamics of marketplace activity are taking new forms and a new logic.

In complex, highly dynamic circumstances like these, marketers and their researchers need to use more explorative and data-driven *interpretive* research techniques to gain a better qualitative understanding of the fundamental changes that are taking place in the market, as well as to re-think and revise their 'best practices' for managing customer relationships and competitive strategies. Instead of applying existing models and translating old theoretically derived knowledge into practical solutions, they often need to tap into the experience and practical knowledge of their customers – and of marketing practitioners who work in close interaction with the customer, such as sales people and customer service specialists – to gain strategic insight and to build new planning models for marketing management (Schultz and Hatch 2005).

Therefore, in the contemporary market environments, interpretive approaches to marketing research are becoming increasingly popular, particularly in the field of consumer marketing (Wirth Fellman 1999). Over the years, an increasing number of interpretive research strategies and methods have emerged for the study of the culturally shared or collective understandings and social practices that give meaning to and guide marketplace activity (Belk 2007). In strategic brand management, for example, it is acknowledged that the success and financial profits of marketers seem to be increasingly dependent upon the ability of marketers and strategy-makers to interpret, understand, anticipate, and control the consumption-related meaning that is relevant for their markets and products (Holt 2004). To carry out successful, innovative, and customer-oriented marketing strategies, marketers need to improve their ability to recognize and understand the prevalent symbols, myths, images, values, and cultural narratives of the culture of their target markets. Such cultural knowledge enables them to design products and services that add value and make sense in the everyday life of their customers.

Douglas Holt (2003), for example, has argued that Nike, Harley-Davidson and many other powerful global brands maintain a firm hold in the marketplace mainly because they have become cultural icons. They do not succeed primarily because they offer distinctive benefits, trustworthy service, or innovative technology, but rather because they forge a deep connection with culture. They invoke powerful cultural narratives and myths, citing culturally shared meanings, norms and values, and thus give people a sense of structure and security in their life. Therefore, these brands continue to add value for their customers, year after year.

Ethnography as an intellectual tool for gaining consumer market insight

In this section we discuss ethnography, which arguably epitomizes interpretive research, as an intellectual tool for gaining consumer market insight (see e.g. Arnould and Wallendorf 1994; Elliott and Jankel-Elliott 2003; Peñaloza and Cayla 2007). Ethnography refers to a research process in which the researcher participates in the daily life of consumers in a particular social setting and collects data using a set of ethnographic fieldwork methods (particularly participant observation and personal, in-context interviews) and then writes accounts of this process. Essentially, ethnography encourages marketers and their researchers to make sense of human social behaviour in terms of cultural patterning. As Harry F. Woolcott has argued:

> To pursue ethnography in one's thinking, doing, and reporting is to engage simultaneously in an ongoing intellectual dialogue about what culture is in general – and how … culture influences without controlling – while attempting to portray specific aspects of the culture of some human group in particular.
>
> (Wolcott 1995: 83–4)

Originally, ethnography was a research strategy developed by cultural anthropologists for the study of 'other' people in faraway places. Anthropologists would typically participate in the everyday life of an exotic tribal community, for example, over an extended period of time, trying to learn the language and cultural traditions of the tribe. But today the fieldwork methods perfected in anthropology are widely used in all areas of interpretive social science, also for the study of cultures and sub-cultures that are more familiar and closer to home.

Recently, leading consumer electronics companies such as Microsoft and Motorola, for example, have hired staff and consultants with anthropological credentials, trained ethnographers and even people with a PhD in anthropology. As a result of globalization and technological development, consumers, consumer markets and consumer culture have changed, and corporations need new knowledge and new ways of gaining insights into not only how consumers have changed but also into the complex social and cultural processes through which this change has taken place. Anthropologists are particularly well suited for studying these changes because the ethnographic methods and techniques that they use are specifically designed for delivering insights into the unfamiliar and the strange.

The task of these anthropologists usually is to immerse themselves in the everyday life of consumers to provide detailed accounts of the patterns of behaviour that the use of specific technologies and devices entails. The customer-centric knowledge that ethnographic methods produce is then injected into the development of technological products. Tracy Lovejoy, for example, describes ethnography and her work as a corporate anthropologist at the Microsoft Corporation in the following way:

> The ultimate goal is to understand the holistic view of the world from our participants' eyes, as opposed to viewing the world from our own perspective. For Microsoft, this translates to understanding how our customers – and potential customers – experience the world and how technology fits into that experience.
>
> Ethnographers at Microsoft study people; look at their behaviors, values and desires, then make recommendations about how technology can better serve people's lives. This translates to feature ideas, product improvements and new potential markets. Our mantra is that technology should conform to people's lives, supporting their existing needs and behaviors, rather than people's lives having to conform to technology, changing their needs and behaviors.
>
> I try to help ground our planning and development in the real-world scenarios and behaviors of our customers. If we can understand our customers' lives, needs and pain points, we can make products that can really help them. This manifests in many ways. In the planning and early milestone phases, I work closely with product-team members across disciplines such as user research, project managers, testers and developers. I try to be the relentless voice of the customer.
>
> (Microsoft Corporation 2009)

While much of the traditional, quantitative research in marketing aims to produce knowledge and information, e.g. law-like generalizations (Hunt 2002), that can be generalized across time and context, ethnography is, first and foremost, the study of social phenomena *in situ* or in particular contexts.

In its basic form, ethnographic fieldwork consists of a researcher spending time in a specific research setting, having direct and sustained contact with the social actors of the setting (Atkinson *et al.* 2001). By entering into close and relatively prolonged face-to-face interaction with people in their everyday lives, ethnographers aim to develop an in-depth understanding of the ways in which consumers use and give meaning to products and brands in their everyday lives. Tracy Lovejoy explains:

> When in the field, I spend full days with my customers. For example, one day in Finland in 2003, I arrived at the family's home at 7.30 a.m., they ate their breakfast, packed up, and I jumped in the car with the mother and father. The father dropped the mother and me off at the metro, where we traveled to her job at the Helsinki Opera House working as a department scheduler. I sat near her desk most of the day, taking notes, photos and video of her behaviors, actions, interactions and conversations. I would follow her to other offices and meetings. At the end of the day, we stopped at the market, then on to

her language class, then home in the evening. The next day, I followed her son to high school.

(Microsoft Corporation 2009)

In the field, the ethnographer thus typically systematically observes and makes notes of the everyday activities and interactions that take place at the site, trying to make sense of the cultural patterning of social action in the setting.

The strength of these observational methods and techniques is that they allow the corporate ethnographer to record the mundane incidents, activities, and practices of everyday life that tend to remain unnoticed as self-evident to consumers themselves. Much of consumer behaviour involves everyday routines and practices that consumers do not actively think about. And when asked, they do not necessarily come to talk about – or do not even know how to talk about – these routines and patterns. The ways in which people use technological devices in their everyday life, for example, may be so habitual and routine-like that in an interview situation it is difficult for them to elaborate on or even describe how they actually use them in their day-to-day work. These types of practices and the associated purposes of use are therefore difficult to capture with traditional survey methods and interview techniques, which are largely based on the assumption that people are conscious of and able to reflect upon their personal motives and behaviours. In focusing on what people actually do, and not on what they claim to do, ethnography thus responds to people's inabilities to talk about and account for habitual and culturally complex behaviours (Arnould and Wallendorf 1994).

As part of their fieldwork, ethnographers typically also do interviews, both in structured and informal forms, as well as keep a diary of their casual conversations with the participants of the study. In ethnographic research, the interview is not so much a method of extracting information from informants but rather a vehicle for producing cultural talk, which can be analyzed to gain cultural knowledge about the marketplace (Moisander and Valtonen 2006). From this perspective, the interviewee is not viewed or treated as a 'passive vessel of answers' or a repository of facts, feelings, and information about the topic under study (Gubrium and Holstein 2003: 31). An interview is rather understood as a collaborative undertaking and as a dialogue that takes place between the interviewer and the interviewee, who actively uses the cultural resources that are available at the setting to construct meaningful accounts of the social reality in that setting (Moisander *et al.* 2009).

Besides these basic methods, ethnographic fieldwork may also involve using various visual research methods, such as taking photographs and video recordings, and gathering material cultural artifacts such as brochures, flyers, business cards, newsletters, or newspapers to obtain detailed information about the setting from multiple perspectives (see e.g. Peñaloza and Gilly 1999; Peñaloza 2001). The study of visuals, things and qualities that appeal to the sense of sight, is important because visual representation is an essential element of contemporary Western consumer culture (Schroeder 2002). Visibilities, not only images but also visible objects and visual arrangements of all kinds, carry meanings in the marketplace. And people routinely draw on these meanings when they communicate and interact with each other in their day-to-day transactions. For marketers, it is therefore important to study visual representation and the meanings that can be read from specific visibilities, such as package designs and brand logos, by the potential customers of their target markets.

Besides new product development, ethnography and ethnographic methods offer valuable information about brand meanings (Brown *et al.* 2003) and consumers' brand relations (Fournier 1998). Ethnographic methods are well suited for exploring how people use brand meanings not only to construct their identities but also to form communities, such as The Holiday Rambler Recreational Vehicle Club[1] or The Harley Owners Group ® (HOG)[2] (see e.g. Schouten and McAlexander 1995). The term brand community refers to a specialized, non-geographically bound group of people, based on a structured set of social relations among admirers of a brand (Muñiz and O'Guinn 2001).

Many corporations are currently actively incorporating these ideas about brand communities into their brand strategies by supporting and nurturing the communities that have emerged around their brands. At the Harley-Davidson website, for example, owners of Harley-Davidson motorcycles are encouraged to join the H.O.G. brand community to form and engage with families that we can choose (Weston 1997): 'Who says you can't choose your family? Become a part of H.O.G., and meet the thousands of brothers and sisters you've always wanted' (The Harley Owners Group ®, H-D Michigan, Inc. 2009).

For marketing and consumer researchers, *virtual brand communities* constitute a particularly interesting source of data for interpretive analysis. At the websites of virtual brand communities, consumers often post messages and engage in lively discussions where they try to inform and influence the opinions of the other community members. This communication provides marketers with important information about brand image and consumer preferences in target markets. In the course of this interaction, the members of the brand community typically also talk about themselves and provide links to their personal blogs and websites, offering marketers a rich source of data on the personal views and values of the potential and actual customers of the brand. A study by Hope Schau and Mary Gilly (2003) shows, for example, that on personal websites consumers construct identities by associating themselves with commercial signs and symbols to construct and express their identities.

To understand and investigate these various online or computer-mediated environments, virtual methods such as virtual ethnography – or netnography – have been developed (Kozinets 2002). Netnography refers to ethnography that is undertaken in computer-mediated environments. As in conventional ethnography, virtual ethnography researchers either participate in the interaction that takes place in the research setting or they can just observe it by 'lurking', for example, monitoring a website through non-participant observation (Maclaran and Catterall 2002: 323–4). Moving ethnography to an online setting, however, brings along a number of challenges that need to be dealt with when studying virtual communities. Online interviewing, for example, is a special kind of interactive situation, which is guided by a set of social rules and conventions that are different, to some extent, from typical face-to-face interaction. While non-verbal cues such as eye contact and body language are crucial ways to create rapport in face-to-face interviews, online interviews must rely on different kinds of paralinguistic cues.

More recent forms of ethnography have also drawn attention to the ways in which all the senses – sight, sound, touch, taste, and smell – are involved in the phenomenon under study and in the process of doing ethnographic fieldwork (Valtonen *et al.* 2010).

Overall, the interpretive approaches to marketing research, such as ethnography, thus constitute a powerful intellectual technology for studying marketplace activity at the grassroots level and for gaining consumer market insight in the contemporary multicultural and rapidly changing cultural environments. Using the basic tools and techniques of interpretive marketing research, marketers are able to gain valuable cultural knowledge about the ways in which consumer experience – and satisfaction – are constructed and negotiated in the marketplace. And this knowledge can then be fed into marketing strategies to design customer-oriented market offerings that are based on orchestrating consumer experience in and through complex encounters between the customer, the service provider and a particular visual and spatial environment (see e.g. Arnould and Price 1993; Kozinets *et al.* 2004).

Next we shall illustrate the benefits of interpretive marketing research with two case examples, discussing the ways in which ethnography can be utilized in brand development and cool hunting.

Ethnography in strategic brand development

The first case in point, which is based on the work of Bernard Cova and Véronique Cova (Cova and Cova 2002), illustrates the ways in which ethnographic methods may be fruitfully employed in brand development. The case is concerned with the brand development of Salomon, famous in winter sport equipment, which repositioned its brand image by applying a *tribal marketing* approach when developing its snowboards and in-line skaters (cf. Chapter 11 in this volume). As we discussed above, more and more marketing scholars and managers have realized that a deep understanding of customers' tribal activities – the way customers form different communities of interest, the way they interact across them, and the way products and brands are involved in the activities of communities – is essential for developing a successful marketing strategy.

For Salomon marketing people, the first task was to gain an understanding of the tribal world of the snowbroaders and in-line rollers. To start with, they needed to explore what was the status of the brand among tribe members. Towards this aim, Salomon people 'went into the field', acting like ethnographers: they observed the users, were present in playgrounds, hung around at cult places, engaged in the hobbyist activities, analyzed the rituals, symbols, and practice codes of the tribes. They also supported tribe members' events and contests, and ended up inviting the tribe members to co-design Salomon products and marketing materials. In doing so, Salomon people succeed in forging a relationship between their products and the tribe members.

As a result, Salomon witnessed a considerable rise in its market share and a new brand position (in 1999 Salomon became number three in the world for in-line products, and also rose to number three in the snowboarding French market). While the figures offer evidence that tribal marketing provides promising marketing opportunities, the eventual success lies in a careful appreciation of specific principles of a tribal approach. As Cova and Cova (ibid.) point out, marketers need to have great respect for the constituent features of the tribe. They need to interpret and understand the structure, ethos, values, and practices of a tribe, and to acknowledge that the role of the marketer is to support, facilitate, and assist the tribe members' activity – to enable the tribe members to connect with each other, in particular. Hence, in a tribal approach the traditional roles and relations of marketers and customers are unsettled: instead of being providers, marketers become facilitators and customers active co-creators and co-marketers (Firat and Dholakia 2006). As a result of these new types of customer–marketer partnership, the traditional boundaries dividing the company and the customers become ever more fluid.

Ethnographic methods, such as employed in this case, allow marketers to gain insights into the ways in which the product and brand meanings are actively produced, mediated, and shaped in the midst of different consumption activities. This viewpoint brings to the fore that meanings are not, and cannot be, fabricated in brand management offices nor in advertising agencies, they are – ultimately – fabricated and deployed in the field. The interpretation of these meanings is the primary managerial task.

Ethnography in coolhunting

The particular logic of coolness – what is 'in' now is 'out' tomorrow – fuels the engines of business and economy in many remarkable ways. It is hence increasingly critical for managers and executives to try to predict the future trends so as to stay ahead the curve. An amounting number of companies have discovered the benefits of *coolhunting* in various domains of business life. As Peter Gloor and Scott Cooper (Gloor and Cooper 2007) discuss, coolhunting principles can be applied by venture capitalists to discover new investment opportunities, by sales executives to create better sales forecasts, by financial analysts to identify market trends, and by marketing managers to predict consumer trends, develop new product and service offerings, or to anticipate the development of customer markets.

Coolhunting principles and techniques are, to a significant extent, based upon a skilful interpretation of the cultural marketplace – and upon the application of ethnographic methods. In anticipating what's next, coolhunters observe people through the Web, blogs, newspapers, magazines, and broadcast media, they hang around in likely and unlikely places, and engage in a range of activities of different customer groups. They employ, in other words, basic ethnographic practices. Yet, the data they gather may take specific forms. The data may appear in pictures, it may be a rumour, a hint that is not yet verbalized, or a heated discussion in a blog.

Importantly, the practices of coolhunting point to the need to intimately understand cultural complexities of marketplace behaviour and, in particular, group behaviour. As discussed by several scholars, the essence of cool cannot be revealed if the marketplace is thought of in individualistic terms (Heath and Potter 2004; McCracken 2009). On the contrary, the process of finding cool and cultivating cool requires a profound understanding of the dynamics of socio-cultural and political environment as well as within-group and between-groups behaviour (see also Moisander *et al.* 2009). Let us exemplify the point in relation to terms of *counter-culture*, *collective mindset*, and *diffusion of cool*.

In their recent book *Nation of Rebels*, Joseph Heath and Andrew Potter (Heath and Potter 2004) discuss how cool is structured by a restless quest for rebellious nonconformity. 'Cool' is, according to them, a cultural stance that is denoted as edgy, alternative and hip, and as such an efficient way for consumers to articulate identities. This take provides us with a better understanding of the way *counter-culture* seeds the emergence of new trends. Roughly put, the rebels of today are the trendsetters of tomorrow. Therefore, in attempting to anticipate what's next, coolhunters and marketers need to draw attention to, analyze and interpret signs of resistance and rebellion, since they may turn out to be key indicators of future trends.

Furthermore, coolhunting is essential to understand how the *collective mindset* works. Therefore, gaining insight into the workings of diverse social networks – how people form groups and networks in sites such as Facebook, how people collaborate and gossip there, and what kind of information they share across different networks – is a prerequisite for efficient coolhunting. In the words of Gloor and Cooper: 'Just like social networks allow people to spread ideas, social network sites allow people to leverage their social networks to spread information, culture, and gossip' (Gloor and Cooper 2007: ix). By paying attention to what kind of cultural information people share, and what their friends share, companies can learn a lot about what is cool.

To describe the collective mindset, Gloor and Cooper use the word 'swarm'. In biology, the term swarm refers to the behaviour of a group of animals travelling in the same direction. In the contemporary virtualized era, the formation of swarms is commonly based on the voluntary collaboration of people who share the same interests – the coolest trends are often the ones that are fed off this collaboration. Importantly, these social networks are at their best when they unfold on their own. Therefore, 'it is critical to keep in mind that the swarms are rightfully distrustful of those who try to regulate, control, or capitalize on their social interactions and identity displays' (ibid.: xiii). Companies may explore what the swarm is creating when collaborating by immersing in the social and cultural milieu of the swarms with the help of netnographic methods described earlier, for instance.

The *diffusion of cool* commonly begins with a small group of people who are followed by a group of early adopters, as widely discussed in the previous marketing literature. In practice, the trendsetters who spread out the new ideas are the most connected people, and it is therefore important for marketers to try to identify them. 'Just as epidemics spread through direct contact between people, so cool moves laterally through peer groups' (ibid.: 216). So as to understand this 'movement of cool', coolhunters and managers need to focus on the social nexus of the customers, not on the single individuals.

Conclusion: the managerial challenges of deploying interpretive analyses

While in the history of marketing research scholars and practitioners alike have tended to rely primarily on the facts and figures that survey analysis and statistics provide, in the current constantly changing market environments marketers are increasingly opting for new tools and techniques that interpretive methods and approaches now offer to gain strategic insight, particularly for consumer marketing. Here we have concentrated on ethnographic methods, but the set of methods and methodologies developed in the field of interpretive marketing research is obviously much broader (see e.g. Belk 2007) and draws on multiple disciplines and theoretical traditions besides anthropology, ranging from literary theory to visual studies. No matter which interpretive tools and techniques are used, however, it is important to remember that the use of interpretive data *per se* does not ensure valuable insights into the cultural complexity of consumer experience and marketplace activity. Only the practitioners and researchers who are able to make insightful *interpretations* of those data may gain knowledge that is valuable for designing customer-oriented strategies and for building competitive advantage in the market.

In practice, moreover, buying and evaluating interpretive marketing research for business purposes may often be challenging because the philosophy of interpretive marketing and consumer inquiry challenges the marketing practitioner to re-think many of the received wisdoms in the trade.

First of all, in setting objectives for interpretive analysis, marketing executives and managers need to reject the idea that there is 'one truth to be discovered' and accept the basic assumption of interpretivism that all empirical phenomena are open to multiple interpretations, which vary with the interpretive frameworks and mindsets that are used in making sense of the phenomena. For this polyphony of social life, it is critically important to carefully reflect upon the managerial mindsets and implicit frameworks that guide the process of inquiry. To fully benefit from interpretive analyses of marketplace activity, marketing practitioners need to unlearn many of the managerial truths about customers as decision-makers and goal-oriented individuals who need to be addressed as demographically defined targets of marketing communication (cf. Chapters 11, 12, and 18 in this volume). Instead, in defining objectives and research designs for interpretive inquiry, the focus should clearly be set on exploring and elaborating the cultural complexities of marketplace phenomena.

Moreover, when evaluating the reports on interpretive analyses, marketing executives and managers need to put aside – at least for a while – their preoccupation with facts and figures, as well as their fixations with accurate measurement and prediction. They need to be able to broaden their views about what constitutes data and appropriate knowledge of marketplace phenomena. Instead of drawing attention merely to issues such as the size of the sample, the accuracy of information, or the generalizability of the results, it is important to evaluate the insightfulness of interpretive frame, the variety and quality of empirical materials, or the creativity in drawing up conclusions. While interpretive research cannot offer quantitative estimates and predictions, it does provide us with other forms of valuable strategic understanding based on rich qualitative analyses of visuals, texts, and the soundscape.

Overall, the set of issues to be considered when making decisions about buying ethnographic market research is often much broader and more complex than when ordering a standard customer survey. To illustrate, when commissioning a market research company to carry out an ethnographic study on shopping behaviour, for example, it is important to carefully reflect upon the selection of the research site (e.g. malls, marketplaces, on-line stores), the timing of the fieldwork (e.g. time of the day, weekend versus weekdays), and the adequacy of the empirical materials (e.g. pictures, observations, interviews) that are to be used in the study. Moreover, before closing the deal, it is also necessary to know something about the individuals who will actually do the fieldwork. In selecting the researchers, it is important to pay attention not only to their analytical skills but also to their social position (e.g. their age, gender, ethnicity) in the community that is being studied, as the position opens up a particular analytical perspective on the research site. A good ethnographer also needs to have good social skills to engage in fruitful inter-personal interaction at the site, as well as an adequate cultural sensitivity for making sense of the socio-cultural order that prevails in the community. Finally, the ethnographic researcher needs to be capable of producing good ethnographies: vivid, sensitive, and down-to-earth descriptions and interpretations of what happens in the field (e.g. in the form of films and stories).

Consequently, to successfully develop and deploy interpretive, consumer market insight, marketing executives and managers may well need to re-think their strategic mindsets and routinized practices. Working with interpretive analyses requires not only a methodological but also epistemological shift in managerial thinking (cf. Chapter 14 in this volume). To gain consumer market insight, it is necessary to not only adopt new techniques of analysis but also new conceptual tools and ways of thinking about marketing and consumer behaviour.

Review and discussion questions

1   Outline and elaborate on characteristic features of an interpretive study. What are, in your opinion, its key strengths and challenges from the perspective of strategic market development?
2   Write an outline for an interpretive marketing research plan for strategic brand development, based on ethnographic methods.

Keywords

branding, consumer market insight, coolhunting, ethnography, interpretivism, market development

Notes

1 The Holiday Rambler RV Club (2009), available at: http://www.hrrvc.org/index.html
2 The Harley Owners Group ®, H-D Michigan, Inc. (2009), available at: http://www.harley-davidson. com/wcm/Content/Pages/HOG/HOG.jsp?locale = en_US

References

American Marketing Association (2009) *AMA Dictionary of Marketing Terms*. Available at: http:// www.marketingpower.com/_layouts/Dictionary.aspx.

Arnould, Eric J. and Price, Linda (1993) 'The River Magic: Extraordinary Experience and the Extended Service Encounter', *Journal of Consumer Research*, 20(June): 24–45.

Arnould, Eric. J. and Wallendorf, Melanie (1994) 'Market-Oriented Ethnography: Interpretation Building and Marketing Strategy Formulation', *Journal of Marketing Research*, 31(Nov.): 484–504.

Atkinson, Paul, Coffey, Amanda, Delamont, Sara, Lofland, John and Lofland, Lyn (eds), (2001) *Handbook of Ethnography*, London: Sage.

Belk, Russell W. (2007) *Handbook of Qualitative Research Methods in Marketing*, Northampton: Edward Elgar Publishing.

Brown, Stephen, Kozinets, Robert W. and Sherry Jr, John F. (2003) 'Teaching Old Brands New Tricks: Retro Branding and the Revival of Brand Meaning', *Journal of Marketing*, 67(July): 19–33.

Cova, Bernard and Cova, Véronique (2002) 'Tribal Marketing: The Tribalisation of Society and Its Impact on the Conduct of Marketing', *European Journal of Marketing*, 36(5/6): 595–620.

Elliott, Richard and Jankel-Elliott, Nick (2003) 'Using Ethnography in Strategic Consumer Research', *Qualitative Market Research: An International Journal*, 6(4): 215–23.

Fay, Brian and Moon, J. Donald (1994) 'What Would an Adequate Philosophy of Social Science Look Like?' in Michael Martin and Lee C. McIntyre (eds), *Readings in the Philosophy of Social Science*, Cambridge, MA: The MIT Press, pp. 21–35.

Firat, A. Fuat and Dholakia, Nikhlesh (2006) 'Theoretical and Philosophical Implications of Post-modern Debates: Some Challenges to Modern Marketing', *Marketing Theory*, 6(2): 123–62.

Fournier, Susan (1998) 'Consumers and Their Brands: Developing Relationship Theory in Consumer Research', *Journal of Consumer Research*, 24(March): 343–73.

Gloor, Peter and Cooper, Scott (2007) *Coolhunting: Chasing Down the Next Big Thing*, New York: AMACOM.

Gubrium, Jaber F. and Holstein, James A. (eds) (2003) *Postmodern Interviewing*, London: Sage.

Heath, Joseph and Potter, Andrew (2004) *Nation of Rebels: Why Counterculture Became Consumer Culture*, New York: Harper Business.

Holt, Douglas B. (2003) 'What Becomes an Icon Most?' *Harvard Business Review*, 81(March): 43–9.

—— (2004) *How Brands Become Icons: The Principles of Cultural Branding*, Boston: Harvard Business School Press.

Hunt, Shelby (2002) *Foundations of Marketing Theory: Towards a General Theory of Marketing*, Armonk, NY: M.E. Sharpe Inc.

Jenkins, Henry (2006) *Fans, Bloggers, and Gamers: Exploring Participatory Culture*, New York: New York University Press.

—— (2008) *Convergence Culture: Where Old and New Media Collide*, New York: NYU Press.

Kozinets, Robert V. (2002) 'The Field Behind the Screen: Using Netnography for Marketing Research in Online Communities', *Journal of Marketing Research*, 39(1): 61–72.

Kozinets, Robert V., Sherry Jr, John F., Storm, Diana, Duhachek, Adam, Nuttavuthisit, Krittinee and Deberry-Spence, Benét (2004) 'Ludic Agency and Retail Spectacle', *Journal of Consumer Research*, 31(3): 658–72.

Maclaran, Pauline and Catterall, Miriam (2002) 'Researching the Social Web: Marketing Information from Virtual Communities', *Marketing Intelligence & Planning*, 20(6): 319–26.

McCracken, Grant (2009) *Chief Culture Office: How to Create a Living, Breathing Corporation*, New York: Basic Books.

Microsoft Corporation (2009) *Making Technology Conform to People's Lives*. Available at: http://www.microsoft.com/presspass/features/2005/apr05/04–04Ethnographer.mspx

Moisander, Johanna (2007) 'Motivational Complexity of Green Consumerism', *International Journal of Consumer Studies*, 31(4): 40–9.

—— (2008) *Representation of Green Consumerism: A Constructionist Critique*, Saarbrucken: VDM Verlag Dr. Müller.

Moisander, Johanna, Peñaloza, Lisa and Valtonen, Anu (2009) 'From CCCT to CCC: Building Consumer Culture Community', in John F. Sherry Jr and Eileen Fischer (eds), *Explorations in Consumer Culture Theory*, New York: Routledge, pp. 7–33.

Moisander, Johanna and Valtonen, Anu (2006) *Qualitative Marketing Research: A Cultural Approach*, London: Sage.

Moisander, Johanna, Valtonen, Anu and Hirsto, Heidi (2009) 'Personal Interviews in Cultural Consumer Research: Poststructuralist Challenges', *Consumption, Markets & Culture*, 12(4): 329–48.

Muñiz, Albert M. Jr, and O'Guinn, Thomas C. (2001) 'Brand Community', *Journal of Consumer Research*, 27(4): 412.

Peñaloza, Lisa (2001) 'Consuming the American West: Animating Cultural Meaning and Memory at a Stock Show and Rodeo', *Journal of Consumer Research*, 28(December): 369–98.

Peñaloza, Lisa and Cayla, Julien (2007) 'Writing Pictures/Taking Fieldnotes: Towards a More Material and Visual Ethnographic Consumer Research', in *Handbook of Qualitative Research in Marketing*, ed. Russel Belk, New York: AMACOM, pp. 279–90.

Peñaloza, Lisa and Gilly, Mary C. (1999) 'Marketer Acculturation: The Changer and the Changed', *Journal of Marketing*, 63(July): 84–104.

Peñaloza, Lisa and Venkatesh, A. (2006) 'Further Evolving the New Dominant Logic of Marketing: From Services to the Social Construction of Markets', *Marketing Theory*, 6(3): 299–316.

Schau, Hope Jensen and Gilly, Mary C. (2003) 'We Are What We Post? Self-Presentation in Personal Web Space', *Journal of Consumer Research*, 30(December): 385–404.

Schouten, John W. and McAlexander, James H. (1995) 'Subcultures of Consumption: An Ethnography of New Bikers', *Journal of Consumer Research*, 22(June): 43–61.

Schroeder, Jonathan E. (2002) *Visual Consumption*, London: Routledge.

Schultz, Majken and Hatch, Mary Jo (2005) 'Building Theory from Practice', *Strategic Organization*, 3(3): 337–48.

Schwandt, Thomas A. (2003) 'Three Epistemological Stances for Qualitative Inquiry: Interpretivism, Hermeneutics, and Social Constructionism', in Norman.K. Denzin and Yvonna S. Lincoln (eds), *The Landscape of Qualitative Research*, London: Sage, pp. 292–31.

Solomon, Michael R. (2003) *Conquering Consumerspace*, New York: AMACOM.

Valtonen, Anu, Markuksela, Vesa and Moisander, Johanna (2010) 'Doing Sensory Ethnography in Consumer Research', *International Journal of Consumer Studies*, 34: 375–80.

Weston, Kath (1997) *Families We Choose: Lesbians, Gays, Kinship*, New York: Columbia University Press.

Wirth Fellman, Michelle (1999) 'Breaking Tradition: "Untraditional" Market Research Techniques from the Social Sciences Are Gaining Ground', *Marketing Research*, 11(3): 20–4.

Wolcott, Harry F. (1995) 'Making a Study "More Ethnographic"', in John van Maanen (ed.), *Representation in Ethnography*, Thousand Oaks, CA: Sage, pp. 79–111.

16 Research methods for innovative cultural marketing management (CMM)

Strategy and practises

Samantha N. N. Cross and Mary C. Gilly

Overview

The search for knowledge about marketing and consumption practises can come from a variety of perspectives. The approaches outlined in this chapter are not necessarily new; someone somewhere has usually tried something similar, as you will see from the examples given. What is different is that the approaches outlined all incorporate a cultural perspective. Cultural influences are often unnoticed by consumers, so creative approaches to research are needed to gain an understanding for marketing decisions.

Our examples come from both practitioner and academic sources, for innovative approaches to understanding marketing practise and consumer behavior stem not from any particular realm or any specific methodological focus. Often it is the combination of methodologies or perspectives that yields new insights, which we emphasize. One of the best ways to sensitize readers to unconventional approaches is through exposure to varied examples of innovation in practise. By the end of this chapter, we hope readers will appreciate that a researcher's approach to understanding marketing or consumption phenomena is limited only by: (1) his/her imagination; (2) constraints of researcher training; (3) research goals; and (4) the nature of the phenomenon itself.

Introduction

What do we mean by innovation in research? Brianna Sylver, founder of Sylver Consulting, a product innovation firm in Chicago notes that "technically, 'innovation' is defined merely as 'introducing something new;' there are no qualifiers of how ground-breaking or world-shattering that something needs to be – only that it needs to be better than what was there before" (Sylver 2006). Thus, innovation in research is more than a creative idea. Creativity is indeed the starting point; however, the innovative approach needs to be useful; to add value; to improve upon what was there before. It needs to assist the researcher in gaining insight into some behavior or practise in marketing that was previously not fully understood.

The chapter has three main sections: (1) data collection; (2) data analysis and presentation; and (3) multi-perspective approaches to understanding consumers. Throughout the sections, three basic tools will be discussed – observation, participant involvement and co-creation – and will draw on a mix of examples as illustrations, providing step-by-step guidance as to what to do or avoid in combining similar approaches. The chapter ends with a set of broad recommendations as to how these and other seemingly novel but simple methods can continue to be used in future research studies in marketing. A sample list of helpful publications is provided.

Data collection

Over the years, companies have come to realize the value of simple observation as fascinating, insightful, profitable and increasingly less complicated, given today's technology. Unlike the stealth tactics employed by companies a few years ago to observe customers without their knowledge, and often without their consent, many of the methods used today start with the full permission of the customer. Companies are asking and consumers are inviting researchers to observe them at work, home and play. While participants are usually rewarded for their cooperation, in many instances the motivation to participate goes beyond financial compensation. Consumers enjoy feeling that they are co-creators in the development process for new products and services.

Observation itself is not new. Ethnographers (cf. Chapter 15 in this volume) have been observing people either individually or in groups for decades. What is new is how consumers are observed, what is observed and who is observing. Increasingly corporate researchers are going directly into the home to see, record and analyze the daily routines of consumers. Ethnographic methods are becoming more important in corporate market research, often as a complement to other research methods. Traditional marketing departments are being renamed and redesigned. Executives now have titles such as VP, Consumer Insights (General Mills), VP, Open Innovation and Investment Strategy (Kraft Foods), and Innovation Manager – Holistic Consumer Communication (P&G). The focus is on understanding the customer in his/her environment and from his/her perspective.

Yet, while researchers are clearly very interested in how consumers use products, they are even more interested in the motivation to consume or purchase products in the first place. What drives consumers to make choices, given the many options available today? Researchers are becoming very creative in answering this age-old question.

A remarkable example utilizing observation and interview techniques with digital technology is a hookah study by three academic researchers. Examining a cultural tradition entering the US and targeting young people, Griffiths, Harmon and Gilly (2011) combine participant observation and interviews with analysis of websites of hookah retailers and lounges (see Figure 16.1). A Middle Eastern tradition, hookah smoking involves burning flavored tobacco heated by charcoal, creating smoke which is filtered through water and ingested through the mouth using a hose. Hookah lounges are increasingly locating around college campuses in the US and websites offering hookah paraphernalia target American high school and college students.

The aim of the research was to investigate consumer beliefs and attitudes toward hookah smoking and the way it is portrayed online. Potential negative health effects are ignored on these websites and in hookah lounges, and college students underestimate the risks involved. Young people believe smoking sweetened tobacco through a hookah is non-addictive and safer than cigarettes. Traditional tobacco warnings are not seen in lounges or on websites. These findings are consistent with research conducted in Middle Eastern countries where hookah smoking has a long tradition. We will now examine the data collection steps and key challenges.

Data collection steps

- Websites for hookah lounges and retail hookah sales were examined. The language (e.g., "The New Chill"), promotions (e.g., student discounts), pictures posted of hookah smokers, and product offerings (e.g., starter packs for newcomers) suggested that college students are the primary target market.

Figure 16.1 Sample photo from a hookah website.
    Source: Griffiths *et al*. (2011).

- Interview participants were college students who self-identified in a short survey as having past or current experience with hookah smoking.
- Interviews took place on college campuses and in hookah lounges.
- Each 30–120-minute interview was transcribed verbatim.
- Analysis revealed several themes across participants: hookah initiation and practise involves socializing with friends; hookah smoking is viewed as less addictive than cigarettes because it is an occasional practise; hookah smoking is believed to be safe because the smoke travels through water.
- The researchers returned to the hookah lounge and retail websites to compare and contrast the messages with participant beliefs about hookah smoking.
- Websites were found to support students' erroneous beliefs in the safety of hookah smoking.

Key challenges

- Hookah smoking is not a common practise in the US and it was not always easy to find students willing to be interviewed about this practise.
- It was necessary to gain the trust of those students who did agree to be interviewed.
- Websites often hide any mention of health concerns about hookah smoking so it was necessary to examine all pages of the sites.
- The iterative process (going from websites to interviews and back to websites) made record keeping of data difficult. It was necessary to capture and store website content as it was updated and altered.

- Studies of hookah smoking in the medical literature focus on the practise in Middle Eastern countries where it has a very different tradition than among US college students.

In a second example, researchers also used technological advances to both observe and involve the consumer as part of their data collection efforts. Researchers Cross and Gilly (2010) used a combination of digital technology and a series of email communications to encourage over 70 participants nationwide to take and transmit photographs of their Thanksgiving celebrations.

By examining the blending strategies used by culturally diverse families in food consumption celebrations, Cross and Gilly show that families in the US have very fixed internalized conceptions of the way this US holiday should be celebrated. Including immigrants helped to crystallize and define what the quintessential American holiday is in terms of food consumption. These are traditions so culturally close to Americans that they are less able to articulate them. The researchers also learned that there are several challenges to using this type of multi-method approach.

To start, the researchers realized that to gather data from multiple celebrations all occurring on the same day, they would need the assistance of their participants. They thus proceeded with the following steps:

Data collection steps

- Approximately two months prior to the annual Thanksgiving holiday, the researchers contacted around 140 personal contacts across the US and asked if they would be willing to participate. They had a 56 percent response rate or around 78 participants over a two-year period.
- Participants were then contacted two weeks prior and again a few days prior to the holiday, reminding them of the project and providing instructions as to the data to be collected on Thanksgiving Day.
- Participants were asked to take detailed photographs of their Thanksgiving meals and to send them to the researcher, along with specific details of the meals.
- The following information was also collected from the participants: (1) countries of origin of the members of the participant household; (2) approximate number of people present; (3) their nationalities or ethnic affiliations; and (4) the town or location of the Thanksgiving celebration.
- This information, along with any other comments made by the participants, was entered into a spreadsheet, with codes created to link the photos received to the appropriate household. Photographic and menu data were then examined and analyzed to pinpoint patterns and linkages.
- Selected follow-up interviews of individual participants were then conducted, ranging from 60 to 90 minutes. The photos they had previously submitted were used to promote the dialogue between researcher and participant.

Key challenges

- While the data collected were rich and varied due to the involvement of participants, the quality of the photographs taken also varied. Having another version of the data (the menu data) became crucial to understanding the data.

- Participants were eager to participate, but it was necessary to provide clear, detailed instructions about the type of data to be collected to retain consistency.
- Responding and following up with participants about missing data, points of clarification and expressing appreciation needed to be done on a timely basis. The researchers had to pre-designate time to do this during the holiday weekend and the following week.
- Using a spreadsheet or some systematic manner to organize and link the textual and visual data was a major task, also best done in as timely a fashion as possible upon receipt.

The next set of examples provides a final illustration of employing unusual methods or combinations of methods in the data collection effort to build knowledge around a particular theme, in this case, food consumption. Marketers and researchers have always been interested in understanding food consumption choices and preferences as a way of understanding cultural issues of taste, identity and brand relationships. However, while there have been many studies involving food purchase and choices, not all studies take into account the particular cultural and personal context of consumers (cf. Chapter 1 in this volume). So, what are researchers, both practitioner and academic, doing to understand how consumers make decisions about the food they purchase and consume?

In October 2005, the book *Hungry Planet: What the World Eats* was published; a compilation of photos of food consumed by 30 families in 24 countries and an interesting example of ethnographic photo-journalism. The authors, a photojournalist and a writer, shopped, ate and lived with each of these families for a week as part of the project. The project began in 2000 and lasted for five years.

Menzel and d'Aluisio (2005) describe their work as a "culinary atlas" and feature families in their homes surrounded by a week's worth of groceries as a global portrait of food consumption practises. These photographs starkly illustrate the differing food consumption practises in the cultures portrayed, contrasting the mainly pre-packaged consumption items of a family in the US, with the grains, fruit, vegetables and nuts that comprise the food purchases for a family in Mali. The participants agreed to be part of the project and be photographed with a week's worth of groceries. The authors, in turn, paid for the groceries for the week.

In their latest book, *What I Eat*, Menzel and d'Aluisio (2010) again examine food consumption behavior in context, with a focus this time not on the family, but on the individual, looking at food consumption in the context of his/her world. They focus on daily caloric requirements and sustenance in the individual home, work and social environments of 80 participants in 30 countries and over a dozen US states.

In the methodology sections of their books, the authors discuss some of the steps and challenges of collecting their data.

Key challenges

- Working on multiple projects simultaneously and the expense of traveling causes additional difficulties and confusion in the photography and reporting.
- The choice of countries, individuals and families was not simple. The authors tended to choose countries if they were already working there, or a country that they had not been to before or a country that balanced their sample. They chose families based on a snowball sample (even if not statistically average) through colleagues and other

encounters, focusing on representative people and proximity to stimulating situations and events.

- Gaining access to participants was difficult, especially in remote locations.
- Gathering and calculating supporting data, such as individual caloric count and ingredient lists for unfamiliar foods, proved challenging.
- A lengthy process of systematically ensuring accuracy of information received was required.

Cross and Gilly (2011a) also used a combination of observation, elicitation techniques and interviews conducted in the kitchens of their participants to better understand the symbolic role of food and the consumption compromise strategies used by spouses of differing cultural backgrounds who unite to create bi-national households. Let us go through the data collection steps.

Data collection steps

- The authors had to begin with a clear definition of the concepts, particularly that of the different types of participant households, helping the reader to understand why these participant households were the focus of the study.
- Data for the study were collected in participants' homes over a one-year period, using a purposive sample.
- Data were gathered through a combination of in-depth interviews, observation and photographic elicitation.
- Data gathered on the families were compiled to form a profile of the interview participants.
- Photographs were taken by participants prior to the interviews and sent to the researchers. Photographs received from each household were compiled into color print collages and used as elicitation tools during the interviews to stimulate discussions.
- The interviewees were actively involved in an ongoing dialogue while initiating the exposure and display of the various food storage areas, which the authors describe as "interactive observation."

Key challenges

- Again, the variability in the quality and clarity of the photographs collected by the participants was a problem. Personal observation by the researcher during the interviews proved to be an important alternate method of verifying the initial photographic data.
- In addition to facilitating data collection, technology was also a challenge in the actual mechanics of gathering the interview data during the interactive observation process. The ongoing dialogue combined with the constant movement of the researcher and participant proved difficult for the audio recording devices at times. Thus, each interview had to be carefully transcribed.

Summary

These data collection examples run the gamut from simple observation of the consumer in his/her environment to the use of online tools. Researchers use observation and differing levels of participant involvement to better understand the consumption patterns and choices of customers. However, companies are seeking not just the cooperation of the consumer, but are engaging them even further, soliciting their ideas for product improvement and the creation of new goods and services. Researchers are increasingly using online environments to reach a wide range of consumers and inviting them to collaborate with the company in the search for a better product (cf. Chapter 12 in this volume).

All the methods share two characteristics. The researchers tried something new – sometimes something a little different, at other times a totally radical approach. They also explicitly include a focus on the cultural perspective in the research design and provide examples of an ethnographic, context-driven approach to data collection. Yet, all research methods have flaws (McGrath 1981), including innovative ones, which need to be minimized or avoided.

- Observation, whether in person or indirectly using video cameras and other sophisticated aids, can be intrusive and can affect the behavior of the participants.
- Consumer involvement can be costly for the researcher, both in terms of time and money.
- There is also the risk of both researcher and participant bias, with the possibility of over-immersion in the project.
- Including a cultural perspective may involve translation services and recruiting a culturally diverse research team.
- Huge amounts of data are often collected and the researcher has the onerous task of deciding what is relevant for a particular decision or insights he/she wishes to share.

Yet, in spite of the cons of collecting data with the cultural perspective in mind, one key advantage underlying all the approaches discussed is that behavior is examined *in context*. Researchers are learning that behavior should not just be studied as isolated events, but that what drives behavior may have as much to do with the social and cultural setting as the personal characteristics of the individual.

The tasks of observing, asking and involving the consumer provide a multi-method approach to collecting data that is intrinsic to ethnographic research. Doing all of these with a cultural twist is aimed at answering not just the question of: (1) what is happening; but (2) how; (3) in what context; and (4) can we learn something new if we look at the consumer through a different lens?

For additional detailed information on the steps, challenges and rewards of using the data collection methods portrayed, the reader is directed to the following references: Kozinets (2009) on netnography; McCracken (1988) on interviews; Lofland, Snow, Anderson and Lofland (2005) and Spradley (1980) on observation.

Data analysis and presentation

The process of data analysis brings to mind the image of the exhausted researcher poring over mounds of textual or numerical data in an effort to make sense of it. However, while analyzing data is still often a lengthy, time-intensive process, it can also be a fascinating one. Analyzing research data need not be a tedious, isolated procedure, but can be enhanced through presentation and collaborative techniques, with the purpose of simplifying and illuminating the data. Levine (1996) stresses that "data analysis is about the world, asking, always asking, 'How does it work?'"

Yet so many researchers, both in academia and corporations, seem confined to a particular way of trying to understand how the world works. Even those who collect data in exciting new ways often seem constrained by the familiar, well-worn techniques of analyzing the data collected. Data analysis does need to be done carefully and systematically always, but as with data collection, innovative approaches to analyzing data can often yield insights that may have been otherwise overlooked. The techniques highlighted in this section focus on research tools used by academics and practitioners to help the researcher better understand and explain the insights revealed by his/her data. There are two broad categories: observation through visualization and researcher/participant collaboration.

Observation through visualization

Donald Hoffman (2000: xi) argues that humans have three types of intelligence: the rational, the emotional and the visual. Yet the visual, which he describes as "so swift and sure, so dependable and informative" that we take it for granted, is often overlooked, both as a source of research information and as a tool in the analytic process. Humans are generally regarded as highly visual animals, yet as researchers we do not always use our full analytical capabilities.

In the previous section, it was shown that data collection is enhanced when an innovative approach is taken. Observation can also be an important tool in data analysis, particularly observation of the data through simple visualization techniques. Looking at data, whether numerical or textual, from a different perspective usually provides insights not previously considered. The traditional use of the image has been as visual stimuli in experimental settings or as corroborative data in ethnographic studies. In this discussion, a simple technique is shared for observing data through visualization, where the image serves as a crucial aid in the analysis of the data.

The feasibility triangle is a perceptual mapping technique originally suggested by Wolfe (1959) and later used by Davis and Rigaux (1974). As with other perceptual mapping techniques, such as multi-dimensional scaling, factor analysis or correspondence analysis – the feasibility triangle represents consumer perceptions in a multi-dimensional space. The vertical axis of the triangle represents the relative influence of the husband and wife in the decision, ranging from husband-dominant = 1, joint = 2, to wife-dominant = 3, as indicated by the respondent. The horizontal axis shows the extent of role specialization as measured by the percentage of families reporting that a decision is jointly made. The two axes then converge at a point 2, 100 percent; the triangular feasibility region reflecting the fact that the axes are non-independent (Davis and Rigaux 1974). The locations of the decisions on the triangle are based upon an average across the differing aspects of the decision process and across the participants.

This method of mapping data allows easy visualization of data versus a table of percentages and means. The researcher can also easily gauge both the average relative influence and extent of role specialization for each decision, as well as the similarity or dissimilarity among decisions with respect to marital roles.

This technique was later adopted in 1987 by corporate researchers, Mandy Putnam and William Davidson, for their study of family purchasing behavior in The RIS Consumer Focus Series reports for Price Waterhouse. Twenty years later, this simple approach to observing decision data in a graphic rather than tabular form has only been used in three published studies. In these studies, the feasibility triangle has been used solely to map

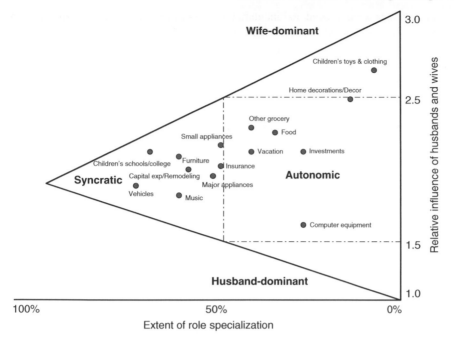

Figure 16.2 The feasibility triangle.
        Source: Cross and Gilly (2011b).

household decision perceptions and thus aid in understanding relative power and influence in the household.

By using the feasibility triangle as an analytical tool in a different context (Figure 16.2) Cross and Gilly (2011b) were able to argue that for bi-national families (families where the spouses were born and raised in different countries and cultures), the sources of conjugal power must be examined from a different perspective. By focusing on a context that explicitly examines cultural interactions within the home, and comparing feasibility triangles for differing household compositions, they demonstrate that expertise, as a source of power, has four different dimensions. A particularly important dimension is expertise based on cultural competence and savvy. The researchers arrived at their findings by using the following steps.

Data analysis steps

- The survey instrument (independently completed by both spouses in each household prior to the actual interview and also discussed during the interview) was based on prior studies and designed to ensure easy extraction and coding of data.
- The data were coded as 1, 2, or 3 depending on the participant's response and entered into a spreadsheet program, like Microsoft Excel, where husband-dominant = 1, joint = 2, to wife-dominant = 3, based on the original Davis and Rigaux (1974) study.
- Once coded, statistical averages across categories and across respondents, and response congruency between spouses were calculated.

- Congruency tables were created and the data averages plotted on the feasibility triangle based on the mappings by Davis and Rigaux (1974).
- Total data were portrayed and mapped, as well as sub-data based on the gender of the immigrant and native spouses.

Key challenges

- After coding the data for the first spouse, reverse coding of the responses was required for the partner spouse's responses, which added a layer of complexity.
- Mapping the data accurately within the original guidelines using a visual presentation software program was necessary.

Thus, Cross and Gilly (2011b) show that cultural competence is a particular form of cultural capital in bi-national and bi-cultural relationships. For the innovative researcher, combining this little-used approach with other data perspectives – tables, figures and/or transcripts – yields additional insights into consumer decision-making.

Researcher/participant collaboration

Examples highlighted above show that participant involvement in data collection fosters cooperation and provides fresh insights and new ideas for products and services. However, participant involvement can take place at any stage of the research process. Involving participants in the data analysis stage can be extremely beneficial for the researcher. Joint efforts of researcher and participant in analyzing data can be a valuable tool in the development of sound, relevant and important research.

Two things are important to note here. First, the researchers in each study recognized that the direct involvement of the participants in the data analysis process would be an enhancement to the research and aid in construct development. Second, in each study, data analysis starts early and overlaps with data collection. There are several techniques that can be used by the innovative researcher to foster researcher/participant collaboration and enhance the findings from the study. The researcher simply needs to start with the question: How can I best work with participants to maximize insights?

Photo elicitation is one technique, which can often foster researcher/participant collaboration. Photo elicitation uses photographs of participant behavior during the interviews to stimulate discussion and examine behavior from another perspective. Photographs are either taken by the researcher as in autodriving (Heisley and Levy 1991) or by the participant as in photovoice or photo novella (Wang and Burris 1994, 1997).

Photo elicitation was used by Cross and Gilly (2010) in their Thanksgiving research, with participants taking photographs at the beginning of the research project and photograph collages later used to enhance the interviews. Collages are often compiled by the participants themselves, but in this study the researchers produced the collages. Figure 16.3 is one example of the photograph collage used to depict the food items consumed in a US household at Thanksgiving.

With modern technology, photo elicitation has been updated, with websites being used as stimuli. Schau and Gilly (2003) see personal websites as a type of collage which represents a conspicuous form of consumer self-presentation. Two examples are shown in Figure 16.4. They find that brands are frequently used as shorthand for describing selves to others. The researchers examined the content of personal websites and also used them to drive

Figure 16.3 Photocollage of Thanksgiving food.
          Source: Cross and Gilly (2010).

interviews with creators of those sites, following up with research participants as they revised the content of their websites. Here are the steps they took to analyze the data collected.

Data analysis steps

- Long interviews, consumer-created documents (personal websites and postings) and co-created documents (electronic exchanges) were analyzed for deep meanings.
- Interviews were coded and themes were distilled.
- The initial interview was analyzed separately and then reinterpreted in a comparative manner. Subsequent interviews were analyzed in the light of previous interviews.
- Using personal websites as consumer-created digital collages to augment the interviews allowed informants to influence researcher interpretation.

Key challenges

- While the internet is global, the face-to-face nature of the interviews required limiting the sample geographically.
- The researchers attempted to have informants create a real collage where they would not be limited by online resources; however, this technique was not as useful as the actual personal websites.
- Informants were constantly revising their pages, sometimes in response to interview questions. Keeping records of website content at various stages was difficult but important to see the evolution of the websites.

Examples in this section demonstrate that data analysis can be an interactive process, not simply an isolated activity. While the bulk of the analysis will still be done by the

Figure 16.4 Personal website page examples.
Source: Schau and Gilly (2003).

researchers, engaging participants in preliminary analytic activities can yield valuable insights. This process can start at the end of the data collection stage. Simply inviting the participant at the end of the interview to provide feedback and comments on the questions asked, the themes raised, the format and approach of the interview is one technique used. Another is member checks, where participants are invited to comment on the findings of the study as the analysis progresses. This approach involves the consumer by inviting them to comment on the analysis to discern if, and how, the research resonates with them.

If the goal of the corporate researcher is to find information that can lead to better products and services for the consumer, then maximizing consumer involvement, whether in data collection or data analysis, can be rewarding for both researcher and participant.

Multi-perspective approaches to research

In his paper on the dilemmas inherent in research design, McGrath (1981) reminds us that all research methods are "seriously flawed." Some methods enhance generalizability (such as surveys and to a lesser extent, experiments) based on the causal nature of their findings, their larger sample sizes and the high level of precision in control and measurement. However, experiments and surveys are seen as low in realism. Other more qualitative methods emphasize behavioral context, focus on underlying meanings and are high in realism. However, qualitative methods are generally lower in generalizability, with smaller sample sizes, and measurement precision. Experimental research settings are often contrived, whereas ethnographic settings are existentially "real." McGrath points out researchers must be aware of tradeoffs between the strengths and weaknesses of a particular method. He advocates the use of multiple observations and multiple perspectives to maximize methodological strengths and counteract methodological weaknesses.

A multiple perspective approach to research is inherent in many culturally based research methods. This convergence of perspectives occurs across methods, disciplines, functional areas and contexts. The goal of this section is to show that innovative ideas often spring from pooling disparate resources, viewpoints, expertise and methods. We will discuss some of the pros and cons of two approaches: the multi-method approach and the cross-disciplinary approach.

Multi-method approach

Ethnographic-based researchers typically combine observation, discussion and interaction in their study of human behavior. Many of the examples given throughout this chapter show a triangulation of techniques to understand consumption. The authors of this chapter use a multi-method approach in much of their research, combining projective techniques with surveys to understand what customers wanted from their online shopping experiences (Wolfinbarger and Gilly 2003); interviews and projectives with network analytic techniques to examine adaptation and blending processes in culturally diverse families in the context of food consumption celebrations (Cross and Gilly 2010); and interviews and experiments with neuro-decision techniques (Childers *et al.* 2011) to understand the effect of diminished and hyper-sensitivity to smell on consumption.

A multi-method approach has both advantages and disadvantages. Multi-method research is generally more time-intensive and usually requires multiple researchers with differing expertise in the particular methodologies employed on a project. Combining multiple methods can sometimes be regarded skeptically, particularly by those with a strong affilia-tion with a particular methology. However, a multi-method approach also addresses and balances the methodological weaknesses of a single method and provides a richer, more holistic view of phenomena. It also allows the consumer behavior researcher to better capture both the overt and latent motivations for behavior in culturally diverse and non-traditional consumers.

Cross-disciplinary approach

Collaboration across disciplines and areas of expertise is another innovative way to approach research studies from multiple perspectives. In 2004 and 2005, a collaborative effort between research firms GfK NOP and Social Solutions, Inc. led to the creation of an unprecedented visual database to study global consumers. Labeled the "Visual Survey of Domestic Space," this project is viewed as the most comprehensive project of its kind. Anthropologists and sociologists spent over a year photographing an average of 20 household interiors in 12 countries and compiled nearly 13,000 comparable photographs. The photographs were then linked to quantitative data to document and examine cultural nuances and consumer preferences across the globe. This project is an amazing example of collaboration across disciplines, companies, contexts and methods (Fielding 2006).

Cross-disciplinary research is also actively encouraged in academic circles. Several campuses have interdisciplinary centers that encourage collaboration on research projects across disciplines. Students value the multi-disciplinary faculty and research projects (particularly those looking at human behavior in context) benefit from the multiple perspec-tives provided. Two such centers are the Center for Human Computer Interaction (HCI) at Iowa State University and the Center for Research on Information Technology and Organizations (CRITO) at the University of California, Irvine. Researchers are given incentives such as grants and awards to collaborate across disciplines. For example, "The Best Idea" grant, from American University's Center for Teaching, Research and Learning (CTRL) provides funding and support to a team of multidisciplinary faculty working together to develop critical knowledge on a research subject. In 2010, a four-person team of researchers from Psychology, Marketing, Philosophy and Global Environmental Politics was awarded the grant for their innovative proposal to examine environmentalism from a different perspective: mindfulness and contemplation.

However, cross-disciplinary research does have its limitations. For academics, inter-disciplinary work can be time-consuming and may not fit neatly into any of the research paradigms or disciplines traversed. For corporate researchers, research projects involving a variety of business units can be a source of frustration. These projects are often large and require a huge commitment and level of support from the organization or corporate leaders. Yet in spite of the limitations, collaborative consumer research embracing multiple approaches can be exciting. Studies have shown that diversity often leads to creativity, which we know is the first step in the innovation process (Amabile *et al*. 1996). Consumers are complex and research must address that complexity.

The multi-perspective examples discussed ranged from academia to corporate practise, from multi-method research to inter-disciplinary and international collaborative projects. There are many other examples, but the ones highlighted give a sample of the kinds of approaches available to researchers.

Conclusion and recommendations for future innovative research

Sunderland and Denny (2007: 48) point out that cultural analysis helps to make "visible the invisible." Cultural aspects can be so tacit and familiar that neither the researcher nor the participant is always aware of their existence. Thus, innovative methods for collecting data are needed that enable researchers to uncover cultural information that will help them better understand consumers and satisfy their customers. Creative ways of analyzing data and involving consumers expose researchers to new ways of thinking about the data they collect. Finally, new ways to present findings aids researchers in conveying information to market-ing decision-makers effectively.

Yet how do researchers move from data analysis to innovative strategic thinking? How are innovative consumer insights used to develop and revise strategy? How do researchers effectively communicate their insightful analyses to clients or managers? These are difficult questions, even for the experienced researcher. We offer a few suggestions to get you started and help you think about this important step.

Contemplating data holistically

- Start by systematically analyzing the data gathered. Software packages appropriate for the type of data gathered are recommended. For example, QSR NVivo or ATLAS.ti are two commonly used software programs for storing, sorting and coding textual data derived from interview transcripts and other data collection sources.
- Contemplate your data deeply, noting points of similarity and contrast, systematically probing to understand what additional strategic insights were gained from the individual and collective research approaches.
- If the research was done within a cross-disciplinary team, analysis is typically done separately, then as a team using discussion, brainstorming and critique as techniques to dig deeper and uncover what the data are trying to reveal. It is important to draw on the strengths of the individuals in the team (or capitalize on the strengths of the methods) while acknowledging the limitations.
- Really listen to the consumers – listen to your data – and what they are trying to com-municate. Listen audibly and visually to seek the underlying meanings behind the words and the behavior.
- Think about the data within its context and then consider what similar behavior in another context might reveal. Thinking out of context forces deeper contemplation.
- Question the data. Is this relevant or not? Is that what this really means or not? Always ask how and why. What are the implications for shifting current strategic thinking? Are suggested actions feasible given the overall organizational strategy?

Communicating data insights: establishing credibility, validity and support

- Establish your qualifications and goals for the research. Outline any research questions or conceptual propositions.
- Describe your approach, ensuring the audience understands the context, importance and motivations for the choice of method(s) and team.
- Give the audience a sense of the data. For example:

- Create a participant profile with demographic and behavioral information using pseudonyms, so your audience has some sense of your sample.
- Include verbatims or comments from your participants to support your analysis and give credibility to your insights.
- Use visual summation methods – tables, figures, charts and photographs, as illustrated in earlier examples – to effectively summarize the data and communicate patterns or trends.
- Be clear, organized, concise and enthusiastic about the insights gained and the advantages of using a multi-perspective innovative approach.

With advances in technology, the door is open for additional innovation in research methods for cultural marketing management. Constructing virtual worlds in which consumers can interact with marketers and their products; tracking consumer-generated content for authentic conversations about products and services; using mobile devices across cultures as a tool for understanding nuances in behavior and preferences; and allowing data to be presented from multiple perspectives within particular cultural contexts are just now being explored by marketers. Technology allows cultural boundaries to be bridged in ways that will enlighten marketing decision-makers and researchers about culture's influences. Analysis of those cultural influences "unpacks and illuminates the implicit" (Sunderland and Denny 2007: 51) helping us as marketing researchers to better understand human consumption.

Review and discussion questions

1   What is innovation? What is innovation in research?
2   What is the difference between innovation and creativity?
3   Why are innovative approaches to studying cultural issues necessary?
4   How does using more than one research method improve the quality of consumer insights? What are the challenges of multi-method research?
5   What are the challenges of using cross-disciplinary research teams?
6   What are the various ways in which consumers can participate in the research process?
7   What is a feasibility triangle? How is it used in visualizing data?
8   Understand the consumer in his/her environment by going grocery shopping with a friend or family member. Ask about each selection, e.g., why that brand, what will it be used for? Compare their shopping style to your own.
9   Consider your friends' use of social network sites by noting mentions of products and brands. How are products and brands used to communicate with others?
10 Go to an ethnic grocery store (different from your own ethnicity). Choose a product category and compare the display, pricing, assortment, etc. to your own grocery store.

Keywords

collage, data analysis, data collection, feasibility triangle, multi-perspective approach, photo elicitation, research methods, visualization

References

Amabile, Teresa M., Conti, Regina, Coon, Heather, Lazenby, Jeffrey and Herron, Michael (1996) "Assessing the Work Environment for Creativity," *Academy of Management Journal*, 39(5): 1154–84.

Ariely, Dan (2008) *Predictably Irrational: The Hidden Forces That Shape Our Decisions*, New York: HarperCollins Publishers.

Belk, Russell (2006) *Handbook of Qualitative Research Methods in Marketing*, Cheltenham: Edward Elgar Publishers.

Bernard, H. Russell (2005) *Research Methods in Anthropology: Qualitative and Quantitative*, Walnut Creek, CA: AltaMira Press.

Brewer, John and Hunter, Albert (2005) *Foundations of Multimethod Research: Synthesizing Styles*, London: Sage.

Childers, Terry L., Lin, Meng-Hsien and Cross, Samantha N. N. (2011) "Individual Differences in Olfactory Function and Decision Making," Working Paper, Iowa State University.

Cross, Samantha N. N. and Gilly, Mary C. (2010) "The Creolization of Family and Society: When Tradition Meets Innovation," Working Paper, University of California, Irvine.

—— (2011a) "Consumption Compromises: Understanding Family Creation through Narratives of Bi-national Families," Working Paper, University of California, Irvine.

—— (2011b) "For Better or for Worse: Cultural Competence and Power Dynamics in Bi-National Households," Working Paper, University of California, Irvine.

Davis, Harry L. and Rigaux, Benny P. (1974) "Perception of Marital Roles in Decision Processes," *Journal of Consumer Research*, 1(1): 51–62.

Feldman, Martha S. (1995) *Strategies for Interpreting Qualitative Data*, London: Sage.

Fielding, Michael (2006) "In One's Element: Global Household Pix Yield Consumer Insights," *Marketing News*, 15–19.

Griffiths, Merlyn, Harmon, Tracy and Gilly, Mary C. (2011) "Hubble Bubble Trouble: The Need for Education and Regulation of Hookah Smoking," *Journal of Public Policy and Marketing*, 30(1): 119–32.

Heisley, Deborah D. and Levy, Sidney J. (1991) "Autodriving: A Photoelicitation Technique," *The Journal of Consumer Research*, 18: 257–72.

Hoffman, Donald (2000) *Visual Intelligence: How We Create What We See*, New York: W.W.Norton & Company, Inc.

Iacobucci, Dawn (1996) *Networks in Marketing*, London: Sage.

Kozinets, Robert V. (2009) *Netnography: Doing Ethnographic Research Online*, London: Sage.

Levine, Joel (1996) *Introduction to Data Analysis*. Available at: http://www.dartmouth.edu/~mss/data%20analysis/Volume%20I%20pdf%20/006%20Intro%20(What%20is%20the%20weal.pdf

Lofland, John D., Snow, David A., Anderson, Leon, and Lofland, Lyn H. (2005) *Analyzing Social Settings: A Guide to Qualitative Observation and Analysis*, London: Wadsworth Publishing.

Mariampolski, Hy (2005) *Ethnography for Marketers: A Guide to Consumer Immersion*, Newbury Park, CA: Sage.

Menzel, Peter and D'Aluisio, Faith (2005) *Hungry Planet: What the World Eats*, Berkeley, CA: Ten Speed Press.

—— (2010) *What I Eat: Around the World in 80 Diets*, New York: Material World.

McCracken, Grant (1988) *Culture and Consumption*, New York: John Wiley & Sons, Ltd.

—— (2005) *Culture and Consumption II: Markets, Meaning and Brand Management*, Bloomington, IN: Indiana University Press.

McGrath, Joseph E. (1981) "Dilemmatics: The Study of Research Choices and Dilemmas," *American Behavioral Scientist*, 25: 179–210.

Pink, Sarah (2001) *Doing Visual Ethnography: Images, Media and Representation in Research*, London: Sage.

Putnam, Mandy and Davidson, William R. (1987) "Family Purchasing Behavior: II Family Roles by Product Category," in *The RIS Consumer Focus Series*, Dublin, OH: Management Horizons.

Rapaille, Clotaire (2007) *The Culture Code: An Ingenious Way to Understand Why People Around the World Live and Buy as They Do*, New York: Broadway Books.

Schau, Hope Jensen and Gilly, Mary C. (2003) "We Are What We Post? Self-Presentation in Personal Web Space," *Journal of Consumer Research*, 30(3): 385–404.

Schwartzman, Helen B. (1992) *Ethnography in Organizations*, London: Sage.

Spradley, James P. (1980) *Participant Observation*, New York: Holt, Rinehart and Winston.

Sunderland, Patricia and Denny, Rita (2007) *Doing Anthropology in Consumer Research*, Walnut Creek, CA: Left Coast Press, Inc.

Sylver, Brianna (2006) "What Does Innovation Really Mean?" *BusinessWeek*, 31 January.

Wang, Caroline and Burris, Mary Ann (1994) "Empowerment through Photo Novella: Portraits of Participation," *Health Education Quarterly*, 21(2): 171–86.

—— (1997) "Photovoice: Concept, Methodology, and Use for Participatory Needs Assessment," *Health Education & Behavior*, 24(3): 369–87.

Wolfe, Donald M. (1959) "Power and Authority in the Family," in Dorwin Cartwright (ed.), *Studies in Social Power*, Ann Arbor, MI: Research Center for Group Dynamics, Institute for Social Research, University of Michigan, pp. 99–117.

Wolfinbarger, Mary and Gilly, Mary C. (2003) "Etail-Q: Dimensionalizing, Measuring and Predicting Etail Quality," *Journal of Retailing*, 79(3): 183–98.

Zaltman, Gerald (2003) *How Consumers Think: Essential Insights Into the Mind of The Market*, Boston: Harvard Business School Press.

17 Action research methods in consumer culture

Julie L. Ozanne and Laurel Anderson

Overview

Action research is an alternative approach to conducting marketing research that works with consumers and producers to co-create empirical findings that are timely, relevant, and implementable. These methods are appropriate when consumption phenomena are culturally-embedded, multifaceted, and involve diverse stakeholders. The action research process is explained and compared with traditional research approaches. We highlight the cultural basis of different methods by offering illustrations that either draw on the local cultural resources or imported cultural resource. The use of local cultural resources is demonstrated through oral histories that leverage the traditional practise of embedded storytelling. But we also explore using Web-based collaboration as a method, which is also a cultural resource native to youths in industrialized countries. Imported cultural tools are examined through the use of expressive collages for individuals to convey their life experiences. Also, the use of cameras is another imported cultural resource that can help people deeply reflect on social problems toward engaging in productive social change. Today's marketplace is dynamic and increasingly global, and new market opportunities exist in subsistence and emerging economies, as well as highly developed economies. The methods discussed here highlight how cultural practices can inform the way managers gather data to better capture insights about diverse consumers.

Introduction

The relationship between the firm and the consumer is generally characterized by control and separation within much of marketing research. The firm creates and coordinates the research processes often in secret; the consumer participates compliantly by filling out opinion surveys or voicing their views in directed focus group discussions. Yet a new model of marketing research is emerging in which many consumers participate in the idea generation, construction, and market testing of new products. Perhaps best exemplified by the creation of the Linux operating system, in this new approach, little clear delineation exists between the producer and the consumer who are both working together using different resources, guided by different agendas, and using different approaches. What may at first blush look like the colorful and noisy chaos of a market bazaar, instead, is an efficient way of developing an innovative and reliable product. In this new model, consumers create, alter, interpret, and give meaning to products and experiences (Visconti *et al.* 2010). Thus, the consumer is both a producer and a consumer – a prosumer (cf. Chapters 9, 10, and 12 in this volume) – who is often part of an energetic community sharing a "creative commons."

While the idea of co-creating products has precedent in the area of services, the online community is opening up additional opportunities such as the case of Web 2.0. Other contributions in this book illuminate the active role played by consumers in the market; here we aim to locate such agency within research and from a specific methodological perspective.

Action research shares a similar approach to co-creating research and is an alternative research method for gathering information about consumers. Action research is defined in numerous ways and utilized in such far-ranging domains as management, education, and economic development among others (cf. Elden and Chisholm 1993; Bailey 1994). We utilize a form of participatory action research (Ozanne and Saatcioglu 2008) that focuses on consumers and has three basic components: (1) the attainment of a deep understanding of a group or community of consumers; (2) the collaboration with consumers in the research process; and (3) the co-development of some marketing action. Action research takes an additional step beyond traditional marketing research to include consumers in the design of marketing action as part of the research. Action research is particularly relevant when the problems investigated are complex, embedded in cultural contexts, and solutions require the involvement of many different stakeholders. In this chapter, we briefly highlight the general differences among traditional marketing research approaches and the action research approach. Next, we explain the steps that are involved in doing action research. Throughout this discussion, we illustrate the process by drawing on our own case study of action research that was done in the area of health services (Ozanne and Anderson 2010). Finally, we delve more deeply into research in this area by focusing on four concrete methods: (1) oral histories; (2) collages; (3) Web-based collaboration; and (4) Photovoice. We demonstrate these methods drawing once again on our health case study but also bring in additional examples to illuminate the strengths of these different methods.

General approaches to research methods

Two general approaches to gathering data about consumers are popular within the field of marketing management: a quantitative and a qualitative research approach. Borrowing from the hard sciences, the quantitative approach involves the researcher controlling the design, collection, and analysis of the data; the goal is to collect precise, numerical data, submit this data to rigorous statistical analysis, and generate an exact answer. An exemplar of this approach would be a controlled laboratory experiment in which different advertising appeals are tested for their impact on consumers' recall of brand attributes. Or two different versions of advertising copy might be tested in identical magazines and consumers' recognition of the brand could be measured. These methods work best when the problems under investigation are narrow and a specific answer to a well-structured problem is sought.

The qualitative approach to gathering data is also very popular and includes such techniques as in-depth interviews, focus groups, and ethnographic field research. In this approach, the researcher also decides the general questions to be examined, the methods used, and the analysis of the data. However, in an effort to generate more in-depth and holistic understandings of the consumer, the qualitative researcher relinquishes more control to the consumer and allows the research process to unfold and emerge. For example, during an in-depth interview, the researcher might plan to examine family decision-making, but new issues will likely emerge that would also be explored, such as managing conflict in family finances. Because these methods allow consumers considerable opportunities to expand upon and explore their ideas, these tools are particularly useful for discovering deeper insights into consumers' motivations and the meanings they attach to different phenomena. Thus, qualitative methods are useful when the marketing manager seeks new insights into less well-defined problems such as developing a profitable brand extension or creating a brand identity for a new product.

While action research methods originally evolved within organizational research to increase worker involvement within decision-making (Lewin 1946), many of the recent innovations have evolved from field research in developing countries (Chambers 1997). In this context, new methodological innovations were needed because many consumers in subsistence markets had low levels of literacy. Despite their lack of formal education and training, these consumers have significant life experiences that can inform the development of strategic interventions. As we will see, action research methods have been extended into a range of situations in both economically developed and undeveloped countries.

All consumer research methods aim to increase the understanding of consumers and their behavior. To this traditional goal of both quantitative and qualitative consumer research, action research adds the explicit goal of increasing consumers' well-being. Action research is unique in that it explicitly researches actions that might change behaviors that affect consumers' well-being. As such, an action research project seeks to create knowledge, propose and implement changes, and improve practise and performance (Stringer 1999). Thus, the ultimate outcome of action research in marketing management is to develop marketing actions that increase consumer well-being, which is particularly relevant for firms that seek to be profitable in the long run by developing more authentic relationships with consumers. For example, this approach would be useful for utility companies trying to decrease energy consumption that can save money for both the firm and the consumer.

While action research approaches may use data gathering techniques from both quantitative methods, such as surveys, or qualitative methods, such as interviews, this research approach differs on two basic assumptions that guide the research process. First, because change in behavior is desired, action researchers assume that the consumers being researched and other stakeholders should be collaborators who are actively involved in the research process (Ozanne and Saatcioglu 2008). This desire to include consumers in the research process means that qualitative methods are often preferred since consumers are sometimes better able to understand these methods (Ozanne and Anderson 2010). Moreover, sometimes new methods need to be customized to the knowledge, skills, and socio-cultural understandings of the consumers. Thus, action research is a hot bed of methodological innovation (see, for example, Mukherjee 1993). Finally, the research findings are collectively shared and used to benefit not only the firm but also the consumers being studied (Lewin 1946; Reason and Bradbury 2001).

In understanding consumers, Calder (2001: 155) emphasizes that for marketing researchers the "crucial thing is to have an explanation ... to start with an explanation ... think about explanations first and data second." This traditional quantitative approach to consumer research is in stark contrast to action research. Action research differs from traditional marketing research in that it does not privilege the position of the marketing researcher to understand consumers, design the research, interpret the results, and develop a marketing action. It is collaborative and strives to include consumers in these processes. This approach works when the product involved is experiential and is thus co-created with the consumer (such as in the case of services). This approach also works well when the product is high involvement and the well-being of the consumer is paramount. It is evident that in these situations culture is fundamental to understanding consumption. For example, relevant cases might include developing retirement facilities and services for the elderly, services for pregnant teenagers, or programs aimed at reducing obesity in children. All of these examples are deeply nested in cultural meanings and discourse.

Overview of the action research process

The action research process can be broadly viewed as three overlapping stages (Ozanne and Anderson 2010). The first stage is building relationships within a consumer group or community where a focal issue arises. The researcher seeks to identify individuals or groups who could be partners in the research process and could offer their help in understanding the issue as well as identifying resources and constraints (Koch and Kralik 2006). Participants from the community are collaborators in the research because it is believed that effective interventions require the consideration and respect of the social and cultural constructions of the people involved (Reason and Bradbury 2001). This view is consistent with core ideas within the field of marketing. For example, the marketing concept is a foundational concept based on the assumption that effective strategy is based on the needs of the consumers. Action researchers believe that if consumers are involved in researching problems that are important to them, then they will be more invested in the research outcome and will produce more reliable findings and enduring changes in behavior. Action researchers' interests align with the rise of companies who seek to be more socially responsible and use more sustainable business practises (Kotler and Lee 2005).

In our own health action research, we studied the problem of diabetes in an economically poor town in south-western United States where 23 percent of the people suffered from the disease, which is three times higher than the national average. This community was primarily composed of immigrant Hispanics and Native Americans. Managerial questions regarding the diabetes problem might include, who is the best service provider? What would a service look like that would have a significant impact on this problem and bring about actions that would change this high rate of diabetes? In the first stages of research, we sought out a range of partners who could provide different insights including the staff at a health clinic, members of a health advocacy group (with representatives from different social and governmental services), staff and students from a community college, and other community members. These groups provided different perspectives on the illness and access to different stakeholders within the community.

The second phase of action research involves collaborating with willing partners who help plan, design, and conduct the research. For example, the director of the health clinic advised us on the locally appropriate methods and arranged interviews with health workers and patients so we could better understand the problem of diabetes. Similarly, we worked with and trained students and faculty from the community college in research methods in order to examine town members' experiences of diabetes through the use of collages and photography (we will discuss these methods later in the chapter and highlight findings from our health study). During this stage, findings are often presented to groups affected by the problem for their reflection and are then used to inspire discussion and the development of deeper insights. Action research benefits consumers and communities when people are able to learn new skills, analyze their social and economic conditions, and then look for solutions and actions. For example, in our study, the photography technique that we employed was adopted by a teacher for use in a tribal educational program. Since this method assumes that two-way learning and sharing will occur, it is a good approach to use when a firm seeks to develop long-term relationships in the community based on respect and trust.

Finally, in collaboration with the research partners, an action plan is implemented based on the emergent findings. Following the implementation of the plan, additional research may be needed to see if the goals were accomplished, which often leads to a new cycle of problem identification, research, and action (Stringer 1999). In our study on diabetes, one of the action plans that emerged from discussions among community stakeholders was the need for a local health worker program. The residents felt that health workers who share a similar social and cultural background would be better able to work with local community members who suffered from diabetes and could help customize more culturally appropriate interventions.

In the next section, some of the interesting methods employed within this broader action research process are explored.

Four different types of action research

Action research is a broad research process and many different methods can be used to gather useful information and improve consumer outcomes. We highlight the diversity of methods by organizing four different action methods along two axes to examine the resources leveraged and the focus of the research insights. To a great degree, the methods used can be based on local embedded cultural resources or they may rely on imported cultural resources. Or, the methods may focus more on insights from individuals or the community at large (Figure 17.1). First, we discuss oral history as a method that explores individual life histories using embedded storytelling traditions. Second, we examine an imported tool, collages, and show how this tool can be used by individuals to express their life experiences. Third, we explore the Web as a method that has deep cultural roots in some communities, such as teenagers in industrialized countries, and can be used to explore community strengths and opportunities. Fourth, Photovoice is examined as an imported method that has considerable power to engage the community in deep reflection, problem solving, and social change.

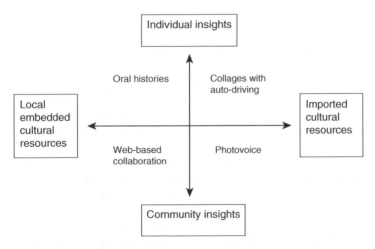

Figure 17.1 Four types of action research.

An embedded cultural tool for understanding individuals: oral history

Within all societies, home-grown ways exist of organizing and representing important local cultural insights and knowledge. Probably the most widespread and ancient form of such transmissions is oral storytelling. While marketing researchers frequently talk directly to consumers using methods, such as interviews and focus groups, an oral history is a first-hand account of a consumer's life story. The method is frequently called a personal narrative, a life history, or a biographical interview (Reinharz 1992). While oral histories were originally used to capture the experiences of elite members of society, such as famous politicians or historical figures, they are now widely used to explore the experiences of ordinary people that are often lost or overlooked as unimportant. For example, Elliot and Davies (2006) use oral histories to understand how ordinary consumers create meaning through their use of brands.

Unlike an autobiography or biography, the researchers and the consumer co-create this account through their dialogue as consumers tell their stories encouraged by the questions and inquiries of the researcher (Reinharz 1992). The researcher might also use the consumers' personal possessions to trigger a memory. Nevertheless, the story teller exerts considerable control in the research process as memories and life events are recalled, selected, and explored. Oral histories are broader in scope than traditional interviews that tend to be more focused. Oral histories capture more than simple narrative lines and also capture the important cultural categories that are worth remembering and preserving. These cultural categories can be used to develop actions focused on the well-being of these consumers. Thus, within traditional societies, oral histories often provide links between the past and the future. Collections of stories can capture diverse and unique experiences of the individual but they can also reveal broader cultural patterns. The rules and norms of storytelling differ among groups and so researchers need to be sensitive to differences within the culture where the method is used. For instance, groups may vary in the extent to which humor and gossip are viewed as an appropriate part of the narrative and often different levels of interactivity are deemed proper between the speaker and the listener (Smith 1999).

Traditional quantitative social scientists often criticize oral histories as overly subjective; and it would certainly be costly to implement this method with large numbers of consumers. But when this focus is on the personal experience of overlooked groups, this method is particularly relevant to marketing managers. These ignored consumers may have unmet needs and wants. Imagine the generative power of hearing the actual voices of consumers for those business clients who have to engage in creative and challenging tasks such as developing new products, forging brand identities, or creating breakthrough advertising.

The usefulness of oral history as a method is well demonstrated by Cheryl Gilkes' (1983) study of African American working-class women who achieved upward mobility into the middle class. Black professionals are a relatively under-researched group. In this study, life histories were created through interviews with "ordinary" community organizers who were identified as being extraordinary for their social activism within their communities. These women successfully gained the educational skills they needed to be able to advance in organizations that were dominated by whites but served African American communities. While receiving significant monetary rewards and recognition, the women were able to maintain their ties and commitment to the black community. All of these women struggled within traditional university environments. They found the university curriculum often irrelevant to the practical and pressing needs of their community, they perceived higher education as a pacifying force that "teaches you not to fight," and they often had conflict with educators whom they perceived as basing their curriculum on inaccurate knowledge of poor black communities (ibid.: 123). Given the failure of many educational institutions to expand services to minority groups, this study offers valuable insights into the educational system's failure to meet the needs of this consumer group by providing more relevant and accurate educational experiences aimed at social change.

An imported cultural tool for understanding individuals: collages

Collages are a technique that is focused on understanding an individual consumer's feelings, motivations, and attributions of meaning. Collages are a projective technique that uses collections of pictures to represent more personal experiences. Consumers are first asked to collect meaningful pictures and then visually arrange the pictures to represent their perceptions on a theme or topic. For many consumers, this method would be a technique relying on "imported" cultural resources since few consumers routinely engage in this type of visual, artistic, and creative process.

The main strength of this technique is that it allows individual consumers to express their feelings and perceptions in a nonverbal way. Most marketing research relies heavily on written language and assumes that consumers are able and willing to verbalize their feelings and experiences in response to the researcher's verbal questions. With visual methods, it is recognized that some experiences exist at a deeper level of consciousness and are more difficult to articulate and examine. Furthermore, verbally based research methods assume a high level of literacy. Thus, the collage is particularly beneficial when the consumers are not highly literate, such as children or new immigrants.

Recent neurological research suggests that we operate at a more visual level than previously recognized and much communication among people is nonverbal (Zaltman and Coulter 1995). Thoughts are often visually based and about two-thirds of stimuli apprehended by our brain are visual (Kosslyn 1994). Thus, a disconnection may arise between how consumers actually think and communicate – which is more visual – and how researchers access this information – which is often verbal. Through the use of collages, the language of visual imagery is activated thereby allowing for richer verbal descriptions of feelings and meanings (Zaltman 2003). Usually, the researcher uses the collages to guide, or "auto-drive," an interview in which the consumer explores the meaning of the visual symbols in the collage (Heisley and Levy 1991).

In our own research discussed earlier, we sought to understand consumers' perceptions and feelings about diabetes through collages (Ozanne and Anderson 2010). Consumers were provided with photographs from the community, magazines, and art supplies and asked to develop a collage on what diabetes is and what it means to be healthy. Diabetes is generally a taboo subject in this community, so the collages provided a powerful stimulus that was used to explore personal emotions and meanings. We found that community members of all ages were highly engaged in this method. The method also had the practical benefit of being able to be accomplished in one meeting since our participants often juggled busy schedules and had two jobs and many family commitments.

Through auto-driving on the collages, it became clear that the consumers who had witnessed the harsh consequences of diabetes in childhood were more likely to maintain healthy habits in adulthood. These harsh consequences included seeing their grandparents in diabetic shock, being with a parent or grandparent during dialysis, or observing the results of an amputation. As we helped develop interventions for a youth educational program on diabetes, these insights were invaluable. Again, collages can provide a powerful revelatory method but this is a labor-intensive process and would be difficult to implement on a large scale.

More managerial uses of collages also exist. For example, Ziba Design utilized collages with bank employees and executives to identify Umpqua Bank's "essence," which emerged as being human-centered. Specifically, customers wanted a more caring style of banking rather than the traditional authoritarian approach to banking (Sella 2004). Similarly, in revising United Airline's ad campaign, Fallon McElligott, a Minneapolis advertising agency, probed their customers' experiences of flying through drawings with different color crayons and collages (Kaufman 1997).

An embedded cultural tool for understanding communities: Web-based collaboration

"Online culture is *the culture*," according to Kevin Kelly, the co-founder of *Wired* magazine and author of the bestseller, *New Rules for the New Economy* (Kelly 2005). With the spread and diffusion of Internet technologies, online collaborative communities are growing rapidly. An important trend is emerging where consumers both research and co-create products, but considerable controversy arises in this context. Social network technology tools certainly qualify as embedded resources in many developed countries, especially among the younger generations. Until the Internet, many forms of collaboration were difficult on a large scale or with dispersed communities. And in the realm of action research, these online communities have demonstrated the challenges of collaboration both in terms of involvement and control.

We see the Internet as a media evolving from mass audiences to a somewhat unruly bazaar-like mode of participation. As we have previously mentioned, considerable co-creation occurs among consumers engaged in action research on the Web. These activities include consumers offering product or advertising ideas, organizations forming online community blogs to monitor consumer attitudes and experiences, and consumers participating in research on an issue or problem. For example, Google's Project 10 (to the 100) sought action plans from consumers by putting out a call for ideas that "change the world by helping as many people as possible." They pledged $10 million to put these ideas into action and the best idea will be determined by a vote of the online community (Google 2008).

HopeLab is an organization whose mission is to "combine rigorous research with innovative solutions to improve the health and quality of life of young people with chronic illness." HopeLab explicitly seeks collaboration with its patients, their families, and nurses throughout its product development process. Through this research and action process, they developed the award-winning video game, *Re-Mission*, for teens with cancer. Teenagers who played *Re-Mission* showed impressive improvement in their adherence to their medication regime. Relative to Google, HopeLab collaborates more deeply with consumers by creating an online community of teen cancer patients through their blog site for the *Re-Mission* game. HopeLab uses this blog to research and better understand their teen consumers and also collaborates with teens to form action plans. They have expanded their focus to obesity through the idea competition called Ruckus Nation, which seeks to tap into "the power of the global community—including kids—to generate new ideas for products that will get kids moving" (HopeLab 2009).

HopeLab draws on the insights and credibility of a community of peers. Teenagers can interact anonymously on potentially sensitive topics such as cancer and obesity without embarrassment or the fear of stigmatization. Moreover, geographically dispersed and diverse people can come together and work easily particularly given the norms on the Internet that encourage collaboration. This technique has the potential not only for developing, in collaboration with the consumers, a deep understanding of the group, but can incorporate rather more easily the action step of this research.

However, this tool is limited to relatively wealthy and electronically connected consumers. This tool also has drawbacks particularly with regards to issues of anonymity and privacy. For example, privacy issues have arisen with Facebook. Many instances exist where email address lists and personal information have been sold. Furthermore, ethical issues of transparency on the part of the marketing researcher require the development of thoughtful policies to avoid alienating consumers. Marketing research in general can be tainted by the actions of a few, such as when covert practices occur that make consumers wary and guarded.

An imported cultural tool for understanding community: Photovoice

Since its invention, photography has been used to document community problems, raise public awareness, and, at times, motivate social action. For example, Roy Stryker's work recorded social problems such as the decline of the rural farm and the rise of urban blight in the United States in the 1930s. Here, trained photographers recorded poignant images that were then presented to the public to generate public awareness and social action. Photovoice has its roots in such documentary photography and similarly takes advantage of the potential power of visual images to inspire people to act. However, cameras are instead placed into the hands of ordinary people to capture the issues that are important to them. While professional photographers might create more artistic and competent work, they will also inescapably see the communities they visit through the prism of their own experiences. Ordinary people are "experts on their own lives" (Wang *et al.* 2004: 911) and have insights that outside photographers might overlook – such as the deeper meaning of seemingly mundane activities that women engage in within their homes. Community members also have wider access into private areas within the community that might be off limits to an outside researcher.

Some groups exist at the margins of society, have less power, and may lack the tools and abilities to make their needs known (e.g., women, the poor, children, and the physically challenged). Photovoice is a method that can help these segments articulate their needs even when they do not read, write, or have formal education. Photovoice (Voicing Our Individual and Collective Experience) in the past has been used to examine health problems but it is a very flexible method that is used globally with a wide variety of groups. For example, Wendy Ewald (1985) gave cameras to youths in Appalachia to document their lives and stories. The nonprofit organization Photovoice has given cameras to children in Sarajevo, immigrant workers in the United States, Iranian earthquake survivors, and homecare residents in London (www.Photovoice.org). These people represent large groups of consumers with special needs that are not being met in the marketplace.

Photovoice was originally inspired to provide citizens with a way to communicate directly with policy-makers through their photos (Wang *et al.* 1996), but this method clearly has managerial implications. Given its focus on identifying unmet needs and also documenting community resources, it could be particularly relevant to marketing managers. Growing interest exists in trying to meet the needs of the millions of consumers who are at the bottom of the economic pyramid (Prahalad 2005). In addition, with companies increasingly heeding

288   *Julie L. Ozanne and Laurel Anderson*

the call to engage in good corporate behavior, Photovoice is another valuable tool for corporate social responsibility and for firms working within their communities to help solve social problems (Kotler and Lee 2005).

The method is fairly straightforward. A community of interest is identified and willing participants are selected. Research facilitators are also needed to help coordinate activities, train the participants, and lead group discussions. The photos are developed and analyzed in a two-stage process. First, the individual photographers select the photos that they believe best capture the needs and resources of the community. Second, these photographs are presented to the group and contextualized by the photographers telling the story of the photograph, what it captures, and what it means. Within this group discussion, other people may offer additional insights and explanations of the photographs; thus, multiple and richly contextualized meanings including any contested issues are constructed from the photograph by the community. Across the analysis of different community photographs, the group critically analyzes the root sources of problems identified. Finally, they prioritize the most pressing needs of the community. These photos may inspire social or policy change when they are displayed in public exhibits or presented to community leaders and politicians (Wang *et al.* 1996). Similarly, these photos could provide powerful evidence of the needs of consumer groups that could be used to initiate marketing innovation such as the development of new products.

When compared to marketing researchers generating data using traditional methods, such as observations, interviews, or focus groups, Photovoice offers unique advantages. First, the participants control the images captured and thus their expertise and perspective are more likely to be captured. The photos capture the rich and multifaceted socio-cultural life that may be hidden from the view of outsiders. Second, as with collages, this method works particularly well with people who are more vulnerable and lack literacy skills; the method is fun and engaging and is a new form for representing their views. Third, the visual images and stories generated by this method are a potent form of communication and provide powerful visual evidence. Finally, the method can be used to both assess the needs and the resources of the community and thus can be used to motivate social change or innovation (Wang *et al.* 2004).

The Photovoice technique does present some challenges. First, the Photovoice research process takes time and requires several points of contact with consumers. This requirement may be prohibitive with economically depressed groups of consumers who may be working two or more jobs in addition to handling their other responsibilities. They have little discretionary time to spend doing marketing research. Second, this is a group process. If community members know one another, they may be reticent to be very forthcoming when compared to more anonymous methods such as focus groups among strangers. Finally, conflict may arise in these group discussions. The meaning of conflict and the methods for handling it are often culturally layered. Collaboration with a member of the consumer community then becomes crucial in the facilitation of these group dynamics.

The original application of Photovoice was among rural Chinese women in dozens of villages in southwestern China. These women lived far away from the decision-making hubs within the local Chinese government or business spheres. Yet decisions were regularly made by business and policy-makers that impacted the lives of these women. The photographs generated gave testimony to the harsh physical realities of rural women and the competing demands they face. For example, since women lacked childcare, infants were brought into the fields and exposed to the elements while their mothers did heavy manual labor. Photographs of young babies on blankets in the fields made vivid this reality. The men making decisions regarding daycare facilities were far removed from these rural realities but the photographs made them aware of the needs of rural families and led to the development of a daycare program (Wang *et al*. 1996).

Managerial implications

Action research strategies offer an alternative set of tools to be used in conjunction with traditional quantitative and qualitative research methods. As marketing managers work within the constant challenges of a dynamic global economy, they will increasingly need more research tools that are culturally sensitive and can be adapted to the needs of the local consumers. Within emerging economies and subsistence markets, consumers often lack literacy skills that make some of the traditional methods less viable. Yet these consumers are experts in their daily lives and are the best source for understanding their needs. Action methods offer a set of flexible research tools that may be particularly relevant in this context.

Methodological tools are flexible resources that can and should be imported and adapted to local cultural needs. Photovoice is an imported technique that offers consumers new ways to collectively and powerfully represent their needs through potent visual images. Likewise, collages provide a way to gain insight into more individual feelings and experiences through visual images. But here the value of the imported technique is based on the ability of the method to access individual consumer emotions that are more difficult to tap through verbal methods. New methods can also be created by leveraging embedded forms of cultural expression. We can respect embedded forms of communication, such as storytelling and oral histories, to learn more about these consumers and their communities. Similarly, we can examine local forms of expressions, such as the social networks of the Web to provide vivid settings for collaboration.

A core underlying assumption across all these methods is to respect that all consumers have a wealth of valuable experience. Considerable ingenuity and creativity may be needed in adapting old methods and creating new methods to tap into this consumer expertise. As the trends toward more consumer co-creation and collaboration in the marketplace grow, it is likely that a parallel need will exist for more collaborative research methods. Action research methods are particularly well suited for collaborative design of goods and the co-creation of services.

It is evident that marketing research and the development of marketing programs are less separate activities in the action research process. This raises a number of managerial implications and questions:

1　How might this approach change the organizational structure and role descriptions?
2　What additional skills are needed by marketing researchers conducting action research?
3　How much control can be ceded to consumers?
4　What expectations does action research create in consumers?
5　What company information will it be necessary to share with consumers to enable high quality collaboration?
6　What training is necessary for consumers in order to participate in action research to their highest level?
7　What guarantees and returns are necessary to encourage consumer participation?
8　How do you develop trust with consumers throughout this process? This is a pressing issue if the firm is seeking to develop authentic relationships.

Finally, marketing managers must recognize that action research is not defined by any specific research technique. Action research is predicated on the goals of improving consumers' outcomes through engaging in collaborative inquiry that results in positive actions and changes in behavior. To exemplify action research, research methods must be used within this broader framework of action research.

Review and discussion questions

1   What managerial problems are best suited to quantitative research methods?
2   What managerial problems are best suited to qualitative research methods?
3   What managerial problems are best suited to action research methods?
4   Explain the steps in the action research process.
5   Discuss the pros and cons of including consumers in the research process.
6   What are the pros and cons of each of the methods discussed: oral histories, collages, Web-based collaboration, and Photovoice?
7   Generate concrete managerial uses for each of the four methods discussed: oral histories, collages, Web-based collaboration, and Photovoice.

Keywords

action research, action research process, collages, oral history, Photovoice, qualitative research approach, quantitative research approach, Web-based collaboration

References

Bailey, K. D. (1994) *Methods of Social Research*, New York: Free Press.
Calder, B. (2001) "Understanding Consumers," in D. Iacobucci (ed.), *Kellog on Marketing*, New York: John Wiley & Sons, Ltd, pp. 155–64.
Chambers, R. (1997) *Whose Reality Counts? Putting the First Last*, London: IT.
Elden, M. and Chisholm, R. F. (1993) "Emerging of Action Research: Introduction to the Special Issue," *Human Relations*, 46: 121–41.
Elliot, R. and Davies, A. (2006) "Using Oral History Methods in Consumer Research," in R. W. Belk (ed.) *Handbook of Qualitative Research Methods in Marketing*, Cheltenham: Edward Elgar Publishing, pp. 244–54.
Ewald, W. (1985) *Portraits and Dreams: Photographs and Stories by Children of Appalachians*, New York: Writers and Readers.
Gilkes, C. (1983) "Going Up for the Oppressed: The Career Mobility of Black Women Community Workers," *Journal of Social Issues*, 39(3): 115–39.
Google (2008) *Project 10 (to the 100)*. Available at: http://www.project10tothe100.com/how_it_works.html (accessed February 24, 2009).
Heisley, D. D. and Levy, S. J. (1991) "Autodriving: A Photoelicitation Technique," *Journal of Consumer Research*, 17: 257–72.
HopeLab (2009) Available at: http://www.hopelab.org/ (accessed January 15, 2009).
Kaufman, L. (1997) "Enough Talk: Focus Groups Are Old News; Today's Marketers Prefer Crayolas, Collages, and Surveillance," *Newsweek*, August 18, p. 48.
Kelly, K. (2005) "We Are the Web." Available at: http://www.wired.com/wired/archive/13.08/tech_pr.html (accessed February 24, 2009).
Koch, T. and Kralik, D. (2006) *Participatory Action Research in Health Care*, Oxford: Blackwell.
Kosslyn, S. M. (1994) *Image and Brain: The Resolution of the Imagery Debate*, Cambridge, MA: MIT Press.

Kotler, P. and Lee, N. (2005) *Corporate Social Responsibility: Doing the Most Good for Your Company and Your Cause*, Hoboken, NJ: John Wiley & Sons.

Lewin, K. (1946) "Action Research and Minority Problems," *Journal of Social Issues*, 2(4): 34–46.

Mukherjee, N. (1993) *Participatory Rural Appraisal: Methodology and Applications*, New Delhi: Concept.

Ozanne, J. L. and Anderson, L. (2010) "Community Action Health Research," *Journal of Public Policy & Marketing*, 29(1): 123–37.

Ozanne, J. L. and Saatcioglu, B. (2008) "Participatory Action Research," *Journal of Consumer Research*, 35: 423–39.

Prahalad, C. K. (2005) *The Fortune at the Bottom of the Pyramid*, Upper Saddle River, NJ: Wharton School Publishing.

Reason, P. and Bradbury, H. (2001) "Introduction: Inquiry and Participation in Search of a World Worthy of Human Aspiration," in P. Reason and H. Bradbury (eds) *Handbook of Action Research*, Thousand Oaks, CA: Sage, pp. 1–14.

Reinharz, S. (1992) *Feminist Methods in Social Research*, Oxford: Oxford University Press.

Sella, J. (2004) "Umpqua Bank Research: Gold, Design Explorations." Available at: http://www.idsa.org/ideas/idea2004/g2024.htm (accessed February 19, 2009).

Smith, L. T. (1999) *Decolonizing Methodologies: Research and Indigenous Peoples*, London: Zed Books.

Stringer, E. T. (1999) *Action Research*, Thousand Oaks, CA: Sage.

Trendwatching.com (2009) "Generation G: That Would Be G for 'Generosity,' Not G for 'Greed')." Available at: http://www.trendwatching.com/briefing/ (accessed February 24, 2009).

Visconti, L. M., Sherry, J. F., Borghini, S., and Anderson, L. (2010) "Street Art, Sweet Art? Reclaiming the 'Public' in Public Places," *Journal of Consumer Research*, 37(3): 511–29.

Wang, C., Burris, M. A. and Ping, X. Y. (1996) "Chinese Village Women as Visual Anthropologists: A Participatory Approach to Reaching Policymakers," *Social Science and Medicine*, 42(10): 1391–400.

Wang, C., Morrel-Samuels, S., Hutchison, P. M., Bell, L. and Pestronk, R. M. (2004) "Flint Photovoice: Community Building among Youths, Adults, and Policymakers," *American Journal of Public Health*, 94(6): 911–13.

Zaltman, G. (2003) *How Customers Think: Essential Insights into the Mind of the Market*, Boston: Harvard Business School.

Zaltman, G. and Coulter, R. H. (1995) "Seeing the Voice of the Customer: Metaphor-Based Advertising Research," *Journal of Advertising Research*, 35(July/August): 35–51.

Appendix: suggested Web resources

1 Oral history

- Baylor University offers a good tutorial on how to go about doing an oral history. Available at: http://www.baylor.edu/oral_history/index.php?id = 23566
- HopeLab has developed a Center for Digital Storytelling in order to understand the needs and interests of teens with cancer. The case studies provide examples of many other well-being initiatives that use this technique. Available at: http://www.hopelab.org/innovative-solutions/digital-storytelling/

2 Collages

- Zaltman Metaphor Elicitation Technique is examined in more depth. Available at: http://www.olsonzaltman.com/downloads/2002%20Harvard%20Business%20Review.pdf

- This article offers more depth on the collage technique. Available at: http://www.fastcompany.com/magazine/14/coffee.html

3 Web

- Google's (2008) *Project 10 (to the 100)* uses consumer-generated ideas to improve well-being. Available at: http://www.project10tothe100.com/how_it_works.html
- Trendwatching (2009) calls the present generation G for generosity, collaboration, and sharing. They note this trend parallels the collaborative aspects of action research. Available at: http://www.trendwatching.com/briefing/
- HopeLab is dedicated to involving its patients and other stakeholders in developing new products for teens with chronic illnesses and the game *Re-Mission* has won awards. Available at: http://www.hopelab.org/

4 Photovoice

- A rich resource is provided by the nonprofit organization Photovoice. This website offers useful help on using the method and has a wide range of examples and applications. Available at: http://www.Photovoice.org
- The Academy Award-winning film for best documentary, by Zana Briski and Ross Kauffman, is an engaging example of how photographs can be used to give vulnerable groups new tools of communication. *Born into Brothels: Calcutta's Red Light Kids* would provide for a provocative class discussion. Available at: http://www.kids-with-cameras.org/bornintobrothels/

Part IV
Refashioning marketing practices

18 Segmentation and targeting reloaded

Luca M. Visconti and Mine Üçok Hughes

Overview

An ancient Latin precept states "divide et impera", basically, "divide and rule". Despite the ambiguity surrounding the attribution of the saying, the Roman dictator Julius Caesar certainly complied with the principle to control the vastness of his reign. By breaking up the whole into smaller chunks, each portion becomes more easily controllable and manageable, as the long reign of the Roman Empire testified.

In our times and for the purposes of the chapter, the foundations of this adage still hold as they describe the motivations behind *market segmentation* as splitting the market into groups of customers, each of them having similar consumption behavior (Peter and Donnelly 2008). From this perspective, the aims of market segmentation parallel Caesar's desire to rule the disparate realms of the Roman Empire by assigning local rulers who had an understanding of the local populations. Identifying and isolating market subgroups help meet customers' needs more effectively, and thereby support companies' market-oriented strategies, since they indicate the customers to be served, the competitors to be faced, the critical resources to possess in order to compete in each segment, and the main actors (Lambin 1998).

By comparing traditional and cultural frames, this chapter critically discusses market segmentation and *targeting*, defined as the selection of one or more segments to be reached by the company by means of specific market offers (Pride and Ferrell 2004). In particular, we aim to illustrate the moment when discontinuity occurred in the marketing discipline due to the overwhelming prevalence of the realist, cognitive view that has developed in the past few decades. We show how the adoption of the cultural perspective has introduced new conceptual models and marketing practices for segmentation and targeting. Specifically, we present segmentation and targeting within the established tradition of marketing studies, i.e. *à la* Kotler, and subsequently compare the cultural approach to them. By contextualizing our discussion with cross-cultural examples drawn from ethnic markets in the USA, Denmark, and Italy, we propose a complementary cultural frame to revisit the understanding and implementation of segmentation and targeting. Managerial implications and generalizations are presented in the closing section.

Segmentation and targeting in the Old World Order

Metaphorically, the Old World Order depicts the marketing tradition as being rooted in cognitivism and realism, according to which market phenomena are objective and knowable entities and comply with the principle of non-contradiction: if something is white, it cannot be black, and its color is given and objectively researchable. From this perspective, market segmentation is made possible by customers' agglomerated preferences (Kerin *et al.* 2006), that is, by stable and widely shared desiderata within each group of customers. By positioning customers' preferences along a continuum, agglomerated preferences are located between the two extremes, both of them identifying states of unfeasible segmentation (McDonald and Dunbar 2004). Actually, when customers show homogeneous needs and reactions to the marketing-mix levers, there is no economic rationale to perform segmentation. Similarly but conversely, when preferences are totally fragmented such that segments are composed of one or a limited number of customers, micro-segmentation and customized market offers replace segmentation.

When possible – indeed, most often, since preferences are seldom truly homogeneous or scattered, market segmentation is a process of stages. First, by leveraging on Abell's three-dimensional model (1980), macro-segmentation allows the isolation of market macro-segments (Figure 18.1) in terms of: (1) groups of potential customers ("who"); (2) types of functions and needs to be satisfied ("what"); and (3) technologies or processes necessary to produce the different market offers ("how"). At this stage, each company must select one or more macro-segments in which to operate. According to this choice, the company is then categorized (Lambin 1998) as: (1) a specialist for a given product-market (the group of customers and the technology are given but the functions met by the company are several); (2) a specialist for a given market solution (the group of customers and the function/need are given but the company provides a wide set of technological and productive solutions); and (3) an industry-driven firm (technology and function/need are given but the company targets various groups of customers).

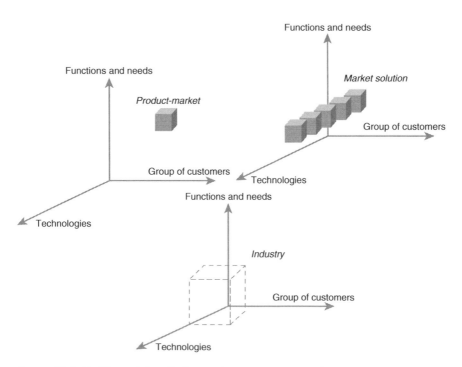

Figure 18.1 Abell's model applied to market macro-segmentation.

At the second stage, micro-segmentation further fragments each macro-segment into smaller portions. This stage is the one usually derived by segmentation and can be performed based on different criteria (Table 18.1; Kotler and Armstrong 2006; Peter and Donnelly 2008). On the one hand, marketers may rely upon indirect segmentation criteria that infers customers' needs and their uses of the company's product/service through one

Table 18.1 The taxonomy of traditional segmentation criteria

	Segmentation criteria	*Definition*
Indirect criteria	Geographical criteria	• Supranational markets (North America and Canada; Far East and Asia; European Union, etc.) • National markets (the USA, Canada, France, etc.) • Regional markets (Rocky Mountains, West Coast, etc.) • Cities • Density of the population (rural, suburban, urban) *Usefulness*: any time the location of consumers impacts their culture, consumption practices, and logistical issues
	Socio-demographic criteria	• Age • Sex • Number of family members • Life stage of the family • Education • Income • Profession • Religion • Ethnicity • Nationality *Usefulness*: easily applicable and often available in official statistics, they identify influential variables impacting consumers' functional and symbolic needs
	Psychographic criteria	• Social class • Personality • Lifestyle *Usefulness*: they trace lifestyle profiles combining different geographical and socio-demographic criteria, and thus tracing values of different groups of clients. There are different examples of psychographic models: VALS II (SRI International) in North America; Europanel (GfK) in Europe; Sinottica (Eurisko) in Italy, etc.
Direct criteria	Behavioral criteria	• Attitudes towards the product/service/brand • Level of awareness (uninformed, informed, interested) • Situations of use • Benefits requested • Stage of use (non-user, user, former user) • Intensity of use (light, intermediate or heavy user) • Loyalty *Usefulness*: they directly connect market segments to different profiles of customers of the product/service/brand of the company

or more external features of the customers (e.g., their geographical location, income, sex, age, generation, lifestyle, religion, and, for b2b contexts, industry or company size, etc.). On the other hand, managers can look for the way customers directly relate to their market offer (direct criteria). In such cases, segmentation is made by acquiring a straightforward understanding of customers' needs, attitudes, consumption behaviors or loyalty, all related to a given brand, product/service category, or supply system. Needless to say, direct criteria are more reliable due to their immediate connection with the company's products or services, but they require deeper customer knowledge and primary research data (i.e., data collected specifically for segmentation purposes). Conversely, indirect criteria are more easily applicable because most of them are already available through secondary data sources (e.g., official statistics, censuses, market research reports, etc.). To balance pros and cons, firms often combine various criteria to segment their markets, and thus give rise to the so-called mixed segmentation (Kotler and Armstrong 2006).

As stated above, the process of market micro- and macro-segmentation is possible in cases of agglomerated preferences. This *condicio sine qua non* is, however, insufficient. As most of the marketing textbooks warn, managers also must honor a lengthy list of additional conditions while performing segmentation that become useful benchmarks to judge the quality of the generated segments. Summing up, the main provisions to be granted (Kerin *et al.* 2006; Kotler and Armstrong 2006; Lambin 1998) include:

1   *Differentiability*. With reference to customers' needs and their sensitivity to the marketing levers, segmentation ought to generate groups of customers internally homogeneous yet externally heterogeneous. As such, this requirement is highly consistent with the notion of agglomerated preferences illustrated above.

2   *Measurability*. For each segment it is necessary to quantify the number of individuals or organizations composing it. This also means measuring their purchasing power and the most relevant traits related to their purchasing and consumption behaviors (e.g., frequency of consumption, amount of single purchase, etc.).

3   *Relevance*. Relying on the aforementioned measures, each segment should be economically profitable so to justify the costs of marketing differentiation. Relevance should be evaluated also in projective terms, taking into account prospective customers and the overall market potential.

4   *Accessibility*. Segments can be differentiated and profitable but sometimes out of reach for the company. Accessibility thus implies the possibility for the firm to reach the segments by circumventing the various gates that impede full admission. In this, the company may lack the resources necessary to compete in a given segment or have trouble applying the selected segmentation criterion (e.g., while it is easier to state the sex or age of a customer, it can be harder to infer the rate of his/her involvement if the information is not collected systematically and/or deliberately). Finally, access may be related to problems with distribution or communication strategies if the aimed segment does not rely upon peculiar and distinctive points of sale or media, and thus cannot be effectively separated from other segments.

5   *Exhaustiveness*. Two additional conditions that most marketing textbooks omit are pointed out by Peter and Donnelly (2008) and are particularly beneficial to our discussion here. Both are deeply rooted in the tradition of realism and cognitivism, and represent a major point of difference when adopting the cultural approach. First and consistent with the principle of non-contradiction, exhaustiveness specifies that each

customer can be attributed to one segment only. Thus, the situation of multiple belonging is excluded.

6   *Stability*. Second, traditional approaches to segmentation postulate that features qualifying each segment are almost preserved over time. This tenet fits the criterion of objectivity, since customers' characteristics and needs are usually defined by customers' personality traits and genes (Arnould *et al.* 2002), thus preventing continuous modification of the segments' features.

Elaborating upon these provisions, each company can identify the segment(s) to target. This stage of the marketing strategy is tautologically known as *targeting*, and implies the attribution to the company of one or more groups of customers to be served. The criteria of self-attribution of macro- and micro-segments can be synthesized as follows (Kotler and Armstrong 2006): (1) the selected segment has to be highly profitable; (2) the targeted segment should not be saturated (i.e., the number of competitors serving the segment are limited); and (3) the resources necessary to compete in the segment are available to the company. Kerin *et al.* (2006) add a fourth criterion that relates to the competitive tensions and to the defensibility of the company's position within the targeted group. According to the decisions taken at the targeting stage, each company gives shape to its marketing strategy that ultimately can be defined as undifferentiated marketing (if the company serves the whole market by means of a single supply system), differentiated marketing (if more segments are targeted but through different supply systems) or concentrated marketing (if a single segment is served through a highly tailored supply).

In the following section, we discuss how segmentation and targeting are revisited in the cultural approach to market segmentation in a way that constitutes an interpretive shift about reality and market phenomena and leads to the reassessment of the relationship between companies and their customers. Metaphorically speaking, we suggest that the cultural approach constitutes a different "hardware" through which marketing strategy can be re-evaluated, and thus "reloaded". In this, we question the traditional conditions for segmentation and show they need to be updated. While the two last provisions have been completely removed (exhaustiveness and stability), the other four (differentiability, measurability, relevance, and accessibility) are partially revisited. Finally, we provide the reader with an extended and updated set of segmentation criteria and an implemented revised definition of targeting.

Towards cultural segmentation and targeting

As discussed in other chapters in this volume, cultural marketing management originates from the acknowledgement of a different ontology (i.e., what is reality) and epistemology (i.e., what kind of knowledge is achievable about reality). In brief, the cultural perspective is consistent with an idea of the world that is culturally constructed (McCracken 1986; Costa and Bamossy 1995). In other words, culture is not only a variable affecting reality and human phenomena from the outside – what Arnould *et al.* (2002: 73) refer to as the "relatively unchanging precursor of individual behavior" – but also culture becomes a variable structuring the world and human life from the inside to the point of framing individual identity projects (Arnould and Thompson 2005). Its pervasiveness is well encapsulated in the reductionist definition given by Firat and Venkatesh (1995) who conceive of culture as everything but nature.

When a cultural view of the world is retained, knowing the world equates to *interpreting* it. So, with the main exception of the aforementioned natural phenomena, all social phenomena are understandable through the elaboration and confrontation of their proposed meanings (McCracken 1986). As such, researchers become interpreters, and interpretation definitely and necessarily is as much subjective as negotiated inter-subjectively. Thus, knowing has been the art of establishing shared, dense, multifaceted interpretations of the meanings incorporated in human experience.

Market dynamics and consumption are no exception. Within the traditional marketing approach, market exchanges and consumption are envisioned as attempts to regulate efficient production and to satisfy consumers' and organizations' functional needs effectively (think of the "*homo œconomicus*" acting as a cognitive subject). As such, no attention is devoted to the interpretation of meanings, since economic actors are all aware of their behavioral motivations that coincide with their functional necessities. Conversely, the postindustrial, postmodern era (Brown 1995) led to the emergence and dominance of symbolic, relational, and experiential needs over functionality. Consequently, market exchanges are no longer readable in the light of cognitivism and this phenomenon asks for more interpretive, cultural lenses. As commented on by Solomon, Bamossy and Askegaard (1999: 443):

> The relationship between consumer behavior and culture is a two-way street. On the one hand, products and services that resonate with the priorities of a culture at any given time have a much better chance of being accepted by consumers. On the other hand, the study of new products and innovations in product design successfully produced by a culture at any point in time provides a window on the dominant cultural ideas of that period.

Segmentation and targeting are part of this interpretive transformation. If customers change and become agentic, social, and communicative subjects computing much more than their marginal utility (i.e., they become *interpretive subjects*), so do their aggregates, including market segments. Therefore, we cannot look at segments in the same way we did in the past, since most of the hypotheses held by traditional segmentation are to be removed or, at least, to be revised. As anticipated at the end of the previous paragraph, the re-examination of the six conditions for segmentation is then telling, indeed. Hereafter, we recall and revisit them to point out the main upheavals stimulated by social and market changes and captured by the cultural paradigm. We start with the two main transformations that have occurred over time and subsequently illustrate their impact on the other conditions:

1   *Exhaustiveness rejected.* Contemporary, postmodern consumers are fragmented subjects who can shift from different subject positions at different moments in time (Firat and Shultz 1997). The emergence of the multiple self is ascribable to the proliferation of rival roles (e.g., parent, son/daughter, friend, worker, member of a club, etc.), different consumption situations (e.g., home *vs* outdoor, individual *vs* group, etc.), belonging to various subcultures (e.g., gender, generational, religious, ethnic subcultures), suspension between real and virtual lives, and different levels of structuring the self (I-self, me-self, looking glass self, etc.). The main implication for segmentation is that postmodern customers cannot be expected to maintain a stable position in the market, nor to comply with the principle of non-contradiction, as suggested by mainstream marketing scholars and managers. Instead, they may swing between different identity positions and enter and leave more segments within limited timeframes. As such, the requisite of exhaustiveness can no longer be supported.

2　*Stability rejected.* Similarly, the tenet of stability also becomes unstable. On the one hand, self-fragmentation accounts for the constant transformation and reconfiguration of the customers' features. On the other hand, however, an even more radical modification has taken place. If customers become interpretive subjects, operating in culturally constructed markets where products, services, brands, and experiences are dense carriers of meanings, their behavior cannot be explained solely (or mainly) in terms of personality traits, genetic imprinting (Arnould *et al.* 2002) or rationality. Their functioning is more likely to conform to cultural categories and principles (McCracken 1986), which are learned by experience and constantly revised through practice. In other words, what characterizes a customer is not written at the outset but steadily updated, thus introducing an element of structural unsteadiness when segmenting the market.

3　*Differentiability reloaded.* The conviction that each segment has to be internally homogeneous and externally heterogeneous is at the very heart of segmentation and cannot be discounted without doing away with segmentation itself. Nonetheless, in light of our discussion, the meaning of differentiability must be revised. Traditional segmentation postulates that consumers are homogeneous inside each market segment because each client is (a) part of a single segment; and (b) behaves consistently with the other parts of the same market group. Cultural segmentation acknowledges the migration of customers across different segments but confirms that their behavior, when part of a given segment, has to be internally consistent. Metaphorically speaking, the traditional approach theorizes that actors are stable in each segment and that they all play the same role, while the cultural view assumes the stability of the role within each segment while actors constantly move back and forth in that role. Hence, the composition of each segment is in a state of transformation while its behavioral features are more steadily maintained.

4　*Measurability and relevance reloaded.* Similarly, the unstable composition of each segment jeopardizes its univocal measurement. Instead of having delineated estimates of the dimensions of each market segment, it is more likely to provide ranges of estimates. Therefore, the economic relevance of each segment is subject to the oscillation embedded in the measurement procedures, which implies some kind of inaccuracy and lack of clarity.

5　*Accessibility reloaded.* As stated, the transition from traditional to cultural marketing has so far increased the unpredictability and complexity of market phenomena, and of segmentation in particular, due to customers' multiple belongingness and high rates of variation and the wobbly measurement and economic calculation. Surprisingly, this transition actually simplifies the way companies interact with their targets with reference to accessibility in that it unlocks some of the gates that usually impede the possibility of reaching a targeted segment. First, the need to identify and utilize large amounts of exclusive media and retailing settings to filter the targeted customers is now attenuated because customers can flow across various segments. This migration of customers across segments, and thus across multiple retailing and communicational formats, expands companies' opportunities to reach the aimed group as well as the locations or mediascapes (Appadurai 1996) that are less consistent with their intended positioning. Second and more relevantly, cultural marketing fully acknowledges the active role played by customers, because the customers participate in the co-creation of the product or service and, thus, in the generation of value (Vargo and Lusch 2004; Borghini and Carù 2008). Consequently, the resources necessary to engender value in a given market segment come to be possessed jointly by the company and its customers. Through the bi-directional participation of managers and customers in the activities of design, production, and consumption, companies can eventually gain access to segments where the requested resources are partially brought in by their customers or are constructed with them. This condition largely is confirmed by empirical evidence, both for the consumer and industrial contexts, and has been shown to reduce the numerous resources that firms must have in order to enter appealing market niches.

When marketing managers confront the market from a cultural perspective, they need to expand their interpretive frames. In particular, with specific reference to the taxonomy of segmentation criteria, a second dimension is added to the classification of criteria. Beyond the distinction between direct and indirect criteria (Table 18.2), it is worth incorporating an additional level wherein segmentation criteria are based on an objective view of the market rather than a co-constructed reading of company–market exchanges. Table 18.2 offers a visual overview of the full set of criteria. In the left column (Q1, Q3), segmentation criteria are associated with the traditional cognitive representation of company–customer relationships, which takes into account adopting indirect or cognitive and behavioral indicators for the purpose of market segmentation. Contrastingly, the two quadrants (Q2, Q4) located on the right incorporate the constructivist view of company–customer exchanges.

Table 18.2 The taxonomy of traditional and cultural segmentation criteria

Typologies	Typologies
Geographical criteria Socio-demographic criteria Psychographic criteria	*Indirect criteria* → Elaboration of the global market culture Elaboration of the national market culture Elaboration of the local market cultures Elaboration of "made in" and "country of origin"
Assumption: Deploy some objective features of the customers that can be used to infer their relation with the product/service	**Assumption:** Deploy the patterns of customers' elaboration of the cultural features of the external market world (extra-somatic culture becoming intra-somatic culture)
Q1	**Q2**
Objective criteria ←	→ Co-constructed criteria
Q3	**Q4**
Behavioral criteria	Consumers' identity projects Consumer tribes and communities Organizational networks *Direct criteria* Market ideologies
Assumption: Deploy some objective cognitive attitudes or behaviors of the customers that are directly referred to the product/service under consideration	**Assumption:** Deploy the patterns customers work out in order to use consumption meanings of a given product/service for their identity projects at individual and/or social level

Co-constructed indirect criteria utilize the cultural features of the market to ground segmentation. More precisely, they use various levels of the market culture – spanning from the global to the local – and question the way different customers have been able to interpret and assimilate these features. Differing from the traditional approach in which global, national and/or local cultures are used for segmentation, culture is never used prescriptively. The cognitive approach postulates that a given culture is always symptomatic of some generalized purchasing and consumption patterns, and can thus be cross-culturally compared to other cultures in order to identify its peculiar traits on which to establish segmentation decisions (see also Geert Hofstede's (n.d.) foundational work). For example, markets can be segmented on the basis of national cultures whenever managers think the behaviors of customers are significantly different at the country level. A company might assume that Chinese are more nationalist than Japanese customers with respect to technological devices, and so prefer local brands to foreign offers. In contrast, the cultural approach does not allow any *a priori* judgement. Individual differences may even exceed cross-cultural ones. From this perspective, managers should be more sensitive to identifying the different patterns of cultural assimilation that various customers exhibit. What matters is the way each customer elaborates the external market culture (i.e., the extra-somatic culture) at an individual or group level (i.e., the intra-somatic culture). As such, the same global, national, or local culture can be variously interpreted and, thus, incorporated by different customers. Therefore, the various interpretive patterns emerging from the company's market configuration ground its real opportunities and boundaries for segmentation.

Furthermore, co-constructed direct criteria focus on the way customers process and utilize the meanings embedded in a given brand, product, or service for their identity building processes. In these ways, managers are not looking widely at the overall cultural landscape and at its appropriation by customers. Rather, they are trying to understand the meanings that customers attach to their specific market offer and how these meanings become part of an identity strategy. Also, identity strategies can be pursued both individually – what Arnould and Thompson (2005) refer to as individuals' identity projects – and collectively within a given group. In the latter case, identity strategies are generated within consumer groups and consumption communities (Cova *et al.* 2007) for business-to-customer (b2c) contexts and within inter-organizational networks in business-to-business (b2b) environments (Nohria and Eccles 1992). Examples are countless. The baby food industry has relied largely on parents' identity projections by offering products that simplify the various role tensions that mothers and fathers often have (e.g., working *vs* nursing, tradition *vs* modernity, masculinity *vs.* femininity, etc.). Brands have also been very powerful tools in marking distinctions within several consumption communities, including bikers (e.g., Ducati *vs.* Harley-Davidson followers), motorists (e.g., Hummer *vs.* city cars) and PC users (e.g., Macintosh *vs.* Windows), among others. For industrial settings, the choice of suppliers can be a powerful lever to communicate the qualities and reliability of its offerings to a company's end customers as it strives to create valid identity positions. For instance, in the building industry the types of construction machinery produced/sold by a company are part of its reputational capital (e.g., having Caterpillar machines means working with a leading provider, with worldwide assistance and integrated know-how, which gives the company a sounder identity position in the industry and makes it more trustworthy to its end clients).

In summary, the underlying effect of cultural marketing on segmentation implies the need for multidimensional approaches to segmentation. Direct/indirect criteria must be matched with objective/co-constructed ones. At the same time, the traditional conditions to perform and assess an effective market segmentation are revised in the light of higher rates of uncertainty, transformation, and fluidity. Overall, the cultural approach confirms the centrality of segmentation for marketing management while adding depth and a new approach to established marketing wisdom. Similarly, cultural targeting is upheld as the evaluation and selection of the market segments to be targeted by the company, with full understanding that targeting should be a bi-dimensional, circular, recursive cultural dialogue involving companies and customers working together.

In the following section we contextualize our discussion of the ethnic market. By comparing three national contexts (the USA, Denmark, and Italy), we show how cognitive and cultural frames modify the segmentation of this market and comment on the necessity of integrating traditional and new criteria.

Segmenting and targeting ethnic consumers: a (cross-)cultural perspective

Cultural segmentation and targeting can be illustrated effectively through the study of ethnic markets because, early on, ethnic consumers were studied in the light of their cultures of reference. In moving from the country of origin to a country of destination, people contextually leave a given cultural environment to enter a different cultural scenario. As such, their process of cultural adaptation (Padilla 1980) is central to understanding the way they reframe their identities, interact with members of their ethnicity as well as the local people, and navigate the meanings of consumption. Predictably, ethnic consumer research first established a strong nexus between the patterns of the customers' cultural patterns and their market behaviors, far beyond any traditional view of culture as a mere external factor affecting human behavior.

Migration flows produce an immense economic phenomenon. With an overall world population reaching almost 7 billion people in 2010, the United Nations forecast an additional demographic boom leading the world population to the dramatic level of 9 billion by 2045. Noteworthy, this jump will be due primarily to the growth of the developing countries, and is thus expected by demographers to expand the already huge stock of immigrants coming from this part of the world significantly. Today, 6.2 percent of the total population in the European Community is immigrant (roughly, 30.8 million people), and approximately 48 million foreigners live in the USA (official and illegal presence as estimated by the Department of Homeland Security in 2009).

In particular, the empirical evidence regarding this market as we present it is based primarily on the three contexts of the USA, Denmark, and Italy, where our research has been conducted over the past decade. Table 18.3 offers a cursory description of these nations and of their different demographic, socio-cultural, institutional, and economic characteristics. For example, the USA has long been acquainted with migration flows, and ethnicity currently is more an issue of second and subsequent generations than of immigration itself. Also, ethnic consumers are socially and economically grouped into ethnic communities, including Latinos, African Americans, Asians, and Native Americans. Conversely, Italy has experienced migration flows from the early 1980s but recently has risen rapidly in the European ranking, scoring third highest in 2010. Its market is unique, since more than 200 different nationalities are present with almost no dominant group. Denmark offers a different pattern. The ethnic population mainly falls into the categories of immigrants and refugees. Immigrants from Turkey, who originally came as guest workers in the 1960s and their

Table 18.3 Ethnic consumers in the USA, Denmark, and Italy

(2010)	USA	Denmark	Italy
Demographics			
Total population	Around 307,000,000*	About 5,500,000**	Around 60,000,000
Foreign residents	Foreign born (37,679,592), Foreign born naturalized (16,028,758), Foreign born not US citizen (21,650,834)	Around 542,000 (this includes immigrants born outside DK and descendants born in DK)	Around 5,000,000
% of total population	15.6	9.8	8.3
First generation	N/A	Around 414,000 (76%)	Around 4,000,000 (80%)
Sex	(49.7% women foreign born, 53.4% women foreign born naturalized, 46.9% women foreign born not US citizens)	40% women	50.5% women
Three main ethnicities/ country of origin	Hispanics or Latino (48,419,324 = 15.7%), Asians (15,989,876 = 5.2%), Black or African American (41,804,073 = 13.6%)	Turkey (59,000 = 10.9%), Germany (30,912 = 5.7%), Iraq (29, 264 = 5.3%)	Romania (18.2%), Albania (11.7%), Morocco (10.7%)
Social context			
Model of integration	Multiculturalism	Government policies are assimilationist. Immigrants hold transnational ties	Mixed and partially inconsistent
Social narratives	Originally an immigrant nation but growing anti-immigration sentiments towards Muslims especially since 9/11, also against the Hispanics mainly crossing from the Mexican border	Existence of negative sentiments concerning the immigrants' alleged exploitation of the welfare system, and bewilderment of the role of Islam in an otherwise secularized society	Mostly negative, related to irregular presences, criminality, Islamism, and competition in the job market
Citizenship	Relatively easy to obtain, can be obtained through naturalization or by birth, *jus sanguinis* and *jus soli*	Can be obtained by birth or by naturalization, *jus sanguinis* and *jus soli*	Hard to obtain; *jus sanguinis*

Continued

Table 18.3 Cont'd

(2010)	USA	Denmark	Italy
Market context			
Value of the ethnic market	Buying power (US$ billion/2009): Hispanics $978; African Americans $910; Asians $509	N/A	Around €40–42 billion/year
Main industries targeting the ethnic market	Food, telecommunication, clothing, housing	Telecommunication, transportation, print and broadcast media, food	Telecommunication, banking, food, retailing
Main brands overtly targeting the ethnic market	Goya, telemundo; also many major brands like McDonald's target different ethnic markets	Lufthansa, Elgiganten	Vodafone, Tim, Western Union, MoneyGram, Coop, IKEA
Main market segments	Mainly organized according to ethnic backgrounds	Mainly organized according to ethnic backgrounds	Seven main segments, according to the rate of acculturation; each ranging from 400,000 to 600,000 people (GfK-Eurisko)
Main targeting problems	Especially the Hispanics and the Asians represent a highly heterogeneous market requiring multiple targeting strategies	Difficult to target ethnic markets due to relatively high heterogeneity	High heterogeneity of the ethnic market (more than 200 nationalities); due to the negative social discourse, risks to impact company's image in case of frontal targeting

Source: *www.uscensus.gov **www.statebank.dk/folk1

descendants, comprise the largest ethnic minority. There also has been an influx of refugees from the former Yugoslavia as well as Somalia.

Segmenting the ethnic market in the three nations is not an easy task. One might be tempted to use nationality or ethnicity to easily trace the boundaries of different consumption patterns. Such an approach equates to using a socio-demographic criterion (i.e., an objective, indirect approach; see Tables 18.1 and 18.2) to infer the particular behaviors of a group of customers on the basis of its ethnic appurtenance. Banco de la Gente, a bank operating in the USA with five branches located in Charlotte, Monroe, and Raleigh (North Carolina), has adopted this strategy since its opening in August 2004. It explicitly targets Hispanics in the United States – both consumers and business entrepreneurs – to the point of having adopted a differentiated marketing strategy. Its website is written in Spanish only (no English version is even available); the bank operates seven days per week, opening hours fit Latino lifestyle (late opening in the morning at 10.30 a.m. and late closing in the evening at 7.30 p.m.), and loud Latin music greets customers who visit the bank offices.

Therefore, the bank's traditional segmentation and targeting decisions are openly ethnic, and may work effectively in the case of: (1) really distinctive behaviors of ethnic consumers; (2) economic relevance of this target; (3) supportive institutional forces, which favor the separation of different ethnic communities within the social arena; and (4) a trusted, distinctive marketing strategy.

However, the same segmentation approach can be disastrous for other products/services in the same geographical market and/or for the same product/service in other geographical locations. Within the USA, and within certain industries, marking an ethnic divide can prove to be counterproductive. While Latinos may have problems accessing banking credit, and, thus, are willing to welcome a dedicated bank facilitating their business, they could be less prone to being addressed as different customers when buying American food or selecting neighborhoods and schools for their children. Here they might feel like other customers in the market, and companies targeting them, should not openly segment the market based on ethnicity. Mattel faced this sort of tradeoff when launching the "black" Barbie. Interestingly, the company went through various stages that relate to the progressive approach of African features in the doll (Figure 18.2). In 1967, Mattel introduced "Colored Francie", a model with dark skin but the same head traits of the traditional Barbie. The following steps were the advent of "Christie" (1968–69), "Black Barbie" (1980), and "So in Style" (2009), eventually incorporating the main features of African-American women. Mattel envisioned these Barbie models as particularly appealing to the prospective African-American target market and also the mainstream girls who might be interested in reproducing the variety of the world in which they live through their collection of dolls.

In the case of Denmark, the ethnic consumers are targeted both by the Danish and the ethnic marketers. The immigrant population can be described as transmigrants that continue to forge and sustain socio-cultural, economic, and political ties with their home countries (Basch *et al.* 1994). Among the forerunners of marketers to this group are transportation and telecommunication companies who offer special rates for the ethnic consumers who travel back to their country of origin and communicate frequently with the family members left behind. Scandinavian Airlines (SAS) established a low-cost subsidiary called Snowflake, and in 2004, among its 12 destinations from Denmark, seven were to destinations in countries and cities of emigration (e.g., Ankara, Istanbul, and Beirut). Similarly, Turkish

Figure 18.2 The transformation of African-American models of Barbie: 1967; 1969; 1980; 2009.

Airlines regularly advertises its direct flights to destinations in Turkey in the Danish media. One Danish telecommunication company, TDC Mobil, printed its ads in Turkish in a Danish newspaper announcing that their customers now could reach the customer service in Turkish.

In Italy, institutional conditions are totally reversed from the USA and those European countries with long migratory traditions (e.g., the UK, France, Germany). First, ethnic consumers have quite recently entered the Italian market. Therefore, the number of offers dedicated to the ethnic market is still limited, and Italian customers are not well acquainted with the emergence of a multicultural market. Second, social representations of immigrants are mostly negative, and messages combine narratives portraying immigrants as deviant with tales of wanting them only provisionally in the country. As such, ethnic consumers are seen neither as stable presences nor presented as a valuable component of the market, despite making up 11.2 percent of the Italian GDP.

Companies are often fearful to overtly target ethnic consumers since they run the risk of reprisals from the mainstream market. Thus, one major Italian bank, UniCredit, launched a specific business network named Agenzia Tu in 2005, through which it originally targeted non-conventional customers (www.agenziatu.it). In theory, non-conventional customers included immigrants as well as young Italian customers and temporary employees. In practice, Agenzia Tu has primarily served an established foreign demand. Nonetheless, its initial communication (advertising and below-the-line) was maintained on the wider representation of the whole customer base, thus not overtly featuring immigrants in the ad (Figure 18.3a). So, no black, Asian or veiled Islamic persons were part of the visual campaign. As such, immigrants could identify with the people in the advertisement due to minor somatic features, whereas Italian customers were more easily deceived. In this way, UniCredit could reach the ethnic market without losing its appeal to its core Italian customer base. To date, the strategy of Agenzia Tu has evolved; 12 agencies are currently operating in Italy, and the bank is now more overtly and significantly involved with migrant customers. It has been training around 300 linguistic and cultural mediators to facilitate the access of foreign customers to its bank services. Also, its communication is now more clearly directed to immigrants (Figure 18.3b), interestingly without losing the support of its various stakeholders.

Sometimes companies may profitably rely upon indirect co-constructed criteria to segment the ethnic market. For example, instead of applying the habitual criterion of nationality/ethnicity (i.e., the socio-demographic approach to market segmentation), they can segment the ethnic market by cutting across nationalities. In this case, companies may provide a trans-cultural market segmentation that stems from the identification of the different acculturation patterns immigrants have achieved (e.g., adaptation, assimilation, resistance and alternation). In effect, former consumer studies document several alternatives that ethnic consumers can adopt to cope with the duality of their cultural references, which can be used as preferable segmentation criteria. Berry (1980) lists and describes eight strategies of cultural adaptation. Peñaloza (1994) restricts her focus to Latinos and shows how people can alternatively: (1) assimilate to the local culture; (2) maintain their original culture; (3) resist adaptation; or (4) segregate. Similarly, in Italy, GfK-Eurisko – the leading market research company – identifies seven market segments (Table 18.3) within the ethnic market, ranging from the so-called "last arrivals", whose consumption patterns are reduced to the minimum and impacted by linguistic differentials, and the "integrated", for whom any form of ad hoc targeting would be irrelevant if not detrimental.

Figure 18.3 Visual communication of Agenzia TU, Italy.

Finally, companies may need to acknowledge the way ethnic consumers interpret and assimilate brand meanings to accomplish their identity projects, individually or collectively. In similar circumstances, only direct co-constructed criteria can account for the meanings attached to the company's market offer. In France, the clothing company Lacoste has experienced difficulties as immigrants have adopted the brand to signal upward social mobility. Given their marginality within the French society, some immigrants have used the well-known, highly reputed brand to force social restructuring and contest their economic segregation. Interestingly, fake Lacoste t-shirts are also used for this purpose, adding complexity to the matter. Similar behavior occurs in the Italian market, where first generation consumers, who usually ignore branded products for their personal shopping, lamenting the superficiality of branding logics, are more likely to buy them for their children. Again, these parents utilize the symbolic potential of branded goods (clothing, food, school garments, etc.) to reduce the social gap between the ethnic Italian kids and their own.

In conclusion, we wish to note that incorporating the centrality of culture to understand ethnic consumers' purchasing and consumption behaviors can be extended to any type of consumer. In other words, ethnic consumers constitute a microcosm in which to analyze culture in action, but most of our ideas can be expanded to include any consumer in the market. Just to quote a case, the financial giant HSBC, founded in Hong Kong but headquartered in London, has long been leveraging cultural heterogeneity beyond the boundaries of ethnicity. Starting from the idea of a multi-ethnic customer base (cf. the HSBC ad "In New York, the whole world is your neighbor"), it rapidly has expanded its identity strategy to include a plurality of customers – both ethnic and local – and their different cultural viewpoints (cf. their ad "The more you look at the world, the more you recognize how people value things differently"). Today, HSBC presents itself as "The world's local bank" (http://www.hsbc.com) and so reconciles the global and the local, the exotic and the familiar, as part of the same whole.

Learning from the field: performing cultural segmentation and targeting

As discussed in the previous section, cultural segmentation and targeting can be extended beyond ethnicity. Whenever customers make sense of consumption through their own cultural lenses and internalize the communication and symbolic potential of products and services to shape their identities, traditional references are not sufficient. As a matter of fact, similar situations are not exclusive to immigrant or ethnic customers but involve the whole market within a scenario we only have just begun to understand.

Table 18.4 proposes a comprehensive summary of the interpretive shift that has occurred during the past few decades, redefining the sense of consumption, the nature of the company–customer relationship, and the marketing practice. Specifically, the peculiar ontological and epistemological starting points held by cultural marketing make consumption readable in more general terms. Consumers' and companies' consumption not only provides a means to meet functional needs, but also (and mainly) is a device to express a sense of identity, establish social and inter-organizational bridges, live unique experiences, and/or indulge in hedonic moments. Grounded in this, marketing strategic decisions must be re-thought. The conditions for segmentation currently are reduced in number, since customers may move fast across segments, thus making it harder to stabilize segment composition and its related measurement. At the same time, the blurring of traditional marketing opens the door to an era of enlarged strategic scenarios.

First, objective criteria for market segmentation are now complemented by co-constructed criteria, which account for the participation of customers in the formulation of the company's offer. Customers can play various roles, including the transfer of technical know-how to the company (think of Ducati bikers participating in the design of the purchased motorcycle), the elaboration of additional or rival expressive meanings, the ritualization of the brand/product's consumption (e.g., the beauty rituals incorporating

Table 18.4 Comparing traditional and cultural perspectives on segmentation and targeting

	Cognitive approach	*Cultural approach*
Ontology	Objective reality and markets	Culturally constructed reality and markets
Epistemology	Objective observation of laws ruling reality	Interpretation of meanings
Consumption	Functional consumption	Symbolic, communicative, identity-making consumption
Segmentation conditions	Differentiability; measurability; relevance; accessibility; exhaustiveness; and stability	Differentiability; measurability; relevance; and accessibility reloaded
Segmentation criteria	Indirect objective criteria Direct objective criteria	Indirect co-constructed criteria Direct co-constructed criteria
Segmentation process	Stage-process: from macro- to micro-segmentation	Dialogical, circular process
Targeting	Defined by the company and closed	Partially defined by the company and open
Positioning	Through brand elements	By means of co-constructed brand narratives

the use of cosmetics), the establishment of social networks around a given brand (e.g., Harley-Davidson, Mac users, *Star Trek*, or the Nutella community), and/or a shared interest (e.g., surfers, climbers, vegans, etc.). As such, the market can be effectively segmented by means of criteria explicitly incorporating the role(s) played by various groups of customers, which ultimately enrich managers' strategic levers.

Second, the scope of strategic marketing is extended since segmentation, targeting, and positioning do not coincide with a sequence of linear steps performed by the company. Instead, they require stable cooperation between the company and its customers, which resembles a dialogue more than a decision chain. However, dialogues are difficult to conduct and are costly. Typically, participation in a dialogue requires reciprocal trust, dependence, respect, and the willingness to invest time and other resources in the process. This means that customers do not only benefit from the dialogue but also are asked to contribute their time and competences, which need to be adequately valued and rewarded to avoid the risk of doubly exploiting customers (by selling them the product/service and benefiting from their work in the dialogue; Cova and Dalli 2009). Since making segmentation, targeting, and positioning a dialogical process is complex, companies should attentively value the returns and customers' availability before undertaking this process.

Finally, the scope of marketing managers' strategic decisions widens in parallel with the broadening of their tools for positioning. Within the traditional perspective, brands and other offerings are positioned by integrating *elements* that jointly gain credence in the minds of the targeted customers. This approach contends that each company drives and controls its positioning by selecting a consistent set of elements. Cultural marketing additionally suggests that positioning can be carried out by leveraging the emotional, social, and expressive valences of the company's brand/supply. Under this assumption, positioning is not achieved by pushing consistent brand elements onto the market but by generating complex and even conflicting brand narratives (Diamond *et al.* 2009) that targeted customers actively interpret.

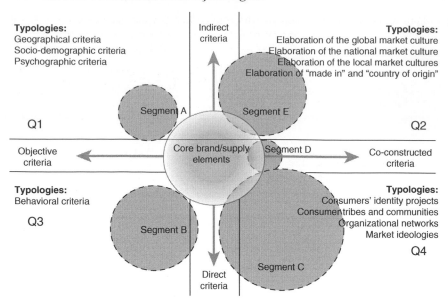

Figure 18.4 Performing cultural segmentation and targeting.
      Source: Photo credits: Luca Visconti.

Conclusion

To systematize our discussion and assist managerial decisions of segmentation and targeting, we offer a recapitulatory model (Figure 18.4). Segmentation and targeting can be defined at the intersection of direct/indirect and objective/co-constructed criteria, as illustrated in Table 18.2. The quadrants on the left (1, 3) describe traditional marketing logics whereas the quadrants on the right (2, 4) complement them with the cultural approach. According to the rate of participation expressed by the company's customers, managers will rely upon objective versus co-constructed criteria, which can be combined whenever different segments show significantly different rates of involvement (mixed segmentation). At the very heart of the model, we locate the company's bundle of brand/supply elements. Also within the cultural perspective, each company must identify the key constituents of its identity.

Within traditional marketing, these core elements are exhaustive and are forced upon the targeted segments. However, within cultural marketing they represent the narrative plot subsequently elaborated on together and supplemented by the company's active audiences. Since no co-construction operates here, the circles describing each segment are tangential to the bundle of brand/supply elements for traditional market segments. Thus, they partially overlap with the company's circle in contexts of co-construction. The larger the overlapping area, the stronger the involvement and participation of the segment represented with the related circle.

Some additional notes help capture the full informative potential of the model. Segments are represented by dotted circles since the composition of segments has become fluid over the past decades (the rejection of exhaustiveness and stability). This means that the same customer can move across segments (here, segment A through E) according to the situation, role, and identity position held at any given time. However, circles representing segments are not overlapping since the condition of differentiability is maintained also within the cultural perspective. Finally, the dimension of these circles indicates the relevance of each segment in terms of the number of customers composing it or the turnover generated.

We hope this chapter has demonstrated that cultural marketing management is particularly receptive to the transformations that have occurred at the social and market level in all the developed economies. With specific reference to strategic marketing, it more distinctively aims at proposing cultural segmentation and targeting as useful complements to cognitive ones.

Review and discussion questions

1   Discuss market segmentation and targeting from the cultural perspective as they differ from the traditional model.
2   Choose a company and discuss its market segmentation and targeting strategies. Discuss whether their strategies adhere more to a traditional model or a cultural one as presented in the chapter.
3   Is there an ethnic market segment in your country? If so, give specific examples of how they are targeted by the marketers.
4   Again, with reference to your country, contrast segmentation strategies of different companies in a given industry and discuss the representation of the markets incorporated in these strategies. You may replicate this analysis with particular reference to immigrant consumers.
5   Give examples of products that are specifically targeted to ethnic consumers. How do the marketing strategies differ from the other products that are targeted to mainstream consumers?
6   Imagine you are the marketing manager of a jeans brand. Describe the criteria you would use to segment your market.
7   Can cultural segmentation and targeting be used for all kinds of products? For what type of products would it not make sense?

Keywords

agglomerated preferences, co-constructed criteria of segmentation, cultural segmentation, cultural targeting, direct criteria of segmentation, homogeneous preferences, indirect criteria of segmentation, macro-segmentation, micro-segmentation, objective criteria of segmentation, segmentation, targeting

References

Abell, D. F. (1980) *Defining the Business*, New York: Prentice Hall.

Appadurai, A. (1996) *Modernity at Large: Cultural Dimensions of Globalization*, Vol. 1, *Public Worlds*, Minneapolis: University of Minnesota Press.

Arnould, E. J. and Thompson, C. (2005) "Consumer Culture Theory (CCT): Twenty Years of Research", *Journal of Consumer Research*, 31: 868–82.

Arnould, E. J., Price, L., and Zinkhan, G. (2002) *Consumers*, New York: McGraw-Hill.

Basch, L. Schiller, N. G., and Blanc, C. S. (1994) *Nations Unbound: Transnational Projects, Postcolonial Predicaments and Deterritorialized Nation-States*, New York: Gordon and Breach.

Berry, J. W. (1980) "Acculturation as Adaptation", in A. M. Padilla (ed.), *Acculturation: Theory, Models, and Some New Findings*, Boulder, CO: Westview Press.

Borghini, S. and Carù, A. (2008) "Co-creating Consumption Experiences: An Endless Innovation", in A. Carù and K. Tollin (eds), *Strategic Market Creation*, Chichester: John Wiley & Sons, Ltd.

Brown, S. (1995) *Postmodern Marketing*, London: Routledge.

Costa, J. A. and Bamossy, G. J. (eds) (1995) *Marketing in a Multicultural World*, Thousand Oaks, CA: Sage.

Cova, B. and Dalli, D. (2009) "Working Consumers: The Next Step in Marketing Theory?", *Marketing Theory*, 9(3): 315–39.

Cova, B., Kozinets, R. V. and Shankar, A. (eds) (2007) *Consumer Tribes*, Oxford: Elsevier.

Diamond, N., Sherry, J. F. Jr., Muñiz, A. M. Jr., McGrath, M. A., Kozinets, R. V. and Borghini, S. (2009) "American Girl and the Brand Gestalt: Closing the Loop on Sociocultural Branding Research", *Journal of Marketing*, 73: 118–34.

Firat, A. F. and Shultz II, C. J. (1997) "From Segmentation to Fragmentation. Markets and Marketing in the Postmodern Era", *European Journal of Marketing*, 31(3/4): 183–207.

Firat, A. F. and Venkatesh, A. (1995) "Liberatory Postmodernism and the Reenchantment of Consumption", *Journal of Consumer Research*, 22: 239–66.

Hofstede, G. (n.d.) Available at: www.geert-hofstede.com

Kerin, R. A., Hartley, S. W., Berkowitz, E. N., and Rudelius, W. (2006) *Marketing*, 8th edn, New York: McGraw-Hill.

Kotler, P. and Armstrong, G. (2006) *Principles of Marketing*, 11th edn, London: Prentice Hall.

Lambin, J. J. (1998) *Le marketing stratégique*, Paris: Ediscience international.

McCracken, G. (1986) "Culture and Consumption: A Theoretical Account of the Structure and Movement of the Cultural Meaning of Consumer Goods", *Journal of Consumer Research*, 13(1): 71–84.

McDonald, M. and Dunbar, I. (2004) *Market Segmentation: How to Do It, How to Profit from It*, New York: Elsevier.

Nohria, N. and Eccles, R. (eds) (1992) *Networks and Organizations*, Boston: Harvard Business School Press.

Padilla, A. M. (ed.) (1980) *Acculturation: Theory, Models, and Some New Findings*, Boulder, CO: Westview Press.

Peñaloza, L. (1994) "Atraversando Fronteras/Border Crossing: A Critical Ethnographic Exploration of the Consumer Acculturation of Mexican Immigrants", *Journal of Consumer Research*, 21(1): 32–54.

Peter, J. P. and Donnelly, J. H. Jr. (2008) *A Preface to Marketing Management*, 11th edn, New York: McGraw-Hill.

Pride, W. M. and Ferrell, O. C. (2004) *Foundations of Marketing*, Boston: Houghton Mifflin Company.

Solomon, M., Bamossy, G. J. and Askegaard, S. (1999) *Consumer Behavior: A European Perspective*, Harlow: Prentice Hall.

Vargo, S. L. and Lusch, R. F. (2004) "Evolving to a New Dominant Logic for Marketing", *Journal of Marketing*, 68(1): 1–17.

19 Driving a deeply rooted brand

Cultural marketing lessons learned from GM's Hummer advertising

Marius K. Luedicke

Overview

This chapter explains how marketers can use netnographic, ethnographic, and historical analysis of a brand's socio-cultural environment to surface local, deeply rooted beliefs and values that influence how a brand resonates with consumers. Drawing from General Motors' (GM) culturally most and least sensitive advertisements for its Hummer brand of vehicles, the chapter discusses how brands can tap into powerful cultural tensions that traditional marketing research, positioning/targeting, and communication methods tend to overlook. It suggests that marketers should carefully study the cultural patterns and ideological conflicts that surround their brands; listen to owners' and critics' definitions of their brands' cultural meanings; and attune their advertising messages to either strengthening their buyers' ideological position, or trying to bridge the socio-cultural divide with conciliatory meanings. This culture-sensitive approach helps commercial and NGO brand managers to connect their brands with powerful cultural patterns rather than wasting advertising dollars on producing socio-cultural backlashes.

Driving a deeply rooted brand

> Every single time I go to the southwest, I get accosted by these monstrosities, these repugnant road beasts, these vile vehicular examples of the greedy, lazy Americans. I hate Hummers. H1, H2 or H3, I hate them with a passion that burns as intensely as a thousand suns. I also have serious questions about the value of Hummer owners as human beings. I'm trying really hard to reserve judgment.
>
> (Csosa, 2005)

When GM first introduced the Hummer line of vehicles in 2002, the brand almost instantly provoked passionate responses from American consumers. The Hummer truck's iconic, boxy design spoke of freedom, capability, and security. No matter how much the Hummer H2 and H3 vehicles departed from the military predecessor, the High Mobility Multi-purpose Wheeled Vehicle ("HUMVEE"), their design and functionality left no doubt that owners were superiorly equipped to escape natural or social threats of any epic dimension. Owing to the brand's prominent role in Operation Desert Storm in 1991, Schwarzenegger's dramatic HUMVEE entrance at the Academy Awards in 1991, the Middle East wars following 9/11, the doomsday movie spectacle *The Day After Tomorrow* in 2004, or the devastating Hurricane Katrina in 2005, Americans found it easy to imagine themselves roaring away from a desolate scene in a Hummer truck, leaving less fortunate drivers behind, stranded or washed away. Unlike most brands, the Hummer was deeply rooted in American culture long before it entered the commercial sport utility vehicle (SUV) market. Only a handful of brands before have been so deeply rooted in their home market's national identity and developed such a strong cultural connection to its identity conflicts. Among them are long-standing national icons such as Harley-Davidson and Coca-Cola, but also newer brands such as Ben and Jerry's ice cream and Sweat-X clothes, or celebrity brands such as Barack Obama and Arnold Schwarzenegger.

What an exceptional asset for managers to be able to build a brand that is already connected to national meanings so strong that some citizens are ready to defend them with their lives! But what if marketers ignore these meanings and push a potentially conflicting idea of what the brand should stand for? When starting and managing the Hummer brand, GM rigorously followed key marketing and branding principles popularized by the influential writings of Philip Kotler and Kevin Lane Keller (2008), Jean-Noël Kapferer (2008), David Aaker (2002), Christian Homburg *et al.* (2009), and many others. These textbooks advised GM with good reason, that in order to build a brand successfully, they must create compelling brand meanings and associations that resonate with a well-defined target group of customers in a specific local environment.

Using the case of GM's advertising for the short-lived Hummer brand as an illustrative example, I will show that these traditional procedures tend to underestimate the extent to which consumers attach meanings to brands that may not overlap with those created by an authoritarian firm. And I will show that the audiences relevant for a brand's success are not only the target groups, but also groups of consumers that love to hate the brand. The Hummer case evidences that neglecting deeply rooted, consumer-made social and cultural connections of a brand with a national identity can produce detrimental marketing decisions that contribute to prematurely killing a brand before its time.

This chapter explains how marketers can study the cultural patterns and ideological conflicts that surround their brands, translate these insights into resonant advertising messages, and thus leverage the equity of their brands. This culture-sensitive approach to positioning a brand in an ideological context helps commercial and NGO brand managers to connect their brands better with existing cultural patterns rather than spending advertising dollars on producing socio-cultural backlashes.

The birth of the Hummer brand

To begin, let us take a step back and sneak into the marketing department of GM on a sunny Detroit day in early 1999. We hear a group of senior marketing executives discussing the latest results from a national market research project that was started to explore opportunities to satisfy customers' rising demands for extra-large SUVs. The research team has confronted potential buyers with a series of prototypes with alternating GM brand labels attached to them. To their surprise, they found that a militaristic, boxy SUV prototype garnished with a fictitious HUMMER logo sparked the most remarkable responses among their respondents. Americans, so the data suggested, wanted a truck that carried the meanings of military ruggedness, security and sophistication. By the end of the day, GM marketers had decided to pitch "Project Maria"[1] to their general management. And they won.

Soon after the board's decision, the team started negotiations with AM General, the producer of the military HUMVEE and the first civilian version of the truck owned by Arnold Schwarzenegger. Their goal was to co-produce a new line of civilian luxury vehicles named

Hummer. About three years later, the first Hummer H2 (Figure 19.1) left the GM production line at Mishawaka, Indiana. The marketing team got it right. In the US market, the brand hit a nerve with its iconic design and its bold message of distinction. Sales sky-rocketed from the start (see Figure 19.2).[2]

Figure 19.1 A Hummer H2.
  Source: Photo credits: Marius Luedicke.

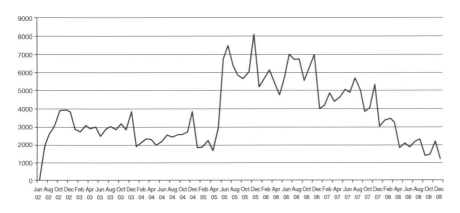

Figure 19.2 Averaged monthly unit sales of Hummer vehicles.
  Note: Hummer H2 sales started in June 2002. The H3 was launched in May 2005.
  Source: GM investor relations website.

The traditional positioning/targeting and communication approach

> At HUMMER our customers can't be labeled by color, gender or creed. HUMMER is a mindset. A mindset of daring, self-assured, entrepreneurial people who see HUMMER as being a reflection of themselves – unique.
>
> (Randy Foutch, Hummer marketing analyst)

Following the prescriptions of the leading branding experts such as Aaker (2002), Keller (2008), and Kapferer (2008), GM marketers targeted the Hummer brand to appeal to affluent consumers who characterize themselves as "rugged individualists," those people who would skydive, mountain climb, trail bike, camp, fish and hunt; but also as "achievers," who wanted to reward themselves for having accomplished ambitious goals in sports, business, or the arts. According to Hummer's marketing management, prospective Hummer drivers identified themselves as "daring, self-assured, entrepreneurial, individualistic" people, who had no problems with defying social conventions.

In the next traditional step, Hummer was positioned against off-road champion and World War I veteran Jeep and the emerging class of luxurious SUVs. Even though Hummer was clearly part of an existing luxury SUV segment, it was positioned as a "class of its own." The Hummer claim readily reflected this ambitious positioning: "Hummer – Like nothing else." For Hummer marketers, this promise was easily fulfilled. Owing to its iconic, militaristic, masculine, and rugged design, the Hummer stood out in the masses of extra large Navigators (Lincoln), Excursions (Ford), Tahoes (Chevrolet), Yukons (GMC), or Escalades (Cadillac). Drawing from the original HUMVEE's cultural legacy, the brand also carried deep meanings of militaristic ruggedness and sophistication that were unique in the SUV market. For Jeep, who has carried such connotations decades earlier, these associations seemed to have long faded.

It seemed that marketers would only need to announce the birth of the Hummer to sell out the dealers' lots. In fact, Hummer introduced the brand with TV commercials that almost entirely ignored the trucks' particular cultural legacy. Marketers aired ads named "Urban Techno" and "Giddyup" that appealed to lovers of computer graphics and club culture, but seemed disconnected from the rugged individual defined as their core target group. Hummer marketers also broadcasted spots such as "Training Day" or "Submarine" that pointed at the functional capabilities of the truck, but not at the cultural meanings of the underlying icon.[3] It seemed the Hummer brand entered the market with enough iconic design and history to find buyers despite these contradictory messages. Customers quickly filled the void opened by the lack of commercial prescriptions and connected in own stories and meanings the Hummer themselves with national myths that have permeated the American cultural context for centuries. These long-standing cultural narratives were well represented by the Hummer trucks, but not related to techno music, or submarine trucks, or training days.

Limitations of the traditional approach

When the smaller H3 model was introduced to the US market in May 2005, it became apparent how little GM's traditional marketing approach accounted for the deep cultural roots of its Hummer brand.

GM marketers again followed classic textbook positioning/targeting and communication procedures when imagining, designing, and communicating the Hummer H3. As a Hummer manager reports, the marketing team learned from customer surveys that 40 percent of the H2 buyers were female, that the truck was considered too expensive for selling to a mass market, that it was too thirsty for not being despised as a gas-guzzler, and that it was too big to be effortlessly parked.

Their conclusions were unambiguous: build a truck that is significantly smaller and lower priced, ecologically friendly, and with a friendlier design that appeals to female buyers. Ironically, the new H3 looked strikingly similar to the 2005 Jeep Grand Cherokee, its main competitor.[4]

If we presume that GM's agency Modernista was briefed to communicate these new features, the campaign was right on target. The agency tried the new H3 ads to be humorous and welcoming to female buyers while highlighting the practical features of the smaller models. For its most straightforward functional ad, Modernista showcased an old-fashioned magician character that showed Americans the "magic" of parking a Hummer in a low-clearance parking garage (obviously pointing at the difficulties that H2 owners experienced with parking). Lance Jenson of Modernista admits: "The parking commercial, that's pretty, like, 'duh.' But we had to do it because being maneuverable is important to a lot of people."[5] This ad not only establishes quite remote and irritating cultural references, but also disobeys McMath and Forbes' (1998) classic rule "Don't mess with your cash cow." These authors remind marketers not to discredit the features of their most successful product (i.e. large size/not easy to park) when introducing a line extension.

From a culture-sensitive branding perspective, GM's traditional positioning/targeting approach got even more bizarre. In an attempt to build cultural capital for the brand, Hummer brand managers created a story of a tofu-eating male who acquires a Hummer H3 to regain the respect of a meatpacking guy that has looked down on him at a supermarket checkout. The spots' punch line read: "Reclaim your manhood." This presumably self-ironic ad made strong references to "compensatory consumption" appeals (Holt and Thompson 2004), by suggesting quite squarely that consumers can make up for a lack of masculinity by driving a Hummer. The online version of this spot surprisingly came with a different claim: "Restore the balance." But that was not much better. The second spot in this series featured a woman who buys a Hummer H3 in response to her child being harassed by the kid of another woman at a public playground. The claim: "Get your girl on" also evoked the unfavorable cultural frame of compensatory consumption. Together, these ads suggested that Hummers are for the weak, which directly contradicts both the traditional goal of targeting self-assured, rugged individualists and the deeper cultural references of the brand. These ads were quickly erased from the public eye (including the internet), most likely owing to massive complaints from Hummer owners and dealers that hated the socio-cultural corner in which they were pushed by these messages (see below).

Lastly, at Superbowl 2006, Modernista married a Godzilla-type monster with a giant low-tech, tin toy robot. These two ugly giants fell in love while devastating a city of apparently Asian style and layout. The two monsters lay together and the Godzilla-type gave birth to a small Hummer H3 that drove off from their hands through the devastated cityscape. The caption: "It's a little monster."[6]

Hummer owners and dealers that I spoke to over the course of our research project expressed little appreciation for these commercials even though they seemed to address the right target group and some even delivered the key messages: practicability, female drivers wanted, and the image of Hummer as more rugged and "mean" than other brands. But how had Hummer owners perceived the "Reclaim your Manhood"[7] and "Get Your Girl on" television spots? A top-selling Californian Hummer dealer explains in our interview:

These spots were just bad marketing. I think that was very bad marketing. They had another H3 and H2 ad out last year or the year before where they had some weird one with techno music on and the car kept changing shape and there was this weird kaleido-scope thing going on. That was annoying. Those were made to drive the younger people to buy the car. But half of those people haven't graduated from college and can't afford to buy the car. They were like "hey, that is a cool little ad" but it had nothing to do with the car really or anything. Then they had the new one where the guy jumps off the pier and kind of goes in the water and his car turns into the submarine and goes into all that stuff. And the Godzilla commercial, that lost me. How you get a car from a robot and Godzilla creature getting together? Poor advertising! I think people looked at it cause it was a funny ad, but they couldn't remember what the ad was for or about. They just remembered it was a monster and a robot.

Such responses show that even for the most devoted Hummer enthusiasts these ads clearly missed the point of the Hummer's deep cultural heritage. The spots insulted existing owners rather than supporting their consumer identity projects. The tofu ad, though intended to be ironically self-critical, mainly delivered the idea to our respondents that Hummer is about attenuating a weak self-confidence, a notion that was insulting the intelligence of both Hummer drivers and (sometimes Hummer-hating) vegetarians. The "little monster" spot also subtly fired the public discourse about Hummer owners being racists and prodigals of American natural resources. The two giants were meeting while carelessly destroying a city of an Asian metropolitan layout and gave birth to the H3 in this foreign country. Apparently, that was not the kind of cultural practice that Hummer owners wanted to be associated with, nor was the city relating particularly well to Hummer's American cultural background.

Despite this heap of "poor advertising," Hummer H2 and H3 trucks sales patterns largely followed the typical lifecycle of GM's extra large mass market SUVs, i.e. the GMC Yukon or the Chevrolet Tahoe (see Figure 19.2 for a comparison). However, in contrast to its sib-lings that have been around for decades (GMC has been around for more than 100 years, Chevrolet for more than 90), the Hummer brand was discontinued after only 7.4 years of market presence.

Could GM have sold more Hummers or significantly extended the length of the brand life cycle, if they had better catered to the brand's deep cultural connections? I cannot give a definite answer here, since market success depends on more than just good positioning/targeting and communication, but in the next sections I offer empirical evidence-based insights that allow for some educated recommendations.

The culture-sensitive approach to positioning/targeting and communication

I have 2 Hummers, an H2 & a SUT. Our experiences:

Love – We get waved to by children like we are driving a fire truck. People are constantly asking us to sit in, look in & even feel it. Many thumbs up and "I wish I had one."

Hates – People actually try and cut us off on the freeway. We have been cussed at, yelled at, given the thumbs down for "killing children" (not sure what that was about). Six times in the last three months people have tried to steal a parking spot from us when we were waiting first. When we confronted one, the guy actually jump out of his truck and acted like he was going to go after my wife. Then I jumped out and he sped off shouting cuss words at us.

This only makes me want to drive a Hummer more. Why be like everyone else, when you can make a statement and cause much hooplah everyday!

(John, email interview)

No doubt, defining the target group's individual attitudes and characteristics such as "daring," "entrepreneurial" and "unconventional" is important for marketers to get a sense of whom to sell to and where to find these potential buyers. But as the Hummer case shows, deeply rooted brands like Hummer thrive on shared cultural narratives, many of which precede the manufacturers' brand-building activities. Hummer touches upon more than just individuals' preferences for distinctly designed, comfortable, parkable, secure, and capable sport utility vehicles. The brand rather evokes a set of almost sacrosanct national identity narratives that matter to a large fraction of American consumers more than any functional, emotional, or social symbolic feature of the brand.

To surface these influential narratives, we can ask very broadly what kinds of tensions the Hummer brand produces in American popular culture. Why have Hummer owners – not owners of equally big and thirsty Ford or Cadillac SUVs – become prime targets of the most passionate brand-mediated social conflicts in recent history? And why are Hummer trucks – not Navigators, Escalades, or Excursions – keyed, spat on, parked in, cut off, and "flipped off" for their owners' presumed "misbehavior" most (Luedicke and Giesler 2008)?

Yet, we may also wonder why so many American consumers passionately love the Hummer brand, even though many of their social peers and international observers rate the vehicle among the most ecologically destructive choice on the consumer market. Do Hummer drivers actually hate the environment? Which cultural models do they use to frame Hummer ownership as true and faithful to the American identity rather than as the vehicle of choice for ignorant, self-absorbed polluters?

The thesis of this chapter is that accurate answers to these questions provide marketers with important cultural knowledge needed for successfully positioning/targeting and communicating brand meanings that are deeply rooted in cultures that lie beyond their direct influence.

The following sections explain how brand managers and anti-brand activists may gain knowledge on these cultural meanings and use it to better achieve their communication goals. I begin by outlining a procedure of culture-sensitive research that has proven useful for understanding the cultural grounds on which the Hummer brand thrived, and then use the Hummer case to detail three cultural positioning/targeting and communication strategies that build communication on cultural tensions, not individual, functional preferences.

Study the cultural nexus of the brand

To resolve the puzzle of what Hummer means for consumers in the US, we drew upon three established consumer culture research methods: netnography, ethnography, and historical research. Inspired by the passionate cultural conflict about the brand, my colleagues Craig J. Thompson, Markus Giesler and I started with netnographic desk research as described by Robert Kozinets (2002) to gain an overview of the diverse discourses that evolved around the Hummer in the US context. This step included searching the internet for websites, forums, and blogs that held discussions about the Hummer brand. We studied and clustered

The ideology of American exceptionalism embraces a set of beliefs and visions that position the American nation as a global cultural and political leader (in metaphoric terms as a "City Upon a Hill"), as a nation of independent, rugged and solidary individuals (the "Cowboy in the White Hat"), and as a nation of forward-looking entrepreneurs and unlimited natural resources (as in the "American Frontier" myth). In addition to and as a result of the nation's idea of an exceptional role in the world's geo-political scheme, many Americans feel not only that they inhabit a superior social system, but also one that (almost naturally) attracts the negativity of terrorists, political activists, environmentalists and social critics that question America's morally leading role in the geo-political scheme and discredit the nation as ruthless, greedy, and hegemonic. Historical research has shown that this feeling of being besieged by other nations or internal critics emerged with the nation claiming the moral high ground as a global social, cultural, and economic leader vis-à-vis the encrusted social systems of old Europe. The myth of being besieged is very strong in American culture and is frequently updated through socio-cultural occurrences. In 2001, the 9/11 terrorist attacks dramatically re-produced the idea of being under siege and, in consequence, brought many American citizens temporarily closer together in their desire to defend endangered American values.

The besiegement motive also allows American consumers to frame environmental, political, and consumerist critics as enemies of American identity. In this view, Americans who critique and try to restrict other people's consumption choices (e.g. by flipping off a Hummer driver) are violating *laissez-faire* and rugged individualism cultural traditions. They are thus metaphorically aligned with the prophet Jeremiah lamenting about the decline of his people's morals and the imminent end of the world. We refer to this form of this critique as the "Jeremiad against consumerism" (Luedicke *et al.* 2010). Framing a social critique of Hummer driving as an expression of the anti-American, anti-consumerist, anti-capitalist "Jeremiad" allows our Hummer informants to experience these historically rooted feelings of being besieged, and to rhetorically and physically defend their consumption choices against their critics (see John's report on his Hummer experiences above).

The myth of the American frontier raises another view of American consumption that is key to understanding Hummer ownership and its critique. We found that Hummer owners have no difficulties in combining environment protection with off-road driving. Other than their critics, owners consider off-road driving an appreciation and consumption of a beautiful yet abundant nature, rather than a destruction of pristine ecosystem.

When our informants are criticized for consuming too much gas and caring too much about their own interest, they are likely to respond with two arguments that draw legitimacy from the ideology of American exceptionalism: "What I buy or drive is none of your business" (*laissez-faire*) and "You do not understand what America is all about. Your behavior is betraying the nation's values" (being besieged). In the light of the besiegement discourse, an anti-Hummer critique as expressed, for instance, through insulting bumper stickers that seek to educate owners about their "excessive" pollution is likely to strengthen the owners' feelings of being besieged and thus strengthen their brand relationships. Some Hummer owners that I have met are biologists, scientists, teachers, and farmers who live far out in the woods and possess extensive knowledge about their surrounding nature. They believe in rugged individualism, self-dependence, and *laissez-faire* as nationally shared cultural ideals that also stretch into the realm of free consumption choices. In their view, Hummer consumption is not a threat to the social or ecological system that they hold dear, but rather serves the local and national community.

Robert's report on the activities of his local Hummer owners group reflects an extreme version of this view:

> Why Hummers are good for the environment? [Our group] donated over 2,000 hours to the SBNFA, donated over $5,000 in cash to SBNFA, donated over $30K in toys to the USMC reserve for Toys for Tots in 2005, donated over 10,000 hours in disaster relief at Katrina and Rita Efforts: Four Wheeling can be good for the environment and its people.
>
> (Robert, interview)

If critiqued for unnecessarily spilling oil, our informants have frequently argued, for instance, that their country has experienced at least three phases of media-made peak oil panic that came and went without any notable impact. Their critics, they find, are hypocrites who care for their own media careers more than for hard science facts.

In summary, the consumers' diverging positions towards morally legitimate contemporary interpretations of the boundless frontier, the rugged individual, the city upon a hill and the besieged/captivity narrative split the American people (squarely) into two camps: those who seek to affirm the traditional tenets of American exceptionalism through their consumption choices and narratives, and those who criticize this identity system and its cheerleaders for their excessive self-interest and greed. Of course, both fractions claim the moral high ground for their own vision of contemporary American identity.

But how does this relate to the Hummer brand and its positioning in the American market? I argue that the positioning of a brand alongside or against one of two oppositional cultural positions – in our context the "affirmative" vs. the "critical" take on American exceptionalism – is a more promising path to crafting culturally resonant brand messages than pursuing a position and target group on the basis of individual character traits and consumers' sociodemographics.

Consider the following GM advertisements in the light of the affirmative and critical views on American exceptionalism: by connecting Hummer owners with insecure vegetarians or fearful mothers, GM first of all insulted rugged individualists and, second, aligned Hummer owners with their social antagonists, i.e., "Jeremiad" activists who critique other consumers for their consumption choices. But Hummer also aired at least two spots that – in contrast to most spots – catered almost perfectly to the tensions produced by the myths of American exceptionalism. In the spot "The Big Race," a boy builds a Hummer-like soapbox vehicle to beat the competing kids by racing down the hill in a direct off-road route instead of following the serpentine trail that all other kids pursued. The cunning, rule-defying behavior of the boy reflected the mindset of an independent, self-reliant American explorer that breaks with cultural conventions for the sake of progress (and fun). For Hummer haters, in turn, this commercial offered food for agitation: though cute and clever, the Hummer-box kid disobeyed the rules of the game and, later down the hill, even blocked the road for the faster kids who tried to pass him at the home stretch.

The second, and culturally-sensitive, Hummer ad called "The Right Tool" shows a series of events in which individuals use life-saving tools under life-threatening circumstances. First, a fire fighter rushes towards a burning wall (caption: "Heat resistant to 1,500°"), then a staggering man fires a light bullet on a deserted mountain ("Visible up to 20 miles"), then a climber falls into his robe from an extreme height ("8,000 LB tensile strength") and lastly a Hummer H3 with full outdoor gear climbs up an almost impossibly steep terrain with engine roaring saying: "Scales 60% inclines." The ad closes with the claim "Purpose built."

This ad is the most culturally-sensitive among all Hummer ads even though it superficially delivers a functional message. The spot makes references to 9/11 besieged motives (the heroic fire fighter), to contemporary versions of the rugged frontier-exploring individual (climbers, mountaineers), and to male fascination with technical achievement. Other than its predecessors, the ad does not focus on references to social class (like "First Day" described below) or cultural styles (like "Techno"). Rather than framing the truck as a toy for self-absorbed urban professionals, GM framed the truck in this ad as a tool that has legitimacy in the American cultural system.

Address cultures, not individuals

How can these kinds of insights be useful for brand managers? Our three-step research, as detailed above, has helped reveal what the brand means for American consumers not only at an individual character traits or demographics level, but at a more deeply rooted level of long-standing, shared, cultural myths and narratives. Before the Hummer SUV hit the road, the HUMVEE was already a cultural icon, reflecting American military achievement and the nation's globally leading role. Later, Hummer owners used their trucks for pleasure and self-reward, but also to help their fellow citizens (e.g. as Hurricane Katrina hit New Orleans in 2005, Hummer owners provided extensive first aid support with their trucks) and to protect the environment (e.g. a group of Hummer owners frequently support Californian park authorities to clean up trails from boulders by use of their capable trucks) in the spirit of affirmative American exceptionalism. Critical consumers, instead, used the brand as a diagnostic tool for questioning American exceptionalism and its detrimental impact on the nation's long-term survival.

Marketers of brands that strike such a powerful ideological chord face a particular challenge: whether they let consumers define the most significant cultural meanings for the brand, to affirm their buyers' cultural beliefs and provoke the brand's antagonists, or to bridge the cultural divide between opposing camps. There are no definite answers to this question, since strategies depend on cultural context, but the following three generic strategies to driving a deeply rooted brand are worth considering for marketers.

Strategy 1: Let consumers do the magic

One option to cater to a brand with a strong cultural nexus is to let consumers lead the creation of brand meaning. As its products and logos already carry powerful references to culture, marketers can announce the launch of the new brand and explain its product's key features largely without trying to define precisely what kind of people are meant to love, buy and hate the brand, what it stands for socially, or what values the brand wishes to promote. If the brand resonates with some cultural corner of the market, consumers will take care of the meaning creation process. The underlying strategy is akin to what Alex Wipperfürth (2005) celebrates as a "serendipitous brand hijack" that is widely discussed in studies concerning the rise of co-production between consumers and producers (Arvidsson 2008; cf. Chapters 11 and 12 in this volume). As with open source brands (Pitt *et al.* 2006), consumers will surround "their" brand with resonant meanings and narratives that they feel align best to their individual and collective identity projects within a given cultural context.

The marketing department is called to observe, follow up, and interpret the meanings, artifacts, and cultural references that consumers make and turn them into culture-sensitive messages. What is it that people see in the brand, and how do they use and frame it? What, if any, contemporary cultural discourses do they connect with this brand?

Hummer initially started with communications akin to this empty canvas strategy. Yet even though they carefully defined their target group and key messages, the first ads came across to our informants at best as obscure. The ad "First Day" can be seen as Hummer marketers' attempt to address consumers' criticism to the brand. The spot highlighted just the opposite view: A caring mother of three children driving her eldest son to school with the other two kids secured on the backseats. As the little boy is observed jumping out of a black Hummer H2 on his first day at a new school, the ad suggests, he is right away endowed with enough social capital to not be bullied by taller kids that await him walking towards the entrance. The ad supports the idea of Hummers being driven by responsible mothers who fully support their daring, individualistic children and contradicts the idea that Hummer owners are selfish, ignorant, and masculinity-compensating males. Of course, antagonists can also use the spot to frame mother and children as insecure consumers who need the support of a brand to compensate for their insecure personalities. This ad fires the brand discourse, as it provides both parties with visual and narrative ammunition to defend their side of the moral divide. In this ad, Hummer supported only one ("their") side, a strategy I detail next.

Strategy 2: Support one side of the cultural divide

A second way of building on the above kinds of cultural knowledge is to position a brand to explicitly leverage one side of the ideological divide and accept it will provoke a cultural uproar. This strategy is closest to the traditional positioning/targeting and communication approach, but does not remain on the level of individual traits or preferences. Instead, it leverages one side of a moral or ideological dispute and thus leverages a powerful social conflict rather than just individual attitudes and lifestyles.

In the case of Hummer, such a strategy would have resulted in marketing messages that celebrate freedom, independence, reward for individual achievement, enjoyment of nature, solidarity, and rugged individualism, while ignoring themes like environmentalism, political criticism, vegetarianism, or social inferiorities. In this vein, Hummer could have tried not to hide the poor gas mileage of the trucks, but rather connected its gas consumption to its functional capability (as implied in "The Right Tool"), a link that is well accepted among Hummer owners and likely provocative for anti-Hummer activists that do not believe in the truck's capability. The benefit of this strategy for a firm is that it can powerfully appeal to one customer segment and create buzz among the opposite camp via negative press.

In the Hummer case, negative publicity has throughout fostered brand awareness and recognition. But if strategically consistent, Hummer marketers would have followed this second strategy better by fostering images of free and independent explorers, rugged individuals who do not care about other people's opinions while exploring the boundless frontier in their Hummers. The spot "Big Race" that I have described above gets closest to this strategy.

Key to successful communication that aspires to leverage the ideology of American exceptionalism (as one among many different potentially influential meaning systems) is to cheer the values of the American nation while avoiding complaints about the citizens' or nation's potential failures. Complaints (or even calls for more ecological consumption) likely result in the type of anti-Jeremiad counter-resistance explained above (Frank 2004).

Strategy 3: Bridge the gap

The third strategy echoes the suggestions put forward by Douglas Holt (2003, 2004) in his work on iconic branding. Holt suggests that brands can gain iconic status if they help individuals to attenuate tensions emerging between their own identity position and the demands directed at them by the surrounding popular world. The key is a rhetorical resolution of an internal tension by implicitly communicating to consumers that the brand celebrates an alternative, almost rebellious identity position that does not try to live up to the dominant social norms. In the Hummer case, there is no clearly dominant or subordinate group. Hence, a bridging strategy would have to situate the brand between the two camps of citizens that share affirmative or critical views towards the tenets of American exceptionalism. This can generally be done by addressing shared national identity projects, such as advancing a path-breaking, fearless, noble, entrepreneurial, and independent nation.

However, the Hummer brand had little currency for adopting such a strategy, unless the brand had credibly managed to combine weight and engine power with social and ecological sustainability. Despite all odds, Governor Arnold Schwarzenegger pursued this strategy with his Hydrogen-Hummer initiative. By promoting the development of a hydrogen drive powerful enough to power (even) a Hummer and by calling for a network of hydrogen stations along Californian highways, Schwarzenegger celebrated the affirmative image of Californians driving the biggest trucks (e.g. *laissez-faire*, rugged individualism) while conserving clean air and pristine natural resources. This strategy allowed Schwarzenegger to subtly address the needs of both parties while only earning disapproval at the extreme ends of the political spectrum. GM and its Hummer division, however, were not equally credible (and comfortable) in the role of the technological and social innovator.

Marketers operating in other American industries or in different cultural contexts may find resonant ways to bridge ideological gaps with technological and communicative means. Bridging, it seems, is the most sustainable option if the brand goes for a mass market, but letting consumers define the meaning of the brand and then supporting one side of the emerging divide seems particularly viable for niche market brands.

Conclusion

This chapter has illustrated how ethnographic, netnographic, and historical research findings can be translated into culture-sensitive positioning/targeting and communication strategies for brands that build upon deeply rooted cultural meanings. Such brands forge particularly strong links to history and culture within a given social context, and often also inherit their socio-cultural conflicts.

Using the Hummer case as illustration, I have argued that managers who want to position/target and communicate a deeply rooted brand are well advised to analyze the social, cultural, and historical narratives underlying their brands and study consumers' contemporary interpretations thereof rather than focusing on individual attitudes, lifestyles, or socio-demographic factors. Such cultural insights may allow marketers to pursue three strategies for cultural positioning/targeting and communication: (1) letting consumers do the magic; (2) supporting one side of a cultural divide; and (3) bridging the gap between opposing camps. In order to position the brand unambiguously on existing cultural grounds, marketers define which deep cultural meanings they wish to leverage, e.g. by speaking to rugged individualistic drivers, or to environmentalists, or rather letting consumers and mass media define the cultural meanings that attach best to their brand before they build upon these emerging discourses.

In the empirical case of Hummer advertising, I have shown that the Hummer brand unfolded a particularly strong cultural resonance right from the start because it crystallized two opposing visions of American national identity, one that seeks affirmation and another that seeks to redress the tenets of the ideology of American exceptionalism. However, Hummer marketers have apparently not chosen to consistently support the affirmative side of the cultural divide that drives the brand system (Luedicke 2005), but by clinging to classic individual targeting procedures have sent ambiguous and sometimes insulting messages to owners and prospective buyers. Adopting a culture-sensitive approach would likely have opened to GM alternative roads for more successful and even iconic communications.

I have discussed one single empirical case in this chapter, but believe that the market-mediated moral conflict that animates the Hummer is not only relevant for American brand managers in the SUV market. In fact, any organization that seeks to sell resource-intensive or resource-conserving goods, services, and messages in the US is well advised to consider this cultural conflict when briefing their agencies. Our thesis is that when Greenpeace, Code Pink, and other social and environmental activist organizations begin to frame their messages in the vocabulary of the Jeremiad against consumerism, e.g. by complaining about American consumption excess or by trying to educate Americans to consume less, they produce a backlash among affirmative American consumers rather than support. A CNN news interview with Adbusters founder and activist author Kalle Lasn about "Buy Nothing Day" amply illustrates this mechanism of an affirmative interviewer winning rhetorically over the agitating activist (see http://www.youtube.com/watch?v = P8uZEjAsR94 [accessed 15 March 2011]). But when these organizations frame their messages in a vocabulary that is more akin to American exceptionalist values, e.g. by calling for creative ideas that remind consumers of the entrepreneurial spirit of the American frontier, or addressing cultural ideals such as American independence from foreign economies (as more frequently done by www.greenpeace.org than by www.alternet.org, for example), marketers are likely to produce more approval among their affirmative American audiences.

To conclude, gaining a better understanding of the deep cultural roots of a brand through netnographic, ethnographic, and historical interpretive research can help brand managers to better support their brands and create more resonant brand narratives that leverage existing cultural meanings and consumer–brand relationships (McCracken 2009). Cultural knowledge of the historical, local, and national cultures that some brands evoke in consumers (willingly or accidentally) is key to designing culture-sensitive products, agency briefings, and advertising messages, not only in the launch phase, but particularly throughout the deeply rooted brand's cultural lifecycle.

Review and discussion questions

1   How can proper traditional segmenting and targeting of potential buyers result in detrimental brand messages?
2   Why is tapping into the "Jeremiad against consumerism" vocabulary dangerous to marketers who want to promote a social or ecological agenda?
3   Watch the spot "The Big Race" on YouTube (Available at: http://www.youtube.com/watch?v = bV65Z7p2Xy8 (accessed 1 November 2010)). How does it express deeply rooted American values for some people but violate them for others?

4   Observe Kalle Lasn and a moderator talk about "Buy Nothing Day" on CNN (Available at: http://www.youtube.com/watch?v = P8uZEjAsR94 (accessed 1 November 2010)) and study if and how they are expressing the Jeremiad logic and the affirmative American exceptionalism logic. What would you recommend Kalle to change if the goal is to convince the moderator and like-minded individuals?

Keywords

American exceptionalism, cultural analysis, cultural branding, Hummer, Jeremiad against consumerism, moral conflict

Notes

1 Named after Maria Shriver, wife of Arnold Schwarzenegger and niece of John F. Kennedy.
2 Source: Interview with Hummer's marketing director in 2005.
3 Some of these spots are available at www.hummer.com (accessed March 15, 2011).
4 Hummer features a series of parallels to the Jeep brand. Jeep was a former military brand acquired by Chrysler in 1985 and offers both off-road and SUV products. The design is distinguished by a massive front grille, the similarity of which to the later H3 grille was the source of legal confrontation among GM and Chrysler in 2003.
5 Source: http://www.nytimes.com/2005/06/28/business/media/28adco.html?_r = 1
6 See http://www.hummer.com/monsters/ (accessed May 6, 2010).
7 The spot is available at http://www.youtube.com/watch?v = lL4ZkYPLN38 (accessed May 6, 2010), however, in an updated version. The original commercial features more pointed characters and ends with the claim "Reclaim your manhood."

References

Aaker, David A. (2002) *Building Strong Brands*, London: Simon & Schuster.
Arvidsson, Adam (2008) "The Ethical Economy of Customer Coproduction," *Journal of Macromarketing*, 28: 326–38.
Csosa (2005) Available at: http://bakersfield.typepad.com
Frank, Thomas (2004) *What's the Matter with Kansas?* New York: Metropolitan Books.
Holt, Douglas B. (2003) "What Becomes an Icon Most?" *Harvard Business Review*, 81(3): 43–50.
—— (2004) *How Brands Become Icons: The Principles of Cultural Branding*, Boston: Harvard Business School Press.
Holt, Douglas B. and Thompson, Craig J. (2004) "Man-of-Action Heroes: The Pursuit of Heroic Masculinity in Everyday Consumption," *Journal of Consumer Research*, 31(2): 425–40.
Homburg, Christian, Kuester, Sabine and Krohmer, Harley (2009) *Marketing Management: A Contemporary Perspective*, New York: McGraw-Hill.
Kapferer, Jean-Noël (2008) *New Strategic Brand Management: Creating and Sustaining Brand Equity Long Term*, London: Kogan Page.
Keller, Kevin Lane (2008) *Strategic Brand Management: Building, Measuring, and Managing Brand Equity*, 3rd edn., Upper Saddle River, NJ: Pearson Education International.
Kozinets, Robert V. (2002) "The Field Behind the Screen: Using Netnography for Marketing Research in Online Communities," *Journal of Marketing Research*, 39(1): 61–73.
Lipset, Seymour Martin (1996) *American Exceptionalism: A Double-Edged Sword*, New York: W.W. Norton and Company.
Luedicke, Marius K. (2005) "Brand Systems: A Conceptual Framework for the Sociological Analysis of Brand Phenomena," in Karin M. Ekström and Helene Brembeck (eds), *European Advances in Consumer Research*, vol. 7, Valdosta, GA: Association for Consumer Research, pp. 520–21.

Luedicke, Marius K. and Giesler, Markus (2008) "Contested Consumption in Everyday Life," in Angela Y. Lee and Dilip Soman (eds), *Advances in Consumer Research*, vol. 35, Duluth, MN: Association for Consumer Research, 812–13.

Luedicke, Marius K., Thompson, Craig J. and Giesler, Markus (2010) "Consumer Identity Work as Moral Protagonism: How Myth and Ideology Animate a Brand-Mediated Moral Conflict," *Journal of Consumer Research*, 36(6): 1016–32.

McCracken, Grant (2009) *Chief Culture Officer: How to Create a Living, Breathing Corporation*, New York: Basic Books.

McMath, Robert M. and Forbes, Thomas (1998) *What Where They Thinking? Marketing Lessons I've Learned from over 80,000 New-Product Innovations and Idiocies*, New York: Crown Business.

Pitt, Leyland F., Watson, Richard T. and Berthon, Pierre (2006) "The Penguin's Window: Corporate Brands from an Open-Source Perspective," *Journal of the Academy of Marketing Science*, 34(2): 115–27.

Wipperfürth, Alex (2005) *Brand Hijack: Marketing Without Marketing*, New York: Portfolio.

20 Value and price

Domen Bajde

Overview

Marketing literature generally considers value and pricing from a narrow perspective: as a matter of profit optimization by managing the fourth element of the marketing mix (the fourth 'P'). Further, it is often suggested that the price represents a virtually costless 'P', the only 'P' that creates revenue (Kotler and Armstrong 2008). A culturally informed consideration of value and price puts both claims under serious question. First, pricing is not merely a short-term profit-maximizing managerial consideration. It is a vital element of the market(ing) system which directly impacts consumers' access to products and services as well as shapes broader social relations. It carries not only vital marketing implications but also produces wide-ranging effects on which and how resources are expended in our societies (i.e., there are important social, political, economic and environmental implications). A well-informed marketer will strive for a holistic understanding of value and price. Price does not 'create revenue' any more than any other element of the marketing mix does. It is merely a culturally accepted way of measuring and formalizing value in market exchanges. Although marketing textbooks often speak of value as something that is created and delivered by companies to consumers in exchange for payment (Kotler 2003), exchange does not occur because of prices, but rather due to the underlying consumer experiences of value resulting from the process of *value co-production*.

The process of value co-production

There is an apocryphal marketing tale about two shoe salesmen, washed up on an isolated island. The island is inhabited by friendly barefoot natives. The first salesman thinks 'No business here, nobody wears shoes!' The second salesman disagrees: 'This is a salesman paradise. They all need shoes!' The tale exposes an interesting difference in perspective, a difference directly related to the question of value. The dominant perspective holds that value is a property of an object (in this case, a shoe). Accordingly, shoes are believed to be inherently valuable, we all have (and want) them and they are not free (they have a price). This view holds that value is created by those who produce (inherently valuable) objects, in our case the shoemakers.

Product-determined value

The economistic view of value as residing-in-the object is at times extended to argue that value resides not in the shoes as such, but in what the shoes 'do' for a person (i.e., the received utility). This way, other types of shoe-related value can also be acknowledged, such as the things that shoemakers do for us so that shoes are more affordable, or the things that shoe-sellers do for us so that we may get easy access to good pairs of shoes and enjoy the process of shopping. Similar derivatives of object-determined value can also be found in the earlier cultural/symbolic consumer research, which holds that products are vessels or vehicles of meaning (see Holt 1995). Here again companies, or more precisely marketers, are viewed as having the power to create meanings and imbue them into products, while consumers are seen primarily as passive recipients of the value inherent in these meanings.

Such reductionist views of value as produced by companies alone, of value as an inherent and universal property of products and services, or even of value as meaning imbued in products, can be quite useful in environments of limited change and complexity. However, as the above example shows, they can become problematic when faced with a less uniform and stable environment. Approaching the islanders as ignorant consumers who simply do not see the value that is there (in the shoe so to speak) will likely result in failure. Is there any other way to think of value?

Co-produced value

First, we need to recognize that value results from consumers interacting with objects (tangible or intangible ones). A comprehensive culturally informed understanding of value stresses that value is a *socially structured and culturally mediated experience* (Holbrook 1999). The experience of value is structured and mediated in the sense of being a product of culture and society. We learn how to interact with objects and how to experience value. This does not mean that consumers are socially programmed machines who uniformly experience value. The constructed experience of value is also *agentic* inasmuch as individuals have a certain degree of freedom in their interpretation of products and experiencing of value.

Value does not exist if not for those who experience it. It occurs when consumers interact with products in particular ways (Holt 1995) and is heavily dependent on consumers' interpretation or *meaning making* constitutive of this interaction. Although there is clearly no value devoid of meaning, meaning does necessarily translate into value. As explained below, only meanings that lead to positive evaluations of products (i.e., preference experiences) contribute toward positive experiences of value. Value production can thus be considered as a co-productive effort involving a host of social and market entities: *companies* who shape the product we interact with and 'guide' our interaction (e.g., through marketing communication), *consumers* who interact with objects and experience value in individual ways, and other *social entities and institutions* (e.g. reference groups, institutions, culture) who mediate the process of value creation. Value is thus not an intrinsic property of objects, but rather is *co-produced* through the culturally mediated practice of interpretation.

Helping the islanders to experience the value of shoes is a complex process that entails more than just delivering the shoes and collecting the money. It also goes beyond merely teaching the natives to appreciate shoes. It demands a careful examination of the cultural setting (e.g., the meanings and rituals related to feet and clothing) and the individual response to this new product. Based on such cultural analysis and consideration of individual differences, the shoe salesman can decide how best to approach the process of facilitating the experience of value. Such insights allow him to form a suitable marketing strategy by determining the potential target segments and by rethinking the product strategy, the pricing strategy, coming up with suitable channels for communication and distribution of shoes, etc.

Further, we need to recognize that value is not just an interactive experience. It is also a *relativistic preference experience* (Holbrook 1999). The value experience is established on a 'value compared to' basis. In other words, value necessitates a distinction, a difference that can only be established when comparing objects. Value equals preference. The relativistic nature of value reaffirms the fact that value is at the same time cultural and idiosyncratic (personal). There is no such thing as a universal or natural value. Were it so, objects would retain their value over time and space. Instead, value is always experienced in context which in term consists of the evaluator (e.g., John Doe), the reference groups (his friends), culture (American), subculture (nerd), specific spatio-temporal setting (waiting in a line at the unemployment office on a Friday afternoon), etc. There will of course be considerable consistency in evaluating an object, when the variation of context is small. Much less consistency can, for instance, be expected in the case of significant cultural variation.

What does an islander compare shoes to? A surface answer would be: probably to bare feet. If wearing shoes is preferred over being barefoot, then shoes are valued. In reality the issue is much more complex. The perception and evaluation of products inevitably involve object organization and categorization. The new object will be fitted into existent classification schemes of the islanders. Familiar categories, concepts and scripts will be used to make sense of this new object. It is essential for the shoe salesman to understand these processes, all the more so because they will likely differ from his own understanding of shoes. Will the islanders interpret this new object as a sacred object, a Western weakness, a functional device, a symbol of prestige? Will they prefer it over other objects of similar 'nature'? In a sense the salesman needs to help the islanders to co-produce the value of shoes within their native socio-cultural setting. Of course the salesman will not be passive in the process of value creation, but neither will the islanders.

The process of price setting

Prices are generally set by companies (that is when they are not regulated by the government or subject to consumer choice). The responsibility for making decisions regarding pricing is seldom limited to marketing executives. There are many cases where these decisions are made by CEOs, manufacturing and engineering executives, etc. Due to its complexity and its impact on various business functions, the process of pricing strategy formation necessitates cross-functional participation. The role of marketing executives is to make sure that the strategic and tactical decisions regarding pricing are aligned with the overall marketing strategy. Whereas operations, engineering and finance executives are likely to apply a more production/cost-oriented perspective, the marketing executives need to balance these views by promoting the central tenet of the marketing philosophy: the consumer orientation.

What does the process of price setting involve? We follow the generic procedure offered in most marketing textbooks extending it with our cultural perspective of value. The generic procedure of price setting involves four basic themes: setting pricing objectives, pricing situation analysis, pricing strategy and price implementation. In providing a sequence of generic steps involved in setting prices we stress the importance of carefully analyzing the underlying pricing situation prior to making any specific choices regarding pricing objectives and strategy. In contrast, many authors start with setting pricing objectives first.

While pricing objectives undoubtedly offer a useful guide in setting the pricing strategy, in the absence of prior analysis they might also involve uninformed decisions. Above all, a careful examination of the product/consumer relationship in all its socio-cultural complexity needs to be conducted prior to shaping a pricing strategy. Box 20.1 presents the pricing of the iPhone.

Box 20.1 iPricing at Apple Inc.

The launch of iPhone has by some commentators been dubbed as one of the most successful market entries in the history of marketing (Faheem 2008). This exemplary convergence product combines the features of a 'mobile phone, a widescreen iPod with touch controls, and a breakthrough Internet communications device with desktop-class email, web browsing, maps, and searching' (Apple Inc.). The product was announced in January 2007 and released on 29 June 2007 (also called the iDay). The company decided on a market skimming strategy, setting a high price with its margin reported at 50 per cent mark-up (Mann 2007).

   The author of the snapshot of Figure 20.1 (also an iDay iPhone buyer) reports of a passerby shopper observing: 'Is that the line for the $500 iPod phone??! For that price, it should dial by itself!' To this, he replied: 'Well, m'am, I believe it actually does that.'

Figure 20.1 The crowd waiting for the iPhone release.
   Source: Kriegsman, retrieved from http://www.flickr.ceom/photos/kriegsman/663122857/

Table 20.1 The iPhone timeline

Period	January 2007	June 2007	September 2007	November 2007	April 2008	June 2008	Summer 2009
Activity	Official announcement of iPhone	iPhone launched	Infamous price cut	Launch in EU	Price cut in EU	Launch of iPhone 3G	Expected price cut for 3G models
Pricing	Price unknown	$499 for 4GB, $599 for 8GB	$399 for 8GB, $499 for 16GB	$415–587 depending on the country	Prices reduced by $200	$199 for 8GB, $299 for 16GB	Expected reduction of $100

Despite the undeniable success of the iPhone, the product's first year on the market raised considerable pricing problems for Apple Inc. In September, just 10 weeks after the launch, the company decided on a significant reduction in price (see the timeline in Table 20.1). For example, an 8GB iPhone bought for $599 in June was $200 cheaper in September. Many consumer responded with a fury, feeling betrayed by the company and the brand. The yesterday's heroes of iDay became today's clowns taken for a ride (abcNEWS 2007). The company responded by apologizing and issuing $100 rebates to the early adopters of iPhone.

A year later, in June 2008, the company released a G3 model at yet a lower price ($199 for 8GB). Now pundits are predicting another price cut. In the summer of 2009 a $99 G3 is expected. Some critics feel that in today's frail economy such a move might be damaging to the industry as well as Apple itself (Caulfield 2009).

The pricing situation analysis

The generic 3 Cs model of analyzing the pricing situation outlines three areas of analysis: Consumer demand, Costs and Competition. A somewhat broader perspective is adopted here by distinguishing between four *spheres of analysis*: the consumption sphere, the internal sphere, the competitor sphere and the socio-legal sphere (Figure 20.2). Each of the four spheres will be discussed in more detail. Due to its pedagogic nature, the model is inescapably simplistic. We have chosen the notion of *sphere* to indicate that the boundaries of the four categories are malleable. There is considerable overlap between the four spheres. The model is reciprocal as a change in one sphere is likely to cause changes in the remaining three spheres. In addition, we once again stress the priority given to the process of value co-production echoed by the central position of the consumption sphere. To avoid some of the limitations of this abstract, generic model, the process of the four-sphere analysis will be applied to the fascinating case of iPhone and its dynamic pricing history (see Box 20.1).

Internal sphere

The pricing situation analysis should include a penetrating gaze inwards. Setting a price for a particular product or service can have a strong impact on related products and services that

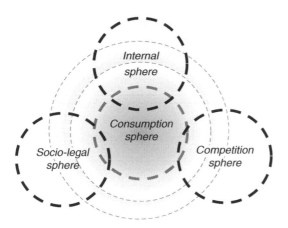

Figure 20.2 The four-sphere analysis of the pricing situation.

the company offers. Before proceeding with price setting, the company needs to explore to what extent and in what manner its products are substitutes or complements. Considerable cannibalization effects can occur when products are priced incongruently to the substitutes offered by the same company. For instance, by simultaneously lowering the price of the iPhone and increasing its storage capacity, Apple might de-stimulate purchases of the iPod. Some critics suggest that a low-priced entry-level iPhone could significantly damage the sales of iPod and high-end iPhones, thus becoming 'a cannibalistic margin killer' for Apple (Caulfield 2009).

Another crucial internal consideration involves the costs of producing, promoting, distributing and selling products. The company needs to carefully examine the costs and its expectations regarding the desired return on its investment. It will want to make sure that at least the average variable costs will be covered by the price. The average variable costs thus represent the floor limit on the price. However, both fixed and variable costs are not independent from the decisions made on pricing. The chosen price can have a vital impact on the quantity of products sold, and companies will of course have different production and distribution costs at different production/distribution levels. Costs should thus not be considered as static information, but rather as a function dependent on the size of the operation and the degree of experience (the so-called learning curve).

As companies put more and more effort in customizing their offerings to specific customers, the cost analysis becomes more complex. The company might well infer different costs from different customers. In these cases calculations of costs associated with actual activities performed in serving specific customers or groups of customers should be conducted. Such *activity-based costing* (ABC), focused on the actual cost of activities, should also be applied in calculating the cost of each product, taking into account the actual cost of activities performed in producing and distributing a product. These calculations provide a sound basis for setting prices and for comparing the company's key costs with those of the competitors.

In addition, cost functions can change as a result of significant efforts put into optimizing the business processes. The principle of *target costing* views costs as a decision variable. Companies using this approach begin with first setting a price, the desired return and forming the product specifications, and then calculate how low the costs must be. Priority is then given to optimizing the product and the processes so that the target cost level is met.

Of course, companies cannot control all their costs. Nor can they expect to retain a permanent level of control over their cost. The company needs to consider what level of control it has over various types of costs and its ability to retain or extend this control in the future.

This brief foray into the analysis of the internal sphere should make it clear that costs are of primary concern in price setting. A comprehensive understanding of costs as a variable dependent on experience, size of operation, customer characteristics, internal efforts and various external factors (e.g., energy prices, governmental interventions, etc.) represents an essential foundation for setting the pricing strategy.

Competition sphere

Conducting a benchmark analysis of the major costs occurred by the company and its chief competitors provides a good starting point for the competition sphere analysis. The demanding task of determining one's true competition has been already discussed (cf. Chapter 18 in this volume). Here let us add that it is within the proposed process of value co-production that competitors should be sought. It is the products and brands that contribute towards similar experiences of value that we compete with, rather than with products that look or sound most similar to ours.

There are many factors in the competition sphere that can influence the pricing strategy. Peter and Olson (2008) list nine:

1   number of competitors
2   cost structure of competitors
3   the market share of competitors
4   the location of competitors
5   conditions of entry into the industry
6   degree of vertical integration of competitors
7   financial strength of competitors
8   number of products and brands sold by each competitor
9   competitors' historical reactions to price change.

The list can be extended to include the competitors' current prices of products and the assessment of their current and future pricing objectives and strategies. It is essential that the competitors' positioning strategies are closely examined in light of pricing, seeking answers to questions such as: how are competitors positioned on a relative price basis? To what extent is pricing used as an active element of each competitor's marketing strategy? What are the probable responses of each competitor to alternative price strategies? (Cravens and Piercy 2006).

To make matters even more complex, pricing strategies are often formed for new products, or products introduced in new markets. Such was the case with Apple's entry into the mobile phone market. By launching the iPhone, Apple completed its transition from a computer company to a consumer electronics company. The iPhone represented the company's first foray into the demanding mobile phone business, known for the fierce competition between traditional brands such as Nokia and Siemens and smart phone brands such as Palm and RIM/BlackBerry. The smart phone market was largely divided between BlackBerry (38 per cent market share) and Palm (23 per cent) (Woods and Carton 2009). In less than a year iPhone had caught up with Palm, eventually overtaking it and ending the year of 2008 with a 23 per cent market share (Palm 9 per cent, RIM/BlackBerry 41 per cent). By lowering its prices and introducing the 3G iPhone, Apple put considerable pressure on its competitors, who have been forced to respond with, among other things, prematurely launching new models (Change Wave 2009).

Socio-legal sphere

A variety of laws and regulations affect pricing decisions. Among the pricing environments that attract most attention from the government, Cravens and Piercy (2006) list: horizontal price fixing (collusion between competitors), price discrimination (different prices for different customers in absence of legitimate basis), deceptive pricing (misleading consumers), vertical price fixing (collusion across the channels of distribution) and price information (requirements on form and availability of price information for consumers). In some cases prices are directly regulated by the government, leaving companies little or no room for manoeuvre.

The social implications of pricing go far beyond the legal and regulative considerations. With the recent socio-economic turmoil surrounding the global economic downturn, the looming environmental crisis and the resentment building up in developing countries, the social implications of business decisions are coming to the fore. As argued earlier, pricing decisions produce wide-ranging effects on which and how resources are expended in our societies. There are important social, political, economic and environmental implications of pricing. Issues ranging from the squeezing out of middle- and lower-class sport fans via prohibitive ticket pricing (Keiser 2009) to the effect of low consumer goods prices on the environment (Leonard 2009) represent popular debate topics.

The breadth and complexity of such issues exceed the scope of this chapter. Instead an example of branding built upon the very premise of broader social implications of pricing is discussed, illustrating the opportunities and responsibilities facing those who form pricing strategies. Box 20.2 presents the Fairtrade Labelling Organization (FTLO) and its efforts in promoting fair trade through alternative pricing and coordination schemes. Although fair trade products essentially cost more than the average products, the price premium comes with a story. In recent years the sale of fair trade products has increased dramatically, peaking at €2.38 billion in 2007 (with an average yearly increase of 40 per cent over the past five years).

In the case of fair trade, the 'fair' price paid to the Third World producer represents a unique source for consumer value co-production. The price premium paid by the Western consumer thus involves special value as it can be construed and experienced as an ethical/political act. Dolan (2005: 369) demonstrates how such ethical consumption provides 'a stage on which myriad discourses of "self" and "other" are played out, as consumers seek to reconcile the gap between the "haves" and "have-nots"' by extending social justice to distant communities.' However, despite the positive overtones, the author warns of the limitations of ethical consumerism, which may 'civilize capitalism for a fraction of [Third World] workers and afford affluent consumers a sort of capitalist redemption, but it also poses no threat to our privileged position in the global hierarchy' (ibid.: 383).

Ethical considerations related to pricing are of course not limited to issues of global inequality and exploitation. The iPhone case provides an illustrative example. As outlined in Box 20.1, the decision to drastically lower the price of the product just ten weeks after its launch stirred considerable resentment among consumers. Many of the early buyers felt betrayed by the company. In his infamous apology to consumers, Apple's then CEO,

Box 20.2 Fairtrade Labelling Organization

Fair trade is an organized social movement advocating fair payment to producers in developing countries as well as social and environmental standards. It focuses on exports from developing countries to developed countries, most notably coffee, cocoa, sugar, tea, bananas, handicrafts, etc. The Fairtrade Labelling Organization International (FTLO) is a non-profit association which develops and reviews fair trade standards and provides support to fair trade producers. According FTLO's website (http://www.fairtrade.net), the fair trade system benefits approximately 6 million people (primarily farmers and workers) in 58 developing countries in Africa, Asia and Latin America. In 2008, fair trade certified sales amounted to approximately €3.4 billion worldwide.

Figure 20.3 Fair trade labelled coffee.
Source: BashaSide7, retrieved from http://www.flickr.com/photos/slowswimmer/2609618343/sizes/o/

As the organization proclaims:

> World market prices for coffee, rice and other commodities are highly volatile and often below the costs of production. A stable price, that covers at least production and living costs, is an essential requirement for farmers to escape from poverty and provide themselves and their families with a decent standard of living.

The Fairtrade label thus ensures fair compensation and sustainable production in developing countries. A study conducted in Costa Rica confirms the beneficial impact of fair pricing and organizational support on producer empowerment and life quality (Ronchi 2009). The minimum price guarantees offered to producers enable them to invest in long-term improvements despite the harsh, volatile environment.

Steve Jobs struggles to combine the business and ethical dimension of Apple's decision:

> Even though we are making the right decision to lower the price of iPhone ..., we need to do a better job taking care of our early iPhone customers as we aggressively go after new ones with a lower price. Our early customers trusted us, and we must live up to that trust with our actions in moments like these.

Jobs is caught between the company's special relationship with its customers and the aggressive tactics that he argues are necessary to succeed in the marketplace.

Consumption sphere

So far the cultural approach to value and pricing has not necessitated any drastic departures from the more traditional approaches in analyzing the pricing situation. To recapitulate, the cultural approach demands a broader examination of the social implications of pricing and provides a value co-production-based criterion to determining competition. The distinction becomes more pronounced when considering the central sphere of analysis: consumption. By posing value as an interactive preference experience, consumer–product interaction is put forward as the fundamental element of pricing situation analysis. Various contributions to understanding the consumer–product interactions have been offered in this book. Rather than repeating them, we turn to those facets of the user–product interaction that are essential to pricing strategy: value co-production and price sensitivity.

Consumers interact with products directly, when they shop, use, display and dispose of products and indirectly, when they think and communicate about them. Subsequently value can be experienced through various consumer–product touch points. Many of the early iPhone buyers first called their friends just to say: 'I have an iPhone!' In this and many other cases, having friends know, increases the *social value* of the product. What is more, the iPhone brand sometimes carries profound *personal meanings* that can significantly contribute toward individual consumers' experience of value. For example, iPhones can become incredibly valuable to persons who experience them as profoundly meaningful. In their video research of another of Apple's cult products, Belk and Tumbat (2005) describe the 'cult of Mac', a set of beliefs about Apple and Mac computers that impart the brand with a quasi-religious character. They show how:

> This religion is based on an origin myth for Apple Computer, heroic and savior legends surrounding its co-founder and current CEO Steve Jobs, the devout faith of its follower congregation, their belief in the righteousness of the Macintosh, the existence of one or more Satanic opponents ... and the hope among cult members that salvation can be achieved by transcending corporate capitalism.

As described by David Levine, a psychologist and a self-professed Mac follower, this brand cult 'provides a community and a common heritage ... a certain common way of thinking, a way of doing things, a certain mindset' (Kahney 2002). These words attest to the commingling of vital social and personal meanings attached to Apple's products and their potential in increasing the value of these products experienced by consumers.

Despite its short history, the story of iPhone is already infused with mythologies and legends (MyphoneWAR 2009). Based on the rich repertoire of ideas associated with

Apple and the iPhone, social distinctions (e.g., between iPhone owners and others) and personal meanings are constructed. People not only use iPhone to make calls, surf the internet and play music. They also use it to make sense of their lives, technology and the ways of the world. This is not to suggest that all products and brands can become profoundly meaningful. Rather, it illustrates the importance of analyzing the broader social and cultural consumption context and the social and personal meanings attached to products. Although products will invariably play different roles in people's lives, there is no consumption outside culture (i.e., outside meaning).

What is the role of price in the social and personal meanings of products and brands? On the one hand, the price can be used as a strategic tool to differentiate products and brands and strengthen product meanings. On the other, prices and other consumers' costs detract from the desirability of the product. Returning to the quasi-religious character of Apple products, religious artefacts are in a sense priceless. This means that while Apple 'worshippers' are prepared to pay a considerable price premium for Apple products, a heavy emphasis on pricing and aggressive salesmanship can detract from the brand's cult status. Pricing decisions need to be considered in light of their impact on the consumer–product interaction and the overall marketing strategy (in particular, the product's positioning).

Of course, consumers not only experience products as beneficial, but their overall experience of value is also shaped by the costs they infer. All four types of consumer costs (money, time, cognitive activity and behavioural effort) play a role in the process of value co-production. Due to their unique devotion to Apple and the iPhone, some consumers were willing to incur considerable monetary, temporal, cognitive and behavioural costs on and prior to iDay. Articles were written to help consumers cope with the anxiety of waiting, offering amusing tips, such as using creative visualization and forming support groups (Maguire 2007). Some consumers waited in line for more than 24 hours to be the first ones to purchase an iPhone for a hefty price. Many of the later buyers did not share this devotion, joining the iPhone waggon only when Apple had reduced the price and made the product more readily available by expanding the distribution of the product and by offering consumers more choice when it came to phone service. These consumers were more sensitive to costs, including the price.

Price sensitivity is an important element of the consumer–product interaction. Economists measure this sensitivity in the form of price elasticity, the percentage change in quantity of demand for a product as per the percentage change in the price of the same commodity. While such analysis can be useful for forecasting, it is important to realize that price sensitivity research often approaches price elasticity on an 'all things being equal' basis. Unfortunately, as proposed earlier, experiences of value that ultimately underlie consumers' interpretation of prices are messy (mediated, relativistic, subject to contextualized personal interpretation). All things being equal, a reduction in the iPhone's price might seem perfectly beneficial to consumers. In reality, such a reduction can result in various realignments of how past and future buyers' attach meaning to Apple's actions and products, and how they subsequently experience the value of iPhone (see Box 20.1).

Pricing objectives

Pricing objectives are meant to provide the process of price setting with a sense of direction and purpose. The objectives will guide those responsible for making decisions related to pricing. There are a number of possible pricing objectives to draw upon. To provide some structure we distinguish between two factors that profoundly shape the setting of pricing objectives: the management preferences and the market situation. *Management preferences* determine the temporal (short-term vs. long-term) orientation of the pricing strategy as well as the axiological orientation (the fundamental values aimed for) in setting the price. The market situation includes the current financial state of the firm, its position relative to competitors, and the market's characteristics.

Among the possible short-term pricing goals, companies often aim for current profit or cash flow maximization, where prices are set so as to earn as much profit or generate as much revenue as possible. Companies who are able to predict the market's response to different prices (the demand curve) and costs at different levels of production (the supply function) will be able to determine prices that maximize profit. Profit can be earned by selling limited quantities at high prices (market skimming) or selling large quantities at relatively low prices (market penetration). Some companies are not in a position to anticipate profit due to their dismal financial performance and/or bleak outlook. Their short-term goal is likely to be one of survival. When being overrun by intensive competition, burdened by excessive production capacities or misguided past investments, the company might elect to lower prices below average total costs. This way the company can at least cover average variable costs and a proportion of fixed costs. Other short-term objectives include demand stimulation, when prices are set so as to encourage new product trial or simply stimulate purchase of existing products (e.g., discount and promotional prices).

An excessive focus on short-term objectives can endanger the company's long-term market position. An excessive exploitation of the market's willingness to pay premium prices will attract competitors or, in cases of socially sensitive markets, result in government intervention (e.g., products related to freedom of expression, education, health, etc.). In these situations, insistence on short-term pricing goals reduces the company's chance of future success. Long-term pricing goals such as market share maximization might instead be adopted. Here, companies forgo current profit in order to secure and improve their market position, thus investing in future profits.

Strengthening the market position does not necessarily involve increasing market share. Some companies forgo a large market share, instead aiming to operate as niche players selling uniquely positioned products. In such circumstances the goal of improving product positioning will guide the process of price setting. Prices will be set so as to increase product awareness and familiarity and improve the product's image. Other long-term pricing goals may include influencing competition. For example, low prices can be set to create entry barriers for potential new entrants or to push a struggling competitor into bankruptcy. Conversely, increases in price can function as an invitation to established competitors to follow suit and raise their prices as well.

Of course, the management's time preferences and the underlying market situation are not the only factors that shape the process of determining pricing objectives. Not all organizations will gear their pricing strategy towards seeking market clout and profit. In some cases priority is given to non-commercial values. As discussed earlier, ethical values represent not only a potential limitation/danger in setting prices, but can also constitute the organization's *raison d'être*. The Fairtrade Labelling Organization (FTLO) sets the following standards for those trading with fair trade products (FTLO 2009; see also Box 20.2):

1   Pay a price to producers that at least covers the costs of sustainable production: the Fairtrade Minimum Price.
2   Pay a premium that producers can invest in development: the Fairtrade Premium.

3   Partially pay in advance, when producers ask for it.
4   Sign contracts that allow for long-term planning and sustainable production
    practices.

Such standards prioritize values of sustainability and fairness as the primary objectives in
determining prices for products obtained from producers in developing countries. Even with
fair trade products other objectives will of course be present in determining the actual price
to suppliers and end customers, but the fair trade values remain an ever-present factor of the
pricing strategy. Other value-related objectives in price settings might include philanthropic
objectives, environmental objectives, etc.

Pricing strategy

Having put considerable effort into analyzing the pricing situation and determining the
pricing objectives, the company now needs to make several strategic decisions regarding
pricing. The company's viable options are constricted by the specifics of the pricing
situation (consumption, competition and socio-legal sphere) and the company's internal
limitations and aspirations (internal sphere). Cravens and Piercy (2006) emphasize
two aspects of the pricing strategy: the price visibility dimension and the positioning
dimension (Figure 20.4). The company needs to decide whether it will use pricing as an
active or passive element of its marketing strategy (the visibility dimension), and whether it
will position its products at the high or low end (positioning dimension).

Based on these dimensions, four basic strategies can be outlined. The *High–Active strategy* will heavily promote the product's higher price, conveying superiority and prestige. The
price premium will be used to establish exceptional consumer–product relationships and
differentiate the product from its potential substitutes. The *High–Passive* strategy also entails
setting a high price. However, in contrast to the active strategy, this time the focus is set on
non-price elements, emphasizing product features and social and personal brand meanings.
Such an approach is necessary when the price alone does not function as a potent indicator
of the product's superiority.

The *Low–Active* strategy aims for the price-sensitive segments, aggressively promoting
competitive prices and consumer savings. It is sustainable only when the company has a
considerable advantage in production, marketing or distribution costs over its competitors
and/or a strong market position. In the case of the *Low–Passive* strategy, the company
does not heavily advertise its competitive prices. In this manner it not only saves

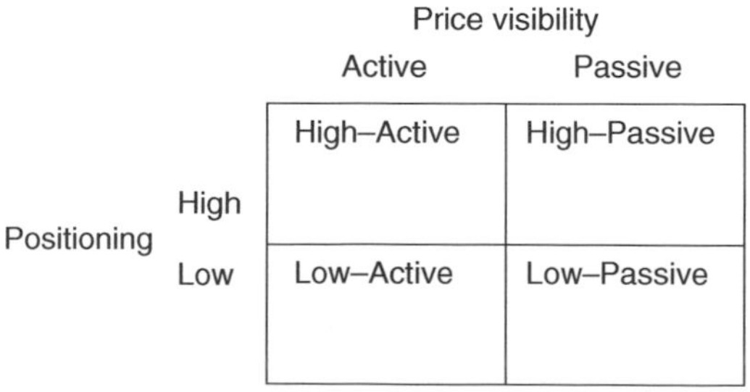

	Active	Passive
High	High–Active	High–Passive
Low	Low–Active	Low–Passive

Figure 20.4 Cravens and Piercy's 2-D model of pricing strategy.
Source: Cravens and Piercy (2006).

money on promotion, but it also reduces the danger of signalling product inferiority. Many companies refrain from aggressively advertising low prices so as to prevent a potential price war.

Competitor response plays an important role in determining the overall pricing strategy. The pricing strategy must provide answers to how the company will respond to competitors' potential price changes. Cressmann and Nagle (2002) compare pricing to playing chess, arguing that 'players who fail to envision a few moves ahead will almost always be beaten'. They offer a systematic framework for decision-making in situations of competitor price changes. When faced with a competitor changing a price, the company must first determine the impact on sales and the cost of responding to competitor's price actions. Eventually, the scope of the potential harm being done to the company's remaining markets and the competitor's anticipated response will determine the suitable course of action to be taken.

Another important strategic consideration relates to the internal and external impact of price. As described earlier, a particular product's price strategy can heavily impact the sale of other products. Among the vital internal concerns, the potential cannibalization effects and the impact on the overall corporate brand image need to be carefully weighed up. External socio-economic impacts can also play an important consideration if a positive corporate image is to be maintained. Here, it suffices to recall the iPhone backlash caused by lowering prices. Needless to say, even more drastic responses to pricing decisions can occur in the case of price increases of products that are vital to well-being (e.g., food, health products) and social development (e.g., education, information).

It should be emphasized that the companies rarely enjoy an absolute control over the price setting process. Government regulation, retailers' strategies and other factors often narrow the company's pricing options. What is more, some companies deliberately pass a proportion of their control over pricing to consumers, setting up auctions where prices are primarily determined based on bidding or deciding upon alternative strategic approaches such as the 'pay what you want' (PWYW) mechanism. PWYW is a participative pricing mechanism in which consumers have control over the price they pay. Whereas participative pricing can increase consumers' intent to purchase, sellers using PWYW also face the risk of consumer exploitation, since consumers might decide to pay nothing at all or a price below the seller's costs (Ju-Young *et al.* 2009).

Price implementation

In this final stage, companies need to determine specific prices and pricing policies that enable a day-to-day management of pricing. Various methods and techniques are available to determine the actual price of a product. These methods often give emphasis to one of the four pricing spheres (corporate, competitor, socio-legal and consumption). Normally, prices are based primarily on internal corporate considerations such as costs and expected return. In this case, prices are usually determined by adding the desired mark-up to the average costs (the cost-plus approach). Competition-oriented pricing methods calculate prices based on competitors' prices. Based on these prices and its positioning strategy, the company can set prices on par (the so-called 'going rate'), lower or higher than competitors.

Socio-legal considerations can also be forefronted when calculating a price. In the case of the FTLO, prices are calculated based on non-profit standards of sustainability and fairness. Other companies must employ a legally predetermined procedure to calculate prices or simply adapt prices determined by the government. The remaining consumption sphere provides price calculation standards that forefront the consumers' response to price. For instance, the PWYW example presented above transfers the process of price calculation to consumers, who themselves decide on the actual price to be paid. In other, more common examples, companies rely on market research. Prices are set based on determined consumer price sensitivity, consumers' willingness to pay a certain price or the overall monetary value attributed to the product by consumers.

Needless to say, any excessive favouring of one of the four pricing spheres at the expense of the others results in questionable pricing decisions that fail to incorporate the full range of pricing considerations. If possible, companies should strive to combine the proposed methods incorporating the vital factors present in all four pricing spheres.

The implementation of the pricing strategy is not an issue that can be dealt with once and for all. It involves a perpetual process of readjusting prices and the marketing elements related to them. Policy guidelines that guide the process of price decision-making and price structure are essential. A pricing policy includes considerations of issues such as discounting, allowances, consumer financing, returns and other operating guidelines. In addition, product–mix guidelines need to be established so as to make sure that price adjustments are not made without considering the full range of company's products (see Box 20.1 on product mix pricing). If Apple decides to change the price of the 16GB model, it must of course consider realigning the price of other iPhones as well.

Another important issue related to price implementation entails decisions on how to communicate prices. The price communication policy involves not only how prices will be conveyed to consumers at the point of purchase (e.g., price tags), but also how pricing information will be integrated in the company's wider marketing communication activities. This is of particular essence when price-active strategies (see above) are adopted.

Unfortunately, companies can never anticipate all the potential future pricing situations. What is more, it takes time, effort and resources to determine, formalize and implement pricing policies. Companies must eventually decide on a viable degree of pricing policy formalization, making sure that the essential pricing scenarios are covered by the existent policies, thus minimalizing the probability of future errors and inconsistencies in implementing the pricing strategy.

Conclusion

The cultural approach to value emphasizes that value is neither an inherent property of the product, nor can products be viewed as hermetic vessels in which marketers can imbue pre-produced meaning. Instead, value is approached as a culturally mediated experience resulting from consumers interacting with products in particular ways. As a result, value is inescapably co-produced by consumers who have an active stake in producing relativistic preference experiences based on the meanings they attach to products. In market exchanges value is measured and formalized through the instrument of price. Marketers can help their companies better formalize value, by insisting that the process of price setting begin with a consumption-centric, culturally informed analysis of the pricing situation. In addition, the subsequent phases of the pricing process should take into account not only that consumers' experiences of value and interpretations of prices are socially constructed and mediated by culture, but also that the company's stake in co-producing and formalizing value bears important social implications.

Review and discussion questions

1 Why would it be wrong to confuse value with price? Explain the difference and connection between these two concepts.
2 What do we mean when we say that value is a *relativistic preference experience*?
3 What does the process of price setting involve?
4 What should managers consider in the pricing situation analysis stage? In which of the proposed areas does the cultural approach hold additional weight?
5 What kind of pricing objectives can managers set? How would you describe the core pricing objective in Fairtrade (see Box 20.2)?
6 Which dimensions does Cravens and Piercy's model of pricing strategy emphasize? Outline the four possible strategies in this 2D model.
7 What should managers pay attention to when implementing prices?

Keywords

price implementation, price setting, price, pricing objectives, pricing situation analysis, pricing strategy, value, value co-production

References

abcNEWS (2007) '[First] Buyers Beware: Price Cut Coming'. Available at: http://abcnews.go.com/GMA (accessed 15 June 2009).

Belk, Russell W. and Tumbat, Gulnur (2005) 'The Cult of Macintosh,' *Consumption, Markets, and Culture*, 8(3): 205–17.

Caulfield, Brian (2009) 'Why A $99 iPhone Is Bad For Apple'. Available at: http://www.forbes.com/

Change Wave (2009) 'BlackBerry vs. iPhone'. Available at: http://www.changewave.com/ (accessed 20 June 2009).

Cravens, D. W. and Piercy, N. F. (2006) *Strategic Marketing*, 8th edn, New York: McGraw-Hill.

Cressmann, George E. and Nagle, Thomas T. (2002) 'How to Manage an Aggressive Competitor', *Business Horizons*, 45 (March–April): 23–30.

Dolan, Catherine S. (2005) 'Fields of Obligation: Rooting Ethical Sourcing in Kenyan Horticulture', *Journal of Consumer Culture*, 5(3): 365–89.

Faheem, Hadiya (2008) 'Apple Inc's iPhone: Can iPhone Maintain Its Initial Momentum?' ICFAI Center for Management Research, Case Study No. 508-117-1.

FTLO (2009) Available at: http://www.fairtrade.net/

Holbrook, Morris B. (1999) *Consumer Value: A framework for Analysis and Research*, London: Routledge.

Holt, Douglas, B. (1995) 'How Consumers Consume: A Typology of Consumption Practices', *The Journal of Consumer Research*, 22(1): 1–16.

Ju-Young, Kim, Natter, Martin and Spann, Martin (2009) 'Pay-What-You-Want: A New Participative Pricing Mechanism', *Journal of Marketing*, 73(1): 44–58.

Kahney, Leander (2002) 'Worshipping at the Altar of Mac'. Available at: http://www.wired.com.

Keiser, Richard A. (2009) 'Take Me Out to the Ball Game, But Only If You're Rich: Stadiums Put Corporate Guests First,' *Le Monde Diplomatique*, July.

Kotler, Philip (2003) *Marketing Management*, 11th edn, New Jersey: Prentice Hall.

Kotler, Philip and Armstrong, Gary (2008) *Principles of Marketing*. 12th edn, London: Pearson Prentice Hall.

Leonard, Annie (2009) 'The Story of Stuff'. Available at: http://www.storyofstuff.com (accessed 5 June 2009).

348   *Domen Bajde*

Maguire, James (2007) 'Waiting for Your iPhone: Five Ways to Handle the Unbearable Stress'. Available at: http://itmanagement.earthweb.com/cnews

Mann, Justin (2007) 'iSuppli Claims iPhone Profit Margin is 50 percent'. Available at: http://www.techspot.com/news (accessed 5 June 2009).

MyphoneWAR (2009) 'iDolatry – The iPhone and the Ever Growing Cult of the Macintosh'. Available at: http://www.myphonewar.com (accessed 15 June 2009).

Peter, J. Paul and Olson, Jerry (2008) *Consumer Behavior and Marketing Strategy*, Boston: McGraw-Hill/Irwin.

Ronchi, Loraine (2009) 'The Impact of Fair Trade on Producers and Their Organisations: A Case Study with Coocafé in Costa Rica,' Prus Working Paper No. 11, Poverty Research Unit at University of Sussex.

Woods, Jim and Carton, Paul (2009) 'BlackBerry vs. iPhone'. Available at: http://www.changewave.com/ (accessed 5 June 2009).

21 Sales promotion

From a company resource to a customer resource

Philippe Odou, Souad Djelassi, and
Isabelle Collin-Lachaud

Overview

For many years, sales promotion has accounted for a large part of companies' marketing budgets. The development of various types of sales promotion is due to their short-term positive effects on sales. While their transactional impacts may be doubtful from a relational standpoint, numerous questions have also arisen about their long-term efficiency, both in terms of sales and customer loyalty. Although these techniques still remain a core element of marketing plans, consumers have started to exhibit negative responses towards them (skepticism, mistrust, and even resistance). Some consumers feel that promotions seek to trick them into buying unwanted and useless products and therefore try to avoid them, while others use them to outsmart the marketers. So it seems that sales promotions, which were initially a company resource to increase sales, can now also be considered as a consumer resource to optimize their purchasing power, achieve an identity project or challenge marketing principles. Marketers must therefore change the way they perceive consumers, who should be viewed not as passive recipients of marketing stimuli, but as people with whom marketers can co-produce or co-create marketing actions. They must supply consumers with resources capable of helping them to fulfill their own objectives and values.

Traditional sales promotion: principles and limitations

Before analyzing the limitations of traditional sales promotions, we will briefly present the principles on which they are based.

Traditional sales promotion principles

Sales promotion is traditionally defined as "an action-oriented marketing event whose purpose is to have a direct impact on the behavior of the firm's consumers" (Blattberg and Neslin 1990: 3). It targets various actors at different stages of the purchasing process: consumers, retailers or sales forces. In this chapter, we will be looking at consumer promotion as initiated by brands or retailers.

Sales promotion is supposed to do the following:

- offer an incentive to purchase;
- have a short-term effect on behavior (or medium-term where the re-purchase is deferred);
- be a temporary phenomenon.

Table 21.1 Promotional objectives

Promotional objectives			
Brand		**Retailer**	
Objectives	*Examples of techniques*	*Objectives*	*Examples of techniques*
Recruit new customers	Trial techniques (free samples, free trial, etc.), cash refund offers, etc.	Increase customer numbers as well as the frequency of visits to sales outlets	Price discounts, coupons, etc.
Develop loyalty among existing customers	Special purchases, games, sweepstakes, premiums, etc.	Increase basket loads, encourage impulse buying	Point-of-purchase demonstrations, price rebates, free tasting, etc.
Increase sales volumes	Multi-product cash refund offers, draws, etc.	Develop loyalty	Offers based on points accumulated
Competitive offers	Rebates	Increase customer traffic for store opening	Special offers, welcome gifts, etc.

The objectives of sales promotions vary according to the source of the promotion – brand or retailer. The promotional technique chosen will depend largely on the objective and also on the nature of the professional, as summarized in Table 21.1.

Traditional promotional practices are based on behavioral learning theory. According to this theory, the individual learns to react, often in a reflex, automatic way without analyzing the situation, in response to an external stimulus (stimulus response). Two types of learning may be distinguished:

1   *Conditioning learning*: unconscious behaviors are induced by the association between an unconditioned stimulus (which is the initial cause of the response) and another conditioned stimulus (which is able, after repeated pairing with the unconditioned stimulus, to produce the original response).
2   *Instrumental learning*: the individual learns to reproduce a behavior for a reward (positive reinforcement) or to avoid punishment (negative reinforcement).

In sales promotion, the most frequently used strategy is positive reinforcement. By providing a benefit for the consumer, the manufacturer or retailer tries to condition consumers and encourage them to buy the product even in the absence of the benefit (e.g. (1) offer a free sample to promote the testing of the product; (2) attach a refund offer to the sample to facilitate an initial purchase; and (3) buy the product at the normal price). In this approach, the consumer is seen as passive, responding mechanistically to the stimulus of the sales promotion. The effectiveness of this transactional approach has its limitations.

Traditional sales promotion limitations

While the effect of the promotion on the increase in short-term sales is indisputable, its long-term effectiveness, both in recruiting new customers and in developing customer loyalty, is now questioned for a variety of reasons.

1 *Negative effects of promotion on the brand's (retailer's) perceived image.* Systematic use of promotions runs the risk of impairing a brand's image by making it appear too "cheap," and has negative effects on brand equity (Yoo *et al.* 2000). Price-related promotions have negative effects on brand preference in the long term.

   The search for a long-term relationship with consumers leads professionals to bet on advantages other than purely monetary benefits, namely more hedonistic advantages. Premiums or prizes are offered to customers, either in the classic framework of short-term promotional operations or possibly in brand or retailer loyalty programs. However, even if the rewards offered to customers are more varied than previously, the way of operating has not changed, since the consumer is still viewed as passive and easily conditioned. A gift can certainly have a significant emotional value, but only on condition that it is appreciated and valued by the consumer. Reactions to a brand can be negative when a promotion does not appear attractive or relevant to consumers. An unattractive premium that the consumer views as having no use or value will have a negative effect on a brand's image and on attitudes towards it (Simonson *et al.* 1994).

2 *Development of price sensitivity and consumer disloyalty.* The objectives of recruiting new consumers and the development of loyalty may be thwarted by the price sensitivity and opportunism of some consumers. Thus the proliferation of promotional offers may lead to increased consumer sensitivity to price and promotions. Instead of accustoming the consumer to buy the brand, the promotion results in him buying only when goods are on promotional offer (i.e., the consumer becomes deal-prone; Lichtenstein *et al.* 1997). He will then tend to attribute his purchase to the promotion rather than to any preference for the product. In this case, new buyers are in reality simply opportunist buyers who will change brand (or retailer) when the promotional offer ends. Moreover, promotional outbidding tactics make the consumer gradually lose the notion of the reference price and this consumer then becomes a sales promotion hunter. Sales promotion and, by extension, loyalty programs may therefore fail to meet their marketing objective of developing loyalty, as a result of fickle purchasers who do not hesitate to switch brands, stores or loyalty programs in accordance with whatever promotion is currently available.

3 *Cultural differences as limitations to the effectiveness of promotions.* The cultural characteristics of individuals influence their attitudes and responses to promotional practices. Standard promotional offers without any distinction between cultural backgrounds may be ineffective. Saving money, an important benefit of sales promotions, does not have the same value for consumers from dissimilar cultural backgrounds. For example, Anglo-American consumers redeem more coupons than African-American consumers (Green 1995), and Hispanic consumers see coupons as a form of charity (Hernandez 1988).

   Promotional techniques can be associated with an image of social status: "in many countries coupons or money-off offers can be associated with low-class status, because the implied price consciousness mediates an image of low purchasing power" (Usunier and Lee 2005: 359). For example, in a cross-cultural study, Huff and Alden (1999) showed that use of both coupons and sweepstakes is substantially lower in Taiwan than Thailand or Malaysia. Among these three countries, Malaysians appear to have a greater fear of embarrassment or losing face when using a coupon. In other cultures, e.g. certain Muslim countries, promotional techniques such as games and lotteries are either forbidden or strictly controlled. These practices are seen as immoral and contrary to religious principles that prohibit easy money and games of chance. Thus, in thinking about sales promotions, it would seem to be essential to take into account the socio-cultural context in which the consumer evolves.

New consumer responses to measures aimed at stimulating sales

For the most part, studies focus on what makes a promotion attractive for consumers. This approach may be logical, but it does have one major disadvantage: it views consumers as passive recipients of the commercial transaction, as if waiting patiently for someone to come along and stimulate their purchases. In most cases, of course, consumers are neither passive nor naïve when it comes to the different promotional tools employed. Their purchasing experience over the years has allowed them to develop a real understanding of the various techniques used by brands and retailers to encourage them to make a purchase. In order to identify the active role played by consumers, we must first decipher their consumption practices in given contexts; doing so will help us understand how they adapt promotions to their behavior, rather than the other way round (looking at a promotion and studying its effect on the consumer). This requires a shift in our point of view, as proposed by the cultural approach.

Sales promotion as a resource for the consumer

To adopt a cultural point of view is to believe that consumers, although influenced to some extent, enjoy a degree of autonomy by using their consumption habits to achieve personal and family objectives. In this respect, promotions can be considered as resources that are provided by brands and retailers and allow the purchaser to realize his/her own projects. Consumers make daily choices based on their resources in terms of finance and time. This means that compromises must be made and products of value must be distinguished from those where savings may be made. As well as their practical aspects, promotions may also be used to satisfy hedonic needs (e.g. treasure hunts) or to express oneself (a smart purchase). Bargain hunting can even be considered a core tendency in consumer practices. From something marginal a few years ago, the search for "great deals" is now becoming a distinctive style of consumption. Consumers are transforming themselves into "smart shoppers." The development of low-cost businesses, hard discounts, special online offers and the success of in-store promotions and sales bear witness to the appetite among consumers for such commercial offers, as well as their ability to find products at the best price.

For a few years, specialists have been able to identify those consumers who display a particular type of behavior: smart shoppers. These consumers have developed a highly opportunistic approach to sales promotion. Once inside the store, they do not hesitate to ask staff about special offers and try to identify the available promotions. They are also more likely to bargain over price. Outside retail outlets, smart shoppers are attentive to the media and advertising; they read consumer magazines and visit consumer websites. For these consumers, searching for the most appealing promotions is akin to a treasure hunt; it makes them feel proud of being craftier than other shoppers who pay the full price. These smart shoppers take advantage of loyalty programs by, for example, lending their loyalty cards to friends in order to accumulate the promised benefits as quickly as possible.

Thus, as well as the economic benefit such behavior provides, there is also a degree of motivation based on self-expression and hedonism (Schindler 1998). Some consumers – cash refund hunters – have taken the principle of smart shopping to an extreme: they will actually exploit sales promotions by only purchasing products that are partially or fully reimbursed (Box 21.1). Others – competition specialists (sometimes from the same category of shoppers) – systematically enter all competitions organized by various brands.

Yet the smart shopper is looking for consumption optimization. The cultural goals linked to consumerist materialism are still predominant, but the smart shopper tries to find innovative ways to satisfy his consumption appetite. In times of economic crisis, the desire for

---

Box 21.1 Refund offer specialists

Although few in number, cash refund hunters in France represent a significant proportion of consumers seeking full or partial reimbursement on their purchases. They therefore have a considerable impact on the profitability of promotional activities and are forcing brands to introduce stricter conditions for the refund. The development of more complex conditions discourages the occasional purchaser and has led to a feeling of defiance among certain consumers towards promotions.

A study of 15 cash refund offer specialists, contacted via a dedicated website, shows that they use promotions as a resource enabling them to realize various projects, particularly in economic terms:

> With the money we get back, as well as what we save through coupons, we've always been able to afford a few treats, such as a meal out or small gifts for the family, etc. I've always budgeted that separately from the family budget. It's really about small pleasures".
>
> (Michèle)

Nevertheless, hunting for refunds occupies a significant amount of time (around 10–15 hours a week) and the time devoted to this activity is justified by many forms of valorization. Using the four "metaphors for consuming" (Holt 1995): consumption as experience, consumption as integration, consumption as play and consumption as classification – we explore the way these bargain hunters make use of sales promotions.

1   *Consumption as experience*: how cash refund consumers make sense of their activity and respond to sales promotions: "It's a real game for me to go looking for the different offers ... I get a certain amount of excitement out of browsing through the shops" (Martin).
2   *Consumption as integration*: how cash refund consumers integrate their activity into their identity: "It's kind of satisfying to outsmart the big shots ... it's silly but I think it's cool to make these big companies lose money" (Sandrine).
3   *Consumption as play:* how cash refund consumers interact with other like-minded consumers (information exchange, comparison with other refund specialists, etc.): "There's a small group of us in the town where I live. We give each other tips, it's pretty friendly ... we meet up in shops and exchange information by e-mail" (Martin).

> 4   *Consumption as classification*: how cash refund consumers differentiate them-
> selves from other people: "People complain a lot but they don't watch what they
> buy. Advertising is okay but it's up to them what they put in their trolley, nobody's
> forcing them. We live in a country full of people with their hand out. Am I too
> harsh? I don't think I'm resisting a consumer society; I'm just respecting my own
> desires, I'm not a sheep who does the same as everyone else" (Athos).
>
> Source: Odou *et al.* (2008).

hyper-consumption is less obvious. Consumers then try to moderate their buying impulse
(Djelassi *et al.* 2009). They assess the ways in which they consume. A phenomenon of
rationalization affects purchases, leading consumers to exploit their knowledge differently.
The problem is less about consuming more with the same budget than about providing for an
anticipated decrease in purchasing power. Such consumers are considered "wise" rather than
"smart" shoppers (see Table 21.2). Rationalizing their consumption practices means that
wise shoppers see promotions differently: they will first ask whether a product is indispen-
sable before finding out whether a good deal is on offer. The utilitarian consumer makes a
return but has retained the experience accumulated over years of purchasing. Like smart
shoppers, wise shoppers are fond of promotions and other advantages offered by their loyalty cards. They keep themselves informed about ongoing promotions and include them in
their shopping list. They maintain an overall positive attitude toward promotions even though
their expertise leads them to systematically check the appeal of each one. By contrast, many
consumers develop a negative attitude toward stimulating techniques involving sales promotion or loyalty program benefits.

Table 21.2 Smart and wise shopping: two different ways of dealing with sales promotion

Smart shopping	Wise shopping
Objective	
To quench the urge to consume by spending the least possible → Active search for the good deal	To control spending in order to respect the budget defined beforehand (even if it means reducing consumption)
Attitude toward retailer offer	
Opportunistic attitude: taking advantage of the system and even sometimes exploiting it in one's own interest	Distrust and questioning of many aspects of the offer (selection, communication, etc.)
Sales promotion use	
Active use of promotional offers even if they do not relate to products which the consumer needs	Use of promotional offers only if items are included in the shopping list. Distrust and caution in the use of promotions
Consumer role	
Active → Considerable time and energy are devoted to bargain-hunting, procurement optimization and thinking about the best way to take advantage of promotional offers	Active and critical thinking on the mode of purchase and consumption, control of purchases. Key behaviors: buy cheaper but also less, try to avoid temptation

*Consumer resistance to programs aiming at stimulating sales: from
skeptical to cynical consumers*

Reactions to sales promotions can be viewed from two angles: interest in the promotion
and a feeling of manipulation. Companies must be careful: by increasing interest in a
promotion (by indicating the value of the offer, for example) they can also heighten the sense
of manipulation and thereby damage their brand image in the long term (Darke and
Dahl 2003). The type of promotion used will influence perceptions of manipulation. For
example, offers that include deferred payment and proof of purchase are perceived as more
manipulative and, similarly, promotional offers that offer very little value or are complex
(e.g. promotions involving various mechanisms) increase consumer mistrust and skepticism.
The same applies to loyalty programs, in which the complexity of reward schemes, as
well as delays before any reward is received, adversely affect the ways in which customers
benefit.

In return, consumers develop new reflexes in response, such as always checking
the true appeal of a promotion in relation to their regular purchases. Typically, consumers
ask themselves the following questions: Is the promotion on this brand really advantageous
compared to the brand I usually buy? Are they trying to make me buy something I don't
really need? Is the quantity appropriate to my consumption habits? (This last question is
very common among single people, one-parent families and the elderly.) Such consumers
are wary of false promotions and can be defined as skeptical or even cynical (if they
doubt whether there is any such thing as corporate altruistic motivation). Consumer
skepticism may be interpreted as a distanciation, a kind of emancipation from
marketing stimulation techniques and even sometimes from the consumer society. In both
cases, the consumer tries to regain control of his consumption in order to achieve
his own goals. The realization of these objectives is not necessarily accompanied by a
negative attitude toward stimulation tools, but is simply a reasoned distrust allowing the
consumer to distinguish a good bargain from a bad one, as is the case for smart and
wise shoppers.

Regaining control of one's consumption can also satisfy other needs, such as remaining
master of one's acts. El Euch Maalej and Roux (2010) have shown, for example, that
consumer reactance is one of the reasons for non-participation in loyalty programs. Other
consumers avoid them by shopping in stores that do not offer loyalty cards, in particular
hard discounters such as Lidl or Aldi, or by providing false contact details when filling out
their subscription forms. Apart from reactance, stimulation techniques may be rejected
for ideological reasons, whether or not such techniques relate to a loyalty program, because
they encourage the individual to consume more and keep him in a consumerist logic
that creates social and environmental problems (cf. Chapter 28 in this volume). Moreover,
promotional techniques and loyalty programs are often seen as intrusive, and their growth
fuels consumers' resistance to such practices.

How can a company's objectives be reconciled with consumer personal identity projects? Some examples of successful campaigns

Many consumers today are looking for new experiences and new social links that are
meaningful. They also have feelings of mistrust towards institutions. It is therefore
particularly difficult to win the loyalty of these customers without taking away their

freedom to choose, try new things and pursue their personal identity projects or without heightening their resistance to marketing. How then can managers secure the loyalty of their customers?

Managers must admit that they have to share power with consumers, and so customer empowerment (Vargo and Lusch 2004) is the first step. Second, they have to develop consumer-centric strategies by providing consumers with resources (promotions, loyalty program benefits, prizes, services, information, games, innovations, personnel, values, myths, symbols and so on) that they can combine with their own resources (economic, ludic, utopian, temporal, social, etc.) to "accomplish the pursuit of their personal identity and communal projects" (Arnould 2005: 89). We will offer some ideas that can help to realize this co-creation process.

Providing consumers with economic and time resources for the pursuit of smart, wise or responsible consumption (consumption as integration)

The proliferation of promotions has led customers to reflect on what is a fair price for products. It can also be perceived as an incitement to consumption during periods when consumers would rather make savings. Both retailers and brands must therefore endeavor to restore trust among consumers. It is better, in such times of economic hardship, to offer everyday low prices (EDLP) (e.g. Aldi, Wal-Mart) in order to make consumers feel that the company is on their side from day to day and that talk about defending their purchasing power is not simply vacuous.

Other retailers are developing promotions on products bought daily. This is the concept of useful promotions (e.g. French supermarket Intermarché's "useful discount"). Similarly, promotional mechanisms should be simplified (cash benefits and immediate payment). Customers become confused by the combination of loyalty card advantages, discounts valid on their next purchase and immediate reductions, and view this negatively. Several brands have also increased the administrative obstacles to full or partial refund, which is seen as unfair and time-consuming by consumers.

Moreover, loyalty programs are meant to simplify life, and provide customers with solutions and help them save money and time. Because of the difficulty for consumers in managing all the loyalty programs to which they belong (losing their card or missing out on the benefits they are due), a website has been created to make life easier for them: the Australian-run www.perkler.com takes care of everything. Users can list their cards and the site will inform them (free of charge) of the advantages offered by each. It can even recommend others, depending on the kind of reward sought: a sort of loyalty coach!

Surprising customers through creativity: mobilizing consumers' ludic resources for consumption as experience

Most promotions display little creativity, recycling the old approach of price reductions which, while effective, usually end up damaging brand image in the long term. The most effective promotions are generally those that show some innovation. Promotions not only stimulate sales, but also favor creative consumer activities and then develop hedonic and affective bonds between the retailer/brand and consumers. Several innovative approaches may be used: creativity in the medium deployed (e-mails, mobile marketing), creativity in the reward on offer (inviting customers to the filming of their favorite television series), or

Box 21.2 Clockwork Orange's "Beat the clock" sale

Sales promotion has a bad reputation because of its effects on brand image. However, if the brand succeeds in deflecting sales promotion from its price reduction focus, it can use it as a way to improve brand loyalty by creating a strong link with its customers. For the opening of a new retail outlet, Clockwork Orange, a Northern Ireland streetwear fashion brand, organized a "Beat the clock" sale. The principle was simple: the cost of the purchased item was calculated according to the time it was bought. At 5am, each item cost only £5, whether the original price was £30 for a t-shirt or £300 for a leather jacket. It was the first time that a fashion retailer had used this technique and it proved very successful. A minimal marketing campaign included e-mail marketing to a 3,000 VIP database, a local radio promotion, a billboard in the retail park, some regional press PR and flyers in other stores. The results far exceeded expectations. Before the opening of the store at 5am, there were 1,000 cars at the retail park and 2,000 customers waiting. By the end of the working day, 6,000 items had been sold (ten times the usual sales). According to the product manager, Will McCooke, interviewed by *UTalkMarketing*, the promotion also raised brand awareness and positioned the brand as a fun retailer.

creativity in the promotional mechanism (games, treasure hunts, price reductions based on the time of purchase; see the Clockwork Orange case study in Box 21.2, and the article from *UTalkMarketing* by Turner (2007) for the full story).

Offering consumers social and utopian resources for consumption as play and classification

Firms can offer consumers social and utopian resources that help them to accomplish their identity project and supra-ordinate goals: family, happiness, community, frugality, charity and so on. Various examples detailed below show how sales promotion and loyalty programs can provide symbolic and affective benefits to consumers that bond them first to their community and consequently to the companies.

Research carried out on Anglo-Pakistanis has shown them to be particularly sensitive to rewards that allow their children to develop intellectually (Jamal *et al.* 2007). These consumers will therefore support promotions that help to educate their children.

In Europe's Latin countries there is real appetite for charity promotions, with five identifiable issues: health, environment, society, hunger and children. There are two fields of application: local solidarity and poorer nations. The probiotic yogurt brand Actimel (Danone) thus decided to develop links with the Pasteur Institute. Consumers could collect coupons for 20 cent donations during a period of six months, and the money collected was then spent on research into ferments and probiotics. Along the same lines, some retailers develop links with charitable or environmental organizations, such as the WWF or the Red Cross, and pay the monetary equivalent of any loyalty points accumulated by their customers. Loyalty programs then become a resource that gives meaning to people's consumption.

In addition, a strong attachment can transform mere behavioral loyalty into a genuine affective bond. A customer's visit to a sales outlet can be made sacrosanct by means of rituals (Belk *et al.* 1989). For example, some families visit McDonald's every Friday night to celebrate the arrival of the weekend and treat the kids, even though the parents may not actually enjoy the experience themselves. An individual's loyalty to a brand/ company can therefore be synonymous with his/her loyalty to family or friends; this constitutes a strong "exit barrier," as commercial loyalty is associated with a higher, non-commercial form of loyalty. The positioning of a brand/company can therefore be based on affective connotations rather than tangible attributes, making for a competitive advantage that is much more difficult to imitate. This generates and propagates a sort of utopian and affective proximity or identification between a company and consumers, thereby reinforcing trust in the company and the intention to frequent it – maybe again and again. Loyalty to brands or commercial activities is just a small part of people's overall loyalty and allegiances. Commercial loyalty only makes sense for customers if it is linked to the allegiance they have to the people, objects and activities that actually mean something for them and are a part of their values or life projects (Arnould *et al.* 2006).

If a company adopts a more sophisticated conception of customer-centered loyalty that takes into account the wider socio-cultural context of the individual lives of its customers, and their values and their life projects, then it leads to a more involved relationship, and thereby strengthens the commitment and attachment of the customer to the brand/company. In the following examples (see Box 21.3), we can see how consumption as play and consumption as classification are fostered by specific and entangled promotional and relational programs.

Box 21.3 Leroy Merlin and Fnac Case studies

An approach now favored by some companies (some category killers such as Fnac or Leroy Merlin in Europe) is to base customer loyalty on the non-trade value of a lasting interpersonal relationship with the retailer, but also to create value among the "best customer" community (Schau *et al.* 2009). The most recent loyalty programs place increasing emphasis on intangible symbolic benefits (sense of belonging, recognition, gratitude) and organize special attention or VIP-type preferential treatment for their best customers. Each of these best customers has a personal salesperson, who responds to any needs he may have. The degree of interpersonal relation is decided by the customer (either very strong and frequent contacts or looser ones). At the same time, events are organized to enable their best customer community to meet and exchange information and best practices. The combination of the retailer's and consumers' resources is then optimized.

These programs have had very positive effects on company–customer relations and loyalty in various sectors (hotels and retailing in particular), both in terms of attitudes and behavior. Since they are less easily imitated by competitors, such intangible and personalized benefits could be significant sources of competitive advantage that will help distinguish brands.

*How can companies activate cultural resources? By customer
empowerment and co-design strategy*

Companies provide consumers with different resources that consumers will freely use and
combine with their own resources. Consumers become actors and companies' results
improve as they offer personalized promotion and loyalty programs that are valuable because
they match consumers' personal goals and projects. Various examples illustrate this
co-creation, in which consumers are constrained to a greater or lesser extent (Vargo and
Lusch 2004).

The development of e-mail and mobile marketing has made personalized promotions
possible. More targeted promotions that take account of customers' individual characteristics are valuable tools in the development of customer relations. Unlike push strategies,
the new trend is to offer consumers the freedom to choose to receive coupons on their
mobile phone, to print the coupons they want and to indicate what sort of promotions they
are interested in. A far cry from standardized price-based promotions, which usually
prove damaging to a brand, personalized promotional strategies lie half-way between sales
stimulation and the development of brand attachment. They are also associated in most cases
with loyalty programs. For example, Ocean Spray, the well-known North American brand
leader in the category of canned and bottled juice and juice drinks, is offering its UK
consumer community the opportunity to get printable coupons with a newsletter. The
marketing objective is to add value to the newsletter so as to keep the consumer engaged
with the company. Results have been very encouraging, with an average 24 percent print-
to-redeem rate.

There are companies that empower more customers and let them choose freely, as in
the case with Carrefour. In 2009, Carrefour launched a new sales promotion program
called "promos libres" or "free promotions." Every week there are two product families
covered by the promotions. The innovation consists in the fact that it is the customer, and no
longer the dealer or the brand, who chooses his favorite products, and then gets a discount
on every third product bought by the family involved in the promotion. For example, one
week promotions may feature all drinks and pet food; the week after, it may be fruit and
cosmetics, and so on. The system is successful because it responds to consumers' concern to
being free to choose. They are actors and not "marketing targets." The dealer provides
them with operand resources that consumers mix with their own operant resources (tastes,
preferences, skills, etc.) and indeed with other consumers' resources. They can exchange
resources that companies offer them. For example, in 2010, Auchan and Carrefour offered
Disney and Pixar cards to their consumers, who spontaneously organized a card exchange
inside the shopping mall. Consumers took over the operation, which became a game
that enabled social interactions.

Conclusion

To conclude, promotional techniques have serious limitations. The most usual criticism,
mentioned in the first section, is linked to the ephemeral nature of their efficiency. The
integration of these techniques into loyalty programs was an initial answer to this problem.
However, both the opportunism of some consumers towards promotional techniques
and loyalty programs and the resistance of other consumers, which is linked to personality
drivers (the desire for independence and control), whether ideological (anti-consumerist
movements) or cultural, lead to a questioning of traditional stimulating techniques. It is thus

necessary to rethink these techniques by reflecting on one of the key principles of the cultural approach: the consumer is not the passive and obedient receptacle of marketing techniques. On the contrary, he neutralizes them, diverts them and sometimes even sets themselves in opposition to them (Roux, 2005).

This chapter shows how sales promotion has moved from a traditional behaviorist approach to a broader and richer cultural perspective in order to suit new consumer behaviors and requirements (see Table 21.3 for a summary).

Thus, if companies want to improve the effects of their sales promotions and loyalty programs in both the short term and the long term, they need to consider consumers as smart partners and co-producers. If the programs are personalized, co-conceptualized and if consumers have the power to choose their rewards, sales promotions and loyalty programs should minimize consumers' opportunism and skepticism.

Adopting such sales promotion techniques and loyalty programs, which combine tangible (monetary) and intangible benefits (hedonic, symbolic) with a high level of personalization, heightens the creation of experiential value by activating the various value sources (intrinsic or extrinsic, active or reactive, etc.).

Review and discussion questions

1   What are the major limitations of the traditional view of sales promotion?
2   Why do sales promotions provoke such negative reactions nowadays?
3   What are the major changes from the traditional to the cultural perspective on sales promotion?
4   Why may we consider sales promotions to be consumers' resources?
5   How can firms ensure that their sales promotion policies respond to consumers' needs?
6   How can co-creation improve the results of sales promotions and loyalty programs?
7   What sort of consumer resources can sales promotion and loyalty programs mobilize?

Table 21.3 Sales promotion: from a traditional behaviorist perspective to a cultural perspective

Sales promotion principles	
Traditional behaviorist approach	*Cultural perspective*
Promotion = brand/retailer resource	Promotion = consumer resource
Consumer = passive target	Consumer = co-producer, partner
Based on behavioral learning theory/ stimulus → response	Based on a broader consumer analysis, experiential, more affective and socio-cultural, etc.
Short term	Medium and long term
Quantitative measures of sales promotion performance	Qualitative approach to sales promotion performance measures
Imposed promotion, chosen by company	Promotions chosen by consumer, consumer freedom (e.g. promos libres by Carrefour)
Firm has power	Power shifted to consumers
Promotion diffusion control belongs to brands/retailers (offer)	Promotion diffusion is influenced by consumers, social networks, word of mouth. Consumer is central to the success of sales promotion (website such as www.radinmalin.com)

Keywords

co-design, consumer resistance, cultural resources, empowerment, loyalty, sales promotion

References

Arnould, E. J. (2005) "Animating the Big Middle," *Journal of Retailing*, 81(2): 89–96.

Arnould, E. J., Price, L. L. and Malshe, A. (2006) "Toward a Cultural Resource-Based Theory of the Customer," in R. F. Lusch, and S. L. Vargo (eds), *The New Dominant Logic in Marketing*, Armonk, NY: M. E. Sharpe.

Belk, R. B., Wallendorf, M. and Sherry, J. F. Jr. (1989) "The Sacred and the Profane in Consumer Behavior: Theodicy on the Odyssey," *Journal of Consumer Research*, 16(June): 1–37.

Blattberg, R. C. and Neslin, S. A. (1990) *Sales Promotion: Concepts, Methods and Strategies*, Englewood Cliffs, NJ: Prentice Hall.

Darke, P. R. and Dahl, D. W. (2003) "Fairness and Discounts: The Subjective Value of a Bargain," *Journal of Consumer Psychology*, 13: 328–38.

Djelassi, S., Collin-Lachaud, I. and Odou P. (2009) "Purchasing Power Crisis: Retailers Facing the Wise Shopping," *Décisions Marketing*, 56: 37–46.

El Euch Maalej, M. and Roux, D. (2010) "Consumer Resistance to Joining Loyalty Programs: An Exploratory Approach," paper presented at European Advances in Consumer Research Conference, London Royal Holloway, June 30–July 3rd.

Green, C. L. (1995) "Differential Responses to Retail Sales Promotion Among African-American and Anglo-American Consumers," *Journal of Retailing*, 71(1): 83–92.

Hernandez, S. A. (1988) "An Exploratory Study of Coupon Use in Puerto Rico: Cultural vs. Institutional Barriers to Coupon Use," *Journal of Advertising Research*, October/November: 40–6.

Holt, D. B. (1995) "How Consumers Consume: A Typology of Consumption Practices," *Journal of Consumer Research*, 22(1): 1–16.

Huff, L. C and Alden, D. L. (1999) "An Investigation of Consumer Response to Sales Promotions in Developing Markets: A Three-Country Analysis," *Advances in Consumer Research*, 26: 41–2.

Jamal, A., Peattie, S. and Peattie, K. (2007) "Consumers' Response to Sales Promotions: An Explorative Study in Junk Food Market," paper presented at the European Advances in Consumer Research Conference, June, Milan.

Lichtenstein, D. R., Burton, S. and Netemeyer, R. G. (1997) "An Examination of Deal Proneness Across Sales Promotion Types: A Consumer Segmentation Perspective," *Journal of Retailing*, 73(2): 283–97.

Odou, P., Djelassi, S. and Belvaux, B. (2008) "Smart Shopping and Cash Refund Offer Subversion," paper presented at the Consumer Culture Theory Conference, Boston, June.

Roux, D. (2005) "Résistance du consommateur: un état de l'art sur les formes de réponses adverses au marché et aux firmes," paper presented at the 4th International Congress on Marketing Trends, Paris, January.

Schau, H. J., Muñiz, A. M. and Arnould, E. J. (2009) "How Brand Community Practices Create Value," *Journal of Marketing*, 73(September): 30–51.

Schindler, R. M. (1998) "Consequences of Perceiving Oneself as Responsible for Obtaining a Discount: Evidence for Smart-Shopper Feelings," *Journal of Consumer Psychology*, 7(4): 371–92.

Simonson, I., Ziv, C. and O'Curry, S. (1994) "Experimental Evidence on the Negative Effect of Product Features and Sales Promotions on Brand Choice," *Marketing Science*, 13(1): 23–40.

Turner, C. (2007) "'Beat the Clock' Sales Promotions Draws Thousands." Available at: http://www.utalkmarketing.com (accessed October 17, 2010).

Usunier, J. -C. and Lee, J. (2005) *Marketing Across Cultures*, 4th edn, Harlow: Pearson Education Limited.

Vargo, S. L. and Lusch, R. F. (2004) "Evolving to a New Dominant Logic for Marketing," *Journal of Marketing*, 68(1): 1–17.

Yoo, B., Dondhu, N. and Lee, S. (2000) "An Examination of Selected Marketing Mix Elements and Brand Equity," *Journal of the Academy of Marketing Science*, 28(2): 195–211.

Internet resources

http://www.cles-promo.com/: this French news site offers case studies, thematic files and numerous information on French sales promotions.

http://promomagazine.com/: many useful insights on promotion marketing are provided on this American website.

http://www.utalkmarketing.com: many case studies are available on this UK website.

22 Product design and creativity

Nacima Ourahmoune

Overview

Product design is an important aspect of the marketing mix and a crucial reflection of brand discourse and positioning. Yet it has often been reduced to systematic descriptions of the innovation process and to functional definitions. More recently, product design has been viewed simply as an aesthetic touch to be added to a product just before commercialization.

This chapter argues that product design should be situated within the flow of socio-cultural and symbolic meanings derived from consumers' experiences, desires and emotions, and as such is able to add brand value to products. It contends that this approach leads to innovation when a co-creation process involving designers, marketers *and* consumers is implemented.

The HOM case study, based on the author's previous research, shows how the brand launched a new and successful product category for men that they termed "men's lingerie". HOM was able to decipher, capture, interpret and transfer to their products the changing societal gender roles and complexities of current masculine norms. Signs and codes conveyed by the products, together with consistent brand communication, allowed the brand to succeed in selling designs, shapes and material of a markedly feminine character to men.

This case study illustrates the power of product design when conceived as a language able to mediate cultural values leading to product attachment and brand desirability. Rather than an aesthetic touch added at the end of the product design process, product creation is optimized as a space of real dialogue and co-creation between brand managers, designers and consumers within a specific socio-cultural context.

Introduction

We have all grown up in a world of relentless industrial and material progress. Product designers have played a part in this – meeting people's material needs with functional, ergonomic and attractive product designs optimized for manufacture. However, society's expectations are changing and so too is the role of the marketing manager and the product designer. Our holistic view of progress now puts human rather than material values at the heart of a society that is striving to be inclusive and sustainable while satisfying its physical and emotional needs. Product design is evolving to meet the needs of people for whom the experience of discovering, buying and making coffee is valued as much as the cup of coffee itself.

Designing is now about people. What they value, how they relate to themselves, each other and their surroundings. Designers and marketing managers must understand this to create complete product experiences for consumers rather than just well-styled products. Our "product-saturated" marketplace means that effective marketing managers need to have more than simply technical skills.

This chapter aims to clarify the strategic importance of product design seen as a window for brand discourse and as a vehicle for cultural values that echo consumers' representations.

Product design: from function to culture

In order to talk about a cultural perspective on design, we should start with the conventional perspective on marketing in product design. Conventional marketing mentions design in books for students and practitioners, but only very briefly. A standard book such as *Marketing Management* (Kotler and Keller 2008) devotes just over a page to it. In it, design is defined as a way of differentiating and placing a brand's products in such a way as to become competitively attractive. It is "the totality of features that affect how a product looks, feels, and functions in terms of consumers' requirements" (ibid.: 365). The book also describes the different ways a designer must think in order to create a successful product design. He must understand the importance of shape, development, performance, conformity, durability, reliability, "reparability" and style for a product. Whereas companies believe that a good design is the one that is easy to make and distribute, consumers like an attractive product, easy to open, set up, repair and so on. Design plays a part in those concerns. The book also proposes, again briefly, that marketers now acknowledge the emotional power of design; and indeed some companies have seen their market share rise since adding a design department to their operations. Finally, design is seen as a way of changing how consumers perceive a brand in a saturated market.

These elements are interesting and give a general view of how important design is in marketing. The product is indeed one of the pillars of the marketing mix. It is a central aspect of marketing research, and is always something that sales-conscious managers pay great attention to. Product launching is on the increase, and there is a race for innovation among competitors, with a very high risk of failure, making it a strategic matter. Moreover, saturated markets and consumers, always on the lookout for something new, make product renewal a major factor in increased sales: it is the "new" label effect.

Nevertheless, the traditional marketing literature is concerned only with some aspects of innovation and too often neglects the symbolic and imaginary dimensions of a product, the issue of the product's appropriation by the consumer, or even the strong emotional power within the product–consumer interaction. This absence derives from the cognitivist tradition of marketing, which minimizes the experiential dimension of the consumer–product relation.

Furthermore, the process of innovation is often described in this perspective as a sort of universal, systematic methodology that is followed by product designers at different stages. Below I summarize the methodology implemented by product designers and their specific skills as proposed by Morris (2009: 23) in *The Fundamentals of Product Design*.

Initial stage

1   Idea generation can be from imagination, observation or research.

2   Need-based generation can be from the need to solve a problem, the need to follow popular trends or the need for a product to do a specific task.

Middle stage

3   Design solutions arise from meeting user requirements, concept development, exploration of different designs, ergonomics, prototyping, materials and technology.
4   Production involves fabrication and manufacturing the design.

Final stage

Marketing involves selling the product. It can either be client-based which means the client buys the design and manufactures it and then sells it to customers. Or it can be user-based where the designer sells the product directly to the user.

This technical and functional representation of product design traces the frontiers and limits among different actors but pays little attention to interactions between marketers and designers. It also views clients and consumers as a means rather than as an end or as partners. Our cultural approach to product design developed in this chapter claims there is a need to go beyond this systematic and conventional approach and therefore to adopt a holistic view of the process of product design engaging designers, marketers and consumers in the co-creation of products that are invested with meaning and add value to consumers' lives while sustaining brand narratives and creating a distinctive and motivating positioning.

To further clarify this cultural view, I begin by situating product design within the functionalist perspective that echoes traditional marketing concepts.

Functionalist product design

The tradition of conventional marketing goes together with a functionalist conception of product design, which prevailed for a long time. Functionalist design sees the product as efficient, adequate, long-lasting and without any particular decorative feature. This perspective reduces the artefact to its function. What matters is not the object but its function. Of course, the product physically exists, but its material specificity is secondary. The physicality of the product concerns only its functionality. The design does not act on the object, but follows and derives from the anticipated functional use. Thus, famously, Le Corbusier did not build houses, but "machines for living in".

What results from functionalism is that if we emphasize the function rather than the object itself, we are less attached to it. When artefacts are created only to fulfil a purpose and to be easily mass-produced, they are devoid of any individual input. Therefore, by focusing on function rather than materiality, functionalism leads to non-attachment to the product, resulting in objects that are not retained for any great length of time. Indeed, in a society where products may be physically long-lasting, if consumers are not attached to them, they can easily be replaced or discarded.

Yet it is interesting to note that the following is a conventional marketing creed: "For the company, a good product design is easy to make and distribute" (Kotler and Keller 2008: 365). Hence the way the company perceives design somehow contributes to this functionalist image. The definition of "good design for the company" lacks the symbolic and meaningful aspects found in product design that must represent the brand and resonate with the consumers' lived experience. The traditional marketing perspective treats the experiential aspect of the consumer–product–brand relationship as a direct reaction to marketer-produced stimuli, and neglects the interpretative and meaningful dimension coming from consumers. But in our cultural marketing perspective, this is a serious lacuna, for we believe that good product design goes beyond solely functional considerations. Rather it generates dialogue between the brand and consumers, and becomes a locus for the sharing of ideas, values and experiences.

The paradigm that has dominated consumer research for 50 years conceives of the consumer as someone constantly searching for information through advertising messages, in order to process them and make choices. This paradigm has been criticized on various grounds: (1) the model fails to explain the transfer of the cultural meanings and values between the advertisement, the product and the consumer; (2) the consumer's role is much too simplified, as also is the interactive nature of advertisements and products. Consumer researchers such as McCracken (1986) or Belk (1988) pointed out that researchers and marketers were wrong in claiming that consumption was the main activity of the consumer and that culture had a limited impact in the process. Moreover, the study of consumer behaviour was carried out independently of other aspects of life, a shortcoming that limited the cultural understanding of product–consumer relations.

McCracken (1986) argues that in reality, consumption has the role of culture creation and protection. In this context, culture is seen as something holistic, in perpetual motion, changing and enhancing meanings. Brand communication also plays a more direct role, in connection with culture, representing a framework of symbols or special meanings that arise from culture and are located in a product or a particular design. This process implies cultural meanings embodied in the product, hence the *produit-signe* (Baudrillard 1996), *fetish product* (in a Marxist sense) or *totem product* in tribal marketing (Maffesoli 1996). I do not wish to describe the object as simply functionality oriented.

The consumer, therefore, perceives meaning in products, which is then used to support both an inner concept of himself/herself and an outer concept of the external world and its role for him/her. Thus consumption becomes a key element in creating meaning (and culture) for the individual constantly seeking to define his/her inner self and to position himself in the socially and culturally established outer world.

Today, this experiential and emotional dimension has become increasingly modish in the eyes of the marketers, at the same time as the purchase decision has become more complex than a purely rational cost/benefit logic. For 20 years, cultural approaches to marketing have encouraged marketers to invest in marketing as the management of codes and signs. Viewed in this way, product design is not only a way of differentiation through style and ergonomics, it is a real language, a complex semiotic logic that needs to be decoded. On the other hand, design conveys an ideology, i.e. a system of values that interacts with the consumer and involves brands. Products and design thus conceived are fully cultural artefacts with complex meaning that managers must repeatedly decode. As we will see, this process is a way for the company to add value.

Product design as embodiment of meaning

Modernism started to decline in the 1950s when contemporary design took off, followed by Pop and, 20 years later, postmodernism. From then on, what mattered was not the use of the object, but its meaning. The product had to fit the culture and its life styles. Products became symbols, signs or icons. There was no longer any need for durability, unlike under the previous paradigm. Products embodied meaning and this perspective led to their conception and design. Even more so than in functionalism, the materiality of the object was not dominant, since postmodernists were less concerned about material things than ideas. If we view attachment to products from that angle, it seems that postmodernist design is a big step forward, for it focuses on the symbolic aspects of the product. The possibility of creating countless different styles in our mass culture stops it resulting in uniformity.

According to this perspective, design gives rise to stories about products and services. Products become topics of conversation. As the successful (product) designer Philippe Starck puts it, he was not interested in designing a juicer but rather that this juicer would be a pretext for people to start conversations and to create social bonds. Products are only seen as objects from the way they look, and immediately become objects of seduction. This is why marketers need to consider products as elements of language, form, product meanings and the relationship between consumers and companies.

One of the ways to do this in order to meet the consumers' expectations is to see consumption itself as an art. Consumers are confronted by an incredible amount and variety of new products. The globalization of industrial trade has intensified this phenomenon. Moreover, products are backed up by numerous tools – advertising, the media, retailing channels, etc. – to such an extent that it is increasingly difficult to ascertain consumers' real needs other than through these external stimuli. As for designers, the truth is that their creations slip out of their hands as soon as they meet this anonymous and complex consumer. For it is consumers who give meaning to products, with which they are closely linked when using them.

Cultural marketing contrasts with a simplistic economic definition of consumption as a process of using goods and resources that can only be carried out by destroying or transforming them. To this is added a dimension of consumption, that is to say of self-sublimation and fulfilment. Meaning-making improves consumption. In concrete terms, consumption is the selection, purchase, utilization, maintenance and repair of products or services. Furthermore, in Western societies, consumption is increasingly seen as an unending quest for perfection, fulfilment and self-construction.

Anthropologists have shown that consumption is understood through the way products suit consumers and through the rituals that people create to transform and convert products into personal possessions (McCracken 1988). Consumption involves a process of conversion and transformation of simple items into "sociable" possessions. Technology-driven innovation has become insufficient compared to proliferating, expensive and easily copied technological innovations. A whole new world of innovation arises with this societal dimension of appropriation.

The notion of appropriation is crucial for the marketer and the designer. Designing and selling a functional and aesthetic high-performance product is not enough; to be successful it must conform to the consumer's world. Appropriation enables the consumer to make a product specific, unsubstitutable, almost sacred: like family heirlooms passed on to children or collectors' items, their intrinsic value is nothing compared to their emotional value. Consumers use their belongings to adapt to the world they live in and impart meaning to it.

Thus consumers play an active role in the appropriation and the consumption of products. Ethnographic studies of consumption show that products are at the heart of interpersonal and societal influences which marketers, designers and consumers cannot escape. The development of collaboration among the main protagonists has become the key factor in success.

Marketers must not only lay emphasis on the competitive dynamics of their area, as they often do, since innovation also comes from a deep understanding of societal trends. This has an impact on how the market is segmented. One must not only capitalize on factors that may be static and do not give a precise representation of emerging trends, but also on cultural values that shape emerging markets and can produce real success for the company that manages to discover them. Regular qualitative studies are therefore essential. They enable us to understand the evolution of consumers' cultural representations in relation to the appropriate product category and the rituals it involves.

The following case study will show how a brand expresses emerging societal values in a successful product design solution that adds value to the brand positioning and conforms to consumers' changing representations.

HOM creates lingerie for men

HOM was founded in 1968 in Marseilles, France. The company was bought in 1986 by the German-Swiss company 'Triumph International', which also owns brands such as Sloggi, Triumph and Valisère. The brand defines itself as innovative, a "creator of men's underwear". Its slogan is "innovation in masculine elegance".

HOM product innovation story

- In 1970, HOM launched the first transparent briefs (flesh-coloured see-through mini-briefs) but without any great success.
- In 1972, it created jersey stretch-fabric pyjamas.
- 1976: launch of Homix, the first briefs without an elastic waistband.
- 1984: the use of the inner brief gave full support in boxer shorts for the first time (registered patent).
- 1995: the launch of *Homsport* (the first briefs specifically for sports).
- More recently, in 1997: the creation of HO1 (horizontally opening briefs for "total comfort"). The garment was exhibited at the Louvre Museum in Paris and has been worn by Bill Clinton among others. The originality of this product lies in its horizontal opening, convenient for both left-handed and right-handed men (registered patent). The materials are very light and moisture-absorbent. A good example would be polyamide microfiber, or Micro Modal, a soft and silky material. This material gives a "skin-to-skin" feeling. Micro Modal is naturally absorbent and made of renewable fibre.
- Sportswear collection. Fine finish and light materials are characteristic of this collection. They are antibacterial and moisture-absorbent.
- 2002: "Seduction Revolution" with *3001* the first male lingerie collection. HOM became market leader because of its innovation in product design. It was the first company to use the word "lingerie" for men (a word that since has been reused by the media), creating a new range of products which competitors soon started to emulate. The semantic shift from "underwear" to "lingerie" reveals and legitimates the appropriation by men of certain codes of seduction, hitherto reserved for women. A new product category, men's fine underwear, was born. This new range consisted of soft-fabric boxer shorts, briefs, underpants and thongs, echoing women's lingerie (fishnet stockings, lace or silk). The see-through fabrics, the shininess or even the crystal stones the logo is made of reinforce the "precious" touch. Daring colours like gold or silver strongly contrast with traditional codes. The cut also changed: tight-fitting or low waist cuts are particularly figure-flattering. These new products constitute a complete break with the standard codes of the male underwear sector and of the brand itself.

How can HOM's success be accounted for?

To understand this major change, the author studied the brand's narratives from 1970 until the present day so as to decode the meanings of these new products. To this end, a semiotic study was performed to analyze the cultural meanings conveyed through the brand's advertising and products. Analysis of semiotic codes around the brand (products, ads, store visuals, HOM website) showed that the company was aware of social changes in regard to the definition of masculinity. In fact in the years following the company's creation, it had depicted a traditional masculinity based on "manliness" only – like most of their competitors – up until their daring innovation in 2002.

One of the brand's oldest ads from the 1970s is headlined: "HomTom (name of the product) by Hom. For men who feel like real men" (1970). In this way, the brand asserted its adherence to a notion of masculinity in which the man's (fully clothed) body was totally and explicitly virile and powerful. At this time, the product itself was physically absent from the brand ads. During the 1980s and 1990s, they began caricaturing the traditional notion of masculinity, making use of humour, with images of crotches and men's need to have comfortable (functional), high-performance products. The last ad with such a traditional image dates back to 2001; the headline "Stay natural", signifies "not artificial". In Baudrillard's reading, the word "artificial" specifically refers to women's seductiveness (1988).

Since 2002, HOM's narratives have become deeper and more complex; highly contrasting values have been put forward, making the brand a leader in men's underwear. Advertisements show very erotic men's bodies, explicitly signifying seduction. The models wear lace and fishnet underwear ("To turn you on", 2005). In HOM's new avant-garde *3001* lingerie collection, colours range from rouge to verdigris and the sexy shapes include g-strings, micro shorts and classic tank tops in daringly see-through fabrics (lace, fishnet) in prints to match, such as camouflage and tiger (see images on Google under "Hom Lingerie"). The brand encourages men to embrace these new practices ("Dare the minimum", 2005) and thus to overcome men's fear of not being "acceptable" as men. The alluring bodies representing the brand have no ambiguities: they are masculine, muscular, athletic, dynamic and controlled. Yet the brand was sometimes perceived as "gay".

However, a close look at the visuals conveyed by the brand clearly shows that there is a complex man/woman dialectic. HOM's man is staged, being both a subject and an object in his relationships. This very masculine character plays a role and has a traditional seductive posture (self-assured position and look in front of a woman, significant signs of social success such as an open tuxedo on top of standard underwear). On another occasion, he (the same character) is wearing fine underwear and has an unusual and suggestive posture; everything around him suggests passion, romanticism and femininity (cosy bedroom, purple velvet curtains, black satin sheets, champagne glasses, etc.). HOM's images coincide with recently analyzed sociological trends in which men express their wish to be more involved in the home while sticking to main traditional masculine values. This same man wearing lingerie practises boxing, appears on the podium after a swimming competition, or in traditional epic images of him controlling nature.

HOM's new man does not give up his manliness or his need for achievement, but adds a new private dimension to his personality and a desire to seduce through his body, something previously limited to women. This complex and "fragmented" man is perfectly embodied through product design. This product design inflects the product according to man's role, situation and mood (seduction, sportswear or casual, institutional or relational fatherhood, etc.). Thus the narrativizing of product design emblemizes HOM's new position. At the same time, the brand's ads and website cleverly reinforce this position by putting it into context and by echoing men's desire to try new products while still being conscious of their manliness. Thus product design is a strategic element that directly conveys the brand's position, in the same way as advertising. Such innovation comes from accurate analysis of emerging social values in relation to gender, which are subtly conveyed in the brand management.

To supplement this analysis of brand discourse, the author also conducted individual phenomenological interviews with consumers of men's lingerie, interpreting the meaning of such consumption in terms of rituals and identity issues (Ourahmoune 2009). A multi-method research not only enables an understanding of what kind of men the brand appeals to, but also why innovation through product design has been a success. The research showed that the interviewees allow themselves not only to shift from male to female values in the private domain of seduction and beauty, but also in the area of fatherhood, which some of them conceive as relational rather than just traditionally authoritarian. The brand successfully assuages men's anxieties, such as the fear of homosexuality, by portraying a woman next to the male character, thus conveying traditional and instrumental male values. Finally, HOM's man, when shown in underwear, is either by himself or standing next to a woman, but never with other men. Our previous research showed that wearing such underwear is a clandestine, even taboo, practice; it is done only within the male–female couple, but is never mentioned to male peers (Ourahmoune *et al.* 2008).

In sum, we can emphasize that the brand moved from a highly functional to a symbolic design conveying complex messages based on an understanding of masculine rituals and taboos.

In contrast, Aubade, the leading women's lingerie brand in France, tried to launch a masculine line for men in 2005. The brand is famous for its very sensual ads displaying "lessons of seduction" portraying sublime female bodies as objects of desire. The company replicated the message by simply putting the man in the woman's position in launching its male products. Aubade's men became passive objects of desire staged in sensual positions, subject to female desires in a seduction game (search for "Aubade homme" images on Google). The evolution of male identity was viewed as a matter of simply reversing gender positions. On one hand, Audabe failed to understand and capture male ambiguities and tensions in relation to this practice. This failure of understanding was manifested in their product design, which lacked the symbolic dimensions needing to be conveyed. The product was far too simple, rather ordinary, common and not sufficiently high quality compared to the female segment, it ran counter to Aubade's established imaginary of fine quality and very sensual lingerie. The brand dropped the male line in 2008.

Hom's product design is strongly connected to the consumer's masculine representations and plays a significant role in its brand management (Table 22.1). This requires a holistic approach to consumption based on the practices and desires of the consumers, so that the designers can understand them and work with marketers. This issue lies at the heart of design, which tries to anticipate how the object is used. On the one hand, the aim is to make marketers and designers engage in more exchange throughout the creative process, in order to balance a sometimes very innovative solution, which as yet may not meet consumers' needs. On the other hand, marketers must go beyond the conventional definition of consumption, which can be too closely linked with a strictly economic and psychological tradition that views design as no more than an aesthetic touch at the end of the process.

Table 22.1 HOM shift in product design from utilitarian/functional to symbolic/cultural perspective

Product	Underwear	Men's lingerie
Product expectation	Instrumental. Able to accomplish the expected task	Aesthetic, emotional needs and desires. Able to activate meaning
Product value	Used to solve a problem A cost/benefit logic	Consumed to express a personal state (self-perceptions, social aspirations) A meaning-based logic
Product innovation process	Innovation through physical/technical processes	Innovation through consumers' rituals, fantasies and representations
Product design actor roles	Top-down logic Experts are designers, sellers are marketers, consumers are evaluators	Co-creative logic Consumers involved to propose appropriate products
Product destination	Individual practical needs	Self and significant other (identity mediation)
Product relation	Utilitarian	Attachment
Brand relation	Transactional	Desirability

HOM also *encourages consumers' participation in the innovation process*. For a competition (via an ephemeral website launched by the brand: www.ousontleshommes.com), men were asked to send in photos of themselves wearing briefs or boxer shorts. In another photo contest, "The ideal man of the 21st century", contestants had to submit a picture of their ideal man, according to set themes – casual, adventurous, chic, sporty, sexy, passionate, committed, visionary, free and dreamer – which are precisely the themes the brand wants to convey through its collections.

But within the complex context of our consumer societies, where "consuming is existing socially" (Baudrillard 1998), companies need to go even further, treating consumers as experts and transforming approaches to design.

Transforming approaches to design

Consumers as co-creators

Obtaining insights from customers in order to develop new products, for example by carrying out market research to identify needs and trends in the market, conducting focus groups to test reactions to concepts and ideas, or asking for feedback on existing product to identify areas for development – this is by no means new. But all of these approaches to innovation are very much held and driven by the brand. They involve looking at what customers do or asking them what they think, prior to developing a new product intended to meet these needs. Co-production has been then developed by some brands as, for instance, the customization of Swatch watches in a build-to-order system where consumers are included in the production process in dedicated workshops in the retail store. But co-creation is more than that. It is *not* plain feedback without an answer, it is not Do-It-Yourself, it is not customization, it is not even personalization, since all of these actions take place after companies have decided what the basics are and which products and services and experiences they are willing to hand over to consumers. Consumer voting campaigns like www.straightupflavor.com are interesting initiatives but still not sufficiently customer-led.

Co-creation is very much customer-led. Brands and customers work together to develop and design new products. The results can be very effective, and some brands, including Lego and Xerox, have worked with customers in this way to create new products. For example, after viewing children as purchasing advisors and then as full consumers, marketing might as well consider them to be product "designers". "MOBI Discovery, the child designers" is the result of a close collaboration between French furnishing industries and the Education Department. Children were asked to create their ideal piece of furniture. A prototype was then developed and exhibited in furniture fairs and the VIA gallery (Valorisation of Furnishing Industries). Another example is Nespresso's 2005 Design Contest. Aimed at imagining the future of coffee rituals, it yielded such gems as the Nespresso InCar coffee machine and the Nespresso Chipcard (which stores coffee preferences for registered individuals and, when inserted into a vending machine, communicates with a central database to brew a personalized cup of coffee).

Involving customers in this way calls for some significant changes in process and attitude at the brand. Traditionally, customers stand outside the firm – they purchase the product and their only relationship with the firm is essentially a transactional one. With new product co-creation, customers are involved at a much deeper level, working with the brand to develop and design products which they may not even want. In new-product co-creation, customers work to improve the product overall and to improve the offering the brand has to make to all customers. This system functions well for three reasons: (1) customers want to help and work with brands they know listen to them; (2) customers want to solve problems; and (3) all too often the solution or idea needed turns out to be really simple for somebody else.

From a business and innovation angle, we would argue that the trend of co-creating with customers is very important to watch – not because everything has to or will be co-created in the future, but because tapping into the collective experiences, skills and ingenuity of hundreds of millions of consumers around the world is a complete departure from the inward-looking, producer-versus-consumer innovation model so common in corporations worldwide.

Another particularly significant challenge from a cultural marketing perspective is the need for sustainable design that emerges from consumers' awareness of global ecology issues.

Sustainable development and product design

In a society where people are becoming increasingly aware of sustainable development (cf. Chapter 28 in this volume) and where over-consumption and waste are being criticized, another semiological aspect of product design is being developed (complementing the postmodern approach), namely the phenomenological aspect. Phenomenology can be summed up to the attempt to understand day-to-day human experience. By focusing on our everyday connection with reality, phenomenology can produce an understanding of the consumer–product relationship. This materialist approach assumes that by leaving aside the non-material aspects of the product, there remains something over and beyond language, the symbol, the function or the icon, namely the object. Therefore, not only do designers try and go beyond the logic of product deconstruction in creating new products, but also to leave something after such a deconstruction.

This approach does not deny non-materiality; indeed, it acknowledges the symbolic aspect. For example, men's deodorants are often dynamic or streamlined in shape, made from hard, cold materials (brushed metal), with dark colours, a large stick for quick and easy use, and arctic or woody scents for a fresh, confident, manly feeling. By contrast, women's deodorants are rounder, pocket-sized, pastel-coloured and florally scented, all of which conveys the image of a stereotypical romantic woman.

Nevertheless, to illustrate a phenomenological and materialist design perspective, we focus on the material aspects of the objects, which are likely to influence consumers' choices. While writing with a fountain pen calls for style and care, a pencil enables you both to write and erase. The product embodies an intention. Not only do we focus on the impact of the product as an artefact, but also as something meaningful. The artefact is seen as capable of changing the relation to the product without eliminating its symbolic and interpretive dimension. For there are no artefacts as such; identity arises from the context of the consumer's relation to the product. Deodorant sticks, for instance, can be transparent, easy to disassemble, repairable, refillable. Most of the consumer goods that surround us are not easily fixed when broken. What is at stake in product design is to make ready-to-use products, and this means ergonomy; or maybe it is to make more repairable products for everyday use.

In fact, from this perspective, brands need to capitalize on *real* product innovation, instead of the current market tendency to promote packaging innovation, for example. In recent years, the great majority of innovations have involved new or improved packaging for products. Product content is minimized in favour of the form. Managers should carefully consider that focusing on the idea of a product rather than on the product itself makes it possible always to rely on this idea, however it may be conveyed, and to forget about the product itself. In a way, it is easy to be attached to a product because of its symbolic image, but if being attached is primarily associated with the immateriality of the product, it may not last long. Therefore product designers should create products not only where solely the idea matters, but where the idea is instantiated in the product's materiality. In a nutshell, meaning should not be dissociated from the object.

What are the appropriate strategies and tools to help design teams create users' demand for sustainability and integrate their participation and creativity in the ecodesign process? Sustainability is not achievable with today's consolidated strategies and behaviours. It will require "jumps" to radically new systems of production and consumption and changes in industry, government and society. One proposal is the EcoLab, "a paradigm creator to help our under-resourced and locked-in industry venture into hitherto unthinkable territory". Others further argue that EcoLab's eco-innovation in "step-changes" can become more powerful and make more of an impact with "participatory eco-design" – by actively involving users (e.g., domestic consumers, business-to-business buyers and government purchasers) who are normally outside the design process. "Co-creative, participatory eco-design" could better capture each user's needs, values and socio-cultural context, and therefore truly engage them in creating, promoting and demanding new sustainable systems of production and consumption.

How can product design drive sustainable consumption through consumer interaction by intuitively communicating sustainability values in the way products are used? Raising users' awareness can ultimately influence sustainable behaviour and consumption. There is an emergent body of research and experimentation investigating the use of product design to influence sustainability awareness and related consumption behaviours. One inspiring example focuses on the user's interaction and visual representation of the consequences of personal energy consumption when using the product. Electroluminescent wires are shaped into a transparent electric cable and produce dynamic patterns of glowing and pulsating colours to indicate the amount of energy being used at a given moment. The intent is to inspire consumers to explore and reflect upon the energy consumption of electrical devices in their home. This device is now commercially available in Europe.

Managerial implications

Conceptualizing

Investigation is called for to define an overall concept that fits both company and consumers' values and capitalizes on a deep understanding of socio-cultural consumption contexts. Generating ideas from cultural settings allows thinking to go further than the product or service itself and to focus on designing an experience for a consumer (not simply a "user" logic).

Managers should break with conventional beliefs such as over-reliance on product functional features, and thinking solutions are invariably technological, minimizing the impact of emotions. Another pitfall is the over-simplification of the socio-cultural contexts, for example, taking for granted that globalization has eliminated local needs. Instead, managers will put individuals and groups at the heart of complex, changing and uncertain socio-cultural contexts and then design *for* people experiencing those uncertainties. Even though managers may not master the context, they still will try to understand it, and through design offer interpretations that emanate from and resonate with consumers' emotions and values. Empathy is a key resource for managers.

Implementation

The concept should be implemented in all its facets. A holistic approach is needed given that managers should design an experience – deliver meanings and feelings – for each contact between the brand and consumers (through products, services, points of sales, websites, etc.). Managers should consider products as cultural artefacts displayed in different settings to be analyzed through innovative methods and a broader investigative approach than simply focus groups and surveys. A variety of competencies and foci on complex consumption phenomena allow the usual processes to be replaced and therefore permit the fostering of imagination and the challenging of cultural beliefs. Product design is part of a whole brand language with its specific signs, codes and meanings, to be staged by managers. For managers to generate creativity and increase brand consistency awareness, a research program can combine different approaches. Analyzing online communities using both netnography and semiotics together with focus groups, for instance, will facilitate consumer-inspired insights and innovations. For instance, Adidas has developed products using netnography (online-communities analysis).

Optimization

Manager should innovate and renovate the business concept by involving consumers at an early stage in the creativity process and not merely as evaluators of solutions designed by the brand. Not all consumers are interested in co-creating with the brand, but there are influential and innovative consumers who are willing to contribute to product development if they are offered attractive opportunities to do so. It is crucial to include critical consumers in the design process. Understanding their specific representations will help identify limitations and possibilities as a basis for design innovation. In my research on male consumption, I interviewed both "pro-" and "anti"-men's lingerie consumers to map the many discourses that support or negate the possibility of men enacting their masculinity through consumption. The goal for managers is to identify any contradictory demands or wishes and to determine whether those can be satisfied in the same product, service or environment, without interfering with the brand positioning and overall objective. A final argument in favour of involving consumers in design, constructing the prototype and testing is simply cost/benefit based. Transferring some competencies in the creation process to consumers costs the company less money and minimizes the risk of failure in interpreting consumers' expectations.

To conclude, the cultural perspective contrasts with the traditional perspective design (Morris 2009) by deconstructing the design process. The cultural perspective emphasizes a plural integration process between several actors conceived as poles of creativity during the upstream and downstream process.

Concept phase

- A holistic view of the project is needed.
- Socio-cultural and design perspective along with consumers willing to participate in the dynamic of co-creation are necessary for a rich ideation.
- A collaborative platform helps the exchange of ideas, feelings and rituals associated with products and services to achieve a deep understanding of the context. Material culture and culture are here strongly embedded.
- Company's management and values adapt this fuzzy front-end process characterized by horizontal and open interactions instead of hierarchical decision chains.

Action phase

- Designing solutions arise from tapping into multiple perspectives and meanings derived from exchanging with the plural and open platform.
- Critical consumers are also involved to capture the diverse and rich possibilities to come up with meaningful solutions that resonate with consumers' representations.
- Marketers ensure product design solutions enrich brand codes and reflect consumers' experiences (consumers as an end and not as simply a mean).

Conclusion

The conventional conception of marketing too often sees design as an "aesthetic touch" at the end of the process of making the product. The marketing-related cultural approach to product design is distinctive by giving product design a wider meaning and a degree of managerial impact. Indeed, we have emphasized that product design is an important factor in conveying both brand aesthetic *and* ethical codes. Product design is one of the best ways for the brand to convey the company's position in relation to consumers and society in general, and helps enhance its corporate image.

In this manner, product design becomes influential in how consumers are attached to the brand. Moreover, whether a brand is or is not appealing depends on how relevant the product design is and whether it can transcend the experiential dimension of consumption. It is also important to think of product design as something capable of conveying cultural values that echo consumers' lives and their deeper desires. In Western societies we are facing supply saturation, an omnipresent consumption emerging from people's identity construction, a quest for meaning and experience sharing in consumption, a real sophistication in the way people interact with products. All these factors require relevant and ongoing analysis of emerging socio-cultural trends in order to make a given product design successful.

All this goes together with consumers being strongly involved in the creation of products. Instead of expecting consumer groups simply to endorse a solution, it is more important to focus on their being fully involved in the creation process. It therefore seems more promising to go beyond the notion of co-production and to encourage a real co-creation. Moreover, from this standpoint, product design must be used throughout the product's creation project, from beginning to end, along with marketing. Clear communication between both functions must be a priority in order for product design to be coherent and successful. For these reasons, marketing training must be more explicit in the analysis of design as a discipline and a set of practices.

Review and discussion questions

1   Describe the traditional conception of design.
2   Contrast the process of creativity according to the cultural perspective.
3   How far can product design mediate brands' positioning?
4   Why should you involve consumers in the co-creation process?
5   Would you agree that design is becoming democratic?
6   How would you explain this phenomenon?
7   How can eco-design influence sustainable consumer awareness?

Keywords

co-creation, functional design, postmodern design, product attachment, product meaning

References

Baudrillard, J. (1988) *De la Séduction*, Paris: Folio.
—— (1996) *The System of Objects*, London: Verso.
—— (1998) *The Consumer Society*, Paris: Gallimard.
Belk, R. W. (1988) "Possession and the Extended Self", *Journal of Consumer Research*, 15: 139–68.
Kotler, P. and Keller, K. L. (2008) *Marketing Management*, 13th edn, New York: Pearson.
Maffesoli, M. (1990) *Au creux des apparences: Pour une éthique de l'esthétique*, Paris: Plon.
—— (1996) *The Time of the Tribes*, Thousand Oaks, CA: Sage.
McCracken, G. (1986) "Culture and Consumption: A Theoretical Account of the Structure and Movement of the Cultural Meaning of Consumer Goods", *Journal of Consumer Research*, 13: 71–84.
—— (1988) *Culture and Consumption: New Approaches to the Symbolic Character of Consumer Goods and Activities*, Bloomington, IN: Indiana University Press.
Morris, R. (2009) *The Fundamentals of Product Design*, Worthing: AVA Publishing.

Ourahmoune, N. (2009) "Intimacy-Related Male Consumption and Masculine Identity Construction: A Consumer Point of View", *Asia-Pacific Advances in Consumer Research*, 8: 130–6.

Ourahmoune, N., Nyeck, S. and Roux, E. (2008) "Male Consumers Entering the Private Sphere: An Exploratory Investigation of Male Rituals and Fears Around Lingerie for Men Consumption", paper presented at Association for Consumer Research, 9th Gender and Consumer Behaviour Conference, Boston, June.

23 When the diffusion of innovation is a cultural evolution

Amina Bécheur and Deniz Atik

Overview

> I do not serve markets, I create them … The companies which drive the market modify our sights and change our civilization by creating new markets, by giving birth to new categories of product, and by transforming rules of the game
>
> (Akio Morito, founder of Sony)

Since Schumpeter's original thesis, technological innovation has widely been considered the key to any company's success, as well as to the economic and social development of a society. Yet for very many new products, diffusion fails. Thus, identifying the best means to move from invention (new idea) to innovation (massive adoption) represents a key question. Prior research has tried to answer it by investigating the marketing of diffusion and adoptions of innovations. Yet this mechanistic approach to diffusion theory is limited and cannot reveal the social and cultural dynamic underlying the origin of ideas, new consumer habits, and the new cultural institutions they engender.

In essence, conceiving of a technological innovation is a synthesis. The company comes up with the new concept, positions it, defines it, and then sends a signal about it to the wider environment. Thus, a cultural approach is needed to understand the connection between the innovative technique and the wider culture that helps define the new product (cf. Chapter 22 in this volume). Yet most innovation-oriented marketing research focuses only on understanding factors that encourage the diffusion of the innovation, without addressing the cultural elements of the technique.

In this chapter, we argue that technique is part of culture, such that any technological innovation (product or process) helps construct the surrounding material universe. We consider the diffusion of innovations to be a form of emergence of a material culture, as represented in new habits. To confirm this approach, we undertake a case study of the perfume industry and investigate an innovation that diffuses as a process of social and cultural change, rather than being represented solely by new products. It relies on social interactions among various agents, similar to fashion theory. On the basis of these considerations, we offer suggestions for strategic implementations of service innovations.

Innovation process

From a classical marketing perspective, innovation differs from invention; it represents the implementation of an invention and its integration into a social milieu. In this process, a social body compares the qualities of the invention with reality and the contingencies of the broader milieu. If the community appropriates the invention, it becomes an innovation and has various implementation effects. The idea of innovation presupposes an act of invention or creation and implies the successful implementation of creative ideas, in which sense creativity goes beyond innovation. It is the incarnation of novelty in a social context. Invention might remain a hidden brilliant idea, but innovation exists only if it is embodied in a social reality. Innovation therefore implies social transformation; creativity stops at social recognition.

Innovation and creative destruction

In *Business Cycles*, published in 1939, Joseph Schumpeter describes economic cycles in terms of innovation clusters: after a radical innovation that results from an (often technological) invention (e.g., steam, integrated circuits, information technology, the internet, nanotechnologies), other innovations emerge. This phenomenon can be expressed in industrial cycles, such that after a major innovation, the economy enters a growth phase that generates employment, followed by a depression and the exit of companies that do not innovate, and then job losses. Transformations in the textile industry and the introduction of the steam engine thus can explain economic development during 1798–1815.

In his second book, *Capitalism, Socialism and Democracy*, Schumpeter (1942) popularized the concept of creative destruction, which describes the process by which business sectors disappear due to the creation of new economic activities. In capitalist economies, all major technological innovations initiate this process. First, people (often designated entrepreneurs) take a risk and elaborate new combinations of resources. Second, when the advantages of these new combinations are clear, clusters of imitators overturn the established order by putting the new notions into general use and developing secondary innovations. Third, order returns, and the gradual definition of new rules sanction the new social order that has resulted from the preceding upheavals. Because innovation implies a continuous process of value destruction, organizations that previously have revolutionized and dominated their market might disappear, such as when competitors achieve a better design or lower manufacturing costs. Creative destruction also can offer a strategy used knowingly to maintain domination. For example, Walmart continually imposes new techniques for stock management, marketing, and human resources management that drive competitors out of the market in a phenomenon referred to as "Walmartization."

Schumpeter's considerable contributions to understanding the process of innovation in turn constitute the basis for sociological research into the process of social change (e.g., Rogers 2007). Sociologists posit that change occurs within a system because the diffusion of successive or joint innovations generate major social transformations. This epidemiological phenomenon follows the metaphor of a virus spreading throughout a given population. Thus, an innovation follows several stages of diffusion shaped in the form of a logistic curve (S-shaped):

1   Only a minority is sensitive to the innovation; they are the pioneers.
2   The process accelerates, reaching new users, known as early adopters.
3   The movement develops, and the majority accepts the innovation. The innovation takes a collective form and is integrated in everyday usage.

However, a minority of potential users resists and adopts only as a last recourse, likely because the old technique has disappeared. This collective phenomenon also parallels imitation or rumor-spreading paths. The duration of each stage varies, depending on the specific rhythms to each innovation, but the dynamics always follow the same paradigm with regard to two conditions: the population is relatively homogeneous, and many social interactions occur to encourage the transmission.

With these criteria, it seems easier to understand why the rate of renewal has been accelerating in contemporary society. Physical and virtual interactions are effectively stimulated by novel modes of transport and new information technologies. It may have taken decades for televisions, cars, or microwave ovens to settle into the Western world, but in just a few years, cell phones have diffused throughout the world.

This schema of innovation diffusion constitutes the basis of marketing thought on the subject, which marketers then use to understand developing phenomena and identify suitable techniques to ensure the success of an innovation.

Traditional marketing approaches to innovation diffusion

Innovation diffusion follows an S-shaped curve (Rogers 2007). Most studies on the diffusion of innovations therefore divide the process into sequences, whose number varies depending on the author and the nature of the case under study (Bass 1980). In marketing, innovation diffusion depends on six factors (Rogers 2007): process of adoption, media and interpersonal influence, social system, marketing actions, innovation characteristics, and innovators' characteristics.

Analyses of the process of adoption largely employ either the hierarchy of effects model or a low involvement model. In the former, the process of adoption is as follows: growing awareness of the innovation, development of knowledge, attitude formation, trial, and adoption. In the latter, the potential user first becomes aware of the innovation, tries it, forms an attitude toward it, then adopts or rejects it. The determinant factors, in both models, are the level of understanding required by the client to adopt the innovation, the cost of switching from old to new practices, and the importance of the social norm. The greater the number of modalities of these variables, the greater the chance that the hierarchy of effects model fits; otherwise, the low involvement model predominates. However, though this model offers a simple representation of new product adoption, it does not clarify the motivations for consumer action. Moreover, it assumes that consumers are subject to psychological mechanisms, in spite of their choices.

To determine how marketers can influence the adoption process, researchers have addressed the role of interpersonal influence and opinion leaders, starting as early as the 1940s (Lazarfeld *et al.* 1944). A two-step model of the diffusion of information suggests that information first gets disseminated from the source to opinion leaders, then from these leaders to followers. Two important concepts explain the role of the opinion leader: his or her perceived level of competence and the degree of homophily between the leader and the follower. Homophily implies similarity in status and values; it thus constitutes a barrier to diffusion beyond the immediate group, whereas heterophilic communication encourages diffusion across social groups. These two factors explain the speed at which a new technique diffuses. Furthermore, the social system in which the diffusion takes place consists of three descriptors: norms and values, system evolution, and system homogeneity. The rate of diffusion and penetration level link positively to the degree of compatibility of the innovation with the values and norms of the social system (Rogers 2007). However, the social system does not necessarily define the size of the potential market, because not all segments of the population are ready to adopt the new concept.

To encourage diffusion, prior research suggests the importance of factors such as the amount of money spent on marketing (Bass 1980), the sensitivity of the segments to marketing action (Robertson and Wind 1980), and the strength of competition (Olshavsky 1980). For example, by playing on price sensitivity, companies can stimulate demand during the launch and growth phases. Legal, economic, and political characteristics also could mandate changes that favor diffusion.

Cross-disciplinary research by Robertson *et al.* (1984) identifies characteristics common to all innovation adopters: higher income and education levels, strong social mobility, positive risk-taking attitudes, active social participation, and opinion leadership. These innovative adopters possess an independent nature.

Furthermore, according to Rogers (2007), adoption depends on the perceived characteristics of the innovation, such that its relative advantage and compatibility with social norms enhance adoption. Conversely, perceived complexity has a negative influence on adoption, and the degree of novelty moderates these relationships, such that the relationship between the degree of novelty and new product adoption is not linear (Béji-Bécheur 1998). An extremely innovative product that calls traditional schemas into question makes it difficult for the consumer to evaluate its relative advantage. Such a complex evaluation task adds to the uncertain environment, in which information about the virtues of the product is incomplete. However, the more the product corresponds to the norms of the environment, the easier it is to evaluate its relative advantage, such that the product likely prompts positive evaluations by most consumers. Yet this new product also may be less innovative, so its relative advantage might disappear, in which case consumer perceptions would be negative overall.

Marketing studies of innovation largely adopt this summary of innovation diffusion and assess diffusion by investigating different factors to identify forms of leverage available to companies. This approach imagines that the characteristics of the new product structure consumers' beliefs and uses, as modified by marketing actions or beliefs derived from the social environment. Thus, marketing literature mostly has reduced the diffusion of innovation to its economic significance (i.e., sales) and the emergence of a new segment of purchasers. This mechanistic approach is insufficient; however, we propose supplementing it with considerations of social change and cultural construction at work in the innovation and creative destruction processes.

Social and cultural approach to innovation diffusion

With a basis in sociology and anthropology, we aim in this section to update the notion of creative destruction by integrating social interactions and the construction of sense in the innovation. To demonstrate this approach, we undertake a case study of the introduction of new, industrially produced perfumes on the French market. With this case study, we examine the phenomenon of innovation as a social interaction that features deviance of a minority, legitimation by the majority, imitation, and social distinction, which support the emergence, development, renewal, or destruction of cultural meanings.

Furthermore, the socio-cultural context and history of perfume in French culture offer a rich setting to interpret innovation. In particular, we note that the symbolic meaning of perfume (e.g., fashion, luxury) has evolved in response to socio-political changes, power structures, and gender ideology.

A case study of such luxury products is ideal for understanding innovation because it relies heavily on the system of meaning production and imagination. In addition to offering a source of social distinction, luxury products give consumers a means to build a singular identity or conform with the elite. It thus illustrates the creative process of value and sensemaking, through distinction and singularization – mechanisms also at the foundation of innovation diffusion that constitute a source of competitive advantage for modern firms.

Technological innovation mediated by cultural context

Eugénie Briot (2007) offers a history of the beginnings of the perfume industry in nineteenth-century France. She notes that technological innovation in the perfume sector came about mainly at the end of the century, when innovation in chemistry lowered production costs and opened up the prospects for large-scale development. In turn, "The economies brought about by the synthesis of artificial fragrances played a large part in the rapid development of the perfume industry in the 19th century" (ibid.: 4). However, even as production costs dropped, some perfumers maintained the same prices, so:

> By disconnecting the intrinsic value of the product from its sales price…they chose to transfer those elements that make the product desirable in the eyes of consumers from the product itself to elements that were external to the product, thereby placing its value on a symbolic level.
>
> (ibid.: 8)

From that point on, the symbolic dimensions of perfume became essential, with an essential role in shaping social and cultural norms. Perfumeries developed marketing resources to enhance the distinctive value of their products and focused on the quality of production to highlight features that clients could not assess without chemical expertise. These arguments, as validated by the respectability and celebrity of the perfumeries, also gained support from popular media. Even the points of sale became "salesrooms":

> The prestige of the point of sale also contributed to justifying the price of these products. The same perfume by Lubin, retailing at 1.85 francs in the Galeries Saint-Martin, sold for 2.25 francs in the perfumer's boutique in the rue Royale. The framework for the sale therefore has a positive effect on the symbolic value of the product, and consequently, on its sale price.
>
> (ibid.: 9)

At the socio-cultural level, the nineteenth century also was a period of radically changing social forces. After the French Revolution, class considerations shifted, producing a conflict between the tendency to abolish privileges and inequalities but the concomitant growth of the bourgeois model as dominant. Money, merchandise, and mass consumption, in Western societies at least, became the primary method of producing sense through the consumption of differentiated products. The resultant concept of luxury gained new meanings: a luxury consumer would pay more to obtain singular, rare, or localized products.

The changing social forces influenced not only the market but also consumers' rituals. For example, the meaning of artificial versus natural categories underwent a notable shift. Furthermore, innovators could construct distinctive elements that prompted social imitation. In this industrial and cultural context, the fashion designer Coco Chanel – one of the first to link her name to a perfume – invented a new way to distinguish between luxury and the mass market by thinking of a perfume in the same terms as a garment:

An artificial perfume and I mean artificial in the same way as a dress, that is to say something that is made. I am an artisan of dressmaking. I don't want perfume that smells of roses or lily-of-the-valley. I want it to be put together.

(Erner 2006)

Chanel therefore joined forces with the perfumer Ernest Beaux, whom she told "I want a woman's perfume that smells of woman" (ibid.). From series of numbered samples presented by Beaux, she chose the fifth, which contained aldehyde and 79 other ingredients that were not being used by perfume manufacturers at the time. Moreover, the alliance of a prestigious fashion name with a perfumery launched a trend that still constitutes a recipe for success. Even the naming method was innovative; Chanel asserted, "I am launching my collection on 5th May, fifth month of the year; let's leave it with the number it already bears, and the number 5 will bring it luck" (ibid.). Thus Chanel No. 5, one of the world's best-selling perfumes and a primary representative of French-style luxury, was born.

As this case illustrates, the industrialization of perfume was accompanied closely by a cultural construction that linked perfume with luxury.

Luxury and perfume, legitimated taste: social imitation and distinction

Alter's (2004) research is useful as a specific perspective for analyzing the diffusion of a cultural point of view. The diffusion process begins with a phase of imitation, followed by deformation when the players adapt the new product to existing constraints. Acculturation occurs when an innovation encounters other cultural spheres; the meeting of two cultural spheres creates a new concept space (ibid.). Therefore, the construction of collective meaning arises from the confrontation of representations, each issuing from a separate cultural sphere.

Consider the example of perfumes: nineteenth-century French manufacturers could respond to reduced manufacturing costs by either lowering their prices and distributing their products widely or investing in the construction of social status for their perfume as a luxury product. From these two directions, two market sectors emerged: the personal hygiene industry, which produces products with low added value, and the cosmetics and perfume industry, with its high added value. Underlying these two strategic orientations are the two socio-cultural systems generated by the French Revolution. That is, the republican ideology embraces "perfume for everyone," whereas an elitist and aristocratic tradition values perfumes as luxury products (e.g., the meaning of perfume in Louis XIV's French court).

Moreover, the diffusion process, as the Chanel example reveals, is initiated with actors who challenge established norms and appear deviant. Merton (1957) defines deviance as nonconforming behavior; innovation is a form of deviance that consists of doing things in a different way. To be recognized as deviant or innovator, the person must transgress certain rules and be recognized for having done so. Therefore, the judgment of others counts; an interactionist approach further means that deviance results from a transaction effected between a social group and an individual, whom the group believes has transgressed a norm (Becker 1985). The project diffuses only when the new transgression is validated. At the moment the new concept gains legitimacy, its diffusion is facilitated, such that the process corresponds to a process of regressive *institutionalization* (Alter 2004), in which deviant behavior gradually gets accepted in conventional norms and public opinion.

The acquisition of legitimacy also increases access to resources. This process therefore leads to reappropriation by leading actors because the logic of the market again applies. Alter's conclusions about the process of innovation in companies thus appear similar to the diffusion of new products, because "At the end of the process …, conscious of the economic advantages of deviance, they transform what was a transgression of the rules into the rules" (ibid.: 73).

The challenge then is to maintain control of the shared representations of legitimacy. The increasing sophistication of communication and professions that implement it appears continuous: in society, people constantly search for new approaches that will constitute the next active source of innovation (Moscovici 1979). Therefore, we derive an enriched view of innovation diffusion theory that connects research in a "naturalist" tradition with studies that consider the players central to the diffusion phenomenon (Alter 2004). This approach emphasizes that the characteristics constructed and perceived by players influence beliefs in an interactive process that leads to the adoption or rejection of the innovation.

The construction of new meanings and practices requires interactions among inventors, designers, and consumers who attempt to resolve social controversy. The interpretation must make the new practice credible and legitimate within a set belief system, so marketing appeals can help reduce the perceived complexity of and skepticism attached to new products. An innovation becomes stable only if actors can create an alliance between an operational framework and the norms of use.

Therefore, companies and marketing researchers argue that to increase a new product's chances of success, the market must be "educated." Companies develop market preparation techniques (e.g., product testing, preliminary advertising, public relations, opinion leaders) to ensure consumers are ready to receive new concepts. For example, film production companies activate various networks before launching a film, known as buzz; before automobile companies launch a new model, they present their prototypes at automobile fairs or leak details of "secret" tests. The clear objective of these different forms of publicity is to solicit positive word-of-mouth reports and gradually construct favorable meanings for the new product so that its attributes become the determinants of its cultural use. Therefore, the organization's interpersonal communication networks must stimulate positive beliefs and shared notions of new practices. The standardization of an innovation results from a process of mutual adjustment and mediation between technical and cultural systems.

In the initial stages, astute, heterophilic networks are most effective for encouraging adhesion to a new concept. The agents of change include avant-garde users who tend to promote new ideas and encourage collective learning through experimentation. Because they sit at the frontier of various spheres of knowledge, these creative users favor new solutions. It therefore seems relevant to envisage their role as co-designers of the innovation and thus as channels for innovation diffusion in the initial stages.

Through more established players, recognized at institutional level, new practices then get accepted and enter into a normalization process. At this point, the original meaning of the innovation may be removed from initial adopters' control if their network is not powerful enough to ensure their vision prevails. The success of an innovation (i.e., high rate of adoption) thus can lead, ironically, to its dilution and assimilation by a system of existing practices. Thus, initial adopters move to the margins of the new system they have helped create.

This cultural approach to innovation raises questions about the role of marketing and agents in the construction of cultural norms. In this respect, fashion theory provides strategic ideas for understanding the construction and diffusion of trends and new products.

Innovation that builds new cultural norms: the theory of fashion

As conceptualized by McCracken (1988), a fashion system comprises all people and organizations involved in creating symbolic meaning and transferring them to cultural goods. To illustrate, the fashion system takes new styles of clothing and associates them with established cultural categories, moving meaning from the culturally constituted world to the consumer good. These cultural categories of meaning can be associated with time (e.g., leisure, work time), space (e.g., public or private), or human communities (e.g., distinctions of class, gender, age, or ethnicity) (ibid.). A modern consumer thus participates in home life, work life, shopping life, recreational life, neighborhood life, and a variety of social lives, and each life sphere requires different forms of attention and individual capabilities (e.g., dressing appropriately for an occasion) (Firat 1994). Different combinations of apparel, with their attendant meanings, can offer sufficiently consistent meanings for wearers and others, and clothing features such as fabric, color, texture, cut, weight, weaving, stitching, and transparency determine how the garment is interpreted by society (Davis 1992). In turn, to add "meaning into things, creative directors and fashion/product designers discover structural equivalents and draw them together in the compass of an advertisement to demonstrate that the meaning that inheres in the advertisement also inheres in the product in question" (McCracken 1988: 120). For example, marketers try to convince consumers that they can secure athletic accomplishments, sex appeal, popularity, or status by consuming certain products (Goldman and Papson 1996).

Yet Thompson and Haytko (1997) suggest that the meaning transfer model is more dynamic and consumer-centered than originally conceptualized by McCracken. During the appropriation of cultural meanings, consumers continuously engage in interpretive dialogues, reworking their localized knowledge and value systems. This active reworking also is shaped by consumers' desire to construct self-identities through fashion discourses. Therefore, meaning transfer is a diffuse, transformative, and consumer-centered undertaking.

In another capacity, the fashion system invents new cultural meanings. In a modest sense, opinion leaders with high standing, such as the social elite or celebrities, may shape or refine existing cultural meanings and encourage reform of cultural categories (McCracken 1988). Opinion leaders also might be regular people, such as the "cool" adolescents whom their peers look up to with respect (Gladwell 1995). In a more radical way, the fashion system can promote total reforms of cultural meanings, such as in the case of hippies, punks, gays, or even anti-fashion movements that end up being fashionable (McCracken 1988). Anti-fashion takes some symbolic device of opposition, rejection, studied neglect, or parody of the fashion of the time (Davis 1992). Yet overall, fashion remains "a cultural production that both limits and enriches symbolic communication, constitutes a site of freedom or restriction, submission or rebellion, eroticism or domination" (Faurschou 1987: 69).

This meaning is not simply a product of a designer's intentions, and it cannot be solely what the designer or innovator says it is. Nor is it the wearer's or the spectator's intention. The real source of meaning stems from the larger context, which represents a mass of intertextual relations that produce and construct fashion (Barnard 2002).

Institutionalized process

Using large textile companies worldwide, Rinallo *et al.* (2005) illustrate highly institutionalized fashion processes, from collective investments in trend forecasting to announcements

of fashion investors. Saviolo and Testa (2002) also show that the complex institutionalization process within the apparel sector entails structure and competition, from the management of creativity to communication processes. The players include:

> fashion designers (independents, or those operating within a fashion-house or industry,
> or retailers), producers (of semi-finished or finished products), distributors, retailers,
> mass media, research and trend institutes (including fairs), consumers (opinion and
> market leaders), product category associations, banks, and government.
>
> (ibid.: 13)

At the invention phase of fashion, the sources and circumstances of creativity are not very
much different from those obtained in the arts generally; designers, especially those aspiring
to international reputation, take pride in being thought of as original and innovative (Davis
1992: 125). Where designers get their ideas from is anywhere and everywhere. Designers
have been known to consult books of costume history for ideas, as well as to borrow from
their own earlier work and that of others, and they are usually in close contact with leading
creative and progressive elements in the arts, sciences, politics, and culture generally (Davis
1992; McCracken 1988). However, a strongly institutionalized motive is in place as the key
players of the fashion world like the fashion press, sustain and reinforce the designer's quest
for originality; also, the massiveness and demand constancy of the apparel market, along
with heavy fixed capital investments in clothing manufacturing and distribution, restrain the
creativity of designers more than in other arts (Davis 1992; Saviolo and Testa 2002).

> The purpose of artistic creativity is not to satisfy the needs of a mass market. Artistic
> creativity is above all the means through which artists express themselves. Commercial
> creativity, on the other hand, does not have this freedom of expression. This is because
> its purpose is to achieve another subject's objective, the firm. The firm's reason for
> existence lies in its ability to satisfy market needs.
>
> (Saviolo and Testa 2002: 23)

In the introduction phase of new collections, not all creations make it to the fall and spring
openings where typically new fashions are introduced. The social construction of seasons,
competition among designers and fashion centers, the fashion choices of buyers for big
department stores, the fashion press, and the merchandising strategies, they all have a great
deal to do with how fashion happens (Davis 1992; Saviolo and Testa 2002). The quote below
from one interview conducted in 2005 in Milan, with a press office director of a major high
fashion company (Atik 2009), illustrates well this complex process of fashion creation
(neither the interviewee nor the company names are revealed, as requested by the informant
and for confidentiality):

> It is important to increase the popularity of the brand, using the right channels of com-
> munication … There are so many details involved in achieving this popularity. For
> example, in fashion shows, we choose the best hair dresser (the most famous in the
> world), for make-up, similarly, the best people to make the hats, so the level of my
> company, each operation, each person (HR), everything has to be at a high level … the
> people who work for you … let's say, if you are working for African market, you try to
> find the person with the best experience, consultants with great experience. There are
> one million synergies. It is too easy to say, for example, I go to the right place, so it is

OK, it works. For example, our store in Paris is located in the best spot (Champs-Elysées), next to a Gucci store; the shop is two floors, elegant, beautiful, but it does not work. Every French ... no ... every Parisian because the reality is Paris ... just buy famous brands, so it does not work, while in Germany, we sell one million shoes, even if we are in a small town ... but also, I must confess that we don't have a big communication budget for France. We go there, we talk to Madame Elle, we get some editorial space, but it depends. There are so many variables ... it is not only the designer ... it is not only the selling point ... it is a mix of everything and if everything is well calibrated ... probably it works ... also during (economic) crisis, even the best, the most famous companies have problems. You can never say, I am there, so it will sell. Everything must be done in a perfect, at a very high level, and even if you do the best work, it is never certain that it will work. You never know in fashion ... maybe it is famous Gucci bags ... it also depends of the age of the company ... also, the pricing strategy .... OK, I have these shoes, I sell them for five euros, maybe you don't succeed; maybe your price is too low, you lose the "allure" of the object; it is very complicated.

(Press office director of a high fashion company, interview, Milan, 2005)

By the time the new collections are displayed to the public, they have already gone through an extensive filtering process; "more gestures are arrested than completed, and more ideas are abandoned than kept" (Davis 1992: 136). How the crafts, skills, and talents are coordinated and integrated have a great role in the introduction of a new fashion and the reception it receives (Saviolo and Testa 2002). These tasks devolve upon the management of the fashion house rather than on the designer *per se*. As with cuisine, where the culinary talent of the chef hardly guarantees the success of the restaurant, so it is for fashion (Davis 1992: 137).

Although creativity is always sought after, designers and producers largely conform to the fashion trends of the moment. There is an inclination toward producing what sells most rather than experimenting with radical creations that involve the risk of not selling. In another 2005 interview (Atik 2009), a high fashion retail director in Milan acknowledged that a minor portion of fashion collections are for the catwalk; the majority is for mass consumption. The really important purchases are made by representatives of firms that can produce vast quantities of any given design at a price accessible to the mass market (Bell 2003). After the process of institutionalization, a period of uncertainty thus follows: will a new fashion be accepted by wider market segments? If the innovation is not widely adopted, it is not likely to become a trend (Solomon *et al.* 2002).

Interagency in the creation of fashion trends

As Kozinets *et al.* (2004: 658) emphasized "consumer and producer interests are embedded in one another in a process of 'interagency.'" Thus, many players are involved in this complex process of fashion, including consumers. The interaction between producers and consumers, from an innovation perspective, may include several circumstances that allow consumers to play a creative role. In particular, success is measured by sales performance, which means producers must take the interests of consumers into consideration when designing their creations.

As illustrated in Figure 23.1, some people with social influence in their surroundings may initiate potential fashion trends, such as cool adolescents (Gladwell 1995; Kotlowitz 1999)

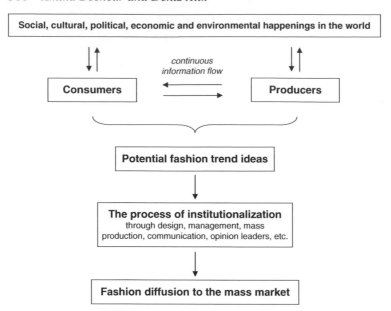

Figure 23.1 Interagency in the creation of fashion trends.

or feminist women who started dressing like men to assert their equal power in the work-place (Wilson 1985). However, mass consumers rarely initiate fashion trends but instead choose from market offerings and exercise creativity by mixing and matching different products. Their greatest power lies in their refusal to accept every new trend or styles that are radically different from what they already wear. Inventions of new fashion trends may be initiated by producers or smaller consumer groups, as in a sub-culture, but mass consumers serve as the jury that decides if a particular new idea eventually will become a socially accepted norm (Atik 2009).

Even if a new fashion trend starts on the street, there must be a process of institutionaliza-tion for fashion diffusion to occur. Trendseekers, journalists, and designers constantly observe social happenings and different consumption patterns and select some new ideas for repackaging for larger market segments, through fashion advertising and mass availability. Thus, the diffusion of fashion is mediated by fashion institutions; for example, the vintage clothing fashion trend, initiated by low-income students' choice of second-hand clothing, now appears in high fashion windows.

Another circumstance that encourages an active role by consumers is when a producer, such as a fashion designer, comes in direct contact with end consumers and asks them what they want or gathers feedback about new creations. This obvious form of interagency allows the consumer essentially to coproduce the new design with the producer.

Finally, though interagency is particularly evident in fashion creation, it is not limited to the efforts of consumers and producers but rather spans the entire context. For example, just as consumers' desires are socially constructed, also designers' artistic inspira-tions are socially constructed. Designers and producers constantly observe the social, cultural, and political events around them; thus a political event like the ongoing war in Iraq might prompt military styles to come into fashion, by affecting both consumers and producers.

Conclusion and implications

A cultural approach to consumption regards innovation as the "co-production of meaning" (Marion 2004) by consumers, companies, and influencers together. These players all participate in the definition of the cultural norm being constituted. Therefore, the diffusion process may no longer be in the control of companies, because of the multitude of influences that enter the consumer's decision process. A multitude of influences and variety of messages mean a multitude of responses on the part of consumers who participate in the process of co-creation of markets.

In the modern economic and social system:

> The marketer is part of the long chain of decisions … from an idea or a vague intuition to the commercialisation of an offer … [They] did not stop at making latent ideas manifest, but steadfastly contributed to constructing, out of the same impulse, solutions and problems.
>
> (ibid.: 269)

Thus, culture, as the basis for interpretation, provides a channel for understanding innovation as a collective phenomenon. In truth, innovation can never be attributed to a particular individual, because after an invention, interpretation invariably follows. The originality of the innovation reflects the complete exchanges among various interpreters, all of whom adopt varied, multicultural, collective perceptions. For new ideas to emerge, the process of interpretation is thus crucial. Science and technology are inextricably linked to society and politics and the culture they constitute. Therefore, to find answers to the questions that continue to confront modern society, we need not only new technologies but also new ways to regard the world and ourselves.

These new ways can be supported by managers' practices. As we have acknowledged, managers are not the only creator of innovation. This implies two major directions when dealing with innovation diffusion: (1) it is relevant to analyze cultural discourses when studying the market in order to understand the emergence of new trends; and (2) management of interagency should be developed so that the firm has a systemic and dynamic view of innovation diffusion.

Review and discussion questions

1   Explain the diffusion of cellular from a classical marketing point of view. Why is this explanation not sufficient to understand the phenomenon?
2   Could the firm control all the diffusion process? Explain.
3   How do deviance, creative destruction and institutionalization operate in the process of diffusion?
4   Who are the main players in the fashion system?
5   How can consumers play a role in fashion creation?
6   How can a brand be creative and trendy at the same time? Give examples.
7   Comment on this sentence by Charles Baudelaire (1846) "The pure designers are philosophers and abstractors of quintessences."
8   Discuss how symbolic meanings transfer to cultural goods such as clothing. Give examples from your own life, such as how you and your friends use certain products to convey meanings.

Keywords

consumer, creation, diffusion, fashion, innovation, institutionalization, interagency, symbolic meaning

References

Alter, N. (2004) "Les composantes d'un processus d'innovation, Croissance et innovation," *Cahiers Français*, 323 (novembre–décembre): 70–3.

Atik, D. (2009) *Consumer Desires in Fashion: The Interagency of Consumers and Producers*, Saarbrück, Germany: VDM.

Barnard, M. (2002) *Fashion as Communication*, London: Routledge.

Bass, F. M. (1980) "The Relationships Between Diffusion Rates, Experience Curves and Demand Elasticities for Consumer Durable Technological Innovations," *Journal of Business*, 53(1): 51–67.

Becker, H. (1985) *Outsiders*, New York: Free Press.

Béji-Bécheur, A. (1998) "Utilisateur leader et degré de novation du produit: une contribution à l'amélioration de l'analyse des tests de produit nouveau," unpublished thesis, Université Paris Dauphine.

Bell, Q. (2003) "Recent History," in R. Boudon, M. Cherkaoui, and P. Demeulenaere (eds), *The European Tradition in Qualitative Research*, London: Sage, pp. 129–46.

Briot, E. (2007) "Le parfum au XIXe siècle, entre luxe et industrie. L'économie du luxe en France et en Italie," paper presented at Comité franco-italien d'histoire économique (AFHE-SISE), Lille, May.

Davis, F. (1992) *Fashion, Culture, and Identity*, Chicago: The University of Chicago Press.

DiMaggio, P. J. and Powell, W. W. (1991) "Introduction," in W. W. Powell and P.J. DiMaggio (eds), *The New Institutionalism in Organizational Analysis*, Chicago: University of Chicago Press, pp. 1–40.

Erner, G. (2006) *Victimes de la mode*, Paris: La Découverte.

Faurschou, G. (1987) "Fashion and the Cultural Logic of Postmodernity," *Body Digest, Canadian Journal of Political and Social Theory*, 6(1–2): 68–82.

Fırat, A. F. (1994) "Gender and Consumption: Transcending the Feminine?," in J. Arnold Costa (ed.), *Gender Issues and Consumer Behavior*, Thousand Oaks, CA: Sage, pp. 205–26.

Gladwell, M. (1995) "The Coolhunt," *The New Yorker*, March 17.

Goldman, R. and Papson, S. (1996) "Advertising in the Age of Accelerated Meaning," in Juliet B. Schor and Douglas B. Holt (eds), *The Consumer Society Reader*, New York: The New Press.

Kotlowitz, A. (1999) "False Connections," in Juliet B. Schor and Douglas B. Holt (eds), *The Consumer Society Reader*, New York: The New Press, pp. 253–8.

Kozinets, R. V., Sherry, J. F. Jr., Storm, D., Duhaheck, A., Nuttavuthisit, K., and Deberry-Spence, B. (2004) "Ludic Agency and Retail Space," *Journal of Consumer Research*, 28(June): 67–89.

Lazarfeld, P., Berelson, B. and Gaudet, H. (1944) *The People's Choice*, New York: Columbia University Press.

Marion, G. (2004) *Marketing Ideology*, Paris: Ed. Eyrolles.

McCracken, G. (1988) *Culture and Consumption: New Approaches to the Symbolic Character of Consumer Goods and Activities*, Bloomington, IN: Indiana University Press.

Merton, R. K. (1957) *Social Theory and Social Structure*, New York: The Free Press.

Moscovici, S. (1979) *Psychologie des Minorités Actives*, Paris: PUF.

Olshavsky, R. (1980) "Time and the Rate of Adoption of Innovations," *Journal of Consumer Research*, 6(March): 425–8.

Rinallo, D., Golfetto, F. and Gibbert, M. (2005) "Representing Markets: The Concertation of Fashion Trends by French and Italian Fabric Companies," Conference paper, 21st IMP Conference, Rotterdam.

Robertson, T. S. and Wind, Y. (1980) "Organizational Psychographics and Innovativeness," *Journal of Consumer Research*, 7(June): 24–31.

Robertson, T. S., Zielinski, J. and Ward, S. (1984) *Consumer Behavior*, Glenview, IL: Scott, Foresman.

Rogers, E. (2007) *Diffusion of Innovations*, 4th edn., New York: The Free Press.

Saviolo, S. and Testa, S. (2002) *Strategic Management in the Fashion Companies*, Milan: Etas.

Schumpeter, J. (1939) *Business Cycles: A Theoretical, Historical and Statistical Analysis of the Capitalist Process*, New York: McGraw-Hill Book Company.

—— (1942) *Capitalism, Socialism and Democracy*, London: Routledge.

Solomon, M. R., Bamossy, G., and Askegaard, S. (2002) *Consumer Behaviour: A European Perspective*, 2nd edn, Englewood Cliffs, NJ: Prentice Hall.

Thompson, C. J. and Haytko, L. D. (1997) "Speaking of Fashion: Consumers' Uses of Fashion Discourses and Appropriation of Countervailing Cultural Meanings," *Journal of Consumer Research*, 24(June): 15–42.

Wilson, E. (1985) "Feminism and Fashion," in J. B. Schor and D. B. Holt (eds), *The Consumer Society Reader*, New York: The New Press, pp. 291–305.

24 Gendered bodies

Representations of femininity and masculinity in advertising practices

Lorna Stevens and Jacob Ostberg

Overview

This chapter introduces the topic of representations of femininity and masculinity in advertising practices. We will show the differences between a common, taken-for-granted understanding of gendered representations in advertising and a cultural perspective, which takes the culturally and socially constructed nature of gender into consideration. We will also demonstrate how marketing managers can adopt a *traditional* approach or a *cultural* approach to their advertising strategies in relation to gender. They may also adopt a *complacent* strategy or a *subversive* strategy. There are therefore four choices available to marketing managers in terms of their advertising strategies. These are *traditional/complacent*, *traditional/subversive*, *cultural/complacent* or *cultural/subversive*. We illustrate these positions with examples from contemporary advertising campaigns. The key implication is that the discussion invites present and future marketing managers to take a more macro and reflective view of gendered representations. By sensitizing managers to wider macro issues, we argue that they can make a more informed choice about whether to sustain the status quo of conventional gendered representations (the *complacent* strategy) or whether to aspire to taking a vanguard position by challenging traditional representations and thereby offering something new instead (the *subversive* strategy).

Introduction

The specific marketing issue to be discussed in this chapter is representations of gendered images in advertising. As consumers, we are bombarded by thousands of commercial messages every day. There is simply no way to avoid being exposed to advertising, and even if we do not necessarily buy the items that are advertised, advertising serves a number of other important functions, which we may not always be consciously aware of. One of the more important functions of advertising is that it provides us with a blueprint of how to live 'the good life'. Among other things, it provides us with images of how 'real' women and 'real' men should be. Often advertisements present us with repeated exposure to representations of men and women which are stereotypical, and these stereotypes give us an implicit assumption of how men and women really are. In particular, we would argue that the different and often opposite ways that men and women are represented might, over time, appear natural and self-evident. While we might be able to critically reflect on an individual advertisement, analyze it, and discuss its implicit values and unrealistic portrayals, the sheer mass of commercial messages has a way of breaking through the barriers of even the most critically conscious consumers. Consequently, advertising portrayals of gender insinuate their way into our collective cultural consciousness, even our individual psyches, normalizing certain traits associated with 'masculinity' and 'femininity', 'men' and 'women', and impacting upon how we frame and define gender and sexual difference in contemporary consumer culture.

Advertisements may reflect, sustain, challenge or even subvert the predominant cultural values of a society. They are myth carriers in our culture, and they may draw on symbolic codes and metaphors to serve up ancient narratives, but often in new and exciting ways. They hold up a mirror to society, reflecting the beliefs and values of it, or they challenge and subvert the norms of society, in order to catch the attention of an intended market. Cultural values are conveyed in advertisements through the language and imagery used in them, and such texts communicate with us at a profound, emotional level, drawing on deep-rooted cultural meanings that are embedded in our shared cultural consciousness and experiences, namely the myths, taboos, rituals and customs that surround us (cf. Chapter 5 in this volume).

Since advertising serves these important social and cultural functions, marketing professionals can benefit from developing a greater awareness of the significance of these more macro dimensions in the marketplace, and how they reflect and indeed impact on both advertising and the consumer behaviour they seek to reflect and influence. Above all, the chapter therefore seeks to explore the dynamics of gender portrayals in contemporary advertising. Insights into the historical, social and cultural constructions of gender in Western culture can be used in order to either uphold the status quo by employing traditional gender stereotypes in advertising campaigns, if one believes this to be the best way to appeal to a target market. We will call this the *complacent* strategy. Both *traditional* (*laissez-faire*) and *cultural* (*playful*) approaches in advertising may employ this complacent strategy. Alternatively, managers might use the power vested in the advertising industry to create a more nuanced and complex view of masculinities and femininities, by either adopting a *traditional* approach (critiquing institutions) or a *cultural* approach (destabilizing ideologies), in order to better reflect the realities of gender in the contemporary marketplace, or even to strive to change perceptions and make us think about what we take for granted in our marketing practices. We refer to this as the *subversive* strategy. We illustrate these two axes in Figure 24.1.

In traditional markcting, consumcr culturc exists 'out there' and is more or less seen as a pre-existing structure in which the company finds itself operating. At each point in time, and in each location, it is up to the marketing department to conjure up an attractive marketing offer suited to a particular target market. Most marketing management textbooks stress the importance of marketing research and robust marketing information systems (see, for example, any edition of Philip Kotler's *Principles of Marketing* texts). Successful marketing management is thus said to be contingent upon a sophisticated understanding of what happens in the company's micro and macro environment. While we do not deny that this type of knowledge is important, we want to challenge the sharp distinction made between the company and the rest of the world. We particularly want to challenge the assumption that consumer culture exists independently of individual companies. One reason for drawing attention to this is that such a view does not place any responsibility on companies for shaping consumer culture (cf. Chapter 28 in this volume). More specifically, it does not place any responsibility on companies in terms of how stereotypical depictions of gender in advertising may serve to reinforce traditional views of what constitutes *real* men and women.

Instead, we want to introduce a cultural approach to consumer culture and advertising. Such a view recognizes that companies are engaged in actively *co-producing* consumer

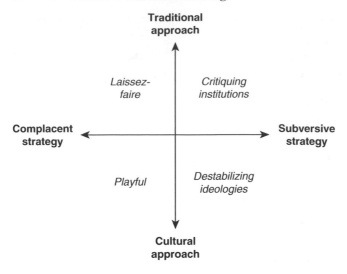

Figure 24.1 Differences between the traditional and the cultural approach.

Table 24.1 Managerial contribution of the cultural approach

	Traditional marketing approach	*Cultural marketing approach*
Consumer culture	"Pre-existing" as an entity separate from companies	Companies and consumer culture exist in a co-constitutive relationship
Role of marketers	Marketing activities do not play a significant role in shaping consumer culture	Marketing activities are co-responsible for creating consumer culture
Responsibility of marketers	None – they merely react to marketing conditions	Considerable – portrayals of idealized gender stereotypes in advertising impinges on consumer culture

culture and the norms and values associated with it. A cultural approach to advertising thus places much more weight, and hence responsibility, on marketing managers' capacity to shape consumer culture. Rather than viewing consumer culture as existing 'out there' as a separate entity, a cultural approach recognizes that company activities, such as advertising, play a part in shaping consumer culture (Table 24.1). What we hope to offer are new approaches for understanding advertising, and especially to critically looking at portrayals of men and women. It should be noted, however, that this sort of critical inquiry into how we portray certain groups of people in advertising could equally be applied to other 'variables' such as age and ethnicity (cf. Chapter 18 in this volume).

Why should a company care about these issues, one might ask? Will it lead to higher revenue in the short run, or even in the long run? Quite possibly, in fitting in with or challenging social constructions of gender. However, our argument situates advertising strategy within the burgeoning management phenomenon of Corporate Social Responsibility (CSR) whereby businesses are conducted along socially and ethically responsible lines (cf. Chapter 28 in this volume). One could argue that CSR is the deliberate inclusion of public interest into corporate decision-making, and indeed the societal marketing concept draws attention to citizens rather than consumers. Most of the time when such public interest is referred to, it has to do with ethics, environmental issues, and labour rights, but we would like to add gender to this agenda. Companies aspiring to contribute not only to their own short-term profits and customer satisfaction but also to long-term profits and public interest and welfare, should, we argue, behave responsibly in terms of how men and women are portrayed in their marketing campaigns, as this is not only an important strategic decision but an important ethical decision.

Marketing managers are thus faced with choices in relation to how they portray gender in their advertising campaigns. They can either sustain gender stereotypes or offer more pluralistic ways of looking at gender. In doing the latter they resist serving up the same old formulaic stereotypes of men and women. These choices acknowledge the profound influence of advertising and how it can reinforce cultural values and, by extension, consumers' values in the marketplace.

Theoretical discussion: gender studies and marketing

We now move on to discuss how stereotypical portrayals of men and women in advertising are based on deep-seated gender dichotomies in culture, such as culture/nature, man/woman, mind/body and so forth, as depicted in Table 24.2. In marketing, a gender dichotomy lies at the heart of its theories and practices. We can illustrate this by offering a brief account of the evolution of marketing as a discipline. The marketing concept places consumers at the centre of the organization, and the traditionally accepted view of consumers in marketing theory was that they were rational and logical human beings, with clear needs that could be met by effective, consumer needs-focused marketing. This focus was very much a micro-managerial one, with an emphasis on identifying consumers' social, psychological and demographic characteristics, and then meeting their needs better than competitors.

It is perhaps curious that early marketing theorists took the view that consumer behaviour and consumer buyer decision-making revolved around a mental process of problem recognition, information searching, evaluation of alternatives and the purchase decision. After all, the word 'consumer' usually describes a physical, bodily act. Joy and Venkatesh (1994) write that this led to the act of consumption being envisaged as a 'disembodied phenomenon'. The wider, cultural context for this emphasis was that the mind was privileged in

Table 24.2 Cultural associations with femininity and masculinity

Concepts associated with femininity	*Concepts associated with masculinity*
Nature	Culture
Body	Mind
Instinct	Logic
Passion	Reason
Carnality	Spirituality
Impulse	Control
Consumer	Producer
Emotion	Discipline
Irrationality	Rationality

Western culture. This so-called *privileging* of the mind had its basis in a modernist value system focused on a perception of man as a rational being, and it led to models of consumer buying behaviour that viewed consumers and the purchase decision-making process as predictable, rational and sequential.

This managerial, modernist focus neglected wider, macro environmental forces, such as cultural, social and political influences. Change was afoot, however. In the 1980s, new theories of consumer behaviour infiltrated the field, originating in other disciplines such as anthropology, the humanities and sociology. These brought with them new perspectives on consumers. Consumers were no longer simply viewed as potential customers of products and services that would satisfy clearly defined needs and solve specific problems. Consumer behaviour was beginning to be understood as being located in a much wider, macro context, and it was acknowledged that it was important to consider issues of cultural, social, personal and gender identity.

Marketers now had a choice: they could rely on models of consumer behaviour that focused on mental processes such as cognition, rationality and logic, or they could consider new concepts of consumer behaviour that focused on the emotions, senses and impulses. Certainly, it is true to say that consumers were increasingly recognized as being driven as much by their senses as by reason, as much by their passions as by logic. Irrespective of which perspective marketers took, experiential and hedonic aspects of consumption had now come to the fore, and the consumer was unlikely to ever again be conceived of as a disembodied problem identifier and solver! (See Holbrook and Hirschman's work (1982) for a full discussion of this paradigmatic shift in consumer behaviour research.)

In this more 'animistic' world the human *body* inevitably took centre stage, and the focus on the body had important implications for how men and women were depicted in advertising. Traditionally men were rational customers who ultimately purchased products and services, and women were the emotional consumers who were targeted by advertisers. This gendered division reflected distinct and different gendered roles and responsibilities in Western society, and furthermore these differences had a long history. In general terms, 'masculinity' was associated with the mind, logic and rationality. Men were traditionally regarded as being 'naturally' more rational than women, and thus they had the ability to transcend their bodily urges; women, however, were not perceived as being able to do this, and were envisaged as being at the mercy of their bodily wants and desires (Joy and Venkatesh 1994).

Women have been associated with nature, carnality, instinct and passion since ancient times, whereas men have been associated with culture, reason, control and spirituality. The feminine thus came to define emotionality, irrationality and sensuality (Bordo 1993). Furthermore, womanhood had a dangerous, appetitive and volatile nature, in contrast to manhood, which was disciplined, rational and controlled. Unlike men, women were therefore at the mercies of their mortal bodies, subject to the body's frailties and vagaries, forever buffeted by their feminine natures.

The traditional privileging of the mind over the body was gradually being challenged, however. The so-called 'turn to the body' is usually associated with postmodernism. Postmodernism is attributed with changing the focus of the consumer as a rational, knowing subject to a communicative subject indulging in subjective experiences. The postmodern consumer is characterized as having a playful attitude to the marketplace, enjoying the games, simulations and fun associated with being a 'fragmented' consumer, leading a 'multi-layered existence' in a liberating and limitless space, where freedom and choice are both expected and demanded (see Brown 1995, for a full discussion of postmodernism and marketing). The postmodernist perspective takes a somewhat ironic view of the meaning and value of things, questioning all that is taken for granted and respecting very little.

Postmodernism gives the body centre stage, and significantly, this body is no longer a female body. The triad of male/producer/mind versus female/consumer/body has now broken down and become fragmented, and the old dichotomy of the marketplace has also been challenged; some might say turned upside down. Postmodernism has paved the way for new conceptualizations, representations and visual spectacles of both men and women in the marketplace, and the marketplace now provides a stage for all kinds of representations of men and women, which shake up traditional ideas about the 'masculine' and the 'feminine', about 'men' and 'women', about 'sexual objects' and 'sexual subjects', about the mind and the body in consumption, and about gender roles in consumer culture. Gender blending and gender bending have thus been thrown into the marketing communication mix alongside traditional gender stereotyping and gender categories, and this has had surprising, challenging, provocative and at times, shocking results.

Aside from the influence of postmodernism, feminist research on the body has also been influential in drawing attention to so-called embodiment issues in the marketplace, challenging how women are portrayed in the media, by focusing on women's experiences with their bodies in terms of beauty practices, fashion, fitness regimes, eating disorders and cosmetic surgery. This research shows how bodies are continually moulded and shaped by societal, cultural and political forces, in order that individuals can achieve normalization in terms of physical appearance. (See Davis 1997 for a full discussion of this.) However, while feminism shares postmodernism's aims of drawing attention to the body in the marketplace, it is also true that feminism or 'feminisms', as they now tend to be called, have an uneasy alliance with postmodernism, as postmodern advertising often resurrects old stereotypes of women and men in order to engage in playful, irreverent depictions that mock so-called political correctness.

In the previous section we highlighted how the values associated with femininity and masculinity emerged in Western culture, briefly outlining the role of history, culture, marketing, postmodernism and feminism on how feminine and masculine values were mapped onto men and women in social and cultural practices, including advertising. We have suggested that a *cultural* approach and a *traditional* approach to advertising are at opposite ends of a continuum. We have also suggested that there is another intersecting axis, with a *complacent* strategy and a *subversive* strategy as the endpoints. In other words, marketing managers can choose to adopt one of four positions: a traditional/complacent, traditional/subversive, cultural/complacent or cultural/subversive position (see Figure 24.1). Furthermore, we will argue that there is a distinct lack of subversive perspectives in marketing communication strategies. In both traditional and cultural approaches the dominance of the postmodern paradigm leads to either a *laissez-faire* attitude on the one hand, or a *playful* attitude on the other.

Femininity and masculinity in advertising

We now offer examples of how contemporary advertising deals with female and male bodies and their representation. The carnal feminine offers an analysis of several advertising campaigns that show a return to the ancient narrative of what we describe as 'the carnal feminine', namely the age-old notion that women are irrational bodies who are prey to their carnal appetites. Sometimes these ads employ postmodern irony when they represent women in stereotypical ways and at other times they assume a more conventional, taken-for-granted tone. The second part explores how the representation of men and masculinity in contemporary advertising campaigns are challenging, yet upholding, conventional norms. Sexual objectification is no longer the preserve of women, it seems, but is becoming increasingly prevalent in advertisements targeting men, specifically in relation to traditional taboos about male sexuality.

The 'carnal feminine'

The main narrative used in advertising depicts women as 'consummate consumers' who are ruled by their bodily appetites and are unable to resist the lure of carnal pleasures. The word carnal is from the Latin *carnalis*, from *carnes* meaning 'flesh'. The definition of 'carnal' is 'of the body or flesh; worldly'. Its secondary meaning is also noteworthy: 'worldly, sensual, sexual'. Most contemporary advertisements targeting women thus adopt what we would define as the *complacent* strategy. In other words, they either adopt a traditional/complacent, *laissez-faire* attitude in terms of gender portrayals, or a cultural/complacent one, employing a postmodern *playfulness* in relation to gender stereotypes. The traditional/complacent *laissez-faire* position is exemplified by advertisements targeting women that emphasize women's animal natures, specifically their carnal appetites. This usually results in advertisements that employ sexually suggestive and erotic narratives which emphasize experiential consumption and sensory pleasures. The narrative is particularly overt in the advertising of products (of which there are many) that are depicted as being endowed with the power to enable women to experience intense physical pleasure from their consumption. Examples of product categories that are depicted as objects of desire for women include food products such as chocolate, ice cream and cream cheese; luxury biscuits; and toiletries and cosmetics, such as shampoo, bath and shower products, and perfume.

Food product advertisements targeting women are usually framed within a carnal (and often erotic) narrative, because these narratives are based on the assumption that eating is women's secret pleasure and secret sin. The association of women's consumption of food and toiletries with their sexual appetites provides advertisers with opportunities to playfully explore 'naughty but nice' narratives. There is also a dark side to this, however, in that giving into the lure of one's appetites can lead to excessive consumption, and this may have undesirable outcomes in our culture, notably in the form of weight gain in the case of high-fat foods such as chocolate. The notion that women's 'animal' appetites are always in danger of spiralling out of control draws on long-standing cultural codes, as we have argued.

Bordo (1993) writes that in Western culture women's appetite for food and women's appetite for sex are often represented as being one and the same thing. There are a number of excellent examples of the conflation of eating and sexual suggestiveness in advertisements targeting women, and its inherent Freudian symbolism is often used to full effect in contemporary advertisements. One of the most famous examples is the 1991 Cadbury's flake ad which features a woman eating a Cadbury's Flake in an over-flowing bubble bath (Figure 24.2). Such ads draw clear parallels between food consumption and sexual surrender. This ad is still considered to be one of the all-time most sexy ads, according to a poll conducted in 2008.

In their study of women's chocolate consumption, Belk and Costa (1998) write that the consumption of luxury foods is gendered as female. They also refer to the 'emotionally charged' environment within which women consume chocolate (ibid.: 189), and they

Figure 24.2 Advertisement for Cadbury's Flake.
Source: Credit: Image Courtesy of the Advertising Archives.

highlight the ambivalence that surrounds women's consumption of such products. Advertisements for chocolate address this ambivalence in their seductive and often tongue-in-cheek narratives about women succumbing to the temptation of eating pleasurable, high calorie, and often luxury food products. In another study, Lupton writes that chocolate signifies 'romance, luxury, decadence, indulgence, reward, sensuousness and femininity' (1996: 35). Chocolate advertisements, reflecting a traditional cultural norm, thus tell us that such animal wants are 'natural' in women and cannot be denied. This being the case, they are thus compelled to offer women a never-ending array of sensually, erotically and emotionally charged advertising narratives, narratives that also point to the bittersweet ambivalence that lies at the centre of such seductive appeals.

Ice cream is another popular product category for depicting the auto-erotic potential of food consumption for advertisers. One recent ad for Wall's Cornetto range of luxury ice creams features an attractive young woman on a balcony slowly consuming her ice cream with a spoon while watching a handsome artist at work in the room opposite. The artist is aware that he is being watched and becomes increasingly distracted from his work and aroused by this spectacle. This is suggested by some auto-erotic body stroking on his part and a noticeable increase in perspiration! Finally, he can bear it no longer and he rushes from the room, presumably in the direction of her apartment, judging by her knowing smile towards the door at the end of the advertisement. Wall's have also recently launched a humorous TV ad campaign for a new range of luxury ice creams in their Cornetto range called 'Love Potion'. The strapline is 'Love at first bite – steer clear of them', and the ad shows the wild, uncontrollable passions that can be unleashed in women by their consumption. HB's Magnum range of luxury ice creams called '7 Deadly Sins', shows a woman who is tempted by Magnum (the devil) who introduces her to her 'sinful selves' and she then embarks on her 'journey…so many sins, so little time'. The television advertising campaign features an ad for each of the seven options available in the range and shows the same woman in seven different guises to represent each of the seven sins: revenge, gluttony, sloth, greed, jealousy, vanity and lust. Words and phrases used include: 'give in', 'let go', 'let gluttony consume you, succumb to true indulgence', 'indulge in the joy of sloth', 'fulfil your heart's deepest desires', 'you know you want to', 'tantalise yourself', 'slide the wrapper off', 'indulge in the uninhibited pleasure of ice cream', 'enjoy the sensation of decadence', and finally, 'lie back, breathe deeply, and continue to relish the sensuous experience'. The campaign clearly draws parallels between ice cream consumption and sexual surrender.

One of the most common ways of underlining women's animalistic sides is to compare them with animals, particularly big cats. These are used to signify women's lustful and dangerous aspects. An advertisement for Dior's Pure Poison perfume shows a dark, predatorial temptress who transforms herself into a black panther, and Lynx toiletry products for young men play on the idea that women have animalistic, lustful natures that are waiting to be unleashed with the right stimulation, in this case the scent of Lynx. A recent television advert shows wild, bikini-clad women descending in their droves from the surrounding hills in order to ravish (we assume) a young man on a deserted beach who has just sprayed himself with some Lynx body spray.

Another important dimension of women's identification with the body in advertising is apparent in ads that show women as a larger than life force of nature that is out of control, and loving it! Such representations of women in advertisements have a humorous and playful tone, as they typically show real, believable women having fun and happily succumbing to their animal appetites. Perhaps the best known example of this theme is the long-standing Terry's Chocolate Orange campaign in the UK. This campaign memorably casts the generously proportioned English comedienne and actress Dawn French as the insatiable chocoholic who can't control her consumption of Terry's Chocolate Orange, and nor does she want to! Above all, she wants to keep the pleasure of eating chocolate to herself: 'It's not Terry's! It's mine!' We are also led to assume that she is supremely indifferent to the bodily consequences of such indulgence, and indeed Dawn French takes a celebratory approach to being a larger woman generally, not least by developing a range of clothing for women with larger than average body shapes. She is a role model in English culture for a woman of excess who delights in excess, whether it is her ribald and outrageous comedy routines or her role as the face of Terry's Chocolate Orange, and the Terry's Chocolate Orange campaign reflects her own flamboyant, comedic style. Dawn French embodies the garrulous, amply-proportioned big woman who is ruled by her appetites and makes no apology for this. In some respects this could be considered to be a difficult position to take in the current climate of concern over the rise in obesity levels in Western societies, and indeed Dawn French ceased to be the face of the campaign in 2007, amidst speculation that Terry's were responding to increasing social pressures in this regard.

Another common strategy in advertising is to deliberately employ 'porn codes' to draw parallels between food consumption and sexual intercourse with 'bad' women. These codes are commonly used when the target markets are men. The pornographic often denotes prostitution and sex for sale, and is rooted in the concept of domination over women. It also commodifies the human body and persistently stereotypes male and female sexual roles (Schroeder and McDonagh 2004). Probyn (2000) suggests that food narratives generally draw on the language of 'soft porn' and thereby equate food consumption with sex consumption. In her study she cites the 'soft porn' antics of celebrity TV cooks in the UK, and she quotes Nigella Lawson's comments that all of us are 'gastropornographers'.

The Kinder Bueno range of chocolate bars provide an excellent exemplar of the pornographic in an advertising campaign, and this brand freely and unapologetically uses 'porn codes'. A recent TV advertising campaign in the UK memorably, and disturbingly, (given that the product range originally targeted children) uses such codes to personify the product as a female prostitute. It features a male customer entering a newsagents' shop in a dirty mac, furtively glancing at the top shelf of the magazine racks for something to buy. His attention is arrested, however, by the voice of a young, high-pitched Far Eastern accented female voice, who urges him to 'bite me, bite me, I'll be whatever you want me to be.' The voice comes from a gyrating chocolate bar. The ad draws on sado-masochistic porn codes to make the product memorable and appealing to its new target market, young adult males, and it clearly hints at sex tourism in its narrative.

In a similar vein, an ad for Pot Noodles shows a man rejecting his wholesome wife's offer of a home-made sandwich so that he can search for 'something dirty' in the local red light district. Having been slapped by a number of indignant ladies of the night by his requests, he eventually finds a 'tart with a heart' who takes him into a dark alley, and there he finds what he's been looking for, a Pot Noodle! More recently, a horse-riding and hunting analogy is used in this series of television ads, with references made to an upper-class lady (with more than a passing resemblance to Lady Chatterley from the notorious novel by DH Lawrence), and her lusty gamekeeper. The campaign currently uses a riding horn ('have you got the horn?') to suggest the product's association with sexual arousal and the sex act itself. A number of Pot Noodle ads have been banned. Their most notorious campaign used the strapline 'the slag of all snacks' to underline the positioning of their product.

This strategy can be perceived as another example of the cultural perception of woman as an insatiable consumer who lures men from the straight and narrow path. In this case she is also the product itself, a commodity that men cannot resist. She is consumed, and, even worse, she is a product that is bad for men's health! The consumption of food and the consumption of sex become one and the same, the common denominator being women, a body to be consumed.

Undesirable and desirable males

Due to changes in conventions of representation of the male body, it has been suggested that men today are being taught, or allowed, to gaze at other men either for pleasure or for anxiety-evoking contrast, and that this makes men increasingly aware of, and dissatisfied with, bodies that do not meet various cultural ideals. When we are faced with admirable bodies in visual representations, such as advertising, the subject being depicted is turned into an admired and admirable object. While female bodies can be portrayed in the nude without too many apologies, the nude, or partially nude, male body typically needs an excuse to be portrayed. The men depicted need to be engaged in some activity rather than just posing. In classical art, war scenes have been the most common excuse to portray eroticized male bodies in action (ripped clothing, bulging muscles, sweat) with neither the subject portrayed, nor the onlooker, having to feel uncomfortable. Today, especially in advertising, sports seem to be the excuse of choice, as there is apparently nothing peculiar about masses of half-naked, well-sculpted, sweaty bodies being seen either on sports courts, or in places connected to sports, such as locker rooms.

Representations of men in advertising have typically been connected to men's traditional role as breadwinners, and this legacy was unchallenged up to the 1970s. During the 1980s, however, this slowly changed, as men started appearing without references to family – shown alone and in close-up. Still, men were typically portrayed as dominant and as actionable, in charge, as if they were creating a sense of identity by extending out from their body to control objects and others. In his classic study of gender in advertisements, Ervin Goffman (1979) found that women are typically represented as cradling or caressing an object but not grasping, holding or manipulating it in a utilitarian way. All in all, it seems that men are active with clear purpose, whereas women just look on admiringly. During the 1990s, men's role as homemakers/breadwinners was further de-emphasized, and contempt for stereotypi-cally unpleasant male behaviours – such as uncleanliness and poor household skills – became a staple of advertising. This open ridicule of masculinity slowly paved the way for an increased erotization of the male body in advertising. In the 1990s men were increasingly portrayed to-be-looked-at, without the protective shelter of humour, degradation or ridicule. Nick Kamen's classic ad for Levi's 501, where he undresses in a 1950s launderette, aired for the first time in 1985, and marks a shift in representations of men in TV ads. About ten years later Calvin Klein took a new turn and introduced a more overtly sexual representation of males in a series of underwear ads that has continued to this day.

While there have been changes in how masculinity is portrayed in advertising, there is still a dominance of fairly traditional modes of representations where men are active, in control and acting upon the world – the *laissez-faire* position in Figure 24.1. Advertisements of this type either address or portray men in a taken-for-granted manner, where stereotypes of how men are – not comfortable in taking care of babies, poor at expressing emotions, or naturally unskilled at household work – are sustained. There is an abundance of these types of advertisements available. There has, however, been an increase in the amount of advertising where men are portrayed in other, non-traditional ways thus occupying the three other positions in Figure 24.1. Most of the time, there is no real subversive potential, rather, we see a cultural/complacent strategy, where a postmodern playfulness in relation to gender stereotypes is employed, but there are tendencies towards change. Here we will look at how men are increasingly being reminded in advertising that they might not be living up to the beauty standards in society, the notion that they might indeed be undesirable is thus played upon. In particular, there is the suggestion that their self-worth is measured by how much attention they are getting from females. This is interesting, as the dominant masculine mode of being judged by what one *does* rather what by how one *looks* is thus challenged. We will also look at how men are shown as objects of sexual desire. Typically, this is described in terms of 'beefcake' ads in addition to the conventional 'cheesecake' ads used in advertis-ing. In all these examples, we will see how men are portrayed as potential objects of desire, but how the ads, in more or less subtle ways, make sure that something more can be detected. It is not merely a picture of a beautiful man or a suggestion that men need certain products in order to be accepted. Instead, there is typically a rational consumption choice that can be made.

Recently, there has been an increase in ads where it is suggested that the purchase of a particular product will result in increased female attention to a man. This marks a shift, as insecurity is inserted in the representations of men. It is no longer self-evident, even in the fantasy world created by advertising, that a good man will find a good woman. Advertising to women has long used this strategy and there are plenty of ads where women are being offered various products or self-help procedures that will help them 'capture' a man. All of a sudden, it has become increasingly common to adopt such an approach in advertising for men. Some of the most vivid examples of these types of advertisements can be seen in the penile enlargement industry, as discussed in detail by Ostberg (2010). There are, however, plenty of less extreme examples, taken from mainstream advertising, pointing towards similar tendencies.

Ever since the breakthrough advertising of Calvin Klein in the 1990s, men's bodies have frequently been shown in advertising as objects of desire. A recent example is the underwear brand Frigo Underwear (www.frigounderwear.se) that has one of their ads featuring a man lounging in a cane chair (Figure 24.3). He is wearing bright white underwear that stands in stark contrast to the grey shades of colour used in the rest of the picture. The man's crotch is in focus of the picture and the rest of the picture becomes increasingly unfocused as one's eyes move away from that area of his body. The man is leaning backwards in the chair, still his abdominal muscles appear tense and flexed, as if he was about to get up from the chair. This is contrasted by the top part of the body that seems exceptionally relaxed and at ease. The man's mouth and eyes are half-open, he is gazing lustily at something outside of the picture. Is he waiting for someone? You perhaps? A lover? Male or female?

These facial features, the half-open eyes and mouth, are a common visual convention in portraits of women as desirable objects. We thus see, in Figure 24.3, how visual conventions of how to portray women are transferred to the portrayal of men. This shows a cultural sensitivity on the behalf of the company; they know that this will not be read negatively by the target group. Eroticized images of men are not new to advertising, but this particular image shows a man that is not actionable, a man that is not engaged in sports, for example, which is the usual excuse for the exposure of partially nude male bodies.

Even though there are to-be-looked-at ads featuring men, this is often regarded as being too overt. There must typically be something more that excuses the presence of the scantily clad man. In the case of Frigo Underwear, the man on the picture is not just stretched out on the cane chair for our pleasure; he is indeed displaying a fantastic invention. The copy reads 'Frigo: A small step for man. A giant step for manhood.' Frigo Underwear is, apparently, the greatest invention in the underwear business since Jockey invented the Y-front in 1935. It is, according to Frigo Underwear's homepage 'more alluring than the wonderbra'. The very masculine traits of science, progression, invention and technology function as a

Figure 24.3 Advertisement for Frigo Underwear.

counterbalance to the picture of the lounging man. The tendency to offset the picture of the lounging man with a more goal-directed reasoning is also found in the statement of the company philosophy:

> When God created man he wanted their genitals to hang loose. The genitals were supposed to stay cool in the gentle breeze, before, after and during the hunt for food. But then things begun to change … And then what happened to their precious genitals? I guess you know. Sweat broke out, it rubbed and hung. But let us establish that we're living in a modern era and stay positive. The men who choose to wear Frigo today is also hunting. It's just the prey that is different.

First and foremost, we see here that the man as breadwinner ethos is restored; men are born, even created, to hunt for food. In today's environment when the hunting might be less eventful, the predatory instincts of men have been transferred to the hunt for a partner. The advertising for Frigo Underwear is playing with ideas of some eternal masculine traits. Still, despite the attempts to hide the invention of Frigo Underwear under the veil of 'restoring things to their natural state', the real benefit of the particular model is that it gives the wearer a more 'shapely package'. The inventor apparently '… equipped his underwear with a sawn pocket in which the whole package was placed which made it easy to ventilate and regulate the body temperature: All parts were kept in place and "voilà" he had invented the first "shape-up" for men.'

So, despite the attempts to cast the marketing of Frigo Underwear in a macho tone, the product is geared towards the insecurities of men. And not just any insecurity, but the most taboo of all insecurities: the insecurity of not being sufficiently well endowed. The advertisers thus utilize the classic technique dispersed in most mainstream branding or advertising textbooks: if you want consumers to act on your marketing offer, make them insecure in their relationships with others and offer your product as the solution.

Frigo continues to play with the conventions in the next ad where they move into slightly more subversive terrain by directly referencing the iconic advertising campaign for Wonderbra where Eva Herzigova is shown with the caption 'Hello boys', suggesting that men cannot keep their eyes off a woman showing off her assets. In the 'Hello girls!' advertisement shown in Figure 24.4 it is implied that women cannot keep their eyes off a man showing off his assets. By placing the man in such an ostentatiously objectified position, albeit with the possibility of a tongue-in-cheek reading, they are using an updated version of the visual repertoire available for the depiction of men.

In these examples we see that even when men are turning themselves into objects to be desired by others, they are given a chance to be in control. We see here a tension between men being insecure and the conventional way of portraying masculinity as a dominant force.

Conclusion: the consuming body in contemporary consumer culture

In this chapter, we have given you a backdrop to the 'brave new world' of more or less conventional representations of femininity and masculinity in advertising. The body, previously represented in a very restrictive and gender-stereotyped way, has now been set free, and this has opened up an arena of carnivalesque humour and previously unimaginable possibilities. Advertisers can engage in a free-for-all bodyfest where almost anything goes,

Figure 24.4 'Hello girls!' advertisement for Frigo Underwear.
    Source: Photo credits: Stevens and Ostberg

and postmodern irony can cover a multitude of sins. The consuming body has become a powerful symbol of twenty-first-century consumer culture, and this concept offers advertising/marketing practitioners the opportunity to engage in tongue-in-cheek theatrics, audacious feats of dare-devilry, slapstick comedy and fantastic flights of fancy that amuse, provoke, move and at times shock their intended target audience(s) as well as those who are not their intended target audience(s)!

One of the issues we have addressed in this chapter is that by turning to the body and postmodernism, we are in danger of being purveyors of the same old stereotypes and indeed the same old taboos about the body, and the gender issues that surround it. No amount of humour or tongue-in-cheek irony can obscure that. We need to be aware of the power issues that lie at the core of dichotomous thinking about gender. While we have demonstrated that change is happening in terms of how the masculine body is represented in current advertising campaigns, and in terms of how women's bodies are represented, we have also shown that these discursive practices may often reproduce long-standing tendencies in marketing strategy to trade in and on the (gendered) body insecurities of consumers.

This chapter suggests that by adopting a more critical and culturally aware approach to the study of advertising, we can better understand where dichotomous thinking originated, how it has evolved over time, and how it currently is manifested in contemporary advertising practices. Furthermore, we argue that a greater awareness of these issues makes for a more nuanced and socially responsible marketing management approach. We have also tried to show that increasingly male and female bodies are represented in advertising as complex, living bodies acting in the marketplace and engaging and interacting with it, rather than stereotypical, gendered objects that are easily manipulated by marketers. This is of course a step in the right direction. While gender stereotypes and dualistic thinking run deep in our society, then, we have argued that new and more varied forms of femininity and masculinity are emerging in the marketplace. We hope we have raised awareness in this chapter of an emerging process in Western society, whereby the dualistic structures surrounding masculinity and femininity are beginning to unravel, the old monochromatic black and white lens is now being replaced by many shades of grey, and indeed we might more accurately say that colour has finally been introduced! As marketers, we now need to rise to the challenge of turning the current idea of the body as the seat of consumer identity into an approach that more accurately reflects the diversity of gendered positions and the multiplicity of gendered identities (and human bodies!) in the marketplace.

Review and discussion questions

1   Browse the internet, thumb through a magazine, or watch TV and try to find examples of advertisements that challenge the status quo of masculine and feminine representations. In what ways do you think these advertisements have the potential to create positive change in society?
2   Are certain types of companies more likely to be successful in the marketplace with non-traditional representations of masculinity and femininity? If so, what are these types of companies and why do you believe that they are more suited?
3   Humour is a very effective means of gaining consumers' attentions and increasing the likeability of a brand. It also enables advertisers to get away with 'political incorrectness', for example, and push the boundaries of good taste. Do you think the end justifies the means? What moral and ethical issues do such strategies raise?

Exercise

While it might be far from a simple and straightforward process to move from a complacent to a subversive strategy regarding the use of gendered representations in advertising, we would like to invite present and future managers to address these issues and to make a conscious choice, rather than just opting for the easy way out, which would typically be the *laissez-faire* position. In order to think more consciously about these issues, here are some questions that one might pose to one's own company:

1   In what ways are we presently portraying women and men – as well as femininity and masculinity – in our marketing communication campaigns?
2   Are we, by portraying women and men in this way, contributing to cementing stereotypes or are we creating positive change?
3   Are there other possible ways, in which we could portray, or address, women and men in our marketing communication campaigns?
4   What would be the possible effects of portraying or addressing women and men in these alternative ways?

Keywords

advertising, body representation, femininity, gender, masculinity

References

Belk, Russell W. and Costa, Janeen A. (1998) 'Chocolate delights: Gender and consumer indulgence', in *Proceedings of the Conference on Gender, Marketing and Consumer Behavior,* San Francisco, CA: Association for Consumer Research, pp. 179–93.

Bordo, Susan (1993) *Unbearable Weight: Feminism, Western Culture, and the Body*, Berkeley, CA: University of California Press.

Bristor, Julia M. and Fischer, Eileen (1993) 'Feminist Thought: Implications for Consumer Research', *Journal of Consumer Research*, 19(March): 518–36.

Brown, Stephen (1995) *Postmodern Marketing*, London: Routledge.

Davis, Kathy (1997) *Embodied Practices: Feminist Perspectives on the Body*, London: Sage.

Goffman, Erving (1979) *Gender Advertisements*, New York: Harper & Row.

Holbrook, Morris B. and Hirschman, Elizabeth C. (1982) 'The Experiential Aspects of Consumption: Consumer Fantasies, Feelings, and Fun', *Journal of Consumer Research*, 9(September): 132–40.

Joy, Annamma and Venkatesh, Alladi (1994) 'Postmodernism, Feminism and the Body: The Visible and the Invisible in Consumer Research', *International Journal of Research in Marketing*, 11(4): 333–57.

Lupton, Deborah (1996) *Food, the Body and the Self*, London: Sage.

Ostberg, Jacob (2010) 'Thou Shalt Sport a Banana in Thy Pocket: Gendered Body Size Ideals in Advertising and Popular Culture', *Marketing Theory*, 10(1): 45–73.

Probyn, Elspeth (2000) *Carnal Appetites: Food, Sex, Identities*, London: Routledge.

Schroeder, Jonathan E. and McDonagh, Pierre (2004) 'The Logic of Pornography in Digital Camera Ads', in *Sex in Promotional Culture; The Erotic Content of Media and Marketing*, New Jersey: Lawrence Erlbaum Associates.

25 The ecology of the marketplace experience

From consumers' imaginary to design implications

*Stefania Borghini, Pauline MacLaran,
Gaël Bonnin, and Véronique Cova*

Overview

In this chapter we explore the role of place from a cultural perspective. More precisely we show how consumers make sense of the spaces and places around them, and how consumptionscapes such as flagships stores, shopping centers, restaurants and bars, and also ordinary stores perform many socio-cultural functions that go unacknowledged in traditional marketing management texts. According to this constructivist view, we propose that the design of commercial spaces should be grounded on a thorough understanding of these psychological, bodily and cultural processes, and of consumers' needs for self-affirmation through a self–place bond fulfillment. The suggested principles of store design are thus based on the use of devices and architectural elements which provide a stage for consumers' experiences (cf. Chapter 10 in this volume) and, at the same time, promote freedom of movement and meaning construction. We illustrate our discussions with many examples of commercial locations and two brief case studies, namely Prada Epicenter and Mama Shelter as interesting points of reference for both theory development and managerial practice.

Introduction

In traditional marketing management approaches, the "P" of place is typically regarded as just another element of the marketing mix, referring to a variety of distribution elements, such as channels, coverage, assortments, locations, inventory and transport. Most commonly, it takes a functional, decision-making approach to assessing the physical logistics of delivering a product or service to the customer. There is some acknowledgement of the importance of servicescapes as environments where sellers and customers interact; and also store atmospherics and their potential sensory appeal to consumers. From a traditional perspective, however, the focus is on the physical, tangible evidence of place and its effects in terms of emotional and behavioral outcomes.

The everyday experience of consumers undoubtedly shows that consumptionscapes can provide deeper symbolic and cultural meanings for their dwellers, thus playing a powerful role in shaping our cultural identity as consumers. Retail outlets, shopping malls and flagship brand stores are places that provide consumers with material and symbolic environments affecting identities and desires. The contemporary thematized and

Table 25.1 Traditional approaches to the study of store design and its impact on consumers' behavior

Approach	Main tenets and foundations	Main contributions
Ecological approach	Physical environment is like a habitat to which consumers try to adapt in order to search various types of benefits	Bloch *et al.* (1994)
Perspectives based on the S.O.R. paradigm	Stimuli from physical environment influence behavior and emotions, see Meharabian and Russel (1974), Lazarus (1991)	For an extended review, see Turley and Milliman (2000), Lyn (2004), Chebat and Michon (2003)
Socio-systemic approach	The combination of both social and physical dimensions of environments' impact on consumer's behavior	Baker *et al.* (1992, 1994)
Experiential shopping approach	Store design influences hedonic dimensions of consumer behavior	Donovan and Rossiter (1982); Babin *et al.* (1994); Babin and Darden (1995); Arnold and Reynolds (2003)

spectacularized commercial venues are able not only to incorporate brand meanings, but also to combine entertainment with therapeutics and spiritual growth, or to enact utopian experiences. Moreover, it is not only spectacular environments that influence us in these ways. We often become very attached to everyday commercial locations such as bars, coffee shops, and even grocery stores.

If we consider the wide range of traditional perspectives which have dealt with the role played by store design (Table 25.1), we can note that they have focused mainly on the physical, sensory and emotional components of consumers' experiences, thus ignoring the cultural and symbolic dimensions. In this chapter we therefore focus on the cultural dimensions of store design and illustrate how different types of commercial venues can provide cultural resources for consumers.

Evoking the imagination: spectacular consumptionscapes

The notion that consumers often visit retail locations for social and emotional reasons, rather than just to make a purchase, is not, in itself, a new concept. Although the more cultural and symbolic dimensions of marketplace experiences are often overlooked by traditional perspectives in marketing and consumer behavior, these dimensions have been evident in retailing practices for many centuries. Indeed, historically the market square was usually a crossroads that served as a focus of community and the point of intersection of different cultures, with merchants from different neighborhoods, regions or even countries, bringing their various wares to sell.

Spectacular consumption environments – for example, flagship brand stores (Nike Town, American Girl Place), sporting complexes (ESPN Zone), shopping malls (West Edmonton Mall), theme parks (Disneyland) and other themed locations (restaurants/hotels/pubs/shops) – are increasingly a significant part of our cityscapes and reflect a growing tendency to blur the boundaries between leisure, entertainment and shopping. Environments such as these awe consumers with their elaborate visual displays designed to evoke desires and imaginings. They invite consumers to enter an illusionary realm where they can fantasize about themselves in multifaceted ways.

Nowadays, the most ubiquitous spectacular consumptionscape is the contemporary shopping mall which is a hybrid of both the arcades and the department stores. The mall shares many of its predecessors' design features, bringing together a large assortment of goods under one roof, and with often spectacular features that attract and enchant consumers. A key principle of shopping mall design is that a distinctive sense of place should be created in order to draw people to visit and identify with the location. Hedonic consumption is encouraged in the mall environment where retailers appeal to multiple senses of sight, sound, scent and taste through sophisticated merchandising techniques. The increasing interpenetration of leisure facilities alongside these techniques mean that malls now often become attractions in their own right. For example, more recent major mall developments, such as the West Edmunton Mall, Canada, and The Mall of America, have maximized this new cultural form in their introduction of major leisure complex elements.

An important part of the fantasy-weaving process in such environments is the concept of retail as a play or drama, a drama in which customers become involved. There are many theatrical and hyper-real qualities of the mall and they have been referred to as "theatres of consumption" (Hopkins 1990). Production at the mall can be likened to a "retail drama" where a fantasy world is managed and orchestrated to persuade customers to buy (Kowinski 1985). The use of theming is common in mall design to enhance the performative aspects and give the mall (and/or particular areas of it) a more distinct identity. For example, the West Edmonton Mall recreates a Parisian Boulevard and Chinatown among its many other simulations. One of Europe's biggest shopping centers, the MetroCentre, Gateshead, England, has themed shopping in the Roman Forum, the Mediterranean Village and the Garden Court to name but a few of its themes. As theming is becoming an increasingly important part of contemporary retailing, we go on to explore its use in more detail in the following section.

The use of themed retail environments

The contemporary use of theming began with well-known consumer attractions such as Disneyland and Las Vegas. As Western society moves more toward an experience economy, the use of theming is becoming increasingly prevalent across many different types of retail environment as marketers appeal to consumers' imaginations and try to better engage them in the overall experience of the product or service they are offering. The use of theming can be found not only in shopping centers and malls, but also in restaurants, hotels, pubs (the "Irish Pub" can now be found around the world) and many other leisure venues. Another recent phenomenon is the themed flagship brand store that encourages consumers to engage in an experience with their brands (Kozinets *et al.* 2002). The term "flagship" denotes the leader of the fleet and flagship stores are to be found in exclusive shopping areas of city centers (for example, Abercrombie & Fitch has flagship stores on Fifth Avenue, New York and Saville Row, London). Flagship stores such as Niketown, Chicago, and Prada, New York (see Box 25.1 for details about its retail strategy), Tokyo, and Los Angeles present brandscapes that encode the symbolic meanings of the brand throughout, enabling consumers to experience the brand's values in a very embodied manner. Niketown has museum-style cases displaying Nike shoes that have been worn by the rich and famous. The architecture of the Prada store in Tokyo connotes luxury and refinement and there are

Box 25.1. Prada Epicenter, New York

The Prada Epicenter in New York, located at the corner of Prince Street and Broadway, was opened on December 15, 2001. Along with the Epicenters in Tokyo and Los Angeles, this store represents a totally new way to interpret the sales outlet, viewing it as a multi-functional place that celebrates the brand image and its creations, the client and the visitor, contemporary artistic productions, and the city in which the Epicenter is located.

The space grew out of the collaboration with the architect Rem Koolhaas and the Office of Metropolitan Architecture (OMA).

From the architectural point of view the Epicenter occupies two parallel, non-aligned spaces located in two adjacent buildings. The two spaces – one located on the ground floor of one building and the other in the cellar of the other – are connected by a small section of the cellar, which represents a focal point of the store in that it influences its architectural character. In fact, the design of the entire structure revolves around the wave shape of the connecting section (see Figure 25.1).

From the street a wide, wave-shaped stairway leads to the lower level, at the same time shaping the subdivision of the space inside the Epicenter and identifying the entrance areas, the steps that display the shoes, a stage and the main display area.

The area around the wave is multifunctional, since it can be modulated based on need. During the day the steps are used to display the shoes but they can be changed when necessary into an auditorium that can hold 200 persons. Moreover, the rising part of the wave can be mechanically controlled and transformed into a platform.

The ground floor is for the display of the merchandise in modulated form. Designed based on the philosophy of "mobile volumes", this surface area contains a series of

Figure 25.1 The wave at the Epicenter in New York.
Source: Courtesy of Prada.

Figure 25.2 The display cages, Epicenter in New York.
Source: Courtesy of Prada.

aluminum mesh cages hung from the ceiling, which can be moved and completed in a flexible way as need requires (Figure 25.2). Set on motorized rails, they can be completed by hangers, mannequins and merchandise, and easily and quickly moved throughout the store, thereby maintaining a uniformity in business communication style. These are true internal show windows which, by means of their unique position and structure, effectively capture the attention of the customer, who is thereby led to follow a path suggested by the products themselves.

The entrance leads to the lower floor through a glass cylindrical elevator which is spacious enough to contain a display area for bags and accessories.

The lower floor, tiled in black and white marble like the Prada boutique in the Galleria in Milan, is divided into a display room and a space dedicated to accessories. The display of products is also achieved through a succession of rooms composed of shelves that bring to mind a library design and which in this case as well is modularly modified according to the display needs. Thus, while guaranteeing a certain uniformity in the display approach, the decision to use several criteria contributes to enlivening the product displays, thereby maintaining the customer's attention at a high level.

From the technological point of view, the Epicenter conceives of the personnel and customers as using and "playing with" the technology and its functionality. The wireless terminals or the "omnipresent displays" located throughout the store can be used to consult the database available to the personnel and carry out other service operations, to show films, provide product information, etc., and also to allow the customers themselves to insert data. In fact, customers can create their own web-account by providing personal information during their visit and can conveniently access this information later at home.

The main fitting rooms, located behind a wall of Privalit opaque glass, represents an important innovation in managing the appropriation of space by the customers, thanks to the displays and terminals. In fact, each article brought into the fitting rooms is scanned and shown on the screen in the room. By simply touching the screen the customer can have access to the product's technical information and to other information he/she wishes to save in his/her personal web-account. In the fitting rooms it is also possible to project on the video screen the effects of a magic mirror that allows customers to see themselves from behind and in slow motion instant replay when turning around. The lights can be adjusted as desired, even making the doors transparent so that customers can be seen by anyone accompanying them.

The principle behind the personalization and recreation of one's own physical and virtual space adheres to the philosophy of having the Epicenter represent a true revolution, the physical center of the relationship with Prada. The investment in the web and in computer technology helps the company build a virtual bond with customers and makes it possible to also see at home what has been tried on in the store, thereby building an "existential" link with the Epicenter.

The Epicenter in New York was created also with the idea of reinterpreting not only the language of shopping, but also the use of commercial space and the relation between brand and society as a whole. Each year the Epicenter organizes cultural events such as exhibitions and film presentations that facilitate the interaction between client and environment, according to a Prada press release.

Just to name a few of those events, in 2002, in collaboration with IFP/New York and Paramount Classics, a preview of the film *Just a Kiss* by Fisher Stevens was shown. In May 2003 the Prada Foundation, together with the Tribeca Film Festival, organized a series of films and discussions with movie directors. In November 2003 the famous jeweller Fred Leighton put on exhibit a collection of antique jewels from various eras for sale at the New York Epicenter.

---

intermittent fashion shows when music, fashion, celebrities and consumers merge. The spiritual aspects of such stores have also been noted. They can be likened to cathedrals, and their displays to shrines, where consumers can come to worship the brand. When Apple opened its San Franciscan flagship store in 2004, more than a thousand people queued to be among the first to enter. Many had even camped overnight. Flagship stores try to make an architectural impact. Apple's new Boston flagship store has a glass façade and minimalist features throughout, with a glass staircase in its center that is acknowledged as a major engineering feat. The three-storey building, which remains lit throughout the night, is now an impressive landmark on the Boston cityscape.

This type of theming, referred to as "high tech urban" by Gottdiener (1997), is designed to overawe consumers and testify to the power of the brand. Commonly used by flagship brand stores, it uses a blend of innovative technology to create stunning visual effects that materialize the power of the brand. Another type of common theming identified by Gottdiener is "ye old kitsch", a theming that harks back to the past and creates a nostalgic atmosphere that recreates elements of a bygone age. This has been very successfully used by various forms of retailing including: pubs and restaurants such as the Singapore Heritage Restaurant that recreates a Singapore in the 1930s; individual retail ventures such as the Pastimes

Gift Shop; historic city center areas such as The Lanes in Brighton, England, where a warren of small antique and craft shops is set in a maze of twisting alleyways; and speciality shopping centers such as the festival marketplace that make use of historic settings and buildings.

Themed environments such as festival marketplaces and flagship brand stores invite consumers to develop a relationship with them as the consumers invest their imaginative energies in the location. Consumers can thus build strong emotional attachments to themed environments, environments that may become interwoven with their identities and sense of self. This can make it difficult for marketers to develop alternative themes that consumers may find inconsistent.

The social role of everyday/mundane consumptionscapes

It is not only fantasy-provoking spectacular environments that develop bonds with consumers. Often everyday consumptionscapes become places that we rely on and give us a sense of security (Borghini *et al.* 2006). They may also perform many social functions, allowing us to reinforce existing relationships and develop new ones. The sociologist Oldenburg (1989) analyzed the home as the "first place", a place that is normal regarded as very private by those of us living in the developed world. He identified where we work as the "second place", a place that can be stressful and pressurized. Both home and work places bring with them expected sets of behaviors to do with particular relationships and commitments. Oldenburg identified a social role for "third places" such as pubs and coffee shops, shopping malls, and even health spas and gyms, because these are places where we are free from our other commitments.

Third places are places where we can relax and be ourselves. They are usually places we take for granted, that are easily accessible, where food and drink are inexpensive and where we can socialize informally. Fast food restaurants and other branded chains that seek a fast turnaround in clientele, cannot be considered third places as they do not encourage sitting around and lingering, behaviors that are essential to the development of a third place ambience. Many of the key happenings in television soap operas and sitcoms take place in third places. Think of the Rovers Return (a pub) in the longstanding English soap opera, *Coronation Street*, or the coffee shop in *Friends*, the famous US sitcom, which both provide a hub from which many comings and goings take place.

Consumer rituals often develop round third places. For example, we may go to a particular coffee shop/restaurant/bar before/during/after work, on a regular basis, expecting to meet certain friends and colleagues there and even taking it in turns to pay. Such rituals may take place on a daily basis or less frequently. There may also be a core group that meets regularly, and others affiliated to it who drop in when it is convenient. Places build their unique sense of place through intangible factors such as atmosphere, both physical and social. This balance is very important and they must be somewhere we feel good and where there are others to share these feelings with us. In city centers book shops such as Borders or Waterstones are trying to encourage this type of use by having coffee shops, where people can comfortably spend time, relaxing over a cup of coffee, alone or with friends, reading and chatting about books.

Both our past and contemporary practices undoubtedly show our deep connection with consumptionscapes and the multiple ways they have been shaping our social life. But why and how have they always been so relevant for our social and individual life? What are the dynamics and the drivers that underpin consumers' behavior within commercial settings?

In the following section we will investigate these issues and unpack both the emotional, cultural and physical bonds with places.

Cultural identity and the role of place

As the history of retail outlets clearly shows and as Bachelard (1994/1969) has suggested, places have always exercised a poetic power on human emotions and on the development of our sense of selves. Our identities are intimately intertwined with our relationship to the physical spaces around us. Environments represent one important component of our material culture, thus reflecting our beliefs and aspirations. As environmental psychologists, human geographers, philosophers and consumer researchers recognize, our self–place connections are influenced not only by the physical reality of spaces but also by the psychological and cultural meanings that environments convey. Indeed, a space only becomes a "place" when it is invested with meanings by those that use it (Casey 1993). We form bonds with the places we know or discover and as places become interwoven with events in our lives, they also come to hold many symbolic associations for us. The special meanings that places hold for us are thus imbued with many emotional and aesthetic values.

Outside the home, commercial locations can provide a sense of security, giving us anchor points that militate against the feelings of displacement and insecurity that we experience from the increased mobility inherent in contemporary life. Conversely, they can infuse energy and enjoyment. We feel comfortable in our favorite grocery store where salespeople know us personally and call us by name. Others may feel bound to a shopping mall where they used to experience happy moments with friends and family.

The same space can even stimulate multiple reactions. While describing their feelings and sensations after visiting one of the Epicenters of Prada, two consumers express completely different reactions (Borghini and Zaghi 2008). Anna, enthusiast and delighted by the Epicenter of Prada in New York, says:

> "It's impossible to be indifferent after the visit. You cannot avoid to feel any emotion. Positive or negative. You are fascinated, seduced or astonished. You fall in love with it or discover that it's not for you. It has an impact on you as it happens with important things in your life."

In a completely different way, Marla, after her visit, declares:

> "It's artificial. You feel it from any point of view. The place is too formal, cold for me. I didn't like it a lot … I like different places where I feel at home, more comfortable and warm."

No matter how varied and subjective these ways of symbolic interaction can be, an ongoing and existential sense of *place* clearly unfolds within the marketplace (e.g., McGrath 1989; Kozinets *et al.* 2002; Maclaran and Brown 2005; Borghini *et al.* 2009) and influences our retail experience. To have customers who are mostly satisfied by this feeling of *being in the place* when visiting a commercial location is becoming a big challenge for retailers. Customers who experience this sensation are consuming the "space" itself, thus transforming it into a meaningful place. Therefore they will spend more time in the store, increase their purchasing intentions and the level of satisfaction related to the quality of the physical environment. But what makes consumers develop strong bonds with a place? From a phenomenological perspective, the development of such bonds relates to the concept of *insideness* (Relph 1976). According to this idea, individuals experience this sensation towards a place if there they feel safe and not threatened, protected and not exposed, relaxed and not under stress. Consumers could experience different levels of insideness depending on their acquaintance and familiarity with place or to an specific bond. Stores can even become points of reference and act as anchor points in consumers' lives because they evoke feelings of reliability, safety and self-confidence in identity construction. Conversely, consumers can also feel a sense of outsideness, apathy or distance towards commercial spaces.

This process is not only a mental activity, a cognitive or intellectual attitude but an embodied practice or action that engages the entire individual. Any sensorial element of the store design, ranging from its layout to its general atmosphere, guides our movements and thus shapes the overall experience. At the same time, our imagination, together with our memories, aspirations and dreams, transforms a place and makes it special or meaningless. What a consumer may dream of when visiting a themed commercial environment is subjective, of a temporary nature and individually stored in his/her mind. His/her own symbolic experience will thus influence the way he/she approaches and spends time in the place. While specific gestures can indicate common sensations and feelings, it is more difficult to give a common interpretation of their meanings. Nonetheless, this complexity and experiential richness represent valuable sources of differentiation for retailers.

In order to understand consumers' appropriation of commercial spaces, and emotional bonds with them, marketers should try to understand consumers' behavior from multiple points of view, and, in particular, focus their research attention on the following dimensions:

- practices that can be analyzed by observing movements and gestures;
- narratives that can be collected by the means of multiple qualitative research (i.e., ethnography, in-depth interviews, collages, etc.).

In the next sections we will give an overview of the key issues that should be taken into account when studying practices and bodily experiences.

Movement, gestures and practices in marketplaces

From a traditional perspective, marketing tends to overlook the importance of body movement and gestures in spaces. They are seen as consequences of internal states and as mere vehicular devices or "instruments" to reach products or services. The body is viewed as a machine (Berthelot 1995). The main marketing response is to calculate the number of actions performed at one specific place in the store (How many times does the shopper stop? How long does he/she stop? How many products does he/she touch? etc.) or of the flows in the space (Where do shoppers go first? Where do they come from? What are their ways in and out?). The goal of the marketing manager is then to try to optimize the flows (e.g. force shoppers to go to specific places).

In contrast, a cultural perspective stresses the role of body movement in the creation of place experience (Sherry 1998; Peñaloza 1999; Joy and Sherry 2003; Kozinets *et al.* 2004).

The body is our vehicle for being in the world (Merleau-Ponty 1962). Accordingly, body movement and gestures are practices and not mere outcomes of internal processes (Mauss 1979/1935; Crossley 1995). They are active processes through which consumers transform a space into a place and co-produce consumption and place experiences. Indeed, if we want to understand and appreciate a sculpture or any other piece of art in a museum we need to move towards it and the way we do this influences the sensorial and symbolic dimensions of our appreciation. Similarly, consumers' behaviors, movements, and gestures are essential parts of spectacular servicescapes (e.g. Nike Town, ESPN Zone, American Girl) and more mundane marketplaces (Wal-Mart, Tesco or Carrefour stores). The experience is performed by consumers who act as both actors and audiences. Understanding the meaning of what people do in space is then a necessity for marketing managers who want to improve the design of marketplaces.

Of particular importance is the concept of *space appropriation through the body*. It is one of the processes through which people construct place experience. It is complementary to the mental and internal processes, be these emotional or cognitive. According to Fischer (1981), we can distinguish two main elementary means of appropriation: visual activity and exploration (based on movement and contact). At this elementary level of the senses, the individual is in a working process of control of the flow in/out and of completion/separation from the surrounding world through closing and opening the body (Falk 1999). The pioneering research of Aubert-Gamet (1996) has shown how these appropriation practices are performed even in the seemingly mundane space of a bank branch (Table 25.2). In this context, appropriation practices can go against the implicit rules and procedures that people are induced to follow and thus they become re-appropriation practices, when a consumer diverts the norms inscribed in space.

Another way to account for appropriation of space is to shift from the micro perspective of appropriation practices to the meso level of appropriation strategies. These result from the combination of appropriation practices (De Certeau 1980). Appropriation strategies are more global ways of exploring the physical environment. Each appropriation strategy is a construction of a person's role in the space, reflecting how a person has experienced the place and the activity they are undertaking (ibid.).

A few empirical studies have identified four ideal-types of these appropriation strategies in different contexts (Véron and Levasseur 1991; Floch 1990; Bonnin 2003). These provide a detailed analysis of body movement and its relationship to specific consumption values and consumer roles (Table 25.3).

Taken together, all these aspects should be considered when designing commercial spaces, especially when retailers aim at setting a stage for consumers' experiences where functionality and aesthetics merge. In the following section we will explore this issue.

Table 25.2 Actions and gestures inside the entry zone of a bank branch

Nesting practices	• Makes her hair in the zone, looking at herself in a window • Puts up his/her money in the wallet in the zone blocking the way in • Hides behind a display, waiting for a machine to be available, so as to avoid the eyes of employees • Hides behind a display to observe safely the "consultancy" zone • Stays still in the zone while the door is open, to read quietly his/her bank information or to put up his/her money
Stamping practices	• Waves "hello" and makes signs to each other from each side of the zone • Unpacks his/her things meticulously at the beginning of the zone
Exploration practices	• Stays in the zone, not in a hurry to get out, to scrutinize the inside of the bank

Source: Aubert-Gamet (1996).

Table 25.3 Examples of descriptions of appropriation strategies in three contexts

Experiences	Neutralization	Playful experience	Utilitarian experience	Stroll experience
Cultural exhibit (Véron and Levasseur 1991)	Walks in the middle of the path away from walls, short time, few stopping, the itinerary looks like a loop	Zigzags, left-right-left-right, semi-long time, about 15 stops, avoids going through empty spaces	Close to the exhibit panels, long time, numerous stops, walks along a wall, follows the chronological order of the exhibition	Jumps from one point to another, short time (5 minutes), few stops
Subway (Floch 1990)	Follows the flow, ignores limits, signs, attraction and events, same posture, same look, same concentration over its knitting or every other activity	Search for and appreciation of rhythms and role playing offered by the environment, tries to delimitate, give rhythm, to segment, to rediscover some places, to oppose other places, at ease and open to the environment	Joins, steps over, anticipates the obstacles to avoid it, minimum, speeds high and strong, zigzags, moves between, linking, transgression	Some breaks, pauses, interruptions
Retail stores (Bonnin 2003)	Minimum exploration of the environment, no touches, no looks at the product, tries to use the shortest way out the environment	Explore all the retail area, many stops, with each time a huge number of actions (touching products, looking at them, …). No differences between walking and stopping	Focus on one particular place in the area. Usually one stop, with many actions, the rest is walking	Walks in the whole area, but without touching products, just looking at them without coming close to them

The design of commercial spaces: the merging of functionality and aesthetics

Designing meaningful places for contemporary consumers is becoming a more and more challenging enterprise that requires taking relevant decisions that will have a broad impact on marketing strategy.

The typical process that can be followed is based on three essential steps:

1 definition of the *concept* of the physical setting;
2 definition of the *theme* which will characterize the place;
3 translation of the concept and the theme into specific architectural features and sensorial cues that will constitute the store atmosphere.

In relation to the definition of the concept, retailers can choose from alternatives that range between two extremes. On one hand, they can choose a strategy of creating spectacular spaces as already discussed above. On the other hand, they can decide to reproduce everyday places, intimate and homely, thus applying and exploiting the concept of third places.

No matter what direction they take, the next decision is related to the definition of the level of *space appropriability*, i.e., the extent to which the store design allows the consumer to perform bodily practices. The structure of the store, the way the designer decides to cut off the space, will frame the interaction between the individual and the space, the type of experience that will be created, the value that will be produced by the consumer (Bonnin 2003). It will encourage a certain type of appropriation or use strategy.

Three archetypes of spaces can guide marketing managers and designers in the conception of marketplaces (Moles and Rohmer 1982):

1 *Functional spaces* aim at the efficiency of the task to be performed within them. Their main characteristic is openness, continuity.
2 *Active ludic spaces* aim at entertaining shoppers. They are generally enclosed, and discontinuous. For example, alcoves, subspaces, and round shapes are all typical of active ludic spaces.
3 *Passive ludic spaces* aim at providing individuals with a soft ludic experience. They allow contemplation (distant seeing) but do not encourage the physical involvement of consumers. The typical museum room with panels on the wall is exemplary of this type of space.

Regarding choice of themes, potentially practitioners have an infinite set of opportunities that include the reproduction of intimate and domestic spaces, the celebration of brands, lifestyles, subcultural ideologies and myths, sports, hobbies, fun, fantasy, evasion and escapism, temporal and spatial journeys. The opportunities for value creation are endless.

Generally, in terms of both concept and themes, there is no definitive best choice. The decision should be based on the so-called *design fit* which aims at matching both retailers' and consumers' desires and goals.

The final step involves the translation of the concept and the theme into specific architectural features and sensorial cues that will constitute the store atmosphere. Here the main decisions are related to:

- *architectural design*: internal and external architecture; layout; logics of visual merchandising;
- *store atmosphere:* sensory dimensions such as *sight* (colors, brightness, form, line, shape, light/dark, dimensions of objects), *touch* (texture, compositions, and other dimensions related to materials), *sound* (volume, tone, tempo, and genre), and *scent* (nature and intensity of odors and perfumes).

All the elements of both architectural design and store atmosphere have to meet the formal requirements of design such as pattern, rhythm, symmetry, balance, contrast, proportion, theme, and unity. Generally speaking, aesthetics appear to be relevant at any level of store design. Aesthetics have thus become popular in commercial spaces.

The aesthetics of servicescapes

Aesthetics deals with the sensory experience elicited by an artifact, and the extent to which this experience matches with individual goals and attitudes. As Arnold Berleant points out (cited in Maclagan 2001: 10), we consider the roots of the adjective "aesthetic", "to the extent that everything, every place, every event is experienced by an aware body with sensory directness and immediate significance ... has an aesthetic element".

Aesthetics have become popular in commercial spaces. Consumers want pleasurable experiences providing a novel and creative escape from everyday life (Venkatesh and Meamber 2008). Customers expect to find aesthetic design in a service place, and are more satisfied when the design of a servicescape is aesthetic rather than unaesthetic (Wagner 2000).

We expect aesthetics to affect customer reactions because customers are likely to have expectations regarding the aesthetics of a servicescape, and customer satisfaction is likely linked to the extent to which these expectations are met (Belfiore and Bennett 2007). Arguing that aesthetics can create tangible value for an organization, Schmitt and Simonson (1997), propose "the 4 Ps of aesthetics":

- *Properties* (e.g., buildings, offices, retail spaces, company vehicles, etc.);
- *Products* (specific attributes of the good or service);
- *Presentations* (e.g., packaging, labeling, tags, etc.);
- *Publications* (e.g., promotional materials, web site, stationery, business cards, etc.).

These tools can be used by firms strategically to create a variety of sensory experiences that will (1) ensure customer satisfaction and loyalty; (2) sustain lasting customer impressions about a brand's or organization's special personality; (3) permit premium pricing; (4) provide legal trade dress protection from competitive attacks; (5) lower costs and raise productivity; and (6) most importantly, create irresistible appeal.

True servicescape design is best achieved with an integrated approach that focuses as much on objects (e.g., spaces, layout, decoration element, ambiant features, etc.) and actors (both customers and employees) as on the way in which they strike up a relationship. So, it is characterized by a threefold focus:

- on uses, actions and functions as much as on meanings, values and symbols;
- on economic actors' strategies and aims (the roles, responsibilities, and intentions which everyone assumes in the system's operation);

- on people's daily experiences (a focus that goes beyond consumption patterns and tries to take into account people's lives as a whole living experience).

This triple focus is the clear expression of design thinking that does not view the world solely as an object but also as a project.

The aesthetic feature stems from the intertwining of each of these three poles in a way as that achieves harmony and coherency. In any event, it will focus on relationships, exchanges. Aesthetics is both a formalization of each of the three poles as well as the interaction among them that brings new possibilities.

With its simultaneous analysis of both uses and meanings, aesthetics imagines and projects forms which can be physical (i.e., architecture, furniture, colors, objects, and space's disposition) or intangible (i.e., atmosphere, fragrance, symbols, senses, emotions, time within the servicescape). The first characteristic in designing the aesthetics of a servicescape is to visualize spatio-temporal situations that blend well. For example, in a restaurant, aesthetics of forms covers the aesthetics of its dining area, furniture, sensorial environment, smells, colors, materials, and acoustics, but also its architecture, physical layout (i.e., of its parking lot, cloakroom, toilets, etc.), lighting, dishes, tablecloth, staff uniforms, corridor decorations, logo, brand, internet site, and even the overall proposition when it involves the aesthetics of the food on offer, until it forms an aesthetics of taste. In other words, it designates all things, objects and elements that can be identified as being forms.

From another perspective, focusing on actors' strategies and objectives design casts a spotlight on competencies that reflect know-how and knowledge of how to act. These competencies are to be found both with the service provider and with the customer. The second design characteristic of the aesthetics of servicescape is that it provides the knowledge that underpins all actors' abilities, including but not limited to customer participation. The market has become a forum in which consumers become a new source of competence for the corporation (Table 25.4). This know-how is a function of the knowledge and skills consumers possess, their willingness to learn and experiment, and their ability to engage in an active dialogue. Individual consumers can address and learn about businesses either on their own or through the collective knowledge of other customers. To provide aesthetic experiences, companies must create opportunities for customers to experiment with and to act on their know-how. Customers' contribution to aesthetics formalization means recognizing their ability to design the servicescape themselves. Aesthetics of know-how follows a co-design logic wherein users also act as designers.

Lastly, by focusing on people's daily experiences, design asks questions about human life in all senses of this term, whether construed individually or collectively. It centers on the

Table 25.4 From participation to competencies

	Participation	*Know-how*
Focus on	Individuals and their actions	The activity that is to be carried out
Orientation	Current situation-oriented	Future-oriented
Approach	Top-down	Bottom-up
Contribution	Getting as close as possible to the conventional model, script or plan that the company has established	An original output, this being a creation of previously unseen associations and elements of the exchange

notion of exchange, be it economic, social or environmental in nature. The third design characteristic of the aesthetics of servicescape is that it hones in on the service provider/ customer relationship in its entirety. The servicescape frames one of many other places where customers and providers can exchange which can be public spaces, internet blogs and forum, social events. For example, the relationship between a salesperson and consumer where the latter has purchased nothing; the relationship between a professor and his/her students outside of the course; the relationship between a banker who happens by chance to run into a client at a mutual friend's dinner party; the relationship on a golf course, or in a plane, between a management consultant and the head of the auditing firm for which s/he works, etc. The aesthetics of exchange involves trying to project the overall relationship between the service provider and the customer – and between one customer and the next.

As such, the three structuring characteristics of the aesthetics of servicescape can be called:

1   the aesthetics of forms in a situational approach;
2   the aesthetics of know-how in an interactional approach;
3   the aesthetics of exchanges in a relational approach.

These constitute the three facets of the aesthetics of servicescapes. Box 25.2 presents an example of the lived reality of these.

At present, the aesthetics of forms is the most widespread facet of servicescape aesthetics; the aesthetics of competencies and exchanges remain relatively vague to most actors. It is therefore with regards to these two latter facets that the greatest theoretical and practical advances are to be expected.

Conclusion

In this chapter we have emphasized the role that commercial places have in consumers' life for different points of view. By analyzing the evolution of different retail locations we have shown how commercial spaces have always represented meaningful places which shape consumers' experiences and identities. Our discussions illustrate the fact that nowadays both spectacular and ordinary consumptionscapes play a relevant role in the construction of consumers' cultural identity and that retailers' attention should be addressed to a multi-dimensional approach which takes into account bodily, emotional, and symbolic components of consumers' experiences.

Relying on these theoretical underpinnings, we have explored how retailers can differentiate strategically using the principles of store design and aesthetics.

Here we briefly outline some practical implications that be drawn from a cultural perspective on commercial places:

- It is very important to understand the social and emotional reasons that often underpin consumers' visits to retail stores and other consumptionscapes. Functionality, loyalty, habits, or hedonic motivations may not represent the main reasons that attract consumers to a specific store. Symbolic meanings, special attachment, and personal memories may be powerful drivers and sources of long-lasting bonds.
- Theming and in-store ambience can help build emotional bonds with consumers; from this perspective, alternative strategies suited for different marketing purposes are available to managers and companies who want to leverage this potential.

Box 25.2 Mama Shelter (Paris)

Located in the bustling Saint Blaise district, a grungy part of Paris, opposite the trendy Flèche d'Or music venue and with plenty of fashionable boutiques nearby, Mama Shelter is an oasis in the urban landscape which transcends any previous definition of hotel.

Designed by Philippe Starck, Mama Shelter offers an eclectic and electric ambiance thanks to its friendly, warm, and casual common areas. Across 7 floors there are 172 rooms in 5 color schemes. Its creators built it on the site of a disused multi-level graffiti-covered garage on a forgotten railway cutting. The garage has been transformed into one of the most exciting concepts opened in Paris for years – the railway cutting has been used to great effect as a backdrop for a long, lazy terrace for balmy spring and summer nights. "We have created a 'shelter', an ambience in which guests are able to think freely and discover the Paris known to locals by experiencing the French capital's urban and cosmopolitan side," said Serge Trigano. Opposite the hotel, more creative re-use: the abandoned Charonne station has been turned into an electro-rock bar. Mama Shelter's terrace looks over the litter-strewn railway which used to feed it. This is hotel life as urban life reinvented.

About the *aesthetics of forms*: The decor is stylish and adds a lot to the experience. Downstairs is the restaurant and bar, a typically Starckian blend of surreal decor elements. In the middle of the tables, columns display screens where one can put up announcements to swap, meet, and discover or just to dream. In an amusement area there is a 4-meter-long football table for 12 players. A forest of truncated, hollow-cast, tree trunk stools lines a lobby. As do glass display cases with high-concept, design-world porn and, inside pink armoires, a collection of Napoleonic hats. In a graffiti-rich *arrondissement*, graffiti covers the ceiling of Mama Shelter's bar, while an enormous, glass-topped communal table has continuous news feeds on horizontal screens. Guests choose from $15m^2$ size rooms to $35m^2$ size rooms. The largest suite, situated on the top floor, has a terrace with a magnificent view. Luxurious bedding, 5 star 100 percent cotton satin sheets, coffee machines, micro-waves, 24-inch IMacs (including TV, radio, CD/DVD, Skype and free internet access), everything adorned with an urban twist. The staff is dressed by the top couturier designer Anne Gelbard. The dining/clubbing/entertainment spaces are a delight and spectacularly different.

Related to the *aesthetics of competencies*: Each room is equipped with a kitchenette. Thrill seekers can rent electric scooters or motorbikes and pick up a Mama Shelter guide to show them the way to the day and night secrets of the 20th *arrondissement* to be discovered at any time of day or night. Automated check-out kiosks exist for the do-it-yourself types.

Concerning the *aesthetics of exchanges*: Mama Shelter's goal is to take into consideration the person and not the social constraints by which he is bound. It is a "shelter", which as opposed to locking one out from the outside world provides him, with food for thought, an ambience in which, he is able to think freely and experience Paris. The staff, friendly and welcoming, is multinational, of mixed age groups and charming. A food counter includes candies, chocolate, biscuits, and assorted sweets prepared with the grace and art of the best mom. The staff use Chinagraph pencils to write messages on huge mirrors. The two lifts have trivia as decoration – one in French, the other English – reminding us that only humans and dolphins actually enjoy sex.

This allows Mama Shelter to be defined as an apartment block rather than a hotel, easing the health and safety obligations. Discreetly alluring, immersed in its surroundings, nothing would suggest that the building is a hotel. The entrance is indicated only by a glass awning and a few shrubs. One doesn't come to Mama Shelter to vegetate in one's room all day; one comes here to share a moment among society.

www.mamashelter.com

- As a caveat we should remember that particular consumptionscapes become interwoven with consumers' identities and sense of self. Changes to a retail environment may thus interfere or even contradict the meanings that consumers have created. Any developments need to be done with sensitivity or else risk creating a strong emotional response and negative reactions from consumers.
- Ongoing marketing research is recommended to monitor the symbolic meanings that consumers create within a retail environment as these may not be the same as meanings intended by marketers.

Review and discussion questions

1 What are the roles that, according to the cultural perspective, commercial places can have in consumers' lives?
2 What are the different retail forms that play a major role in shaping consumers' experiences?
3 What are the main features of themed retail settings?
4 In your opinion, what benefits are consumers seeking in a servicescape like Prada's Epicenter?
5 How can we understand consumers' practices and gestures in commercial locations?
6 Why should we study those practices?
7 How is it possible to design meaningful places?
8 Can you give examples of commercial locations that fit well with the aesthetic approaches we have outlined?
9 Can you compare different retail settings using a cultural perspective?
10 What are the most relevant drivers for a strong bond between places and people?

Keywords

aesthetics of places, commercial spaces, consumers' bonds with places, consumers' practices in commercial places, gestures in commercial spaces, servicescape, store design, themed retail settings

References

Arnold, M. J. and Reynolds, K. E. (2003) "Hedonic Shopping Motivations", *Journal of Retailing*, 79: 77–95.

Aubert-Gamet, V. (1996) "Le design d'environnement dans les services : appropriation et détournement par le client", Thèse pour le doctorat en Science de Gestion, Langeard E. dir., Université de Droit, d'Economie et des Sciences d'Aix-Marseille III.

Babin, B. J. and Darden, W. R. (1995) "Consumer Self-Regulation in a Retail Environment", *Journal of Retailing*, 71: 47–70

Babin, B. J., Darden, W. R. and Griffin, M. (1994) "Work and/or Fun: Measuring Hedonic and Utilitarian Shopping Value", *Journal of Consumer Research*, 20(4): 644–56.

Bachelard, G. (1969) *La poétique de l'espace*; trans. (1994) *The Poetics of Small Places*, Boston: Beacon Press.

Baker, J., Grewal, D. and Levy, M. (1992) "An Experimental Approach to Making Retail Store Environmental Decisions", *Journal of Retailing*, 68(4): 445–60.

Baker, J., Grewal, D. and Parasuraman, A. (1994) "The Influence of Store Environment on Quality Inferences and Store Image", *Journal of the Academy of Marketing Science*, 22(4): 328–39.

Belfiore, E. and Bennett, O. (2007) "Determinants of Impact: Towards a Better Understanding of Encounters with the Arts", *Cultural Trends*, 16(3): 225–75.

Berthelot, J.-M. (1995) "The Body as a Discursive Operator: Or the Aporias of a Sociology of the Body", *Body & Society*, 1: 13–23.

Bonnin, G. (2003) "La mobilité du consommateur en magasin: une étude exploratoire de l'influence de l'aménagement spatial sur les stratégies d'appropriation des espaces de grande distribution", *Recherche et Applications en Marketing*, 18(3): 7–29.

Borghini, S. and Zaghi, K. (2008) "I consumatori e i negozi favoriti. Fenomenologia dell'attaccamento agli spazi commerciali", in K. Zaghi (ed.), *Atmosfera e visual merchandising: ambienti, relazioni ed esperienze*, Milan: FrancoAngeli, pp. 231–44.

Borghini, S., Diamond, N., Kozinets, R. V., McGrath, M. A., Muñiz, A. Jr. and Sherry, J. F. Jr (2009) "A Consumate Host: Home Away from Home at American Girl", *Journal of Retailing*, 85(3): 363–75.

Borghini, S., Sherry, J. F. Jr. and Joy, A. (2006) "Marketplace Attachment in the Realm of Ordinary Spaces", paper presented at Consumer Culture Theory Conference.

Casey, E. S. (1993) *Getting Back into Place*, Bloomington, IN: Indiana University Press.

Chebat, J. and Michon, R. (2003) "Impact of Ambient Odors on Mall Shoppers' Emotions, Cognition, and Spending", *Journal of Business Research*, 56: 529–39.

Crossley, N. (1995) "Body Techniques, Agency and Intercorporeality: On Goffman's Relations in Public", *Sociology*, 29(2): 133–49.

Csikszentmihalyi, M. and Robinson, R. E. (1990) *The Art of Seeing: An Interpretation of the Aesthetic Encounter*. Los Angeles: J. Paul Getty Museum.

De Certeau, M. (1980) *L'invention du quotidien. L'arts de faire*, Paris: Gallimard.

Donovan, R. J. and Rossiter, J. R. (1982) "Store Atmosphere: An Environmental Psychology Approach", *Journal of Retailing*, 58: 34–57.

Falk, P. (1999) *The Consuming Body*, London: Sage.

Fischer, G. N. (1981), *La psychosociologie de l'espace*, Paris: PUF.

Floch, J. M. (1990) "Etes-vous arpenteur ou somnambule? L'élaboration d'une typologie comportementale des voyageurs dans le métro", in J. M. Floch (ed.), *Sémiotique, marketing et communications*, Paris: PUF, pp. 19–48.

Gottdiener, M. (1997) *The Theming of America*, Boulder, CO: Westview Press.

Hopkins, J. S. P. (1990) "West Edmunton Mall: Landscape of Myths and Elsewhereness", *The Canadian Geographer*, 34: 2–17.

Joy, A. and Sherry, J. F. Jr. (2003) "Speaking of Art as Embodied Imagination: A Multisensory Approach to Understanding Aesthetic Experience", *Journal of Consumer Research*, 30: 259–82.

Kowinski, W. S. (1985) *The Malling of America*, New York: William Morrow & Co.

Kozinets, R. V., Sherry, J. F. Jr., DeBerry-Spence, B., Duhachek, A., Nuttavuthisit, K. and Storm, D. (2002) "Themed Flagship Brand Stores in the New Millennium: Theory, Practice, Prospects", *Journal of Retailing*, 78: 17–19.

Kozinets, R. V., Sherry, J. F., Jr., Storm, D., Duhachek, A., Nuttavuthisit, K. and DeBerry-Spence, B. (2004) "Ludic Agency and Retail Spectacle", *Journal of Consumer Research*, 31: 658–72.

Lazarus, R. S. (1991) *Emotion and Adaptation*, New York: Oxford University Press.

Lefebvre, H. (1974) *La production de l'espace*, Paris: Anthropos

Lyn, I. Y. (2004) "Evaluating a Servicescape: The Effect of Cognition and Emotion", *International Journal of Hospitality Management*, 23: 163–78.

Maclagan, D. (2001) *Psychological Aesthetics: Painting, Feeling and MakingSsense*, London: Jessica Kingsley Publishers.

MacLaran, P. and Brown, S. (2005) "The Center Cannot Hold: Consuming the Utopian Marketplace", *Journal of Consumer Research*, 32: 311–23.

Mauss, M. (1979/1935) "Techniques of the Body", *Economy and Society*, 2(1): 70–88.

McGrath, M. A. (1989) "An Ethnography of a Gift Store: Trappings, Wrappings, and Rapture", *Journal of Retailing*, 65(4): 421–49.

Meharabian, A. and Russel, J. A. (1974) *An Approach to Environmental Psychology*, Cambridge, MA: MIT Press.

Merleau-Ponty, M. (1962) *Phenomenology of Perception*, London: Routledge.

Moles, A. and Rohmer, E. (1982) *Labyrinthes du vécu. L'espace: matière d'actions*, Paris: Librairie des méridiens.

Oldenburg, R. (1989) *The Great Good Place*, New York: Marlowe.

Peñaloza, L. (1999) "Just Doing It: A Visual Ethnographic Study of Spectacular Consumption Behavior at Nike Town", *Consumption, Markets and Culture*, 2(4): 337–400.

Relph, E. (1976) *Place and Placelessness*, London: Pion Ltd.

Schmitt, B. H. and Simonson, A. (1997) *Marketing Aesthetics: The Strategic Management of Branding, Identity and Image*, New York: Simon & Schuster.

Sherry, J. F. Jr. (1990) "Dealers and Dealing in a Periodic Market: 'Informal' Retailing in Ethnographic Perspective", *Journal of Retailing*, 66(2): 174–200.

—— (1998) "Introduction", in J. F. Sherry Jr (ed.), *ServiceScapes: The Concept of Place in Contemporary Markets*, Chicago, NTC Business Books, pp. 1–24.

Turley, L. W. and Milliman, R. E. (2000) "Atmospheric Effects on Shopping Behavior: A Review of the Experimental Evidence", *Journal of Business Research*, 49: 193–211.

Venkatesh, A. and Meamber, L. (2008) 'The aesthetics of consumption and the consumer as an aesthetic subject', *Consumption Markets and Culture*, 11(1):45–70.

Véron, E. and Levasseur, M. (1991) *Ethnographie de l'Exposition: l'Espace, le Corps et le Sens*, Paris: BPI Centre George Pompidou.

Wagner, J. (2000) "A Model of Aesthetic Value in the Servicescape", in T. A. Swartz and D. Iacobbucci (eds), *Handbook of Services Marketing & Management*, Thousand Oaks, CA: Sage Publications, pp. 69–85.

26 Second-hand markets

Alternative forms of retailing

Dominique Roux and Denis Guiot

Overview

> When I set out to a second-hand market, I say to myself, 'I'm inevitably going to find clothes that aren't standard.' The shops are full of standard clothes. But when you go to a second-hand market, it's like Ali Baba's cave, like your grandmother's attic. You search around and suddenly you say, 'There's a jacket I like' or 'these trousers are exactly what I'm looking for'. The fact of coming across an object can trigger the desire to buy it, to match it with an outfit. Or the fact of coming across it at a moment when you've decided that it would be good to have it. It's like they're in league…. In shops, there isn't this element of surprise. You find the fashionable items you see in magazines and that's as far as it goes.
>
> (Paul, male, age 48)

This chapter examines the emergence of parallel retail channels and how they challenge traditional notions of retailing. The reasons consumers shop in second-hand outlets offer an important source of cultural lessons for retail marketing overall. They show how socially integrated persons adopt a form of acquisition on the periphery of mass retailing, a system whose principles are fundamentally challenged. They demonstrate that consumers act as interpretive agents (Arnould and Thompson 2005) who deliberately choose to patronize alternative channels to resist uniformity, predictability and ephemerality of mass production, waste and ecological consequences of consumption and lack of social contact in conventional retailing. They bring to light rationales for a new culture of consumption that stands on the margins of the conventional system and on the cast-offs of the primary market. As a result, one should not be surprised, if mindful, to observe that flea markets, garage sales, second-hand shops, antique dealers, auctions and Web sites are becoming legion, and the proliferation of such venues testifies to a growing phenomenon in most Western, affluent societies. Far from an archaism, rooted in traditional exchange practices such as bartering or haggling (Belk *et al.* 1988), parallel retailing systems reflect consumer expectations. They oppose on the one side predictable, organized, standardized offerings and atmospheres (Figure 26.1), and on the other, unexpected, ludic and exhilarating settings (Figure 26.2).

This chapter examines how and why classical approaches to retailing management fail to account for second-hand markets. That is, the growth of second-hand exchanges reflects the desire of a growing number of consumers to find alternative kinds of offerings – both products and channels – that leads them to bypass and evade traditional retailing. Whereas marketing management mostly focuses on the ways producers can reach consumers and what this reach implies in terms of the choices, organization and structure of various market

Figure 26.1 Standardization: buying in a supermarket.
       Source: Photo credits: Roux and Guiot.

Figure 26.2 Alternative: shopping in a flea market.
       Source: Photo credits: Roux and Guiot.

intermediaries (Kotler and Keller 2008), we provide a new perspective on how consumers become retailers of their own goods, as well as how innovative actors operate as intermediates. Our cultural reading emphasizes the crucial role of experience, atmospherics and unexpectedness in consumers' shopping preferences; these factors often integrate recreational motivations with economic and societal concerns about waste and harmful outcomes. In line with interpretive contributions that portray active consumers as producers (prosumer; cf. Chapters 11 and 12 in this volume), we identify the active role of the consumer as a retailer (protailer). Our interpretive approach thus provides insightful contributions, both for MBAs who consider emerging trends in retailing and consumer behaviour, and for managers operating in conventional and second-hand systems.

In documenting the evolution of second-hand markets, we trace the absence of entry barriers and shoppers' motivations to go outside traditional marketing systems. We provide evidence of consumer expectations using data collected throughout France over a period of three years pertaining to second-hand channels. We conclude with a summary of the issues that these new forms of exchanges raise for retailing, including the potential need for a reconfiguration of strategic thinking.

The second-hand market: a research blind spot?

Marketing theories that apply to retailing reflect the growth of modern commerce, which has evolved over approximately 150 years, featuring various types of sales outlets, facilities and layouts, as well as new ways to select, manage and present offerings to consumers. For example, in one stream of research, theories about intermediaries appear to parallel the growing complexity of this function in retailing. However, with this focus, such studies tend to consider the retailing system only according to the objectives of producers, such that they investigate optimal organizations of retail channels, means to lower transaction costs between producers and consumers and ways to arbitrate physical versus virtual or mixed ('clicks and mortar') retailing.

In accordance with this research, retailers have developed strategies and tools to stimulate and maintain their relationships with customers. Even as they continue to compete on price, retailers have sought other forms of differentiation, such as through stock selection, private labels, extended services or loyalty strategies. Another stream of research, derived from sociology, thus elaborates on the role of retail functions from a consumption (rather than production) standpoint (e.g. Tauber 1972; Ritzer 1999), focusing on some non-economic dimensions of retailing.

Yet a simple dichotomy between retailers as intermediaries (between producers and consumers) and shopping as a social function fails, because marketing practices cannot totally prevent customers from choosing alternative shopping channels. Apparently without the awareness of researchers or traditional retailers, many transactions occur outside of organizations, such as in second-hand markets. Theoretical frameworks currently offered by retail marketing research (e.g. wheel of retailing, multi-channel retailing, relational versus transactional marketing) ignore the specificities of the second-hand market – if they notice its existence at all.

To investigate second-hand markets, we argue for extending beyond the principles of modernity and adopt postmodernism and hypermodernity perspectives (Giddens, 1990; Firat and Venkatesh, 1995). These views emphasize fragmentation, loss of bearings and discontinuity rather than homogeneity, predictability and linearity that characterize a modern approach of retailing. In second-hand markets, disorder prevails over order, the unexpected over the planned purchase, the sudden find over the conventional search, bargaining over fixed prices, social interaction over individualism and the merging functions of producers, retailers, consumers and intermediates instead of clear-cut definition of roles. The inversion of characteristics of the formal sector constitutes the interstices of a freedom that 'liberatory postmodernism' depicts and consecrates (Firat and Venkatesh 1995). Therefore, we next outline certain theoretical elements that can help us clarify the key operational features of second-hand markets and exchanges.

Reversal of trade principles

The concept of the market usually gets viewed from the standpoint of sellers – whether producers or retailers. A linear producer–retailer–consumer schema grants all initiative in the process to producers. But the second-hand market voids such an approach, because it prioritizes a consumer–consumer schema, in which consumers bring their own goods to market. The usual linear form of the market therefore is replaced by an informal, circular relationship. Although a lack of official statistics makes it difficult to measure this phenomenon, in terms of volume or value, several convergent estimations indicate that consumers prefer second-hand markets in ever-increasing numbers. Estimates suggest that individual consumers account for half the total sellers in second-hand markets in France (Beauhain-Roux and Guiot 2001). Considering more formal outlets that are subject to income taxes, Solomon and Rabolt (2004: 458) report that 'the number of used-merchandise retail establishments has grown at about ten times the rate of other stores' in the United States.

Proliferation of sellers

A second basic characteristic of second-hand markets is the shift in actors' roles. Both consumers and retailers can be sellers as well as buyers of second-hand products. In these new market dealings, the presence of intermediaries is justified only if they add value to the transaction. By bringing sellers and buyers into contact, new intermediaries such as specialist boutiques, second-hand stores or second-hand market organizers facilitate trade. Consequently, we can segment second-hand market sellers into two main types of channels:

- A consumer-to-consumer 'direct channel' provides the opportunity for sales through mutual agreement. The buyer carries all the risk and, as compensation, asks for a considerable price reduction from the seller. Price is the key variable and basis of the exchange. Thus, second-hand markets are particularly volatile, subjective and dependent on the assessments of both parties.
- An indirect channel includes at least one intermediary, which might represent one of three groups, depending on the functions they fulfil:
    - Relational (e.g. small ads, press, radio, the internet): The channel simply places the seller and buyer in contact by providing a permanent information channel. It does not grant buyers any expertise or guarantees for the exchanges, which physically take place outside the information medium.
    - Organizational (e.g. discount centres, second-hand markets, fairs, attic sales): These channels provide sellers with an (often temporary) location to display and sell their goods. They also organize physical and even legal aspects of the event. Again the buyer receives no expertise or guarantees, but the transactions occur in a visible manner during the event.

- Multipurpose and specialist (e.g. antique dealers, second-hand goods dealers, sale rooms). These channels manage the transaction, using an expert or qualified sales-person who provides buyers with information, advice, evaluation, certification and guarantees. Some dealers expand systematically and in a structured way through retail chains. Small resale outlets specializing in a particular kind of products, which might sell new products too, fall into this channel, along with second-hand hypermarkets.

Extension of product lives

A second-hand market supports the potentially repeated circulation of the same object among several actors, based on a notion of product 'rotation'. The object may be used and returned to the market as many times as there are buyers who attach value to it. The second-hand market thus institutes a productive trade in products commonly considered 'dead' but whose post-death lifetime can be long. Such trade threatens traditional producers *and* retailers, who may thus regard second-hand markets as parasitic toward conventional retailing. That is, second-hand markets do not destroy but rather cannibalize traditional markets.

Absence of real barriers to entry

The barriers to entry that limit traditional markets are less applicable in a second-hand market. For example, the producer who first introduced the product in a new sale setting has borne the development costs. The financial assets and stock levels are regulated by demand for one product or another. Commercial barriers do not really apply, because any offering can be specific and locally adapted. Furthermore, a lack of extensive regulation eliminates most institutional barriers. Even in France, which places some restrictions on private selling, people remain free to sell their personal belongings several times yearly in their place of residence, and they can do so without any restriction in channels such as the internet or second-hand stores. However, the sale of second-hand items officially is subject to commercial law pertaining to the display of prices, advertising, product safety and parental permission (for purchases by youths under 18 years of age). Specific local and regional regulations bind sellers and organizers of flea markets and other such settings, generally through by-laws that require permission to occupy public property, registration of sellers and appropriate positioning of stalls in the public space.

Contractual barriers might arise when a second-hand market develops a structure, depending on the nature of its retailing procedure. Thus many modern second-hand goods chains have organized into franchise networks (e.g. Cash Converter, Easy Cash, Cash Express), which concentrate the activities of traditionally isolated second-hand dealers. Physical interactions also may retain a local dimension, though the growth of the internet has largely overcome such limits and created a global marketplace where people can quickly search for, locate, evaluate and negotiate for items they would have no chance of finding within easy reach of their homes. The internet also plays a key role for traditional retailers who take advantage of it to dispose of their unsold stock.

New motivations for unconventional products and channels

The emergence of new intermediaries simultaneously responds to two related desires: a wish to sell by households, which have too many possessions and want to exchange some possessions to obtain more space and money, and the wish to buy, as expressed by consumers or dealers who can obtain acceptable quality and perhaps nearly new merchandise at reasonable prices.

Previous research has investigated shoppers' motivations and the economics of exchanges in second-hand markets (Belk *et al.* 1988), flea markets (Gregson and Crewe 1997a, 1997b; Sherry 1990a, 1990b; Stone *et al.* 1996) and garage sales (Soiffer and Herrmann 1987). These studies reveal two main categories of motives that influence shoppers: economic and hedonic. First, second-hand markets give economically disadvantaged groups a means to meet their consumption needs at a low cost (Williams and Paddock 2003; Williams and Windebank 2000). Second, independent of any financial necessity, some consumers enjoy second-hand channels as places to wander around and engage in recreational shopping. These venues offer different attractions than found in traditional channels, especially the potential opportunity of finding unusual items that lack an equivalent in new retail markets.

We considered these elements in developing our qualitative, ethnographic study of nearly two dozen shoppers, as well as our quantitative study of the shopping motivations of a sample of 708 people. As this chapter shows, these studies enrich understanding of the various motivations for participating in second-hand provisioning, as well as its consequences for retailing. We therefore present our findings from these two studies, thereby illuminating consumers' expectations and their critiques of traditional retailing.

Consuming elsewhere and differently: a challenge to traditional retailing

Two broad data collections were conducted among French second-hand shoppers. First, we undertook a qualitative data collection in Paris and its surrounding region with 22 second-hand shoppers – specifically, a focus group followed by 15 semi-structured, in-depth interviews. Second, in a quantitative study with 708 respondents, we defined and measured consumers' second-hand shopping motivations. Although these respondents vary greatly in their practices – including shopping frequency, type and number of products bought, and channels frequented – they all express familiarity with second-hand buying.

Our findings suggest a typology of four second-hand consumer segments, characterized by their different scores on three broad motivation measures (Guiot and Roux 2010):

1   Critical motivations express the desire to avoid ostentation, bypass traditional retailing and its inducement to consume, and combat waste through ethical and ecological practices.
2   Recreational motivations testify to a need for social contact, stimulation and treasure-hunting while shopping.
3   Economic motivations articulate a wish to pay less, search for fair prices, hunt for bargains and smooth budgetary allocations across different kinds of expenditures.

We provide illustrations of these four profiles – which we label 'polymorphous enthusiasts', 'thrifty critics', 'nostalgic hedonists', and 'regular specialist shoppers' – and summarize their main features in Table 26.1.

Table 26.1 Main features of second-hand shoppers' profiles

	Main motivations	Demographics	Determinants/effects
Polymorphic enthusiasts	Distance from the system Gratifying role of price Ethics and ecology Originality Nostalgic pleasure Treasure hunting Social contact	Age 35+ Average high income level	Frugality Browsing Recycling High frequency of shopping second-hand Preferences for flea markets, discount stores, charity Stores, antique stores Collectables, decorative items, clothing, TV, hi-fi
Thrifty critics	Ethics and ecology Gratifying role of price Search for fair price	Age 35– Low income level	Materialism Frugality Moderate frequency of shopping second-hand Preferences for internet sites and direct sales Cars, video games, cells phones, computers, printers
Nostalgic hedonists	Nostalgic pleasure Treasure hunting Social contact Originality	Age 35– Low-middle income level	Predisposition to nostalgia Browsing Impulsive buying Recycling High frequency of shopping second-hand Preferences for flea markets, discount stores, antique stores Books, furniture, collectables, decorative items, crockery, knick-knacks, games, toys
Regular specialists	Gratifying role of price Distance from the system	Age 35– Low-middle income level	Low frequency of shopping second-hand Preferences for discount stores, direct sales Video games and consoles, cell phones, bikes, cars

Polymorphous enthusiasts

This profile, with its higher-than-average income and age, expresses a strong interest in many types of second-hand products and channels (Table 26.1). It is characterized by a strong propensity to recycle, browsing behaviours in different places and venues and high scores for all three types of motivations. Psychologically, these enthusiasts exhibit high levels of frugality and a need to be unique. Romain (male, 45 years) is a typical example: A middle manager in a large information technology company, he has been a second-hand shopper since he first started working and now has become a 'more or less exclusively second-hand shopper'. He uses new retail channels only to acquire specific products, specifically, those for which the time spent finding a 'bargain' or difficulties or risks in obtaining them from second-hand sources make conventional retailing preferable. He notes a refrigerator as an example, because its issues involving its transport and potential condition make acquiring it second-hand a risky solution.

Romain visits Sunday second-hand markets near where he lives, as well as dedicated second-hand stores or specialist shops for specific purchases – such as furniture or photographic equipment, which he looks for in the Bastille neighbourhood of Paris. He further uses the internet frequently to buy second-hand books, CDs and other cultural products. Romain's main motivations are very clearly functional, economic and critical: what is the point of paying more for objects that are no better than those sold second-hand? He directs these criticisms and his refusal to buy new at traditional retailers:

> If I need to buy a microcomputer, I won't go to a retailer like Carrefour because their equipment is too pricey for what there is inside it. I'm familiar with the components and there is always something that's not quite right. There's not enough memory, the sound card isn't right, or the graphics board, the screen isn't the best. I find that they're selling an average overall package for undemanding buyers. If I don't have a good screen on my computer, or the right hard disk, I won't take it. It's a question of standards for a given piece of equipment.

Similarly, Romain often browses in traditional bookshops near his Paris office to learn about the latest literary publications, then goes home and orders them on the second-hand sites he frequents (PriceMinister.com, 2xMoinsCher.com). Through such opportunism, Romain has developed an acute ability to 'poach' from retail networks (*braconnage* in de Certeau's (1984) terminology), such that he is an elusive target for traditional marketing strategies. He does not own any loyalty cards; he goes to the supermarket near where he lives, once a week, with a largely unchanging shopping list; and he spends a minimal amount on clothing, largely acquired through garage sales. Yet he owns a wide range of household and leisure goods, all bought in second-hand stores. Thus, he clearly expresses a multi-faceted way of escaping classical retailing, even as traditional retailers unsuccessfully try to attract him through offerings and marketing devices.

Thrifty critics

This profile is mainly characterized by its strong propensity toward frugality and high score on the economic and critical dimensions (Table 26.1). Informants in this cluster try to reuse and recycle products, in line with their ecological concerns and efforts to avoid waste. Although this group contains a higher proportion of men, people with low income levels and an average age of 30 years, Catherine offers an excellent example of this profile. A 59-year-old project leader at the Ministry of Culture, she exemplifies the habits of saving that she inherited by growing up in a low-income family, immersed in a culture of used and second-hand objects. Both her mother and grandmother 'had no hesitation in climbing up with her stool into the great salvage containers to hunt for things'. She remains constantly on the look-out for whatever people throw out and often picks up items from the sidewalk on days that garbage collectors designate for the disposal of bulky objects. She also gets indignant about the fate of products that appear in perfect condition:

> I say to myself: 'The things people can throw out and waste!' Objects that have been put out on the sidewalk to go into the garbage that are new! When one thinks about it, after all, it's really strange to throw stuff out, because it's throwing out the past and throwing out people too. It's a matter of respect for previous generations, respect for workers, respect for farmers.

Catherine's sensitivity to used objects exemplifies her respect for the preservation of resources and concerns about paying a debt of gratitude to those who produced them. Such objects are not simply things; still less are they merchandise. Instead, they are, above all, the fruits of someone's labour, of the effort invested in them and of the know-how of skilled workers. These nearly anthropomorphic considerations of discarded objects are accompanied by her extreme critical distance from producers and retailers of new products.

Just like Catherine, Vincent, a 38-year-old technical after-sales manager, often buys second-hand for ideological but also strong economic reasons. He sees no reason to pay the price equivalent to a value that he no longer finds in new items often perceived as less durable than used ones. As an expert in computers, mobile phones and other various electronic equipment, he thinks retailers are selling average offerings for 'people who are not very demanding'. Besides, his sensitivity to waste and concern about ecological consequences of consumption lead him to inspect waste bins and recover discarded objects:

> Getting something second hand is a matter of principle. I am pro recycling. You've seen everything that people throw away? So I will not buy new in principle but only if I can not find something second-hand. I find it ridiculous all that is put into the category of waste.

Both Catherine and Vincent finally accuse producers of encouraging the proliferation of products and squandering resources, and believe retailers stimulate demand through devious methods to seduce people into buying.

Nostalgic hedonists

Joëlle (female, 39) defines herself as a passionate antique hunter. Similar to the other mainly middle-income respondents in this cluster (Table 26.1), her motivations are less critical and economic than recreational: she looks for places and products that arouse her nostalgic feelings and prompt browsing. As a keen antique hunter for 20 years, she has observed the proliferation of second-hand markets in the Paris region. For example, she visited antique dealers as a child with her mother, then she was delighted by the growth of attic sales in

Paris in the 1980s – a format she knew from her time in the provinces, which used small displays of goods and village markets. An administrative manager in a bank and a married woman with two children, Joëlle practises what she describes as her 'passion': On Saturday or Sunday, 'a tour of the second-hand markets' represents her form of leisure activity, as well as a motive for discovering nearby villages. Her husband is more inclined to look for functional and utilitarian items, and her children prefer games and cultural products, but Joëlle seeks out the unexpected and hopes to come across 'must-have' objects:

> I think it's like falling in love with something. It's an encounter with an object, even for things that don't have any particular use. It's because they have a charm, or because they have something special about the way they're made or because they may be very unusual. But even if they aren't worth very much, they are rare because in fact they are things we don't use any longer today and one can use them for decoration or embellishment. I really like things that are old, things that have a soul. I don't like new stuff.

Joëlle firmly contrasts the uniformity and banality of new channels with nostalgic objects found in second-hand markets. She uses the former only for functional purchases, such as the household and leisure equipment she and her husband refuse to buy second-hand for fear that they will not work properly. Yet she also notes that these functional items do not provide her with as much pleasure as finding a knick-knack that recalls past times:

> When I buy new, I buy because I need to, but I don't get a kick from it in the same way. For example, we've just replaced the TV, which was getting old. We had to do it. It was an essential purchase. But it gave me no pleasure. My husband, yes. He buys the latest thing, technological, modern, and it makes him really happy. Whereas me, no. I don't like buying new things.

Joëlle's relations with the traditional market are limited to 'duty purchases', which in her case include items that other people might consider pleasurable purchases, such as a DVD player or stereo system (Babin *et al.* 1994). Yet because Joëlle expresses nostalgic and hedonic expectations, she prefers attic sales, flea markets and antique dealers. Such channels provide her simultaneously with products, venues and ambience that all contribute to satisfying her motives in a way that conventional retailing cannot match.

Regular specialist shoppers

This mostly young and moderate income group scores low on all motivations and buys specific second-hand products in a very targeted way (Table 26.1). For example, Daniel (male, 35 years), a plastic arts teacher in a high school, has shopped second-hand for a long time. This kind of selective browser typifies the fourth cluster. He recently found a Mercedes for 4,500 euros and notes his delight with his acquisition. After careful negotiation with a couple of sellers, he even managed to reduce the price by 500 euros:

> The car matched the market price and it was a bargain. If I hadn't accepted that price, it would have taken a long time to find another. At that price, it was very reasonable, and

I'd have been an idiot not to have bought it. Even if I don't keep it for very long, I've fixed myself up with a vehicle that's got a really good image. At least now I know what it's worth.

Daniel patronizes second-hand channels only occasionally and sees them as an advantageous solution in the right circumstances. He became interested in them at a young age because of his interest in photography. For certain products, which were very expensive or reserved for elite photographers, buying second-hand was the only way he could acquire items. His access to second-hand markets also seemed easy and natural, because many conventional stores included a second-hand section. His experiences with sales of photography equipment have always been positive, yet Daniel has not expanded his second-hand buying to all categories of goods. Rather, before he will buy second-hand, he must have good knowledge of the products; for example, he does not believe it possible to find recent or the very latest products second-hand, so for these, he turns to conventional retailers. Faced with the tension between his frequent wish to buy impulsively and the guilt associated with the cost, Daniel uses second-hand markets as a distraction from his urges too:

> When you buy something new, it's true that you have it straightaway. But if you can wait, you'll get it cheaper. Because the goal is really to have it in the end. When there's no great hurry, I buy second-hand. And I tell myself that when all is said and done, it's not often that a purchase is so urgent that I have to go and find it immediately – except for the kind of utilitarian things you buy for your daily life. In the end, if I wait, I'll find it cheaper.

Thus, Daniel arbitrates between his needs and his budget, between what waiting can bring him financially and what it costs him psychologically. He constantly puts new and second-hand markets in tension with each other, according to the nature of this balance and the type of products. Buying certain functional objects requires him to follow a course in which new channels set the standards for quality, functionality and price; then if necessary, he can compensate for the impossibility of finding them second-hand with an advantageous price. The complex decisions that prompt him to buy a second-hand product in one instance but purchase a new product in another scenario depend on a vast number of factors, including the key role of opportunity.

Marketing recommendations

According to the targeted segments, both traditional and second-hand retailers should design new strategies and new outlet concepts. If polymorphous enthusiasts, thrifty critics, nostalgic hedonists, and regular specialist shoppers can be directly targeted, other standard profiles could emerge from breaking down the shopping motivation scores by level, threshold, globally, by dimension, and/or by mixing or blending the dimensions. In turn, retailers could determine a retailing mix to appeal to their own customer segments. Research in retail purchasing behaviour distinguishes between experiential approaches (based on differentiation strategies) and the rise of hard discounting (which obeys a logic of cost domination). It thus suggests separate positioning types, whereas this empirical study of second-hand shopping motives reveals that the forms of exchange can answer both types of expectations simultaneously. This requires the retailing mixes to be adapted to outlets and segments.

Therefore, we distinguish three series of managerial implications associated with the retail offerings generally provided by the new and second-hand sectors.

A competitive strategy focused on price, information, and second-hand extension for traditional retailers

Information and price primarily define the competition between new and second-hand sectors. In this sense, by studying second-hand markets, we enrich analyses of the wheel of retailing. That is, increased entry of used goods into retail sectors will displace the reference point established by a clear-cut division of stores. By combining both advantages, second-hand retailers challenge existing theories about the total separation of strategic arguments and their supposed irreconcilability. Retailers of new products thus need to find a way to 'recover' those consumers who oscillate between new and second-hand markets. Some shoppers, such as Romain, glean information through the former but buy in the latter. This tendency appears to vary according to product category, such that in some cases, the perceived risk is too high to buy in second-hand markets (e.g. household appliances, leisure equipment, brown products) – a concern mentioned by respondents in all four consumer profiles.

In the second-hand market, information from the seller appears untrustworthy; therefore, if they hope to recover consumers, traditional retailers need to offer well-developed mechanisms that increase consumers' trust, such as technical documentation and guarantees. These retailers should emphasize three main elements in their strategic arguments: the reliability of products; compliance with standards, such that their lifetime potential reduces the risk of malfunction; and guarantee extensions that are absent or limited in the used goods sector, especially for products with a heightened risk of failure or breakdown. However, retailers should make sure they offer these forms of reassurance without making any consequential price differential appear as a way to boost profits artificially.

Specifically, pricing policies for new products and promotional offers should be adjusted to account for the interconnection of new and second-hand sectors. For example, selective browsers use a new product price as a yardstick for assessing the utility of an equivalent item they find second-hand. In traditional commerce settings, prices generally reflect manufacturing costs and competition, but new retailers also might consider the price levels associated with second-hand articles, to determine the real perceived value of the new object in the most rational way. This approach has the advantage of taking into account both competition and demand, based on the attributes of the new article and those of a parallel second-hand product. In particular, selective browsers should be very sensitive to this kind of price policy, especially for products such as books and audio-visual media, for which competition between the sectors is particularly strong.

A 'flash sale' promotional technique could complement this price mechanism. Often limited to food sales, a temporary price reduction that lasts just a few minutes might stimulate impulse buys across all browser categories, without having a major impact on the retailer's overall margin. It therefore might be applied beneficially to household and leisure equipment products – markets in which the consumer profiles we delineate appear reluctant to buy second-hand.

To compensate for purchasers who strongly favour used goods, retailers of new products could mimic the marketing approaches used by second-hand channels. For example, in addition to standard offering ranges, they might dedicate sections of their stores to second-hand goods. Another promising idea is to organize swap meets, attic sales and trade-in events, as Decathlon, a specialist sports goods retailer present in 14 countries, has done. Its Trocathlon operation, held once or twice per year over a weekend, allows customers to sell and recycle their used material with the assistance of the venue, which provides them with vouchers they can spend in the store. In the leisure sector especially (e.g. CDs, books, videos), such events could attract a substantial number of shoppers to engage in a treasure hunt, offering the sort of social interactions often ignored by traditional retailing. These actions could allow private sellers to obtain additional resources, which the retailer then immediately captures.

The shopping experience: a communication strategy for second-hand sellers

Advertising through the shopping experience is triggered by recreational motivations that we highlight in the empirical study. Yet it has to be adapted to segments.

To attract simultaneously both polymorphous enthusiasts and moderate and selective browsers, specialist retailers should adopt a communication strategy that does not simply call attention to attractive prices; it must highlight the pleasure of hunting around and the overall shopping experience, in line with the particular features of the retail outlet. This approach might be implemented by focusing certain advertising messages on the shopping experience as an adventure or citing the opportunity to visit a discount store, second-hand store or specialist second-hand outlet with friends or family (Arnold and Reynolds 2003). Such an approach already has been adopted by the Troc.com franchise, a European second-hand retail leader.

More specific actions directed at certain profiles also are possible. For example, because a high proportion of polymorphous enthusiasts visit second-hand stores and antique dealer Web sites, it seems that these second-hand retailers could increase their market penetration considerably, especially among segments corresponding to multi-channel buyers and nostalgic hedonists, if they created synergy between their physical outlets and Web sites (e.g. by putting all or part of their catalogue online or publicizing special offers). Such complementarity could appeal to the treasure hunting motive of all these shoppers and globally optimize browsing across the conventional and virtual outlets, without privileging one or the other form of access to products. This strategy is notably used by the world's largest flea market, *Les Puces de Paris-Saint-Ouen* (http://www.parispuces.com/en/).

Stimulating nostalgia and recycling policies: two strategies for both types of channels

Yet implemented differently, two distinct policies can be considered for both types of retailers. For product presentations, the use of nostalgia is effective, such as that aroused by products such as vinyl records, films, gadgets, books and other items associated with childhood or adolescence. Although the second-hand sections of conventional retailers attract few second-hand shoppers (only 27.1 per cent of our sample frequent them), new product retail channels still can take advantage of this motivation. For both new and second-hand channels, sophisticated sensorial marketing, such as colours or perfumes associated with a certain period, can stimulate nostalgic links. To optimize this approach, retailers should make their offering theatrical and engage in experiential marketing that engages all five senses (cf. Chapters 10 and 25 in this volume). Such actions lend themselves particularly well to outlets that specialize in household decorations, cultural products and clothing. However, these methods should be tested carefully in advance, so that the 're-enchantment' does not seem artificial to nostalgic consumers, who are particularly sensitive to the authenticity of products and channels.

Consumers' sensitivity to waste and recycling offers another area for strategic reflection. Waste and the 'throw-away' society have provoked counter-reactions, such that consumers search for functional objects at the best price. In response, supermarkets could offer bulk sales, such that consumers package products purchased by weight – including sugar, milk or cereals, as well as certain products or components that seem to call for reduced packaging. Along similar lines, traditional retailers might embrace recycling by taking back depleted products and packaging (e.g. batteries, drink containers). Trade-in discounts on new cars when drivers scrap their old cars have received strong support from the French government, and retailers should take simultaneous economic and ecological concerns pro-actively into account.

In the same way, the ecological concerns stimulate consumers to search for used objects that can fulfil a function through repair or restoration, which in turn becomes highly gratifying. Restoring and personalizing recovered objects is a consumption trend, as exemplified by 'do-it-yourself' products, stores and magazines – something that critical sociologists were noting 30 years ago (Baudrillard, 1998). The contemporary illustration of the 'shabby chic' movement involves repairing old furniture by repainting it or altering its original function creatively (e.g. using a garden bench as a living room table). Such trends can provide new retail second-hand or 'hybrid' concepts offering both newly produced articles and original products resulting from the restoration of used objects for sale.

These implications overall take account of the interconnection between new and second-hand markets, as well as the potential for new independent actors and major retail groups to adapt their existing shopping centres or launch new sites that feature new products and second-hand items side by side. Such a system, through a fine-tuning of the retailing mixes, would tend to attract all the second-hand segments this study identifies.

Finally, such developments challenge the basic Porterian (Porter 1985) logic: stick to the middle, rather than viewing differentiation and cost advantages as exclusive. This conclusion also highlights the remarkable interest second-hand markets have for ongoing research. They not only represent a critical form of competition for new markets, but they also open stellar opportunities for finding new answers in retailing.

Review and discussion questions

1   What, in the mind of certain consumers, are the main aspects in which making use of secondhand retail channels is opposed, favourably or unfavourably, to the use of traditional ones?

2   Which alternative retail channels among those that you know can answer to some motivations rather than to others? Which features answer best to which orientations?

3   In what respects can second-hand exchanges between consumers be said to enhance their power? In your opinion does this constitute a long-term threat to traditional channels?

4   Discuss the strengths and weaknesses of lifestyle segmentation criteria if applied to the second-hand markets.

5   What are the positioning themes that traditional retailers could adopt from the second-hand motivations?

6   How should merchandising be implemented in outlets which sell both new and second-hand items?

7   Could second-hand shoppers' segments define subcultures? What are the other cultural issues of second-hand markets? Compare and discuss these notions and issues.

Keywords

alternative retail settings, consumers' interpretive strategies, second-hand markets, second-hand shopping motivations

References

Arnold, M. J. and Reynolds, K. E. (2003) 'Hedonic Shopping Motivations', *Journal of Retailing*, 79(1): 77–95.

Arnould, E. J. and Thompson, C. J. (2005) 'Consumer Culture Theory (CCT): Twenty Years of Research', *Journal of Consumer Research*, 31(4): 868–82.

Babin, B. J., Darden, W. R., and Griffin, M. (1994) 'Work and/or Fun: Measuring Hedonic and Utilitarian Shopping Value', *Journal of Consumer Research*, 20: 644–56.

Bardhi, F. and Arnould, E. J. (2005) 'Thrift Shopping: Combining Utilitarian Thrift and Hedonic Treat Benefits', *Journal of Consumer Behavior*, 4(4): 223–33.

Baudrillard, J. (1998) *The System of Objects*, trans. J. Benedict, London: Verso Books.

Bauhain-Roux, D. and Guiot, D. (2001) 'Le développement du marché de l'occasion. Caractéristiques et enjeux pour le marché du neuf', *Décisions Marketing*, 24 (Sept–Déc): 25–35.

Belk, R., Sherry, J., and Wallendorf, M. (1988) 'A Naturalistic Inquiry into Buyer and Seller Behavior at a Swap Meet', *Journal of Consumer Research*, 14(March): 449–69.

De Certeau, M. (1984) *The Practice of Everyday Life*, Berkeley, CA: University of California Press.

Firat, A. F. and Venkatesh, A. (1995) 'Liberatory Postmodernism and the Reenchantment of Consumption', *Journal of Consumer Research*, 22(3): 239–67.

Giddens, A. (1990) *The Consequences of Modernity*, Cambridge: Polity.

Gregson, N. and Crewe, L. (1997a) 'The Bargain, the Knowledge, and the Spectacle : Making Sense of Consumption in the Space of the Car-Boot Sale', *Environment and Planning D: Society and Space*, 15(1): 87–112.

—— (1997b) 'Performance and Possession. Rethinking the Act of Purchase in the Light of the Car Boot Sale', *Journal of Material Culture*, 2(2): 241–63.

Guiot, D. and Roux, D. (2010) 'A Second-Hand Shoppers' Motivation Scale: Antecedents, Consequences, and Implications for Retailers', *Journal of Retailing*, 86(4): 383–99, doi:10.1016/j.jretai.2010.08.002.

Kotler, P. and Keller, K. L. (2008) *Marketing Management*, Englewood Cliffs, NJ: Pearson Education.

Mano, H. and Elliott, M. T. (1997) 'Smart Shopping: The Origins and Consequences of Price Savings', in M. Brucks and D. MacInnis (eds), *Advances in Consumer Research*, vol. 24, Provo, UT: Association for Consumer Research, pp. 504–10.

Porter, M. E. (1985) *Competitive Advantage: Creating and Sustaining Superior Performance*, New York: Free Press.

Ritzer, G. (1999) *Enchanting a Disenchanted World, Revolutionizing the Means of Consumption*. Thousand Oaks, CA: Pine Forge Press.

Sherry, J. F (1990a) 'A Sociocultural Analysis of a Midwestern American Flea Market', *Journal of Consumer Research*, 17: 13–30.

—— (1990b) 'Dealers and Dealing in a Periodic Market: Informal Retailing in Ethnographic Perspective', *Journal of Retailing*, 66: 174–200.

Soiffer, S. M. and Herrmann, G. M. (1987) 'Visions of Power: Ideology and Practice in the American Garage Sale', *Sociological Review*, 35(1): 48–83.

Solomon, M. R. and Rabolt, N. J. (2004) *Consumer Behavior in Fashion*, Englewood Cliffs, NJ: Prentice Hall.

Stone, J., Horne, S. and Hibbert, S. (1996) 'Car Boot Sales: A Study of Shopping Motives in an Alternative Retail Format', *International Journal of Retail & Distribution Management*, 24(11): 4–15.

Tauber, M. (1972) 'Why Do People Shop?', *Journal of Marketing*, 36(October): 46–59.

Williams, C. C. (2000) 'Beyond Formal Retailing and Consumer Services: An Examination of How Households Acquire Goods and Services', *Journal of Retailing and Consumer Services*, 7: 129–36.

Williams, C. C. and Paddock, C. (2003) 'The Meanings of Informal and Second-Hand Retail Channels: Some Evidence from Leicester', *International Review of Retail, Distribution and Consumer Research*, 13(July): 317–36.

Williams, C. C. and Windebank, J. (2000), 'Beyond Formal Retailing and Consumer Services: an Examination of How Households Acquire Goods and Services,' Journal of Retailing and Consumer Services, 7, 129–136

27 Strategic database marketing

Customer profiling as new product development

Detlev Zwick and Nikhilesh Dholakia

Overview

The fundamental question we pose in this chapter is, how should we understand marketing in the age of increasingly integrated and networked customer databases? This chapter draws on cultural theories adapted from Deleuze and Foucault to argue that new forms of database marketing are best described as customer production processes that rely on the valorization of the multitude of consumer life. We suggest that the recent increase in available consumer data, computational power, and analytical skills have led to a reorganization of the gaze of marketers and increasingly reverse the Fordist organization of production and consumption. More specifically, instead of flexibly adjusting production regimes to shifting consumption patterns (what we conventionally refer to as marketing orientation), database marketers collapse the production–consumption dichotomy by manufacturing customers as the actual product (which could be seen as a return to the production concept). Importantly, stating that databases configure customers as products does not mean that we reject the notion of consumer agency and empowerment. Rather, both of these processes – the performance of consumer agency and the manufacturing of consumers based on the data gleaned by observing the agentic consumer – are going on at the same time. Hence, consumer agency, empowerment, and creativity, on the one hand, and consumer surveillance and manufacturing, on the other, are not opposite concepts but in fact two sides of the same coin. Put differently, in information capitalism, surveillance and control become valuable tools only insofar as they record and analyze difference, which requires an always changing, adapting, creating, and even cunning consumer. The result of our undertaking is a model of customer databases that foregrounds the far-reaching effect of potent simulational capabilities intersecting with constantly increasing computational power to transform the database into the factory of the twenty-first century.

Introduction to database marketing

The task of acquiring, satisfying, and retaining customers has become an uphill battle in massified consumer markets of the affluent world. Building lasting relationships with customers becomes at once more important for ensuring continued profits, yet less likely to occur. To further complicate matters, the 1990s brought about what some commentators have described as the heady days of hypercompetition, a condition characterized by excess capacities of progressively more – and more alike – brands and products vying for the same consumer dollar (see also Barber 2007). Under such circumstances, merely satisfying consumers is an insufficient barrier to prevent customer defection. Rather, securing future business from capricious, unfaithful, and demanding buyers now requires nothing less than customer delight, which is a difficult task to accomplish when market exchanges are characterized by a significant lack of social interaction, growing anonymity, and an ever increasing alienation from the social, cultural, and material processes of production (Seth and Seth 2005). The challenge of delighting and retaining customers, therefore, elicits the predictable response from the corporate offices: to somehow reconstruct the type of relationship that used to characterize customer–marketer/seller interactions of an idyllic era – before the brand started to mediate between the shopkeeper and the customer, production went offshore, and dozens of identical products crowded the shelves in supersized stores. In other words, corporate marketers often nostalgically aspire to a relationship between the firm (i.e., the brand or the product) and the customer that is based on traditional and premodern notions of intimacy, mutual recognition, and trust (Vandermerwe 2004).

Lasting customer commitment to a brand, a product, or a company has become more difficult to obtain in the era of post-modern markets characterized by impersonal mass selling and what could be called structural disloyalty of an unmanageable and fickle consumer (Firat and Dholakia 1998; Gabriel and Lang 1995). Advertising agencies and "trend scouts" provide us with ample evidence of consumers' growing weariness and increasingly cynical attitude toward all forms of overt marketing and advertising assaults. This mercurial consumer is deemed impervious to most forms of marketing control and delights in the playful and ingenious subversion of corporate marketing communication and dominant meanings to suit her or his own individual and collective political projects (Frank 1999; Holt 2006). Consequently, the most recent models posit a market populated by consumers whose tastes and patterns are increasingly fluid, fragmented, heterogeneous, and less amenable to categorization, management, and direction.

In recent years, fuelled by decreasing costs of information technology, data storage systems, and analytical power, data-driven marketing has emerged as a powerful response to the condition of post-modern markets. By capturing consumer activities in a ubiquitous fashion and in minute detail, databases become rich repositories of the fast-changing tastes and fluid identities of post-modern consumers. By making contemporary consumer behavior available as coded, standardized, and manipulable data, it can be studied and become known to the marketer at the microscopic level (Zwick and Dholakia 2004b). The hope is that by regaining the intimate customer knowledge akin to that of the traditional shopkeeper, relating to each individual customer on a more meaningful level is again within reach – even for an anonymous corporation selling to the masses. Hence, the rise of database marketing and its positioning as a powerful competitive weapon for companies, especially large ones, are rooted in the idyllic "small business" philosophy of being close to the customers, understanding and meeting their needs, and treating them well after the sale.

More than a decade ago, the National Center of Database Marketing in New York defined database marketing as:

> Managing a computerized relational database system, in real time, of comprehensive, up to date, relevant data on customers, inquiries, prospects and suspects, to identify our most responsive customers for the purpose of developing a high-quality, long-standing relationship of repeat business by developing predictive models which enable us to send desired messages at the right time in the right form to the right people – all with the result of pleasing our customers, increasing our response per marketing dollar, lowering our post per order, building our business, and increasing our profits.

An updated version was provided by Blattberg *et al.* (2008: 4) who define database marketing as "the use of customer databases to enhance marketing productivity through more effective acquisition, retention, and development of customers". In the final analysis, database marketing as defined by the National Center of Database Marketing and Blattberg *et al.* is part of a company's marketing research function that, when well integrated, underlies other strategic and tactical marketing activities such as communication, product development, pricing, and channel selection. Hence, database marketing represents the revival of a long-standing business maxim that copious knowledge of individual customers is essential in developing a more interactive, exclusive, and deeper relationship. In short, via technology-enabled marketing a customer is "developed" from a one-time buyer to a regular patron. "Development means enhancing the volume of business the retained customer does with the company" (Blattberg *et al.* 2008: 5). Examples the authors give of database marketing performances are:

- An internet portal trying to understand which customer profile is most likely to use its service and which profiles are not.
- A bank trying to decide which of its many financial products should be marketed to which of its current customers.
- A wireless carrier using a model to identify customers that are most likely to leave the contract and to develop a "churn management program" to make them stay.

Database marketing shares a lot of common goals and features with "its close cousins" (Blattberg *et al.* 2008: 5), direct marketing and customer relationship management (CRM). The main difference is that database marketing emphasizes the use of customer information for the support of a broad range of marketing activities, while direct marketing and CRM are more closely associated with a company's communication strategies. We will return to this observation below as it is central to our reconceptualization of database marketing from a cultural marketing theory perspective.

In sum, from a mainstream marketing perspective database marketing is defined as a way to improve marketing communications, channel strategies, and product offerings in an effort to satisfy consumers and build lasting relationships (Blattberg *et al.* 2001; Drozdenko and Drake 2002); in short, "database marketing is about [improving] marketing productivity" (Blattberg *et al.* 2008: 4) and the rejection of the production concept, which favors the company's capability to produce certain goods and services rather than the identification and satisfaction of customer needs. We do not actually contest this claim nor the nature and usefulness of the many examples of database marketing in action. Rather what we will argue in this chapter is that Blattberg *et al.*'s perspective of database marketing as support function for other marketing tasks gets us only halfway to understanding the growing significance of database marketing as part of the post-Fordist production systems of twenty-first-century information capitalism. Thus, against Blattberg *et al.*'s non-theoretical account, we formulate a theory of post-Fordist database marketing that ultimately reformulates (indeed, reverses) their dictum: database marketing is about *improving production* (see Table 27.1).

In fact, as indicated in Table 27.1, we suggest that under conditions of post-Fordism, database marketing represents a return to the much maligned production concept, with the key difference that the new virtualized production is organized akin to the informal and experimental processes of technology-intensive innovation and artistic imagination characteristic of the creative industries; and what is developed and produced – in the sense

Table 27.1 Contrasting traditional and post-Fordist database marketing (DBM) approaches

	Traditional DBM	*Post-Fordist DBM*
Function	Marketing Research	New Product Development
Concept/philosophy	Radical marketing concept (relationship marketing)	Production concept (manufacture of customers)
Objective	Providing new marketing solutions (new products, positioning, channels, etc.) to existing customer needs (relationship through satisfaction)	Finding new customers for existing marketing solutions (profits through transactions)
Approach	Strategic (differentiating and positioning of products; segmenting and targeting of customers)	Experimental (trial and error: sifting, sorting, separating, and grading of customers)

of new product development – is a new customer for an existing product. Hence, contrary to prevalent claims in the literature that database marketing is about building better customer relationships, we argue that post-Fordist database marketing represents a highly production- and transaction-oriented philosophy to marketing where the objective is to drive up sales numbers by "producing customers" rather than generating deep relationships.

To develop our argument, we employ a research strategy that combines material garnered from conversations with professionals working in database marketing and theories generally discussed under the headings of information capitalism, post-industrial capitalism, and post-Fordism (Castells 1996; Gorz 2004; Hardt and Negr 2004; Liagouras 2005; Neilson and Rossiter 2005). The majority of conversations occurred as part of a two-year-long ethnographic study inside a database marketing company called Insight,[1] where one of the authors at times spent several workdays per week as a participant observer. Supplemental exchanges with database marketers outside the field site were also recorded and used in this study, including professionals working in market analytics departments of large financial institutions, insurance companies, and retailing. We use quotes from these conversations for the purpose of providing illustrations from the "field of practice", to use Bourdieu's (1990) well-known term, and to underscore the central theoretical points we are developing.

The result of our undertaking is a model of customer databases as a site for new product development rather than merely knowledge production and marketing research (see table 27.1). The "product" developed with the customer database is a set of customers with certain desired propensities to buy a specific product or service and the nature of the production process is experimental and playful rather than primarily strategic and scientific. Current conceptualizations that maintain the separation between product/service (to be manufactured) and customer (to be sold/communicated/marketed to) need to be updated to acknowledge the evolution of database marketing and customer intelligence (marketing support) services into a central site of creative and flexible production processes in information capitalism. In the final analysis we propose visualizing customer databases and database-driven marketing not primarily as a tool for relationship-driven marketing strategies but as a tool whose simulational capabilities and always increasing computational power turn it into the info-factory of the twenty-first century.

The context of production

Insight, the site of our ethnography, is one of a fast growing breed of businesses that offers to its clients – typically marketers at larger consumer product manufacturers, retailers of all sorts, financial institutions, etc. – "micro-marketing" services, which claim to enable "direct to consumer marketing with pinpoint accuracy and unprecedented results" (quoted from Insight's marketing material). The company is a little more than ten years old and has sales offices in three major cities in the US and Canada. The overall value proposition that companies like Insight present to clients consists of promising "total market information", granting marketers "intimate access to every consumer's life", and turning this intimacy into "real profits". This transformation of massive amounts but still "raw" market information into actionable consumer intelligence requires the perceptive deployment of highly sophisticated analytical tools and statistical techniques, which is Insight's area of expertise.

A look at the amount of data the company hosts on consumers lends credibility to the total market information claim. For example, the company's flagship asset is a micro-marketing database that contains data on every household in the US and Canada at the zip and postal code level respectively, boasting thousands of data points on geographic, demographic, psychographic, behavioral, attitudinal, life style-related, and expenditure-related aspects of the households. Perhaps somewhat hyperbolically, the company declares that this database is 20 to 25 times more finely targeted than typical consumer databases. Insight's significant investments of time and money to continuously grow the amount of, and maintain the accuracy and relevance of, consumer data stored in this database do make it an important and valuable aspect of the company's business. Furthermore, Insight has made a name for itself among its corporate clients as a supplier of fast analytics and data mining services, which the company claims is based on its employees' superior mathematical, statistical, and software engineering skills.

A micro-marketing project typically begins with a visit from a brand manager of a client firm facing a particular marketing task. This could be the launching of a promotional campaign to encourage product trial which may require winning over consumers of, for example, body wash for men, from a competitor's brand or convincing men who do not use body wash that their lives would be improved if they did, particularly by using the promoted brand. Alternatively, a brand manager may feel the need to alert consumers of a specific new attribute that has been added to the original product, such as the whitening feature of a toothpaste. Initially, then, various members of the Insight team join the client for an exploratory needs assessment meeting to discuss the nature of the promotion and to develop a list of specifications with regards to the customer information required for a successful execution of the campaign.

Among its employees, Insight distinguishes between technical staff – those trained in mathematics, statistics, and software engineering – and business staff – trained as managers, marketers, and sales people. While research and development is the responsibility of the technical division at Insight, managing customers and developing new business lies in the hands of those holding MBA degrees. They are, as one chief technician put it, "closer to the customer". Accordingly, during needs assessment meetings the client, who often possesses little technical expertise, considers Insight's business person in the room as the translator between the client's marketing needs and the information products required for the job. The two or three technical staff members also attending the meeting are far from inept on the business side of things; nevertheless they too look to the team's marketing expert to reconcile available information production capabilities with the client's product needs and demands for actionable clarity. Once needs have been assessed and everyone in the room is satisfied with the plan, however, the project gravitates to and remains almost exclusively in the hands of Insight's mathematicians and statisticians. They take the specific information requirements that the client desires and begin their work of database mining, customer profiling, and list generation in front of powerful computers in the back rooms of the company. The client liaison on Insight's project team then retreats from the ensuing arcane, if not esoteric, production process until that time when the results need to be put in a more presentable format for the client. This task of translating the results of the data mining efforts into a meaningful marketing language typically results in a 20-page report containing a range of standard tools for visualizing statistical analyses, such as the obligatory pie and bar charts as well as a range of commercially acquired and strategically placed photos representing typical exemplars of a specific consumer type.[2]

The challenge of producing such documents lies in the act of delicately balancing the client's need for easy access to the results with the firm's interest in reinforcing a perception of the marketplace as a tremendously complex battleground full of traps, mystery, and ambiguity that requires the services of Insight to ensure victory for the brand in the war for market share.

The process of generating such a report and its contents represents an important element in the production of customers, just as the symbolic work of generating a client-specific language with which to make up the marketplace in ways that allow the performance of marketing practice is important. This process of constructing, disseminating, and eventual translating of a specific kind of marketing language into practice no doubt is fascinating and ripe for theoretical scrutiny. The scope of this chapter, however, does not permit a comprehensive treatment of this specific aspect of the general cycle of production of customers, markets, marketing language, and, vicariously, marketing practice. Instead, we will focus our attention on the work of data technicians, analysts, and data miners whose productive labor represents the key to understanding database marketing from a cultural theory perspective as a site of new product development *qua* the production of customers.

The mode of flexible production

Marketing's use of panoptic market research techniques for maintaining control over increasingly mobile and seemingly capricious consumer subjects has a history that goes back to at least the 1950s (see e.g. Miller and Rose 1997; Arvidsson 2004). Nevertheless, the sheer amount of data produced by contemporary electronic consumer surveillance, the computer power available to analyze information, and the speed with which differences, distinctions, and commonalities among customers can be detected are historically new and qualitatively radically different from any previous forms of market research. For the first time in history, according to Arvidsson (2004: 457), it is now possible to capture, store, and retrieve the "physical, social and cultural mobility of social life, the moving about between environments and activities that has become a key characteristic of post-modern life." In other words, the ability to monitor and describe virtually all of consumers' consumption and non-consumption activities ensures that fewer and fewer elements of everyday life escape the electronic super-panopticon, thus increasingly turning everything consumers do into raw material (as encoded, decoded, and recoded information) for the production of consumer representations.

It is important to recall that databases are made up of symbols in data fields. They embody a specific mode of representing the world, what Bolter (2001) calls numeric inscription. As Poster (1995: 278) puts it, "one does not eat them, handle them, or kick them, at least one hopes not. Databases are configurations of language; the theoretical stance that engages them must take at least this ontological fact into account." Poster has in mind a post-structuralist analysis when he points to the database as a repository for linguistic power. Yet theories approaching information and communication technologies via an analysis of the informatization of production also benefit from this insight because it speaks directly to some of the fundamental features of a post-Fordist economic system: the nature of the technological base, the nature of commodities, and time–space compression (see e.g. Harvey 1989).

Many authors have pointed to the shift from an energy-intensive to an information-intensive production system as a key element of the transition from Fordism to post-Fordism. The electronic and information revolutions of the past two decades not only affect how work gets done but what kind of work generates the bulk of economic value. The emphasis is no longer on the development of technologies that have the ability to replicate and replace hard physical labor but on machines that allow for the manipulation of symbols and for the production and representation of information (Kumar 1995). In short, postindustrial technologies do not replicate manual labor as much as they enable and automate knowledge work. Consequently, the dominant strategy of value creation under post-Fordism is focused on expanding, proliferating, and improving symbolic and communicative systems, rather than on the mass production of physical goods. As a consequence, the manufacturing of material components of products declines in economic importance, and thus in strategic importance; while the production of emotional, intellectual, communicative, and aesthetic components become increasingly significant (Lash and Urry 1994). When value generation is the outcome of informationalized production processes, economic value becomes a function of the degree to which time and space can be compressed, i.e., sped up, in the production cycle (Harvey 1989).

Usually notions of time–space compression refer to the discussion about the acceleration of global capitalism. As Castells (1996: 92) puts it, "[T]he informational economy is global…It is an economy with the capacity to work as a unit in real time on a planetary scale." While the new realities brought about by the worldwide real-time interconnectivity of complex and spatially dispersed production systems have garnered most of the attention of theorists of information capitalism, there are other ways in which post-Fordist economies rely on time and space compression to produce valuable commodities. They are related to the shift from the production of capital-intensive, tangible commodities to the production of knowledge-intensive, intangible value such as market information, business intelligence, patents, brands, and community. The focus here is on the accelerated interaction between consumption and production expressed in management concepts such as fast fashion, Toyotaism, just-in-time, and lean manufacturing (Lane and Probert 2009; Thrift 2005), and more recently in marketing practices that use the internet to establish more immediate relationships with consumers (Zwick *et al.* 2008). The speed at which, for example, symbolic goods like brands are fabricated, launched (often globally), positioned, repositioned, and made obsolete is historically unprecedented and points to the relevance of theorizing the nature of goods, the technological base, and time–space compression for the production of intangible goods in post-Fordism. It is against this backdrop of post-Fordist capitalism and its continuous search for increased efficiencies in connecting production and consumption and its pursuit of more flexible value strategies that the database has moved into the center of value creation today.

Databases have come to represent the dispersed and largely surreptitious repositories of our lives. They constitute, according to Haggerty and Ericson (2000: 606), massive computer-assisted classification systems that operate "by abstracting human bodies from their territorial settings and separating them into a series of discrete flows. These flows are then reassembled into distinct 'data doubles' which can be scrutinized and targeted for intervention." Robert, a senior data analyst at Insight, explains how this process looks in practice:

> Once we get the specifics on a new job, we talk to the client to get all the information that they have stored somewhere in their existing databases. They have tons of transactional and sometimes even personalized information [e.g. demographical, geographical, and lifestyle data] that they collected at some point themselves. With most clients we have a standing relationship so they know what we need for the job, so it's no problem. We take their data, clean it up a little, usually, and then add it to our own database. Depending on the client we may be able to develop customer lists of more than a hundred thousand individuals each consisting of 300 or more data points.

Now, the consumer can be converted into a digital assemblage and as an assemblage she or he exists and acquires meaning (in the sense of market value, or what Pridmore and Lyon (2011) and Deighton (2005) refer to as "consumer brands") only in connection with other assemblages. As a consequence, database marketing becomes deeply functional because database marketers never really ask what a particular data flow means, nor do they look for anything to interpret in the data. What they want to know is what they can do with the data. Consider Robert's description of Insight's value proposition to its clients. The company does not promise a hermeneutics of the digital text to excavate deep-seated truths about consumers. Rather, Insight delivers customers "that work":

> Most of our work now deals with identifying customers for whatever it is companies want to promote and sell. This is really where we see our value added to the client and so we push that capability on to them. Basically, we tell them, "Look, we don't care what you're trying to sell, you know, how good or bad or whatever it may be, we will find you customers with the highest probability of success."

Implied in Robert's promise to find "high-probability customers" is the ability of the database to create purely functional hierarchies that set desirable targets apart from undesirable ones for a specific product or marketing message. In other words, meaning emerges from the data only when a customer profile is put in relation to another. Herein lies the challenge (but also the opportunity) for the database marketer because the production of meaning, or more accurately the creation of customer knowledge with market value, depends on continuously and creatively de- and re-assembling sets of consumer representations by establishing always new and productive relationships between data points.

Importantly, the notion of assemblage produces a model of the database as a curiously static representation of the world "out there" that ignores the circular, or as Elmer (2004) calls it, cybernetic dimension of the technology, specifically "the manner in which the signifieds and the process of signification are continuously reconstituted by each other" (ibid.: 48). Elmer offers a more dynamic perspective that focuses on the feedback loop between the nature of customer data coming in and the marketing actions taken to influence customer behavior. Hence, the recurring generation of economic value through the production of customer assemblages is not based primarily on the accuracy of data storage and categorization but on the continuous obsolescence of previous customer productions as well as the constant refinement of the data mining technique. Miro Kundra, who holds a doctorate in statistics and founded Insight in the early 1990s, explains:

> Our job is *not* to tell our clients "this is how your market looks like" and "this is who your customers are". We tell them "This is what your market looks like *right now* but soon it will be different again because everything changes because you act, your competitors react and do their own marketing, then your marketing strategy changes, and then consumers react to the new product selection out there, and everyone does new advertising as a result, and so on." We *know* consumers change all the time because we see the data coming in. In addition, *we* change here at Insight because we always work on our analytics and try to improve the accuracy of our forecasts and profiles … So we never promise a stable world but we promise the most accurate view of the world as it is right now.

Kundra's comment points to the fact that the signified (the consumer) and the process of signification (targeted marketing interventions) always act on each other, thereby ensuring the ongoing variation of data flows. In addition, data mining techniques constantly change because the mathematical algorithm used to analyze (or here, recode) customer behavior, wants, needs, and desires is always under construction and even small changes in the code can make a significant difference in how consumer representations are assembled. This combination of always changing data flows, and permanent upgrading of data analytical capabilities, form the basic building blocks for the flexible production of heterogeneous sets of customers, where each manufactured data assemblage can further be reduced to a single index of propensity of desire. Gary, a data marketing specialist at a large bank, describes this production of assemblages, what he calls targets, as his main activity:

Gary:	What do we do all day? [laughs] Good question. Well, I guess, much of what we do here, … we help our product managers identify customers so they can go out and sell them something they don't know yet they need. [laughs].
Interviewer:	Can you explain?
Gary:	Well, often it starts when …, OK, let's say, a product manager would come in with this new product he wants to get out there. Could be a new type of personal savings account or whatever. Anyway, so they have their product and now they need customers for it, right? So we ask them a few questions like who they think would want this and why, which gives us some idea what variables to include in our model. Then we run the model and generate a list of high-probability targets for them to go after.

Recoding in the context of database marketing, then, refers to the ongoing production of relationships and associations. Put differently, marketers find in the database a tool to manufacture customer sets with specified desires always already "built in" via specific algorithms and statistical models at work.[3]

Hence database marketers do not aim at producing complete and authentic consumer identities or holistic representations of the consumer's inner consciousness. Rather, seen from a modernist perspective on identity, the process of consumer recoding in databases

yields extremely selective and partial identities, which are – in the tradition of lean manufacturing and just-in-time delivery – stripped of anything that might distract from addressing
the specific functional needs of marketers. This is the crux of the "score," a numeric
that demarcates the final result of a complex data mining, simulation, and decoding
process. Sunil Handa, an-analytics expert at Insight, describes the role of the "score" from
the perspective of the economics of customer production:

> For our clients, it's of course important to know who is likely to respond to *their*
> message and buy *their* products. For them, talking to someone who won't buy their
> products no matter what is a big waste. So they come to us, [expecting us] to tell them
> which is which by ranking thousands of individuals according to a model we prepare for
> the client. Each individual gets a "score" and then we provide the client with deciles[4] to
> make it easier for them to compare the different segments of the market for their specific
> product. Our database is huge so we believe we can really parcel out the true scores
> for each member of the population we look at and the client has a lot of confidence in
> the targets and non-targets we provide them with.

The score, then, rank-orders consumers according to the mathematically generated relative
intensity of their desires for a specific product or brand at a specific time and in a specific
place – from ice-cream, to toothpaste, to mutual funds, to lifestyle magazines. In other words,
the score is the outcome of fast data mining processes that recodes consumer habits,
routines, idiosyncrasies, and trajectories into relationships and associations that signal
each consumer's potential economic value within the specified field of consumption.

The score, then, responds perfectly to the imperatives of modern marketing because it
creates instant comparability and calculability of the economic value of a consumer, allowing for the identification of those that have more value and those that have less. Simulating
the economic value of consumers through scoring is a dynamic process that ultimately wants
to operate in real time. With the emergence of computerized informational networks that
increasingly automate data collection, diagnosis, and production, the speed at which scores
are assembled has increased steadily. Banks, for example, owners of arguably the most
sophisticated mining operations and concerned about all sorts of risk associated with the
business of lending and investing money, make use of a wide range of different analytical
and simulation techniques to determine the probability of a credit-seeking customer default-
ing on his or her loan. To build their simulation and profiling models, banks can rely on
millions of customer records from disparate sets of archives of information located across
many sites, collected with diverse processes, and stored via numerous techniques of input.
Yet, in the hands of a bank's frontline employees, the process of customer profiling becomes
an automated, real-time calculation exercise aimed at generating a single number called
the individual risk score (see also Vargha 2009). This is how Gary explains the dynamic
decoding and recoding process at his bank:

> We take historical data to build this risk model and what it is ... is a mathematical
> formula that spits out a number. It could be a, you know, a combination of models. Our
> fraud protection process uses four different techniques, but the ultimate output of that is
> a number ... We had up to a million records to build this model. But when we put it in
> the hands of our frontline employees who interact directly with customers that may ask
> them for some credit, for example, they apply it in real time. They can see immediately
> what the risk level is of *that* customer and suggest an appropriate product. And as new

records come in from the customer, or any customer we have, we take the mathematical formula, run that new data record daily or monthly or weekly, however frequently we apply it, and update the risk score immediately.

The individual risk score simulates only risk, which is a key piece of information for the bank to determine the profit potential of each customer for a specific product. The model itself could be considered very comprehensive, pooling a vast range of historical and personal (sometimes very personal) data about each applying customer. Yet, in the final analysis, the task of the model is to generate a comparable number – a numerical common denominator to rank riskiness of customers. For the model to work efficiently it ought not to say anything else about the individual seeking a loan, nor should it because any other piece of information could distract the employee from matching the score generated by the system with an "appropriate" response from the institutional repertoire of available responses.

As information becomes the core substance driving value creation in contemporary capitalism, consumers inserted in seamless technological networks of surveillance are made a key resource for the (re)production of information. As Sunil Handa from Insight explains:

> Consumer behavior is always changing but when that happens, that's not a problem but actually pretty good because we are the first ones to know about it, right? We even know it before they [the observed population] know it [laughs]. So we can go out and run our analyses on the new data that comes in from the market and, if we see changes, we make a nice report and sell them to our clients. So for us at least, we need that change. It's good for us. The more the better.

Hence marketers, previously concerned with controlling consumers in time and space, are learning to exploit the capacities of electronic surveillance networks to follow "free" consumers everywhere, turning the mobility of everyday life into input for the "more diffuse and expanded systems of production that characterize post-Fordism" (Arvidsson 2005: 237). In other words, within the logic of information capitalism the production of customers as commodities with exchange value requires in the first instance the flexible reproduction of *new* information (through novel behavior) from a more or less autonomous, spatially dispersed, and socio-culturally diverse mass of consumers. Indeed, as Virilio (1995) proposed some time ago, it is precisely dynamic and fast-changing information that holds the most value. Speed of information production, then, becomes an important added dimension in the valorization of customers as products because "speed guarantees the secret and hence the value of all information" (ibid.: 53). This is what Insight does: speeding up the process of decoding, recoding, and communicating information to such an extent that the production of information, whether by consumers in the market or by the database marketers in front of their computers, constitutes the communication it claims to capture. Post-Fordism therefore foregrounds the productive role of the circulation of information, or as Arvidsson (2005: 240) puts it, "[T]he 'information economy' is thus one important example of the fusion of communication and production."

Until recently economists and marketers considered information about the market as a means of controlling volume of production and of determining desired product features. From this perspective, product customization through digital "versioning" – e.g. producing a customized version of the daily newspaper based on a customer's previously specified preferences – lies at the core of the creation of value where information about consumers is said to improve the matching of product features with consumer desires. Increasingly, database marketing is turning this established relationship between market knowledge and the production of goods on its head because the informationalization of consumption has created a situation in which digital versioning can most effectively be achieved via the flexible and rapid production of customer sets. Hence, rather than adjusting product features to match existing customer desires, marketers can now adjust, at very little cost and in real time, customer features to match an existing product. As Miro Kundra explains, Insight pushes the logic of flexible, modular production of targets to its extreme:

> It takes us a few minutes to generate – out of more than 100,000 data profiles – a nice set of customers with extremely high specificity. But the next step is to put this capability online so our clients can do it on their own time, on their own computer. That is what we are working on right now. The result is that a brand manager can produce his own set of customers based on his own requirements whenever he needs to. He can do it online and it will take him 2 minutes to find out … who might be a good target for his brand.

Understanding the reversal in the production of value in information economies has implications for how we theorize the role of the databases in a firm's value creation strategies. Concretely, we may see costly and relatively lengthy efforts to redesign supply chains, products, and production processes replaced by the much speedier, cost-effective, and flexible production of customers.

In sum, then, theorizing technologies such as the customer database in terms of production requires us to re-evaluate from where these technologies derive their unique power. The dominant focus in the current literature on consumer surveillance and management technologies has been on the spatial aspect of consumption that attempts to locate and map information to generate marketing insights and applications. A "production of customers" perspective proposes that the importance of the database for the creation of economic value is derived less from its capacity to identify and map consumers, although these elements are important (e.g. Zwick and Dholakia 2004a). Rather, the ability to produce modular (flexible and reflexive) sets of consumer facsimiles in real time or nearly instantly is what has elevated the customer database from a technology of knowledge production and marketing productivity (Blattberg *et al.* 1994) to a technology of production *tout court*.

Hence, recent gains in speed and the flexibility of production processes, premised on the unfolding of increasingly powerful data mining techniques, are central to our argument of how the customer database leads to a reversal of Fordist organizations of production and consumption that pervade the writings of Blattberg *et al.* (2008) and others in the marketing field. Indeed, even comprehensive theorizations of the informatization of production (Castells 1996) fall short of grasping the extent to which communicative action has informationalized production in late capitalism because these accounts exclude the informatization of consumers.

Conceptualizing the database as a technology of production foregrounds the expanded *strategic* possibilities of market informatization in post-Fordism. We suggest that the economic strength of databases rests with their ability to continuously produce novel sets of consumers. The database's capacity to spot and turn into value creative, nonconforming, and unexpected forms of consumer life has not been lost to marketing executives who understand very well that future market opportunities often evolve out of the social and cultural innovations generated in *un*controlled and *un*disciplined spaces of consumer culture (Frank 1999; Holt 2004; Arvidsson 2005).

Conclusion: marketing strategy implications

In this chapter, we have explored from a cultural theory perspective the increasingly important, yet in the literature largely overlooked, relationship between growing customer databases, modern marketing practice, and contemporary strategies of value creation in information capitalism. We argue that the emergence and proliferation of the customer database have given rise to techniques, competences, expert systems, and productive units aiming not only at the supervision and control of consumption (*qua* better marketing productivity, to use Blattberg *et al.*'s term) but at the flexible production of customers as information products. In other words, the capabilities of the database allow for the restructuring of the strategic gaze of marketers who recognize that new instruments of knowledge also contain the possibility for new forms of production, valorization, and accumulation.

Reducing the effect of customer databases to improvements in market control (typically expressed as improved market segmentation and targeting capabilities, customization, one-on-one relationships, interactivity, etc.) ignores the economic innovations brought about by the integration of database technology into existing post-Fordist modes of production. We argue that the constant and compounding growth in the volume of data coupled with the rising analytical powers of computers has endowed the customer database with an immediate strategic importance in a company's economic value creation process. In short, because of the massive informatization of consumers it is now more efficient (faster, more flexible, and cheaper) to manufacture customers – as modular configurations of propensities, as calculations of possible future values, and as purified groupings of selective homogeneity – than to adjust the manufacturing processes of goods. Database marketing thus emerges as a value creation strategy for the firm that competes directly with more traditional forms of production.

Arvidsson (2003) suggests that database marketing should be regarded as a response to the twin condition of marketing modernity: the increasingly mobile (spatially, economically, culturally) consumer and the disappearing consumer body. The ability of the customer database to capture what Arvidsson (ibid.: 467) calls "the communicative action of life in all its walks" effectively turns increasingly complex and mutable consumer practices into value. In other words, ubiquitous information gathering transforms what has previously been seen as a practical marketing problem in need of more control – the mobile, creative, and unpredictable consumer – into a productive and economically important force. Now, action and inaction, movement and inertia, indeed all of life, has value when inscribed as digital information and rematerialized, packaged, and sold as an information good. Put differently, marketers' continuous quest to create demand and satisfy consumers finds its latest frontier in the manufacturing of customers from the material created by the "labor" of consumers themselves. Other methods to minimize the distance between supply and demand, such as product customization and one-on-one marketing, cannot compete with the complete implosion of consumption into production, represented by the overall reversal of the production process.

The implications of a cultural marketing management approach to database marketing are significant. For starters, database marketing should be considered as a site for new product development and resources should be directed into data collection, mining, and customer production accordingly. Furthermore, marketers need to develop a mindset that rejects the dominant premise that database marketing is a technical and scientific tool. Rather than thinking of database marketing as dominated by complex algorithms and statistical analysis, marketers need to approach this tool from the informal and imaginative culture of the creative industries, where artistic experimentation leads to breakthrough product innovation. Finally, marketers who understand the strategic value, conceptual revolution, and marketing functionality offered by database marketing will be able to embrace the fickleness of consumers as the essential prerequisite for future innovation in customer production. In the era of post-Fordist capitalism, flexible production of information has come to dominate value creation and extraction strategies. Therefore the process of continuously analyzing masses of digitized customer information to discover hidden truths and layers of desire can no longer be reduced to a supporting role of marketing production. Rather, database marketing produces a product with economic value that is itself in need of marketing, turning the customer databases into the factory of the twenty-first century.

Review and discussion questions

1   Describe the conventional relationship between customer intelligence and market orientation and what that relationship is based on.
2   How does the post-Fordist database marketing model differ from the conventional DM approach and what are the changes (social, cultural, economic, technological, etc.) that have made this change possible?
3   What are the implications of post-Fordist database marketing for marketing strategy?
4   What are the implications of post-Fordist database marketing for organizational strategy?
5   Where do you see post-Fordist database marketing going from here?

Keywords

analytics, customer production, databases, Deleuze, Foucault, marketing, post-Fordism, surveillance

Notes

1 The names of the company and all informants for this study have been changed to protect their anonymity.
2 The company eschews speaking of these "types" as "segments" because the whole point of their production work is to do away with segmentation thinking. They aim to individualize consumers to allow for modular control.
3 Obviously, this is a rather essentialist notion of desire, which we reject, but that is the view prevalent among our informants.
4 This term refers to the organization of large computer-generated customer lists into ten equal parts where, for example, the top deciles represent the 10 percent of consumers with the highest score for the respective product and the lowest deciles assemble the bottom 10 percent.

References

Arvidsson, A. (2003) *Marketing Modernity: Italian Advertising from Fascism to Postmodernity*, London: Routledge.

—— (2004) "On the 'Pre-History of the Panoptic Sort': Mobility in Market Research," *Surveillance and Society*, 1(4): 456–74.

—— (2005) "Brands: A Critical Perspective," *Journal of Consumer Culture*, 5(2): 235–58.

Barber, B. R. (2007) *Consumed: How Markets Corrupt Children, Infantilize Adults, and Swallow Citizens Whole*, New York: W.W. Norton and Co.

Blattberg, R. C., Getz, G., and Thomas, J. S. (2001) *Customer Equity: Building and Managing Relationships as Valuable Assets*, Boston: Harvard Business School Press.

Blattberg, R. C., Glazer, R., and Little, J. D. C. (1994) *The Marketing Information Revolution*, Boston: Harvard Business School Press.

Blattberg, R. C., Kim, P. O. -D. and Neslin, S. A. (2008) *Database Marketing: Analyzing and Managing Customers*, New York: Springer.

Bolter, J. D. (2001) *Writing Space: Computers, Hypertext, and the Remediation of Print*, Mahwah, NJ: Lawrence Erlbaum Associates.

Bourdieu, P. (1990) *The Logic of Praxis,* Stanford, CA: Stanford University Press.

Castells, M. (1996) *The Rise of the Network Society*, Malden, MA: Blackwell.

Deighton, J. (2005) "Consumer Identity Motives in the Information Age," in S. Ratneshwar and D. G. Mick (eds), *Inside Consumption: Consumer Motives, Goals, and Desires*, New York: Routledge, pp. 233–50.

Drozdenko, R. G. and Drake, P. D. (2002) *Optimal Database Marketing: Strategy, Development, and Data Mining*, Thousand Oaks, CA: Sage.

Elmer, G. (2004) *Profiling Machines: Mapping the Personal Information Economy*, Cambridge, MA: MIT Press.

Firat, A. F. and Dholakia, N. (1998) *Consuming People: From Political Economy to Theaters of Consumption*, London: Routledge.

Frank, T. (1999) *The Conquest of Cool*, Chicago: The University of Chicago Press.

Gabriel, Y. and Lang, T. (1995) *The Unmanageable Consumer: Contemporary Consumption and its Fragmentations*, London: Sage.

Gorz, A. (2004) *Wissen, Wert und Kapital: Zur Kritik der Wissensökonomie*, Zürich: Rotpunktverlag.

Haggerty, K. D. and Ericson, R. V. (2000) "The Surveillant Assemblage," *British Journal of Sociology*, 51(4): 605–22.

Hardt, M. and Negri, A. (2004) *Multitude: War and Democracy in the Age of Empire*, New York: The Penguin Press.

Harvey, D. (1989) *The Condition of Postmodernity*, Cambridge, MA: Blackwell.

Holt, D. B. (2004) *How Brands Become Icons: The Principles of Cultural Branding*, Boston: Harvard Business School Press.

—— (2006) "Jack Daniel's America: Iconic Brands as Ideological Parasites and Proselytizers," *Journal of Consumer Culture*, 6(3): 355–77.

Kumar, K. (1995) *From Post-Industrial to Post-Modern Society*, Oxford: Blackwell.

Lane, C., and Probert, J. (2009) *National Capitalisms, Global Production Networks: Fashioning the Value Chain in the UK, USA, and Germany*, Oxford: Oxford University Press.

Lash, S., and Urry, J. (1994) *Economies of Signs and Space*, London: Sage.

Liagouras, G. (2005) "The Political Economy of Post-Industrial Capitalism," *Thesis Eleven*, 81(1): 20–35.

Miller, P. and Rose, N. (1997) "Mobilizing the Consumer," *Theory, Culture, and Society*, 14(1): 1–36.

Neilson, B. and Rossiter, N. (2005) "From Precarity to Precariousness and Back Again: Labour, Life and Unstable Networks," *Fibreculture*, 5. Available at: http://journal.fibreculture.org/issue5/neilson_rossiter.html

Poster, M. (1995) "Databases as Discourse, or Electronic Interpellations," in P. Heelas, S. Lash and P. Morris (eds), *Detraditionalization*, Oxford: Blackwell, pp. 277–93.

Pridmore, J. and Lyon, D. (2011) "Marketing as Surveillance: Assembling Consumers as Brands," in D. Zwick and J. Cayla (eds), *Inside Marketing: Practices, Ideologies, Devices*, Oxford: Oxford University Press.

Seth, R. and Seth, K. (2005) *Creating Customer Delight: The How and Why of CRM*, Thousand Oaks, CA: Response Books.

Thrift, N. J. (2005) *Knowing Capitalism*, London: Sage.

Vandermerwe, S. (2004) "Achieving deep customer focus," *MIT Sloan Management Review*, 45(3): 26–34.

Vargha, Z. (2009) "Markets from Interactions: The Technology of Mass Personalization in Consumer Banking." Available at: SSRN: http://ssrn.com/abstract = 1351624

Virilio, P. (1995) *The Art of the Motor*, Minneapolis: University of Minnesota Press.

Zwick, D., Bonsu, S. K., and Darmody, A. (2008) "Putting Consumers to Work: 'Co-Creation' and New Marketing Govern-mentality," *Journal of Consumer Culture*, 8(2): 163–96.

Zwick, D. and Denegri-Knott, J. (2009) "Manufacturing Customers: The Database as New Means of Production,"*Journal of Consumer Culture*, 9(2): 221–47.

Zwick, D. and Dholakia, N. (2004a) "Consumer Subjectivity in the Age of Internet: The Radical Concept of Marketing Control through Customer Relationship Management," *Information and Organization*, 14(3): 211–36.

—— (2004b) "Whose Identity is it Anyway? Consumer Representation in the Age of Database Marketing," *Journal of Macromarketing*, 24(1): 31–43.

Part V

Institutional issues in the marketing organization and the academy

28 (Re)thinking distribution strategy
Principles from sustainability

Susan Dobscha, Andrea Prothero and
Pierre McDonagh

Overview

This chapter will show how consumers have created new strategies for dealing with those goods and services they no longer need or reclaim those goods that may to the untrained eye appear to be worthless (broken, disfigured, out of style, for example). Why are distribution channel members less interested in participating in the reclamation process when consumers are increasingly clamouring for it and indeed are finding their own creative ways of redistributing goods? It is in this context we ask what can channel members learn from consumer-to-consumer distribution processes? We will present *The Inverted Pyramid of Sustainability* (TIPS) and discuss specific marketing strategies that relate to each section. We will then look at examples of these redistribution channels to see how consumers in these markets are using these channels to enact values of sustainability or charity. Next, we consider how corporations also are now tackling these issues, oftentimes in response to grassroots consumer actions. Finally, we end our chapter with exercises designed to incorporate the concepts from the chapter.

Introduction

Cultural perspectives afford marketers the opportunity to comment on marketing domains to determine if the application of a traditional approach has contributed to global problems such as pollution and waste. A cultural approach differs from the traditional approach by giving greater emphasis to the creativity of the consumer across global markets. Distribution is one of those key marketing activities that would benefit from an updated vision that reflects shifts in consumer values, increased visibility of global environmental concerns, and changes in the way the world produces, distributes, consumes and disposes of goods. At first glance, distribution strategy seems to be the most staid of all the marketing functions, yet it is fundamental to business success. The basic ideas that govern a firm's choices on how to distribute their goods and services have not changed that much, even in light of advances in database and other information system technologies.

The idea of environmental sustainability pushes our thinking much further than previous conceptualizations of environmental issues ever did. Prior work in this area lacked the 'stickiness' that environmental sustainability has in terms of promoting global awareness of such issues as over-consumption, waste disposal, pollution and tainted food supplies. Global concern for the natural environment is at an all-time high. Developed nations therefore see the environmental crisis as something that all countries must respond to. While there are differences within and across cultures as to how to best respond to environmental issues, what is clear is that the destruction of the environment is a crisis which must be tackled. The truly global nature of the problem means that while local cultures may respond differently to the issue, it is agreed that a global response will be much more effective. There is an opportunity to learn from cultures which enact sustainability more actively or distinctively than others. How do these cultures distribute the environmental sustainability ethos? How do those nations not currently wrapped in the cycle of hyperconsumption avoid or resist the desire to become like those nations whose consumption has contributed significantly to the problem? The global nature of the environmental problem therefore means that from a cultural marketing perspective, we must be cognizant of the fact that we need to explore cultural responses to a global phenomenon. Like hunger and AIDS, environmental degradation is a problem that affects the entire planet in disproportionate amounts.

Putting the (re) into distribution

Distribution emerged as one of the first strategic domains within the fledgling field of marketing in the 1950s, and forms one of the four cornerstones of the marketing mix, which is the mainstay of introductory marketing textbooks. Mass distribution of goods was perfected by retailers such as Sears and Woolworth's in the USA once it was realized that centralized distribution of goods facilitated exchange much more efficiently. The mathematics is fairly simple: the presence of one intermediatory increases market efficiency as measured by total number of transactions (X producers × Y buyers) by 50 per cent (16 to 8). Overall, the goal of distribution was to improve efficiency and reduce total product cost, thus improving profit.

What is notably absent from Figure 28.1 is the story of the item once it leaves the efficient distribution channel. In fact, as early as 1972, researchers found that distribution channels were not designed to take goods back from the consumer once they were finished with them. For example, retailers who sell newspapers are not equipped to take them back once they have been read. Clumsy intermediaries emerged to perform this function. Early on, those

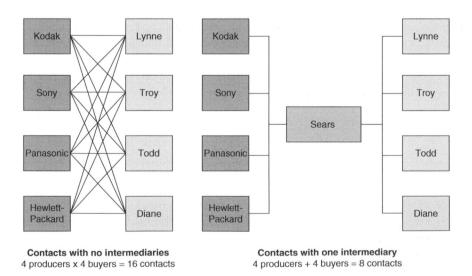

Contacts with no intermediaries
4 producers x 4 buyers = 16 contacts

Contacts with one intermediary
4 producers + 4 buyers = 8 contacts

Figure 28.1 Distribution efficiency diagram.
Source: Kerin *et al.* (2006).

intermediaries were local church and civic groups who created collection boxes and sites and then voluntarily performed the intermediary function. They also found that distribution channels were not equipped nor particularly interested in becoming part of the waste stream solution because these functions did not serve the previously held goals of distribution to: (1) improve efficiency or (2) lower cost. While broadly speaking there have been recent initiatives to green the supply chain and work toward sustainable supply chain management (Vermeulen and Seuring 2009), this philosophy still holds true today. As a consequence, sufficient focus has not been given to consumer-led initiatives in the performance of consumer-citizenship nor how this can be incorporated into governance of distribution (supply chain) strategy. Intermediaries are not equipped to reclaim goods that have ultimately been distributed to the consumer. Old cellular phones become children's play toys; old cars are abandoned in quarries.

In the absence of market innovation, consumers have tenaciously created their own distribution channels to move goods and services around. For example, several new distribution channels, including eBay, Craigslist and Freecycle, emerged so that consumers could redistribute the already purchased goods they no longer need, due to changes in family structures, age, economic conditions or geographic relocation. While it's unclear whether these consumers use these channels in the spirit of environmental sustainability, what is clear is that redistribution of goods decreases landfill sizes and staves off (only fractionally) purchasing new.

Much like their predecessors, the Depression-era generation, this generation of consumers think about their consumer goods in a cradle-to-cradle way: they purchase goods not just with the motivation of needs satisfaction but also sustainable disposition. Many marketers have long ignored this portion of the consuming public as fringe or radical. As a result, they have missed the opportunity to incorporate consumer disposition into their overall marketing strategy. While eBay generates millions in revenue, marketers stuck in their traditional vision of distribution strategy as a one-way street have missed out on potential revenue streams and, perhaps more importantly, the creation of goodwill that would result from partnering with consumers in the reverse distribution chain.

A field of logistics management, named reverse logistics, has emerged to shed some light on the benefits of implementing a "process of moving product from its point of consumption to point of origin to recapture value or for proper disposal" (Tibben-Lembke 1998: 54). In a book on the subject, Rogers and Tibben-Lembke advocate strongly for the positive effects of implementing a reverse logistics system into current logistics and supply chain strategy. It is in the post-transaction phase that Rogers and Tibben-Lembke (1999) see the potential for a positive environmental impact. They cite asbestos removal and computer monitor reclamation as examples where the consumer may use a reverse logistics system to rid themselves of potentially hazardous products. The question then becomes, *why* have more firms not adopted a cultural marketing or consumer perspective toward reverse logistics strategies if, in fact, "they can achieve the goals of sustainable development" (Dowlatshahi 2000: 144) and can save an estimated "40 to 60 percent of the cost of manufacturing a new product" (ibid.: 144)? If implemented properly, reverse logistics systems provide a long-term cost saving and establish and maintain strong customer relationships.

However, due to firms' slow movement in creating reclamation processes, some governments have aimed to tackle this problem with national programs; others have focused on a more supra-national bloc approach. The European Union, for instance, introduced its EU Directive on Waste from Electrical and Electronic Equipment (WEEE) in 2005, with policies focusing on the recycling, reuse, and recovery of electrical goods (classified as the fastest growing waste stream in the EU). The Directive places emphasis on the manufacturers of goods to be responsible for their products once they come to the end of their useful lives. The Directive is currently under review to tackle issues of companies flouting policy. Meanwhile, consumers themselves have been looking for alternative means for disposing their e-waste.

The immediate success of consumer-to-consumer distribution channels highlights a shift in how consumers view the goods they purchase. It also shows a willingness to confront what some have labeled the "'Hidden Mountain" and the "social avoidance of waste" (de Coverly *et al.* 2008). Instead of viewing these goods as waste to be disposed of after they have squeezed every last use from them (cf. Arnould 2003), consumers are viewing them as potentially having a *new life*, inhabiting a new space, serving a new function, or, in fact, making someone else happy. The immediate success of eBay is testament to the consumer desire to dispose of goods they no longer need, can no longer afford or no longer want. In fact eBay stepped in as the one intermediary that connected millions of producers and millions of consumers in a virtual marketplace. And while small distributors flourished, the large channel members ignored this new distribution channel in favor of bigger stores in more locations.

Achieving success through environmental sustainability: the inverted pyramid of sustainability (TIPS)

We submit that TIPS (Figure 28.2) helps us better understand the cultural approach of being a consumer citizen. Using a cultural approach it becomes possible to take the best practices of sustainability from all the different cultures around the world and develop them as a best practice toolkit.

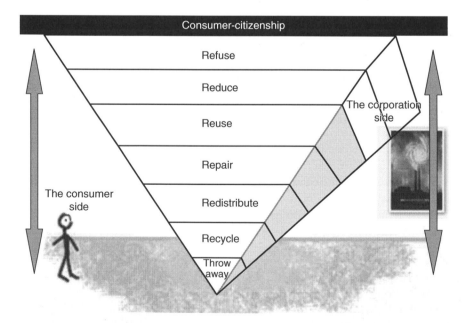

Figure 28.2 The Inverted Pyramid of Sustainability.

(Cultural) strategies related to each stage of TIPS

Imagine you are looking at an upside-down pyramid which is balancing somehow on its apex; it appears to be an optical illusion and you expect it to fall over. How can this be? Is something holding it in place? Perhaps you do not initially recognize what it is. Upon reflection you note that the upside-down pyramid is actually firmly attached to something at its base which holds it in place. This is how we visualize TIPS. TIPS places certain behaviors above others, thus creating a *hierarchy of behaviors*. This ultimately leads to a preferred state of consumer-citizenship. This explanation differs from the traditional 3 R's triangle in that the three original behaviors – *reduce, reuse, recycle* – were *equally* valued even though the impact of each on the environment was very different. TIPS is galvanized by the notion of consumer-citizenship, which we argue is a re-awakening of our civic-mindedness. While some authors have talked about citizen-consumers (Trentmann 2007; Jubas 2007), we actually feel a better descriptor for the present day is consumer-citizens. This is because the seduction of being a consumer seems to have taken precedence in recent times. Addressing the cultural role of the consumer-citizen in their distribution strategy organizations can better manage their relationship with the end user. Please note we argue consuming in itself is not a bad thing; it is a necessary and often enjoyable part of the human condition, but it is *what* and *how* we consume, and also how we dispose of our goods once we no longer want them, that are important. In other words, how people perform and balance their roles of consumer-citizenship in the area of disposition is a neglected focus of the supply chain.

Continuing with our illustration, if we were to do nothing but stare at the pyramid, ignore warnings, and continue throwing away objects, consumer goods, and industrial residue, then the pyramid would, if left alone, fall on one side. It might even cause us harm. Instead, if consumers and corporations would change perspective (here we acknowledge there are more institutions in society or, as we would argue, sides to the pyramid, but for purposes of this chapter we limit it to two sides), move up a gear, wake up to the realities of global climate change, in how they change their activities and lifestyles, then we can argue meaningful change is possible. In such a scenario people and organizations progress from levels *recycle, redistribute, repair, reuse* and *reduce*, to *refuse*, where they proactively begin to perform their roles as consumer-citizens within civic society. Each of the levels may also interact and cross-over; so, for example, one could redistribute a piece of clothing to a friend, who may wear it for a number of months, and who then recycles it by passing it on to a local charity retailer. At this stage the inverted pyramid has a better overall cohesiveness, glue or "stickiness" – it sticks to the performance of consumer-citizenship and is much less likely to topple, ecologically speaking.

Applying cultural perspectives to environmental problems allows marketers to view the entire marketing system as a reflection of cultural values and not "fixed" or "immobile" as previously conceived. Re-conceiving distribution strategy to include more cultural principles will do much to move our thinking away from a system fraught with waste to one that serves consumers and the environment equally.

TIPS reflects this shift toward a more cultural perspective by emphasizing the global nature of consumption and how hyperconsumption is reflective of certain societies and is being quickly exported toward those societies currently engaging in more sustainable practices. Also, consumers and entrepreneurs are innovating within the sustainable distribution space at a disproportionate pace as large, multinational companies.

Refuse

Sustainable consumers rethink the very role of consumption in their everyday lives and are very mindful of their civic and ecological responsibilities. They begin the process of acquisition by first entertaining the notion that they may be able to do without the product in the first place. There have been numerous examples of consumers opting out of the market for many decades now, with voluntary simplifiers being the most oft cited example. In recent years there have also been illustrations of everyday consumers deciding to opt out of the market in various guises. *Buy Nothing Day*, originally established in Canada and the US, and held annualy in November, is one such example, where consumers voice their unhappiness with a consumerist culture, on a typically busy shopping day. What started off as a small movement has now turned into what the organizers call "a global holiday from consumerism," and is held in 65 countries; 2012 will be the twenty-first year of the event. Another illustration is the group *The Compact*, based in San Francisco and set up by a marketing executive and eight of his friends. This group decided to buy nothing other than essentials such as food, medicines and toiletries for a year. All other purchases had to be borrowed, bartered or second-hand goods. Judith Levine also decided to buy nothing but essential items for a year and documents her story in her 2004 book *Not Buying It: My Year Without Shopping*. British supermarkets were severely criticized for importing air-freighted 'organic' produce (Tibbetts 2007) and in the same year Claire and Holden (2007) recommended that citizens take the radical step of not shopping in supermarkets but using local farmer markets instead.

Refusing to consume within hyperconsuming societies reflects a shift in values that could be exported much like the multinational brands that have previously come from these same societies. This shift in values could short-circuit the alarming trend in developing nations to abandon frugality in favor of hyperconsumption.

Reduce

Consumers are also beginning to question the amount of goods that they purchase and are attempting to do more with less. Reducing the amount of goods purchased is part of the current recycling triangle, yet in our pyramid it is placed above other options as part of a hierarchal process that values certain behaviors over others. As recently as summer 2008, consumers responded to rising fuel costs by attempting to drive less, while others switched to greener transportation alternatives such as biking or taking public transportation. Easy-to-use calculators on the internet have emerged that allow consumers to calculate their "carbon footprint." These calculators often provide strategies for reducing this ecological imprint by presenting consumers with options on how to reduce their overall consumption.[1] Some consumers have also opted to fly less frequently and/or have a holiday in their home country rather than fly overseas. Termed "staycations," holidaying at home has become a fashionable thing to do. Other examples of consumers reducing their purchases have focused on the recognition that items do not necessarily need to be replaced as often as they have been. This applies to many consumer items, from new cars to new electrical goods, and to new versions of computer software. Consumers are suddenly asking themselves, "Do I *really* need to upgrade my car every three years?", or "Do I need the latest Microsoft software?" for instance.

As with the *refuse* illustration above, while we would not expect corporations to encourage consumers to reduce their consumption, we do in fact see examples of companies doing just this by reconciling the firm's and consumers' interests. The *Power of One*[2] campaign in Ireland, for instance, runs in conjunction with energy suppliers and encourages consumers to reduce their energy bills by engaging in various environmental initiatives. In the UK, food companies are also supporting the government-led *LoveFoodHateWaste*[3] campaign which encourages and also advises consumers on the means to avoiding throwing away food they have purchased, with the organization estimating that a third of all food bought in the UK is thrown away. Providing advice on how to reduce this can have a significant impact on landfill sizes. Companies such as Marks and Spencer are also setting targets to reduce the amount of food waste occurring at its stores and distribution centers. The company also had a *No to Bags* scheme where it aimed to reduce the use of plastic carrier bags in its store by 33 percent in 2010.

Reducing consumption also reflects a cultural shift away from materialism and conspicuous consumption. Distribution channels should embrace this shift by presenting "better" options on the shelves, not merely "more" options.

Reuse

Another very popular trend that is borne largely from consumer innovation is the option to reuse goods in ways for which the product was not originally intended. Consumers are finding many unique ways to reuse products so that they may avoid putting these otherwise worthless products into the waste stream and also so they can enact the previous tactic of reduction of overall waste. Consumers are making innovative and creative choices to reuse goods that would normally be considered "convenience" or "one-use" goods. Things such as plastic carrier bags that would normally be thrown away after being used or soiled are washed out and used again. Aluminum foil that may be used once and then recycled is cleaned and put away for future use. Children can be particularly good at reuse – making plastic containers homes for playing cards, or cutting up cereal boxes to be used as box files in an office, for example.

Reusing reflects the "one man's trash is another man's treasure" adage very well. In one study, participants built an entire greenhouse from reclaimed "trash" by fabricating a heating element out of old 2-liter plastic bottles, fashioning a door from an old shower door and constructing the walls and roof from reclaimed materials. This greenhouse was then used to grow produce for self-consumption and community sales. Reclaimers are often ridiculed by their neighbors for challenging the strictly held cultural prescription of buying new.

Recognizing consumer initiatives in this area, companies are also now beginning to encourage the reuse of products. Marks and Spencer's PlanA[4] environmental program, for instance, is developing programs to further reuse and recycle the millions of clothes hangers they use in-store every year. In an effort to both reuse and redistribute products, the company also teamed with Oxfam to launch a *Clothes Exchange* program, where customers who took used Marks and Spencer's items to Oxfam for resale to other consumers received a free £5 Marks and Spencer voucher. As they state on their website "we're doing this because it's what you want us to do," illustrates how companies are engaging in various sustainable practices, including those of distribution, as a direct consequence of consumer actions.

Repair

Repairing broken goods is another strategy that consumers are employing in order to live more sustainable lives. Due to the lower cost of consumer electronics, for example, many consumers are finding it more convenient and cheaper to dispose of broken items than to have them repaired. Most consumer electronics stores have discontinued the repair function by outsourcing it or placing it back in the hands of the manufacturer. Many consumers who wish to repair their consumer good rather than replace it are often spurned by the original retailer, are shuffled off to the manufacturer, or are forced to find a third party who will do the repairs, but points out that buying a new product may actually be cheaper than repairing it. The Twentieth Century Fox children's movie, *Robots*, is a good illustration of the demise of the repair culture that used to prevail. With a tagline, *Repair for Adventure*, the movie, set in the future, shows what happens to a society when repairing skills are lost within that society. This is a phenomenon now being witnessed in many cultures. The loss of the repairman who could fix your washing machine, fridge, dishwasher, TV etc., has been replaced in favor of simply buying a new machine, when the old one no longer works. Designed in obsolescence is the industry term used so that new models of product are seen to be more attractive. With movies such as *Robots*, and consumers now questioning the merits of the throwaway society, we would expect to see a greater and more creative role for repair services in the future.

Repair itself is something that consumers are also taking into their own hands, after being frequently frustrated by the poor market system currently in place. For example, repair and reuse groups get 19 hits on the social networking site Facebook, and repair stories are actively sought out by Facebook users. For instance the *We Hate Dead Gadgets* group celebrates repair stories. The cell (mobile) phone market is a prime example of the "throw it away" culture. Most cell (mobile) phones have very short product lives; the carcasses of old cell phones litter family playrooms, office spaces and, unfortunately, landfills. There are now some formal means of recycling unwanted items for charitable purposes. The *Jack and Jill Children's Foundation*, for example, collects unwanted mobile phones, repairs those that are repairable for redistribution in Third World countries, and recycles those that are not repairable in a responsible manner. Some cell (mobile) phone recycling schemes openly acknowledge the consumer-driven nature of the scheme:

> Recycle your mobile for recycling rewards. Our customers have told us that green issues are important to them, and they're just as important to us, which is why we're always looking for ways to make it easier to be a little greener. Did you know you can recycle mobile phones? Most people have old mobiles lying around the house, so why not get rid of the clutter, put them to good use and recycle them?
>
> (http://www.tescomobilerecycle.com/ accessed 20 Feb. 2009)

Big box retailers could capitalize on this cultural shift toward repairing by offering space within the store to allow consumers to bring their broken items to fix themselves or to drop off for the retailer to fix for a fee.

Redistribute

Second-hand shops and stores also offer the consumer a chance to pass on their items to others (cf. Chapter 26 in this volume). Not only are stores helpful but many people also feel creative enough to set up their own stores and feel they benefit from the autonomy this gives them and the ability to choose what items they wish to sell. As the recession bites in the former Celtic Tiger, second hand stores in Ireland, for example, are all of a sudden chic again and, from a nostalgia point of view, people are discussing how much they used to love these stores and that now there are more than ever.[5] One current global trend has been the "*swishing*" phenomenon, which even had its own prime time television show, *Frock Exchange*, hosted by the former 1960s supermodel, Twiggy, in the UK. As *The Swishing Website* states, "The art of swishing involves getting your friends together to swap gorgeous clothes and party at the same time." On the *Frock Exchange* program, friends were not only swapping clothes, but were also shown how to re-style them with consumers using great creative and innovative skills. Swishing parties have been a great success, with friends who attend emphasizing they are a great way to continue to enjoy shopping without spending money, in an environment very different to the shopping mall. Those who give away clothes that have been sitting in their wardrobe, often unworn, feel great about someone else using something they have no need for, and those who receive new items feel great about consuming without spending money. One report in the UK in 2008 estimated that over 46 percent of the clothes in people's wardrobes remained unworn for over a year, and a significant number of these are items that consumers have never actually worn. The potential for the successful redistribution of goods, in this case, clothing items and accessories which would otherwise remain unworn, is phenomenal.

Companies are beginning to recognize the importance of redistribution with events such as the *Visa Swap* program (Visa 2007) and the combined *Clothes Exchange* program, discussed earlier being good illustrations of companies beginning to get involved in such activities. An interesting development is the potential partnership that customers are afforded in their efforts by many non-profit organizations such as county boards in the USA and local county councils in Ireland. For example, in Ireland, Limerick County Council[6] is promoting redistribution as a more sustainable way of dealing with certain types of household waste – to reduce the amount of waste going to landfill and to help people clear their clutter. In this case reusing is promoted as a step up the waste hierarchy and is a preferred alternative to recycling. Posters ask consumers "Why not check out your local charity shops which sell second-hand goods that might otherwise be thrown away or check out some of the Online Reuse Websites – examples listed below." These websites usually operate on the basis that people can offer or use second-hand goods free of charge. Another example of redistribution is the Waste Matchers (http://www.wastematchers.com) initiative in Cork, Ireland. This free exchange website is a joint venture between Cork County Council's Environmental Awareness and Research Unit, Cork City Council, South Cork Enterprise Board and Macroom E. The scheme allows both the general public and businesses to pass on unwanted items to others.

One industry example of both redistributing and recycling products in an innovative manner is the not-for-profit social enterprise *Green Works* in the UK. The social enterprise redistributes unwanted used office furniture to charitable organizations, schools, and small businesses and also makes new furniture from old thus saving landfills from accruing thousands of items of unwanted office furniture and creating jobs in the process. Again, we would expect to see further illustrations of corporate responses to these issues in future.

Recycle

Recycling is the most common environmentally responsible behavior since initiatives began in the early 1970s. Some countries, such as Scandinavia, have also had recycling schemes in existence for many decades; in others recycling is still a relatively recent phenomenon. In England, for example, around 90 percent of all waste was sent to landfill sites as recently as 2000, in comparison to 59.9 percent in 2008.[7] In the late 1980s and early 1990s, recycling was seen as an environmental savior, but suffered much criticism after this period as news of recycled goods such as newspapers and plastic bottles being sent to landfills in poorer nations emerged. Some environmentalists argued that simply recycling products did not solve environmental problems and more attention ought to be given to issues such as reducing packaging, reusing goods, and our waste culture as a whole. In more recent times, however, recycling has become more sophisticated, and while issues of a throwaway society and poor recycling schemes[8] still exist, there are many recycling initiatives that have received support and praise from environmental organizations. It is now widely accepted that, while we should look to refuse, reduce, reuse, repair, and redistribute goods first, the recycling industry itself is now better organized and more sophisticated than in previous years, and as such provides an outlet for the sustainable innovators in our communities.

Examples of turning unwanted and worn items into new recycled products are abundant. Examples include children's pencil cases from worn tires, cat litter from recovered sawdust, clothing from used carrier bags, purses from recycled juice packs, bottle openers from discarded spoons and dog leads from worn bicycle inner tubes. The list is endless, and also recycled products derive from small one-person businesses to large-scale international projects. Consumers themselves participate by spending more time sorting their waste for recycling and also contribute to the purchase of innovative recycled products and again have been viewed as catalysts for change in this field. Facebook, for example, has over 500 groups devoted to recycling issues.

Recycling is the one area of our pyramid where we see many examples of recycling activity by corporations. In part, this is due to the fact that recycling has simply been on the environmental agenda longer and as a result of various legislative policies. As such, many large-scale organizations have successful recycling initiatives. Dell has free recycling programs for all its computers; the Sharp Electronics Company introduced a free recycling program for all its consumer television, audio, and video products in October 2008, and in 2009 at the International Consumer Electronics Show, Motorola introduced a cell (mobile) phone made from post-consumer polyethylene terephthalate plastic that is also 100 percent recyclable. Organizations as diverse as universities, NGOs, large multinationals, and smaller SMEs, also have more sophisticated recycling schemes in place for the recycling of products as diverse as paper, batteries, organic compostable matter, and printer cartridges. There are numerous examples of companies recycling waste and also using recycled and recyclable materials in their products. While environmentalists still question what happens to all this material, many commentators agree that today's recycling schemes, in their more sophisticated and organized formats, are good environmental initiatives as long as we also consider other sustainable practices.

Throw away

The "throw it away" culture is one that has built up over many decades and is directly related to the consumer society that is so popular in our global culture. As discussed earlier, sometimes we have no choice but to simply throw things away. We all get our garbage routinely collected, and while some consumers copiously sort their waste into composting and recycling piles, things must inevitably be disposed of. However, for the many reasons outlined in this chapter, we are on a global scale continuously questioning this throwaway culture, and slowly making strides in moving toward a more sustainable society.

How much we throw away does indeed vary between countries, and some cultures have more of a waste-prone culture than others, but while the response to waste does vary between cultures, all cultures are recognizing and addressing the problems it presents to us all. In this regard TIPS puts forward consumers as the core innovators who can help respond to our "throw it away" culture and, in particular, co-create distribution strategies that can address this. More cultural perspectives are needed to shift our "throw it away" society to a TIPS-driven society. By adopting TIPS, distributors, like the large retailers, could become part of the solution to global waste instead of perpetually contributing to the problem.

Cultural implications of TIPS

TIPS echoes other work by Dixon (2001) that underscores wastefulness as a consequence and an inherent part of what is called conspicuous consumption, as well as work that highlights the fact that people juggle two forms of existence as humans, one of being a consumer and the other of being a citizen. Conspicuous consumption has been labeled a cultural problem for all developed nations, in so far as developed nations consume most of the world's resources and equally produce most of the world's waste. This global problem requires a global response and this chapter has provided details as to how consumers and corporations, following consumers' lead, can, and have, contributed to solving this problem through various distribution strategies. Jubas (2007) argued that resistance to the normal form of transaction in a free market could be conceived as an act of citizenship. As consumers we "want it all" and as citizens we perform civic "duties of conscience" related acts. Trentmann (2007) emphasizes that hyperconsumption has brought back the "political." Micheletti and Follesdal (2007) call this "political consumerism" within certain societies. What our illustration of TIPS adds to this discussion is how sustainable consumers actually perform their roles as green citizens, challenge the traditional approach to distribution, and demonstrate how meaningful change can be enacted in their everyday lives. We submit that the consumer-citizen actions within TIPS are integral to the success of what Shultz (2007) terms marketing as "constructive engagement" and as a result his definition needs to be developed to reflect a more creative consumer in rethinking distribution governance.

Managerial implications

Environmental sustainability affords every member of the distribution channel a new way of thinking about their role in the consumption process. Instead of viewing themselves as mere distributors, channel members may now view themselves in a real partnership role with consumers. Such partnerships require structural changes to occur. Some new initiatives may be worth considering. For example, channel members might reward consumer participation and innovation in distribution much like the Centre for Sustainable Fashion that London College of Fashion currently does by running the Fashioning the Future Awards. These are the leading international cross-disciplinary platforms for celebrating innovative initiatives toward fashion design for sustainability. Consumers clamor for assistance with the disposal of goods and in fact have innovated greatly in order to facilitate the disposal process, yet, many channel members remain awkwardly silent, insolent, or ignorant to their potential participation in this process. Channel members very often view the product once it leaves their hands as no longer their responsibility and it is this form of distribution which is currently highlighted in key marketing texts. There is great potential for change here.

For example, it could be argued that if channel members were more involved in the disposition process, they would stand to gain more customers in the long run vis-à-vis the goodwill produced by the relationship formed. For instance, Apple is willing to take back all broken laptops for free and will even pay for shipping (http://www.apple.com/environment/recycling/). This program benefits both company and consumer. If this program were extended to include drop-off sites at retail outlets, it would foster even more goodwill as well as reduce the waste involved. Apple, along with dozens of other companies, has teamed with eBay to promote the *Rethink* initiative that focuses attention on the problem of e-waste.[9] In conjunction with industry, governments, and environmental organizations, the aim of the *Rethink* initiative is to bring together the buyers and sellers of eBay to reuse and redistribute electronic goods unwanted by buyers who are upgrading, but possibly wanted by other members of the community. There is also potential to creatively use social media to enable key actors in the distribution process to better engage consumers in the importance of environmental sustainability.

Conclusion

This chapter illustrates the cultural shift with regard to conspicuous consumption has been one that has seen global attention, and which applies to all developed nations, albeit to varying degrees. This cultural shift can be attributed to three separate but related global phenomena: (1) the increasingly widespread acceptance of global environmental degradation; (2) the most recent global recessions; and (3) the recognition by many consumers that consumption does not necessarily make you happy. These three forces combined have seen consumers, often at a grassroots level, respond to these issues in various ways. One global response to a global cultural issue has been in the area of waste and, in particular, distribution. What we have shown in this chapter is how consumers globally have been leading the way in changing, an otherwise accepted mainstay of marketing practice, to incorporate these concerns. While actions and activities vary within and across cultures, we still see how consumers globally respond to a global issue and have provided one concrete illustration, in the form of our TIPS pyramid, of the role consumers are playing in contributing to a change in a mainstay marketing activity, in this case distribution.

Review and discussion questions

1   Consider the current American Marketing Association's definition of marketing and compare it to Shultz's (2007) definition of marketing as "constructive engagement." Which do you feel better explains the consumer actions in The Inverted Pyramid of Sustainability? Why is this? Discuss.

2   Debate the usefulness of the phrase "conspicuous consumption". Is this an historical term or does it apply nowadays?

3   Reflect on how you have been a "consumer" and a "citizen" over the past three months – are these conflicting or complementary roles? Illustrate to the class.

4   Imagine you are to be employed in a new television show called *CSI-Waste*. Try to watch and track what happens to your trash or garbage once it leaves your home – how much do you know about what happens? Do the same for the organization where you work.

5   Go online and search for the different waste exchange and disposal options in your area. Look for ways to legally dispose of: (a) your company's waste; and (b) your personal domestic waste.

6 Consider the phrase "Where's the money in waste?" What entrepreneurial opportunities emerged after reading this chapter?

7 How can "hyperconsuming" nations export the ideas in this chapter to stave off the adoption of this type of consumption ethos in developing nations?

Keywords

consumer initiatives, cultural approaches to distribution, global perspectives, hyper-consumption, materialism, recycling, retailing, sustainable consumption, sustainable distribution

Notes

1 http://www.kedco.com/option,com_carbon/Itemid,663/?gclid = CIHMyZWm6pgCFZSB3godQz
2 http://www.powerofone.ie/index.html
3 http://www.lovefoodhatewaste.com/
4 http://plana.marksandspencer.com/
5 http://www.boards.ie/vbulletin/showthread.php?threadid = 2055488726
6 http://www.limerickrecyclingcentres.ie/PosterOnReuseWebsites1.pdf
7 http://www.guardian.co.uk/environment/2009/feb/26/recycling-waste-environment
8 http://www.guardian.co.uk/environment/2009/feb/26/recycling-waste-environment
9 http://pages.ebay.com/rethink/index.html

References

Arnould, E. (2003) "'Good to the Last Drop'™: Perspectives on Thrift and Frugality," in D. Turley and S. Brown (eds), *European Advances in Consumer Research*, 6, Valdosta, GA: Association for Consumer Research, pp. 321–4.

Claire, H. and Holden, C. (eds) (2007) *The Challenge of Teaching Controversial Issues*, Stoke-on-Trent: Trentham Books.

de Coverly, E, McDonagh, P., O'Malley, L. and Patterson, M. (2008) "Hidden Mountain: The Social Avoidance of Waste," *Journal of Macromarketing*, 28(3): 289–303.

Dixon, D. F. (2001) "Conspicuous Consumption versus the Protestant Ethic: The View from Pepys's Diary," *Journal of Macromarketing*, 21(2): 146–55.

Dowlatshahi, S. (2000) "Developing a Theory of Reverse Logistics", *Interfaces* 30(3): 143–55.

Hicks, D. (2007) "Education for Sustainability: How Should We Deal with Climate Change?" in H. Claire and C. Holden (eds), *The Challenge of Teaching Controversial Issues*, Stoke-on-Trent: Trentham Books.

Jubas, K. (2007) "Conceptual Con/fusion in Democratic Societies: Understandings and Limitations of Consumer-Citizenship", *Journal of Consumer Culture* 7: 231–54.

Kerin, R. A., Berkowitz, S. W., Hartley, E. N. and Rudelius, W. (2006) *Marketing*, 8th edn, New York: McGraw-Hill.

Micheletti, M. and Follesdal, A. (2007) "Shopping for Human Rights," *Journal of Consumer Policy*, 30: 167–75.

Rogers, D., and Tibben-Lembke, R. (1999) "Reverse Logistics: Strategies and Techniques," *Logistique & Management*, 7(2): 15–26.

Shultz, C. J. (2007) "Marketing as Constructive Engagement," *Journal of Public Policy & Marketing*, 26(2): 293–301.

Tibben-Lembke, R. (1998) "The Impact of Reverse Logistics on Total Cost of Ownership," *Journal of Marketing Theory and Practice*, 6(4): 51–60.

Tibbetts, G. (2007) "Food Miles: Organic Food's Air Miles Are Catastrophic," *The Telegraph*, 17 July (accessed 12 Feb. 2010).

Trentmann, F. (2007) "Citizenship and Consumption," *Journal of Consumer Culture* 7: 147–58.

UNEP/Sustainability (2008) *Unchaining Value: Innovative Approaches to Sustainable Supply*. New York: UN.

Vermeulen, W. J. V. and Seuring, S. (2009) "Sustainability Through the Market: The Impacts of Sustainable Supply Chain Management: Introduction," *Sustainable Development*, 17: 269–73.

Visa (2007) "Visa UK Announces Visa Swap in Association with TRAID", London, 23 March. Available at: http://www.visaeurope.com/pressandmedia/newsreleases/press286_pressreleases.jsp (accessed 19 Feb. 2009).

29 Institutionalization of the sustainable market

A case study of fair trade in France

Nil Toulouse

Overview

Traditionally, companies are encouraged to commit to sustainable development solely because it can be of benefit to the company, because a segment of consumers views sustainability as important. This demand should thus be catered to. However, the market is judged to be really attractive where a company sees itself as competitive in that market with regard to its customers, suppliers, competitors, potential entrants and substitute products. This chapter proposes to address the sustainable market from a neo-institutional perspective and encourages managers to get involved in the sustainable market, not for reasons of profitability but because there are institutional restrictions to be met. Any company seeking social legitimacy must respect the value and belief systems and social standards in force.

Defining the sustainable market

The market is traditionally defined in economics as the interaction between demand and supply. Marketing refines this definition via two perspectives: that of demanding (by consumers) and that of offering a product/service (by companies). The sustainable market is thus usually studied through the dyadic relationship between (1) consumers and (2) companies.

Within the traditional *consumer perspective* (1), a market is defined as all consumers who have in the past bought the given product/service. The *sustainable market* is then seen as composed of segments that should be better known and whose needs should be better met. Initially, traditional marketing aimed to assess the degree of people's social responsibility. Some authors describe the profile of the consumer adopting purchasing behavior consistent with the conservation of ecosystems as a younger person with a high level of education, higher socio-economic and occupational status, and a more cosmopolitan and less conservative and dogmatic personality than average. Other authors, such as Roberts, define the socially responsible consumer as someone "who purchases products and services which he or she perceives to have a positive (or a less negative) impact on the environment and uses his/her purchasing power to express current social concerns" (1995: 98). Subsequently, demand is viewed as the expression of an attitude measured by the willingness to buy ethical products. Based on decisional models such as the "theory of reasoned action" or the "theory of planned behavior", the consumer engages in sustainable consumption because s/he has a positive attitude toward the products or companies that s/he views as environmentally friendly and socially responsible. Yet this traditional view of demand may be criticized, for several reasons.

First, most writings situate sustainable consumption only in the act of buying. The sphere of consumption goes beyond the actual purchase and includes the whole consumption cycle (production, acquisition, consumption and disposal) (cf. Chapter 28 in this volume). Sustainable consumption is a complex phenomenon characterized by a wide diversity of practices. Although studies show that consumers feel strongly involved in their behavior and give it a meaning over and beyond the intrinsic quality of consumption practices, the traditional approach does not deeply question the meaning that consumers assign to sustainable consumption. The second criticism concerns the lack of socio-political and societal contexts in the traditional approach to sustainable consumption. Nowadays the environment is increasingly an issue for consumers. This growing environmental awareness may be explained by the recent health scares (e.g. "mad cow disease") and the crisis of confidence in relation to industry (the Chernobyl disaster, worries about GMOs, etc.), as well as the impact of opinion-leaders (e.g. Al Gore) and media coverage of political forums (the Kyoto Agreement, Earth Summits, etc.). Alongside this growing environmental awareness, the rise of consumers' social concerns is expressed by the rejection of child labor and sensitivity to employees' working conditions or relocation. The expansion of sustainable development is also associated with manifest deficiencies and shortcomings (social, ecological, etc.) in the present functioning of the globalized economic system. Globalization is thus seen as an accelerating exploitation of resources, the collapse of ecosystems and increased inequality between the global North and South.

According to the company perspective (2), a market is defined as all the interconnected products and services viewed as substitutes by the consumer. The sustainable market is seen as the positioning of the company in terms of products and as a competitive advantage for companies (Kotler and Keller 2006). Ever since consumers have been displaying environmental and social awareness, companies have been obliged to develop a range of green products. From this perspective, companies need to avoid the threats linked to the emergence of criticisms of consumer society, and seize the opportunities offered by new types of consumer, who are aware of the environmental damage caused by human activity and who want to buy products consistent with sustainable development. But before committing themselves to the sustainable market, companies have to evaluate its long-term attraction. According to Porter (1980), there are five forces that act collectively on the appeal of the market. Let us recapitulate these. *The bargaining power of customers* (1) is manifested through the latter's influence on prices and conditions of sale (terms of payment, associated services) and their demand for quality determines the profitability of the market. Customers' degree of concentration gives them a greater or lesser degree of power. Customer power is all the greater when suppliers are numerous and dispersed, when there are alternative sources of supply, and when the transfer cost (the cost that a customer must bear in order to change a supplier) is low and foreseeable. The *bargaining power of suppliers* (2) concerns the ability of suppliers to impose their conditions on a market (in terms of cost or quality). A small number of suppliers, a strong brand and highly differentiated products are all factors that increase the cost of changing suppliers and hence increase their power. A market is less attractive if there are alternatives, whether today or in the near future. *Substitute products* (3) represent an alternative to the offering. These may be different products meeting the same need or products affecting demand (hybrid vehicles / fossil fuel vehicles). *Competitors* (4) strive to increase or simply maintain their market share. Among firms there is a more or less intense balance of power, depending on the attractiveness of the market, its development prospects, the existence of barriers and the intensity of competition (number of companies, size and diversity of competitors, etc.). If barriers to entry are low, the market is less attractive.

The *threat of new entrants* (5) is offset by the existence of barriers to the placement of initial investments and the time needed to obtain returns on them, existing patents, technical norms and standards, protectionist measures, the image of the industry and of already established companies, cultural barriers, etc. All these factors make entry more difficult for new firms. The competitors already in the market generally try to strengthen barriers to entry.

From this perspective the attractiveness of the sustainable market comes down to the fact that the competitive forces are weak, and engaging in sustainable business is an effective way of confronting changes in environmental or technical conditions and a means of adapting to threats and opportunities. Although the five forces were useful in the 1980s, the model is today inadequate for understanding the concepts of competitive advantage and market entry. First, it presupposes a simple market structure, composed solely of consumers, competitors, new entrants and suppliers. However, it is necessary to understand the complexity of the market and the functional, symbolic and social interactions among the various stakeholders. The five forces model has a static view of the market, whereas the market is in fact dynamically structured, under the influence of consumer empowerment and political interactions between actors. The model is based on the idea of competition but does not take into account the imitation that occurs between companies and non-governmental organizations.

Institutionalization of the sustainable market

Cultural research proposes studying the sustainable market through its *institutions* and, by extension, its *institutionalization* – two basic notions for understanding social organizations. Neo-institutional theory explains a market's institutionalization process, focusing on cultural influences on organizational decision-making and market structuring. Although institutions are traditionally viewed as sites where ends and means are defined, enabling actors to determine their interests, the neo-institutional approach recognizes the centrality of the meanings and interpretations that the actors attach to organizational practices. Powell and DiMaggio (1991) thus underline the importance of taking account of actors' intrinsic representations, their motivations, their orientations in action and the contexts in which they operate. Norms and values are not taken as given, but are constructed within the subjectivity of organizational practices.

According to this approach, organizations are influenced by a set of values, norms and organizational models of their structures and management methods (Meyer and Rowan 1977). This perspective views markets as embedded in a social context (Granovetter 1985), interconnected (Powell and DiMaggio 1991) and socially constructed by their environment (Berger and Luckmann 1996). Sustainable market is then studied not as the consequence of the interactions between consumers' demand and companies' supply such as in the traditional perspective, but as the product of a system of values, norms and beliefs that shape the actors' objectives and practices and define the way in which the economic world exists and ought to exist (Meyer and Rowan 1977).

In this globalized world, new actors enter the market and interconnect with consumers and companies. They are bearers of humanitarian values, and social and environmental concerns, and promote sustainable development and the creation of a sustainable market. There are many such stakeholders, of different kinds: civil society, investors, employees and their unions, consumerist movements, etc. Pressure on companies to offer products and operate in a way that respects sustainable development creates both (formal) constraining obligations and (informal) voluntary approaches. These stakeholders help bring into existence institutions such as organizations for monitoring and checking corporate behavior, audit firms, consultancies, non-financial rating agencies, etc. In particular they create sustainable development measurement procedures and instruments. Thus, these actors have significant power to legitimize (Humphreys 2010) symbolic forms such as brand reputation (Holt and Cameron 2010), a resource essential to the survival of the companies.

This chapter relies on the case of fair trade in France to show how a sustainable market is constructed and becomes an institution. The text below begins with an account of the history of fair trade. Here, I will underline the isomorphic effects between the organizations that were instrumental in the institutionalization of fair trade. The chapter will then set out the legitimation strategies used by two major actors on the French market: Artisans du Monde, a historic fair trade association, and Alter Eco, the first private enterprise specializing in fair trade. It will then stress the importance of the notion of transparency and its definition as a means of legitimation for the actors.

Analyzing the institutionalization of fair trade in France

Fair trade is an alternative approach to conventional international commerce. It arose in the United States in the years following the Second World War, with the aim of helping the disadvantaged countries of the global South. From the outset, it strove for greater "solidarity" in trading practices and a partnership dedicated to the sustainable development of excluded or disadvantaged producers. In essence, it is opposed to traditional theories of international trade that extol the use of advantage, whether endogenous or exogenous. Fair trade, by contrast, introduces the idea of the "relative disadvantage" of producers (compared to relative advantage of companies).

Whereas fair trade arose as a vision of trade, the emergence of the concept of sustainable development contributed to its legitimacy and its institutionalization. Sustainable development stresses the need to foster a growth model that does not jeopardize the ability of future generations to meet their needs. Like fair trade, it is based on three foundations: social equity, the environment and the economy. Fair trade is an interesting example for the realization of a sustainable market, since it involves the sustainable and rational use of resources to meet current needs as well as the capacity of future generations to benefit from local wealth (Box 29.1).

Timeline of the institutionalization of fair trade

The first phase, running from the 1950s to the early 1970s, involved experimentation with new ideas by NGOs. These organizations had realized the ineffectiveness of the conventional international trade system in terms of the development needs of the producers of the South. These organizations included religious communities and political groups concerned about Third World poverty, as well as producers wanting to control their own destiny. It was a matter of dispersed development of practices marked by a strong parochial commitment, based on principles of aid and international charity (Nicholls and Opal 2005). The first projects were tried out by people most often organizing locally in the form of local networks, associations and cooperatives. This first phase involved developing prototype forms of trade, the success of which then encouraged institutionalization. These prototypes were gradually improved over the course of their implementation.

Box 29.1. Reloaded 4Ps of fair trade

Products: The sale of fair trade products today is mostly centered around some 20 food products – particularly coffee and tea – and craft products. The product concepts are defined by the producers and validated by the central buying offices, which ensure the existence of outlets in Western markets. Producers may receive help in terms of the design of the products. Regular feedback is arranged to identify any quality problems. Production methods respect the workers' health and the concept of a sustainable environment. The main labeling organization, Max Havelaar, plays no part in designing the products, but puts the producers of the South in contact with intermediaries or retailers from the North. The narrowness of the product range offered compared to that of the sector as a whole is offset by two factors: on the one hand, its ethical character; and, on the other, the history of the product presented on the packaging (along with the origin of the product).

Place: Supermarkets can be considered as "non-places" (Augé 1992), whereas alternative networks selling fair trade products are "anthropological places". Three opposing features distinguish "non-places" from "anthropological places", and therefore supermarkets from specialist fair trade shops. Specialist shops like Artisans du Monde (cf. later in this chapter) are *identity places* whereas supermarkets are less so or not at all. It is above all a matter of strong social identity: consumers who frequent these shops see themselves as actors in the process of balancing international trade. Next, they are *relational places,* since they are also sources of information (more so than standard retail outlets). Each sale is accompanied by information on the origin of the product, production techniques and conditions, the producers, etc. Thus the relationship created between the seller and the buyer also creates a relationship between the producer and the consumer. In contrast, in supermarkets, shopping is largely transactional rather than relational. Finally, they are *historical places*, on the one hand because going there is more the expression of "a wish to act together" than a simple wish to satisfy particular needs; and on the other because they are places where the story of products and of the producers' lives is recounted.

Fair trade specialist shops are places where purchasing or simply browsing become experiences in themselves. They combine market and non-market elements, products and leaflets or petitions. Consumers and sales staff – very often volunteers – frequently discuss and share their experiences; a social link is established. The regular organizing of fair trade tastings in these shops is also a way of creating a social link between consumers, based on solidarity with the countries of the South. These shops are as much information points as they are sales outlets. Every sale is accompanied by documentation on the producers or growers of the product, its country of origin, etc. There are also photographs of the producers, accounts of the history of the products, and so forth. Thus, specialty shops want to work for "decommodification", paradoxically even in the context of a selling situation. Consequently, it is not merchandise that is sold but products, that is to say, goods with a story to tell.

Pricing: Fair trade seeks to correct an economic system the functioning of which does not secure decent living conditions for a large number of producers, since the market sets prices largely on the basis of the interaction of supply and demand. In the classical view, the equity of the price is linked to its effectiveness: it should not lead to discrimination among contracting parties, so that the risks run are equivalent and the continuity of transactions is ensured. As has already been pointed out in Chapter 20 in this volume on value and price, pricing in fair trade is not solely based on costs. Fair trade prices are discussed between producers and NGOs to ensure a margin giving producers a decent standard of living and the opportunity to improve their working and living conditions as well as allowing the environment to be conserved. Fair pricing is seen as necessary to allow the most disadvantaged fringe of the population to benefit from actions that restore social justice. Social value is obtained through a transparent definition of the price between actors, in a sustainable trading relationship characterized by advance payment and the certainty of fixed prices.

Promotion: Communication on fair trade is centered on a discourse combining alter-globalization, the strengthening of international solidarity, criticism of marketing and social marketing. Advertising costs are kept low to cover the additional price paid to producers. The product and the producer are the main vehicles for the promotion of fair trade. These underline the need to make the connection with production, since the product promoted comes from an alternative system of exchange that reduces the social distance between the consumer and the producer. For example, the Max Havelaar label has long been represented by a drawing of a mustachioed farmer carrying a bag of coffee on his back. This logo has often been accompanied by slogans such as "a great coffee, a great cause", "great coffee from small producers", etc. Drawing a parallel between "coffee" and "cause" links physical and personal pleasure to the collective and moral issue.

The packaging and the information it gives offer, at a first level of interpretation, arguments centered around pleasure – an original, high-quality, certified organic product – and, at a second level, lead the consumer to think about the implications of his or her purchase for the producer. It is thus possible to speak of an axiological register that orients the product toward consumer commitment.

In the second, limited market phase (early 1970s to late 1980s), reserved for an activist clientele frequenting specialist stores (World Shops such as Artisans du Monde in France or Oxfam in UK, etc.), fair trade remained extremely marginal. Alternative trade gradually established itself in the sphere of international solidarity and developed through small-scale networks bringing together people who had similar concerns and outlooks, but it also began penetrating networks of a very different order and involving people of varied outlooks, which encouraged the spread of new ideas. People's decisions are explained by their social ties. And the weaker these ties – where people joined large heterogeneous networks – the more effective were the results (Granovetter 1973). It was here that the beginning of the professionalization of alternative exchange through the empowering of small producers (in the South), freed from the power of local middlemen and international buyers, was observed. This was reflected in the North by the progressive organization of integrated marketing channels.

The third phase covers the period from 1988 to 1999. At the end of the 1980s, the Max Havelaar label (called also Transfair in some countries) was created, in order to allow the sale of fair trade products in large stores that did not specialize in this form of trade. The creation of the Max Havelaar label led to new communication channels becoming involved and playing a major role in terms of dissemination and the emergence of new actors, such as Alter Eco in France. In this phase the major actors were governments, international institutions and conventional businesses. Fair trade became topical in the media and attracted young, business school-graduate entrepreneurs. Via lobbying, and through opinion-leaders, community groups and the media, fair trade gradually reached new segments of the population well beyond the activists of its early days. The visibility of Max Havelaar and the support of public authorities that participated in the promotion of fair trade also contributed to a favorable socio-cultural and political climate. From then on, fair trade became normalized, adopting increasingly strict and controlled regulation standards.

The fourth phase of the spread of fair trade – from the late 1990s onwards – was marked by the entry of new actors into the sector as well as by the emergence of new opinion leaders. Fair trade is gradually becoming attractive to actors who had previously rejected it. Its organization into more conventional, certified channels, which has extended the market by involving mass retail, has resulted for the first time in tensions emerging among actors, while at the same time sharply altering the sector's institutional configuration. The actors concerned have gradually accepted the principle of written texts formalizing the definition of fair trade to specify exactly what it means. Within this perspective, one definition in particular has been generally accepted, that of FINE, an informal association of the four main fair trade networks:[1]

> Fair trade is a trading partnership, based on dialogue, transparency and respect, that seeks greater equity in international trade. It contributes to sustainable development by offering better trading conditions to, and securing the rights of, marginalized producers and workers – especially in the South. Fair trade organizations, backed by consumers, are engaged actively in supporting producers, raising awareness and campaigning for changes in the rules and practice of conventional international trade.

The various existing fair trade organizations exert pressure on international, European and national institutions to change the rules of international trade. In France, they have tried to establish a common standard. An initial French project failed in 2005 due to strong disagreement between representatives of the retail sector and fair trade associations and businesses. This setback underscores the existence of two views of the future of fair trade in France: the first is held by long-established actors who wish to maintain the founding principles of fair trade, the second by government and business representatives who want to regulate and control fair trade channels through a standardization process, even if this means settling for less. The problem lies in the clash of ideals held up by these two categories of actors. The idea of standardization, however, generates resistance from activists. Some believe that the standardization process goes against the very principles of fair trade, and tends towards a uniformization of trading practices. Others fear that government standards impose less stringent criteria than the existing guarantee systems. In view of the possible confusion of roles, there is bound to be mistrust on the part of the "historical" fair trade advocates toward government officials.

According to neo-institutional theory, it is possible to analyze the fair trade market not only as the meeting place of supply and demand but as a space where institutionalized myths (seen as self-evident) regardless of their impact, meet. When institutional myths and beliefs emerge in already existing fields, existing organizations change to become isomorphic with those new myths and beliefs. Three mechanisms are then used by organizations (DiMaggio and Powell 1983): (1) *coercive isomorphism* results from formal pressures (governments, international agreements, etc.) and informal pressures (civil society, consumer expectations, criticism by NGOs); (2) *mimetic isomorphism* occurs when an organization finds itself in a situation of uncertainty or limited rationality. The organization begins imitating those organizations that seem to be most successful and on which they model themselves; (3) *normative isomorphism* draws on recruitment, professionalism and training, which generate a knowledge base and a set of shared norms and expectations. It concerns professional standards. These three types of isomorphism emphasize the need to study organizations in their cultural and social context. They can be observed in the history of fair trade as a social construct.

The beginnings of fair trade were marked by *coercive isomorphism*, chiefly originating from informal pressure. By offering an exchange initially referred to as 'charitable' and then as 'alternative', fair trade organizations sought to put pressure on multinationals whose trade practices were criticized. The aim was to change behaviors and to regulate the actions of actors who did not share the same values. This informal pressure gradually transformed, with the arrival of new actors on the market, into a more formal pressure, via the adoption of a shared definition by fair trade organizations internationally (cf. FINE) and of a specific law to that end in France. This law sets out the establishment of a National Fair Trade Commission, responsible for ensuring that the people and agencies who enforce exchanges of goods and services within fair trade are recognized. This formalization therefore applies pressure to conventional companies, in favor of more 'historic' actors (Artisans du Monde, Max Havelaar, etc.). Thus, contrary to what is happening in the organic agriculture sector in France, fair trade is less about the products and more about getting the organizations involved to commit to fair trade as a principle.

Mimetic isomorphism appeared shortly afterwards. The spread of fair trade occurs only through the gradual legitimation of its ideas. In this regard, it was perceived as legitimate by private firms (Suchman 1995) only when its financial viability was demonstrated. Here we find the minimum criterion of necessary economic responsibility for a private economic actor to engage in socially responsible action (Carroll 1995). A process of "regressive" institutionalization may be observed, with alternative behavior, through its gradual acceptance by conventional actors and public opinion, becoming a standard. It should be noted, however, that there is a race to define this standard according to the beliefs of each category of actor. We can therefore observe the development of labels and certification methods. Thus the institutionalization process is also in a way a process of reappropriation by the sector's most powerful actors. Alter's conclusions regarding the analysis of the innovation process in companies can be extended to the spread of fair trade. "At the end of the process ... conscious of the economic advantages of deviance, they [company managements] adopt a rule that was previously a question of transgressing of rules" (2004: 73). The issue for the various actors is one of controlling the legitimacy of the shared representations and the beliefs of the fair trade partners of the North and South.

Finally, because conventional companies are acquiring progressively greater influence in fair trade, the historic actors of fair trade such as NGOs are learning how conventional companies do things. In this phase, which is akin to normative isomorphism, professionalization plays a major role. Thus, fair trade NGOs strive for greater operationality and efficiency in order to be better able to handle the increased number and technicality of their tasks. They work on coordinating their activities and their "voluntary labor". Furthermore, the recruitment procedures for voluntary workers are diversifying above and beyond cooptation and mutual acquaintance (Ozcaglar-Toulouse *et al.* 2010). For example, voluntary workers are taken on via "job interviews" in order to identify which skills and know-how they have. Training programs for voluntary staff are becoming more and more numerous. Predominant marketing norms are adopted. For example, Artisans du Monde recently changed all its packaging designs and applied a standardized visual style to all its shops. Thus, the aim of fair trade NGOs in making their organization, their operation and their staff more professional is to become more competitive; in so doing, they come closer to embodying the structure of conventional companies, even if it costs them some of their specificity.

From this analysis it seems possible to contrast legitimacy linked to the competitive advantage of fair trade, based on the search for efficiency, against institutional legitimacy, which reflects a desire for recognition by society.

Legitimacy of fair trade organizations

Organizations are social structures composed of cultural-cognitive, normative and regulative elements that give stability and meaning to social life (Humphreys 2010; Scott 1995). They rely on these elements to manage the conformity of their behavior and to gain or maintain their legitimacy. Suchman defines "legitimacy [as] a generalized perception or assumption that the actions of an entity are desirable, proper, or appropriate within some socially constructed system of norms, values, beliefs and definitions" (1995: 574). He distinguishes three forms of legitimacy:

- *Pragmatic legitimacy*: the organization satisfies the interests of its partners. Here we must take account of the coercive role taken by shareholders, markets and customers, which sanction the organization if it does not conform to institutionalized behavior. There are three sources of pragmatic legitimacy: exchange with auditors in order to obtain their adherence to the organizational behavior; influencing the auditors in order to have their support with the strategy; and obtaining a favorable attitude from the auditors by engaging in behavior promoting their interests.
- *Moral legitimacy*: the organization focuses on social welfare rather than on satisfying its partners. There are four sources of moral legitimacy: consequences of what the organization has managed to achieve; procedures socially admitted and accepted by the organization; structure of the organization; and finally the personality, i.e. the charisma of the leaders of the organization.
- *Cognitive legitimacy*: the organization adopts practices that are understood and accepted. Here, organizations adopt behavior that conforms to the expectations of their market environment in order to enhance their reputation. There is one single source of this legitimacy: this is legitimacy "taken for granted".

To illustrate the various strategies for legitimation, two cases are discussed in this chapter: Artisans du Monde and Alter Eco.

Artisans du Monde was founded in 1981 as an association within the Third World movement. One of the fair trade pioneers in France, Artisans du Monde rapidly opened shops where all products originated from fair trade while maintaining a profoundly educational approach to the subject. Three issues lie at the heart of their vision: selling products, educating people about fair trade and running public opinion campaigns/advocacy. They distribute their products via their 170 shops and are the largest network of specialist fair trade shops in France. They are furthermore open about their wish to avoid distributing their products in supermarkets and hypermarkets, which they see as opposed to the vision and values of fair trade. The resources of their shops are, additionally, used solely for fair trade projects. In order to acquire a more professional image, Artisans du Monde also began to apply marketing techniques, including for its packaging, by adopting a logo and a thematic color. The aim of this is to secure recognition for the difference and the added value represented by fair trade and to remain focused on sustainability, where ethics are the most important consideration, but also to give it a more professional image. Artisans du Monde owes its continued existence to its voluntary staff in particular. This approach is moreover fundamental, and makes it possible to set them apart from the other approaches on the market.

Founded by a charismatic leader, Tristan Lecomte, in 1998, Alter Eco is among the recent companies that take a pragmatic approach to fair trade. However, launching the project was difficult, since the brand had trouble establishing its legitimacy as a player on the fair trade market: investors were cautious and the shop, opened to distribute the brand's products, did not attract the desired clientele, despite major media coverage. In 2002, Alter Eco decided to focus on distributing its products via supermarkets. It finally became profitable and gained real credibility. Given that it is possible for fair trade to become integrated into mainstream consumption, which is furthermore a requirement for its development and its survival, Alter Eco is pursuing two competitive objectives. The former of these is economic: Alter Eco pays 20 percent of the price paid for each product to its producers. The latter is social: the company runs humanitarian projects in producing countries. Alter Eco feels that being able to support small producers is possible only as part of a general approach aimed at profitability. It therefore does not hesitate to use managerial techniques to optimize the way its products are marketed, such as by using the accreditations and labels that act as genuine identifying tools (Max Havelaar among others), and on relying on a multichannel distribution strategy (online store and supermarkets) (Table 29.1).

According to the neo-institutionalist approach, management tools and concepts used in organizations are influenced by their cultural context (DiMaggio and Powell 1983; Powell and DiMaggio 1991). To meet social expectations and to ensure their survival through

Table 29.1 Summary of the sources of legitimacy for two fair trade organizations in France

	Artisans du Monde	*Alter Eco*
Basis of commercial activities	Pragmatic legitimacy based on influence. Each stakeholder (consumers, producers and fair trade shops) assumes their role as an advocate for international solidarity and fairness in international trade.	Pragmatic legitimacy based on exchange. To increase sales, it is necessary to go via traditional sales channels.
Definition of fair trade	Moral legitimacy based on associative structure and its historical position in fair trade	Moral legitimacy based on the charismatic leader of the company
Impact of the organization on fair trade	Cognitive legitimacy based on social and political performance (associative structure making it possible to integrate into other activist networks)	Cognitive legitimacy based on economic performance (corporate structure to enable sales of fair trade products to be increased)

Source: Adapted from Ramonjy (forthcoming).

isomorphism, companies adopt managerial practices that do not always involve actual change but may simply introduce new rituals (Meyer and Rowan 1977). One of the major requirements of fair trade is transparency, to ensure the legitimacy of organizations. All fair trade stakeholders are committed to transparency in the exchange process (information in both directions on working conditions, wages, duration of relationships, prices, margins, projects supported by products, production processes and distribution). This is possible only by making the entire value chain visible through access to complete and audited information. However, the degree of commitment to transparency on the part of the actors of the North (importers, companies, retailers, etc.) is often left to their discretion. Transparency is a source of legitimacy for companies seeking to express their social and environmental commitment, and requires introducing technologies that, after the institutionalization process has been completed, should remain stable, permanent and communicable.

Transparency imposes new terms on competition in the sustainable market. The competition between producers (of the South) and companies (of the North) emphasized by Porter (1980) is not totally taken into account. But in reality, the spread of the labeling principle and the introduction of fair trade into supermarkets has led to two new forms of competition: between producers of the South, to be selected by importers and labelers, since supply generally exceeds demand; and between the labels themselves, to provide products that are as fair as possible. But what guarantees that the information provided is accurate? There are three types of guarantee used in fair trade: product guarantees, organization guarantees, and sector guarantees (PFCE 2008).

Product guarantees are generally the most well known, since they can be seen on the packaging in the form of a logo. It mainly applies to food products. The certification process takes place in two stages. (1) With regard to the production of raw materials, the certification body checks regularly with producers that the specifications are being properly implemented (fair price, pre-financing, compliance with ILO conventions, etc.). (2) With regard to imports, processing and distribution, the certification body ensures that companies buy and sell fair trade-certified materials, which gives them the right to use the logo or warranty system mark on the product. This right to use the logo is generally granted in exchange for a fee.

Organization guarantees apply mainly to historical structures whose core business is fair trade. The repository concerned specifies the organization's commitments and these commitments are compared against its actual practices. Internationally, the organization guarantee is implemented by the WFTO (World Fair Trade Organization), which includes fair trade organizations (FTOs) across all sectors, from production through to distribution. Compliance with the WFTO's specifications confers the right to use the (W)FTO logo.

Sector guarantees ensure that all of a product's stages of production are compliant with fair trade standards.

Artisans du Monde and Alter Eco both use the Max Havelaar labeling organization's standards (product guarantee) to ensure that self-accredited producer organizations are transparent and democratic, that the decision-making process is properly formalized and shared among producer cooperatives, and that the documents needed by certifying bodies for testing purposes are formalized and made available to inspectors. In the North, in order for the labeling process to be possible, Max Havelaar licensees must declare the quantities bought and sold. However, providing information on their organization and sales, and on all corporate practices, remains optional and varies according to the brand. In most cases, transparency becomes a sales argument: detailed information on the producers is provided on the packaging, and is supplemented by further information on websites and at points of sale.

Managerial implications

The example of fair trade, as an experience of a more sustainable market, shows how a utopia is gradually becoming economic reality. Non-profit-making organizations are progressively being imitated by private organizations. Figure 29.1. summarizes the processes currently occurring.

The neo-institutional approach set out in this chapter illustrates how a minority practice can become generalized over time via a phenomenon of interaction between organizations. Some companies may wonder whether it is advisable to enter the sustainable market, above and beyond the issue of satisfying consumer demand.

First of all, the company as an institution is currently experiencing a crisis of legitimacy produced by the ecological, health and financial crises it caused at the beginning of the century. Sustainable development may be the source of a renewed legitimacy. Today, the institutionalization of certain values shared by the parties involved is forcing brands and companies to consider these expectations actively, at the risk of losing their reputation and consumer trust if they fail to do so. Conversely, sustainable development can be a value creator.

Second, understanding the sources of legitimacy can result in different positionings within the market. The example of Artisans du Monde and Alter Eco shows how two major actors on the French market have adopted different positionings.

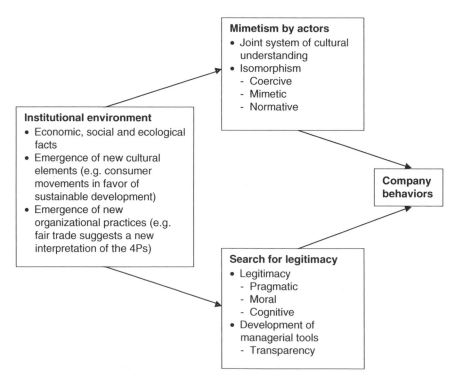

Figure 29.1 Analyzing the sustainable market with regard to its institutionalization.

Review and discussion questions

1. In 2009, Starbucks Coffee Company doubled the amount of the coffee it bought from fair trade sources and became the world's largest buyer of certified fair trade coffee (cf. http://www.starbucks.com/responsibility/learn-more/goals-and-progress/coffee-purchasing). Go to the Starbucks website and identify the sources of legitimation that the company uses.
2. Labels make it possible to evaluate the transparency of a given sustainable approach. (a) List the labels you know from the sustainable development sector. (b) Identify and compare the undertakings guaranteed by these labels and the structures responsible for enforcing those engagements. (c) List the most and least transparent among these engagements. Give reasons for your choice.
3. The market for organic products also contributes to sustainable development. Describe the institutionalization of organic products in your country. Who are the major actors? Which labels are used?
4. The most hardline fair trade activists refuse to integrate fair trade into the mainstream, indicating the lack of "fairness" in mass retail distribution. Find arguments for and against integrating it into mass retail distribution.
5. Read the 4Ps of fair trade. How are they different from the traditional 4Ps?

Keywords

4P, competitive advantage, fair trade, isomorphism, legitimization, mimetism, neo-institutional theory, sustainable development, transparency

References

Alter, N. (2004) "Les composantes d'un processus d'innovation – Croissance et innovation" , *Les Cahiers Français*, 323(Novembre–Décembre): 70–3.

Augé, M. (1992) *Non-lieux*, Paris: Seuil.

Berger, P. L. and Luckmann, T. (1967) *The Social Construction of Reality: A Treatise in the Sociology of Knowledge*, New York: Anchor.

Carroll, A. B. (1995) "Stakeholder Thinking in Three Models of Management Morality: A Perspective with Strategic Implications", in J. Näsi (ed.), *Understanding Stakeholder Thinking*, Gummerus Kirpajaino: Oy.

DiMaggio, P. J. and Powell, W. W. (1983) "The Iron Cage Revisited: Institutional Isomorphism and Collective Rationality In Organizational Fields", *American Sociological Review*, 48: 147–60.

Holt, D. B. and Cameron, D. (2010) *Cultural Strategy: Using Innovative Ideologies To Build Breakthrough Brands*, Oxford: Oxford University Press.

Humphreys, A. (2010) "Semiotic Structure and the Legitimation of Consumption Practices: The Case of Casino Gambling", *Journal of Consumer Research*, 37(October): 490–510.

Granovetter, M.(1973) "The Strength of Weak Ties", *American Journal of Sociology*, 78(6): 1360–80.

—— (1985) "Economic Action and Social Structure: The Problem of Embeddedness", *American Journal of Sociology*, 91: 481–510.

Kotler, P. and Keller, K. L. (2006) *Marketing Management*, New Jersey: Pearson/Prentice-Hall.

Meyer, J. W. and Rowan, B. (1977) "Institutional Organizations: Formal Structure as Myth And Ceremony", *American Journal of Sociology*, 83: 340–63.

Nicholls, A. and Opal, C. (2005) *Fair Trade: Market-Driven Ethical Consumption* London: Sage Publications.

Ozcaglar-Toulouse, N., Béji-Bécheur, A., Gateau M. and Robert-Desmontrond, P. (2010) "Demythicising Fair Trade in France: History of an Ambiguous Construction", *Journal of Business Ethics*, 92(2), 205–16.

PFCE (2008) "Mémento: Etude comparée de différents systèmes de garantie", April. Available at: http://www.commercequitable.org/ressources/les-garanties.html

Porter, M. (1980) *Competitive Strategy*, New York: Free Press.

Powell, W. W. and DiMaggio, P. J. (1991) *The New Institutionalism in Organizational Analysis*, Chicago: The University of Chicago Press.

Ramonjy, D. (Forthcoming) "Dynamiques d'un champ institutionnel et stratégies des organisations: le cas des organisations du commerce équitable en France, PhD thesis, Université Dauphine-Paris.

Roberts, J. A. (1995) "Profiling Levels of Socially Consumer Behavior: A Cluster Analytic Approach and its Implications for Marketing", *Journal of Marketing Theory and Practice*, 3(4): 97–117.

Scott, R. W. (1995) *Institutions and Organizations*, Thousand Oaks, CA: Sage.

Suchman, M. C. (1995) "Managing Legitimacy: Strategic and Institutional Approaches", *Academy of Management Review*, 20(3): 571–610.

30 Catering to consumers or consuming the caterers

A bridge too far …, way too far

Morris B. Holbrook

Overview

This chapter recalls the danger of a military disaster that resulted from pushing too far behind enemy lines and suggests, by analogy, that a comparable catastrophe might result from pushing too far in the adoption of a commercial ethos and the privileging of a customer orientation in the administration of the university in general and of business schools in particular. Extending old concerns expressed by President Dwight D. Eisenhower, the chapter warns of threats posed by an emerging educational-industrial complex. In short, pressures from commercial corporations tend to warp intellectual priorities in the direction of subverting academic values. As gloomily prophesied by Veblen, the university comes to be run like a business and students come to be treated like customers, the pleasing of whom comes to entail the maximization of job opportunities through career-enhancing vocational training in the spirit of a trade-school mentality. This wayward customer orientation can prove disastrous in many areas of endeavor – the judicial system, penitentiaries, medicine, religious institutions, arts organizations, and so forth – but it seems especially ill-advised in the domain of education. All this is illustrated by a case study that pertains to the misadventures of one Professor M.B.H. and that appears to indicate the pitfalls of focusing the academic enterprise on serving the desires of students as customers by the provision of satisfying consumption experiences without adequate attention to issues of whether such experiential marketing leads toward the (co-)creation of a full range of the most desirable types of customer value. After briefly reviewing a conceptual typology of customer value and proposing a new set of "eight E's" – that is, eight key value types – the chapter suggests that running the university according to a business model tends to elevate three of the E's (Entertainment, Exhibitionism, and Efficiency) above the other five (Excellence, Elitism, Esthetics, Ethics, and Ecstasy) with a consequent sacrifice in educational quality (excellence), scholarly integrity (elitism), intellectual honesty (esthetics), social responsibility (ethics), and spiritual enlightenment (ecstasy). This threat to academic values – pursued by school administrators in the name of building bridges between theory and practice – suggests that the university has built "A Bridge Too Far, … Way Too Far."

Introduction: a bridge too far

In his film entitled *A Bridge Too Far* (1977), Sir Richard Attenborough depicts the painful misadventures of a military action called Operation Market Garden. In 1944, after the success of the Normandy Invasion, the Allies attempted to attack the Germans behind enemy lines in Holland. Toward that end, they invaded the Netherlands but failed in this ambitious campaign, with consequences that turned out to be disastrous for the Allied troops. From the failure of Operation Market Garden, I conclude that – whether waging war or undertaking some other mission; whether building bridges, crossing bridges, or destroying bridges – it does not pay to go too far, no matter how confident one might be in the merits of one's own strategic posture. Indeed, by analogy, the contemporary university has pursued what we might call Operation Market Orientation to a degree that I would regard as too far … way too far … and therefore dangerous-bordering-on-disastrous to the academic enterprise.

I like Ike

On leaving office in 1961, President Dwight D. "Ike" Eisenhower – a former military hero during World War II – delivered a justifiably famous speech in which he warned against the dangers of what he called the *military-industrial complex*. Essentially, Eisenhower (1961) worried that industry (weapons manufacturers, munitions dealers, arms distributors) had much to gain economically from the conduct of warfare and that the military establishment existed in part to support and fulfill that economic and political mission. In retrospect, Ike appears rather clairvoyant in anticipating the militaristic extremes to which American foreign policy has devolved during the intervening years.

But beyond cautioning about the dangers of the military-industrial complex, Eisenhower – who, before serving in the US's highest political office, had been the President of Columbia University and who therefore knew something about the administration of academic institutions – warned of another looming debacle via a perceptive prophecy for which he has received less credit. Specifically, like the military-industrial complex, an *educational-industrial complex* also threatens to prove catastrophic to the American value system in general and to the conduct of the university in particular:

> The free university, historically the fountainhead of free ideas and scientific discovery, has experienced a revolution in the conduct of research. Partly because of the huge costs involved, a government contract [or, we might add, a consulting opportunity] becomes virtually a substitute for intellectual curiosity … The prospect of domination of the nation's scholars by … the power of money is ever present … and is gravely to be regarded.
>
> (Eisenhower 1961)

In short, economic pressures increasingly are forcing academics to conduct their inquiries in ways that attract supporting funds from various public and private agencies. As elsewhere, such agencies seek to serve their own self-interests by influencing academic inquiry in ways intended to prove beneficial or lucrative to the sources of funds. Such pressures potentially corrupt the ideals of academic freedom by biasing the priorities that guide scholarly research. This clash with academic values cannot help but damage the intellectual ethos that guides aspirations in the community of scholars (Holbrook 2009).

Prophecy fulfilled

Had Eisenhower lived another fifty years, he would have witnessed the fulfillment of his discouraging prophecy with spectacularly devastating results in the halls of our nation's academic institutions. Here – in ways that have prompted my frequent lamentations in the past (reviewed by Holbrook 2007a, 2009) – I refer to the insidious incursions via which the *business model* provides the basic guidelines according to which an academic institution is administered. With penetrating insight, as long ago as the early part of the last century, Veblen (1918) warned about the dangers inherent in running a university like a business. Veblen believed that intellectual curiosity – rather than monetary gain – should serve as the guiding light for educational achievement. But he realized, all too well, that the self-interested free-enterprise system in general or, in a word, greed tends all too often to take precedence in the American way of doing things so that education – like every other American institution – comes all too easily to be governed by the dictates of commerce. As any number of recent commentators have vociferously pointed out, Veblen's worst nightmares have become an entrenched reality from which there appears to be little hope of escape (*RARA* – meaning "*R*eferences *A*vailable by *R*equest from the *A*uthor").

The customer is king

In a nutshell, the business model – as universally embraced by academic administrators – places a premium on the wisdom of the *marketing orientation* in general or, misunderstanding the meaning of the marketing orientation, on *customer orientation* in particular. Though influentially touted by Drucker (1954), Levitt (1960), and their followers, an over-zealous customer orientation represents a dangerously simplistic way of running *any* enterprise – *especially* in the instances of such endeavors as the judicial system, penitentiaries, hospitals, religions, arts organizations, and other areas where customers may not know what is best for them. As a conspicuously egregious example of consumer centricity pushed to its most unfortunate extremes, the contemporary university has come to think of itself as catering to two major sorts of customers: (1) businesses as prospective clients for consulting services or employers of graduates; and (2) students or their parents as consumers of the educational offering.

Businesses as prospective clients for consulting services or employers of graduates

It has long been true that many college teachers in general and business school professors in particular supplement their otherwise modest incomes by means of extensive consulting activities whereby they sell their industry-relevant knowledge to the highest bidder. To say that such consulting activities distract the faculty member from pursuits governed by intellectual curiosity rather than lucrative marketability would be the understatement of the century. Further, corporate recruiters think of themselves as customers for the services of university graduates as employees. Again, this perspective emphasizes the ascendancy of business interests that come to rule activities in the classroom.

Students or their parents as consumers of the educational offering

Further – as encouraged by the ubiquitous magazine polls conducted by *Business Week, U.S. News & World Report, The Wall Street Journal*, and other industry-oriented publications – students and their parents have come increasingly to think of themselves as *consumers* of the school's offering, with professors viewed as some sort of subordinate education providers. During the college years – encouraged by such university-sanctioned policies as teacher ratings or course evaluations – this adoption of *customer orientation* may manifest itself in an obeisance to the immature student's appreciation for entertainment at the expense of knowledge. Thus, undergraduate teachers had better be funny and charming if they know what's good for them. Later, graduate students abandon their childish ways and focus their customer-oriented mentality on a demand for job-relevant career-enhancing vocation-building tools of the sort that they can use on the jobs that they very much hope to get by virtue of their MBA degrees or other job-related diplomas. In short, catering to the student as a customer evolves over time from a focus on *edutainment* to a preoccupation with what in the old days, as an intentional insult, we used to call the *trade-school mentality*.

Irony abounding

Thus, as a supremely ironic paradox, universities and their business schools have increasingly come to think of themselves as producing *products* intended for sale on the *job market* – namely, graduates in search of lucrative career opportunities as the immanent employees of some future employers – where those employable products are themselves *customers* for the relevant training provided. In this, however paradoxically, students become *both* products *and* consumers at the same time. And so blinded are they by career aspirations and monetary greed that they fail to notice how an embrace of the former status diminishes or dilutes their potential dignity in the latter capacity. Indeed, in my experience, students appear oblivious to the implicitly insulting way in which their embodiment as marketable commodities – at their own insistence – demeans their stature as consumers of education.

Please notice, Dear Readers, that – in focusing on business students – I refer to *you*. In other words, *you* are the *targets* of my comments – but in ways that I fully expect you to find disagreeable or even intolerable. Please feel free to amuse yourselves by carefully analyzing all the many ways in which you disagree with me.

Case study: Professor M.B.H.

Permit me to illustrate the disadvantages of the educational model just described with a brief story that might appeal to those dedicated to the virtues of the case method and that chronicles the somewhat autobiographical adventures of Professor M.B.H.

Early in his career (1977–92), Professor M.B.H. taught the introductory course in marketing strategy, four times a year, with some degree of success. His teaching style was a bit unusual, full of strange metaphors and fanciful stories intended to convey the essence of strategic thinking in marketing. In those days, the marketing-strategy course was optional, and students had a variety of teachers from which to choose. Some instructors used Harvard-inspired cases; others math-and-modeling approaches; still others a textbook such as Kotler. Professor M.B.H. told stories and focused on analogies drawn from ecology, aesthetics, and other seemingly tangential sources of wisdom. Many students had no use for Prof. H.'s methods and took sections taught by other professors. Others – many of them former liberal arts majors – seemed to enjoy Prof. H.'s unusual material, flocked to his section voluntarily, and rewarded his eccentricities with consistently high ratings in the course evaluations.

Eventually, there came a time when a new administration decided that the school's curriculum needed changing. According to the new plan, the school would offer a core curriculum of required courses – marketing strategy among them. Further, to facilitate networking, students would be clustered into groups of about 60 each that would take all ten required core courses together. This clustering system meant, of course, that each cluster would be assigned to a particular instructor about whom they would have no choice whatsoever. From this, it followed that the various faculty members would have to coordinate their offerings to produce identical material in each section. In other words, each core course – including the basic marketing-strategy class – would need to be standardized with the same materials, same lectures, same readings, same problem sets, and same PowerPoint slides used by each instructor. In this, the administration correctly perceived that the school's students – that is, its customers – valued the opportunity to network with their peers far more highly than they cared about any such esoteric concepts as academic freedom in the classroom.

When Professor M.B.H. heard about this plan, he first responded by arguing to the fullest extent of his capabilities that it represented a truly terrible idea. He pointed out that the *standardization* of a product offering or the *mass marketing* of a commodity in hopes that it will appeal to the average customer represents the *single greatest marketing fallacy* that it is possible to commit – that is, the egregious error of assuming that "one size fits all."

With delicious irony, the new curriculum created a required standardized course in marketing strategy that itself embodied the ultimate marketing fallacy. And all this reflected the school's commitment to serving the preferences of students-as-customers who preferred the opportunity to interact with a cluster of fellow networkers (as this cluster wandered from class to class like a herd of dim-witted cows) far more than they cared about any freedom of academic choice (on the part of either students or teachers).

Professor M.B.H. realized that he was not suited – intellectually, temperamentally, or viscerally – to participate in this new core curriculum. Accordingly, he requested and received permission to develop two new elective courses – one on Consumer Behavior, the other on Commercial Communication in the Culture of Consumption – which he taught for ten years (1993–2002) with good results in terms of student ratings and course evaluations, but with only modest class sizes and way too many students from other parts of the university (journalism, law, social sciences, education, and so forth). Due largely to these small enrollments, pressure grew to force Prof. H. to return to teaching the now-required, now-clustered, now-standardized, now-commoditized marketing-strategy core course. He resisted this pressure, of course, often pointing out that he had been the sole individual in the school to campaign vigorously against this required-clustered-standardized-and-commoditized monstrosity. Prof. H. knew full well that his efforts to teach such a course would fail miserably. And he was right.

In 2003, the school's administration forced Professor M.B.H. to teach the core course in marketing strategy. He tried with every ounce of his energy to make his version of this course a good one. But – despite his best efforts, as he had feared – his class received a mediocre set of teacher ratings and course evaluations.

One member of the administration responded by conducting focus groups to ascertain what was wrong with Professor M.B.H. The answer, it appeared, was that Prof. H. still did things a bit differently from other professors in a school where standardization reminiscent of Henry Ford's Model "T" had become the watchword to success. At this point, Prof. H. surmised that the school had cleverly managed to bypass all concerns about the fallacy of mass marketing. Specifically, it had apparently found a way to recruit precisely those students who – in their eagerness to network with their peers and their complete indifference to the merits of academic freedom – actually *want* to take required-clustered-standardized-and-commoditized courses from intellectually hog-tied instructors.

So Professor M.B.H. – with sad reluctance – decided that he had no choice but to standardize his offering even more. He redoubled his efforts and put every ounce of his strength and energy into creating a version of the course that mirrored the sections taught by his colleagues to the greatest extent humanly possible. He worked harder on this venture than he had ever worked on anything in his life. And it appeared to him that most of the students seemed to enjoy his resulting course offering. They spoke to him pleasantly. They smiled at him in the hallways. They called upon him to offer all sorts of extracurricular help on various group projects and personal concerns. So – despite his deep sense of selling out intellectually – Professor M.B.H. felt half-way reconciled to the whole sad academic compromise in which he had been forced to participate.

Then came the course evaluations. To put it mildly, these turned out to be as cruel and insulting as it is possible to imagine, amounting to nothing so much as a heartless form of character assassination. In brief, the students – roughly 180 of them in three sections – had conspired to create a list of six or seven grievances (the party line) that they repeated in virtually every one of their course evaluations (like a lynch mob) en route to compiling what must surely be the lowest average student ratings in the history of the school (down around 1.5 on a 5-point scale).

Blinded by the fact that he had tried so hard to make this an enjoyable class for his student customers and fooled by the dissimulations of class members who had persuasively but misleadingly feigned friendly attitudes toward him, Professor M.B.H. was surprised, shocked, dismayed, heartbroken, and humiliated by this turn of events. He read these course evaluations with a sense of despair unprecedented by anything in his former experience at the university. After this punishment, Prof. H found that he could not sleep at night. And when he did manage to fall asleep, he had terrible nightmares. His first response was a deep sense of inadequacy and shame. Later, he felt that he had been trapped into something of a no-win situation. Eventually, he began to allow himself to feel some degree of anger over the astonishing hypocrisy evinced by a large number of people acting collectively but duplicitously to ruin his life.

After his humiliation in the core course (2004), Prof. H. returned to teaching Consumer Behavior – happily and thankfully, with acceptable results in the course evaluations and teacher ratings (albeit in small classes consisting of only a few MBAs plus "too many" students from other parts of the university). Ultimately, however, he moved as quickly as possible in the direction of retirement (2009).

This being a case example – in the spirit of all good cases – I shall mostly allow you, Dear Readers, to draw your own conclusions from the sad story of Professor M.B.H., which many of you may interpret as an illustration of well-deserved punishment. My main point at the moment is that this is the sort of thing that happens when a school subscribes uncritically to an ill-conceived customer orientation; when it compromises academic values in the service of providing a pleasant or lucrative consumption experience; and, most importantly, when it limits its view of the consumption experience to just a few arguably inadequate aspects of customer value. Facets of the latter issue will concern us in what follows.

Consumption experiences

No one should imagine that the school where Professor M.B.H. teaches and countless others like it have steered their policies toward obeisance to job recruiters, corporate donors, and students as customers by accident or happenstance. Rather, the push toward *customer orientation* in the halls of ivy reflects the conscious and, indeed, the insistent adoption of a desire to please the relevant consumers. Most conspicuously, this mission now manifests itself in a devotion to the objective of maximizing *student satisfaction* with the *consumption experience* attained while pursuing a degree at the relevant institution. For example, the administration at Prof. H.'s school recently circulated an e-mail memo that began:

> Dear [Addressees], ... I want to update you on the progress that we are making to improve [the school's] student experience – a topic that remains top of mind for the administration – and to request your help by providing feedback on ideas that we have generated over the past months.

The message continued by describing "past student satisfaction surveys"; the deployment of a "strategy consulting firm ... to assist us"; and the school's dedication to "identifying customer needs and maximizing customer satisfaction" so as to develop "initiatives that could enhance the overall ... student experience." It concluded with an appeal to participate in "a short, 15- to 20-minute online survey" intended to "help us obtain a clear perspective on which of these initiatives ... will have the greatest positive impact on the student experience": "Once we have analyzed the results of the survey, we will begin implementing the initiatives that have the highest likelihood of improving student satisfaction." Shortly thereafter, this follow-up message arrived:

> A few days ago I requested your help in providing feedback on ... an initiative to improve the student experience ... Our work included a review and analysis of the student satisfaction surveys ... We also enlisted the support of [a] strategy consulting firm ... Together, we developed a comprehensive list of potential initiatives that address...the student experience ... Therefore, we request your participation in a short 20-minute survey by clicking on the link below.

In catering to students-as-customers, with every effort geared toward maximizing their satisfaction with their education-related consumption experiences, Professor M.B.H.'s school and others like it attempt rather transparently to emulate the conventional wisdom espoused by any number of successful businesses that have come to regard *experiential marketing* as their ticket to profits and prosperity. Having participated in a trend toward celebrating the importance of consumption experiences (Hirschman and Holbrook 1982; Holbrook and Hirschman 1982; *RARA*), I cannot help but feel some sense of self-defeating bemusement to note that a viewpoint I once championed has come to be applied in ways that I now regret (Holbrook 2009).

Others had proclaimed the importance of consumption experiences long before we got around to it (Abbott 1955; *RARA*). More recently, the implications of consumption experiences for the practice of experiential marketing have served as the major theme for any number of managerial self-help books (Pine and Gilmore 1999; Schmitt 1999; *RARA*). During the new millennium, I have amused myself by writing book reviews of at least fifteen such entries in the management-guru sweepstakes (Holbrook 2007b, 2007c; *RARA*). Fundamentally, these treatises on experiential marketing share two main characteristics in common. First – with one conspicuous exception (LaSalle and Britton 2002) – they show their authors to be totally oblivious to the intellectual origins of the concepts they espouse, relying instead on a breathlessly excited expression of ideas that are about as new as rediscovering the wheel of retailing. Second – as if by some sort of unintentional postmodern self-parody – they worship the success of experience-oriented firms that have subsequently encountered profound problems in the marketplace – for example, JetBlue, Krispy Kreme, Microsoft, and Starbucks. Indeed, in retrospect, I have come to regard representation in one of these self-help experiential-marketing books as tantamount to the kiss of death.

Multiple aspects of customer value

What all these mainstream best-selling books on customer-oriented experiential marketing, as well as applications of their principles by the bamboozled administrators of academic institutions, share in common is their reliance on a simplistic version of the experiential view that celebrates the importance of "Fantasies, Feelings, and Fun" (Holbrook and Hirschman 1982) or other pleasure-related aspects of "Hedonic Consumption" (Hirschman and Holbrook 1982). Back in the day, we soon came to realize that consumption experiences matter for one and only one reason – namely, their inextricable role as the central element in the creation or co-creation of customer value (Holbrook 1999; *RARA*). Thus, I define customer value as an *interactive relativistic (comparative, personal, situational) preference experience* – meaning that some product has value *only* by virtue of the *services* that it performs in providing some desirable consumption experience(s). In this sense, by the way, all products are services, and there is no reason to invent a terminology that says otherwise.

To elaborate briefly on the conceptualizations provided at greater length elsewhere (ibid.; *RARA*), by "interactive," I mean that customer value always entails a relationship between some object (a product) and some subject (a consumer). By "relativistic," I mean that the nature of customer value is "comparative" (based on a comparison between one product and another); "personal" (differing among individuals); and "situational" (depending on the context in which the evaluation occurs). By "preference," I mean that value reflects an overall evaluation or preference judgment. And by "experience" – as already noted – I mean that value hinges *not* on some tangible good or intangible service but *rather* on the experience that one derives therefrom. Or, as expressed by my favorite economist, Abbott: "The thesis may be stated quite simply. What people really desire are *not products but satisfying experiences*…People want products because they want the *experience-bringing services* they hope the products will render" (1955: 40, emphasis added).

Building on the earlier work that had characterized the relevant consumption experiences as "fantasies, feelings, and fun" (Holbrook and Hirschman 1982) or "hedonic satisfaction" (Hirschman and Holbrook 1982), subsequent analyses developed a broader and more systematic consideration of the relevant types of customer value (Holbrook 1999; *RARA*). Thus, my ultimate Typology of Customer Value recognizes at least eight major types of consumer value in the consumption experience. The problem, put briefly, is that school administrators and other conventional, naïve, or careless disciples of experiential marketing have failed to notice that all types of consumption experiences are fundamental to the (co-)creation of multiple aspects of consumer value in ways that encourage high levels of satisfaction or that inspire elevated degrees of brand loyalty (Holbrook 2006; *RARA*).

The eight key types of customer value

Briefly, the recommended conceptualization focuses on three key distinctions or dimensions that underlie the relevant types of customer value. Specifically, *extrinsic versus intrinsic value* refers to the difference between an object prized for its ability to function as a means to some end (extrinsic value) and an experience valued for its own sake as a self-justifying end in itself (intrinsic value). Meanwhile, *self- versus other-oriented value* refers to the contrast between something prized for my own sake, for how I respond to it, or for the effect it has on me (self-oriented) and something valued for the sake of others, how others responds to it, or the effect it has on them (other-oriented) where the "other" may refer to all levels from the most micro (family, friends) to the most macro (Mother Nature, the Deity). And *active versus reactive value* refers to the distinction between the active manipulation of some physical or mental object in the attainment of value (active) and the process of responding to the object as it acts upon oneself (reactive). Combining these three distinctions into all possible combinations produces the Typology of Customer Value with the relevant names (shown in capital letters) and with various examples (shown parenthetically) in Figure 30.1.

After discussing these various value types for the past three decades, it now occurs to me that a more easily-remembered or reader-friendly mnemonic would result from re-naming the various value categories in a way that uses only words beginning with the letter "E" so that we might replace the original terminology with a new set of names that better capture the full set of experience-based value types by means of their designation as the eight E's (Figure 30.2).

In what follows, by means of examples drawn from what I view as the misapplication of experiential marketing to the case of academic institutions, I shall suggest ways in which an

		Extrinsic	**Intrinsic**
Self-oriented	*Active*	EFFICIENCY (O/I ratio: EVC)	PLAY (Fun)
	Reactive	EXCELLENCE (Quality)	AESTHETICS (Beauty)
Other-oriented	*Active*	STATUS (Impression management)	ETHICS (Justice, virtue, morality)
	Reactive	ESTEEM (Materialism)	SPIRITUALITY (Ecstasy, rapture)

Figure 30.1 Typology of customer value.

		Extrinsic	**Intrinsic**
Self-oriented	*Active*	EFFICIENCY (O/I ratio: EVC)	ENTERTAINMENT (Play, fun)
	Reactive	EXCELLENCE (Quality)	ESTHETICS (Beauty)
Other-oriented	*Active*	EXHIBITIONISM (Status, impression management)	ETHICS (Justice, virtue, morality)
	Reactive	ELITISM (Esteem, materialism)	ECSTASY (Spirituality, rapture)

Figure 30.2 The eight E's of customer value.

excessive preoccupation with only a few types of customer value (Entertainment, Exhibitionism, and Efficiency) has limited the university's focus on other aspects of customer value (Excellence, Elitism, Esthetics, Ethics, and Ecstasy) in ways that have damaged or even destroyed the abilities of schools to sustain their dedication to fostering what was once known as a community of scholars.

The eight E's, misplaced customer orientation, and the death of academic values

Impoverished preoccupations

Let us first consider the three main types of customer value that have preoccupied academic institutions in their eagerness to apply the conceptually shaky but pedagogically persuasive principles of customer-oriented experiential marketing as preached by the aforementioned management gurus. I shall argue that – in each case – the narrow focus of school administrators represents a distortion or abandonment of worthwhile academic values.

Entertainment refers to the active manipulation of a self-oriented experience in a manner that is enjoyed intrinsically for its own sake as an end in itself. Here, we think of play, fun, or other aspects of leisure activities as key examples. In the classroom – especially at the undergraduate level – a key criterion of success involves the degree to which the students are entertained or amused, as reflected in the happiness registered on their teacher-rating forms. Probably, no instructor wants to be dull or dreary on purpose. But the sad fact is that some important course material often entails a certain amount of drudgery – taking derivatives, for example, or learning the Amendments to the Constitution. Hence, I conclude that play or fun in the classroom and the glowing teacher ratings that they inspire should not be equated with pedagogic success.

Exhibitionism refers to the active manipulation of one's own consumption as the extrinsic means to achieving some other-oriented end such as an elevation in status, a favorable impression, or a job offer. By the time students reach their postgraduate years – especially in MBA programs or other professional schools – the focus of customer orientation has shifted from mere entertainment to an emphasis on the role of the school as an engine of career advancement. In essence, newly minted graduates use their academic degrees as a form of exhibitionism, status enhancement, or impression management that – like wearing an Armani suit or carrying a Gucci attaché case to a job interview – elevates their standings on the job market and insures them the most lucrative possible employment opportunities. Such students may understandably come to view the whole academic enterprise as nothing more than an extended job search in which any aspect of the curriculum is valued only for its ability to improve performance in an entry-level position or, more accurately, to secure access to the biggest possible paycheck. Only someone who has suffered through the chore of teaching a class filled with students dedicated to this perspective can fathom how completely such an attitude destroys any hint of intellectual curiosity or scholarly integrity among those few class members who manage to find time to attend class rather than participating in job interviews. The idea that some concept or theory might be worth studying just because it is interesting or of potential relevance to some moment in the distant future has completely died in the MBA classroom. Obsessed with immediate practical relevance – that is, tools of use in the job search – the typical MBA (with only rare exceptions) can think of no more damning condemnation than to opine that a course is "too theoretical." Nowhere has this anti-intellectual attitude taken root more firmly than at the famous Harvard Business

School (HBS), noted for its dedication to the case-study method where this teaching device appears to be prized in part by virtue of its implicit associations with a form of sugar-coated on-the-job training. Yet I know of no self-confession more pitiable than that of a recent HBS grad who wrote an Op-Ed piece for the *New York Times* just after the bursting of the dot.com bubble a few years ago to say that – having taken all of his courses at HBS on topics of direct hands-on real-world tools-of-the-trade relevance to various aspects of e-commerce – he now found himself virtually unemployable and without hope for prospects on the job market (Buchanan 2000). Specifically, at the height of the financial euphoria surrounding the much-ballyhooed dot.com companies, HBS had "overhauled its curriculum to emphasize ... e-commerce entrepreneurship," viewing these curriculum changes as "responding to the demands of its customers," where "The customers are the school's ... students, of course" (ibid.: A33). The unfortunate problem is that, by "listening to these customers," this school's eager-to-please professoriate had prepared its students for jobs that had suddenly vanished. As the deeply disillusioned author concedes:

> The problem is, platitudinous business maxims notwithstanding, the customer isn't always right. The customers – and I include myself here – do not have the perspective to see the big picture, to identify what remains important in the midst of the change occurring in the economy.
>
> (ibid.: A33)

This example spectacularly illustrates the cataclysmic fallacy of pursuing practice at the expense of theory while still ensconced in a graduate-degree program that might otherwise offer some useful conceptual underpinnings before it is too late.

Efficiency refers to the active manipulation of one's own consumption as a means of achieving self-oriented ends such as those measurable by calculating the ratio of one's outputs to inputs (O/I Ratio) or computing the cumulative difference between the two (Economic Value to the Customer or EVC). Most MBA students and those instructors who pander to their sensibilities tend to focus rather obsessively on EVC – that is, the Net Present Value (NPV) of all future cash flows resulting from the opportunity in question (say, future salaries and bonuses less tuition expenses and costs of foregone earnings, all discounted to current dollars). For example, a cover story for *Business Week* by Merritt (2003) asks the probing question, "What's an MBA Really Worth?" But – instead of concerning herself with issues pertaining to the assimilation of knowledge, wisdom, or insights – Merritt gives a dollars-and-cents answer framed in the terms that communicate best with those devoted to maximizing EVC. Thus, *Business Week* has surveyed 1,500 graduates from a large number of MBA programs in the Class of 1992 and reports that these spokespeople are highly satisfied with their graduate degrees:

> Today, members of the class earn an average salary of more than $155,000 ... Add in the $232,400 in average bonus and other compensation ... and compensation for the class last year was $387,600 on average. Compare that to today's average salary for a person with only a college degree – about $43,400 – and the MBA premium comes into focus.
>
> (ibid.: 4, 92)

So – as elsewhere with *Business Week*, other like-minded publications, and professors who espouse similar values – the "focus" of education-related commentary revolves around the dollars-and-cents issues of salaries, bonuses, job offers, career expectations, and other greed-inflected aspects of the consumer-centric university. And why not? How, in our current climate of customer-oriented vocationalism, could it be different?

Missing values

From what I have said, it should be clear that several of the eight E's are conspicuous by their absence from the misguided preoccupations that currently steer universities in general and that shape business education in particular.

Excellence refers to the reactive appreciation of some product or consumption experience as a potential extrinsic means toward achieving a self-oriented end. A clear example appears in the case of Quality – where we admire some product for its capacity to perform well in some desirable function (without necessarily deploying it for that purpose). Once upon a time, the quality of education – that is, the speed of conveying profound knowledge and the sharpness of analytic skills developed in the classroom – assumed the greatest possible importance for faculty and students alike. But nowadays, the quality of the learning experience is the farthest thing from the minds of education providers and their student customers. An instructor cares less about such academic values as truth, honesty, and intellectual integrity than about the sorts of classroom tricks that will win approval in the teacher ratings. Indeed, a popular marketing teacher once confided to me that his secret in leading class discussions of a particularly problematic case was to wait until his students asked "What really happened?" and then to deliver a completely fictitious answer that he had fabricated out of thin air in order to bolster his pat solution. As I argued in a recent diatribe on this and related topics, "Bullshit Happens" (Holbrook 2005b; see also Frankfurt 2005).

Elitism refers to the reactive appreciation of one's own consumption as the potential extrinsic means to produce some response such as Esteem from others (again, without necessarily flaunting this consumption in the manner that would produce this effect). Though the term implies some sort of justifiable pride in one's own estimable possessions or accomplishments, the word "Elitism" carries some of the most negative connotations to be found in the English language. Almost no pejorative epithet carries more vituperative venom than to accuse someone of being elitist. Yet the writer Henry (1994) has argued persuasively in favor of certain benefits of elitism – for example, in those circumstances where rewards reflect the achievement of excellence or the display of unusual merit. I would like to think that certain aspects of education might aspire to sharing in these not-to-be-denigrated aspects of the elitist perspective. Thus, attending a prestigious school, earning a high grade-point average, graduating *summa cum laude*, and/or winning a place in the Phi Beta Kappa or Beta Gamma Sigma Society strike me as accomplishments worthy of esteem from both oneself and others. Yet the current academic regime undermines such traditionally elitist sources of esteem. Grades are withheld from corporate recruiters, who apparently consider them irrelevant. But, in such a situation, the only possible reason to strive for excellence would be the quiet pride of knowing that one performed well academically. And with the prevailing emphasis on success in the job market, why should anybody care about that? The answer, of course, is that few do.

Esthetics refers to the reactive appreciation of one's own self-oriented consumption experience as an intrinsically valued end in itself. The typical example of esthetic value involves the admiration of Beauty in a work of art or perhaps in a scene drawn from nature. Certainly, such experiences have their place in education – as when taking a course on

Baroque music or Renaissance painting. But, in the business or marketing context, another source of esthetic value would lie in the acquisition of knowledge prized purely for its own sake. Thus, even in business, we find aspects of beauty – well-written essays, clever analyses, elegant solutions to otherwise inconsequential problems – that deserve to be admired purely as self-justifying ends in themselves. Yet few MBA candidates would bother to stop and smell the roses in this fashion. No matter how exquisite, such aspects of beauty would be regarded as impractical, useless, or trivial. And such, alas, is the pitiable condition of anti-intellectualism into which the current state of business education has fallen.

Ethics refers to the active manipulation of one's consumption experiences for the intrinsically valued impacts that they have on others – where "others" could imply a more micro-level focus (family, friends) or a more macro-level perspective (society, the planet). Obviously, such ethical aspects (Virtue, Justice, Morality) imply a large set of issues of interest to those concerned with studying the impact of business on society, the role of commerce in the environment, sustainability, ecological aspects of the firm as a dynamic open complex adaptive system, the promise of green marketing, and so forth. Yet – despite the obvious importance of such ethics-related issues – the sad fact is that they fail to interest business educators in general or academic marketing researchers in particular (Wilkie and Moore 2003). Elsewhere, I have suggested that:

> one plausible explanation ... stems from the rise of the customer orientation in academic institutions – whereby marketing professors feel pressured to focus on topics of value to advancing the careers of their students. In such an ethos, ... larger concerns about the role of marketing in society get neglected.
>
> (Holbrook 2005a: 143)

In other words – in this age of obsessing about practical applications (at the expense of theoretical conceptualizations) and career-enhancing job opportunities (at the expense of attention to larger social issues) – what rational professor would devote time or effort to a focus on ethical questions of potential relevance to ecological concerns, long-run sustainability, or macro-marketing solutions that might work toward saving the planet? The answer, I fear, is very few professors and certainly not those with a propensity toward rational self-interest.

Finally, *Ecstasy* refers to the reactive appreciation of consumption experiences valued intrinsically for aspects that involve the disappearance of the self–other dichotomy in ways associated with Spirituality or Rapture. As in a moment of religious exaltation (Unity with God) or esthetic transcendence (one-ness with a work of art), one seems to become part of that which one consumes in ways that produce a loss of Self in the Other. Even though it might be too much to hope that such exalted moments of transcendent rapture would occur routinely in the MBA classroom, it does seem reasonable to wish that occasional aspects of education would lead in the direction of some sort of spiritual fulfillment – as when one attains a worldview that fits one's own paltry contributions into some sort of larger-level scheme with a resulting sense of participation in a kind of Grand Design. Aspects of complexity theory appear to search in that direction – with deeply moving consequences for students thereof – and also to carry profound relevance to the future of business as an evolving system of interconnections with the surrounding ecology (Holbrook 2003). In the aforementioned case study of academic failure, Professor M.B.H. found that a large group of otherwise intelligent MBA students had no interest in such matters. Indeed, on the day when he had scheduled a discussion of complexity theory, they used up large chunks of class time to complete their singularly nasty and hurtful course evaluations in a manner that sabotaged all hope of including a discussion of ecological aspects of the firm as a dynamic open complex adaptive system. Clearly, their behavior did not seem to reflect a spiritual attunement with larger aspects of the universe or any sort of sympathetic vibration with the cosmos.

Conclusion

In public announcements and private pronouncements at the school where Professor M.B.H. once taught, members of the administration frequently proclaim the student-satisfying objective of "building…a culture promoting ideas bridging theory and practice." By this, they mean to advocate research with real-world applications and the presentation of these useful findings in the classroom via teaching anchored in on-the-job managerial relevance. From everything I have said, it should be clear that the construction of such bridges between theory and practice proves pleasing to the students-as-customers who populate the MBA program and wins popularity for the instructors who best display these bridge-building talents and habits.

Yet – from everything I have said – it should also be clear that creating an institutional culture in which theory is valued only if it is linked to practice tends to subvert most or even all of the "missing values" described in the preceding section. In brief, such a customer-oriented culture denigrates the values of Excellence, Elitism, Esthetics, Ethics, and Ecstasy – placing the importance of these below that of Entertainment, Exhibitionism, and Efficiency. In this, such considerations as educational quality (excellence), scholarly integrity (elitism), intellectual honesty (esthetics), social responsibility (ethics), and spiritual enlightenment (ecstasy) – in other words, types of academic values that used to form a bedrock foundation for the community of scholars who once inhabited the university – are subverted in favor of catering to students viewed as customers of the professors who now serve as knowledge providers, subservient to the whims of their predominantly self-interested job-hungry greed-inspired clientele. Thus, the project of building bridges between theory and practice in accord with a business model for how to run an academic institution – which sounds so innocent on the surface – can actually damage the intellectual quality, scholarly integrity, and academic freedom of the university. Progress in that direction has already proceeded far enough. In the metaphor based on warfare that never lurks far below the surface of business discourse (pro-motional campaign, advertising slogan, positioning strategy, competitive attack, marketing firepower, box-office blockbuster, corporate mission, and all the rest), it appears that univer-sity administrations have already moved much too aggressively in the direction of building bridges between education and industry, between scholarship and commerce, between theory and practice, between God and Mammon. Indeed, recalling the title of this chapter, we stand on the brink of a disaster caused by building "A Bridge Too Far …, Way Too Far."

Review and discussion questions

1   Assuming that "Professor M.B.H." is actually the author, how and why might this chapter reflect conscious or unconscious authorial biases?
2   In what ways does the present book illustrate or contradict the problems identified by this chapter?
3   To what extent do you, Dear Readers, (dis)agree that academic values have been sacrificed to commercial success in your own education?

4   To what extent has the author – in emphasizing the importance of consumption experiences – been hoist with his own petard?

5   Please explain the author's statement that "all products are services."

Keywords

edutainment, military-industrial-educational complex, misguided business model applied to the university, misplaced customer orientation, threats to academic values, trade-school mentality

References

Abbott, Lawrence (1955) *Quality and Competition*, New York: Columbia University Press.

Buchanan, Phill (2000) "The E-Mania at the B-Schools," *New York Times*, December 12, p. A33.

Drucker, Peter F. (1954) *The Practice of Management*, New York: Harper and Row.

Eisenhower, Dwight D. (1961) "Military-Industrial Speech." Available at: coursesa.matrix.msu.edu/~hst306/documents/indust.html

Frankfurt, Harry G. (2005) *On Bullshit*, Princeton, NJ: Princeton University Press.

Henry, William A., III, (1994) *In Defense of Elitism*, New York: Doubleday.

Hirschman, Elizabeth C. and Holbrook, Morris B. (1982) "Hedonic Consumption: Emerging Concepts, Methods, and Propositions," *Journal of Marketing*, 46(Summer): 92–101.

Holbrook, Morris B. (ed.) (1999) *Consumer Value – A Framework for Analysis and Research*, London: Routledge.

—— (2003) "Adventures in Complexity....," *Academy of Marketing Science Review*, book-length monograph. Available at: www.amsreview.org/articles/holbrook06–2003.pdf

—— (2005a) "Marketing Education as Bad Medicine for Society: The Gorilla Dances," *Journal of Public Policy & Marketing*, 24(1): 143–5.

—— (2005b) "Marketing Miseducation and the MBA Mind: Bullshit Happens," *Marketing Education Review*, 15(3): 1–5.

—— (2006) "ROSEPEKICECIVECI versus...the Concept of Customer Value: 'I Can Get It For You Wholesale,'" in Robert F. Lusch and Stephen L. Vargo (eds), *The Service-Dominant Logic of Marketing: Dialog, Debate, and Directions*, Armonk, NY: M. E. Sharpe, pp. 208–23.

—— (2007a) "Five Phases in a Personal Journey through the Troubled Waters of Academic Values in a World of Business: Where's the Beef?" *Journal of Public Policy & Marketing*, 26 (1): 135–8.

—— (2007b) "The Consumption Experience – Something New, Something Old, Something Borrowed, Something Sold – Part 3," *Journal of Macromarketing*, 27(2): 173–83.

—— (2007c) "The Consumption Experience – Something New, Something Old, Something Borrowed, Something Sold – Part 4," *Journal of Macromarketing*, 27(3): 303–19.

—— (2009) "Manufacturing Memorable Consumption Experiences From Ivy and Ivory: The Business Model, Customer Orientation, and the Distortion of Academic Values in the Post-Millennial University," in Adam Lindgreen, Joëlle Vanhamme, and Michael B. Beverland (eds), *Memorable Customer Experiences*, Burlington, VT: Gower Publishing Company, pp. 267–90.

Holbrook, Morris B. and Hirschman, Elizabeth C. (1982) "The Experiential Aspects of Consumption: Consumer Fantasies, Feelings, and Fun," *Journal of Consumer Research*, 9(September): 132–40.

LaSalle, Diana and Britton, Terry A. (2002) *Priceless: Turning Ordinary Products into Extraordinary Experiences*, Boston: Harvard Business School.

Levitt, Theodore (1960) "Marketing Myopia," *Harvard Business Review*, 37(July–August): 45–56.

Merritt, Jennifer (2003) "What's an MBA Really Worth?" *Business Week*, September 27, pp. 90–102.

Pine, B. Joseph, II, and Gilmore, James H. (1999) *The Experience Economy: Work Is Theatre & Every Business a Stage*, Boston: Harvard Business School Press.

Schmitt, Bernd H. (1999) *Experiential Marketing: How to Get Customers to Sense, Feel, Think, Act, and Relate to Your Company and Brands*, New York: The Free Press.

Veblen, Thorstein (1918) *The Higher Learning in America*, New Brunswick, NJ: Transaction.

Wilkie, William L. and Moore, Elizabeth S. (2003) "Scholarly Research in Marketing: Exploring the '4 Eras' of Thought Development," *Journal of Public Policy & Marketing*, 22(Fall): 116–46.

31 Ethics

Lisa Peñaloza

Can it be believed that the democracy which has overthrown the feudal system and vanquished kings will retreat before tradesman and capitalists?

(Alexis de Tocqueville)

Overview

According to noted expert O.C. Ferrell (2005: 3), organizational ethics is "one of the most important, yet overlooked and misunderstood concepts in corporate America and schools of business". Traditional approaches emphasize psychological and economic dimensions of ethics and direct attention to the ethical principles guiding the decisions and techniques that marketers engage in as individuals in organizations. Such approaches view ethics as part of individual self-development and consider culture as an influence on such individual ethical principles and decisions within organizations.

Cultural approaches build upon traditional approaches by drawing from sociology, anthropology, and the humanities in directing attention to the social representations, discourses, and practices of actors within various fields in producing and enacting what becomes recognized as ethical and unethical within market systems. Such actors include marketers, suppliers, and distributors in business networks; consumers in social groups such as families and communities; competitors, other businesses, and non-profit organizations; other stakeholders; government representatives and appointees; and even the natural environment. The cultural approach views ethics as emergent and negotiated within market systems as members specify, evaluate, and enforce ethics using particular codes, symbol systems, and practices. In their most explicit form such specification consists of laws, codes, and customs, yet it also includes more subtle patterns of interaction, gesture, gossip, and innuendo and less subtle sanction and punishment in social and market fields including firms, families, and governing bodies in cities and nations. *Members determine what is ethical as they define and regulate unethical practices.*

Two examples illustrate the fundamentally social nature of markets. Social media is creating a whole new arena for market ethics as it enlarges the scale of negotiation from regional to national, from national to international, and from international to global dimensions (cf. Chapters 1 and 2 on globally scaled market activity; cf. Chapters 3, 4, 6, and 7 for regionally scaled market activity).

- Everywhere we go, there we are! Members of social media speak of their connections with others and the convenience of many apps in making their lives easier. And yet, as the numbers of users approach the populations of good-sized countries, emerging ethical concerns include privacy, harassment, even violence. Facebook employs a "Hate and Harassment Team" to police their site. Team member David Willner, 26, relates that the H&H Team regularly deals with bullying, gay-bashing, suicide pacts, religious intolerance, and fake "troll" profiles posting violent messages (Helft 2010).

- Freedom and Oppression? Laura LeNoir, 42, office manager, Birmingham, AL., expressed her concerns with privacy, since her friends can send her messages to their friends (cited in Della Cava 2010). Dustin Blythe, 35, "felt compelled to update my page every hour or so, even if there really was nothing new to write or show," while Leana Fry, 32, from Provo, Utah, described social media as "time sucking" and "taking the real out of life," only to discover "I don't have to know what hundreds of people are doing. Now I have more time for people who really matter in my life" (ibid.). The desire to unplug underlies the success of Freedom (http://macfreedom.com/), Suicide Machine (http://suicidemachine.org/) and Les Liens Invisible (http://www.lesliensinvisibles.org/).

Given the increasing interpenetration of social and market phenomena, it is imperative that marketing managers gain knowledge and understanding of the market system(s) in which they operate to do their job effectively and ethically. As we shall see, emerging ethical issues of privacy, safety, and addiction in social media merge with longstanding ethical concerns in such marketing activities as production, distribution, pricing, and advertising, to name a few.

- *Supplier Oversight and Responsibility*. In its annual supplier audit Apple reported child labor, suicides, chemical poisoning, and excessive work schedules (Moore 2011). The company reported 91 children under the age of 16 working in 10 of their Chinese suppliers' factories in 2010, up from 11 workers in 2009. The company terminated a supplier contract after their audit confirmed 42 children working on their assembly line. In another case, after learning that 137 workers had been poisoned using the chemical n-hexane to clean iPod and iPhone screens, Apple requested the supplier stop using the chemical. According to their last audit 46 percent of suppliers were compliant in limiting work schedules to 60 hours per week with one day off within each 7-day period (Moore 2011).

- *Environmental Issues in Production and Distribution*. In February 2010, Chevron was fined $8.6 billion by an Ecuadorian court for pollution committed by its 2001 acquisition, Texaco, in the course of their extraction and distribution of oil (Adams 2011). The charges were for "billions of gallons of waste oil and water dumped into open pits, fouling fishing grounds, damaging crops, killing farm animals, and leading to an increase in cancer cases among residents of villages in the region" (Pyper 2011). Texaco had worked oil fields in the area from 1969–92 in a joint venture with Petroecuador and had agreed to pay $40 million for cleaning up some of the damage. The initial lawsuit was filed against Texaco in 1992 in a New York court shortly after the company's departure from the country. Experts appointed by the Ecuadorian courts have calculated that the pollution from the oil wells has since killed at least 1,400 people. Chevron plans to appeal and has the resources to do so; its 2010 earnings were $19 billion. In Ecuador this is a politically charged case; current president Rafael Correa has made nationalization of the oil company part of his presidential platform (ibid.).

- *The Price of Work: A downward trend in compensation for the design and advertising profession?* Quirky.com offers "crowdsourcing" to innovators who pay $99 for a panel of participants to evaluate the idea. Crowdspring.com has paid $2.5 million in "awards" to an army of creatives for product design ideas. LG electronics paid $80k for what the mobile phone will look like in the future. Barilla paid $1,000 to three winners for the next pasta design. In exchange, the companies get a free, perpetual, non-exclusive license to practice every idea submitted. John Winsor, of Victors and Spoils, uses crowdsourcing to "bring down advertising agency fees" (Frazier 2010). In contrast, the t-shirt company Threadless professes fair distribution of resources to designers and ethical procurement and disposition of materials (http://collectivehunch.com/threadless/).

- *The Fair Price of an MBA.* "The dirty secret of online education is the appallingly low completion rate. Fewer than one in four students who begin an online MBA ever graduate, and it didn't seem ethical to me to take someone's money up front, knowing that most of them won't finish," says Aaron Etingen, founder and chief executive of the MBA Facebook app at The London School of Business and Finance. He started LSBF in 2003 with two rooms and four students. The school has grown to 15,000 students; each pays separately for modular classes in marketing, finance, business law, and accounting, for a total of £14,500 (US$23,000). The school combines distance learning with bricks and mortar locations in London, Birmingham, Manchester, and Toronto, for a completion rate the school claims is 90 percent. In 2012, half a million students are expected to take a free online test run, watching lectures, participating in study groups, and taking interactive tests (Guttenplan 2010).

- *Truth in Advertising.* Groupon, recently listed by *Forbes* as the "fastest growing company in the world" was chastised for misleading advertising claims by the UK-based Advertising Standards Authority in 2010. To date, founder Andrew Mason has expanded the enterprise to 500 cities, 35 countries, and 50 million users on a win-win-win proposition for local businesses to offer customers more than half off their regular prices, with the company taking half of the money that changes hands. The incident in question entailed the company's claim of a 74 percent discount on the purchase of a £24 ($38.7) meal voucher. The claim was misleading since the 74 percent had been calculated against the most expensive meal on the menu. In effect, savings on most menu choices would cost much less. Groupon agreed it would add the phrase *up to* 74 percent savings in their future advertisements (Foley 2011).

Defining cultural market ethics begins by appreciating what the previous vignettes have in common: collective cultural ideas, customs, and standards for evaluating and regulating what is right, fair, and/or just. Such ideas, customs, and standards are negotiated in market practices by various agents (marketers, consumers, competitors, other stakeholders) and in market systems comprised of multiple "fields" including organizations, families, friendship groups, governments, and the natural environment. The chapter proceeds with traditional conceptualizations and principles of marketing ethics. It then discusses cultural approaches useful in grasping the dynamic and negotiated nature of ethics as technological and institutional advances reverberate through contemporary social-market systems. Together, understanding the traditional *and* cultural views better prepares readers for the ethical challenges they will face as marketing managers.

Conceptualizing ethics

The term ethics comes from the Greek, *ēthikē*, most broadly conceived as the philosophy of human conduct (*Webster's Ninth New Collegiate Dictionary* 1986). Distinctions are made between ethical and legal matters. While both rest on cultural ideals and practices, ethics are more informal and feature normative principles of what people should/should not do, as compared to more formal codified laws and standards, fines, and punishments through which people govern what they allow people to do legally.

Ethics stem from a person's and a community/society's sense of right and wrong, morals, fairness, and equity. These principles are conveyed and reinforced through *socialization* in personal contact among family members, at school, at work, at church, and in clubs/social organizations. Socialization occurs as well across a realm of online, broadcast, and printed forms in websites, blogs, newspapers, and magazines, film and television, etc., and in institutional activities in meetings and other outreach by religious and political organizations, statements by elected officials and governmental and nonprofit organizations, and even lobbying of political representatives by business and non-profit organizations.

Some of the most *explicit* ethical teachings are found in religious writings, legal codices and precedents, and business and other organizational codes of conduct, mission statements, and operating procedures. Examples include the Ten Commandments, the Quran, and the teachings of Confucius and Buddha, to name a few religious texts. Nations, states, and cities establish laws and legal precedents. Companies have more or less explicit codes guiding work.

Yet just as important are the *implicit* ethics in fables, movies, children's stories, popular phrases, music, and ritualized holiday customs and traditions. Take a moment, list a few current examples of phrases, and try to extract the meaning, with attention to the ethical lesson each "teaches." Here are a few: Whoever dies with the most toys wins. Too big to fail. Make my day. Privatize the profits; socialize the risk.

This chapter emphasizes explicit codes as well as implicit, generally accepted ideals and standards that guide managers in word and deed in social-marketing fields. In this sense ethics goes beyond traditional normative principles and codices encompassing what should and should not be done and said to include discourse and activities as they are rewarded, punished, or ignored in virtual and bricks-and-mortar social and market contexts. In the academic discipline of marketing the most recent terminology is sustainability in referring to business activity that has a positive or at least neutral effect on society and the environment (cf. Chapters 28 and 29 of this volume). Before that, the appropriate term was corporate social responsibility, in documenting the emerging social obligations of organizations to have a positive impact. In the 1970s, the term social marketing referred to the application of marketing techniques for social goals. In this chapter references will be made to all of these terms as parts of marketing ethics.

In 2003, Richard L. Schmalensee, Dean of the Sloan School of Management, Massachusetts Institute of Technology, charged business schools as being partly responsible for producing a cadre of managers more focused on short-term gains to beat the market than building lasting value for shareholders and society (Schmalensee 2003). As readers involved in business practices, take a moment to consider your interactions in and outside business field with others – colleagues, teachers, family, strangers. What is "tested" in financial statements, short-term or long-term gain? Profit? Shareholder wealth? Other goals, such as CEO/employee pay ratio? Contributions to community development and to the natural environment? What do you do if you see a colleague who doesn't do their share of work, takes credit for the work of others on a group project or other assignment, or cheats on an exam? Does the end goal, be it grades, a job, social acceptance, companionship, and/or money, justify the means? Does the field matter – whether someone takes credit for others' work or shortchanges another at school, work, home, with friends?

Among the key ethical violations Ferrell (2005) listed are conflicts of interest, fraud, and discrimination. *Conflicts of interest* entail a failure to separate and partition interests, be they those of the individual from the organization, or of one organization in its dealings with others. Ferrell cites the example of Arthur Anderson in serving as outside auditor for Waste Management Inc. while providing consulting services to the firm. An investigation by the Securities and Exchange Commission ruled that consulting fees compromised the independence of the firm's financial audits. To settle the ruling Arthur Anderson agreed to pay a $7 million fine, and later paid $100 million to Waste Management shareholders (ibid.: 15).

Fraud consists of deceptive practices that advance individual or corporate interests over the organization or some other group. Fraudulent practices include inaccurate information provided by a company to try to influence its stock price or convince a supplier to buy its products over those of a competitor. Ferrell noted that the passing of the *Sarbanes–Oxley Act* in 2002 replaced longstanding, club-like industry practices of self-regulation with regulation by the Securities and Exchange Commission. The act holds both organizations and their employees responsible for misconduct (ibid.: 15).

Discrimination in hiring and promotion is illegal in many countries, and yet racial and gender differences persist in earnings, in management, and in boardrooms worldwide. Gabriel (1994) presents a case study contrasting the equal opportunity position of McDonald's with its challenges in dealing with racial and gender discrimination among employees and between employees and managers in the UK in the 1990s. In the US Title IV of the Civil Rights Act 1964 made it illegal to discriminate on the basis of race, national origin, color, religion, and gender (Ferrell 2005: 17). Businesses, such as Coors Brewing (http://query. nytimes.com/gst/fullpage.html?res = 990CE7D81F3AF93BA35754C0A963958260), cities, such as Salt Lake City (http://www.slcgov.com/ndo/), and universities, such as the University of California (http://www.universityofcalifornia.edu/regents/policies/4402.html) have added sexual orientation to their non-discrimination clauses.

Traditional views

Ferrell (2005) views individual ethics as primarily a matter of *personal* moral development (Figure 31.1). Ferrell's model draws from the work of Rest (1986) and Kohlberg (1975). Rest (1986) mapped out a sequence of moral awareness, moral judgment, moral intent, and moral behavior. Kohlberg (1975) emphasized three developmental stages:

- The first stage emphasizes an individual's focus on their own needs and desires.
- The second stage features the ability to acknowledge and conform to group values and expectations.
- The third stage is characterized by a person's conformity and concern with upholding the basic rights, values, and rules of society.

Ferrell's model adds to Kohlberg's and Rest's work in two ways. First, he draws attention to the varying importance of the issue at hand. Second, Ferrell includes such organizational factors as organizational culture, the influence of co-workers and superiors, and opportunity

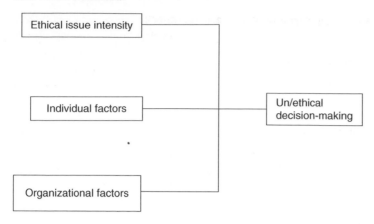

Figure 31.1 A model of ethical decision-making.
    Source: Ferrell (2005).

within the organization. The author cites the example of Enron employee Lynn Brewer to show that organizations can influence people's ethical decisions with rewards/punishments, codes of conduct, and organizational values. Brewer charged that many managers and employees knew about, and were rewarded for illegal and unethical activities, such as over-stating revenue, while those not going along were punished in being alienated from the group or let go (Brewer and Hanson 2002).

Second, for Ferrell (2005), individual factors including personal moral philosophy and stages of moral development are directly important in determining individual ethical decisions, while organizational factors have indirect effects on individual ethical/unethical decision making. And yet, early studies in marketing contexts by the author (Ferrell and Gresham 1985) pointed to the primacy of organizational factors in determining ethics at work. How can we reconcile these findings with the model? Ferrell (2005) openly challenges the view that ethics is for those with an unacceptable level of personal moral development. Instead, he suggests that a high level of personal moral development may not be enough to prevent people from breaking the law while at work in their organizations. He explains the importance of "special considerations for business" to balance their legitimate concern with profit with the needs/desires of society (ibid.). Recognizing that pressures, opportunities, and incentives may sway employees to make unethical *decisions*, the author lists a chilling example of how tenuous ethical concerns can be when managers/ employees' livelihoods are at stake. Betty Vinson, a mid-level accountant, was asked to account for profit for Worldcom, and eventually agreed to record a $3.7 billion overage (Pullman 2003).

Considering the ways the organization influences individual ethical decisions clearly is important. At the level of employees, Ferrell (2005) lists such character traits as honesty, fairness, and openness that are often assumed to be self-evident and accepted among employees (ibid.: 7). At the level of managers, Ferrell notes that even experienced managers may need training to reach agreement and communicate clear expectations as to what constitutes legal and ethical conduct since ethical concerns are always evolving. He empha-sizes *proactive leadership* together with *formal training* to produce an *ethical organiza-tional climate.*

Ethics in marketing: element by element

In the field of marketing ethical concerns pertain to all of the marketing functions. While not exhaustive, this section strives to acquaint readers with some of the major ethical issues relevant to a subset of marketing activities – sales, marketing research, advertising, and pricing – in dealing with consumers and organizational partners, such as suppliers and distributors:

- *Sales*. Dubinsky (1985) lists such ethical concerns as truthfulness and avoiding pressure sales tactics, differential pricing (not grounded in quantity or other legitimate bases), preferential treatment, making knowingly wrong promises for delivery, limiting available merchandise, and taking sales credit or clients away from associates. (cf. Chapter 21 in this volume).
- *Marketing research*. Tull and Hawkins (1985) discuss the unethical collection and use of information against people's wishes, not giving accurate and sufficient information about the use of the research to enable participation to opt in and out of a study, misleading reporting of results, paying for data, using research as a guise to sell products, not treating people with dignity, and invading privacy. This area becomes increasingly important as markets globalize (cf. Chapters 14, 15, 16, and 17 in this volume).
- *Advertising*. Ferrell (1985) emphasizes unethical practices including false claims, manipulation of human hopes and desires, and stimulating undesirable purchases. In another work Scott (1993) notes the widespread use of images in advertisements, for which "truthfulness" is less a matter of provable claims and more a matter of credibility for imaginative and metaphorical connections to products and firms (cf. also Chapters 5 and 24 in this volume).
- *Pricing*. Kehoe (1985) discusses the ethical importance of computing a fair price, and notes unethical activities, such as altering merchandise quality, price discrimination, excessive markups, and collusion (cf. Chapter 20 in this volume).

The cultural approach to market ethics

Markets are powerful institutions supported by a web of cultural beliefs, organizational practices, and means of governance as illustrated in Figure 31.2. The figure represents ethics in the market system as the negotiation of meanings and values within the fields of consumption, business organizations, financial trading, and government, all encircled in a large blue circle representing the natural environment.

The cultural approach to market ethics builds upon the work discussed so far. Ferrell (2005: 3) acknowledges the relevance of society in advocating a "societal" approach to organizational ethics, although his model emphasizes *individual* ethical decisions. Laczniak's (1983) framework for analyzing marketing ethics is socially oriented as well, in distinguishing between utilitarianism, in giving consideration to minimum levels of satisfaction and standards, and justice protecting the interests and seeking the greatest possible balance of value for all persons involved. Individual decisions and philosophical considerations are indeed important, yet leave gaps in understanding how complex concepts of justice, value, standards, outcomes, even satisfaction are produced in market systems.

Cultural approaches to ethics emphasize representations, discourses, and practices as the means through which a plurality of members of social and organizational groups *specify*, *enact*, and *police* ethical and unethical meanings and values in various fields that

512   *Lisa Peñaloza*

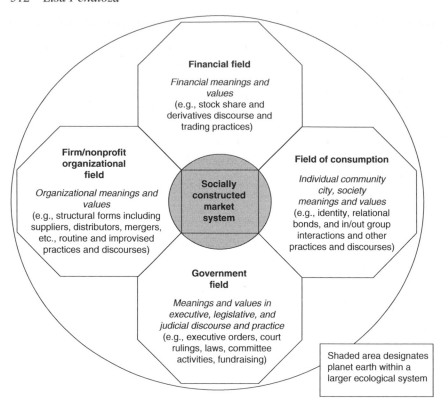

Figure 31.2 Various fields of negotiation for ethical meanings and values in a market system.
Source: Lisa Peñaloza

comprise a market system. Such work emphasizes the relational, dialogic, and negotiated nature of ethics. Thus, ethics is misunderstood as a matter of *either* the individual subject or the macro system. Instead, what is important is how ethics is: conceptualized and enacted by individuals; explicated in formal and informal collective customs, laws and traditions; and manifest in terms of overall comprehension of a particular social-market system. Together, the traditional and cultural approaches yield a more complete picture of ethics in markets.

Representations are the specific symbols carrying meaning. Such symbols include linguistic codes, images, and photographs. Market ethics are communicated subtly in signs, such as product logos and colors, as well as in gestures, activity, and innuendo. An example is the political campaign marketing website posted in 2008 by Republican former Vice Presidential candidate Sarah Palin featured democratic politicians in a bull's-eye, which is an image of a dark circle surrounded by a series of gradually larger rings. In its most general sense the image can signify focusing efforts on attaining a goal, and yet it is also commonly used as a shooting target at weapons ranges. On January 8, 2011 Gabrielle Giffords, a Democratic member of the House of Representatives from Arizona was among 13 people wounded, another 6 persons were killed, by the gunfire of a zealous citizen, Jared Loughner, whose online videos and writings contained anti-government messages (McKinnon 2011). The image was taken down immediately after the shooting (http://www.talksy.com/83221/the-palin-website-with-a-bullseye-over-gabrielle-gifford-s-district-is-down-now).

As this example illustrates, signs are used to position companies and to build iconic brands, including political candidates. Because signs convey cultural meanings important to people and because they do so online in previously unimaginable numbers, signs can generate dramatic, even violent reactions and responses (cf. Chapter 8 on the use of semiotic signs in advertising and Chapter 19 for the strong reactions of consumers to changes in advertising for Hummer).

Discourse consists of organized ideas and speech patterns (Davies and Harré 1990). Market ethics are communicated in intentional, spoken and written directives, such as mission statements and operating procedures. The term discourse refers to the ways in which topics are discussed and whether they can be discussed at all. As an example, the *free market* is a discursive phrase of much importance in understanding contemporary market ethics. Take a minute to specify the various representations, ideals, actors, and activities for this discourse and compare it to the *socially responsible market*. Note the multiple and contested meanings and values.

Practice consists of human action, especially acts that are repeated, follow in a sequence and become routine (Warde 2005). Examples include making a sales call for managers, or using a credit card for consumers. Statler, Roos, and Victor (2007) contrast the emphasis on *individual* cognition, rationality, information processing, and decision-making (i.e., the traditional view) with their emphasis on the *habituated ethical performances* of members as configured within particular social and market systems. In drawing attention to tacit, bodily knowledge and cultural customs and expectations in marketing ethics, their work converges with what Polanyi (1976) described as a form of human understanding not reflected upon explicitly as such, rather learned over time through embodied practice.

Statler and Oppegaard (2005) agree that implicit and habit-based patterns of thought and behavior are fundamental in marketing ethics. They are particularly concerned with requirements for a measurable and instrumental relationship between ethics and efficiency. This seemingly reasonable requirement has a deleterious effect: where ethics do not pay, they are rendered ineffective and illegitimate. Further, the focus on the individual can detract from understanding the ways in which organizational reinforcements and rewards stem from and become generalized in markets and in society.

Statler and Oppegaard also point to the diffusion globally of discourses of the free market: of business activity being guided by an invisible hand, with the sole responsibility of organizations to create wealth, and the unfettered actions in the market of innumerable persons pursuing their own interests to bring about the best in society. This view – most often attributed to Adam Smith from his eighteenth-century text, *Wealth of Nations*, and popularized by Milton Friedman in the 1970s – seldom mentions Smith's concerns at the time that markets eroded communities and social traditions. Weber (1958) later developed the "Protestant Ethic and the Spirit of Capitalism" to track the elevation of monetary gain into a more general social goal, even a measure of divine favor in Western Europe in the nineteenth century. Bell (1976) elaborated the sense of entitlement that people developed in Western Europe and in the US in the twentieth century when accustomed to a high standard of living.

Cultural work emphasizes that *social and market processes together negotiate what is ethical and unethical in word and deed. Such processes are rife with contradictions and contestations.* Margolis and Walsh (2003) noted that people in organizations struggle when they cannot reconcile normative ethical principles with those of profit and efficiency that drive firms. Such difficulties may be fairly common. According to a classic study, only

15 percent of people surveyed claimed they kept same ethical standards at and away from work (Fraedrich and Ferrell 1992).

Cultural approaches direct further attention to how social and organizational fields display an authority that imposes upon their members and is carried out and reinforced via individual decisions and judgment to the point that ethical practice may well run counter-cultural to the organization and even to society. Sternberg (1998: 356) proposes three courses of ethical action in balancing multiple and conflicting interests: (1) adaptation of oneself or others to existing environments; (2) shaping of environments in order to render them more compatible with oneself or others; and (3) selection of new environments to achieve a desired fit between self and environmental characteristics.

In their study of Triple Bottom Line firms (TBL) oriented to social, environmental, and economic objectives, Peñaloza and Mish (2011) note that managers followed each of these options, in leaving conventional businesses to orient their firms to sustainable goals, shaping standards for more sustainable industry practices, and adapting novel technologies to compete with non-sustainable businesses. As examples, for New Vision Bank, goals of developing the community and financing environmentally sustainable buildings are as important as profitability. Earthly Eating shared technological innovations that have become industry standards in supply chain management to make healthier food more available. Future Friendly discloses all ingredients on household cleaner labels to safeguard water quality. Broadened social and environmental goals, measurable standards in reaching these goals and transparency are exemplary of ethical leadership in the market system.

Such practices contrast with Friedman's (1970) view that the sole responsibility of business is to increase its profits. Key in his argument is responsibility as an individual quality. Friedman described corporate executives as employees of their organizations, and limited their responsibilities to their employers, in this case stockholders, while conforming to the law. For Friedman, attention to social issues went against the interests of employers, and was comparable to taxation without representation.

John Mackey, C.E.O. of Whole Foods, takes a systemic view to sustainability that is quite compatible with the cultural approach to ethics explicated in this chapter. In a debate with Friedman, Mackey elaborated his contrasting views:

> I believe that the enlightened corporation should try to create value for *all of its constituencies*. From an investor's perspective, the purpose of the business is to maximize profits. But that's not the purpose for other stakeholders – for customers, employees, suppliers, and the community. Each of those groups will define the purpose of the business in terms of its own needs and desires, and each perspective is valid and legitimate. My argument should not be mistaken for a hostility to profit. I believe I know something about creating shareholder value. When I co-founded Whole Foods Market 27 years ago, we began with $45,000 in capital; we only had $250,000 in sales our first year. During the last 12 months we had sales of more than $4.6 billion, net profits of more than $160 million, and a market capitalization over $8 billion. But we have not achieved our tremendous increase in shareholder value by making shareholder value the primary purpose of our business ... In the profit-centered business, customer happiness is merely a means to an end: maximizing profits. In the customer-centered business, customer happiness is an end in itself, and will be pursued with greater interest, passion, and empathy than the profit-centered business is capable of.
>
> (Macky 2005: 3)

Global market ethics

Work in international business has noted differences in negotiation strategies, acceptable levels of profit, fixed prices, and usury laws. In general, such work calls for cultural sensitivity in adapting to local cultural practices, while adhering to organizational policies and strategies. The cultural perspective holds that people's understandings of markets are not fixed; instead they are a dynamic and ongoing construction that builds upon social and market tradition and ritualized understandings. As illustrated in the following vignette, ethical understandings derive from and contradict the practices in which they are experienced.

> *In the US markets are fair!* In doing fieldwork, the author was puzzled at hearing Victor Fuentes, a Mexican immigrant working in the US, talk about buying a car in the US. He went on and on, saying he couldn't understand how one person could sell a car for one price; another could sell the same car for another price. The same car, he said, repeatedly! Having taught marketing, the author tried to account for the pricing differences. Perhaps you, the reader, can assist her in offering an explanation. Like her, you might explain differences in seller sales volume, differences in the risk of the buyers, differences in the salesperson's quota, and the dealer's targeted profits. But the man does not yield. He does not accept these explanations. Exasperated, the author asked him how he could not understand the price differences. He's from Mexico, after all. There they negotiate many things – at least in some markets. And finally, he said, "It's not right, it's not fair. *In the US things are fair!"*

Perhaps you have experiences living, working, and/or traveling in other countries. Take a moment and exchange a memorable foreign market experience with your neighbor. People's sense of markets is a comparative activity, produced in comparison with other nations and historically at various points in time. Compare Señor Fuentes' idealized sense of market fairness in the US to stereotypes of highly developed and lesser developed nations.

Much can be learned from stereotypes. Rhodes and Westwood (2007) assert that the "foreign" is misrepresented when reduced to Western terms. These scholars of ethics challenge the essentialized, exoticized, and denigrated representation of foreign others, for example, the Chinese reduced to Confucianism, Germans to authoritarians, British as aristocrats, and African managers as primitive. Instead, the authors draw from the work of Lithuanian philosopher Emmanuel Levinas (1969/1991: 42) in explaining that the self exists in relation to others.

For Levinas (who lived from 1906 to 1995), the self is fundamentally misunderstood as a "knower" of another because that reduces the other to a creation of the self. Such creation is philosophically and practically untenable, and tends to produce the other as an inferior creation, a projection, and to produce the self as a self-evident, superior being. Rhodes and Westwood (2007) add that this logic continues to justify unjust treatment of others and degradation of the natural environment and instead pose *the ethical subject as responding to ongoing and mutual acts of creation.* For the self, ethical interactions with others are responses to them for their recognition of the self; such recognition by others is fundamental to self in its very being (ibid.: 78) (Figure 31.3).

Case study: market financialization in the US

Viewing market representations, discourses, and practices at the level of the system helps provide a framework for managers to better comprehend ethics from the perspective

Figure 31.3 "We are not markets in the hands of politicians and bankers." Festival of St. Ignacio, Patron Saint of Madrid, 15 May 2011.
Source: Photo: Lisa Peñaloza.

of multiple actors and fields. For example, at the system level, marketing elements becomes more than a matter of bilateral exchange. Instead generalized exchanges are applicable for agents concerned with, and acting to support, even defend the interests of other people and the natural environment. Relevant in promotion is resonance, dissonance, and appropriation in meaning transfer for agents with multiple and at times competing interests. For distribution, material delivery remains important, extended to encompass fair and just distribution of resources, with transparency essential in product and service logistics.

The case that follows compiles various perspectives and incidents regarding the financial crisis in the US to illustrate the ongoing, relational, and dialogic nature of ethics, as members negotiate in representation, discourse, and practice; and as their representations, discourses, and practices reverberate through the market system. Readers are invited to take part as individuals or in groups in a role-playing exercise, in taking one of the agents – consumers, CEO, marketing manager, banker, trader, regulator, etc., and considering their particular position and field in relation to the other fields in the market system.

Consumption

• *Individual greed and stupidity.* On Denver's Talk Radio Station, AM 630, Tom Martino listed a few contributing factors (the Clinton Administration's belief that home ownership should be for *everyone* and the mortgage industry's "funny money" loans that required no money as down payment, subprime loans, 125 percent loan to value loans, and adjustable rate mortgages), before putting blame squarely on consumers. Martino recounted key events,

> Suddenly people who had been in their homes for years found themselves with thousands of dollars in equity! Whoopee they thought! Let's refinance and pull the cash out! And that's what many Americans did. They pulled cash from their homes and bought new cars, trucks, appliances and boats. Many of them went on vacations and did home improvements. Some of them paid off credit cards, which ironically lead to MORE credit card spending!
>
> WHO IS REALLY TO BLAME? WHY did people "cash in" on their equity? WHY did they charge up credit cards, WHY did they buy, buy, buy? And WHY did they not honor their obligations? The answer: GREED AND STUPIDITY.
>
> Now ask yourself: Are the people who lost their homes victims?
>
> No. They are sellers.
>
> In almost every case they took ALL of their equity out of the home BEFORE they lost it.
>
> No, they did not lose their home. THEY SOLD IT IN ADVANCE AND SPENT ALL THE MONEY!
>
> (Martino 2008: 23)

- *Living in foreclosure and liking it.* Streitfeld (2010) gives an account of Alex Pemberton and Susan Reboyras, 46, who owe $280,000 on a house now worth less than half of that, and insist that amount would be their starting point in future negotiations with their lender. "If they took the house from us, that's all they would end up getting for it anyway" says Susan (ibid.: 21), who uses the $1,837 to publicize their restoration business. Streitfeld explains that "any ethical qualms are overshadowed by a conviction that the banks created the crisis by taking advantage of homeowners with loans that got them in over their heads" (ibid.: 21). Alex describes their loan as "a stupid move by their lender. They went outside their own guidelines on debt to income, and when they did they put themselves in jeopardy" (ibid.). Streitfeld writes that foreclosure was initiated against 1.7 million US households in 2009, with the average borrower being evicted after being delinquent 438 days. Kyle Lundstedt, managing director at LPS, a company that services the mortgage industry, calls the Pemberton/Seboyras move "dangerous," because there is a legal process in many states to go after those who have substantial assets after foreclosure (cited in Streitfeld 2010: 21).
- *Credit cards.* When credit cards first appeared in the 1960s, "They were very hard to get, almost status symbols." And now "It's harder to get a higher limit. It's harder even to get a card at all," says Carol Kaplan, spokeswoman for the American Bankers' Association (quoted in Abate 2008: A10). In the early 2000s, common were "aggressive teaser rates with 12 months of zero percent and no fees" and US households were solicited with about 26 offers per year, notes Curtis Arnold, of CardRatings.com, a watchdog on the industry who labels the cards, "life preservers to manage debt" (quoted in Abate 2008: A10). Abate compares credit as a convenience with discounts and benefits for those who pay their balances at the end of every month to the higher fees and interest rates of 50 million Americans whose "rollover" balances make them the industry's most profitable customers.

Peñaloza and Barnhart (2011) detail how credit and debt have become *normalized* in US society. Ava (25 years old) put it this way,

> There's (*sic*) things you have to borrow money for, and you're going to be in debt if you want to get things, unless you have millions of dollars. That's just the way it is. So, it's acceptable. I think you have to accept it because, you know, most people don't have cash to buy a house or cash to buy a car. But you have to buy one. So, I've just accepted it.

The authors note that the US consumer credit market has evolved such that a credit history is *required* for many job and housing rental applications, and to access telephone, utility, and travel services.

Also contributing to credit use is the increased cost of living. In congressional testimony, Harvard University Professor of Law, Elizabeth Warren, stated that a typical American family has seen its income fall more than $1,000 between 2000 and 2007 while gas, food, health care, and housing prices have increased over $4,000 (cited in Abate 2008: A10).

By designating some debt as good (especially that with earnings potential, such as loans for a house and education), consumers are changing previous norms and heuristics to use credit only in emergencies and to pay it back as soon as possible, note Peñaloza and Barnhart (2011). In addition, consumers "work" their credit cards to qualify for higher credit limits and mortgages, as Jennifer (46 years old) explains,

> I will probably keep the Citibank, because I am thinking, from what I have been reading, they are saying that having a bank card, there are different kinds of credit cards. The mass mailing kind are less useful for your credit report, so I think what I will do is talk my credit union into giving me a line of credit or a credit card, and just use them, and then close the US bank account, and maybe find a nicer or smaller bank, because I think you have to have like two or four. That's like the optimal number of cards. I read different things. It is so confusing, the information you get, compared to what's logical … you know, you are not to use more than 20 percent. I've heard that. So, I'm just trying to do things to try to get myself back. I'm going to have to manipulate it to do that.
>
> (quoted in Peñaloza and Barnhart 2011: 2011)

In getting and using her credit cards this way Jennifer was able to qualify for a mortgage.

Finance

In 2007, Fair Isaac Corp, maker of the FICO score used by 90 percent of the largest 100 banks to rate consumer risk, updated their score to be "more forgiving of occasional slips" and "take a harder line on repeat offenders" noted Kim (2007). The company was pressured by lenders to help them deal with rising loan defaults, subprime mortgages, and falling housing prices, and predicts that the new system will help lenders reduce defaults between 5 and 15 percent.

By 2008, the most profitable instruments were credit cards, payday loans, loans on car titles, loans on income tax refunds, and subprime mortgage – i.e., the low initial rates that quickly ballooned driving some middle-class mortgage holders to foreclosure (Coy 2008; Abate 2008). That same year the Federal Reserve Bank, the European Central Bank, the

Banks of England and Germany, and sovereign wealth funds infused billions to stabilize global credit markets (Leonhardt 2008).

In 2009, Merrill Lynch went under, General Motors filed bankruptcy, and Goldman Sachs and Chase banks were nationalized (Connelley 2009). December of that same year Goldman Sach's reported $1.8 billion quarterly profit (Norris 2009). Reviewing the $100 million in insurance the company had taken out in the event that American International Group (AIG) would default (it did and they collected), company sales of $5 billion in new stock at a triple digit share price, an accounting feat in reporting losses in December that would have been part of the quarter had the firm not changed its fiscal year (according to tables on p. 10 of the companies' news release), a $10 billion government "investment" under the Troubled Asset Relief Program, a loan of $28 billion with a guarantee from the Federal Deposit Insurance Corporation (FDIC), and Goldman Sachs' CFO, David Viniar's expectation to borrow up to $35 billion (the limit), Norris sees no contradiction, only "confusion" about whether bailouts are "the corporate equivalent of welfare checks aimed at invigorating the financial system, with the money going to banks to use to increase lending," or "benefits bailouts for the undeserving rich" (2009: 18).

- *What good is Wall Street?* asks Cassidy (2010), asserting that the sector has paid little for bringing the world to near collapse and even received a bailout from taxpayers. Historically the industry has made a valuable social contribution in distributing money where it is needed and keeping an account of how it is used, he observes, comparing large banks to utilities whose commanding position in the market can benefit customers and the economy at large.

  Frank Capra's film, *It's a Wonderful Life* (voted "most inspirational American film of all time" by the American Film Institute), dramatically compares the goals of financing community development and profit. George Bailey (Jimmy Stewart) is trying to keep the Building and Loan afloat. Depositors are pressing to withdraw their funds, having heard a rumor that the bank is on the brink of failure. Across town, investor/developer Henry Potter has offered them 50 cents on the dollar. George pleads,

  > You're thinking of this place all wrong. As if I had the money back in a safe. The money's not here. Your money's in Joe's house … right next to yours. And in the Kennedy house, and Mrs. Macklin's house, and a hundred others. Why, you're lending them the money to build, and then, they're going to pay it back to you as best they can. Now what are you going to do? Foreclose on them? … Ed. You know, you remember last year when things weren't going so well, and you couldn't make your payments. You didn't lose your house, did you? Do you think Potter would have let you keep it? Can't you understand what's happening here? Don't you see what's happening? Potter isn't selling. Potter's buying! And why? Because we're panicky and he's not. That's why. He's picking up some bargains. Now, we can get through this thing all right. We've got to stick together, though. We've got to have faith in each other.

  > Over time banks have transformed into "immense trading houses" notes Cassidy (2010: 4). Buying and selling securities and derivatives now dominate bank earnings, with the financial industry accounting for more than a quarter of American business profits, up from 14 percent 25 years ago. Business development now makes up only 13 percent of the revenue of Goldman Sachs, with 63 percent of its revenue from trading. For Morgan Stanley the figures are 15 per cent and 36 per cent (ibid).

- *A trader speaks out.* Michael Kubin (2010: 9) remembers feeling "gutted, humiliated, deeply shaken" December 11, 2008, the day they arrested Bernie Madoff. Two weeks earlier he had doubled his investment. How did this happen? He had an MBA, had read about ponzi schemes, played cards, and knew about bluffing. His connection to the fund came through a wealthy family who kept millions in Madoff's funds for years. He expressed anger at "someone who stole so much from so many," "at the SEC for not having uncovered the scheme sooner," at the family who "put me into the investment," at his own family for "not talking him out of it," and ultimately angry at himself, "a fool and his money are soon parted and I was the fool" (ibid.: 9). Months later Kubin came to see his Madoff experience as "the penalty for sloppy judgment" and was "scratching his way back" (ibid.: 9). In 2009, he received the "biggest tax refund in his life," and slowly returned to investing with new rules: "make sure the accountants are reputable, the results transparent, insist on meeting the managers in person. Keep in mind that risk and reward always travel together, that if something sounds too good to be true it usually is" (ibid.: 9).

- *Transparency for derivatives trading?* Story (2010) reports on the secret monthly meetings of Intercontinental Exchange, ICE, one of several clearinghouses set up in response to the Dodd–Frank financial regulation bill requiring that many derivatives be traded through a clearinghouse. "Clearing" involves keeping track of trades and providing a central repository for money backing the wagers to help reduce risks in the market.

  As incentives to persuade the banks to join their efforts, the clearinghouses offered membership on their risk committees Story (2010) reports, listing ICE members: Athanassis Diplas, Deutsche Bank, Paul Hamill UBS, Andy Hubbard, Credit Suisse, Oliver Frankel, Goldman Sachs, Paul Mitrokostas, Barclays, Ali Balali, Bank of America, Biswarup Chaterjee, Citigroup, Thomas Benison, JP Morgan Chase, James J. Hill, and Morgan Stanley.

  The committees help decide the prices for clearing trades, the fees the banks receive for matching buyers and sellers, and which trades will be exempt. Millions of dollars are traded daily in credit default swaps, one of several types of derivative instruments used by pension funds, power companies, municipalities, and airlines to hedge risk by shifting it from one party to another. The author estimates a cost of $25,000 for $25 million in insurance coverage, noting the real figures are unknown – buyers are told only what they pay for the derivative contract, sellers are told only the amount they will receive, and the difference goes to the banks.

  The banks have incentives to protect their revenues and secrecy enables such large profits, notes Darrell Duffie, a Stanford University professor who studies the derivatives market with other researchers from the Federal Reserve Board (quoted in Story 2010: 15). Gary Gensler, Chairman of the US Commodity Futures Trading Commission, a regulatory body whose scope includes derivatives trading, wants to make prices more transparent and limit banks' control over clearinghouses, such as the ICE (ibid.). Banks have lobbied heavily to limit the regulation. At the time of this writing a US Department of Justice antitrust unit was conducting an investigation into "the possibility of anti-competitive practices in the credit derivatives clearing, trading, and information services industries" (ibid.: 15).

Government

Years before the crisis was officially recognized, politicians, such as Comptroller General David Walker, Texas Congresswoman Sheila Jackson Lee, and former Georgia Governor

Roy Barnes, and scholars, such as Robert Manning (2000), warned that the US economy might collapse, drawing comparisons to the large scale of speculation and high interest rates of the 1920s and portraying debt levels as a threat to the nation, as depicted in film (Schechter 2006, http://www.google.fr/search?q = In+Debt+We+Trust:+America+Before+ the+Bubble+Bursts&hl = fr&sa = G&prmd = ivns&source = univ&tbs = vid:1&tbo = u&ei = 5FKUTbX7Lse44gaEsfH_Cw&oi = video_result_group&ct = title&resnum = 1&ved = 0CBcQqwQwAA).

In 1999, Republican Chairman of the Senate Banking Committee under the Clinton Administration, Phil Gramm, brokered bipartisan support for bank deregulation that dissolved former market distinctions between banks, insurance companies, and securities traders, such that they all competed in the markets for banking, home financing, trading securities and derivatives, insurance, and consulting.

In 2008, James Lockhart, director of the Federal Housing Finance Agency (FHFA), placed Fannie Mae and Freddie Mac (agencies long associated with affordable housing), under the agency's conservatorship. In effect this provided government guarantees for middle-class housing that had risen and fallen in value in what would later be described as a burst housing bubble.

In 2009, the Credit Card Accountability Responsibility and Disclosure Act (CARD) was passed that requires financial institutions to post the time it will take to pay off a card and how much interest will accrue when consumers pay only the minimum payment (Connelly 2009). White House advisor Larry Summers summed up the concerns of the Obama administration,

> Individuals are going to have to save more. That's why savings incentives are so impor-
> tant. That's why we need to do things to stop the marketing of credit in ways that addicts
> people to it so that our households are again saving and families are again preparing to
> send their kids to college.
>
> (Associated Press 2009)

In a highly charged column that referenced an infamous Wall Street party in which a former Morgan Stanley trader handcuffed himself to a hired dwarf, Rich (2010) compared Wall Street to the trader and the US to the dwarf! Industries such as finance and health care can buy politicians as easily as dwarfs, he charges, pointing to their record profits. What concerns Rich is the recent US Supreme Court case ruling, Citizen's United, allowing non-profit groups to front for those who prefer to donate anonymously. The passage of this law legally circumvents campaign contributions previously held to be illegal he asserts, citing the money laundering conviction of former House Majority Leader, Tom Delay. Delay was charged with funneling funds to seven Republican candidates through the Republican National Committee (Ratcliffe and Fikac 2010). Both political parties are implicated, Rich (2010) charges, citing a Bloomberg news report tallying $86 million in contributions by the insurance lobby to the US Chamber of Commerce "Anti-Democratic War Chest" and a report by the investigative news organization, ProPublica, calling the New Democratic Coalition 69 lawmakers "one of the most successful money machines" (ibid.: 9). Neither party appears in synch with public opinion, he concludes, citing a Times-CBS poll in which 92 percent of Americans supported full disclosure of campaign contributions (ibid.). Soliciting funds has become a major political activity as campaigns can cost millions of dollars.

The past four years have been an economic trial for many nations. Iceland became "the 2008 global financial crisis' worst casualty" (Quinn 2010). At the time of this writing an 80-billion-euro "rescue package" was being proposed for Portugal by European finance ministers working with the European Commission, the European Central Bank and the International Monetary Fund (Castle 2010). If brokered, the package will be the third, following those of Ireland and Greece, with some concerns that Italy and Spain may follow.

Free markets, responsible markets

Some economists and politicians contend that markets operate properly only when unfettered by government regulation. Ron Paul is one, notes Zernike (2010). Representative 14th District in Texas and current Chairman of the House Subcommittee on Domestic Monetary Policy, which oversees the Fed and national currency policy, he is known as the "godfather" of the Tea Party for his strong views on government regulation of business and monetary policy. Representative Paul decorates his office with photos of Ludwig von Mises and Murray Rothbard, renowned founders of the Austrian school of economic theory that argues for no central bank and against centralized economic and monetary policy (ibid.).

For the Austrian school, failure is a vital and necessary corrective in markets. The Austrian school is not alone in asserting the importance of failure. Noted Richard Brodhead, President of Duke University, at his address to the school's Kenan Institute for Ethics, "True leaders understand the importance of making mistakes and learning from them" (cited in Cohan 2010: 8). Learning from failure was the theme of Steve Jobs' legendary graduation speech at Stanford University in 2005, in which he recalls being fired at Apple as "the best thing that could have ever happened to me ... The heaviness of being successful was replaced by the lightness of being a beginner again, less sure about everything. It freed me to enter one of the most creative periods of my life" (ibid).

Cohan's message is sobering, "Wall Street has failed us, time and time again. Worse, its top executives refuse to admit their mistakes – and, therefore, cannot possibly learn from them. They prefer to speak about once in a lifetime tsunamis or complain about taxpayers bailing out other firms but not Lehman Brothers" (2010: 8). The author attributes part of the financial crisis to American society and its citizens, specifically our infatuation with bankers and traders and the exalted position we give them in movies and books. "Why does the American public tolerate such questionable morality and behavior," he asks? "Why excuse the financial calamities, insider trading, pay for play scandals?" He answers his own question, "Finance is the top destination for our best and brightest ... because we're always striving to achieve, to be the best ... When you imbibe a culture of aspiration from someone else, do you really care about the values that are driving you so hard?" (ibid.: 8). Cohan answers with another question, "Wall Street has been making a lot of mistakes lately. Will it bother to ever learn about them?" (ibid.: 8).

To the point of this chapter, will *we* have the courage and conviction to do what is ethical at home and at work in ways that contribute to a healthy balance for markets in society, as Sternberg (1998) and Laczniak (1983) encourage? Does the end goal of wealth justify the means – any means? Has making money truly become the path to heavenly salvation that Max Weber anticipated in his classic work, *The Protestant Ethic and the Spirit of Capitalism?*

These questions apply to everyone in marketing systems in the US and in other nations as markets develop globally – marketing managers competing for capital with financial derivatives, consumers in building identity and making family and friendship, suppliers and distributors in meeting production challenges and enacting services, government in seeking to facilitate trade that is so important to social development while minimizing its detrimental impacts.

Many companies are finding strategic footing in making their operations more ethical and sustainable. Porter and Kramer suggest that business is not nearly as productive as they could be in their efforts to improve the social and environmental consequences of their activities because they continue to pit business against society, when "clearly the two are interdependent" (2006: 78). Former chair of the Texas Railroad Commission, Jim Hightower, would agree. He has written extensively about the corporate charters granted by states as a proxy for their people that give corporations the right to exist. The legitimacy of business stems from this charter, and companies do well to remember that their right to exist and to act is, and always has been, social.

Review and discussion questions

1   Distinguish the traditional and the cultural approach to marketing ethics. Discuss the strengths and the weaknesses of each approach.
2   Compare and contrast ethics with laws. Account for their discrepancy.
3   Return to the phrase, "Too big to fail." What happens to failure when risk is marketized and managed via insurance, hedging, derivatives trading, lobbying, and government bailouts? Is failure then a matter of price? Is such failure ethically priced in the risk management discourses and practices animating contemporary markets?
4   For the case: You make the call. What is ethical and unethical? For whom? Take a position and explicate its interests and ethical challenges.
5   Now take the position of a marketing manager. The case has focused on consumers, on financial market activity, and on government. Discuss the degree to which marketing managers in small and large firms are impacted by: (1) financial market activity in the trading of their shares, in competing for capital, etc.; and (2) by consumer credit – its tightening, impacts on living standards and expectations, current levels of in-home valuation.

Keywords

conflict of interest, credit, discourse, discrimination, ethics, financialization of markets, fraud, practice, representation, sustainability

References

Abate, Tom (2008) "It's a Matter of Balance as Credit Card Rules Change," *San Francisco Chronicle*, October 26, pp. A1, A10.
Adams, Guy (2011) "A Dirty Fight," *The Independent*, 16 February, pp. 1, 4.
Associated Press (2009) "Obama to Host Credit-Card CEOs meeting, Pledges New Rules," April 23 Available at: http://news.yahoo.com/s/ap/20090423/ap_on_go_pr_wh/us_obama_credit_cards
Bell, Daniel (1976) *The Contradictions of Capitalism*, New York: Basic Books.
Brewer, Lynn and Hanson, Matthew Scott (2002) *House of Cards: Confessions of an Enron Executive*, College Station, TX: Virtualbookworm.com Publishing.
Cassidy, John (2010) "What Good is Wall Street? Much of What Investment Bankers Do is Socially Worthless," *New Yorker*, November 29.
Castle, Stephen (2010) "Rescue Offer to Portugal Estimated at 80 Billion Euros," *International Herald Tribune*, April, p. 1.

Cohan, William D. (2010) "The Power of Failure," *International Herald Tribune*, 30 November 8.

Connelly, Eileen (2009) "New Credit Card Rules May Reveal Unwelcome Details," Associated Press. Available at: http://www.heralddemocrat.com/hd/News/National/BC-US – Credit-Cards-Mixed-Blessing-1st-Ld-Writethru-981

Coy, Peter (2008) "Sinking Credit," *Businessweek*, 18 February pp. 33, 38.

Davies, Bronwyn and Harré, Rom (1990) "Positioning: the Discursive Production of Selves," *Journal for the Theory of Social Behavior*, 20: 43–63.

Della Cava, Marco (2010) "Friends No More: For Some Social Networking Has Become Too Much of a Good Thing," *USA Today*, 10 February pp. 1, 2.

Dubinsky, Alan J. (1985) "Studying Field Salespeople's Ethical Problems: An Approach for Designing Company Policies," in Laczniak and Murphy, 41–53.

Ferrell, O. C. (1985) "Implementing and Monitoring Ethics in Advertising," in Laczniak and Murphy, pp. 27–40.

—— (2005) "A Framework for Understanding Organizational Ethics" in Robert A. Peterson and O. C. Ferrell (eds), *Business Ethics: New Challenges for Business Schools and Corporate Leaders*, Armonk, NY: M.E. Sharpe, pp. 3–17.

Ferrell, O. C. and Gresham, Larry G. (1985) "A Contingency Framework for understanding Ethical Decision Making in Marketing," *Journal of Marketing*, 49(Summer): 87–96.

Foley, Stephen (2011) "Underpriced and Over Here," *The Independent*, Viewspaper, pp. 10–11.

Fraedrich, John P. and Ferrell, O. C. (1992) "Cognitive Consistency of Marketing Managers in Ethical Situations," *Journal of the Academy of Marketing Science*, 20(Summer): 245–52.

Frazier, Mya (2010) "Crowdsourcing," *Delta Sky Magazine*, February, pp. 70–4, 90.

Friedman, Milton (1970) "The Social Responsibility of Business is to Increase Its Profits," *New York Times Magazine*, 13 September.

Gabriel, John (1994) "Underneath the Arches: McDonald's, Markets, and Equality," in J. Gabriel, *Racism, Culture, Markets*, London: Routledge, pp. 98–126, 197, 198.

Guttenplan, D. D. (2010) "Poking, Tagging, and Now Landing an MBA" *International Herald Tribune*, 29 November, p. 6.

Helft, Miguel (2010) "Delete it or Leave it? Drawing a Line on Facebook Comments" *International Herald Tribune*, 13 December, p. 14.

Kehoe, William J. (1985) "Ethics, Price Fixing, and the Management of Price Strategy," in Laczniak and Murphy, pp. 71–83.

Kim, Jane J. (2007) "Default Lines: The New Math of Credit Scores," *Wall Street Journal*, Personal Finance section, November p. 1.

Kohlberg, Lawrence (1975) "Moral Stages and Moralization: The Cognitive-Development Approach to Socialization," in Thomas Lickona (ed.), *Moral Development and Behavior: Theory, Research, and Social Issues*, New York: Holt, Rinehard and Winston, pp. 31–53.

Kubin, Michael (2010) "Madoff Opened My Eyes," *New York Times Global Edition*, 13 December, p. 9.

Laczniak, Gene R. (1983) "Framework for Analyzing Marketing Ethics," *Journal of Macromarketing*, Spring, 7–18.

Leonhardt, David (2008) "Deep Roots, Long Reach of a Crisis," *Le Monde/New York Times Insert*, 22 March, p. 1.

Levinas, E. (1969/1991) *Totality and Infinity*, Dordrecht: Kluwer.

Mackey, John (2005) "Profit is the Means, Not End" and "Putting Customers Ahead of Investors" in *Rethinking the Social Responsibility of Business: A Reason Debate featuring Milton Friedman, Whole Foods, John Mackey, and Cypress Semiconductor's T. J. Rodgers*. Available at: http://reason.com/archives/2005/10/01/rethinking-the-social-responsibility

Manning, Robert (2000) *Credit Card Nation: The Consequences of America's Addiction to Credit*, New York: Basic Books.

Margolis, J. D. and Walsh, J. P. (2003) "Misery Loves Companies: Rethinking Social Initiatives by Business," *Administrative Science Quarterly*, 48: 268–305.

Martino, Tom (2008) "The Greed and Stupidity Crisis," 630 KHOW, Denver Talk Radio, 7 October.

McKinnon, Scott (2011) "Arizona Congresswoman Wounded in Shooting," *The Arizona Republic*, 9 January. Available at: http://www.azcentral.com/news/articles/2011/01/09/20110109gabrielle-giffords-arizona-shooting.html#ixzz1Av9S5oI1

Moore, Malcolm (2011) "Apple Hit by Child Labor at Chinese Suppliers," *The Daily Telegraph*, 16 February, B3.

Norris, Floyd (2009) "Goldman Can't Expect to Be Popular," *International Herald Tribune*, 17 April, p. 18.

Peñaloza, Lisa and Barnhart, Michelle (2011) "Living US Capitalism: The Normalization of Credit/Debt," *Journal of Consumer Research*, December.

Peñaloza, Lisa and Mish, Jenny (2011) "Leveraging Insights from Consumer Cultural Theory in Services Logic: Value Co-Creation in Sustainable Businesses," *Marketing Theory*, March.

Polanyi, M. (1976) "Tacit Knowledge," in M. Marx and F. Goodson (eds), *Theories in Contemporary Psychology*, New York: Macmillan, pp. 330–44.

Porter, Michael E. and Kramer, Mark R. (2006) "Strategy and Society: The Link between Competitive Advantage and Corporate Social Responsibility," *Harvard Business Review*, December, pp. 78–92.

Pullman, Susan (2003) "A Staffer Ordered to Commit Fraud Balked, Then Caved," *Wall Street Journal*, 23 June, p. A1.

Pyper, Neil (2011) "A Messy Affair – and It's Hard to See It Ending Cleanly," *The Independent*, 16 February, p. 4.

Quinn, Ben (2010) "Amid Greek Debt Crisis, Ireland Still Recovering from Its own," *Christian Science Monitor*, 11 February 2010.

Ratcliffe, R.G. and Fikac, Peggy (2010) "Delay Convicted of Money Laundering Charges," *Houston Chronical*, 24, November Available at: http://www.chron.com/disp/story.mpl/metropolitan/7308000.html.

Rest, J. R. (1986) *Moral Development: Advances in Research and Theory,* New York: Praeger.

Rich, Frank (2010) "Government for Sale," *Global Edition of the New York Times*, November 29, p. 9.

Rhodes, Carl and Westwood, Bob (2007) "Letting Knowledge Go: Ethics and Representation of the Other in International and Cross-Cultural Management," in Chris Carter, Stewart Clegg, Martin Kornberger, Stephan Laske, and Martin Messner (eds), *Business Ethics as Practice*, Cheltenham, UK: Edward Elgar, pp. 68–83.

Schechter, Danny (2006) *In Debt We Trust: America Before the Bubble Bursts*, New York: Globalvision Film.

Schmalensee, Richard L. (2003) "The 'Thou Shalt' School of Business," *Wall Street Journal*, 30 December A4.

Scott, Linda (1993) "Spectacular Vernacular: Literacy and Commercial Culture in the Postmodern Age, *International Journal of Research in Marketing*, 10(Winter): 251–75.

Statler, Matt and Oppegaard, Karin (2005), "Practical Wisdom: Integrating Ethics and Effectiveness in Organizations," in Chris Carter, Stewart Clegg, Martin Kornberger, Stephan Laske, and Martin Messner (eds), *Business Ethics as Practice*, Cheltenham: Edward Elgar, pp. 169–89.

Statler, Matt, Roos, Johan, and Victor, Bart (2007) "Dear Prudence: An Essay on Practical Wisdom in Strategy-Making," *Social Epistemology*, 21(2): 151–67.

Sternberg, R.J. (1998) "A Balance Theory of Wisdom," *Review of General Psychology*, 2(4): 347–65.

Streitfeld, David (2010) "Living in Foreclosure, and Liking it," *International Herald Tribune*, 2 June, p. 21.

Story, Louise (2010) "Secret Group Keeps Grip on Trading Derivatives," *International Herald Tribune*, 13 December, pp. 1, 15.

Tull, Donald S. and Hawkins, Del, I. (1985) "Ethical Issues in Marketing Research", in Laczniak and Murphy, pp. 55–70.

Warde, Alan (2005) "Consumption and Theories of Practice," *Journal of Consumer Culture*, 5(2): 131–53.

Weber, Max (1958) *The Protestant Ethic and the Spirit of Capitalism*, trans. Talcott Parsons, New York: Scharles Scribner's Sons.

Webster's (1986) *Webster's Ninth New Collegiate Dictionary*, Springfield, MA: Merriam-Webster Inc.

Zernike, Kate (2010) "A Republican Loner Gets a Seat of Power," *New York Times Global Edition*, 14 December, p. 5.

Index

Note: page numbers in *italic* type refer to Figures; those in **bold** type refer to Tables and Boxes.